PYTHON

IN A NUTSHELL

Third Edition

Alex Martelli, Anna Ravenscroft, and Steve Holden

Beijing • Boston • Farnham • Sebastopol • Tokyo

Python in a Nutshell

by Alex Martelli, Anna Ravenscroft, and Steve Holden

Published by O'Reilly Media, Inc., 1005 Gravenstein Highway North, Sebastopol, CA 95472.

O'Reilly books may be purchased for educational, business, or sales promotional use. Online editions are also available for most titles (*http://oreilly.com/safari*). For more information, contact our corporate/institutional sales department: 800-998-9938 or *corporate@oreilly.com*.

Editor: Dawn Schanafelt
Production Editor: Kristen Brown
Copyeditor: Kim Cofer
Proofreader: Rachel Monaghan
Indexer: Judith McConville
Interior Designer: David Futato
Cover Designer: Karen Montgomery
Illustrator: Rebecca Demarest

April 2017: Third Edition

Revision History for the Third Edition

2017-04-06: First Release

See *http://oreilly.com/catalog/errata.csp?isbn=9781449392925* for release details.

978-1-449-39292-5

[LSI]

Table of Contents

Part II. Core Python Language and Built-ins

Part III. Python Library and Extension Modules

Part IV. Network and Web Programming

Part V. Extending, Distributing, v2/v3 Migration

Preface

The Python programming language reconciles many apparent contradictions: both elegant and pragmatic, both simple and powerful, it's very high-level yet doesn't get in your way when you need to fiddle with bits and bytes, and it's suitable for programming novices as well as great for experts, too.

This book is aimed at programmers with some previous exposure to Python, as well as experienced programmers coming to Python for the first time from other languages. The book is a quick reference to Python itself, the most commonly used parts of its vast standard library, and a few of the most popular and useful third-party modules and packages, covering a wide range of application areas, including web and network programming, XML handling, database interactions, and high-speed numeric computing. The book focuses on Python's cross-platform capabilities and covers the basics of extending Python and embedding it in other applications.

How This Book Is Organized

This book has five parts, as follows.

Part I, Getting Started with Python

Chapter 1, Introduction to Python
: Covers the general characteristics of the Python language, its implementations, where to get help and information, how to participate in the Python community, and how to obtain and install Python on your computer(s).

Chapter 2, The Python Interpreter
: Covers the Python interpreter program, its command-line options, and how to use it to run Python programs and in interactive sessions. The chapter mentions text editors for editing Python programs and auxiliary programs for checking your Python sources, along with some full-fledged integrated devel-

opment environments, including IDLE, which comes free with standard Python. The chapter also covers running Python programs from the command line.

Part II, Core Python Language and Built-ins

Chapter 3, The Python Language
: Covers Python syntax, built-in data types, expressions, statements, control flow, and how to write and call functions.

Chapter 4, Object-Oriented Python
: Covers object-oriented programming in Python.

Chapter 5, Exceptions
: Covers how to use exceptions for errors and special situations, and logging.

Chapter 6, Modules
: Covers how Python lets you group code into modules and packages, how to define and import modules, and how to install third-party Python packages. The chapter also covers working with virtual environments to isolate project dependencies.

Chapter 7, Core Built-ins and Standard Library Modules
: Covers built-in data types and functions, and some of the most fundamental modules in the standard Python library (roughly, the set of modules supplying functionality that, in some other languages, is built into the language itself).

Chapter 8, Strings and Things
: Covers Python's string-processing facilities, including Unicode strings, byte strings, and string literals.

Chapter 9, Regular Expressions
: Covers Python's support for regular expressions.

Part III, Python Library and Extension Modules

Chapter 10, File and Text Operations
: Covers how to deal with files and text processing using many modules from Python's standard library and platform-specific extensions for rich text I/O. The chapter also covers issues of internationalization and localization, and the specific task of defining interactive text-mode command sessions with Python.

Chapter 11, Persistence and Databases
: Covers Python's serialization and persistence mechanisms, as well as Python's interfaces to DBM databases and relational (SQL-based) databases, particularly the handy SQLite that comes with Python's standard library.

Chapter 12, Time Operations
Covers how to deal with times and dates in Python, using the standard library and popular third-party extensions.

Chapter 13, Controlling Execution
Helps you to achieve advanced execution control in Python, including execution of dynamically generated code and control of garbage collection. The chapter also covers some Python internal types, and the specific issue of registering "clean-up" functions to execute at program-termination time.

Chapter 14, Threads and Processes
Covers Python's functionality for concurrent execution, both via multiple threads running within one process and via multiple processes running on a single machine. The chapter also covers how to access the process's environment, and how to access files via memory-mapping mechanisms.

Chapter 15, Numeric Processing
Shows Python's features for numeric computations, both in standard library modules and in third-party extension packages; in particular, the chapter covers how to use decimal numbers or fractions, instead of the default binary floating-point numbers. The chapter also covers how to get and use pseudorandom and truly random numbers, and how to speedily process whole arrays (and matrices) of numbers.

Chapter 16, Testing, Debugging, and Optimizing
Deals with Python tools and approaches that help ensure your programs are correct (i.e., that your programs do what they're meant to do), find and fix errors in your programs, and check and enhance your programs' performance. The chapter also covers the concept of "warning" and the Python library module that deals with it.

Part IV, Network and Web Programming

Chapter 17, Networking Basics
Covers the basics of networking with Python.

Chapter 18, Asynchronous Alternatives
Covers alternatives for asynchronous (event-driven) programming, particularly modern coroutine-based architectures and lower-level multiplexing, with standard library modules.

Chapter 19, Client-Side Network Protocol Modules
Covers modules in Python's standard library to write network client programs, particularly for dealing with various network protocols from the client side, sending and receiving emails, and handling URLs.

Chapter 20, Serving HTTP
: Covers how to serve HTTP for "web applications" in Python, using popular third-party lightweight Python frameworks leveraging Python's WSGI standard interface to web servers.

Chapter 21, Email, MIME, and Other Network Encodings
: Covers how to process email messages, and other network-structured and encoded documents, in Python.

Chapter 22, Structured Text: HTML
: Covers popular third-party Python extension modules to process, modify, and generate HTML documents.

Chapter 23, Structured Text: XML
: Covers Python library modules and popular extensions to process, modify, and generate XML documents.

Part V, Extending, Distributing, v2/v3 Migration

Chapter 24, Extending and Embedding Classic Python
: Covers how to code Python extension modules using Python's C API and Cython.

Chapter 25, Distributing Extensions and Programs
: Covers popular tools and modules to package and distribute Python extensions, modules, and applications.

Chapter 26, v2/v3 Migration and Coexistence
: Covers modules and best practices to help you code for both v2 and v3, how to best migrate existing code from v2 to v3, and how to retain portability between versions.

Conventions Used in This Book

The following conventions are used throughout this book.

Reference Conventions

In the function/method reference entries, when feasible, each optional parameter is shown with a default value using the Python syntax *name*=*value*. Built-in functions need not accept named parameters, so parameter names may not be significant. Some optional parameters are best explained in terms of their presence or absence, rather than through default values. In such cases, we indicate that a parameter is optional by enclosing it in brackets (`[]`). When more than one argument is optional, brackets can be nested.

Version Conventions

This book covers Python 3.5, referred to as v3, and Python 2.7, referred to as v2. Highlights of Python 3.6 (released as this book was about to go to print) are called out as 3.6. All examples in the book assume you have run `from __future__ import print_function` if you are using v2 (see the note Imports from __future__ on page 711).

Typographic Conventions

Italic
: Used for filenames, program names, URLs, and to introduce new terms.

Bold italic
: Used for New in 3.6 highlights.

`Constant width`
: Used for code examples, as well as for all items that appear in code, including keywords, methods, functions, classes, and modules.

`Constant width italic`
: Used to show text to be replaced with user-supplied values in code examples.

`Constant width bold`
: Used for commands to be typed at a system command line and to indicate code output.

How to Contact Us

We have tested and verified the information in this book to the best of our ability, but you may find that features have changed (or even that we have made mistakes!). Please let the publisher know about any errors you find, as well as your suggestions for future editions, by writing to:

O'Reilly Media, Inc.
1005 Gravenstein Highway North
Sebastopol, CA 95472
800-998-9938 (in the United States or Canada)
707-829-0515 (international or local)
707-829-0104 (fax)

We have a web page for this book, where we list errata, examples, and any additional information. You can access this page at *http://bit.ly/pythonNutshell_3E*.

To comment or ask technical questions about this book, send email to *pythonian3d@gmail.com*.

For more information about our books, courses, conferences, and news, see our website at *http://www.oreilly.com*.

Find us on Facebook: *http://facebook.com/oreilly*

Follow us on Twitter: *http://twitter.com/oreillymedia*

Watch us on YouTube: *http://www.youtube.com/oreillymedia*

O'Reilly Safari

Safari (formerly Safari Books Online) is a membership-based training and reference platform for enterprise, government, educators, and individuals.

Members have access to thousands of books, training videos, Learning Paths, interactive tutorials, and curated playlists from over 250 publishers, including O'Reilly Media, Harvard Business Review, Prentice Hall Professional, Addison-Wesley Professional, Microsoft Press, Sams, Que, Peachpit Press, Adobe, Focal Press, Cisco Press, John Wiley & Sons, Syngress, Morgan Kaufmann, IBM Redbooks, Packt, Adobe Press, FT Press, Apress, Manning, New Riders, McGraw-Hill, Jones & Bartlett, and Course Technology, among others.

For more information, please visit *http://oreilly.com/safari.*

Acknowledgments

Thanks to our thorough and conscientious reviewers and editor! All errors that remain are entirely our own.

Many thanks to our editor, Dawn Schanafelt, for gently guiding, nudging, and pushing us along to get this done! Also, thanks to Kim Cofer, our excellent copyeditor, whose eye for detail caught not just grammatical issues, but also some technical errors.

Thanks to our hard-working tech reviewers: Brett Cannon, Luciano Ramalho, and Victoria Wong, who read through every explanation and example in the book's draft. Without them, this book would not have been nearly as clear or accurate.

Thanks as well to our several unofficial reviewers: Tim Golden, for his invaluable help with Python for Windows coverage; Nick Coghlan and Donald Stufft, for their help untangling the intricacies of Python packaging; Łukasz Langa, for his copious feedback on asynchronous programming; Peter Norvig, for his precious, detailed feedback and advice about the entire book; Daniel Pyrathon, for his review of the chapter on HTTP serving frameworks; and George Gillan, for reporting many typos and unclear explanations in Early Release editions of this book.

And finally, thanks to Google for its useful Hangouts app and other G Suite online collaboration tools, without which our intense communication and coordination among authors in different continents would have been far less easy and efficient.

I

Getting Started with Python

1
Introduction to Python

Python, a general-purpose programming language, has been around for quite a while: Guido van Rossum, Python's creator, started developing Python back in 1990. This stable and mature language is very high-level, dynamic, object-oriented, and cross-platform—all very attractive characteristics. Python runs on all major hardware platforms and operating systems, so it doesn't constrain your choices.

Python offers high productivity for all phases of the software life cycle: analysis, design, prototyping, coding, testing, debugging, tuning, documentation, deployment, and, of course, maintenance. Python's popularity has seen steady, unflagging growth over the years. Today, familiarity with Python is an advantage for every programmer, as Python has infiltrated every niche and has useful roles to play as a part of any software solution.

Python provides a unique mix of elegance, simplicity, practicality, and sheer power. You'll quickly become productive with Python, thanks to its consistency and regularity, its rich standard library, and the many third-party packages and tools that are readily available for it. Python is easy to learn, so it is quite suitable if you are new to programming, yet is also powerful enough for the most sophisticated expert.

The Python Language

The Python language, while not minimalist, is spare, for good pragmatic reasons. Once a language offers one good way to express a design idea, adding other ways has, at best, modest benefits, while cost, in terms of language complexity, grows more than linearly with the number of features. A complicated language is harder to learn and master (and to implement efficiently and without bugs) than a simpler one. Complications and quirks in a language hamper productivity in software development and maintenance, particularly in large projects, where many developers cooperate and often maintain code originally written by others.

Python is simple, but not simplistic. It adheres to the idea that, if a language behaves a certain way in some contexts, it should ideally work similarly in all contexts. Python also follows the principle that a language should not have "convenient" shortcuts, special cases, ad hoc exceptions, overly subtle distinctions, or mysterious and tricky under-the-covers optimizations. A good language, like any other well-designed artifact, must balance such general principles with taste, common sense, and a high degree of practicality.

Python is a general-purpose programming language: Python's traits are useful in just about any area of software development. There is no area where Python cannot be part of a great solution. "Part" is an important word here; while many developers find that Python fills all of their needs, it does not have to stand alone: Python programs can cooperate with a variety of other software components, making it an ideal language for gluing together components written in other languages. One of the language's design goals was that it should "play well with others."

Python is a very high-level language (VHLL). This means that Python uses a higher level of abstraction, conceptually further from the underlying machine, than do classic compiled languages such as C, C++, and Fortran, which are traditionally called "high-level languages." Python is simpler, faster to process (both for human brains and for programmatic tools), and more regular than classic high-level languages. This enables high programmer productivity and makes Python an attractive development tool. Good compilers for classic compiled languages can generate binary machine code that runs faster than Python code. However, in most cases, the performance of Python-coded applications is sufficient. When it isn't, apply the optimization techniques covered in "Optimization" on page 479 to improve your program's performance while keeping the benefit of high productivity.

Somewhat newer languages such as Java and C# are slightly higher-level than classic ones such as C and Fortran, and share some characteristics of classic languages (such as the need to use declarations) as well as some of VHLLs like Python (such as the use of portable bytecode as the compilation target in typical implementations, and garbage collection to relieve programmers from the need to manage memory). If you find you are more productive with Java or C# than with C or Fortran, try Python (possibly in the Jython or IronPython implementations, covered in "Python Implementations" on page 5) to become even more productive.

In terms of language level, Python is comparable to other powerful VHLLs like JavaScript, Ruby, and Perl. The advantages of simplicity and regularity, however, remain on Python's side.

Python is an object-oriented programming language, but lets you develop code using both object-oriented and procedural styles, and a touch of functional programming, too, mixing and matching as your application requires. Python's object-oriented features are conceptually similar to those of C++, but simpler to use.

Intro to Python

The Python Standard Library and Extension Modules

There is more to Python programming than just the Python language: the standard library and other extension modules are nearly as important for effective Python use as the language itself. The Python standard library supplies many well-designed, solid, 100 percent pure Python modules for convenient reuse. It includes modules for such tasks as representing data, processing text, interacting with the operating system and filesystem, and web programming. Because these modules are written in Python, they work on all platforms supported by Python.

Extension modules, from the standard library or from elsewhere, let Python code access functionality supplied by the underlying operating system or other software components, such as graphical user interfaces (GUIs), databases, and networks. Extensions also afford maximal speed in computationally intensive tasks such as XML parsing and numeric array computations. Extension modules that are not coded in Python, however, do not necessarily enjoy the same automatic cross-platform portability as pure Python code.

You can write special-purpose extension modules in lower-level languages to achieve maximum performance for small, computationally intensive parts that you originally prototyped in Python. You can also use tools such as Cython and CFFI to wrap existing C/C++ libraries into Python extension modules, as covered in "Extending Python Without Python's C API" on page 681. Last but not least, you can embed Python in applications coded in other languages, exposing existing application functionality to Python scripts via app-specific Python extension modules.

This book documents many modules, both from the standard library and from other sources, in areas such as client- and server-side network programming, databases, manipulation of text and binary files, and interaction with the operating system.

Python Implementations

Python currently has four production-quality implementations (CPython, Jython, IronPython, PyPy) and a new high-performance implementation in early development, Pyston (*https://blogs.dropbox.com/tech/2014/04/introducing-pyston-an-upcoming-jit-based-python-implementation/*), which we do not cover further. We also mention a number of other, more experimental, implementations in a following section.

This book primarily addresses CPython, the most widely used implementation, which we usually refer to as just "Python" for simplicity. However, the distinction between a language and its implementations is an important one.

CPython

Classic Python (AKA CPython, often just called Python) is the most up-to-date, solid, and complete production-quality implementation of Python. It can be considered the "reference implementation" of the language. CPython is a compiler, interpreter, and set of built-in and optional extension modules, all coded in standard C. CPython can be used on any platform where the C compiler complies with the ISO/IEC 9899:1990 standard (i.e., all modern, popular platforms). In "Installation" on page 18, we explain how to download and install CPython. All of this book, except a few sections explicitly marked otherwise, applies to CPython. CPython supports both *v3* (version 3.5 or better) and *v2* (version 2.7).

Jython

Jython (*http://www.jython.org*) is a Python implementation for any Java Virtual Machine (JVM) compliant with Java 7 or better. Such JVMs are available for all popular, modern platforms. As of this writing, Jython supports v2, but not yet v3. With Jython, you can use all Java libraries and frameworks. For optimal use of Jython, you need some familiarity with fundamental Java classes. You do not have to code in Java, but documentation and examples for Java libraries are couched in Java terms, so you need a nodding acquaintance with Java to read and understand them. You also need to use Java-supporting tools for tasks such as manipulating *.jar* files and signing applets. This book deals with Python, not with Java. To use Jython, you should complement this book with *Jython Essentials*, by Noel Rappin and Samuele Pedroni (O'Reilly), *Java in a Nutshell*, by David Flanagan (O'Reilly), and/or *The Definitive Guide to Jython (Open Source Version)* by Josh Juneau, Jim Baker, et al. (Apress, available on O'Reilly's Safari (*https://oreilly.com/safari*) and on Jython.org (*http://www.jython.org/jythonbook/en/1.0/*)), as well as some of the many other Java resources available.

IronPython

IronPython (*http://ironpython.net*) is a Python implementation (as of this writing, only v2, not yet v3) for the Microsoft-designed Common Language Runtime (CLR), most commonly known as .NET, which is now open source (*https://github.com/dotnet/coreclr*) and ported to Linux and macOS. With IronPython, you can use all CLR libraries and frameworks. In addition to Microsoft's own implementation, a cross-platform implementation of the CLR known as Mono (*http://www.mono-project.com/*) works with other, non-Microsoft operating systems, as well as with Windows. For optimal use of IronPython, you need some familiarity with fundamental CLR libraries. You do not have to code in C#, but documentation and examples for existing CLR libraries are often couched in C# terms, so you need a nodding acquaintance with C# to read and understand them. You also need to use CLR supporting tools for tasks such as making CLR assemblies. This book deals with Python, not with the CLR. For IronPython usage, you should complement this book with IronPython's own online documentation, and, if needed, some of the many other resources available about .NET, the CLR, C#, Mono, and so on.

PyPy

PyPy (*http://pypy.org/*) is a fast and flexible implementation of Python, coded in a subset of Python itself, able to target several lower-level languages and virtual machines using advanced techniques such as type inferencing. PyPy's greatest strength is its ability to generate native machine code "just in time" as it runs your Python program. PyPy implements v2 and, at this writing, Python 3.5 support is being released in alpha. PyPy has substantial advantages in speed and memory management, and is seeing production-level use.

Choosing Between CPython, Jython, IronPython, and PyPy

If your platform, as most are, is able to run all of CPython, Jython, IronPython, and PyPy, how do you choose among them? First of all, don't choose prematurely: download and install them all. They coexist without problems, and they're all free. Having them all on your development machine costs only some download time and a little extra disk space, and lets you compare them directly.

The primary difference between the implementations is the environment in which they run and the libraries and frameworks they can use. If you need a JVM environment, then Jython is your best choice. If you need a CLR (AKA ".NET") environment, take advantage of IronPython. If you need a custom version of Python, or need high performance for long-running programs, consider PyPy.

If you're mainly working in a traditional environment, CPython is an excellent fit. If you don't have a strong preference for one or the other, start with the standard CPython reference implementation, which is most widely supported by third-party add-ons and extensions, and offers the highly preferable v3 (in full 3.5 glory).[1]

In other words, when you're experimenting, learning, and trying things out, use CPython, most widely supported and mature. To develop and deploy, your best choice depends on the extension modules you want to use and how you want to distribute your programs. CPython applications are often faster than Jython or IronPython, particularly if you use extension modules such as NumPy (covered in "Array Processing" on page 446); however, PyPy can often be even faster, thanks to just-in-time compilation to machine code. It may be worthwhile to benchmark your CPython code against PyPy.

CPython is most mature: it has been around longer, while Jython, IronPython, and PyPy are newer and less proven in the field. The development of CPython versions tends to proceed ahead of that of Jython, IronPython, and PyPy: at the time of writing, for example, the language level supported is, for v2, 2.7 for all of them; for v3, 3.5 and 3.6 are now available in CPython, and PyPy has 3.5 in alpha.

However, Jython can use any Java class as an extension module, whether the class comes from a standard Java library, a third-party library, or a library you develop yourself. Similarly, IronPython can use any CLR class, whether from the standard CLR libraries, or coded in C#, Visual Basic .NET, or other CLR-compliant

1 Throughout this book, we'll mention some highlights of Python 3.6, just barely released as we write—while 3.6 may not yet be mature enough for you to use in production releases, knowing what's coming as 3.6 does mature can't fail to be helpful to your technical choices.

languages. PyPy is drop-in compatible with most standard CPython libraries, and with C-coded extensions using Cython, covered in "Cython" on page 682, and CFFI, mentioned in "Extending Python Without Python's C API" on page 681.

A Jython-coded application is a 100 percent pure Java application, with all of Java's deployment advantages and issues, and runs on any target machine having a suitable JVM. Packaging opportunities are also identical to Java's. Similarly, an IronPython-coded application is entirely compliant with .NET's specifications.

Jython, IronPython, PyPy, and CPython are all good, faithful implementations of Python, reasonably close to each other in terms of usability and performance. Since each of the JVM and CLR platforms carries a lot of baggage, but also supplies large amounts of useful libraries, frameworks, and tools, any of the implementations may enjoy decisive practical advantages in a specific deployment scenario. It is wise to become familiar with the strengths and weaknesses of each, and then choose optimally for each development task.

Other Developments, Implementations, and Distributions

Python has become popular enough that there are a number of other groups and individuals who have taken an interest in its development and provided features and implementations outside the core development team's focus.

Programmers new to Python used to often find it troublesome to install. Nowadays almost all Unix-based systems include a v2 implementation, and recent releases of Ubuntu include v3 as the "system Python." If you are serious about software development in Python, the first thing you should do is *leave your system-installed Python alone!* Quite apart from anything else, Python is increasingly used by the operating system itself, so tweaking the Python installation could lead to trouble.

Therefore, consider installing one or more Python implementations that you can freely use for your development convenience, sure in the knowledge that nothing you do affects the operating system. We also recommend the use of *virtual environments* (see "Python Environments" on page 188) to isolate projects from each other, allowing them to make use of what might otherwise be conflicting dependencies (e.g., if two of your projects require different versions of the same module).

Python's popularity has led to the creation of many active communities, and the language's ecosystem is very active. The following sections outline some of the more interesting recent developments, but our failure to include a project here reflects limitations of space and time rather than implying any disapproval on our part.

Intro to Python

Pyjion

Pyjion (*https://github.com/Microsoft/Pyjion*) is an open source project from Microsoft whose primary goal is to add an API to CPython for managing just-in-time (JIT) compilers. Secondary goals include the creation of a JIT compiler for Microsoft's core CLR environment, which although at the heart of the .NET environment is now open sourced, and a framework for the development of JIT compilers. It is therefore not an implementation of Python, but we mention it because it offers the potential to translate CPython's bytecode into highly efficient code for many different environments. Integration of Pyjion into CPython will be enabled by PEP 523 (*https://www.python.org/dev/peps/pep-0523/*), which was implemented in Python 3.6.

IPython

IPython enhances standard CPython to make it more powerful and convenient for interactive use. IPython extends the interpreter's capabilities by allowing abbreviated function call syntax, and extensible functionality known as *magics* introduced by the percent (`%`) character. It also provides shell escapes, allowing a Python variable to receive the result of a shell command. You can use a question mark to query an object's documentation (two question marks for extended documentation); all the standard features of Python are also available.

IPython has made particular strides in the scientific and data-focused world, and has slowly morphed (through the development of IPython Notebook, now refactored and renamed the Jupyter Notebook and shown in the following figure) into an interactive programming environment that, among snippets of code, also lets you embed commentary in literate programming (*https://en.wikipedia.org/wiki/Literate_programming*) style (including mathematical notation) and show the output of executing code, with advanced graphics produced by such subsystems as `matplotlib` and `bokeh`. An example of `matplotlib` graphics is shown in the bottom half of the figure. Reassuringly grant-funded in recent years, Jupyter/IPython is one of Python's most prominent success stories.

Moving Window Average

```
In [6]: np.random.seed(0)
        t = np.linspace(0, 10, 300)
        x = np.sin(t)
        dx = np.random.normal(0, 0.3, 300)

        kernel = np.ones(25) / 25.
        x_smooth = np.convolve(x + dx, kernel, mode='same')

        fig, ax = plt.subplots()
        ax.plot(t, x + dx, linestyle='', marker='o',
                color='black', markersize=3, alpha=0.3)
        ax.plot(t, x_smooth, '-k', lw=3)
        ax.plot(t, x, '--k', lw=3, color='blue')

        display_d3(fig)
Out[6]:
```

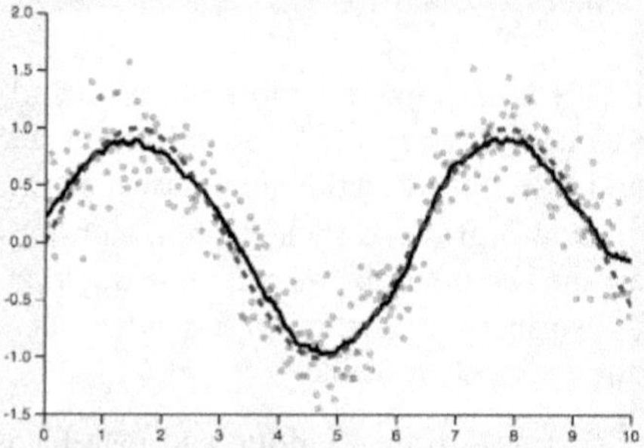

MicroPython: Is your child already a programmer?

The continued trend in miniaturization has brought Python well within the range of the hobbyist. Single-board computers like the Raspberry Pi (*https://www.raspberrypi.org/*) and the Beagle Board (*https://beagleboard.org/*) let you run Python in a full Linux environment. Below this level, there is an interesting class of devices known as *microcontrollers*, programmable chips with configurable hardware. This extends the scope of hobby and professional projects—for example, by making analog and digital sensing easy, enabling such applications as light and temperature measurements with little additional hardware.

Typical examples at the time of writing were the Adafruit Feather (*https://www.adafruit.com/feather*) and the WiPy (*https://www.pycom.io/product/wipy-2-0/*), but new devices appear (and disappear) all the time. Thanks to the MicroPython (*http://micropython.org/*) project, these devices, some of which come with advanced functionality like WiFi, can now be programmed in Python.

MicroPython is a Python 3 implementation that can produce bytecode or executable machine code (though many users will be happily unaware of the latter fact). It implements the syntax of v3, but lacks most of the standard library. Special hardware control modules allow configuration and driving of the various pieces of built-in configurable hardware, and access to Python's socket library lets devices be clients for Internet services. External devices and timer events can trigger code.

A device typically offers interpreter access through a USB serial port or over the Telnet protocol (we aren't aware of any `ssh` implementations yet, though, so take care to firewall these devices properly: *they should not be directly accessible across the Internet without proper precautions!*). You can program the device's power-on bootstrap sequence in Python by creating a *boot.py* file in the device's memory, and this file can execute arbitrary Python code of any complexity.

Thanks to MicroPython, the Python language can be a full player in the Internet of Things. At the time of writing the Python-capable BBC *micro:bit* device (*https://www.microbit.co.uk/*) is being distributed to every year-7 schoolchild in the UK (roughly one million in number). Are you sure your children don't already know some Python?

Anaconda and Miniconda

One of the more successful Python distributions in recent years is Anaconda (*https://www.continuum.io/anaconda-overview*) from Continuum Analytics. This open source package comes with an enormous number of preconfigured and tested modules in addition to the standard library. In many cases you might find that it contains all the necessary dependencies for your work. On Unix-based systems it installs very simply in a single directory: to activate it, just add the Anaconda *bin* directory at the front of your shell `PATH`.

Anaconda is a Python distribution based on a packaging technology called `conda`. A sister implementation, Miniconda (*http://conda.pydata.org/miniconda.html*), gives access to the same libraries but does not come with them preloaded, making it more suitable for creating tailored environments. Conda does not use the standard virtual environments but contains equivalent facilities to allow separation of the dependencies for multiple projects.

Nuitka: Convert your Python to C++

Nuitka is an alternative compiler that converts your Python code to C++, with support for v2 and v3. Nuitka allows convenient optimization of your code, with current speeds over twice as fast as CPython. Future milestones include better type inferencing and even more speed. The Nuitka homepage (*http://nuitka.net/*) has more information.

Grumpy: A Python-to-Go transpiler

Grumpy is an experimental compiler that converts your Python code to Go, with support for v2 only; the Go code then compiles to a native executable, allowing the import of Go-coded modules (though not of normal Python extensions) and high scalability. Grumpy is optimized for serving large parallel workloads with many lightweight threads, one day potentially replacing CPython as the runtime used to serve YouTube's millions of requests per second, as explained on the Google Open

Source blog (*https://opensource.googleblog.com/2017/01/grumpy-go-running-python.html*). Grumpy's maintained on the GitHub Grumpy project (*https://github.com/google/grumpy*).

Transcrypt: Convert your Python to JavaScript

Many attempts have been made to determine how Python could become a browser-based language, but JavaScript's hold has been tenacious. The Transcrypt (*http://www.transcrypt.org/*) system is a pip-installable Python package to convert Python code into browser-executable JavaScript. You have full access to the browser's DOM, allowing your code to dynamically manipulate window content and use JavaScript libraries.

Although it creates minified code, Transcrypt provides full sourcemaps that allow you to debug with reference to the Python source rather than the generated JavaScript. You can write browser event handlers in Python, mixing it freely with HTML and JavaScript. Python may never make it as a first-class browser language, but Transcrypt means you might no longer need to worry about that.

Another (more mature but very active) project to let you script your web pages with Python is Brython (*https://brython.info/*), and there are others yet. To help you pick among them, you can find useful info and links on this Stack Overflow thread (*http://stackoverflow.com/questions/30155551/python-in-browser-how-to-choose-between-brython-pypy-js-skulpt-and-transcrypt*).

Licensing and Price Issues

CPython is covered by the Python Software Foundation License Version 2 (*https://docs.python.org/3/license.html*), which is GNU Public License (GPL) compatible, but lets you use Python for any proprietary, free, or other open source software development, similar to BSD/Apache/MIT licenses. Jython's, IronPython's, and PyPy's licenses are similarly liberal. Anything you download from the main Python, Jython, IronPython, and PyPy sites won't cost you a penny. These licenses do not constrain what licensing and pricing conditions you can use for software you develop using the tools, libraries, and documentation they cover.

However, not everything Python-related is free from licensing costs or hassles. Many third-party Python sources, tools, and extension modules that you can freely download have liberal licenses, similar to that of Python itself. Others are covered by the GPL or Lesser GPL (LGPL), constraining the licensing conditions you can place on derived works. Some commercially developed modules and tools may require you to pay a fee, either unconditionally or if you use them for profit.

There is no substitute for careful examination of licensing conditions and prices. Before you invest time and energy into any software tool or component, check that you can live with its license. Often, especially in a corporate environment, such legal matters may involve consulting lawyers. Modules and tools covered in this book, unless we explicitly say otherwise, can be taken to be, at the time of this writing, freely downloadable, open source, and covered by a liberal license akin to Python's.

However, we claim no legal expertise, and licenses can change over time, so double-checking is always prudent.

Python Development and Versions

Python is developed, maintained, and released by a team of core developers led by Guido van Rossum, Python's inventor, architect, and Benevolent Dictator For Life (BDFL). This title means that Guido has the final say on what becomes part of the Python language and standard library. Python's intellectual property is vested in the Python Software Foundation (PSF), a nonprofit corporation devoted to promoting Python, described in "Python Software Foundation" on page 16. Many PSF Fellows and members have commit privileges to Python's reference source repositories (currently Mercurial, but transitioning to git (*https://github.com/python*), as documented in the Python Developer's Guide (*https://docs.python.org/devguide/*)), and most Python committers are members or Fellows of the PSF.

Proposed changes to Python are detailed in public docs called Python Enhancement Proposals (PEPs (*https://www.python.org/dev/peps/pep-0001/*)), debated (sometimes an advisory vote is taken) by Python developers and the wider Python community, and finally approved or rejected by Guido (or his delegates), who take debates and votes into account but are not bound by them. Hundreds of people contribute to Python development through PEPs, discussion, bug reports, and patches to Python sources, libraries, and docs.

The Python core team releases minor versions of Python (3.*x* for growing values of *x*), also known as "feature releases," currently at a pace of about once every 18 months. Python 2.7, first released in July 2010, was the last feature release of the 2.x series. Current and future releases of v2 are and will be bug-fix point releases only, not adding any features. As of this writing, the current bug-fix release of 2.7.13 is available. There will never be a 2.8 release: we recommend migrating to v3.

Each v3 minor release (as opposed to bug-fix point release) adds features that make Python more powerful and simpler to use, but also takes care to maintain backward compatibility. Python 3.0, which was allowed to break backward compatibility in order to remove redundant "legacy" features and simplify the language, was first released in December 2008. Python 3.5 (the version we cover as "v3") was first released in September 2015; 3.6 was released in December 2016, just as we are finishing writing this book.

Each minor release 3.*x* is first made available in alpha releases, tagged as 3.*x* a0, 3.*x* a1, and so on. After the alphas comes at least one beta release, 3.*x* b1, and after the betas, at least one release candidate, 3.*x* rc1. By the time the final release of 3.*x* (3.*x*.0) comes out, it is quite solid, reliable, and tested on all major platforms. Any Python programmer can help ensure this by downloading alphas, betas, and release candidates, trying them out, and filing bug reports for any problems that emerge.

Once a minor release is out, part of the attention of the core team switches to the next minor release. However, a minor release normally gets successive point releases (i.e., 3.*x*.1, 3.*x*.2, and so on) that add no functionality, but can fix errors, port Python to new platforms, enhance documentation, and add optimizations and tools.

This book focuses on Python 2.7 and 3.5 (and all their point releases), the most stable and widespread releases at the time of this writing (with side notes about the highlights of the newest release, 3.6). Python 2.7 is what we call v2, while 3.5 (with its successors) is what we call v3. We document which parts of the language and libraries exist in v3 only and cannot be used in v2, as well as v3 ones that can be used in v2—for example, with `from __future__ import` syntax (see Imports from __future__ on page 711). Whenever we say that a feature is *in v3*, we mean it's in Python 3.5 (and presumably all future versions, including 3.6, but not necessarily in, say, 3.4); saying that a feature is *in v2* means it's in Python 2.7.x (currently 2.7.13) but not necessarily in 2.6 or earlier. In a few minor cases, we specify a point release, such as 3.5.3, for language changes where the point release matters.

This book does not address older versions of Python, such as 2.5 or 2.6; such versions are more than five years old and should not be used for any development. However, you might have to worry about such legacy versions if they are embedded in some application you need to script. Fortunately, Python's backward compatibility is quite good within major releases: v2 is able to properly process almost every valid Python program that was written for Python 1.5.2 or later. As mentioned, however, Python 3 was a major release that *did* break backward compatibility, although it is possible to write code that works in both v2 and v3 if care is taken. Please see Chapter 26 for more on migrating legacy code to v3. You can find code and documentation online (*https://www.python.org/doc/versions/*) for all old releases of Python.

Python Resources

The richest Python resource is the web. The best starting point is Python's homepage (*https://www.python.org/*), full of interesting links to explore. The Jython (*http://www.jython.org*)site is a must if you're interested in Jython. IronPython has a .net site (*http://ironpython.net/*). PyPy is documented at the PyPy site (*http://pypy.org/*).

Documentation

Python, Jython, IronPython, and PyPy all come with good documentation. The manuals are available in many formats, suitable for viewing, searching, and printing. You can read CPython's manuals online (we often refer to these as "the online docs"): both v2 (*https://docs.python.org/2.7/*) and v3 (*https://docs.python.org/3/*) are available. You can also find various downloadable formats for v2 (*https://docs.python.org/2.7/download.html*) and v3 (*https://docs.python.org/3.5/download.html*).The Python Documentation (*https://www.python.org/doc/*) page has links to a large variety of documents. The Jython Documentation (*http://www.jython.org/docs/*) page has links to Jython-specific documents as well as general Python ones; there are also documentation pages for IronPython (*http://ironpython.net/documentation/*) and for PyPy (*http://doc.pypy.org/en/latest/*). You can also find Frequently

Asked Questions (FAQ) documents for Python (*https://docs.python.org/2/faq/*), Jython (*https://wiki.python.org/jython/JythonFaq*), IronPython (*http://ironpython.codeplex.com/wikipage?title=FAQ*), and PyPy (*http://doc.pypy.org/en/latest/faq.html*) online.

Python documentation for nonprogrammers

Most Python documentation (including this book) assumes some software-development knowledge. However, Python is quite suitable for first-time programmers, so there are exceptions to this rule. Good introductory online texts for nonprogrammers include:

- Josh Cogliati's "Non-Programmers Tutorial For Python," available online in two versions: for v2 (*http://oopweb.com/Python/Documents/easytut/VolumeFrames.html*), and for v3 (*https://en.wikibooks.org/wiki/Non-Programmer%27s_Tutorial_for_Python_3*)
- Alan Gauld's "Learning to Program," available online (*http://alan-g.me.uk/*) (covers both v2 and v3)
- "Think Python, 2nd edition," by Allen Downey, available online (*http://greenteapress.com/wp/think-python-2e/*) (covers primarily v3, with notes for v2 usage)

An excellent resource for learning Python (for nonprogrammers, and for less experienced programmers too) is the Beginners' Guide wiki (*https://wiki.python.org/moin/BeginnersGuide*), which includes a wealth of links and advice. It's community-curated, so it will likely stay up-to-date as available books, courses, tools, and so on keep evolving and improving.

Extension modules and Python sources

A good starting point to Python extensions and sources is the Python Package Index (*https://pypi.python.org/pypi*) (still fondly known to old-timers as "The Cheese Shop," and generally referred to now as PyPI), which at the time of this writing offers over 95,000 packages,[2] each with descriptions and pointers.

The standard Python source distribution contains excellent Python source code in the standard library and in the Demos and Tools directories, as well as C source for the many built-in extension modules. Even if you have no interest in building Python from source, we suggest you download and unpack the Python source distribution for study purposes; or, if you choose, peruse it online (*https://github.com/python/cpython/tree/master/Lib*).

Many Python modules and tools covered in this book also have dedicated sites. We include references to such sites in the appropriate chapters in this book.

2 By the time you read this, there will likely be more than 100,000 packages.

Books

Although the web is a rich source of information, books still have their place (if we didn't agree on this, we wouldn't have written this book, and you wouldn't be reading it). Books about Python are numerous. Here are a few we recommend, although some cover older versions rather than current ones:

- If you're just learning to program, *Python for Dummies*, by Stef and Aahz Maruch (For Dummies), while dated (2006), is a great introduction to programming, and to elementary Python (v2) in particular.
- If you know some programming, but are just starting to learn Python, *Head First Python*, 2nd edition, by Paul Barry (O'Reilly), may serve you well. Like all Head First series (*http://shop.oreilly.com/category/series/head-first/formula.do*) books, it uses graphics and humor to teach its subject.
- *Dive Into Python* and *Dive Into Python 3*, by Mark Pilgrim (APress), teach by example, in a fast-paced and thorough way that is quite suitable for people who are already expert programmers in other languages. You can also freely download the book, in any of several formats, for either v2 (*http://www.diveintopython.net*) or v3 (*http://www.diveintopython3.net/*).
- *Beginning Python: From Novice to Professional*, by Magnus Lie Hetland (APress), teaches both by thorough explanations and by fully developing 10 complete programs in various application areas.
- *Python Essential Reference*, by David Beazley (New Riders), is a complete reference to the Python language and its standard libraries.
- For a concise summary reference and reminder of Python's essentials, check out *Python Pocket Reference*, by Mark Lutz (O'Reilly).

Community

One of the greatest strengths of Python is its robust, friendly, welcoming community. Python programmers and contributors meet f2f[3] at conferences, "hackathons" (often known as *sprints* in the Python community), and local user groups; actively discuss shared interests; and help each other on mailing lists and social media.

Python Software Foundation

Besides holding the intellectual property rights for the Python programming language, a large part of the mission of the Python Software Foundation (PSF) is to "support and facilitate the growth of a diverse and international community of Python programmers." The PSF sponsors user groups, conferences, and sprints, and provides grants for development, outreach, and education, among other activities.

---

3 Face-to-face (i.e., in-person).

The PSF has dozens of Fellows (nominated for their contributions to Python, and including all of the Python core team, as well as all authors of this book); hundreds of members who contribute time, work, and money; and dozens of corporate sponsors. Under the new *open membership model*, anyone who uses and supports Python can become a member of the PSF. Check out the membership page (*https://www.python.org/psf/membership/*) for information on becoming a member of the PSF. If you're interested in contributing to Python itself, see the Python Developer's Guide (*https://docs.python.org/devguide/*).

Python conferences

There are lots of Python conferences worldwide. General Python conferences include international and regional ones, such as PyCon (*https://us.pycon.org/2016/*) and EuroPython (*https://ep2015.europython.eu/en/*), and other more localized ones such as PyOhio (*http://www.pyohio.org/*) and Pycon Italia (*https://www.pycon.it/en/*). Topical conferences include SciPy (*http://conference.scipy.org/*), PyData (*http://pydata.org/events.html*), and DjangoCon (*https://2016.djangocon.us/*). Conferences are often followed by coding sprints, where Python contributors get together for several days of coding focused on particular open source projects and on abundant camaraderie. You can find a listing of conferences at the Community Workshops (*https://www.python.org/community/workshops/*) page. Videos of talks from previous conferences can be found at the pyvideo site (*http://pyvideo.org/*).

User groups and Meetups

The Python community has local user groups in every continent except Antarctica, as listed at the Local User Groups wiki (*https://wiki.python.org/moin/LocalUserGroups*). In addition, there are Python Meetups (*https://www.meetup.com/topics/python/*) listed for over 70 countries. Women in Python have an international PyLadies group (*http://www.pyladies.com/*), as well as local PyLadies chapters.

Special Interest Groups

Discussions on some specialized subjects related to Python take place on the mailing lists of Python Special Interest Groups (SIGs). The SIGS (*https://www.python.org/community/sigs/*) page has a list, and pointers to general and specific information about them. Over a dozen SIGs are active at the time of this writing. Here are a few examples:

- cplusplus-sig (*https://www.python.org/community/sigs/current/cplusplus-sig/*): Bindings between C++ and Python
- mobile-sig (*https://www.python.org/community/sigs/current/mobile-sig/*): Python on mobile devices
- edu-sig (*https://www.python.org/community/sigs/current/edu-sig/*): Python in Education

Social media

For an RSS feed of Python-related blogs, see planetpython (*http://planetpython.org/*) or follow them on Twitter @planetpython (*https://twitter.com/planetpython*). On Twitter, you can also follow @ThePSF (*https://twitter.com/ThePSF*). FreeNode on IRC hosts several Python-related channels: the main one is `#python`. On Facebook, you can join the Python Software Developers (*https://www.facebook.com/groups/2249498416/*) public group; on Google+, the Unofficial Python Community (*https://plus.google.com/communities/103393744324769547228*); on LinkedIn, check its Python page (*https://www.linkedin.com/topic/python*) for more. Technical questions and answers about Python can also be found and followed on stackoverflow.com under a variety of tags, including python (*http://stackoverflow.com/questions/tagged/python*), python-2.7 (*http://stackoverflow.com/questions/tagged/python-2.7*), python-3.x (*http://stackoverflow.com/questions/tagged/python-3.x*), and others. Python is an actively curated topic on Stack Overflow, where many useful answers with illuminating discussions can be found.

Mailing lists and newsgroups

The Community lists (*https://www.python.org/community/lists/*) page has links to Python-related mailing lists and newsgroups. The Usenet newsgroup for Python discussions is comp.lang.python (*https://groups.google.com/forum/#!forum/comp.lang.python*). The newsgroup is also available as a mailing list; to subscribe, fill out the form (*https://mail.python.org/mailman/listinfo/python-list*). Python-related official announcements are posted to python announce (*https://groups.google.com/forum/#!forum/comp.lang.python.announce*), or its mailing-list equivalent (*https://mail.python.org/mailman/listinfo/python-announce-list*). To ask for individual help with specific problems, write to *help@python.org*. For help learning or teaching Python, write to *tutor@python.org* or join the list (*https://mail.python.org/mailman/listinfo/tutor*). For issues or discussion about porting between v2 and v3, join the python-porting (*https://mail.python.org/mailman/listinfo/python-porting*) list.

For a useful weekly round-up of Python-related news and articles, you can subscribe to the *Python Weekly (http://www.pythonweekly.com/)*.

In 2015, the Python Software Foundation created a community-oriented mailing list (*https://mail.python.org/mailman/listinfo/psf-community*) to support its new open membership model, which you can subscribe to.

Installation

You can install Python in classic (CPython), JVM (Jython), .NET (IronPython), and PyPy versions, on most platforms. With a suitable development system (C for CPython, Java for Jython, .NET for IronPython; PyPy, coded in Python itself, only needs CPython installed first), you can install Python versions from the respective source code distributions. On popular platforms, you also have the (highly recommended!) alternative of installing from prebuilt binary distributions.

Installing Python if it comes preinstalled

If your platform comes with a preinstalled version of Python, you're still best advised to install another, independent, updated version. When you do, you must *not* remove or overwrite your platform's original version—rather, install the other version "side by side" with the first one. This way, you make sure you are not going to disturb any other software that is part of your platform: such software might rely on the exact Python version that came with the platform itself.

Installing CPython from a binary distribution is faster, saves you substantial work on some platforms, and is the only possibility if you have no suitable C compiler. Installing from source code gives you more control and flexibility, and is a must if you can't find a suitable prebuilt binary distribution for your platform. Even if you install from binaries, it's best to also download the source distribution, as it includes examples and demos that may be missing from prebuilt binaries.

Installing Python from Binaries

If your platform is popular and current, you'll find prebuilt, packaged binary versions of Python ready for installation. Binary packages are typically self-installing, either directly as executable programs, or via appropriate system tools, such as the RedHat Package Manager (RPM) on some versions of Linux and the Microsoft Installer (MSI) on Windows. After downloading a package, install it by running the program and choosing installation parameters, such as the directory where Python is to be installed. In Windows, select the option labeled "Add Python 3.5 to PATH" to have the installer add the install location into the PATH in order to easily use Python at a command prompt (see "The python Program" on page 25).

To download "official" Python binaries, visit the Python site (*https://www.python.org/*), click Downloads, and on the next page, click the button labeled Python 2.7 or Python 3.x to download the binary suitable for the browser's platform.

Many third parties supply free binary Python installers for other platforms. Installers exist for Linux distributions, whether your distribution is RPM-based (*http://rpmfind.net*) (RedHat, Fedora, Mandriva, SUSE, etc.), or Debian and Ubuntu (*http://www.debian.org*). The Other Downloads page (*https://www.python.org/download/other/*) provides links to binary distributions for now-somewhat-exotic platforms such as OS/2, RISC OS, IBM AS/400, and so forth.

Anaconda (*https://www.continuum.io/downloads*) is a binary distribution including either v2 or v3, plus the conda (*http://conda.pydata.org/docs/*) package manager, and hundreds of third-party extensions, particularly for science, math, engineering, and data analysis. It's available for Linux, Windows, and macOS. The same package, but without all of those extensions (you can selectively install subsets of them with `conda`), is also available, and is known as Miniconda (*http://conda.pydata.org/miniconda.html*).

macOS

Apple's macOS comes with v2 (text-mode only), as of this writing. Nevertheless, we recommend you install the latest version and enhancements by following the instructions and links on the Python site under Downloads (*https://www.python.org/downloads/*); due to Apple's release cycles, the Python version included with your version of macOS may be out of date or incomplete. Python's latest version installs in addition to, not instead of, Apple's supplied one; Apple uses its own version of Python and proprietary extensions to implement some of the software it distributes as a part of macOS, so it's unwise to risk disturbing that version in any way.

The popular third-party macOS open source package manager Homebrew (*http://brew.sh/*) offers, among many other packages, excellent versions of Python (*https://github.com/Homebrew/brew/blob/master/docs/Homebrew-and-Python.md*), both v2 and v3. Beware, though, that usually only one release of each is available.

Installing Python from Source Code

To install CPython from source code, you need a platform with an ISO-compliant C compiler and tools such as `make`. On Windows, the normal way to build Python is with Visual Studio (ideally both VS2008 *and* VS2010 for v2, or VS 2015 for v3).

To download Python source code, visit the Python site (*https://www.python.org/*), click Downloads, then pick v2 or v3. For more options, hover on Downloads, and use the menu that shows.

The *.tgz* file extension under the link labeled "Gzipped source tarball" is equivalent to *.tar.gz* (i.e., a *tar* archive of files, compressed by the powerful and popular `gzip` compressor). Alternatively, use the link labeled "XZ compressed source tarball" to get a version with an extension of *.tar.xz* instead of *.tgz*, compressed with the even more powerful *xz* compressor, if you have tools that can deal with XZ compression.

Microsoft Windows

On Windows, installing Python from source code can be a chore unless you are already familiar with Visual Studio and are used to working in the text-oriented windows known as the command prompt.

If the following instructions give you any trouble, stick with "Installing Python from Binaries" on page 19. It's best to do a separate installation from binaries anyway, even if you also install from source. If you notice anything strange while using the version you installed from source, double-check with the installation from binaries. If the strangeness goes away, it must be due to some quirk in your installation from source, so you know you must double-check the latter.

In the following sections, for clarity, we assume you have made a new folder called *%USERPROFILE%\py*, (e.g., *c:\users\tim\py*). Open this folder by typing, for example, `%USERPROFILE%` in the address bar of a Windows Explorer window and going from there. Download the source *tgz* file—for example, *Python-3.5.2.tgz* (or other Python version of your choice) to that folder. Of course, name and place the folder as it best suits you: our name choice is just for expository purposes.

Intro to Python

Uncompressing and unpacking the Python source code

You can uncompress and unpack a *.tgz* or *.tar.xz* file, for example, with the free program 7-Zip (*http://www.7-zip.org/*). Download and install 7-Zip from the download page (*http://www.7-zip.org/download.html*), and run it on the sources' *tgz* file (e.g., *c:\users\tim\py\Python-3.5.2.tgz)* you downloaded. (The *tgz* file may have downloaded to *%USERPROFILE%\downloads*, in which case you need to move it to your *\py* folder before unpacking it with 7-Zip.) You now have a folder *%USERPROFILE%\py \Python-3.5.2* (or other version originally downloaded), the root of a tree that contains the entire standard Python distribution in source form.

Building the Python source code

Open the text file *%USERPROFILE%\py\Python-3.5.2\PCBuild\readme.txt* (or whichever version of Python you downloaded) with the text editor of your choice, and follow the detailed instructions found there.

Unix-Like Platforms

On Unix-like platforms, installing Python from source code is generally simple. In the following sections, for clarity, we assume you have created a new directory named *~/Py* and downloaded the sources' *tgz* file—for example, *Python-3.5.2.tgz* (or other Python version of your choice)—to that directory. Of course, name and place the directory as it best suits you: our name choice is just for expository purposes.

Uncompressing and unpacking the Python source code

You can uncompress and unpack a *.tgz* or *.tar.xz* file with the popular GNU version of *tar*. Just type the following at a shell prompt:

```
$ cd ~/Py
$ tar xzf Python-3.5.2.tgz
```

You now have a directory *~/Py/Python-3.5.2*, the root of a tree that contains the entire standard Python distribution in source form.

Configuring, building, and testing

Detailed notes are in *~/Py/Python-3.5.2/README* under the heading "Build instructions," and we recommend studying those notes. In the simplest case, however, all you need may be to give the following commands at a shell prompt:

```
$ cd ~/Py/Python-3.5.2
$ ./configure
    [configure writes much information - snipped here]
$ make
    [make takes quite a while, and emits much information]
```

If you run **make** without first running **./configure**, **make** implicitly runs **./configure**. When **make** finishes, check that the Python you have just built works as expected:

```
$ make test
    [takes quite a while, emits much information]
```

Usually, **make test** confirms that your build is working, but also informs you that some tests have been skipped because optional modules were missing.

Some of the modules are platform-specific (e.g., some may work only on machines running SGI's ancient Irix operating system), so don't worry about them. However, other modules are skipped because they depend on other open source packages that are not installed on your machine. For example, module `_tkinter`—needed to run the Tkinter GUI package and the IDLE integrated development environment, which come with Python—can be built only if **./configure** can find an installation of Tcl/Tk 8.0 or later on your machine. See *~/Py/Python-3.5.2/README* for more details and specific caveats about different Unix and Unix-like platforms.

Building from source code lets you tweak your configuration in several ways. For example, you can build Python in a special way that helps you track down memory leaks when you develop C-coded Python extensions, covered in "Building and Installing C-Coded Python Extensions" on page 647. **./configure --help** is a good source of information about the configuration options you can use.

Installing after the build

By default, **./configure** prepares Python for installation in */usr/local/bin* and */usr/local/lib*. You can change these settings by running **./configure** with option **--prefix** before running **make**. For example, if you want a private installation of Python in subdirectory *py35* of your home directory, run:

```
$ cd ~/Py/Python-3.5.2
$ ./configure --prefix=~/py35
```

and continue with **make** as in the previous section. Once you're done building and testing Python, to perform the actual installation of all files, run:

```
$ make install
```

The user running **make install** must have write permissions on the target directories. Depending on your choice of target directories, and permissions on those directories, you may need to **su** to *root*, *bin*, or some other user when you run **make install**. A common idiom for this purpose is **sudo make install**: if **sudo** prompts for a password, enter your current user's password, not root's. An alternative, and recommended, approach is to install into a virtual environment, as covered in "Python Environments" on page 188.

Intro to Python

Installing Jython

To download Jython, visit the Jython homepage (*http://www.jython.org*) and follow the link labeled *Download*. The latest version, at the time of this writing, is Jython 2.7.0, which supports Python 2.7 and comes as two executable JARs: one for just running Jython and one for embedding it in Java applications. Perform the installation by following the installation instructions (*https://wiki.python.org/jython/InstallationInstructions*).

Installing IronPython

To install IronPython, you need to have a current Common Language Runtime (CLR, AKA .NET) implementation installed on your machine. Both Mono (*http://www.mono-project.com*) and the Microsoft .NET Framework work fine with IronPython. To download IronPython, visit the IronPython homepage (*http://ironpython.net*), and click the arrow-shaped icon labeled *Download IronPython 2.7*; this gives you an executable installer—run it to install IronPython.

Installing PyPy

To install PyPy, download (*http://pypy.org/download.html*) your chosen version of PyPy's sources (the latest version, at the time of this writing, is PyPy 5.6.0, but don't let its numbering confuse you—it fully supports Python 2.7, which we call v2 in this book!), then follow the instructions (*http://pypy.org/download.html#building-from-source*) if you want to build PyPy from sources. Alternatively, download a binary installer for your platform (if supported), uncompress it from its *.zip* or *.tar.bz2* format, and then run the resulting executable file.

2
The Python Interpreter

To develop software systems in Python, you write text files that contain Python source code and documentation. You can use any text editor, including those in Integrated Development Environments (IDEs). You then process the source files with the Python compiler and interpreter. You can do this directly, or within an IDE, or via another program that embeds Python. The Python interpreter also lets you execute Python code interactively, as do IDEs.

The python Program

The Python interpreter program is run as **`python`** (it's named *python.exe* on Windows). **`python`** includes both the interpreter itself and the Python compiler, which is implicitly invoked, as and if needed, on imported modules. Depending on your system, the program may typically have to be in a directory listed in your `PATH` environment variable. Alternatively, as with any other program, you can give a complete pathname to it at a command (shell) prompt, or in the shell script (or shortcut target, etc.) that runs it.[1]

PEP 397

On Windows, since PEP 397 (*https://www.python.org/dev/peps/pep-0397/*), *py.exe*, the launcher, installs in the system area of Windows and is therefore guaranteed—barring deliberate further manipulation on your part—to be always on the PATH.

1 This may involve using quotes if the pathname contains spaces—again, this depends on your operating system.

On Windows, press the Windows key and start typing **python**: "Python 3.5 (command-line)" (if you have installed v3) appears, along with other choices, such as "IDLE (Python GUI)." Alternatively, if you have the *py.exe* launcher installed (that's automatic with v3; with v2, you need to install the standalone launcher (*https://bitbucket.org/vinay.sajip/pylauncher/downloads*)), at a command prompt, typing **py** launches Python. If you have more than one version of Python installed, then the most recent v2 gets run, unless you override that default via a config file or a command-line parameter (e.g., **py -3**).

Environment Variables

Besides PATH, other environment variables affect the **python** program. Some environment variables have the same effects as options passed to **python** on the command line, as documented in the next section. Several environment variables provide settings not available via command-line options. The following list covers only the basics of a few frequently used ones; for all details, see the online docs (*https://docs.python.org/3/using/cmdline.html#environment-variables*).

PYTHONHOME
: The Python installation directory. A *lib* subdirectory, containing the standard Python library, must exist under this directory. On Unix-like systems, the standard library modules should be in *lib/python-2.7* for Python 2.7, *lib/python-3.5* for Python 3.5, and so on. If not set, the Python executable uses some heuristics to locate the installation directory.

PYTHONPATH
: A list of directories, separated by colons on Unix-like systems, and by semicolons on Windows. Python can import modules from these directories. This list extends the initial value for Python's sys.path variable. We cover modules, importing, and sys.path in Chapter 6.

PYTHONSTARTUP
: The name of a Python source file to run each time an interactive interpreter session starts. No such file runs if this variable is not set or if it is set to the path of a file that is not found. The PYTHONSTARTUP file does not run when you run a Python script; it runs only when you start an interactive session.

How to set and examine environment variables depends on your operating system. In Unix, use shell commands, often within persistent startup shell scripts. On Windows, press the Windows key and start typing **environment var** and a couple of shortcuts appear, one for user env vars, the other for system ones. On a Mac, you can work like in other Unix-like systems, but there are other options, including a MacPython-specific IDE. For more information about Python on the Mac, see Using Python on a Mac (v2) (*https://docs.python.org/2/using/mac.html*) or Using Python on a Mac (v3) (*https://docs.python.org/3.5/using/mac.html*).

Command-Line Syntax and Options

The Python interpreter command-line syntax can be summarized as follows:

```
[path]python {options} [-c command | -m module | file | -] {args}
```

Here, brackets ([]) enclose what's optional, braces ({}) enclose items of which zero or more may be present, and vertical bars (|) mean a choice among alternatives. Python consistently uses a slash (/) for file paths, as in Unix.

Running a Python script at a command line can be as simple as:

```
$ python hello.py
Hello World
```

If the script is not in the current working directory, provide the path to the script:

```
$ python ./hello/hello.py
Hello World
```

The filename of the script can be any absolute or relative file path, and need not have any specific extension (though it is conventional to use a *.py* extension). Each operating system has its own ways to make the Python scripts themselves executable, but we do not cover those details here.

Options are case-sensitive short strings, starting with a hyphen, that ask **python** for a nondefault behavior. **python** accepts only options that start with a hyphen (-), not with a slash. We list the most frequently used options in Table 2-1. Each option's description gives the environment variable (if any) that, when set, requests the same behavior. Many options have longer versions beginning with two hyphens, as documented in the help available from **python -h.** For all details, see the online docs (*https://docs.python.org/3/using/cmdline.html#command-line*).

Table 2-1. Python frequently used command-line options

Option	Meaning (and equivalent environment variable, if any)
-B	Don't save compiled bytecode files to disk (PYTHONDONTWRITEBYTECODE)
-c	Specifies Python statements as part of the command line
-E	Ignores all environment variables
-h	Prints a full list of options and summary help, then terminates
-i	Runs an interactive session after the file or command runs (PYTHONINSPECT)
-m	Specifies a Python module or package to run as the main script

Option	Meaning (and equivalent environment variable, if any)
`-O`	Optimizes generated bytecode (`PYTHONOPTIMIZE`)—note that this is an uppercase letter `O`, not the digit `0`
`-OO`	Like `-O`, but also removes documentation strings from the bytecode
`-Q arg`	Controls the behavior of division operator `/` on integers (v2 only)
`-S`	Omits the implicit `import site` on startup (covered in "The site and sitecustomize Modules" on page 381)
`-t`	Issues warnings about inconsistent tab usage (`-tt` issues errors)
`-u`	Uses unbuffered binary files for standard output and standard error (`PYTHONUNBUFFERED`)
`-v`	Verbosely traces module import and cleanup actions (`PYTHONVERBOSE`)
`-V`	Prints the Python version number, then terminates
`-W arg`	Adds an entry to the warnings filter (covered in "Filters" on page 477)
`-x`	Excludes (skips) the first line of the main script's source

Use `-i` when you want to get an interactive session immediately after running some script, with top-level variables still intact and available for inspection. You do not need `-i` for normal interactive sessions, although it does no harm. `-t` and `-tt` ensure that you use tabs and spaces consistently in Python sources (see "Lines and Indentation" on page 37 for more information about whitespace usage in Python).

`-O` and `-OO` yield small savings of time and space in bytecode generated for modules you import, turning `assert` statements into no-operations, as covered in "The assert Statement" on page 171. `-OO` also discards documentation strings.[2] In v2, only, `-Q` determines the behavior of division operator `/` when used between two integer operands (we cover division in "Division" on page 60). `-W` adds an entry to the warnings filter (we cover warnings in "The warnings Module" on page 476).

In v2, `-u` forces binary mode for standard input, output, and error (not for other file objects). Some platforms, mostly Windows, distinguish binary and text modes. You need binary mode to emit binary data to standard output. `-u` also ensures that such output happens immediately, without buffering. You need this when delays due to buffering could cause problems, as in some Unix pipelines. In v3, `-u` forces unbuf-

2 This may affect code that tries to introspect docstrings for semantically meaningful purposes; we suggest you avoid writing such code.

fered output for standard output's and error's binary layer (available from their `.buffer` attribute), not their text layer.

After the options, if any, comes an indication of which Python script to run. A file path is that of a Python source or bytecode file to run, complete with file extension, if any. On any platform, you may use a slash (/) as the separator between components in this path. On Windows only, you may alternatively use a backslash (\). Instead of a file path, you can use **`-c command`** to execute a Python code string **`command`**. **`command`** normally contains spaces, so you need quotes around it to satisfy your operating system's shell or command-line processor. Some shells (e.g., **`bash`**) let you enter multiple lines as a single argument so that **`command`** can be a series of Python statements. Other shells (e.g., Windows shells) limit you to a single line; **`command`** can then be one or more simple statements separated by semicolons (;), as discussed in "Statements" on page 42.

Another way to specify which Python script to run is **`-m module`**. This option tells Python to load and run a module named **`module`** (or the *__main__.py* member of a package or ZIP file named **`module`**) from some directory that is part of Python's `sys.path`; this is useful with several modules from Python's standard library. For example, as covered in "The timeit module" on page 489, **`-m timeit`** is often the best way to perform micro-benchmarking of Python statements and expressions.

A hyphen, or the lack of any token in this position, tells the interpreter to read program source from standard input—normally, an interactive session. You need an explicit hyphen only if arguments follow. **`args`** are arbitrary strings; the Python application being run can access these strings as items of the list `sys.argv`.

For example, on a standard Windows installation, you can enter the following at a command prompt to have Python print the current date and time:

```
C:\> py -c "import time; print(time.asctime())"
```

On Cygwin, Linux, OpenBSD, macOS, and other Unix-like systems, with a default installation of Python from sources, enter the following at a shell prompt to start an interactive session with verbose tracing of module import and cleanup:

```
$ /usr/local/bin/python -v
```

You can start the command with just **`python`** (you do not have to specify the full path to the Python executable) if the directory of the Python executable is in your PATH environment variable. (If you have multiple versions of Python installed, you can specify the version, with, for example, **`python2`**, **`python2.7`**, **`python3`**, or **`python3.5`**, as appropriate; in this case, the version used if you just say **`python`** is generally the one you installed most recently.)

Interactive Sessions

When you run **`python`** without a script argument, Python starts an interactive session and prompts you to enter Python statements or expressions. Interactive sessions are useful to explore, to check things out, and to use Python as a powerful, extensible interactive calculator. (IPython, mentioned in "IPython" on page 9, is like "Python on steroids" specifically for interactive-session usage.)

When you enter a complete statement, Python executes it. When you enter a complete expression, Python evaluates it. If the expression has a result, Python outputs a string representing the result and also assigns the result to the variable named _ (a single underscore) so that you can immediately use that result in another expression. The prompt string is `>>>` when Python expects a statement or expression and `...` when a statement or expression has been started but not completed. In particular, Python prompts you with `...` when you have opened a parenthesis on a previous line and have not closed it yet.

You terminate an interactive session with an end-of-file on standard input (Ctrl-Z on Windows, Ctrl-D on Unix-like systems). The statement `raise SystemExit` also ends the session, as does a call to `sys.exit()`, either interactively or in code being run (we cover `SystemExit` and `raise` in Chapter 5).

Line-editing and history facilities depend in part on how Python was built: if the optional `readline` module was included, the features of the GNU readline library are available. Windows has a simple but usable history facility for interactive text-mode programs like *python*. You can use other line-editing and history facilities by installing pyreadline (*https://pypi.python.org/pypi/pyreadline/2.0*) for Windows, or pyrepl (*https://pypi.python.org/pypi/pyrepl/0.8.4*) for Unix.

In addition to the built-in Python interactive environment, and those offered as part of richer development environments covered in the next section, you can freely download other alternative, powerful interactive environments. The most popular one is IPython (*http://ipython.org/*), covered in "IPython" on page 9, which offers a dazzling wealth of features. A simpler, lighter-weight, but still quite handy up-and-coming alternative read-line interpreter is bpython (*https://bpython-interpreter.org/*).

Python Development Environments

The Python interpreter's built-in interactive mode is the simplest development environment for Python. It is a bit primitive, but it is lightweight, has a small footprint, and starts fast. Together with an appropriate text editor (as discussed in "Free Text Editors with Python Support" on page 31), and line-editing and history facilities, the interactive interpreter (or, alternatively, the much more powerful IPython/Jupyter command-line interpreter) offers a usable and popular development environment. However, there are a number of other development environments that you can also use.

IDLE

Python's Integrated DeveLopment Environment (IDLE) comes with the standard Python distribution on most platforms. IDLE is a cross-platform, 100 percent pure Python application based on the Tkinter GUI toolkit. IDLE offers a Python shell similar to interactive Python interpreter sessions but richer in functionality. It also includes a text editor optimized to edit Python source code, an integrated interactive debugger, and several specialized browsers/viewers.

For even more functionality in IDLE, you can download and install IdleX (*http://idlex.sourceforge.net*), a substantial collection of free third-party extensions to it.

To install and use IDLE in macOS, follow these specific instructions (*https://www.python.org/download/mac/tcltk/*).

Other Python IDEs

IDLE is mature, stable, easy to use, fairly rich in functionality, and extensible. There are, however, many other IDEs—cross-platform and platform-specific, free and commercial (including commercial IDEs with free offerings, especially if you're developing open source software yourself), standalone and add-ons to other IDEs.

Some of these IDEs sport features such as static analysis, GUI builders, debuggers, and so on. Python's IDE wiki page (*https://wiki.python.org/moin/IntegratedDevelopmentEnvironments*) lists over 30 of them, and points to over a dozen external pages with reviews and comparisons. If you're an IDE collector, happy hunting!

We can't do justice to even a tiny subset of those IDEs, but it's worth singling out the popular cross-platform, cross-language modular IDE Eclipse (*http://www.eclipse.org/*): the free third-party plug-in PyDev (*http://www.pydev.org/*) for Eclipse has excellent Python support. Steve is a long-time user of Wingware IDE (*https://wingware.com/*) by Archaeopteryx, the most venerable Python-specific IDE. The most popular third-party Python IDE today may be PyCharm (*https://www.jetbrains.com/pycharm/*).

If you use Visual Studio, check out PTVS (*https://github.com/Microsoft/PTVS/wiki/PTVS-Installation*), an open source plug-in that's particularly good at allowing mixed-language debugging in Python and C as and when needed.

Free Text Editors with Python Support

You can edit Python source code with any text editor, even simplistic ones such as Notepad on Windows or *ed* on Linux. Powerful free editors support Python with extra features such as syntax-based colorization and automatic indentation. Cross-platform editors let you work in uniform ways on different platforms. Good programmers' text editors also let you run, from within the editor, tools of your choice on the source code you're editing. An up-to-date list of editors for Python can be found on the Python wiki (*https://wiki.python.org/moin/PythonEditors*), which currently lists many dozens of them.

The very best for sheer editing power is probably still classic Emacs (*https://www.gnu.org/software/emacs/*) (see the Python wiki (*https://wiki.python.org/moin/EmacsEditor*) for many Python-specific add-ons). However, Emacs is not easy to learn, nor is it lightweight. Alex's personal favorite is another classic, vim (*http://www.vim.org/*), Bram Moolenaar's modern, improved version of the traditional

Unix editor *vi*, perhaps not *quite* as powerful as Emacs, but still well worth considering—fast, lightweight, Python-programmable, runs everywhere in both text-mode and GUI versions. See the Python wiki (*https://wiki.python.org/moin/Vim*) for Python-specific tips and add-ons. Steve and Anna also use *vim*. When it's available, Steve also uses the commercial editor *Sublime Text 2*, with good syntax coloring and enough integration to run your programs from inside the editor.

Tools for Checking Python Programs

The Python compiler does not check programs and modules thoroughly: the compiler checks only the code's syntax. If you want more thorough checking of your Python code, you may download and install third-party tools for the purpose. Pyflakes (*https://pypi.python.org/pypi/pyflakes*) is a very fast, lightweight checker: it's not thorough, but does not import the modules it's checking, which makes using it safer. At the other end of the spectrum, PyLint (*https://www.pylint.org/*) is very powerful and highly configurable. PyLint is not lightweight, but repays that by being able to check many style details in a highly configurable way based on customizable configuration files.

Running Python Programs

Whatever tools you use to produce your Python application, you can see your application as a set of Python source files, which are normal text files. A *script* is a file that you can run directly. A *module* is a file that you can import (as covered in Chapter 6) to provide functionality to other files or to interactive sessions. A Python file can be *both* a module (exposing functionality when imported) *and* a script (suitable for being run directly). A useful and widespread convention is that Python files that are primarily intended to be imported as modules, when run directly, should execute some simple self-test operations, as covered in "Testing" on page 456.

The Python interpreter automatically compiles Python source files as needed. Python source files normally have the extension *.py*. In v2, Python saves the compiled bytecode file for each module in the same directory as the module's source, with the same basename and extension *.pyc* (or *.pyo* when you run Python with option `-O`). In v3, Python saves the compiled bytecode in subdirectory *__pycache__* of the directory containing the module's source, with a version-specific extension, and annotated to denote optimization level.

Run Python with option `-B` to avoid saving compiled bytecode to disk, which can be handy when you import modules from a read-only disk. Also, Python does not save the compiled bytecode form of a script when you run the script directly; rather, Python recompiles the script each time you run it. Python saves bytecode files only for modules you import. It automatically rebuilds each module's bytecode file whenever necessary—for example, when you edit the module's source. Eventually, for deployment, you may package Python modules using tools covered in Chapter 25.

You can run Python code interactively with the Python interpreter or an IDE. Normally, however, you initiate execution by running a top-level script. To run a script, give its path as an argument to **python**, as covered earlier in "The python Program" on page 25. Depending on your operating system, you can invoke **python** directly from a shell script or command file. On Unix-like systems, you can make a Python script directly executable by setting the file's permission bits `x` and `r` and beginning the script with a so-called *shebang* line, which is a first line such as:

```
#!/usr/bin/env python
```

or some other line starting with `#!` followed by a path to the *python* interpreter program, in which case you can optionally add a single word of options, for example:

```
#!/usr/bin/python -O
```

On Windows, you can now use the same style `#!` line, in accordance with PEP 397 (*https://www.python.org/dev/peps/pep-0397/*), to specify a particular version of Python, so your scripts can be cross-platform between Unix-like and Windows systems. You can also run Python scripts with the usual Windows mechanisms, such as double-clicking their icons. When you run a Python script by double-clicking the script's icon, Windows automatically closes the text-mode console associated with the script as soon as the script terminates. If you want the console to linger (to allow the user to read the script's output on the screen), ensure the script doesn't terminate too soon. For example, use the following (in v3) as the script's last statement:

```
input('Press Enter to terminate')
```

(use `raw_input` in v2). This is not necessary when you run the script from a command prompt.

On Windows, you can also use extension *.pyw* and interpreter program *pythonw.exe* instead of *.py* and *python.exe*. The *w* variants run Python without a text-mode console, and thus without standard input and output. These variants are useful for scripts that rely on GUIs or run invisibly in the background. Use them only when a program is fully debugged, to keep standard output and error available for information, warnings, and error messages during development. On a Mac, you need to use interpreter program **pythonw**, rather than **python**, when you want to run a script that needs to access any GUI toolkit, rather than just text-mode interaction.

Applications coded in other languages may embed Python, controlling the execution of Python for their own purposes. We examine this briefly in "Embedding Python" on page 687.

The jython Interpreter

The *jython* interpreter built during installation (see "Installing Jython" on page 23) is run similarly to the *python* program:

```
[path]jython {options} [ -j jar | -c command | file | - ] {args}
```

-j *jar* tells Jython that the main script to run is *__run__.py* in the *.jar* file. Options **-i**, **-S**, and **-v** are the same as for **python**. **--help** is like **python**'s **-h**, and **--version** is like **python**'s **-V**. Instead of environment variables, *jython* uses a text file named *registry* in the installation directory to record properties with structured names. Property `python.path`, for example, is the Jython equivalent of Python's environment variable `PYTHONPATH`. You can also set properties with **`jython`** command-line options in the form **`-D`** *`name=value`*.

See the Jython homepage (*http://www.jython.org*) for complete, up-to-date information.

The IronPython Interpreter

IronPython may be run similarly to the *python* program:

```
[path]ipy {options} [-c command | file | - ] {args}
```

See the IronPython homepage (*http://ironpython.net*)for complete, up-to-date information.

The PyPy Interpreter

PyPy may be run similarly to the *python* program:

```
[path]pypy {options} [-c command | file | - ] {args}
```

See the PyPy homepage (*http://pypy.org/*) for complete, up-to-date information.

II

Core Python Language and Built-ins

3
The Python Language

This chapter is a guide to the Python language. To learn Python from scratch, we suggest you start with the appropriate links from *https://www.python.org/about/gettingstarted/*, depending on whether you're a programming beginner or already have some programming experience. If you already know other programming languages well, and just want to learn specifics about Python, this chapter is for you. However, we're not trying to teach Python: we cover a lot of ground at a pretty fast pace. We focus on the rules, and only secondarily point out best practices and style; as your Python style guide, use PEP 8 (*https://www.python.org/dev/peps/pep-0008/*) (optionally augmented by extra guidelines such as The Hitchhiker's Guide's (*http://docs.python-guide.org/en/latest/writing/style/*), CKAN's (*http://docs.ckan.org/en/latest/contributing/python.html*), and/or Google's (*https://google.github.io/styleguide/pyguide.html*)).

Lexical Structure

The *lexical structure* of a programming language is the set of basic rules that govern how you write programs in that language. It is the lowest-level syntax of the language, specifying such things as what variable names look like and how to denote comments. Each Python source file, like any other text file, is a sequence of characters. You can also usefully consider it a sequence of lines, tokens, or statements. These different lexical views complement each other. Python is very particular about program layout, especially regarding lines and indentation: pay attention to this information if you are coming to Python from another language.

Lines and Indentation

A Python program is a sequence of *logical lines*, each made up of one or more *physical lines*. Each physical line may end with a comment. A hash sign # that is not inside a string literal starts a comment. All characters after the #, up to but excluding the line end, are the comment: Python ignores them. A line containing only whitespace, possibly with a comment, is a *blank line*: Python ignores it.[1]

In Python, the end of a physical line marks the end of most statements. Unlike in other languages, you don't normally terminate Python statements with a delimiter, such as a semicolon (`;`). When a statement is too long to fit on a physical line, you can join two adjacent physical lines into a logical line by ensuring that the first physical line has no comment and ends with a backslash (`\`). However, Python also automatically joins adjacent physical lines into one logical line if an open parenthesis (`(`), bracket (`[`), or brace (`{`) has not yet been closed: take advantage of this mechanism to produce more readable code than you'd get with backslashes at line ends. Triple-quoted string literals can also span physical lines. Physical lines after the first one in a logical line are known as *continuation lines*. Indentation issues apply to the first physical line of each logical line, not to continuation lines.

Python uses indentation to express the block structure of a program. Unlike other languages, Python does not use braces, or other begin/end delimiters, around blocks of statements; indentation is the only way to denote blocks. Each logical line in a Python program is *indented* by the whitespace on its left. A *block* is a contiguous sequence of logical lines, all indented by the same amount; a logical line with less indentation ends the block. All statements in a block must have the same indentation, as must all clauses in a compound statement. The first statement in a source file must have no indentation (i.e., must not begin with any whitespace). Statements that you type at the interactive interpreter primary prompt >>> (covered in "Interactive Sessions" on page 29) must also have no indentation.

v2 logically replaces each tab by up to eight spaces, so that the next character after the tab falls into logical column 9, 17, 25, and so on. Standard Python style is to use four spaces (*never* tabs) per indentation level.

Don't mix spaces and tabs for indentation, since different tools (e.g., editors, email systems, printers) treat tabs differently. The **`-t`** and **`-tt`** options to the v2 Python interpreter (covered in "Command-Line Syntax and Options" on page 27) ensure against inconsistent tab and space usage in Python source code. In v3, Python does not allow mixing tabs and spaces for indentation.

Use spaces, not tabs

We recommend you configure your favorite editor to expand tabs to four spaces, so that all Python source code you write contains just spaces, not tabs. This way, all tools, including Python itself, are consistent in handling indentation in your Python source files. Optimal Python style is to indent blocks by exactly four spaces, and use no tabs.

1 In an interactive interpreter session, you must enter an empty physical line (without any whitespace or comment) to terminate a multiline statement.

Character Sets

A v3 source file can use any Unicode character, encoded as UTF-8. (Characters with codes between 0 and 127, AKA *ASCII characters*, encode in UTF-8 into the respective single bytes, so an ASCII text file is a fine v3 Python source file, too.)

A v2 source file is usually made up of characters from the ASCII set (character codes between 0 and 127).

In both v2 and v3, you may choose to tell Python that a certain source file is written in a different encoding. In this case, Python uses that encoding to read the file (in v2, you can use non-ASCII characters only in comments and string literals).

To let Python know that a source file is written with a nonstandard encoding, start your source file with a comment whose form must be, for example:

```
# coding: iso-8859-1
```

After `coding:`, write the name of a codec known to Python and ASCII-compatible, such as `utf-8` or `iso-8859-1`. Note that this *coding directive* comment (also known as an *encoding declaration*) is taken as such only if it is at the start of a source file (possibly after the "shebang line," covered in "Running Python Programs" on page 32). The *only* effect of a coding directive in v2 is to let you use non-ASCII characters in string literals and comments. Best practice is to use `utf-8` for all of your text files, including Python source files.

The Python Language

Tokens

Python breaks each logical line into a sequence of elementary lexical components known as *tokens*. Each token corresponds to a substring of the logical line. The normal token types are *identifiers*, *keywords*, *operators*, *delimiters*, and *literals*, which we cover in the following sections. You may freely use whitespace between tokens to separate them. Some whitespace separation is necessary between logically adjacent identifiers or keywords; otherwise, Python would parse them as a single, longer identifier. For example, `ifx` is a single identifier; to write the keyword `if` followed by the identifier `x`, you need to insert some whitespace (e.g., `if x`).

Identifiers

An *identifier* is a name used to specify a variable, function, class, module, or other object. An identifier starts with a letter (in v2, `A` to `Z` or `a` to `z`; in v3, other characters that Unicode classifies as letters are also allowed) or an underscore (_), followed by zero or more letters, underscores, and digits (in v2, `0` to `9`; in v3, other characters that Unicode classifies as digits or combining marks are also allowed). See this website (*https://www.dcl.hpi.uni-potsdam.de/home/loewis/table-3131.html*) for a table identifying which Unicode characters can start or continue a v3 identifier. Case is significant: lowercase and uppercase letters are distinct. Punctuation characters such as `@`, `$`, and `!` are not allowed in identifiers.

Normal Python style is to start class names with an uppercase letter, and other identifiers with a lowercase letter. Starting an identifier with a single leading underscore indicates by convention that the identifier is meant to be private. Starting an identifier with two leading underscores indicates a *strongly private* identifier; if the identifier also ends with two trailing underscores, however, this means that the identifier is a language-defined special name.

Single underscore _ in the interactive interpreter

The identifier _ (a single underscore) is special in interactive interpreter sessions: the interpreter binds _ to the result of the last expression statement it has evaluated interactively, if any.

Keywords

Python has keywords (31 of them in v2; 33 in v3), which are identifiers that Python reserves for special syntactic uses. Keywords contain lowercase letters only. You cannot use keywords as regular identifiers (thus, they're sometimes known as "reserved words"). Some keywords begin simple statements or clauses of compound statements, while other keywords are operators. We cover all the keywords in detail in this book, either in this chapter or in Chapters 4, 5, and 6. The keywords in v2 are:

`and`	`continue`	`except`	`global`	`lambda`	`raise`	`yield`
`as`	`def`	`exec`	`if`	`not`	`return`	
`assert`	`del`	`finally`	`import`	`or`	`try`	
`break`	`elif`	`for`	`in`	`pass`	`while`	
`class`	`else`	`from`	`is`	`print`	`with`	

In v3, `exec` and `print` are no longer keywords: they were statements in v2, but they're now functions in v3. (To use the `print` function in v2, start your source file with `from __future__ import print_function`, as mentioned in "Version Conventions" on page xiii.) `False`, `None`, `True`, and `nonlocal` are new, additional keywords in v3 (out of them, `False`, `None`, and `True` were already built-in constants in v2, but they were not technically keywords). Special tokens `async` and `await`, covered in Chapter 18, are not currently keywords, but they're scheduled to become keywords in Python 3.7.

Operators

Python uses nonalphanumeric characters and character combinations as operators. Python recognizes the following operators, which are covered in detail in "Expressions and Operators" on page 57:

```
+  -  *  /  %   **  //  <<  >>  &

|  ^  ~  <  <=  >   >=  <>  !=  ==
```

In v3 only, you can also use `@` as an operator (in matrix multiplication, covered in Chapter 15), although the character is technically a delimiter.

Delimiters

Python uses the following characters and combinations as delimiters in expressions, list, dictionary, and set literals, and various statements, among other purposes:


```
(   )   [   ]   {   }

,   :   .   `   =   ;   @

+=  -=  *=  /=   //=  %=

&=  |=  ^=  >>=  <<=  **=
```

The period (`.`) can also appear in floating-point literals (e.g., `2.3`) and imaginary literals (e.g., `2.3j`). The last two rows are the augmented assignment operators, which are delimiters, but also perform operations. We discuss the syntax for the various delimiters when we introduce the objects or statements using them.

The following characters have special meanings as part of other tokens:

```
'  "  #  \
```

' and " surround string literals. # outside of a string starts a comment. \ at the end of a physical line joins the following physical line into one logical line; \ is also an escape character in strings. The characters `$` and ?, all control characters[2] except whitespace, and, in v2, all characters with ISO codes above 126 (i.e., non-ASCII characters, such as accented letters) can never be part of the text of a Python program, except in comments or string literals. (To use non-ASCII characters in comments or string literals in v2, you must start your Python source file with a *coding directive* as covered in "Character Sets" on page 39.)

2 Control characters are nonprinting characters such as \t (tab) and \n (newline), both of which count as whitespace; and \a (alarm, AKA beep) and \b (backspace), which are not whitespace.

Literals

A *literal* is the direct denotation in a program of a data value (a number, string, or container). The following are number and string literals in Python:

```
42                          # Integer literal
3.14                        # Floating-point literal
1.0j                        # Imaginary literal
'hello'                     # String literal
"world"                     # Another string literal
"""Good
night"""                    # Triple-quoted string literal
```

Combining number and string literals with the appropriate delimiters, you can build literals that directly denote data values of container types:

```
[42, 3.14, 'hello']     # List
[]                      # Empty list
100, 200, 300           # Tuple
()                      # Empty tuple
{'x':42, 'y':3.14}      # Dictionary
{}                      # Empty dictionary
{1, 2, 4, 8, 'string'} # Set
# There is no literal to denote an empty set; use set() instead
```

We cover the syntax for literals in detail in "Data Types" on page 43, when we discuss the various data types Python supports.

Statements

You can look at a Python source file as a sequence of simple and compound statements. Unlike some other languages, Python has no "declarations" or other top-level syntax elements: just statements.

Simple statements

A *simple statement* is one that contains no other statements. A simple statement lies entirely within a logical line. As in many other languages, you may place more than one simple statement on a single logical line, with a semicolon (`;`) as the separator. However, one statement per line is the usual and recommended Python style, and makes programs more readable.

Any *expression* can stand on its own as a simple statement (we discuss expressions in "Expressions and Operators" on page 57). When working interactively, the interpreter shows the result of an expression statement you enter at the prompt (>>>) and binds the result to a global variable named _ (underscore). Apart from interactive sessions, expression statements are useful only to call functions (and other *callables*) that have side effects (e.g., perform output, change global variables, or raise exceptions).

An *assignment* is a simple statement that assigns values to variables, as we discuss in "Assignment Statements" on page 53. An assignment in Python is a statement and can never be part of an expression.

Compound statements

A *compound statement* contains one or more other statements and controls their execution. A compound statement has one or more *clauses*, aligned at the same indentation. Each clause has a *header* starting with a keyword and ending with a colon (`:`), followed by a *body*, which is a sequence of one or more statements. When the body contains multiple statements, also known as a *block*, these statements are on separate logical lines after the header line, indented four spaces rightward. The block lexically ends when the indentation returns to that of the clause header (or further left from there, to the indentation of some enclosing compound statement). Alternatively, the body can be a single simple statement, following the `:` on the same logical line as the header. The body may also consist of several simple statements on the same line with semicolons between them, but, as we've already mentioned, this is not good Python style.

Data Types

The operation of a Python program hinges on the data it handles. Data values in Python are known as *objects*; each object, AKA *value*, has a *type*. An object's type determines which operations the object supports (in other words, which operations you can perform on the value). The type also determines the object's *attributes* and *items* (if any) and whether the object can be altered. An object that can be altered is known as a *mutable object*, while one that cannot be altered is an *immutable object*. We cover object attributes and items in "Object attributes and items" on page 53.

The built-in `type(obj)` accepts any object as its argument and returns the type object that is the type of *obj*. The built-in function `isinstance(obj, type)` returns `True` when object *obj* has type *type* (or any subclass thereof); otherwise, it returns `False`.

Python has built-in types for fundamental data types such as numbers, strings, tuples, lists, dictionaries, and sets, as covered in the following sections. You can also create user-defined types, known as *classes*, as discussed in "Classes and Instances" on page 102.

Numbers

The built-in numeric types in Python include integers (`int` and `long`, in v2; in v3, there's no distinction between kinds of integers), floating-point numbers, and complex numbers. The standard library also offers decimal floating-point numbers, covered in "The decimal Module" on page 444, and fractions, covered in "The fractions Module" on page 443. All numbers in Python are immutable objects; therefore, when you perform an operation on a number object, you produce a new number object. We cover operations on numbers, also known as arithmetic operations, in "Numeric Operations" on page 59.

Numeric literals do not include a sign: a leading + or -, if present, is a separate operator, as discussed in "Arithmetic Operations" on page 60.

Integer numbers

Integer literals can be decimal, binary, octal, or hexadecimal. A decimal literal is a sequence of digits in which the first digit is nonzero. A binary literal is `0b` followed by a sequence of binary digits (`0` or `1`). An octal literal, in v2 only, can be `0` followed by a sequence of octal digits (`0` to `7`). This syntax can be quite misleading for the reader, and we do *not* recommend it; rather, use `0o` followed by a sequence of octal digits, which works in both v2 and v3 and does not risk misleading the reader. A hexadecimal literal is `0x` followed by a sequence of hexadecimal digits (`0` to `9` and `A` to `F`, in either upper- or lowercase). For example:

```
1, 23, 3493                    # Decimal integer literals
0b010101, 0b110010             # Binary integer literals
0o1, 0o27, 0o6645              # Octal integer literals
0x1, 0x17, 0xDA5               # Hexadecimal integer literals
```

Integer literals have no defined upper bound (in v2 only, if greater than `sys.maxint`, integer literals are instances of built-in type `long`; v3 does not draw that distinction, but rather uses `int` as the type of all integers).

Floating-point numbers

A floating-point literal is a sequence of decimal digits that includes a decimal point (`.`), an exponent suffix (an `e` or `E`, optionally followed by `+` or `-`, followed by one or more digits), or both. The leading character of a floating-point literal cannot be `e` or `E`; it may be any digit or a period (`.`). For example:

```
0., 0.0, .0, 1., 1.0, 1e0, 1.e0, 1.0e0  # Floating-point literals
```

A Python floating-point value corresponds to a C `double` and shares its limits of range and precision, typically 53 bits of precision on modern platforms. (For the exact range and precision of floating-point values on the current platform, see `sys.float_info`: we do not cover that in this book—see the online docs (*https://docs.python.org/3.5/library/sys.html#sys.float_info*).)

Complex numbers

A complex number is made up of two floating-point values, one each for the real and imaginary parts. You can access the parts of a complex object `z` as read-only attributes `z.real` and `z.imag`. You can specify an imaginary literal as a floating-point or decimal literal followed by a `j` or `J`:

```
0j, 0.j, 0.0j, .0j, 1j, 1.j, 1.0j, 1e0j, 1.e0j, 1.0e0j
```

The j at the end of the literal indicates the square root of -1, as commonly used in electrical engineering (some other disciplines use i for this purpose, but Python has chosen j). There are no other complex literals. To denote any constant complex number, add or subtract a floating-point (or integer) literal and an imaginary one. For example, to denote the complex number that equals one, use expressions like 1+0j or 1.0+0.0j. Python performs the addition or subtraction at compile time.

New in 3.6: Underscores in numeric literals

To assist visual assessment of the magnitude of a number, from 3.6 onward numeric literals can include single underscore (_) characters between digits or after any base specifier. As this implies, not only decimal numeric constants can benefit from this new notational freedom:

```
>>> 100_000.000_0001, 0x_FF_FF, 0o7_777, 0b_1010_1010
(100000.0000001, 65535, 4095, 170)
```

The Python Language

Sequences

A *sequence* is an ordered container of items, indexed by integers. Python has built-in sequence types known as strings (bytes and Unicode), tuples, and lists. Library and extension modules provide other sequence types, and you can write yet others yourself (as discussed in "Sequences" on page 45). You can manipulate sequences in a variety of ways, as discussed in "Sequence Operations" on page 61.

Iterables

A Python concept that generalizes the idea of "sequence" is that of *iterables*, covered in "The for Statement" on page 74 and "Iterators" on page 76. All sequences are iterable: whenever we say you can use an iterable, you can in particular use a sequence (for example, a list).

Also, when we say that you can use an iterable, we mean, usually, a *bounded* iterable: an iterable that eventually stops yielding items. All sequences are bounded. Iterables, in general, can be unbounded, but if you try to use an unbounded iterable without special precautions, you could produce a program that never terminates, or one that exhausts all available memory.

Strings

A built-in string object (bytes or Unicode) is a sequence of characters used to store and represent text-based information (byte strings, also known as *byte objects*, store and represent arbitrary sequences of binary bytes). Strings in Python are *immutable*: when you perform an operation on strings, you always produce a new string object, rather than mutating an existing string. String objects provide many methods, as discussed in detail in "Methods of String and Bytes Objects" on page 233.

Different string types in v2 and v3

In v2, unadorned string literals denote *byte strings*; such literals denote *Unicode* (AKA *text*) strings in v3.

A string literal can be quoted or triple-quoted. A quoted string is a sequence of 0+ characters within matching quotes, single (') or double ("). For example:

```
'This is a literal string'
"This is another string"
```

The two different kinds of quotes function identically; having both lets you include one kind of quote inside of a string specified with the other kind, with no need to escape quote characters with the backslash character (\):

```
'I\'m a Python fanatic'          # a quote can be escaped
"I'm a Python fanatic"           # this way is more readable
```

Other things equal, using single quotes to denote string literals is better Python style. To have a string literal span multiple physical lines, you can use a \ as the last character of a line to indicate that the next line is a continuation:

```
'A not very long string \
that spans two lines'      # comment not allowed on previous line
```

To make the string contain two lines, you can embed a newline in the string:

```
'A not very long string\n\
that prints on two lines'  # comment not allowed on previous line
```

A better approach is to use a triple-quoted string, enclosed by matching triplets of quote characters (''' or, more commonly, """):

```
"""An even bigger
string that spans
three lines"""              # comments not allowed on previous lines
```

In a triple-quoted string literal, line breaks in the literal remain as newline characters in the resulting string object. You can start a triple-quoted literal with a backslash immediately followed by a newline, to avoid having the first line of the literal string's content at a different indentation level from the rest. For example:

```
the_text = """\
First line
Second line
"""  # like 'First line\nSecond line\n' but more readable
```

The only character that cannot be part of a triple-quoted string is an unescaped backslash, while a quoted string cannot contain unescaped backslashes, nor line ends, nor the quote character that encloses it. The backslash character starts an *escape sequence*, which lets you introduce any character in either kind of string. We list Python's string escape sequences in Table 3-1.

Table 3-1. String escape sequences

Sequence	Meaning	ASCII/ISO code
\<newline>	Ignore end of line	None
\\	Backslash	0x5c
\'	Single quote	0x27
\"	Double quote	0x22
\a	Bell	0x07
\b	Backspace	0x08
\f	Form feed	0x0c
\n	Newline	0x0a
\r	Carriage return	0x0d
\t	Tab	0x09
\v	Vertical tab	0x0b
\ *DDD*	Octal value *DDD*	As given
\x *XX*	Hexadecimal value *XX*	As given
\ *other*	Any other character: a two-character string	0x5c + as given

A variant of a string literal is a *raw string*. The syntax is the same as for quoted or triple-quoted string literals, except that an r or R immediately precedes the leading quote. In raw strings, escape sequences are not interpreted as in Table 3-1, but are literally copied into the string, including backslashes and newline characters. Raw string syntax is handy for strings that include many backslashes, especially regular expression patterns (see "Pattern-String Syntax" on page 254). A raw string cannot end with an odd number of backslashes: the last one would be taken as escaping the terminating quote.

In Unicode string literals you can use \u followed by four hex digits, and \U followed by eight hex digits, to denote Unicode characters, and can also include the same escape sequences listed in Table 3-1. Unicode literals can also include the escape sequence \N{*name*}, where *name* is a standard Unicode name, as listed at *http://www.unicode.org/charts/*. For example, \N{Copyright Sign} indicates a Unicode copyright sign character (©).

Raw Unicode string literals in v2 start with `ur`, not `ru`; raw byte string literals in v2 start with `br`, not `rb` (in v3, you can start them with either `br` or `rb`).

Raw strings are not a different type from other strings

Raw strings are *not* a different type from ordinary strings; they are just an alternative syntax for literals of the usual two string types, byte strings and Unicode.

New in 3.6, *formatted string literals* let you inject formatted expressions into your strings, which are therefore no longer constants but subject to evaluation at execution time. We cover these new literals in "New in 3.6: Formatted String Literals" on page 246. From a syntactic point of view, they can be regarded just as another kind of string literal.

Multiple string literals of any kind—quoted, triple-quoted, raw, bytes, formatted, Unicode—can be adjacent, with optional whitespace in between (except that, in v3, you cannot mix bytes and Unicode in this way). The compiler concatenates such adjacent string literals into a single string object. In v2, if any literal in the concatenation is Unicode, the whole result is Unicode. Writing a long string literal in this way lets you present it readably across multiple physical lines and gives you an opportunity to insert comments about parts of the string. For example:

```
marypop = ('supercalifragilistic' # Open paren->logical line continues
           'expialidocious')      # Indentation ignored in continuation
```

The string assigned to `marypop` is a single word of 34 characters.

Tuples

A *tuple* is an immutable ordered sequence of items. The items of a tuple are arbitrary objects and may be of different types. You can use mutable objects (e.g., lists) as tuple items; however, best practice is to avoid tuples with mutable items.

To denote a tuple, use a series of expressions (the *items* of the tuple) separated by commas (`,`); if every item is a literal, the whole assembly is a *tuple literal*. You may optionally place a redundant comma after the last item. You may group tuple items within parentheses, but the parentheses are necessary only where the commas would otherwise have another meaning (e.g., in function calls), or to denote empty or nested tuples. A tuple with exactly two items is also known as a *pair*. To create a tuple of one item, add a comma to the end of the expression. To denote an empty tuple, use an empty pair of parentheses. Here are some tuple literals, all in the optional parentheses (the parentheses are not optional in the last case):

```
(100, 200, 300)             # Tuple with three items
(3.14,)                     # Tuple with 1 item needs trailing comma
()                          # Empty tuple (parentheses NOT optional)
```

You can also call the built-in type `tuple` to create a tuple. For example:

```
tuple('wow')
```

This builds a tuple equal to that denoted by the tuple literal:

```
('w', 'o', 'w')
```

`tuple()` without arguments creates and returns an empty tuple, like `()`. When *x* is iterable, `tuple(x)` returns a tuple whose items are the same as those in *x*.

Lists

A *list* is a mutable ordered sequence of items. The items of a list are arbitrary objects and may be of different types. To denote a list, use a series of expressions (the *items* of the list) separated by commas (`,`), within brackets (`[]`); if every item is a literal, the whole assembly is a *list literal*. You may optionally place a redundant comma after the last item. To denote an empty list, use an empty pair of brackets. Here are some example list literals:

```
[42, 3.14, 'hello']         # List with three items
[100]                       # List with one item
[]                          # Empty list
```

You can also call the built-in type `list` to create a list. For example:

```
list('wow')
```

This builds a list equal to that denoted by the list literal:

```
['w', 'o', 'w']
```

`list()` without arguments creates and returns an empty list, like `[]`. When *x* is iterable, `list(x)` creates and returns a new list whose items are the same as those *x*. You can also build lists with list comprehensions, covered in "List comprehensions" on page 78.

Sets

Python has two built-in set types, `set` and `frozenset`, to represent arbitrarily ordered collections of unique items. Items in a set may be of different types, but they must be *hashable* (see `hash` in Table 7-2). Instances of type `set` are mutable, and thus, not hashable; instances of type `frozenset` are immutable and hashable. You can't have a set whose items are sets, but you can have a set (or frozenset) whose items are frozensets. Sets and frozensets are *not* ordered.

To create a set, you can call the built-in type `set` with no argument (this means an empty set) or one argument that is iterable (this means a set whose items are those of the iterable). You can similarly build a frozenset by calling `frozenset`.

Alternatively, to denote a (nonfrozen, nonempty) set, use a series of expressions (the items of the set) separated by commas (`,`) and within braces (`{}`); if every item is a literal, the whole assembly is a *set literal*. You may optionally place a redundant comma after the last item. Some example sets (two literals, one not):

```
{42, 3.14, 'hello'}       # Literal for a set with three items
{100}                     # Literal for a set with one item
set()                     # Empty set (can't use {}—empty dict!)
```

You can also build nonfrozen sets with set comprehensions, as discussed in "List comprehensions" on page 78.

Dictionaries

A *mapping* is an arbitrary collection of objects indexed by nearly[3] arbitrary values called *keys*. Mappings are mutable and, like sets but unlike sequences, are *not* (necessarily) ordered.

Python provides a single built-in mapping type: the dictionary type. Library and extension modules provide other mapping types, and you can write others yourself (as discussed in "Mappings" on page 132). Keys in a dictionary may be of different types, but they must be *hashable* (see `hash` in Table 7-2). Values in a dictionary are arbitrary objects and may be of any type. An *item* in a dictionary is a key/value pair. You can think of a dictionary as an associative array (known in some other languages as an "unordered map," "hash table," or "hash").

To denote a dictionary, you can use a series of colon-separated pairs of expressions (the pairs are the items of the dictionary) separated by commas (`,`) within braces (`{}`); if every expression is a literal, the whole assembly is a *dict literal*. You may optionally place a redundant comma after the last item. Each item in a dictionary is written as *`key`*`:`*`value`*, where *`key`* is an expression giving the item's key and *`value`* is an expression giving the item's value. If a key's value appears more than once in a dictionary expression, only an arbitrary one of the items with that key is kept in the resulting dictionary object—dictionaries do not allow duplicate keys. To denote an empty dictionary, use an empty pair of braces.

Here are some dictionary literals:

```
{'x':42, 'y':3.14, 'z':7}    # Dictionary with three items, str keys
{1:2, 3:4}                   # Dictionary with two items, int keys
{1:'za', 'br':23}            # Dictionary with mixed key types
{}                           # Empty dictionary
```

You can also call the built-in type `dict` to create a dictionary in a way that, while usually less concise, can sometimes be more readable. For example, the dictionaries in the preceding snippet can equivalently be written as:

```
dict(x=42, y=3.14, z=7)      # Dictionary with three items, str keys
dict([(1, 2), (3, 4)])       # Dictionary with two items, int keys
dict([(1,'za'), ('br',23)])  # Dictionary with mixed key types
dict()                       # Empty dictionary
```

---

3 Each specific mapping type may put constraints on the type of keys it accepts: in particular, dictionaries only accept hashable keys.

`dict()` without arguments creates and returns an empty dictionary, like `{}`. When the argument *x* to `dict` is a mapping, `dict` returns a new dictionary object with the same keys and values as *x*. When *x* is iterable, the items in *x* must be pairs, and `dict(x)` returns a dictionary whose items (key/value pairs) are the same as the items in *x*. If a key value appears more than once in *x*, only the *last* item from *x* with that key value is kept in the resulting dictionary.

When you call `dict`, in addition to, or instead of, the positional argument *x*, you may pass *named arguments*, each with the syntax *name=value*, where *name* is an identifier to use as an item's key and *value* is an expression giving the item's value. When you call `dict` and pass both a positional argument and one or more named arguments, if a key appears both in the positional argument and as a named argument, Python associates to that key the value given with the named argument (i.e., the named argument "wins").

You can also create a dictionary by calling `dict.fromkeys`. The first argument is an iterable whose items become the keys of the dictionary; the second argument is the value that corresponds to each and every key (all keys initially map to the same value). If you omit the second argument, it defaults to `None`. For example:

```
dict.fromkeys('hello', 2)   # same as {'h':2, 'e':2, 'l':2, 'o':2}
dict.fromkeys([1, 2, 3])    # same as {1:None, 2:None, 3:None}
```

You can also build dicts with dict comprehensions, as discussed in "List comprehensions" on page 78.

None

The built-in `None` denotes a null object. `None` has no methods or other attributes. You can use `None` as a placeholder when you need a reference but you don't care what object you refer to, or when you need to indicate that no object is there. Functions return `None` as their result unless they have specific `return` statements coded to return other values.

Callables

In Python, callable types are those whose instances support the function call operation (see "Calling Functions" on page 89). Functions are callable. Python provides several built-in functions (see "Built-in Functions" on page 201) and supports user-defined functions (see "The def Statement" on page 83). Generators are also callable (see "Generators" on page 96).

Types are also callable, as we already saw for the `dict`, `list`, `set`, and `tuple` built-in types. (See "Built-in Types" on page 198 for a complete list of built-in types.) As we discuss in "Python Classes" on page 102, `class` objects (user-defined types) are also callable. Calling a type normally creates and returns a new instance of that type.

Other callables are *methods*, which are functions bound to class attributes, and instances of classes that supply a special method named `__call__`.

Boolean Values

Any data value in Python can be used as a truth value: true or false. Any nonzero number or nonempty container (e.g., string, tuple, list, set, or dictionary) is true. `0` (of any numeric type), `None`, and empty containers are false.

Beware using a float as a truth value

Be careful about using a floating-point number as a truth value: that's like comparing the number for exact equality with zero, and floating-point numbers should almost never be compared for exact equality.

The built-in type `bool` is a subclass of `int`. The only two values of type `bool` are `True`and `False`, which have string representations of `'True'` and `'False'`, but also numerical values of `1` and `0`, respectively. Several built-in functions return `bool` results, as do comparison operators.

You can call `bool(x)` with any *x* as the argument. The result is `True` when *x* is true and `False` when *x* is false. Good Python style is not to use such calls when they are redundant, as they most often are: *always* write `if x:`, *never* any of `if bool(x):`, `if x is True`, `if x==True:`, `if bool(x)==True`. However, you can use `bool(x)` to count the number of true items in a sequence. For example:

```
def count_trues(seq): return sum(bool(x) for x in seq)
```

In this example, the `bool` call ensures each item of *seq* is counted as `0` (if false) or `1` (if true), so `count_trues` is more general than `sum(seq)` would be.

When we write "`expression` is true," we mean that `bool(expression)` would return `True`.

Variables and Other References

A Python program accesses data values through *references*. A *reference* is a "name" that refers to a value (object). References take the form of variables, attributes, and items. In Python, a variable or other reference has no intrinsic type. The object to which a reference is bound at a given time always has a type, but a given reference may be bound to objects of various types in the course of the program's execution.

Variables

In Python, there are no "declarations." The existence of a variable begins with a statement that *binds* the variable (in other words, sets a name to hold a reference to some object). You can also *unbind* a variable, resetting the name so it no longer holds a reference. Assignment statements are the most common way to bind variables and other references. The `del` statement unbinds references.

Binding a reference that was already bound is also known as *rebinding* it. Whenever we mention binding, we implicitly include rebinding (except where we explicitly exclude it). Rebinding or unbinding a reference has no effect on the object to which the reference was bound, except that an object goes away when nothing refers to it. The cleanup of objects with no references is known as *garbage collection*.

You can name a variable with any identifier except the 30-plus reserved as Python's keywords (see "Keywords" on page 40). A variable can be global or local. A *global variable* is an attribute of a module object (see Chapter 6). A *local variable* lives in a function's local namespace (see "Namespaces" on page 92).

Object attributes and items

The main distinction between the attributes and items of an object is in the syntax you use to access them. To denote an *attribute* of an object, use a reference to the object, followed by a period (`.`), followed by an identifier known as the *attribute name*. For example, `x.y` refers to one of the attributes of the object bound to name `x`, specifically that attribute whose name is `'y'`.

The Python Language

To denote an *item* of an object, use a reference to the object, followed by an expression within brackets (`[]`). The expression in brackets is known as the item's *index* or *key*, and the object is known as the item's *container*. For example, `x[y]` refers to the item at the key or index bound to name `y`, within the container object bound to name `x`.

Attributes that are callable are also known as *methods*. Python draws no strong distinctions between callable and noncallable attributes, as some other languages do. All rules about attributes also apply to callable attributes (methods).

Accessing nonexistent references

A common programming error is trying to access a reference that does not exist. For example, a variable may be unbound, or an attribute name or item index may not be valid for the object to which you apply it. The Python compiler, when it analyzes and compiles source code, diagnoses only syntax errors. Compilation does not diagnose semantic errors, such as trying to access an unbound attribute, item, or variable. Python diagnoses semantic errors only when the errant code executes—that is, *at runtime*. When an operation is a Python semantic error, attempting it raises an exception (see Chapter 5). Accessing a nonexistent variable, attribute, or item—just like any other semantic error—raises an exception.

Assignment Statements

Assignment statements can be plain or augmented. Plain assignment to a variable (e.g., `name=value`) is how you create a new variable or rebind an existing variable to a new value. Plain assignment to an object attribute (e.g., `x.attr=value`) is a request to object `x` to create or rebind attribute `'attr'`. Plain assignment to an item in a container (e.g., `x[k]=value`) is a request to container `x` to create or rebind the item with index or key `k`.

Augmented assignment (e.g., *name*+=*value*) cannot, per se, create new references. Augmented assignment can rebind a variable, ask an object to rebind one of its existing attributes or items, or request the target object to modify itself. When you make a request to an object, it is up to the object to decide whether and how to honor the request, and whether to raise an exception.

Plain assignment

A plain assignment statement in the simplest form has the syntax:

```
target = expression
```

The target is known as the lefthand side (LHS), and the expression is the righthand side (RHS). When the assignment executes, Python evaluates the RHS expression, then binds the expression's value to the LHS target. The binding does not depend on the type of the value. In particular, Python draws no strong distinction between callable and noncallable objects, as some other languages do, so you can bind functions, methods, types, and other callables to variables, just as you can numbers, strings, lists, and so on. This is part of functions and the like being *first-class objects*.

Details of the binding do depend on the kind of target. The target in an assignment may be an identifier, an attribute reference, an indexing, or a slicing:

An identifier
: Is a variable name. Assigning to an identifier binds the variable with this name.

An attribute reference
: Has the syntax `obj.name`, where `obj` is an arbitrary expression, and `name` is an identifier, known as an *attribute name* of the object. Assigning to an attribute reference asks object `obj` to bind its attribute named `'name'`.

An indexing
: Has the syntax `obj[expr]`. `obj` and `expr` are arbitrary expressions. Assigning to an indexing asks container `obj` to bind its item indicated by the value of `expr`, also known as the index or key of the item in the container.

A slicing
: Has the syntax `obj[start:stop]` or `obj[start:stop:stride]`. `obj`, `start`, `stop`, and `stride` are arbitrary expressions. `start`, `stop`, and `stride` are all optional (i.e., `obj[:stop:]` and `obj[:stop]` are also syntactically correct slicings, equivalent to `obj[None:stop:None]`). Assigning to a slicing asks container `obj` to bind or unbind some of its items. Assigning to a slicing such as `obj[start:stop:stride]` is equivalent to assigning to the indexing `obj[slice(start, stop, stride)]`. See Python's built-in type `slice` in (Table 7-1), whose instances represent slices.

We'll get back to indexing and slicing targets when we discuss operations on lists, in "Modifying a list" on page 64, and on dictionaries, in "Indexing a Dictionary" on page 70.

When the target of the assignment is an identifier, the assignment statement specifies the binding of a variable. This is *never* disallowed: when you request it, it takes place. In all other cases, the assignment statement specifies a request to an object to bind one or more of its attributes or items. An object may refuse to create or rebind some (or all) attributes or items, raising an exception if you attempt a disallowed creation or rebinding (see also `__setattr__` in Table 4-1 and `__setitem__` in "Container methods" on page 134).

A plain assignment can use multiple targets and equals signs (=). For example:

```
a = b = c = 0
```

binds variables `a`, `b`, and `c` to the same value, `0`. Each time the statement executes, the RHS expression evaluates just once, no matter how many targets are part of the statement. Each target, left to right, is bound to the single object returned by the expression, just as if several simple assignments executed one after the other.

The target in a plain assignment can list two or more references separated by commas, optionally enclosed in parentheses or brackets. For example:

```
a, b, c = x
```

This statement requires `x` to be an iterable with exactly three items, and binds `a` to the first item, `b` to the second, and `c` to the third. This kind of assignment is known as an *unpacking assignment*. The RHS expression must be an iterable with exactly as many items as there are references in the target; otherwise, Python raises an exception. Each reference in the target gets bound to the corresponding item in the RHS. An unpacking assignment can also be used to swap references:

```
a, b = b, a
```

This assignment statement rebinds name *a* to what name *b* was bound to, and vice versa. In v3, exactly one of the multiple targets of an unpacking assignment may be preceded by `*`. That *starred* target is bound to a list of all items, if any, that were not assigned to other targets. For example, in v3:

```
first, *middle, last = x
```

when *x* is a list, is the same as (but more concise, clearer, more general, and faster than):

```
first, middle, last = x[0], x[1:-1], x[-1]
```

Each of these assignments requires *x* to have at least two items. The second form, compatible with v2, requires the values in *x* to be a sequence, accessible by numeric index; the first, v3-only, form, is fine with *x* being any iterable with at least two items. This v3-only feature is known as *extended unpacking*.

Augmented assignment

An *augmented assignment* (sometimes also known as an *in-place assignment*) differs from a plain assignment in that, instead of an equals sign (=) between the target and the expression, it uses an *augmented operator*, which is a binary operator followed by =. The augmented operators are +=, -=, *=, /=, //=, %=, **=, |=, >>=, <<=, &=, and ^= (and, in v3 only, @=). An augmented assignment can have only one target on the LHS; augmented assignment doesn't support multiple targets.

In an augmented assignment, just as in a plain one, Python first evaluates the RHS expression. Then, when the LHS refers to an object that has a special method for the appropriate *in-place* version of the operator, Python calls the method with the RHS value as its argument. It is up to the method to modify the LHS object appropriately and return the modified object ("Special Methods" on page 126 covers special methods). When the LHS object has no appropriate in-place special method, Python applies the corresponding binary operator to the LHS and RHS objects, then rebinds the target reference to the operator's result. For example, `x+=y` is like `x=x.__iadd__(y)` when `x` has special method `__iadd__` for in-place addition. Otherwise, `x+=y` is like `x=x+y`.

Augmented assignment never creates its target reference; the target must already be bound when augmented assignment executes. Augmented assignment can rebind the target reference to a new object, or modify the same object to which the target reference was already bound. Plain assignment, in contrast, can create or rebind the LHS target reference, but it never modifies the object, if any, to which the target reference was previously bound. The distinction between objects and references to objects is crucial here. For example, `x=x+y` does not modify the object to which name `x` was originally bound. Rather, it rebinds the name `x` to refer to a new object. `x+=y`, in contrast, modifies the object to which the name `x` is bound, when that object has special method `__iadd__`; otherwise, `x+=y` rebinds the name `x` to a new object, just like `x=x+y`.

del Statements

Despite its name, a `del` statement *unbinds references*—it does *not*, per se, delete objects. Object deletion may automatically follow as a consequence, by garbage collection, when no more references to an object exist.

A `del` statement consists of the keyword `del`, followed by one or more target references separated by commas (`,`). Each target can be a variable, attribute reference, indexing, or slicing, just like for assignment statements, and must be bound at the time `del` executes. When a `del` target is an identifier, the `del` statement means to unbind the variable. If the identifier was bound, unbinding it is never disallowed; when requested, it takes place.

In all other cases, the `del` statement specifies a request to an object to unbind one or more of its attributes or items. An object may refuse to unbind some (or all) attributes or items, raising an exception if you attempt a disallowed unbinding (see also `__delattr__` in "General-Purpose Special Methods" on page 126 and `__delitem__` in "Container methods" on page 134). Unbinding a slicing normally has the same effect as assigning an empty sequence to that slicing, but it is up to the container object to implement this equivalence.

Containers are also allowed to have `del` cause side effects. For example, assuming `del C[2]` succeeds, when *C* is a dict, this makes future references to `C[2]` invalid (raising `KeyError`) until and unless you assign to `C[2]` again; but when *C* is a list, `del C[2]` implies that every following item of *C* "shifts left by one"—so, if *C* is long enough, future references to `C[2]` are still valid, but denote a distinct item than they did before the `del`.

Expressions and Operators

An *expression* is a "phrase" of code, which Python evaluates to produce a value. The simplest expressions are literals and identifiers. You build other expressions by joining subexpressions with the operators and/or delimiters listed in Table 3-2. This table lists operators in decreasing order of precedence, higher precedence before lower. Operators listed together have the same precedence. The third column lists the *associativity* of the operator: L (left-to-right), R (right-to-left), or NA (non-associative).

The Python Language

Table 3-2. Operator precedence in expressions

Operator	Description	Associativity
`{ key : expr ,...}`	Dictionary creation	NA
`{ expr ,...}`	Set creation	NA
`[ expr ,...]`	List creation	NA
`( expr ,...)`	Tuple creation or just parentheses	NA
`f( expr ,...)`	Function call	L
`x[ index : index ]`	Slicing	L
`x[ index ]`	Indexing	L
`x . attr`	Attribute reference	L
`x ** y`	Exponentiation (*x* to the *y*th power)	R
`~ x`	Bitwise NOT	NA
`+x, -x`	Unary plus and minus	NA
`x*y, x/y, x//y, x%y`	Multiplication, division, truncating division, remainder	L

<table>
<tr><th>Operator</th><th>Description</th><th>Associativity</th></tr>
<tr><td>x+y, x-y</td><td>Addition, subtraction</td><td>L</td></tr>
<tr><td><i>x</i><<<i>y</i>, <i>x</i>>><i>y</i></td><td>Left-shift, right-shift</td><td>L</td></tr>
<tr><td>x & y</td><td>Bitwise AND</td><td>L</td></tr>
<tr><td>x ^ y</td><td>Bitwise XOR</td><td>L</td></tr>
<tr><td>x | y</td><td>Bitwise OR</td><td>L</td></tr>
<tr><td><i>x</i><<i>y</i>, <i>x</i><=<i>y</i>, <i>x</i>><i>y</i>, <i>x</i>>=<i>y</i>, <i>x</i><><i>y</i> (v2 only), <i>x</i>!=<i>y</i>, <i>x</i>==<i>y</i></td><td>Comparisons (less than, less than or equal, greater than, greater than or equal, inequality, equality)[a]</td><td>NA</td></tr>
<tr><td>x is y, x is not y</td><td>Identity tests</td><td>NA</td></tr>
<tr><td>x in y, x not in y</td><td>Membership tests</td><td>NA</td></tr>
<tr><td>not x</td><td>Boolean NOT</td><td>NA</td></tr>
<tr><td>x and y</td><td>Boolean AND</td><td>L</td></tr>
<tr><td>x or y</td><td>Boolean OR</td><td>L</td></tr>
<tr><td>x if expr else y</td><td>Ternary operator</td><td>NA</td></tr>
<tr><td>lambda arg,...: expr</td><td>Anonymous simple function</td><td>NA</td></tr>
</table>

[a] In v2, <> and != are alternate forms of the same operator. != is the preferred version; <> is obsolete, and not supported in v3.

In Table 3-2, *expr*, *key*, *f*, *index*, *x*, and *y* indicate any expression, while *attr* and *arg* indicate any identifier. The notation ,... means commas join zero or more repetitions. In all such cases, a trailing comma is optional and innocuous.

Comparison Chaining

You can *chain* comparisons, implying a logical and. For example:

```
a < b <= c < d
```

has the same meaning as:

```
a < b and b <= c and c < d
```

The chained form is more readable, and evaluates each subexpression at most once.[4]

Short-Circuiting Operators

The `and` and `or` operators *short-circuit* their operands' evaluation: the righthand operand evaluates only when its value is necessary to get the truth value of the entire `and` or `or` operation.

In other words, *x* `and` *y* first evaluates *x*. When *x* is false, the result is *x*; otherwise, the result is *y*. Similarly, *x* `or` *y* first evaluates *x*. When *x* is true, the result is *x*; otherwise, the result is *y*.

`and` and `or` don't force their results to be `True` or `False`, but rather return one or the other of their operands. This lets you use these operators more generally, not just in Boolean contexts. `and` and `or`, because of their short-circuiting semantics, differ from other operators, which fully evaluate all operands before performing the operation. `and` and `or` let the left operand act as a *guard* for the right operand.

The ternary operator

Another short-circuiting operator is the ternary operator `if`/`else`:

```
whentrue if condition else whenfalse
```

Each of *`whentrue`*, *`whenfalse`*, and *`condition`* is an arbitrary expression. *`condition`* evaluates first. When *`condition`* is true, the result is *`whentrue`*; otherwise, the result is *`whenfalse`*. Only one of the subexpressions *`whentrue`* and *`whenfalse`* evaluates, depending on the truth value of *`condition`*.

The order of the subexpressions in this ternary operator may be a bit confusing. The recommended style is to always place parentheses around the whole expression.

Numeric Operations

Python offers the usual numeric operations, as we've just seen in Table 3-2. Numbers are immutable objects: when you perform operations on number objects, you produce a new number object, never modify existing ones. You can access the parts of a complex object `z` as read-only attributes `z.real` and `z.imag`. Trying to rebind these attributes raises an exception.

A number's optional `+` or `-` sign, and the `+` that joins a floating-point literal to an imaginary one to make a complex number, is not part of the literals' syntax. They are ordinary operators, subject to normal operator precedence rules (see Table 3-2). For example, `-2**2` evaluates to `-4`: exponentiation has higher precedence than unary minus, so the whole expression parses as `-(2**2)`, not as `(-2)**2`.

---

4 Note that, perhaps curiously, *`a!=b!=c`* does not imply *`a!=c`*, just like the longer-form equivalent expression *`a!=b`* `and` *`b!=c`* wouldn't.

Numeric Conversions

You can perform arithmetic operations and comparisons between any two numbers of Python built-in types. If the operands' types differ, *coercion* applies: Python converts the operand with the "smaller" type to the "larger" type. The types, in order from smallest to largest, are integers, floating-point numbers, and complex numbers. You can request an explicit conversion by passing a noncomplex numeric argument to any of the built-in number types: `int`, `float`, and `complex`. `int` drops its argument's fractional part, if any (e.g., `int(9.8)` is `9`). You can also call `complex` with two numeric arguments, giving real and imaginary parts. You cannot convert a `complex` to another numeric type in this way, because there is no single unambiguous way to convert a complex number into, for example, a `float`.

You can also call each built-in numeric type with a string argument with the syntax of an appropriate numeric literal, with small extensions: the argument string may have leading and/or trailing whitespace, may start with a sign, and—for complex numbers—may sum or subtract a real part and an imaginary one. `int` can also be called with two arguments: the first one a string to convert, and the second the *radix*, an integer between 2 and 36 to use as the base for the conversion (e.g., `int('101', 2)` returns `5`, the value of `'101'` in base `2`). For radices larger than 10, the appropriate subset of letters from the start of the alphabet (in either lower- or uppercase) are the extra needed "digits."

Arithmetic Operations

Python arithmetic operations behave in rather obvious ways, with the possible exception of division and exponentiation.

Division

If the right operand of `/`, `//`, or `%` is `0`, Python raises a runtime exception. The `//` operator performs truncating division, which means it returns an integer result (converted to the same type as the wider operand) and ignores the remainder, if any.

When both operands are integers: in v3, the `/` operator performs true division, returning a floating-point result (or a complex result if either operand is a complex number); in v2, `/` performs truncating division, like `//`. To perform truncating division in v3, use `//`. To have `/` perform true division on integer operands in v2, use option **`-Qnew`** on the Python command line (*not* recommended), or, better, begin your source file or interactive session with the statement:

```
from __future__ import division
```

This statement ensures that the operator `/` (within the module that starts with this statement) works without truncation on operands of any type.

To ensure that the behavior of division does *not* depend on the exact version of Python you're using, always use `//` when you want truncating division. When you do *not* want truncation, use `/`, but also ensure that at least one operand is *not* an integer. For example, instead of using just *a/b*, code `1.0*a/b` (`float(a)/b` is marginally slower, and fails when *a* is complex) to avoid making any assumption on the types of *a* and *b*. To check whether your v2 program has version dependencies in its use of division, use the option **`-Qwarn`** on the Python command line to get runtime warnings about uses of / on integer operands.

The built-in `divmod` function takes two numeric arguments and returns a pair whose items are the quotient and remainder, so you don't have to use both // for the quotient and % for the remainder.

Exponentiation

The exponentiation ("raise to power") operation, *a****b*, in v2, raises an exception when *a* is less than zero and *b* is a floating-point value with a nonzero fractional part, but, in v3, it returns the appropriate complex number in such cases.

The built-in `pow(a, b)` function returns the same result as *a****b*. With three arguments, `pow(a, b, c)` returns the same result as `(a**b)%c` but is faster.

Comparisons

All objects, including numbers, can be compared for equality (==) and inequality (!=). Comparisons requiring order (<, <=, >, >=) may be used between any two numbers, unless either operand is complex, in which case they raise runtime exceptions. All these operators return Boolean values (`True` or `False`). Beware comparing floating-point numbers for equality, as the online tutorial (*https://docs.python.org/3.5/tutorial/floatingpoint.html*) explains.

Bitwise Operations on Integers

Integers can be interpreted as strings of bits and used with the bitwise operations shown in Table 3-2. Bitwise operators have lower priority than arithmetic operators. Positive integers are conceptually extended by an unbounded string of `0` bits on the left. Negative integers, as they're held in two's complement (*https://en.wikipedia.org/wiki/Two's_complement*) representation, are conceptually extended by an unbounded string of `1` bits on the left.

Sequence Operations

Python supports a variety of operations applicable to all sequences, including strings, lists, and tuples. Some sequence operations apply to all containers (including sets and dictionaries, which are not sequences); some apply to all iterables (meaning "any object over which you can loop," as covered in "Iterables" on page 45; all containers, be they sequences or not, are iterable, and so are many objects that are not containers, such as files, covered in "The io Module" on page 273, and generators, covered in "Generators" on page 96). In the following we use the terms *sequence*, *container*, and *iterable* quite precisely, to indicate exactly which operations apply to each category.

Sequences in General

Sequences are ordered containers with items that are accessible by indexing and slicing. The built-in `len` function takes any container as an argument and returns the number of items in the container. The built-in `min` and `max` functions take one argument, a nonempty iterable whose items are comparable, and return the smallest and largest items, respectively. You can also call `min` and `max` with multiple arguments, in which case they return the smallest and largest arguments, respectively. The built-in `sum` function takes one argument, an iterable whose items are numbers, and returns the sum of the numbers.

Sequence conversions

There is no implicit conversion between different sequence types except that Python, in v2 only, converts byte strings to Unicode strings if needed. (We cover string conversion in detail in "Unicode" on page 250.) You can call the built-ins `tuple` and `list` with a single argument (any iterable) to get a new instance of the type you're calling, with the same items, in the same order, as in the argument.

Concatenation and repetition

You can concatenate sequences of the same type with the + operator. You can multiply a sequence *S* by an integer *n* with the * operator. *S**n or *n***S* is the concatenation of *n* copies of *S*. When *n*<=0, *S**n is an empty sequence of the same type as *S*.

Membership testing

The *x* `in` *S* operator tests to check whether object *x* equals any item in the sequence (or other kind of container or iterable) *S*. It returns `True` when it does and `False` when it doesn't. The *x* `not in` *S* operator is equivalent to `not (`*x* `in` *S*`)`. For dictionaries, *x* `in` *S* tests for the presence of *x* as a key. In the specific case of strings, though, *x* `in` *S* is more widely applicable; in this case, *x* `in` *S* tests whether *x* equals any *substring* of *S*, not just any single *character*.

Indexing a sequence

To denote the *n*th item of a sequence *S*, use an *indexing*: *S*`[`*n*`]`. Indexing is zero-based (*S*'s first item is *S*`[0]`). If *S* has *L* items, the index *n* may be `0`, `1`…up to and including *L*`-1`, but no larger. *n* may also be `-1`, `-2`…down to and including `-`*L*, but no smaller. A negative *n* (e.g., `-1`) denotes the same item in *S* as *L*+*n* (e.g., `L + -1`) does. In other words, *S*`[-1]`, like *S*`[L-1]`, is the last element of *S*, *S*`[-2]` is the next-to-last one, and so on. For example:

```
x = [1, 2, 3, 4]
x[1]                    # 2
x[-1]                   # 4
```

Using an index >=*L* or <-*L* raises an exception. Assigning to an item with an invalid index also raises an exception. You can add elements to a list, but to do so you assign to a slice, not an item, as we'll discuss shortly.

Slicing a sequence

To indicate a subsequence of *S*, you can use a *slicing*, with the syntax `S[i:j]`, where *i* and *j* are integers. `S[i:j]` is the subsequence of *S* from the *i*th item, included, to the *j*th item, excluded. In Python, ranges always include the lower bound and exclude the upper bound. A slice is an empty subsequence when *j* is less than or equal to *i*, or when *i* is greater than or equal to *L*, the length of *S*. You can omit *i* when it is equal to `0`, so that the slice begins from the start of *S*. You can omit *j* when it is greater than or equal to *L*, so that the slice extends all the way to the end of *S*. You can even omit both indices, to mean a shallow copy of the entire sequence: `S[:]`. Either or both indices may be less than `0`. Here are some examples:

```
x = [1, 2, 3, 4]
x[1:3]                  # [2, 3]
x[1:]                   # [2, 3, 4]
x[:2]                   # [1, 2]
```

A negative index *n* in a slicing indicates the same spot in *S* as *L+n*, just like it does in an indexing. An index greater than or equal to *L* means the end of *S*, while a negative index less than or equal to -*L* means the start of *S*. Slicing can use the extended syntax `S[i:j:k]`. *k* is the *stride* of the slice, meaning the distance between successive indices. `S[i:j]` is equivalent to `S[i:j:1]`, `S[::2]` is the subsequence of *S* that includes all items that have an even index in *S*, and `S[::-1]`[5] has the same items as *S*, but in reverse order. With a negative stride, in order to have a nonempty slice, the second ("stop") index needs to be *smaller* than the first ("start") one—the reverse of the condition that must hold when the stride is positive. A stride of `0` raises an exception.

```
y = list(range(10))
y[-5:]            # last five items
[5, 6, 7, 8, 9]
y[::2]            # every other item
[0, 2, 4, 6, 8]
y[10:0:-2]        # every other item, in reverse order
[9, 7, 5, 3, 1]
y[:0:-2]          # every other item, in reverse order (simpler)
[9, 7, 5, 3, 1]
y[::-2]           # every other item, in reverse order (best)
[9, 7, 5, 3, 1]
```

5 A slicing that's also whimsically known as "the Martian smiley."

Strings

String objects (byte strings, as well as text, AKA Unicode, ones) are immutable: attempting to rebind or delete an item or slice of a string raises an exception. The items of a string object (corresponding to each of the characters in the string) are themselves strings of the same kind, each of length 1—Python has no special data type for "single characters" (except for the items of a `bytes` object in v3: in that case, indexing produces an `int`). All slices of a string are strings of the same kind. String objects have many methods, covered in "Methods of String and Bytes Objects" on page 233.

Tuples

Tuple objects are immutable: therefore, attempting to rebind or delete an item or slice of a tuple raises an exception. The items of a tuple are arbitrary objects and may be of different types; tuple items may be mutable, but we don't recommend this practice, as it can be confusing. The slices of a tuple are also tuples. Tuples have no normal (nonspecial) methods, except `count` and `index`, with the same meanings as for lists; they do have some of the special methods covered in "Special Methods" on page 126.

Lists

List objects are mutable: you may rebind or delete items and slices of a list. Items of a list are arbitrary objects and may be of different types. Slices of a list are lists.

Modifying a list

You can modify a single item in a list by assigning to an indexing. For instance:

```
x = [1, 2, 3, 4]
x[1] = 42                    # x is now [1, 42, 3, 4]
```

Another way to modify a list object *L* is to use a slice of *L* as the target (LHS) of an assignment statement. The RHS of the assignment must be an iterable. When the LHS slice is in extended form (i.e., the slicing specifies a stride`!=1`), then the RHS must have just as many items as the number of items in the LHS slice. When the LHS slicing does not specify a stride, or explicitly specifies a stride of `1`, the LHS slice and the RHS may each be of any length; assigning to such a slice of a list can make the list longer or shorter. For example:

```
x = [1, 2, 3, 4]
x[1:3] = [22, 33, 44]        # x is now [1, 22, 33, 44, 4]
x[1:4] = [8, 9]              # x is now [1, 8, 9, 4]
```

Here are some important special cases of assignment to slices:

- Using the empty list `[]` as the RHS expression removes the target slice from *L*. In other words, `L[i:j]=[]` has the same effect as `del L[i:j]` (or the peculiar statement `L[i:j]*=0`).

- Using an empty slice of *L* as the LHS target inserts the items of the RHS at the appropriate spot in *L*. For example, `L[i:i]=['a','b']` inserts `'a'` and `'b'` before the item that was at index *i* in *L* prior to the assignment.
- Using a slice that covers the entire list object, `L[:]`, as the LHS target, totally replaces the contents of *L*.

You can delete an item or a slice from a list with `del`. For instance:

```
x = [1, 2, 3, 4, 5]
del x[1]                    # x is now [1, 3, 4, 5]
del x[::2]                  # x is now [3, 5]
```

The Python Language

In-place operations on a list

List objects define in-place versions of the `+` and `*` operators, which you can use via augmented assignment statements. The augmented assignment statement `L+=L1` has the effect of adding the items of iterable *L1* to the end of *L*, just like `L.extend(L1)`. `L*=n` has the effect of adding `n-1` copies of *L* to the end of *L*; if `n<=0`, `L*=n` empties the contents of *L*, like `L[:]=[]`.

List methods

List objects provide several methods, as shown in Table 3-3. *Nonmutating methods* return a result without altering the object to which they apply, while *mutating methods* may alter the object to which they apply. Many of a list's mutating methods behave like assignments to appropriate slices of the list. In Table 3-3, *L* indicates any list object, *i* any valid index in *L*, *s* any iterable, and *x* any object.

Table 3-3. List object methods

Method	Description
Nonmutating	
`L.count(x)`	Returns the number of items of *L* that are equal to *x*.
`L.index(x)`	Returns the index of the first occurrence of an item in *L* that is equal to *x*, or raises an exception if *L* has no such item.
Mutating	
`L.append(x)`	Appends item *x* to the end of *L*; like `L[len(L):]=[x]`.

Method	Description
L.extend(*s*)	Appends all the items of iterable *s* to the end of *L*; like *L*[len(*L*):]=*s* or L += s.
L.insert(*i*, *x*)	Inserts item *x* in *L* before the item at index *i*, moving following items of *L* (if any) "rightward" to make space (increases len(*L*) by one, does not replace any item, does not raise exceptions; acts just like *L*[*i*:*i*]=[*x*]).
L.remove(*x*)	Removes from *L* the first occurrence of an item in *L* that is equal to *x*, or raises an exception if *L* has no such item.
L.pop(*i*=-1)	Returns the value of the item at index *i* and removes it from *L*; when you omit *i*, removes and returns the last item; raises an exception if *L* is empty or *i* is an invalid index in *L*.
L.reverse()	Reverses, in place, the items of *L*.
L.sort(cmp=cmp, key=None, reverse=False)	Sorts, in-place, the items of *L*, comparing items pairwise via—v2, only —the function passed as *cmp* (by default, the built-in function cmp). When argument *key* is not None, what gets compared for each item *x* is *key*(*x*), not *x* itself. For more details, see "Sorting a list" on page 66. Argument cmp is deprecated in v2 (we recommend *never* using it) and does not exist at all in v3.

All mutating methods of list objects, except pop, return None.

Sorting a list

A list's method sort causes the list to be sorted in-place (reordering items to place them in increasing order) in a way that is guaranteed to be stable (elements that compare equal are not exchanged). In practice, sort is extremely fast, often *preternaturally* fast, as it can exploit any order or reverse order that may be present in any sublist (the advanced algorithm (*https://en.wikipedia.org/wiki/Timsort*) sort uses, known as *timsort* to honor its inventor, great Pythonista Tim Peters, is a "non-recursive adaptive stable natural mergesort/binary insertion sort hybrid"—now *there's* a mouthful for you!).

In v2, the sort method takes three optional arguments, which may be passed with either positional or named-argument syntax. The argument *cmp* (deprecated), when present, must be a function that, when called with any two list items as arguments, returns -1, 0, or 1, depending on whether the first item is to be considered less than, equal to, or greater than the second item for sorting purposes (when not present, it defaults to the built-in function `cmp`, which has exactly these semantics). The argument *key*, if not `None`, must be a function that can be called with any list item as its only argument. In this case, to compare any two items *x* and *y*, Python uses `cmp(key(x),key(y))` rather than `cmp(x,y)` (internally, Python implements this in the same way as the decorate-sort-undecorate idiom presented in "Searching and sorting" on page 491, but substantially faster). The argument *reverse*, if `True`, causes the result of each comparison to be reversed; this is not the same thing as reversing *L* after sorting, because the sort is stable (elements that compare equal are never exchanged) whether the argument *reverse* is true or false.

The Python Language

v3's `sort` works just like v2's, but the previously deprecated argument *cmp* is now simply nonexistent (if you try passing it, Python raises an exception):

```
mylist = ['alpha', 'Beta', 'GAMMA']
mylist.sort()                    #  ['Beta', 'GAMMA', 'alpha']
mylist.sort(key=str.lower)       #  ['alpha', 'Beta', 'GAMMA']
```

Python also provides the built-in function `sorted` (covered in Table 7-2) to produce a sorted list from any input iterable. `sorted`, after the first argument (which is the iterable supplying the items), accepts the same arguments as a list's method `sort`.

The standard library module `operator` (covered in "The operator Module" on page 438) supplies higher-order functions `attrgetter` and `itemgetter`, which produce functions particularly suitable for the `key=` optional argument of lists' method `sort` and the built-in function `sorted`. The identical `key=` optional argument also exists for built-in functions `min` and `max`, and for functions `nsmallest` and `nlargest` in standard library module `heapq`, covered in "The heapq Module" on page 224.

Set Operations

Python provides a variety of operations applicable to sets (both plain and frozen). Since sets are containers, the built-in `len` function can take a set as its single argument and return the number of items in the set. A set is iterable, so you can pass it to any function or method that takes an iterable argument. In this case, iteration yields the items of the set in some arbitrary order. For example, for any set *S*, `min(`*S*`)` returns the smallest item in *S*, since `min` with a single argument iterates on that argument (the order does not matter, because the implied comparisons are transitive).

Set Membership

The *k* `in` *S* operator checks whether object *k* is one of the items of set *S*. It returns `True` when it is, `False` when it isn't. *k* `not in` *S* is like `not (`*k* `in` *S*`)`.

Set Methods

Set objects provide several methods, as shown in Table 3-4. Nonmutating methods return a result without altering the object to which they apply, and can also be called on instances of `frozenset`; mutating methods may alter the object to which they apply, and can be called only on instances of `set`. In Table 3-4, *S* denotes any set object, *S1* any iterable with hashable items (often but not necessarily a `set` or `frozenset`), *x* any hashable object.

Table 3-4. Set object methods

Method	Description
Nonmutating	
`S.copy()`	Returns a shallow copy of *S* (a copy whose items are the same objects as *S*'s, not copies thereof), like `set(S)`
`S.difference( S1 )`	Returns the set of all items of *S* that aren't in *S1*
`S.intersection( S1 )`	Returns the set of all items of *S* that are also in *S1*
`S.issubset( S1 )`	Returns `True` when all items of *S* are also in *S1*; otherwise, returns `False`
`S.issuperset( S1 )`	Returns `True` when all items of *S1* are also in *S*; otherwise, returns `False` (like `S1.issubset(S)`)
`S.symmetric_difference( S1 )`	Returns the set of all items that are in either *S* or *S1*, but not both
`S.union( S1 )`	Returns the set of all items that are in *S*, *S1*, or both
Mutating	
`S.add( x )`	Adds *x* as an item to *S*; no effect if *x* was already an item in *S*
`S.clear()`	Removes all items from *S*, leaving *S* empty
`S.discard( x )`	Removes *x* as an item of *S*; no effect when *x* was not an item of *S*
`S.pop()`	Removes and returns an arbitrary item of *S*
`S.remove( x )`	Removes *x* as an item of *S*; raises a `KeyError` exception when *x* was not an item of *S*

All mutating methods of set objects, except `pop`, return `None`.

The pop method can be used for destructive iteration on a set, consuming little extra memory. The memory savings make pop usable for a loop on a huge set, when what you want is to "consume" the set in the course of the loop. A potential advantage of a destructive loop such as

```
while S:
    item = S.pop()
    ...handle item...
```

in comparison to a nondestructive loop such as

```
for item in S:
    ...handle item...
```

is that, in the body of the destructive loop, you're allowed to modify *S* (adding and/or removing items), which is not allowed in the nondestructive loop.

Sets also have mutating methods named difference_update, intersection_update, symmetric_difference_update, and update (corresponding to non-mutating method union). Each such mutating method performs the same operation as the corresponding nonmutating method, but it performs the operation in place, altering the set on which you call it, and returns None. The four corresponding non-mutating methods are also accessible with operator syntax: where *S2* is a set or frozenset, respectively, *S*-*S2*, *S*&*S2*, *S*^*S2*, and *S*|*S2*; the mutating methods are accessible with augmented assignment syntax: respectively, *S*-=*S2*, *S*&=*S2*, *S*^=*S2*, and *S*|=*S2*. Note that, when you use operator or augmented assignment syntax, both operands must be sets or frozensets; however, when you call named methods, argument *S1* can be any iterable with hashable items, and it works just as if the argument you passed was set(*S1*).

Dictionary Operations

Python provides a variety of operations applicable to dictionaries. Since dictionaries are containers, the built-in len function can take a dictionary as its argument and return the number of items (key/value pairs) in the dictionary. A dictionary is iterable, so you can pass it to any function that takes an iterable argument. In this case, iteration yields only the keys of the dictionary, in arbitrary order.[6] For example, for any dictionary *D*, min(D) returns the smallest key in *D*.

Dictionary Membership

The *k* in *D* operator checks whether object *k* is a key in dictionary *D*. It returns True when it is, False when it isn't. *k* not in *D* is like not (*k* in *D*).

6 ***New in 3.6***: dictionaries have been reimplemented; keys are now iterated in insertion order until the first noninsertion mutator on the dict. To keep your code solid, do not rely on this new, non-guaranteed behavior until Python's official docs explicitly ensure it.

Indexing a Dictionary

To denote the value in a dictionary *D* currently associated with key *k*, use an indexing: `D[k]`. Indexing with a key that is not present in the dictionary raises an exception. For example:

```
d = {'x':42, 'y':3.14, 'z':7}
d['x']                          # 42
d['z']                          # 7
d['a']                          # raises KeyError exception
```

Plain assignment to a dictionary indexed with a key that is not yet in the dictionary (e.g., `D[newkey]=value`) is a valid operation and adds the key and value as a new item in the dictionary. For instance:

```
d = {'x':42, 'y':3.14}
d['a'] = 16                    # d is now {'x':42, 'y':3.14, 'a':16}
```

The `del` statement, in the form `del D[k]`, removes from the dictionary the item whose key is *k*. When *k* is not a key in dictionary *D*, `del D[k]` raises a `KeyError` exception.

Dictionary Methods

Dictionary objects provide several methods, as shown in Table 3-5. Nonmutating methods return a result without altering the object to which they apply, while mutating methods may alter the object to which they apply. In Table 3-5, *D* and *D1* indicate any dictionary object, *k* any hashable object, and *x* any object.

Table 3-5. Dictionary object methods

Method	Description
Nonmutating	
`D.copy()`	Returns a shallow copy of the dictionary (a copy whose items are the same objects as *D*'s, not copies thereof), like `dict(D)`
`D.get(k[, x])`	Returns `D[k]` when *k* is a key in *D*; otherwise, returns *x* (or `None`, when *x* is not given)
`D.items()`	In v2, returns a new list with all items (key/value pairs) in *D*; in v3, returns an iterable `dict_items` instance, not a list
`D.iteritems()`	Returns an iterator on all items (key/value pairs) in *D* (v2 only)
`D.iterkeys()`	Returns an iterator on all keys in *D* (v2 only)
`D.itervalues()`	Returns an iterator on all values in *D* (v2 only)

Method	Description
`D.keys()`	In v2, returns a new list with all keys in *D*; in v3, returns an iterable `dict_keys` instance, not a list
`D.values()`	In v2, returns a new list with all values in *D*; in v3, returns an iterable `dict_values` instance, not a list
Mutating	
`D.clear()`	Removes all items from *D*, leaving *D* empty
`D.pop(k[, x])`	Removes and returns `D[k]` when *k* is a key in *D*; otherwise, returns *x* (or raises a `KeyError` exception when *x* is not given)
`D.popitem()`	Removes and returns an arbitrary item (key/value pair)
`D.setdefault(k[, x])`	Returns `D[k]` when *k* is a key in *D*; otherwise, sets `D[k]` equal to *x* (or `None`, when *x* is not given) and returns *x*
`D.update(D1)`	For each *k* in mapping *D1*, sets `D[k]` equal to `D1[k]`

The `items`, `keys`, and `values` methods return their resulting lists (in v2; `dict_...` iterable instances in v3) in arbitrary order.[7] If you call more than one of these methods without any intervening change to the dictionary, the order of the results is the same for all. The `iteritems`, `iterkeys`, and `itervalues` methods (v2 only) return iterators equivalent to these lists (we cover iterators in "Iterators" on page 76).

Never modify a dict's set of keys while iterating on it

An iterator or `dict_...` instance consumes less memory than a list, but you must never modify the set of keys in a dictionary (i.e., you must never either add or remove keys) while iterating over any of that dictionary's iterators.

Iterating on the lists returned by `items`, `keys`, or `values` in v2 carries no such constraint (in v3, for the same purpose, you can explicitly make lists, such as `list(D.keys())`). Iterating directly on a dictionary `D` is exactly like iterating on `D.iterkeys()` in v2, on `D.keys()` in v3.

v3's `dict_...` types are all iterable. `dict_items` and `dict_keys` also implement `set` nonmutating methods and behave much like `frozenset`s; `dict_values` doesn't,

7 In 3.6, as mentioned in the previous note, insertion order until a noninsertion mutator...but, to make your code robust, don't take advantage of this new constraint.

since, differently from the others (and from sets), it may contain some duplicate items.

The `popitem` method can be used for destructive iteration on a dictionary. Both `items` and `popitem` return dictionary items as key/value pairs. `popitem` is usable for a loop on a huge dictionary, when what you want is to "consume" the dictionary in the course of the loop.

`D.setdefault(k, x)` returns the same result as `D.get(k, x)`, but, when *k* is not a key in *D*, `setdefault` also has the side effect of binding `D[k]` to the value *x*. (In modern Python, `setdefault` is rarely used, since type `collections.defaultdict`, covered in "defaultdict" on page 219, offers similar functionality with more elegance and speed.)

The `pop` method returns the same result as `get`, but, when *k* is a key in *D*, `pop` also has the side effect of removing `D[k]` (when *x* is not specified, and *k* is not a key in *D*, `get` returns `None`, but `pop` raises an exception).

The `update` method can also accept an iterable of key/value pairs, as an alternative argument instead of a mapping, and can accept named arguments instead of—or in addition to—its positional argument; the semantics are the same as for passing such arguments when calling the built-in `dict` type, as covered in "Dictionaries" on page 50.

Control Flow Statements

A program's *control flow* is the order in which the program's code executes. The control flow of a Python program depends on conditional statements, loops, and function calls. (This section covers the `if` conditional statement and `for` and `while` loops; we cover functions in "Functions" on page 82.) Raising and handling exceptions also affects control flow; we cover exceptions in Chapter 5.

The if Statement

Often, you need to execute some statements only when some condition holds, or choose statements to execute depending on mutually exclusive conditions. The compound statement `if` —comprising `if`, `elif`, and `else` clauses—lets you conditionally execute blocks of statements. The syntax for the `if` statement is:

```
if expression:
    statement(s)
elif expression:
    statement(s)
elif expression:
    statement(s)
...
else:
    statement(s)
```

The `elif` and `else` clauses are optional. Note that, unlike some languages, Python does not have a "switch" statement. Use `if`, `elif`, and `else` for all conditional processing.

Here's a typical `if` statement with all three kinds of clauses (not in optimal style):

```
if x < 0: print('x is negative')
elif x % 2: print('x is positive and odd')
else: print('x is even and non-negative')
```

When there are multiple statements in a clause (i.e., the clause controls a block of statements), place the statements on separate logical lines after the line containing the clause's keyword (known as the *header line* of the clause), indented rightward from the header line. The block terminates when the indentation returns to that of the clause header (or further left from there). When there is just a single simple statement, as here, it can follow the `:` on the same logical line as the header, but it can also be on a separate logical line, immediately after the header line and indented rightward from it. Most Python programmers prefer the separate-line style, with four-space indents for the guarded statements. Such a style is more general and more readable, and recommended by *PEP 8 (https://www.python.org/dev/peps/pep-0008/#indentation)*. So, a generally preferred style is:

```
if x < 0:
    print('x is negative')
elif x % 2:
    print('x is positive and odd')
else:
    print('x is even and non-negative')
```

You can use any Python expression as the condition in an `if` or `elif` clause. Using an expression this way is known as using it *in a Boolean context*. In a Boolean context, any value is taken as either true or false. As mentioned earlier, any nonzero number or nonempty container (string, tuple, list, dictionary, set) evaluates as true; zero (of any numeric type), `None`, and empty containers evaluate as false. To test a value *x* in a Boolean context, use the following coding style:

```
if x:
```

This is the clearest and most Pythonic form. Do *not* use any of the following:

```
if x is True:
if x == True:
if bool(x):
```

There is a crucial difference between saying that an expression *returns* `True` (meaning the expression returns the value `1` with the `bool` type) and saying that an expression *evaluates as* true (meaning the expression returns any result that is true in a Boolean context). When testing an expression, for example in an `if` clause, you only care about what it *evaluates as*, not what, precisely, it *returns*.

When the `if` clause's condition evaluates as true, the statements after the `if` clause execute, then the entire `if` statement ends. Otherwise, Python evaluates each `elif` clause's condition, in order. The statements after the first `elif` clause whose condition evaluates as true, if any, execute, and the entire `if` statement ends. Otherwise, when an `else` clause exists it is executed, and then the statements after the entire `if` construct execute.

The while Statement

The `while` statement repeats execution of a statement or block of statements, controlled by a conditional expression. Here's the syntax of the `while` statement:

```
while expression:
    statement(s)
```

A `while` statement can also include an `else` clause, covered in "The else Clause on Loop Statements" on page 81, and `break` and `continue` statements, covered in "The break Statement" on page 80 and "The continue Statement" on page 80.

Here's a typical `while` statement:

```
count = 0
while x > 0:
    x //= 2           # truncating division
    count += 1
print('The approximate log2 is', count)
```

First, Python evaluates *`expression`*, which is known as the *loop condition*. When the condition is false, the `while` statement ends. When the loop condition is true, the statement or statements that make up the *loop body* execute. Once the loop body finishes executing, Python evaluates the loop condition again to check whether another iteration should execute. This process continues until the loop condition is false, at which point the `while` statement ends.

The loop body should contain code that eventually makes the loop condition false; otherwise, the loop never ends (unless the body raises an exception or executes a `break` statement). A loop within a function's body also ends if the loop body executes a `return` statement, since in this case the whole function ends.

The for Statement

The `for` statement repeats execution of a statement, or block of statements, controlled by an iterable expression. Here's the syntax of the `for` statement:

```
for target in iterable:
    statement(s)
```

The `in` keyword is part of the syntax of the `for` statement; its purpose here is distinct from the `in` operator, which tests membership.

Here's a typical for statement:

```
for letter in 'ciao':
    print('give me a', letter, '...')
```

A for statement can also include an else clause, covered in "The else Clause on Loop Statements" on page 81, and break and continue statements, covered in "The break Statement" on page 80 and "The continue Statement" on page 80. *iterable* may be any Python expression suitable as an argument to built-in function iter, which returns an iterator object (explained in detail in the next section). In particular, any sequence is iterable. *target* is normally an identifier that names the *control variable* of the loop; the for statement successively rebinds this variable to each item of the iterator, in order. The statement or statements that make up the *loop body* execute once for each item in *iterable* (unless the loop ends because of an exception or a break or return statement). Note that, since the loop body may contain a break statement to terminate the loop, this is one case in which you may use an *unbounded* iterable—one that, per se, would never cease yielding items.

You can also have a target with multiple identifiers, like in an unpacking assignment. In this case, the iterator's items must be iterables, each with exactly as many items as there are identifiers in the target (in v3 only, precisely one of the identifiers can be preceded by a star, in which case the starred item is bound to a list of all items, if any, that were not assigned to other targets). For example, when *d* is a dictionary, this is a typical way to loop on the items (key/value pairs) in *d*:

```
for key, value in d.items():
    if key and value:             # print only true keys and values
        print(key, value)
```

The items method returns a list (in v2; another kind of iterable, in v3) of key/value pairs, so we use a for loop with two identifiers in the target to unpack each item into key and value. Although components of a target are commonly identifiers, values can be bound to any acceptable LHS expression as covered in "Assignment Statements" on page 53:

```
prototype = [1, 'placemarker', 3]
for prototype[1] in 'xyz': print(prototype)
# prints [1, 'x', 3], then [1, 'y', 3], then [1, 'z', 3]
```

The Python Language

Don't alter mutable objects while looping on them

When an iterable has a mutable underlying object, don't alter that object during a `for` loop on it. For example, the preceding key/value printing example cannot alter *d* in v3 (and couldn't in v2 if it used `iteritems` instead of `items`). `iteritems` in v2 (and `items` in v3) return iterables whose underlying object is *d*, so the loop body cannot mutate the set of keys in *d* (e.g., by executing `del d[key]`). `d.items()` in v2 (and `list(d.items())` in v3) return new, independent lists, so that *d* is not the underlying object of the iterable; therefore, the loop body could mutate *d*. Specifically:

- When looping on a list, do not insert, append, or delete items (rebinding an item at an existing index is OK).
- When looping on a dictionary, do not add or delete items (rebinding the value for an existing key is OK).
- When looping on a set, do not add or delete items (no alteration permitted).

The control target variable(s) may be rebound in the loop body, but get rebound again to the next item in the iterator at the next iteration of the loop. The loop body does not execute at all if the iterator yields no items. In this case, the control variable is not bound or rebound in any way by the `for` statement. However, if the iterator yields at least one item, then, when the loop statement terminates, the control variable remains bound to the last value to which the loop statement has bound it. The following code is therefore correct only when `someseq` is not empty:

```
for x in someseq:
    process(x)
print('Last item processed was', x)
```

Iterators

An *iterator* is an object *i* such that you can call `next(i)`. `next(i)` returns the next item of iterator *i* or, when iterator *i* has no more items, raises a `StopIteration` exception. Alternatively, you can call `next(i, default)`, in which case, when iterator *i* has no more items, the call returns *default*.

When you write a class (see "Classes and Instances" on page 102), you can allow instances of the class to be iterators by defining a special method `__next__` (in v2 the method must be called `next`—this was eventually seen as a design error) that takes no argument except `self`, and returns the next item or raises `StopIteration`. Most iterators are built by implicit or explicit calls to built-in function `iter`, covered in Table 7-2. Calling a generator also returns an iterator, as we'll discuss in "Generators" on page 96.

The `for` statement implicitly calls `iter` to get an iterator. The statement:

```
for x in c:
    statement(s)
```

is exactly equivalent to:

```
_temporary_iterator = iter(c)
while True:
    try: x = next(_temporary_iterator)
    except StopIteration: break
    statement(s)
```

where *_temporary_iterator* is an arbitrary name not used elsewhere in the current scope.

Thus, when `iter(c)` returns an iterator *i* such that `next(i)` never raises `StopIteration` (an *unbounded iterator*), the loop `for x in c` never terminates (unless the statements in the loop body include suitable `break` or `return` statements, or raise or propagate exceptions). `iter(c)`, in turn, calls special method `c.__iter__()` to obtain and return an iterator on *c*. We'll talk more about the special method `__iter__` in "Container methods" on page 134.

Many of the best ways to build and manipulate iterators are found in the standard library module `itertools`, covered in "The itertools Module" on page 228.

range and xrange

Looping over a sequence of integers is a common task, so Python provides built-in functions `range` (and, in v2, `xrange`) to generate integer sequences. The simplest way to loop *n* times in Python is:

```
for i in range(n):
    statement(s)
```

In v2, `range(x)` returns a list whose items are consecutive integers from `0` (included) up to *x* (excluded). `range(x, y)` returns a list whose items are consecutive integers from *x* (included) up to *y* (excluded). The result is the empty list when *x* is greater than or equal to *y*. `range(x, y, stride)` returns a list of integers from *x* (included) up to *y* (excluded), such that the difference between each two adjacent items is *stride*. If *stride* is less than `0`, `range` counts down from *x* to *y*. `range` returns the empty list when *x* is greater than or equal to *y* and *stride* is greater than `0`, or when *x* is less than or equal to *y* and *stride* is less than `0`. When *stride* equals `0`, `range` raises an exception.

While `range`, in v2, returns a normal list object, usable for any purpose, `xrange` (v2 only) returns a special-purpose object, intended just for use in iterations like the `for` statement shown previously (`xrange` itself does not return an iterator; however, you can easily obtain such an iterator, should you need one, by calling `iter(xrange(...))`). The special-purpose object returned by `xrange` consumes less memory (for wide ranges, *much* less memory) than the list object `range` returns;

apart from such memory issues, you can use `range` wherever you could use `xrange`, but not vice versa. For example, in v2:

```
>>> print(range(1, 5))
[1, 2, 3, 4]
>>> print(xrange(1, 5))
xrange(1, 5)
```

Here, `range` returns a perfectly ordinary list, which displays quite normally, but `xrange` returns a special-purpose object, which displays in its own special way.

In v3, there is no `xrange`, and `range` works similarly to v2's `xrange`. In v3, if you need a `list` that's an arithmetic progression of `int`s, call `list(range(...))`.

List comprehensions

A common use of a `for` loop is to inspect each item in an iterable and build a new list by appending the results of an expression computed on some or all of the items. The expression form known as a *list comprehension* or *listcomp* lets you code this common idiom concisely and directly. Since a list comprehension is an expression (rather than a block of statements), you can use it wherever you need an expression (e.g., as an argument in a function call, in a `return` statement, or as a subexpression of some other expression).

A list comprehension has the following syntax:

```
[ expression for target in iterable lc-clauses ]
```

`target` and *`iterable`* are the same as in a regular `for` statement. When *`expression`* denotes a tuple, you must enclose it in parentheses.

`lc-clauses` is a series of zero or more clauses, each with one of the two forms:

```
for target in iterable
if expression
```

`target` and *`iterable`* in each `for` clause of a list comprehension have the same syntax and meaning as those in a regular `for` statement, and the *`expression`* in each `if` clause of a list comprehension has the same syntax and meaning as the *`expression`* in a regular `if` statement.

A list comprehension is equivalent to a `for` loop that builds the same list by repeated calls to the resulting list's `append` method. For example (assigning the list comprehension result to a variable for clarity):

```
result1 = [x+1 for x in some_sequence]
```

is (apart from the different variable name) the same as the `for` loop:

```
result2 = []
for x in some_sequence:
    result2.append(x+1)
```

Here's a list comprehension that uses an `if` clause:

```
result3 = [x+1 for x in some_sequence if x>23]
```

This list comprehension is the same as a for loop that contains an if statement:

```
result4 = []
for x in some_sequence:
    if x>23:
        result4.append(x+1)
```

And here's a list comprehension that uses a nested for clause to flatten a "list of lists" into a single list of items:

```
result5 = [x for sublist in listoflists for x in sublist]
```

This is the same as a for loop with another for loop nested inside:

```
result6 = []
for sublist in listoflists:
    for x in sublist:
        result6.append(x)
```

As these examples show, the order of for and if in a list comprehension is the same as in the equivalent loop, but, in the list comprehension, the nesting remains implicit. If you remember "order for clauses as in a nested loop," it can help you get the ordering of the list comprehension's clauses right.

Don't build a list if you don't need to

If you are simply going to loop on the values, rather than requiring an actual, indexable list, consider a generator expression instead (covered in "Generator expressions" on page 97). This lets you avoid list creation, and takes less memory.

List comprehensions and variable scope

In v2, target variables of for clauses in a list comprehension remain bound to their last value when the list comprehension is done, just like they would if you used for statements; so, remember to use target names that won't trample over other local variables you need. In v3, a list comprehension is its own scope, so you need not worry; also, no such worry, in either v2 or v3, for generator expressions, set comprehensions, and dict comprehensions—only for listcomps.

Set comprehensions

A *set comprehension* has exactly the same syntax and semantics as a list comprehension, except that you enclose it in braces ({}) rather than in brackets ([]). The result is a set, so the order of items is not meaningful. For example:

```
s = {n//2 for n in range(10)}
print(sorted(s))  # prints: [0, 1, 2, 3, 4]
```

A similar list comprehension would have each item repeated twice, but, of course, a `set` intrinsically removes duplicates.

Dict comprehensions

A *dict comprehension* has the same syntax as a set comprehension, except that, instead of a single expression before the `for` clause, you use two expressions with a colon `:` between them—*`key`*`:`*`value`*. The result is a `dict`, so, just as in a `set`, the order of items (in a `dict`, that's key/value pairs) is not meaningful. For example:

```
d = {n:n//2 for n in range(5)}
print(d)  # prints: {0:0, 1:0, 2:1, 3:1, 4:2] or other order
```

The break Statement

The `break` statement is allowed only within a loop body. When `break` executes, the loop terminates. If a loop nests inside other loops, a `break` terminates only the innermost nested loop. In practice, a `break` is usually within a clause of an `if` in the loop body, so that `break` executes conditionally.

One common use of `break` is in the implementation of a loop that decides whether it should keep looping only in the middle of each loop iteration (what Knuth called the "loop and a half" structure in his seminal 1974 paper (*http://www.kohala.com/start/papers.others/knuth.dec74.html*), in which he also first proposed using "devices like indentation, rather than delimiters" to express program structure—just as Python does). For example:

```
while True:             # this loop can never terminate naturally
    x = get_next()
    y = preprocess(x)
    if not keep_looping(x, y): break
    process(x, y)
```

The continue Statement

The `continue` statement can exist only within a loop body. When `continue` executes, the current iteration of the loop body terminates, and execution continues with the next iteration of the loop. In practice, a `continue` is usually within a clause of an `if` in the loop body, so that `continue` executes conditionally.

Sometimes, a `continue` statement can take the place of nested `if` statements within a loop. For example:

```
for x in some_container:
    if not seems_ok(x): continue
    lowbound, highbound = bounds_to_test()
    if x<lowbound or x>=highbound: continue
    pre_process(x)
    if final_check(x):
        do_processing(x)
```

This equivalent code does conditional processing without `continue`:

```
for x in some_container:
    if seems_ok(x):
        lowbound, highbound = bounds_to_test()
        if lowbound <= x < highbound:
            pre_process(x)
            if final_check(x):
                do_processing(x)
```

Flat is better than nested

Both versions work the same way, so which one you use is a matter of personal preference and style. One of the principles of The Zen of Python (*https://www.python.org/dev/peps/pep-0020/*) (which you can see at any time by typing `import this` at an interactive Python interpreter prompt) is "Flat is better than nested." The `continue` statement is just one way Python helps you move toward the goal of a less-nested structure in a loop, if you so choose.

The Python Language

The else Clause on Loop Statements

`while` and `for` statements may optionally have a trailing `else` clause. The statement or block under that `else` executes when the loop terminates *naturally* (at the end of the `for` iterator, or when the `while` loop condition becomes false), but not when the loop terminates *prematurely* (via `break`, `return`, or an exception). When a loop contains one or more `break` statements, you often need to check whether the loop terminates naturally or prematurely. You can use an `else` clause on the loop for this purpose:

```
for x in some_container:
    if is_ok(x): break  # item x is satisfactory, terminate loop
else:
    print('Beware: no satisfactory item was found in container')
    x = None
```

The pass Statement

The body of a Python compound statement cannot be empty; it must always contain at least one statement. You can use a `pass` statement, which performs no action, as an explicit placeholder when a statement is syntactically required but you have nothing to do. Here's an example of using `pass` in a conditional statement as a part of somewhat convoluted logic to test mutually exclusive conditions:

```
if condition1(x):
    process1(x)
elif x>23 or condition2(x) and x<5:
    pass  # nothing to be done in this case
elif condition3(x):
    process3(x)
```

```
else:
    process_default(x)
```

Empty def or class statements: use a docstring, not pass

As the body of an otherwise empty `def` or `class` statement, you should use a docstring, covered in "Docstrings" on page 87; when you do write a docstring, then you do not need to also add a `pass` statement (you can do so if you wish, but it's not optimal Python style).

The try and raise Statements

Python supports exception handling with the `try` statement, which includes `try`, `except`, `finally`, and `else` clauses. Your code can explicitly raise an exception with the `raise` statement. As we discuss in detail in "Exception Propagation" on page 155, when code raises an exception, normal control flow of the program stops, and Python looks for a suitable exception handler.

The with Statement

A `with` statement can be a much more readable and useful alternative to the `try`/`finally` statement. We discuss it in detail in "The with Statement and Context Managers" on page 153.

Functions

Most statements in a typical Python program are part of functions. Code in a function body may be faster than at a module's top level, as covered in "Avoid exec and from ... import *" on page 491, so there are excellent practical reasons to put most of your code into functions, in addition to the advantages in clarity and readability. On the other hand, there are *no* disadvantages to organizing your code into functions versus leaving the code at module level.

A *function* is a group of statements that execute upon request. Python provides many built-in functions and allows programmers to define their own functions. A request to execute a function is known as a *function call*. When you call a function, you can pass arguments that specify data upon which the function performs its computation. In Python, a function always returns a result value, either `None` or a value that represents the results of the computation. Functions defined within `class` statements are also known as *methods*. We cover issues specific to methods in "Bound and Unbound Methods" on page 112; the general coverage of functions in this section, however, also applies to methods.

In Python, functions are objects (values), handled just like other objects. Thus, you can pass a function as an argument in a call to another function. Similarly, a function can return another function as the result of a call. A function, just like any other object, can be bound to a variable, can be an item in a container, and can be an attribute of an object. Functions can also be keys into a dictionary. For example, if you need to quickly find a function's inverse given the function, you could define a dictionary whose keys and values are functions and then make the dictionary bidirectional. Here's a small example of this idea, using some functions from module math, covered in "The math and cmath Modules" on page 433, where we create a basic inverse mapping and add the inverse of each entry:

```
def make_inverse(inverse_dict):
    for f in list(inverse_dict):
        inverse_dict[inverse_dict[f]] = f
    return inverse_dict
inverse = make_inverse({sin:asin, cos:acos, tan:atan, log:exp})
```

The fact that functions are ordinary objects in Python is often expressed by saying that functions are *first-class* objects.

The def Statement

The def statement is the most common way to define a function. def is a single-clause compound statement with the following syntax:

```
def function_name(parameters):
    statement(s)
```

function_name is an identifier. It is a variable that gets bound (or rebound) to the function object when def executes.

parameters is an optional list of identifiers that get bound to the values supplied when you call the function, which we refer to as *arguments* to distinguish between definitions (parameters) and calls (arguments). In the simplest case a function doesn't have any parameters, which means the function won't accept any arguments when you call it. In this case, the function definition has empty parentheses after *function_name*, as must all calls to the function.

When a function does accept arguments, *parameters* contains one or more identifiers, separated by commas (,). In this case, each call to the function supplies values, known as *arguments*, corresponding to the parameters listed in the function definition. The parameters are local variables of the function (as we'll discuss later in this section), and each call to the function binds these local variables in the function namespace to the corresponding values that the caller, or the function definition, supplies as arguments.

The nonempty block of statements, known as the *function body*, does not execute when the def statement executes. Rather, the function body executes later, each time you call the function. The function body can contain zero or more occurrences of the return statement, as we'll discuss shortly.

Here's an example of a simple function that returns a value that is twice the value passed to it each time it's called:

```
def twice(x):
    return x*2
```

Note that the argument can be anything that can be multiplied by two, so the function could be called with a number, string, list, or tuple as an argument, and it would return, in each case, a new value of the same type as the argument.

Parameters

Parameters (more pedantically, *formal parameters*) name, and sometimes specify a default value for, the values passed into a function call. Each of the names is bound inside a new local namespace every time the function is called; this namespace is destroyed when the function returns or otherwise exits (values returned by the function may be kept alive by the caller binding the function result). Parameters that are just identifiers indicate *positional parameters* (also known as *mandatory parameters*). Each call to the function must supply a corresponding value (argument) for each mandatory (positional) parameter.

In the comma-separated list of parameters, zero or more positional parameters may be followed by zero or more *named parameters* (also known as *optional parameters*, and sometimes—confusingly, since they do not involve any keyword—as *keyword parameters*), each with the syntax:

```
identifier=expression
```

The `def` statement evaluates each such *`expression`* and saves a reference to the expression's value, known as the *default value* for the parameter, among the attributes of the function object. When a function call does not supply an argument corresponding to a named parameter, the call binds the parameter's identifier to its default value for that execution of the function.

Note that Python computes each default value precisely once, when the `def` statement evaluates, *not* each time the resulting function gets called. In particular, this means that exactly the *same* object, the default value, gets bound to the named parameter whenever the caller does not supply a corresponding argument.

Beware using mutable default values

A mutable default value, such as a list, can be altered each time you call the function without an explicit argument corresponding to the respective parameter. This is usually not the behavior you want; see the following detailed explanation.

Things can be tricky when the default value is a mutable object and the function body alters the parameter. For example:

```
def f(x, y=[]):
    y.append(x)
    return y, id(y)
print(f(23))                  # prints: ([23], 4302354376)
print(f(42))                  # prints: ([23, 42], 4302354376)
```

The second `print` prints `[23, 42]` because the first call to `f` altered the default value of `y`, originally an empty list `[]`, by appending `23` to it. The `id` values confirm that both calls return the same object. If you want y to be bound to a new empty list object each time you call f with a single argument, use the following idiom instead:

```
def f(x, y=None):
    if y is None: y = []
    y.append(x)
    return y, id(y)
print(f(23))                # prints: ([23], 4302354376)
prinf(f(42))                # prints: ([42], 4302180040)
```

Of course, there are cases in which you explicitly want to alter a parameter's default value, most often for caching purposes, as in the following example:

```
def cached_compute(x, _cache={}):
    if x not in _cache:
        _cache[x] = costly_computation(x)
    return _cache[x]
```

Such caching behavior (also known as *memoization*), however, is usually best obtained by decorating the underlying function with `functools.lru_cache`, covered in Table 7-4.

At the end of the parameters, you may optionally use either or both of the special forms **args* and ***kwds*.[8] There is nothing special about the names—you can use any identifier you want in each special form; *args* and *kwds* or *kwargs*, as well as *a* and *k*, are just popular identifiers to use in these roles. If both forms are present, the form with two asterisks must come second.

**args* specifies that any extra positional arguments to a call (i.e., those positional arguments not explicitly specified in the signature, defined in "Function signatures" on page 86 below) get collected into a (possibly empty) tuple, and bound in the call namespace to the name *args*. Similarly ***kwds* specifies that any extra named arguments (i.e., those named arguments not explicitly specified in the signature, defined in "Function signatures" on page 86 below) get collected into a (possibly empty) dictionary[9] whose items are the names and values of those arguments, and bound to the name *kwds* in the function call namespace (we cover positional and named *arguments* in "Calling Functions" on page 89).

For example, here's a function that accepts any number of positional arguments and returns their sum (also showing the use of an identifier other than **args*):

```
def sum_args(*numbers):
    return sum(numbers)
print(sum_args(23, 42))          # prints: 65
```

8 Also spelled **kwargs.

9 ***New in 3.6***: the mapping to which *kwds* is bound now preserves the order in which you pass extra named arguments in the call.

Function signatures

The number of parameters of a function, together with the parameters' names, the number of mandatory parameters, and the information on whether (at the end of the parameters) either or both of the single- and double-asterisk special forms are present, collectively form a specification known as the function's *signature*. A function's signature defines the ways in which you can call the function.

"Keyword-only" Parameters (v3 Only)

In v3 only, a `def` statement also optionally lets you specify parameters that *must*, when you call the function, correspond to named arguments of the form *`identifier=expression`* (see "Kinds of arguments" on page 90) if they are present at all. These are known as (confusingly, since keywords have nothing to do with them) as *keyword-only parameters*. If these parameters appear, they must come after `*args` (if any) and before `**kwargs` (if any).

Each keyword-only parameter can be specified in the parameter list as either a simple identifier (in which case it's mandatory, when calling the function, to pass the corresponding named argument), or in *`identifier=default`* form (in which case it's optional, when calling the function, whether to pass the corresponding argument—but, when you pass it, you *must* pass it as a named argument, not as a positional one). Either form can be used for each different keyword-only parameter. It's more usual and readable to have simple identifiers, if any, at the start of the keyword-only parameter specifications, and *`identifier=default`* forms, if any, following them, though this is not a requirement of the language.

All the keyword-only parameter specifications come *after* the special form *`*args`*, if the latter is present. If that special form is not present, then the start of the sequence of keyword-only parameter specifications is a null parameter, consisting solely of an `*` (asterisk), to which no argument corresponds. For example:

```
def f(a, *, b, c=56):  # b and c are keyword-only
    return a, b, c
f(12,b=34)  # returns (12, 34, 56)—c's optional, having a default
f(12)       # raises a TypeError exception
# error message is: missing 1 required keyword-only argument: 'b'
```

If you also specify the special form *`**kwds`*, it must come at the end of the parameter list (after the keyword-only parameter specifications, if any). For example:

```
def g(x, *a, b=23, **k):  # b is keyword-only
    return x, a, b, k
g(1, 2, 3, c=99)  # returns (1, (2, 3), 23, {'c': 99})
```

Attributes of Function Objects

The `def` statement sets some attributes of a function object. Attribute `__name__` refers to the identifier string given as the function name in the `def`. You may rebind the attribute to any string value, but trying to unbind it raises an exception.

Attribute __defaults__, which you may freely rebind or unbind, refers to the tuple of default values for optional parameters (an empty tuple, if the function has no optional parameters).

Docstrings

Another function attribute is the *documentation string*, also known as the *docstring*. You may use or rebind a function's docstring attribute as __doc__. If the first statement in the function body is a string literal, the compiler binds that string as the function's docstring attribute. A similar rule applies to classes (see "Class documentation strings" on page 105) and modules (see "Module documentation strings" on page 176). Docstrings usually span multiple physical lines, so you normally specify them in triple-quoted string literal form. For example:

```
def sum_args(*numbers):
    """Return the sum of multiple numerical arguments.

    The arguments are zero or more numbers.
    The result is their sum.
    """
    return sum(numbers)
```

Documentation strings should be part of any Python code you write. They play a role similar to that of comments, but their applicability is wider, since they remain available at runtime (unless you run your program with **python -OO**, as covered in "Command-Line Syntax and Options" on page 27). Development environments and tools can use docstrings from function, class, and module objects to remind the programmer how to use those objects. The doctest module (covered in "The doctest Module" on page 459) makes it easy to check that sample code present in docstrings is accurate and correct, and remains so, as the code and docs get edited and maintained.

To make your docstrings as useful as possible, respect a few simple conventions. The first line of a docstring should be a concise summary of the function's purpose, starting with an uppercase letter and ending with a period. It should not mention the function's name, unless the name happens to be a natural-language word that comes naturally as part of a good, concise summary of the function's operation. If the docstring is multiline, the second line should be empty, and the following lines should form one or more paragraphs, separated by empty lines, describing the function's parameters, preconditions, return value, and side effects (if any). Further explanations, bibliographical references, and usage examples (which you should check with doctest) can optionally follow toward the end of the docstring.

Other attributes of function objects

In addition to its predefined attributes, a function object may have other arbitrary attributes. To create an attribute of a function object, bind a value to the appropriate attribute reference in an assignment statement after the def statement executes. For example, a function could count how many times it gets called:

```
def counter():
    counter.count += 1
    return counter.count
counter.count = 0
```

Note that this is *not* common usage. More often, when you want to group together some state (data) and some behavior (code), you should use the object-oriented mechanisms covered in Chapter 4. However, the ability to associate arbitrary attributes with a function can sometimes come in handy.

Function Annotations and Type Hints (v3 Only)

In v3 only, every parameter in a `def` clause can be *annotated* with an arbitrary expression—that is, wherever within the `def`'s parameter list you can use an identifier, you can alternatively use the form *`identifier:expression`*, and the expression's value becomes the *annotation* for that parameter name.

You can annotate the return value of the function, using the form `->`*`expression`* between the `)` of the `def` clause and the `:` that ends the `def` clause; the expression's value becomes the annotation for name `'return'`. For example:

```
>>> def f(a:'foo', b)->'bar': pass
...
>>> f.__annotations__
{'a': 'foo', 'return': 'bar'}
```

As shown in this example, the `__annotations__` attribute of the function object is a `dict` mapping each annotated identifier to the respective annotation.

You can use annotations for whatever purpose you wish: Python itself does nothing with them, except constructing the `__annotations__` attribute.

The intention is to let future, hypothetical third-party tools leverage annotations to perform more thorough static checking on annotated functions. (If you want to experiment with such static checks, we recommend you try the mypy project (*http://mypy-lang.org/*).)

Type hints (Python 3.5 only)

To further support hypothetical third-party tools, Python 3.5 has introduced a complicated set of commenting conventions, and a new *provisional* module called `typing` in the standard library, to standardize how annotations are to be used to denote typing hints (again, Python does nothing with the information, but third-party tools may eventually be developed to leverage this now-standardized information).

A provisional module is one that might change drastically, or even disappear, as early as the next feature release (so, in the future, Python 3.7 might not have the module `typing` in its standard library, or the module's contents might be different). It is not yet intended for use "in production," but rather just for experimental purposes.

As a consequence, we do not further cover type hints in this book; see PEP 484 (*https://www.python.org/dev/peps/pep-0484/*) and the many links from it for much, much more. (The mypy (*http://mypy-lang.org/*) third-party project does fully support PEP 484–compliant v3 Python code).

New in 3.6: Type annotations

Although the conventions defined in PEP 484 could help third-party static analysis tools operate on Python code, the PEP does not include syntax support for explicitly marking variables as being of a specific type; such type annotations were embedded in the form of comments. PEP 526 (*https://www.python.org/dev/peps/pep-0526/*) now defines syntax for variable type annotations.

Guido van Rossum has cited anecdotal evidence (*https://mail.python.org/pipermail/python-dev/2016-September/146282.html*) that type annotations can be helpful, for example, when engineering large legacy codebases. They may be unnecessarily complicated for beginners, but they remain completely optional and so can be taught as required to those with some Python experience. While you can still use PEP 484–style comments, it seems likely that PEP 526 annotations will supersede them. (The mypy (*http://mypy-lang.org/*) third-party project, at the time of this writing, only partially supports PEP 526–compliant Python 3.6 code.)

The return Statement

The `return` statement in Python can exist only inside a function body, and can optionally be followed by an expression. When `return` executes, the function terminates, and the value of the expression is the function's result. A function returns `None` if it terminates by reaching the end of its body or by executing a `return` statement that has no expression (or, of course, by explicitly executing `return None`).

Good style in return statements

As a matter of good style, *never* write a `return` statement without an expression at the end of a function body. When some `return` statements in a function have an expression, then all `return` statements in the function should have an expression. `return None` should only ever be written explicitly to meet this style requirement. Python does not enforce these stylistic conventions, but your code is clearer and more readable when you follow them.

Calling Functions

A function call is an expression with the following syntax:

```
function_object(arguments)
```

`function_object` may be any reference to a function (or other callable) object; most often, it's the function's name. The parentheses denote the function-call operation itself. *`arguments`*, in the simplest case, is a series of zero or more expressions separa-

ted by commas (`,`), giving values for the function's corresponding parameters. When the function call executes, the parameters are bound to the argument values, the function body executes, and the value of the function-call expression is whatever the function returns.

Don't forget the trailing () to call a function

Just *mentioning* a function (or other callable object) does *not*, per se, call it. To *call* a function (or other object) without arguments, you *must* use `()` after the function's name (or other reference to the callable object).

The semantics of argument passing

In traditional terms, all argument passing in Python is *by value* (although, in modern terminology, to say that argument passing is *by object reference* is more precise and accurate; some, but not all, of this book's authors also like the synonym *call by sharing*). For example, if you pass a variable as an argument, Python passes to the function the object (value) to which the variable currently refers, not the variable itself, and this value is bound to the parameter name in the function call namespace. Thus, a function cannot rebind the caller's variables. However, if you pass a mutable object as an argument, the function may request changes to that object, because Python passes the object itself, not a copy. Rebinding a variable and mutating an object are totally disjoint concepts. For example:

```
def f(x, y):
    x = 23
    y.append(42)
a = 77
b = [99]
f(a, b)
print(a, b)                   # prints: 77 [99, 42]
```

`print` shows that `a` is still bound to `77`. Function `f`'s rebinding of its parameter `x` to `23` has no effect on `f`'s caller, nor, in particular, on the binding of the caller's variable that happened to be used to pass `77` as the parameter's value. However, `print` also shows that `b` is now bound to `[99, 42]`. `b` is still bound to the same list object as before the call, but that object has mutated, as `f` has appended `42` to that list object. In either case, `f` has not altered the caller's bindings, nor can `f` alter the number `77`, since numbers are immutable. However, `f` can alter a list object, since list objects are mutable. In this example, `f` mutates the list object that the caller passes to `f` as the second argument by calling the object's `append` method.

Kinds of arguments

Arguments that are just expressions are known as *positional arguments*. Each positional argument supplies the value for the parameter that corresponds to it by position (order) in the function definition. There is no requirement for positional arguments to match positional parameters—if there are more positional arguments that positional parameters, the additional arguments are bound by position to named parameters, if any, and then (if the function's signature includes a *args special form) to the tuple bound to *args*. For example:

```
def f(a, b, c=23, d=42, *x):
    print(a, b, c, d, x)
f(1,2,3,4,5,6)  # prints (1, 2, 3, 4, (5, 6))
```

In a function call, zero or more positional arguments may be followed by zero or more *named arguments* (sometimes confusingly known as *keyword arguments*), each with the following syntax:

```
identifier=expression
```

In the absence of any **kwds parameter, the *identifier* must be one of the parameter names used in the def statement for the function. The *expression* supplies the value for the parameter of that name. Many built-in functions do not accept named arguments: you must call such functions with positional arguments only. However, functions coded in Python accept named as well as positional arguments, so you may call them in different ways. Positional parameters can be matched by named arguments, in the absence of matching positional arguments.

A function call must supply, via a positional or a named argument, exactly one value for each mandatory parameter, and zero or one value for each optional parameter. For example:

```
def divide(divisor, dividend):
    return dividend // divisor
print(divide(12, 94))                        # prints: 7
print(divide(dividend=94, divisor=12))       # prints: 7
```

As you can see, the two calls to divide are equivalent. You can pass named arguments for readability purposes whenever you think that identifying the role of each argument and controlling the order of arguments enhances your code's clarity.

A common use of named arguments is to bind some optional parameters to specific values, while letting other optional parameters take default values:

```
def f(middle, begin='init', end='finis'):
    return begin+middle+end
print(f('tini', end=''))                    # prints: inittini
```

Using named argument end='', the caller specifies a value (the empty string '') for f's third parameter, end, and still lets f's second parameter, begin, use its default value, the string 'init'. Note that you may pass the arguments as positional arguments, even when the parameters are named; for example, using the preceding function:

```
print(f('a','c','t'))                       # prints: cat
```

At the end of the arguments in a function call, you may optionally use either or both of the special forms **seq* and ***dct*. If both forms are present, the form with two asterisks must be last. **seq* passes the items of *seq* to the function as positional arguments (after the normal positional arguments, if any, that the call gives with the usual syntax). *seq* may be any iterable. `**dct` passes the items of *dct* to the function as named arguments, where *dct* must be a dictionary whose keys are all strings. Each item's key is a parameter name, and the item's value is the argument's value.

Sometimes you want to pass an argument of the form `*seq` or `**dct` when the parameters use similar forms, as covered earlier in "Parameters" on page 84. For example, using the function `sum_args` defined in that section (and shown again here), you may want to print the sum of all the values in dictionary *d*. This is easy with `*seq`:

```
def sum_args(*numbers):
    return sum(numbers)
print(sum_args(*d.values()))
```

(Of course, `print(sum(d.values()))` would be simpler and more direct.)

You may also pass arguments `*seq` or `**dct` when calling a function that does not use the corresponding forms in its signature. In that case, of course, you must ensure that iterable *seq* has the right number of items, or, respectively, that dictionary *dct* uses the right identifier strings as its keys; otherwise, the call operation raises an exception. As noted in ""Keyword-only" Parameters (v3 Only)" on page 86, keyword-only parameters in v3 *cannot* be matched with a positional argument (unlike named parameters); they must match a named argument, explicit or passed via `**dct`.

In v3, a function call may have zero or more occurrences of `*seq` and/or `**dct`, as specified in PEP 448 (*https://www.python.org/dev/peps/pep-0448/*).

Namespaces

A function's parameters, plus any names that are bound (by assignment or by other binding statements, such as `def`) in the function body, make up the function's *local namespace*, also known as *local scope*. Each of these variables is known as a *local variable* of the function.

Variables that are not local are known as *global variables* (in the absence of nested function definitions, which we'll discuss shortly). Global variables are attributes of the module object, as covered in "Attributes of module objects" on page 175. Whenever a function's local variable has the same name as a global variable, that name, within the function body, refers to the local variable, not the global one. We express this by saying that the local variable *hides* the global variable of the same name throughout the function body.

The global statement

By default, any variable that is bound within a function body is a local variable of the function. If a function needs to bind or rebind some global variables (*not* a good practice!), the first statement of the function's body must be:

```
global identifiers
```

where *`identifiers`* is one or more identifiers separated by commas (`,`). The identifiers listed in a `global` statement refer to the global variables (i.e., attributes of the module object) that the function needs to bind or rebind. For example, the function `counter` that we saw in "Other attributes of function objects" on page 87 could be implemented using `global` and a global variable, rather than an attribute of the function object:

```
_count = 0
def counter():
    global _count
    _count += 1
    return _count
```

Without the `global` statement, the `counter` function would raise an `UnboundLocalError` exception because `_count` would then be an uninitialized (unbound) local variable. While the `global` statement enables this kind of programming, this style is inelegant and unadvisable. As we mentioned earlier, when you want to group together some state and some behavior, the object-oriented mechanisms covered in Chapter 4 are usually best.

Eschew global

Never use `global` if the function body just *uses* a global variable (including mutating the object bound to that variable, when the object is mutable). Use a `global` statement only if the function body *rebinds* a global variable (generally by assigning to the variable's name). As a matter of style, don't use `global` unless it's strictly necessary, as its presence causes readers of your program to assume the statement is there for some useful purpose. In particular, never use `global` except as the first statement in a function body.

Nested functions and nested scopes

A `def` statement within a function body defines a *nested function*, and the function whose body includes the `def` is known as an *outer function* to the nested one. Code in a nested function's body may access (but not rebind) local variables of an outer function, also known as *free variables* of the nested function.

The simplest way to let a nested function access a value is often not to rely on nested scopes, but rather to pass that value explicitly as one of the function's arguments. If necessary, the argument's value can be bound at nested function `def` time, by using the value as the default for an optional argument. For example:

```
def percent1(a, b, c):
    def pc(x, total=a+b+c):
        return (x*100.0) / total
    print('Percentages are:', pc(a), pc(b), pc(c))
```

Here's the same functionality using nested scopes:

```
def percent2(a, b, c):
    def pc(x):
        return (x*100.0) / (a+b+c)
    print('Percentages are:', pc(a), pc(b), pc(c))
```

In this specific case, `percent1` has at least a tiny advantage: the computation of *a+b +c* happens only once, while `percent2`'s inner function `pc` repeats the computation three times. However, when the outer function rebinds local variables between calls to the nested function, repeating the computation can be necessary: be aware of both approaches, and choose the appropriate one case by case.

A nested function that accesses values from outer local variables is also known as a *closure*. The following example shows how to build a closure:

```
def make_adder(augend):
    def add(addend):
        return addend+augend
    return add
```

Closures are sometimes an exception to the general rule that the object-oriented mechanisms covered in Chapter 4 are the best way to bundle together data and code. When you need specifically to construct callable objects, with some parameters fixed at object-construction time, closures can be simpler and more effective than classes. For example, the result of `make_adder(7)` is a function that accepts a single argument and adds `7` to that argument. An outer function that returns a closure is a "factory" for members of a family of functions distinguished by some parameters, such as the value of argument *augend* in the previous example, and may often help you avoid code duplication.

In v3 only, the `nonlocal` keyword acts similarly to `global`, but it refers to a name in the namespace of some lexically surrounding function. When it occurs in a function definition nested several levels deep, the compiler searches the namespace of the most deeply nested containing function, then the function containing that one, and so on, until the name is found or there are no further containing functions, in which case the compiler raises an error.

Here's a v3-only nested-functions approach to the "counter" functionality we implemented in previous sections using a function attribute, then a global variable:

```
def make_counter():
    count = 0
    def counter():
        nonlocal count
        count += 1
        return count
    return counter

c1 = make_counter()
c2 = make_counter()
```

```
print(c1(), c1(), c1())     # prints: 1 2 3
print(c2(), c2())           # prints: 1 2
print(c1(), c2(), c1())     # prints: 4 3 5
```

A key advantage of this approach versus the previous ones is that nested functions, just like an OOP approach, let you make independent counters, here *c1* and *c2*—each closure keeps its own state and doesn't interfere with the other.

This example is v3-only because it requires `nonlocal`, since the inner function `counter` needs to rebind free variable `count`. In v2, you would need a somewhat nonintuitive trick to achieve the same effect without rebinding a free variable:

```
def make_counter():
    count = [0]
    def counter():
        count[0] += 1
        return count[0]
    return counter
```


Clearly, the v3-only version is more readable, since it doesn't require any trick.

lambda Expressions

If a function body is a single `return` *`expression`* statement, you may choose to replace the function with the special `lambda` expression form:

```
lambda parameters: expression
```

A `lambda` expression is the anonymous equivalent of a normal function whose body is a single `return` statement. Note that the `lambda` syntax does not use the `return` keyword. You can use a `lambda` expression wherever you could use a reference to a function. `lambda` can sometimes be handy when you want to use an extremely simple function as an argument or return value. Here's an example that uses a `lambda` expression as an argument to the built-in `filter` function (covered in Table 7-2):

```
a_list = [1, 2, 3, 4, 5, 6, 7, 8, 9]
low = 3
high = 7
filter(lambda x: low<=x<high, a_list)    # returns: [3, 4, 5, 6]
```

(In v3, `filter` returns an iterator, not a list.) Alternatively, you can always use a local `def` statement to give the function object a name, then use this name as an argument or return value. Here's the same `filter` example using a local `def` statement:

```
a_list = [1, 2, 3, 4, 5, 6, 7, 8, 9]
def within_bounds(value, low=3, high=7):
    return low<=value><high
filter(within_bounds, a_list)            # returns: [3, 4, 5, 6]
```

While `lambda` can at times be handy, `def` is usually better: it's more general, and makes the code more readable, as you can choose a clear name for the function.

Generators

When the body of a function contains one or more occurrences of the keyword `yield`, the function is known as a *generator*, or more precisely a *generator function*. When you call a generator, the function body does not execute. Instead, the generator function returns a special iterator object, known as a *generator object* (sometimes, somewhat confusingly, also referred to as just "a generator"), that wraps the function body, its local variables (including its parameters), and the current point of execution, which is initially the start of the function.

When you call `next` on a generator object, the function body executes from the current point up to the next `yield`, which takes the form:

```
yield expression
```

A bare `yield` without the expression is also legal, and equivalent to `yield None`. When a `yield` executes, the function execution is "frozen," with current point of execution and local variables preserved, and the expression following `yield` returned as the result of `next`. When you call `next` again, execution of the function body resumes where it left off, again up to the next `yield`. When the function body ends or executes a `return` statement, the iterator raises a `StopIteration` exception to indicate that the iteration is finished. In v2, `return` statements in a generator cannot contain expressions; in v3, the expression after `return`, if any, is an argument to the resulting `StopIteration`.

`yield` is an expression, not a statement. When you call `g.send(value)` on a generator object *g*, the value of the `yield` is *value*; when you call `next(g)`, the value of the `yield` is `None`. We cover this in "Generators as near-coroutines" on page 98: it's the elementary building block to implement coroutines (*https://en.wikipedia.org/wiki/Coroutine*) in Python.

A generator function is often a very handy way to build an iterator. Since the most common way to use an iterator is to loop on it with a `for` statement, you typically call a generator like this (with the call to `next` implicit in the `for` statement):

```
for avariable in somegenerator(arguments):
```

For example, say that you want a sequence of numbers counting up from `1` to *N* and then down to `1` again. A generator can help:

```
def updown(N):
    for x in range(1, N):
        yield x
    for x in range(N, 0, -1):
        yield x
for i in updown(3): print(i)                    # prints: 1 2 3 2 1
```

Here is a generator that works somewhat like built-in `range`, but returns an iterator on floating-point values rather than on integers:

```
def frange(start, stop, stride=1.0):
    while start < stop:
        yield start
        start += stride
```

This `frange` example is only *somewhat* like `range` because, for simplicity, it makes arguments `start` and `stop` mandatory, and assumes `step` is positive.

Generators are more flexible than functions that return lists. A generator may return an *unbounded* iterator, meaning one that yields an infinite stream of results (to use only in loops that terminate by other means, e.g., via a `break` statement). Further, a generator-object iterator performs *lazy evaluation*: the iterator computes each successive item only when and if needed, just in time, while the equivalent function does all computations in advance and may require large amounts of memory to hold the results list. Therefore, if all you need is the ability to iterate on a computed sequence, it is most often best to compute the sequence in a generator, rather than in a function that returns a list. If the caller needs a list of all the items produced by some bounded generator `g(arguments)`, the caller can simply use the following code to explicitly request that a list be built:

```
resulting_list = list(g(arguments))
```


yield from (v3-only)

In v3 only, to improve execution efficiency and clarity when multiple levels of iteration are yielding values, you can use the form `yield from expression`, where *`expression`* is iterable. This yields the values from *`expression`* one at a time into the calling environment, avoiding the need to `yield` repeatedly. The `updown` generator defined earlier can be simplified in v3:

```
def updown(N):
    yield from range(1, N)
    yield from range(N, 0, -1)
for i in updown(3): print(i)                    # prints: 1 2 3 2 1
```

Moreover, the ability to use `yield from` means that, in v3 only, generators can be used as full-fledged *coroutines*, as covered in Chapter 18.

Generator expressions

Python offers an even simpler way to code particularly simple generators: *generator expressions*, commonly known as *genexps*. The syntax of a genexp is just like that of a list comprehension (as covered in "List comprehensions" on page 78), except that a genexp is within parentheses (`()`) instead of brackets (`[]`). The semantics of a genexp are the same as those of the corresponding list comprehension, except that a genexp produces an iterator yielding one item at a time, while a list comprehension produces a list of all results in memory (therefore, using a genexp, when appropriate, saves memory). For example, to sum the squares of all single-digit integers, you could code `sum([x*x for x in range(10)])`; however, you can express this even better, coding it as `sum(x*x for x in range(10))` (just the same, but omitting the brackets), and obtain exactly the same result while consuming less memory. Note that the parentheses that indicate the function call also "do double duty" and enclose the genexp (no need for extra parentheses).

Generators as near-coroutines

In all modern Python versions (both v2 and v3), generators are further enhanced, with the possibility of receiving a value (or an exception) back from the caller as each `yield` executes. This lets generators implement coroutines, as explained in PEP 342 (*https://www.python.org/dev/peps/pep-0342/*). The main change from older versions of Python is that `yield` is not a statement, but an expression, so it has a value. When a generator resumes via a call to `next` on it, the corresponding `yield`'s value is `None`. To pass a value *x* into some generator *g* (so that *g* receives *x* as the value of the `yield` on which it's suspended), instead of calling `next(g)`, call `g.send(x)` (`g.send(None)` is just like `next(g)`).

Other modern enhancements to generators have to do with exceptions, and we cover them in "Generators and Exceptions" on page 155.

Recursion

Python supports recursion (i.e., a Python function can call itself), but there is a limit to how deep the recursion can be. By default, Python interrupts recursion and raises a `RecursionLimitExceeded` exception (covered in "Standard Exception Classes" on page 160) when it detects that the stack of recursive calls has gone over a depth of 1,000. You can change the recursion limit with function `setrecursionlimit` of module `sys`, covered in Table 7-3.

However, changing the recursion limit does not give you unlimited recursion; the absolute maximum limit depends on the platform on which your program is running, particularly on the underlying operating system and C runtime library, but it's typically a few thousand levels. If recursive calls get too deep, your program crashes. Such runaway recursion, after a call to `setrecursionlimit` that exceeds the platform's capabilities, is one of the very few ways a Python program can crash—really crash, hard, without the usual safety net of Python's exception mechanisms. Therefore, beware "fixing" a program that is getting `RecursionLimitExceeded` exceptions by raising the recursion limit with `setrecursionlimit`. Most often, you're better advised to look for ways to remove the recursion or, at least, limit the depth of recursion that your program needs.

Readers who are familiar with Lisp, Scheme, or functional programming languages must in particular be aware that Python does *not* implement the optimization of "tail-call elimination," which is so important in these languages. In Python, any call, recursive or not, has the same cost in terms of both time and memory space, dependent only on the number of arguments: the cost does not change, whether the call is a "tail-call" (meaning that the call is the last operation that the caller executes) or any other, nontail call. This makes recursion removal even more important.

For example, consider a classic use for recursion: "walking a tree." Suppose you have a "tree" data structure where each node is a tuple with three items: first, a payload value as item 0; then, as item 1, a similar tuple for the left-side descendant, or `None`; and similarly as item 2, for the right-side descendant. A simple example might be: `(23, (42, (5, None, None), (55, None, None)), (94, None,None))` to represent the tree where the payloads are:

```
        23
     42    94
   5  55
```

We want to write a generator function that, given the root of such a tree, "walks the tree," yielding each payload in top-down order. The simplest approach is clearly recursion; in v3:

```
def rec(t):
    yield t[0]
    for i in (1, 2):
        if t[i] is not None: yield from rec(t[i])
```

However, if a tree is very deep, recursion becomes a problem. To remove recursion, we just need to handle our own stack—a list used in last-in, first-out fashion, thanks to its `append` and `pop` methods. To wit, in either v2 or v3:

```
def norec(t):
    stack = [t]
    while stack:
        t = stack.pop()
        yield t[0]
        for i in (2, 1):
            if t[i] is not None: stack.append(t[i])
```

The only small issue to be careful about, to keep exactly the same order of `yield`s as `rec`, is switching the `(1, 2)` index order in which to examine descendants, to `(2, 1)`, adjusting to the reverse (last-in, first-out) behavior of *`stack`*.

The Python Language

4
Object-Oriented Python

Python is an object-oriented (OO) programming language. Unlike some other object-oriented languages, Python doesn't force you to use the object-oriented paradigm exclusively: it also supports procedural programming with modules and functions, so you can select the best paradigm for each part of your program. The object-oriented paradigm helps you group state (data) and behavior (code) together in handy packets of functionality. It's also useful when you want to use some of Python's object-oriented mechanisms covered in this chapter, such as *inheritance* or *special methods*. The procedural paradigm, based on modules and functions, may be simpler and more suitable when you don't need the pluses of object-oriented programming. With Python, you can mix and match paradigms.

Python today has an object model different from that of many years ago. This chapter exclusively describes the so-called *new-style*, or *new object model*, which is simpler, more regular, more powerful, and the one we recommend you *always* use; whenever we speak of classes or instances, we mean new-style classes or instances. However, for backward compatibility, the default object model in v2 is the *legacy object model*, also known as the *classic* or *old-style* object model; the new-style object model is the only one in v3. For legacy information about the old style, see some ancient online docs (*https://docs.python.org/release/2.1.3/ref/datamodel.html*) from 2002.

This chapter also covers *special methods*, in "Special Methods" on page 126, and advanced concepts known as *abstract base classes*, in "Abstract Base Classes" on page 135; *decorators*, in "Decorators" on page 140; and *metaclasses*, in "Metaclasses" on page 142.

Classes and Instances

If you're familiar with object-oriented programming in other OO languages such as C++ or Java, you probably have a good intuitive grasp of classes and instances: a *class* is a user-defined type, which you *instantiate* to build *instances*, meaning objects of that type. Python supports these concepts through its class and instance objects.

Python Classes

A *class* is a Python object with several characteristics:

- You can call a class object as if it were a function. The call, often known as *instantiation*, returns an object known as an *instance* of the class; the class is known as the *type* of the instance.
- A class has arbitrarily named attributes that you can bind and reference.
- The values of class attributes can be *descriptors* (including functions), covered in "Descriptors" on page 106, or normal data objects.
- Class attributes bound to functions are also known as *methods* of the class.
- A method can have a special Python-defined name with two leading and two trailing underscores (commonly known as *dunder names*, short for "double-underscore names"—the name `__init__`, for example, is often pronounced as "dunder init"). Python implicitly calls such *special methods*, if a class supplies them, when various kinds of operations take place on instances of that class.
- A class can *inherit* from other classes, meaning it delegates to other class objects the lookup of attributes that are not found in the class itself.

An instance of a class is a Python object with arbitrarily named attributes that you can bind and reference. An instance object implicitly delegates to its class the lookup of attributes not found in the instance itself. The class, in turn, may delegate the lookup to classes from which it inherits, if any.

In Python, classes are objects (values), handled like other objects. Thus, you can pass a class as an argument in a call to a function. Similarly, a function can return a class as the result of a call. A class, just like any other object, can be bound to a variable (local or global), an item in a container, or an attribute of an object. Classes can also be keys into a dictionary. The fact that classes are ordinary objects in Python is often expressed by saying that classes are *first-class* objects.

The class Statement

The `class` statement is the most common way to create a class object. `class` is a single-clause compound statement with the following syntax:

```
class classname(base-classes):
    statement(s)
```

`classname` is an identifier. It is a variable that gets bound (or rebound) to the class object after the `class` statement finishes executing.

`base-classes` is a comma-delimited series of expressions whose values must be class objects. These classes are known by different names in different programming languages; you can, at your choice, call them the *bases*, *superclasses*, or *parents* of the class being created. The class being created can be said to *inherit* from, *derive* from, *extend*, or *subclass* its base classes, depending on what programming language you are familiar with; in this book, we generally use *extend*. This class is also known as a *direct subclass* or *descendant* of its base classes. In v3 only, base-classes can include a named argument `metaclass=...` to establish the class's *metaclass*, as covered in "How Python v3 Determines a Class's Metaclass" on page 143.

Syntactically, `base-classes` is optional: to indicate that you're creating a class without bases, you can omit `base-classes` (and, optionally, the parentheses around it), placing the colon right after the classname. However, in v2, a class without bases, for backward compatibility, is an old-style one (unless you define the `__metaclass__` attribute, covered in "How Python v2 Determines a Class's Metaclass" on page 142). To create a new-style class *C* without any "true" bases, in v2, code `class C(object):`; since every type extends the built-in `object`, specifying `object` as the value of `base-classes` just means that class *C* is new-style rather than old-style. If your class has ancestors (if any) that are all old-style, and does not define the `__metaclass__` attribute, then your class is old-style; otherwise, a class with bases is always new-style (even if some of the bases are new-style and some are old-style). In v3, *all* classes are new-style (you can still "inherit from `object`" quite innocuously, if you wish, to make your code backward compatible with v2). In our examples, for uniformity, we always specify `(object)` as a base rather than leaving a class "base-less"; however, if you're programming in and for v3 only, it's more elegant, and recommended, to leave such "fake subclassing" out.

The subclass relationship between classes is transitive: if *C1* extends *C2*, and *C2* extends *C3*, then *C1* extends *C3*. Built-in function `issubclass(C1, C2)` accepts two arguments that are class objects: it returns `True` if *C1* extends *C2*; otherwise, it returns `False`. Any class is a subclass of itself; therefore, `issubclass(C, C)` returns `True` for any class *C*. We cover the way in which base classes affect a class's functionality in "Inheritance" on page 115.

The nonempty sequence of indented statements that follows the `class` statement is known as the *class body*. A class body executes immediately as part of the `class` statement's execution. Until the body finishes executing, the new class object does not yet exist, and the `classname` identifier is not yet bound (or rebound). "How a Metaclass Creates a Class" on page 144 provides more details about what happens when a `class` statement executes.

Finally, note that the `class` statement does not immediately create any instance of the new class, but rather defines the set of attributes shared by all instances when you later create instances by calling the class.

The Class Body

The body of a class is where you normally specify the attributes of the class; these attributes can be descriptor objects (including functions) or normal data objects of any type (an attribute of a class can also be another class—so, for example, you can have a `class` statement "nested" inside another `class` statement).

Attributes of class objects

You normally specify an attribute of a class object by binding a value to an identifier within the class body. For example:

```
class C1(object):
    x = 23
print(C1.x)                                    # prints: 23
```

The class object *C1* has an attribute named *x*, bound to the value 23, and *C1.x* refers to that attribute.

You can also bind or unbind class attributes outside the class body. For example:

```
class C2(object): pass
C2.x = 23
print(C2.x)                                    # prints: 23
```

Your program is usually more readable if you bind, and thus create, class attributes only with statements inside the class body. However, rebinding them elsewhere may be necessary if you want to carry state information at a class, rather than instance, level; Python lets you do that, if you wish. There is no difference between a class attribute created in the class body, and one created or rebound outside the body by assigning to an attribute.

As we'll discuss shortly, all instances of the class share all of the class's attributes.

The `class` statement implicitly sets some class attributes. Attribute `__name__` is the *classname* identifier string used in the `class` statement. Attribute `__bases__` is the tuple of class objects given as the base classes in the `class` statement. For example, using the class *C1* we just created:

```
print(C1.__name__, C1.__bases__)
# prints: C1 (<type 'object'>,)
```

A class also has an attribute `__dict__`, the mapping object that the class uses to hold other attributes (AKA its *namespace*); in classes, this mapping is read-only.

In statements that are directly in a class's body, references to attributes of the class must use a simple name, not a fully qualified name. For example:

```
class C3(object):
    x = 23
    y = x + 22                                # must use just x, not C3.x
```

However, in statements in *methods* defined in a class body, references to attributes of the class must use a fully qualified name, not a simple name. For example:

```
class C4(object):
    x = 23
    def amethod(self):
        print(C4.x)  # must use C4.x or self.x, not just x!
```

Note that attribute references (i.e., an expression like `C.s`) have semantics richer than those of attribute bindings. We cover these references in detail in "Attribute Reference Basics" on page 110.

Function definitions in a class body

Most class bodies include `def` statements, since functions (known as *methods* in this context) are important attributes for most class objects. A `def` statement in a class body obeys the rules presented in "Functions" on page 82. In addition, a method defined in a class body has a mandatory first parameter, conventionally named `self`, that refers to the instance on which you call the method. The `self` parameter plays a special role in method calls, as covered in "Bound and Unbound Methods" on page 112.

Here's an example of a class that includes a method definition:

```
class C5(object):
    def hello(self):
        print('Hello')
```

A class can define a variety of special methods (methods with names that have two leading and two trailing underscores—these are also occasionally called "magic methods," and frequently referenced verbally as "dunder" methods, e.g., "dunder init" for `__init__`) relating to specific operations on its instances. We discuss special methods in detail in "Special Methods" on page 126.

Class-private variables

When a statement in a class body (or in a method in the body) uses an identifier starting with two underscores (but not *ending* with underscores), such as `__ident`, the Python compiler implicitly changes the identifier into `_classname__ident`, where `classname` is the name of the class. This lets a class use "private" names for attributes, methods, global variables, and other purposes, reducing the risk of accidentally duplicating names used elsewhere, particularly in subclasses.

By convention, identifiers starting with a *single* underscore are meant to be private to the scope that binds them, whether that scope is or isn't a class. The Python compiler does not enforce this privacy convention: it's up to programmers to respect it.

Class documentation strings

If the first statement in the class body is a string literal, the compiler binds that string as the documentation string for the class. This attribute, named `__doc__`, is the *docstring* of the class. See "Docstrings" on page 87 for more information on docstrings.

Descriptors

A *descriptor* is any object whose class supplies a special method named `__get__`. Descriptors that are class attributes control the semantics of accessing and setting attributes on instances of that class. Roughly speaking, when you access an instance attribute, Python gets the attribute's value by calling `__get__` on the corresponding descriptor, if any. For example:

```
class Const(object):        # an overriding descriptor, see later
    def __init__(self, value):
        self.value = value
    def __set__(self, *_):  # ignore any attempt at setting
        pass
    def __get__(self, *_):  # always return the constant value
        return self.value

class X(object):
    c = Const(23)

x=X()
print(x.c)  # prints: 23
x.c = 42
print(x.c)  # prints: 23
```

For more details, see "Attribute Reference Basics" on page 110.

Overriding and nonoverriding descriptors

If a descriptor's class also supplies a special method named `__set__`, then the descriptor is known as an *overriding descriptor* (or, by an older, more widespread, and slightly confusing terminology, a *data descriptor*); if the descriptor's class supplies only `__get__` and not `__set__`, then the descriptor is known as a *nonoverriding* (or *nondata*) *descriptor*.

For example, the class of function objects supplies `__get__`, but not `__set__`; therefore, function objects are nonoverriding descriptors. Roughly speaking, when you assign a value to an instance attribute with a corresponding descriptor that is overriding, Python sets the attribute value by calling `__set__` on the descriptor. For more details, see "Attributes of instance objects" on page 107.

Instances

To create an instance of a class, call the class object as if it were a function. Each call returns a new instance whose type is that class:

```
an_instance = C5()
```

You can call built-in function isinstance(*i*, *C*) with a class object as argument *C*. isinstance returns True when object *i* is an instance of class *C* or of any subclass of *C*. Otherwise, isinstance returns False.

__init__

When a class defines or inherits a method named __init__, calling the class object implicitly executes __init__ on the new instance to perform any needed per-instance initialization. Arguments passed in the call must correspond to the parameters of __init__, except for parameter self. For example, consider:

```
class C6(object):
    def __init__(self, n):
        self.x = n
```

Here's how you can create an instance of the *C6* class:

```
another_instance = C6(42)
```

As shown in the *C6* class, the __init__ method typically contains statements that bind instance attributes. An __init__ method must not return a value other than None; if it does, Python raises a TypeError exception.

The main purpose of __init__ is to bind, and thus create, the attributes of a newly created instance. You may also bind, rebind, or unbind instance attributes outside __init__, as you'll see shortly. However, your code is more readable when you initially bind all attributes of a class instance in the __init__ method.

When __init__ is absent (and is not inherited from any base), you must call the class without arguments, and the new instance has no instance-specific attributes.

Object-Oriented Python

Attributes of instance objects

Once you have created an instance, you can access its attributes (data and methods) using the dot (.) operator. For example:

```
an_instance.hello()                      # prints: Hello
print(another_instance.x)                # prints: 42
```

Attribute references such as these have fairly rich semantics in Python; we cover them in detail in "Attribute Reference Basics" on page 110.

You can give an instance object an arbitrary attribute by binding a value to an attribute reference. For example:

```
class C7: pass
z = C7()
z.x = 23
print(z.x)                              # prints: 23
```

Instance object *z* now has an attribute named *x*, bound to the value 23, and *z.x* refers to that attribute. Note that the __setattr__ special method, if present, intercepts every attempt to bind an attribute. (We cover `__setattr__` in Table 4-1.) When you attempt to bind on an instance an attribute whose name corresponds to an overriding descriptor in the class, the descriptor's `__set__` method intercepts the attempt: should *C7.x* be an overriding descriptor, the assignment *z.x*=23 would execute `type(z).x.__set__(z, 23)`.

Creating an instance implicitly sets two instance attributes. For any instance *z*, `z.__class__` is the class object to which *z* belongs, and `z.__dict__` is the mapping that *z* uses to hold its other attributes. For example, for the instance *z* we just created:

```
print(z.__class__.__name__, z.__dict__)    # prints: C7 {'x':23}
```

You may rebind (but not unbind) either or both of these attributes, but this is rarely necessary.

For any instance *z*, any object *x*, and any identifier *S* (except `__class__` and `__dict__`), *z.S*=*x* is equivalent to `z.__dict__['S']=x` (unless a `__setattr__` special method, or an overriding descriptor's `__set__` special method, intercepts the binding attempt). For example, again referring to the *z* we just created:

```
z.y = 45
z.__dict__['z'] = 67
print(z.x, z.y, z.z)                        # prints: 23 45 67
```

There is no difference between instance attributes created by assigning to attributes and those created by explicitly binding an entry in `z.__dict__`.

The factory-function idiom

It's often necessary to create instances of different classes depending on some condition, or to avoid creating a new instance if an existing one is available for reuse. A common misconception is that such needs might be met by having `__init__` return a particular object, but such an approach is unfeasible: Python raises an exception if `__init__` returns any value other than `None`. The best way to implement flexible object creation is by using a function, rather than calling the class object directly. A function used this way is known as a *factory function*.

Calling a factory function is a flexible approach: a function may return an existing reusable instance, or create a new instance by calling whatever class is appropriate. Say you have two almost interchangeable classes (*SpecialCase* and *NormalCase*) and want to flexibly generate instances of either one of them, depending on an argument. The following *appropriate_case* factory function, as a "toy" example, allows you to do just that (we cover the role of the `self` parameter in "Bound and Unbound Methods" on page 112):

```
class SpecialCase(object):
    def amethod(self): print('special')
class NormalCase(object):
    def amethod(self): print('normal')
def appropriate_case(isnormal=True):
```

```
    if isnormal: return NormalCase()
    else: return SpecialCase()
aninstance = appropriate_case(isnormal=False)
aninstance.amethod()                    # prints: special
```

__new__

Each class has (or inherits) a class method named __new__ (we cover class methods in "Class methods" on page 120). When you call *C(*args,**kwds)* to create a new instance of class *C*, Python first calls *C.__new__(C,*args,**kwds)*. Python uses __new__'s return value *x* as the newly created instance. Then, Python calls *C.__init__(x,*args,**kwds)*, but only when *x* is indeed an instance of *C* or any of its subclasses (otherwise, *x*'s state remains as __new__ had left it). Thus, for example, the statement *x=C(23)* is equivalent to:

```
x = C.__new__(C, 23)
if isinstance(x, C): type(x).__init__(x, 23)
```

object.__new__ creates a new, uninitialized instance of the class it receives as its first argument. It ignores other arguments when that class has an __init__ method, but it raises an exception when it receives other arguments beyond the first, and the class that's the first argument does not have an __init__ method. When you override __new__ within a class body, you do not need to add __new__=classmethod(__new__), nor use an @classmethod decorator, as you normally would: Python recognizes the name __new__ and treats it specially in this context. In those extremely rare cases in which you rebind *C.__new__* later, outside the body of class *C*, you do need to use *C.__new__=classmethod(whatever)*.

__new__ has most of the flexibility of a factory function, as covered in "The factory-function idiom" on page 108. __new__ may choose to return an existing instance or make a new one, as appropriate. When __new__ does need to create a new instance, it most often delegates creation by calling object.__new__ or the __new__ method of another superclass of *C*. The following example shows how to override class method __new__ in order to implement a version of the Singleton design pattern:

```
class Singleton(object):
    _singletons = {}
    def __new__(cls, *args, **kwds):
        if cls not in cls._singletons:
            cls._singletons[cls] = super(Singleton, cls).__new__(cls)
        return cls._singletons[cls]
```

(We cover built-in super in "Cooperative superclass method calling" on page 117.)

Any subclass of *Singleton* (that does not further override __new__) has exactly one instance. If the subclass defines __init__, the subclass must ensure its __init__ is safe when called repeatedly (at each creation request) on the one and only class instance; that is because __init__, on any subclass of *Singleton* that defines it, executes repeatedly, each time you instantiate the subclass, on the one and only instance that exists for each subclass of *Singleton*.

v3 allows simple, cleaner coding for this example

We coded this example to work equally well in v2 and v3. In v3, you could code it more simply and cleanly by giving *Singleton* no superclasses, and calling `super` without arguments.

Attribute Reference Basics

An *attribute reference* is an expression of the form `x.name`, where *x* is any expression and *name* is an identifier called the *attribute name*. Many kinds of Python objects have attributes, but an attribute reference has special rich semantics when *x* refers to a class or instance. Remember that methods are attributes too, so everything we say about attributes in general also applies to attributes that are callable (i.e., methods).

Say that *x* is an instance of class *C*, which inherits from base class *B*. Both classes and the instance have several attributes (data and methods), as follows:

```
class B(object):
    a = 23
    b = 45
    def f(self): print('method f in class B')
    def g(self): print('method g in class B')
class C(B):
    b = 67
    c = 89
    d = 123
    def g(self): print('method g in class C')
    def h(self): print('method h in class C')
x = C()
x.d = 77
x.e = 88
```

A few attribute dunder-names are special. `C.__name__` is the string `'C'`, the class's name. `C.__bases__` is the tuple `(B,)`, the tuple of *C*'s base classes. `x.__class__` is the class *C*, the class to which *x* belongs. When you refer to an attribute with one of these special names, the attribute reference looks directly into a dedicated slot in the class or instance object and fetches the value it finds there. You cannot unbind these attributes. You may rebind them on the fly, to change the name or base classes of a class, or to change the class of an instance, but this advanced technique is rarely necessary.

Both class *C* and instance *x* each have one other special attribute: a mapping named `__dict__`. All other attributes of a class or instance, except for the few special ones, are held as items in the `__dict__` attribute of the class or instance.

Getting an attribute from a class

When you use the syntax `C.name` to refer to an attribute on a class object *C*, the lookup proceeds in two steps:

1. When *'name'* is a key in C.__dict__, C.*name* fetches the value *v* from C.__dict__['*name*']. Then, when *v* is a descriptor (i.e., type(*v*) supplies a method named __get__), the value of C.*name* is the result of calling type(*v*).__get__(*v*, None, *C*). When *v* is not a descriptor, the value of C.*name* is *v*.
2. When *'name'* is *not* a key in C.__dict__, C.*name* delegates the lookup to *C*'s base classes, meaning it loops on *C*'s ancestor classes and tries the *name* lookup on each (in *method resolution order*, as covered in "Method resolution order" on page 115).

Getting an attribute from an instance

When you use the syntax x.*name* to refer to an attribute of instance *x* of class *C*, the lookup proceeds in three steps:

1. When *'name'* is found in *C* (or in one of *C*'s ancestor classes) as the name of an overriding descriptor *v* (i.e., type(*v*) supplies methods __get__ and __set__)
   - The value of x.*name* is the result of type(*v*).__get__(*v*, *x*, *C*)
2. Otherwise, when *'name'* is a key in x.__dict__
   - x.*name* fetches and returns the value at x.__dict__['*name*']
3. Otherwise, x.*name* delegates the lookup to *x*'s class (according to the same two-step lookup used for C.*name*, as just detailed)
   - When a descriptor *v* is found, the overall result of the attribute lookup is, again, type(*v*).__get__(*v*, *x*, *C*)
   - When a nondescriptor value *v* is found, the overall result of the attribute lookup is just *v*

When these lookup steps do not find an attribute, Python raises an AttributeError exception. However, for lookups of x.*name*, when *C* defines or inherits the special method __getattr__, Python calls C.__getattr__(*x*,'*name*') rather than raising the exception. It's then up to __getattr__ to either return a suitable value or raise the appropriate exception, normally AttributeError.

Consider the following attribute references, defined previously:

```
print(x.e, x.d, x.c, x.b, x.a)              # prints: 88 77 89 67 23
```

x.e and *x.d* succeed in step 2 of the instance lookup process, since no descriptors are involved, and 'e' and 'd' are both keys in x.__dict__. Therefore, the lookups go no further, but rather return 88 and 77. The other three references must proceed to step 3 of the instance process and look in x.__class__ (i.e., *C*). *x.c* and *x.b* succeed in step 1 of the class lookup process, since `'c'` and `'b'` are both keys in `C.__dict__`. Therefore, the lookups go no further but rather return `89` and `67`. `x.a` gets all the way to step 2 of the class process, looking in `C.__bases__[0]` (i.e., `B`). `'a'` is a key in `B.__dict__`; therefore, `x.a` finally succeeds and returns `23`.

Setting an attribute

Note that the attribute lookup steps happen as just described only when you *refer* to an attribute, not when you *bind* an attribute. When you bind (on either a class or an instance) an attribute whose name is not special (unless a `__setattr__` method, or the `__set__` method of an overriding descriptor, intercepts the binding of an instance attribute), you affect only the `__dict__` entry for the attribute (in the class or instance, respectively). In other words, for attribute binding, there is no lookup procedure involved, except for the check for overriding descriptors.

Bound and Unbound Methods

The method `__get__` of a function object can return an *unbound method object* (in v2) or the function object itself (in v3), or a *bound method object* that wraps the function. The key difference between unbound and bound methods is that an unbound method (v2 only) is not associated with a particular instance, while a bound method is.

In the code in the previous section, attributes `f`, `g`, and `h` are functions; therefore, an attribute reference to any one of them returns a method object that wraps the respective function. Consider the following:

```
print(x.h, x.g, x.f, C.h, C.g, C.f)
```

This statement outputs three bound methods, represented by strings like:

```
<bound method C.h of <__main__.C object at 0x8156d5c>>
```

and then, in v2, three unbound ones, represented by strings like:

```
<unbound method C.h>
```

or, in v3, three function objects, represented by strings like:

```
<function C.h at 0x102cabae8>
```

Bound versus unbound methods

We get bound methods when the attribute reference is on instance `x`, and unbound methods (in v3, function objects) when the attribute reference is on class `C`.

Because a bound method is already associated with a specific instance, you call the method as follows:

```
x.h()                          # prints: method h in class C
```

The key thing to notice here is that you don't pass the method's first argument, `self`, by the usual argument-passing syntax. Rather, a bound method of instance *x* implicitly binds the `self` parameter to object *x*. Thus, the body of the method can access the instance's attributes as attributes of `self`, even though we don't pass an explicit argument to the method.

An unbound method (v2 only), however, is not associated with a specific instance, so you must specify an appropriate instance as the first argument when you call an unbound method. For example:

```
C.h(x)                          # prints: method h in class C
```

You call unbound methods far less frequently than bound methods. One important use for unbound methods is to access overridden methods, as discussed in "Inheritance" on page 115; even for that task, though, it's usually better to use the `super` built-in covered in "Cooperative superclass method calling" on page 117. Another frequent use of unbound methods is in higher-order functions; for example, to sort a list of strings alphabetically but case-insensitively, `los.sort(key=str.lower)` is fine.

Object-Oriented Python

Unbound method details (v2 only)

As we've just discussed, when an attribute reference on a class refers to a function, a reference to that attribute, in v2, returns an unbound method object that wraps the function. An unbound method has three attributes in addition to those of the function object it wraps: `im_class` is the class object supplying the method, `im_func` is the wrapped function, and `im_self` is always `None`. These attributes are all read-only, meaning that trying to rebind or unbind any of them raises an exception.

You can call an unbound method just as you would call its `im_func` function, but the first argument in any call must be an instance of `im_class` or a descendant. In other words, a call to an unbound method must have at least one argument, which corresponds to the wrapped function's first formal parameter (conventionally named `self`).

Bound method details

When an attribute reference on an instance, in the course of the lookup, finds a function object that's an attribute in the instance's class, the lookup calls the function's `__get__` method to get the attribute's value. The call, in this case, creates and returns a *bound method* that wraps the function.

Note that when the attribute reference's lookup finds a function object in `x.__dict__`, the attribute reference operation does *not* create a bound method: in such cases Python does not treat the function as a descriptor, and does not call the function's `__get__` method; rather, the function object itself is the attribute's value. Similarly, Python creates no bound method for callables that are not ordinary functions, such as built-in (as opposed to Python-coded) functions, since such callables are not descriptors.

A bound method is similar to an unbound method in that it has three read-only attributes in addition to those of the function object it wraps. Like in an unbound method, `im_class` is the class object that supplies the method, and `im_func` is the wrapped function. However, in a bound method object, attribute `im_self` refers to *x*, the instance from which you got the method.

You use a bound method just like its `im_func` function, but calls to a bound method do not explicitly supply an argument corresponding to the first formal parameter (conventionally named `self`). When you call a bound method, the bound method passes `im_self` as the first argument to `im_func` before other arguments (if any) given at the point of call.

Let's follow in excruciating low-level detail the conceptual steps involved in a method call with the normal syntax `x.name(arg)`. In the following context:

```
def f(a, b): ...              # a function f with two arguments

class C(object):
    name = f
x = C()
```

x is an instance object of class *C*, `name` is an identifier that names a method of *x*'s (an attribute of *C* whose value is a function, in this case function *f*), and *arg* is any expression. Python first checks if `'name'` is the attribute name in *C* of an overriding descriptor, but it isn't—functions are descriptors, because their type defines method `__get__`, but not overriding ones, because their type does not define method `__set__`. Python next checks if `'name'` is a key in `x.__dict__`, but it isn't. So Python finds `name` in *C* (everything would work in just the same way if `name` was found, by inheritance, in one of *C*'s `__bases__`). Python notices that the attribute's value, function object *f*, is a descriptor. Therefore, Python calls `f.__get__(x, C)`, which creates a bound method object with `im_func` set to *f*, `im_class` set to *C*, and `im_self` set to *x*. Then Python calls this bound method object, with *arg* as the only argument. The bound method inserts `im_self` (i.e., *x*) as the first argument, and *arg* becomes the second one, in a call to the bound method's `im_func` (i.e., function `f`). The overall effect is just like calling:

```
x.__class__.__dict__['name'](x, arg)
```

When a bound method's function body executes, it has no special namespace relationship to either its `self` object or any class. Variables referenced are local or global, just as for any other function, as covered in "Namespaces" on page 92. Variables do not implicitly indicate attributes in `self`, nor do they indicate attributes in any class object. When the method needs to refer to, bind, or unbind an attribute of its `self` object, it does so by standard attribute-reference syntax (e.g., `self.name`). The lack of implicit scoping may take some getting used to (simply because Python differs in this respect from many other object-oriented languages), but it results in clarity, simplicity, and the removal of potential ambiguities.

Bound method objects are first-class objects: you can use them wherever you can use a callable object. Since a bound method holds references to the function it wraps and to the `self` object on which it executes, it's a powerful and flexible alternative to a closure (covered in "Nested functions and nested scopes" on page 93). An instance object whose class supplies the special method `__call__` (covered in Table 4-1) offers another viable alternative. Each of these constructs lets you bundle some behavior (code) and some state (data) into a single callable object. Closures are simplest, but limited in their applicability. Here's the closure from "Nested functions and nested scopes" on page 93:

```
def make_adder_as_closure(augend):
    def add(addend, _augend=augend): return addend+_augend
    return add
```

Bound methods and callable instances are richer and more flexible than closures. Here's how to implement the same functionality with a bound method:

```
def make_adder_as_bound_method(augend):
    class Adder(object):
        def __init__(self, augend): self.augend = augend
        def add(self, addend): return addend+self.augend
    return Adder(augend).add
```

And here's how to implement it with a callable instance (an instance whose class supplies the special method `__call__`):

```
def make_adder_as_callable_instance(augend):
    class Adder(object):
        def __init__(self, augend): self.augend = augend
        def __call__(self, addend): return addend+self.augend
    return Adder(augend)
```

From the viewpoint of the code that calls the functions, all of these factory functions are interchangeable, since all of them return callable objects that are polymorphic (i.e., usable in the same ways). In terms of implementation, the closure is simplest; the bound method and the callable instance use more flexible, general, and powerful mechanisms, but there is no need for that extra power in this simple example.

Inheritance

When you use an attribute reference `C.`*`name`* on a class object `C`, and `'`*`name`*`'` is not a key in `C.__dict__`, the lookup implicitly proceeds on each class object that is in `C.__bases__` in a specific order (which for historical reasons is known as the *method resolution order*, or MRO, but applies to all attributes, not just methods). `C`'s base classes may in turn have their own bases. The lookup checks direct and indirect ancestors, one by one, in MRO, stopping when `'`*`name`*`'` is found.

Method resolution order

The lookup of an attribute name in a class essentially occurs by visiting ancestor classes in left-to-right, depth-first order. However, in the presence of multiple inheritance (which makes the inheritance graph a general Directed Acyclic Graph rather than specifically a tree), this simple approach might lead to some ancestor class being visited twice. In such cases, the resolution order leaves in the lookup sequence only the *rightmost* occurrence of any given class.

Each class and built-in type has a special read-only class attribute called `__mro__`, which is the tuple of types used for method resolution, in order. You can reference `__mro__` only on classes, not on instances, and, since `__mro__` is a read-only attribute, you cannot rebind or unbind it. For a detailed and highly technical explanation of all aspects of Python's MRO, you may want to study an online essay by Michele Simionato, The Python 2.3 Method Resolution Order (*https://www.python.org/download/releases/2.3/mro/*), and GvR's history note at the Python History site (*http://python-history.blogspot.com/2010/06/method-resolution-order.html*).

Overriding attributes

As we've just seen, the search for an attribute proceeds along the MRO (typically, up the inheritance tree) and stops as soon as the attribute is found. Descendant classes are always examined before their ancestors, so that, when a subclass defines an attribute with the same name as one in a superclass, the search finds the definition in the subclass and stops there. This is known as the subclass *overriding* the definition in the superclass. Consider the following:

```
class B(object):
    a = 23
    b = 45
    def f(self): print('method f in class B')
    def g(self): print('method g in class B')
class C(B):
    b = 67
    c = 89
    d = 123
    def g(self): print('method g in class C')
    def h(self): print('method h in class C')
```

In this code, class `C` overrides attributes `b` and `g` of its superclass `B`. Note that, unlike in some other languages, in Python you may override data attributes just as easily as callable attributes (methods).

Delegating to superclass methods

When a subclass `C` overrides a method `f` of its superclass `B`, the body of `C.f` often wants to delegate some part of its operation to the superclass's implementation of the method. This can sometimes be done using what, in v2, is an unbound method (in v3, it's a function object, but works just the same way), as follows:

```
class Base(object):
    def greet(self, name): print('Welcome', name)
class Sub(Base):
```

```
    def greet(self, name):
        print('Well Met and', end=' ')
        Base.greet(self, name)
x = Sub()
x.greet('Alex')
```

The delegation to the superclass, in the body of *Sub.greet*, uses an unbound method (in v2; in v3, with this same syntax, it's a function object, which works just the same way) obtained by attribute reference *Base.greet* on the superclass, and therefore passes all arguments normally, including `self`. Delegating to a superclass implementation is the most frequent use of unbound methods in v2.

One common use of delegation occurs with special method `__init__`. When Python creates an instance, the `__init__` methods of base classes are not automatically called, as they are in some other object-oriented languages. Thus, it is up to a subclass to perform the proper initialization of superclasses, by using delegation, if necessary. For example:

```
class Base(object):
    def __init__(self):
        self.anattribute = 23
class Derived(Base):
    def __init__(self):
        Base.__init__(self)
        self.anotherattribute = 45
```

If the `__init__` method of class *Derived* didn't explicitly call that of class *Base*, instances of *Derived* would miss that portion of their initialization, and thus such instances would lack attribute *anattribute*. This issue does *not* arise if a subclass does not define `__init__`, since in that case it inherits it from the superclass. So there is *never* any reason to code:

```
class Derived(Base):
    def __init__(self):
        Base.__init__(self)
```

Never code a method that just delegates to the superclass

Never define a semantically empty `__init__` (i.e., one that just delegates to the superclass): rather, just inherit `__init__` from the superclass. This advice applies to *all* methods, special or not, but, for some reason, the bad habit of coding such semantically empty methods occurs most often for `__init__`.

Cooperative superclass method calling

Calling the superclass's version of a method with unbound method syntax is quite problematic in cases of multiple inheritance with diamond-shaped graphs. Consider the following definitions:

```
class A(object):
    def met(self):
```

```
        print('A.met')
class B(A):
    def met(self):
        print('B.met')
        A.met(self)
class C(A):
    def met(self):
        print('C.met')
        A.met(self)
class D(B,C):
    def met(self):
        print('D.met')
        B.met(self)
        C.met(self)
```

In this code, when we call `D().met()`, `A.met` ends up being called twice. How can we ensure that each ancestor's implementation of the method is called once and only once? The solution is to use built-in type `super`. In v2, this requires calling `super(aclass, obj)`, which returns a special superobject of object *obj*. When we look up an attribute in this superobject, the lookup begins *after* class *aclass* in *obj*'s MRO. In v2, we can therefore rewrite the previous code as:

```
class A(object):
    def met(self):
        print('A.met')
class B(A):
    def met(self):
        print('B.met')
        super(B,self).met()
class C(A):
    def met(self):
        print('C.met')
        super(C,self).met()
class D(B,C):
    def met(self):
        print('D.met')
        super(D,self).met()
```

In v3, while the v2 syntax is still OK (and so the preceding snippet runs fine), `super`'s semantics have been strengthened so you can replace each of the calls to it with just `super()`, without arguments.

Now, `D().met()` results in exactly one call to each class's version of `met`. If you get into the habit of always coding superclass calls with `super`, your classes fit smoothly even in complicated inheritance structures. There are no ill effects if the inheritance structure instead turns out to be simple.

The only situation in which you may prefer to use the rougher approach of calling superclass methods through the unbound-method syntax is when the various classes have different and incompatible signatures for the same method—an unpleasant situation in many respects, but, if you do have to deal with it, the unbound-method syntax may sometimes be the least of evils. Proper use of multiple inheritance is seriously hampered—but then, even the most fundamental properties of OOP, such as polymorphism between base and subclass instances, are seriously impaired when you give methods of the same name different and incompatible signatures in the superclass and subclass.

"Deleting" class attributes

Inheritance and overriding provide a simple and effective way to add or modify (override) class attributes (such as methods) noninvasively (i.e., without modifying the base class defining the attributes) by adding or overriding the attributes in subclasses. However, inheritance does not offer a way to delete (hide) base classes' attributes noninvasively. If the subclass simply fails to define (override) an attribute, Python finds the base class's definition. If you need to perform such deletion, possibilities include:

- Override the method and raise an exception in the method's body.
- Eschew inheritance, hold the attributes elsewhere than in the subclass's `__dict__`, and define `__getattr__` for selective delegation.
- Override `__getattribute__` to similar effect.

The last of these techniques is shown in "__getattribute__" on page 124.

The Built-in object Type

The built-in `object` type is the ancestor of all built-in types and new-style classes. The `object` type defines some special methods (documented in "Special Methods" on page 126) that implement the default semantics of objects:

`__new__` `__init__`
: You can create a direct instance of `object` by calling `object()` without any arguments. The call implicitly uses `object.__new__` and `object.__init__` to make and return an instance object without attributes (and without even a `__dict__` in which to hold attributes). Such instance objects may be useful as "sentinels," guaranteed to compare unequal to any other distinct object.

`__delattr__` `__getattribute__` `__setattr__`
: By default, any object handles attribute references (as covered in "Attribute Reference Basics" on page 110) using these methods of `object`.

`__hash__` `__repr__` `__str__`
: Any object can be passed to the functions `hash` and `repr` and to the type `str`.

A subclass of `object` may override any of these methods and/or add others.

Class-Level Methods

Python supplies two built-in nonoverriding descriptor types, which give a class two distinct kinds of "class-level methods": *static methods* and *class methods*.

Static methods

A *static method* is a method that you can call on a class, or on any instance of the class, without the special behavior and constraints of ordinary methods, bound or unbound, with regard to the first parameter. A static method may have any signature; it may have no parameters, and the first parameter, if any, plays no special role. You can think of a static method as an ordinary function that you're able to call normally, despite the fact that it happens to be bound to a class attribute.

While it is never necessary to define static methods (you can always choose to instead define a normal function, outside the class), some programmers consider them to be an elegant syntax alternative when a function's purpose is tightly bound to some specific class.

To build a static method, call the built-in type `staticmethod` and bind its result to a class attribute. Like all binding of class attributes, this is normally done in the body of the class, but you may also choose to perform it elsewhere. The only argument to `staticmethod` is the function to call when Python calls the static method. The following example shows one way to define and call a static method:

```
class AClass(object):
    def astatic(): print('a static method')
    astatic = staticmethod(astatic)
an_instance = AClass()
AClass.astatic()                    # prints: a static method
an_instance.astatic()               # prints: a static method
```

This example uses the same name for the function passed to `staticmethod` and for the attribute bound to `staticmethod`'s result. This naming is not mandatory, but it's a good idea, and we recommend you always use it. Python also offers a special, simplified syntax to support this style, covered in "Decorators" on page 140.

Class methods

A *class method* is a method you can call on a class or on any instance of the class. Python binds the method's first parameter to the class on which you call the method, or the class of the instance on which you call the method; it does not bind it to the instance, as for normal bound methods. The first parameter of a class method is conventionally named *`cls`*.

While it is never necessary to define class methods (you can always choose to instead define a normal function, outside the class, that takes the class object as its first parameter), class methods are an elegant alternative to such functions (particularly since they can usefully be overridden in subclasses, when that is necessary).

To build a class method, call the built-in type classmethod and bind its result to a class attribute. Like all binding of class attributes, this is normally done in the body of the class, but you may choose to perform it elsewhere. The only argument to classmethod is the function to call when Python calls the class method. Here's one way you can define and call a class method:

```
class ABase(object):
    def aclassmet(cls): print('a class method for', cls.__name__)
    aclassmet = classmethod(aclassmet)
class ADeriv(ABase): pass
b_instance = ABase()
d_instance = ADeriv()
ABase.aclassmet()                # prints: a class method for ABase
b_instance.aclassmet()           # prints: a class method for ABase
ADeriv.aclassmet()               # prints: a class method for ADeriv
d_instance.aclassmet()           # prints: a class method for ADeriv
```

This example uses the same name for the function passed to classmethod and for the attribute bound to classmethod's result. This naming is not mandatory, but it's a good idea, and we recommend that you always use it. Python offers a special, simplified syntax to support this style, covered in "Decorators" on page 140.

Object-Oriented Python

Properties

Python supplies a built-in overriding descriptor type, which you may use to give a class's instances *properties*.

A property is an instance attribute with special functionality. You reference, bind, or unbind the attribute with the normal syntax (e.g., print(*x.prop*), x.*prop*=23, del *x.prop*). However, rather than following the usual semantics for attribute reference, binding, and unbinding, these accesses call on instance *x* the methods that you specify as arguments to the built-in type property. Here's one way to define a read-only property:

```
class Rectangle(object):
    def __init__(self, width, height):
        self.width = width
        self.height = height
    def get_area(self):
        return self.width * self.height
    area = property(get_area, doc='area of the rectangle')
```

Each instance *r* of class *Rectangle* has a synthetic read-only attribute *r.area*, computed on the fly in method *r.get_area*() by multiplying the sides. The docstring *Rectangle.area*.__doc__ is 'area of the rectangle'. Attribute *r.area* is read-only (attempts to rebind or unbind it fail) because we specify only a get method in the call to property, no set or del methods.

Properties perform tasks similar to those of special methods __getattr__, __setattr__, and __delattr__ (covered in "General-Purpose Special Methods" on page 126), but are faster and simpler. To build a property, call the built-in type prop erty and bind its result to a class attribute. Like all binding of class attributes, this is normally done in the body of the class, but you may choose to do it elsewhere. Within the body of a class *C*, you can use the following syntax:

```
attrib = property(fget=None, fset=None, fdel=None, doc=None)
```

When *x* is an instance of *C* and you reference *x.attrib*, Python calls on *x* the method you passed as argument *fget* to the property constructor, without arguments. When you assign *x.attrib* = *value*, Python calls the method you passed as argument *fset*, with *value* as the only argument. When you execute `del` *x.attrib*, Python calls the method you passed as argument *fdel*, without arguments. Python uses the argument you passed as *doc* as the docstring of the attribute. All parameters to `property` are optional. When an argument is missing, the corresponding operation is forbidden (Python raises an exception when some code attempts that operation). For example, in the *Rectangle* example, we made property *area* read-only, because we passed an argument only for parameter *fget*, and not for parameters *fset* and *fdel*.

A more elegant syntax to create properties in a class is to use `property` as a *decorator* (see "Decorators" on page 140):

```
class Rectangle(object):
    def __init__(self, width, height):
        self.width = width
        self.height = height
    @property
    def area(self):
        '''area of the rectangle'''
        return self.width * self.height
```

To use this syntax, you must give the getter method the same name as you want the property to have; the method's docstring becomes the docstring of the property. If you want to add a setter and/or a deleter as well, use decorators named (in this example) *area.setter* and *area.deleter*, and name the methods thus decorated the same as the property, too. For example:

```
class Rectangle(object):
    def __init__(self, width, height):
        self.width = width
        self.height = height
    @property
    def area(self):
        '''area of the rectangle'''
        return self.width * self.height
    @area.setter
    def area(self, value):
        scale = math.sqrt(value/self.area)
        self.width *= scale
        self.height *= scale
```

Why properties are important

The crucial importance of properties is that their existence makes it perfectly safe (and indeed advisable) for you to expose public data attributes as part of your class's public interface. Should it ever become necessary, in future versions of your class or other classes that need to be polymorphic to it, to have some code executed when the attribute is referenced, rebound, or unbound, you know you will be able to change the plain attribute into a property and get the desired effect without any impact on any other code that uses your class (AKA "client code"). This lets you avoid goofy idioms, such as *accessor* and *mutator* methods, required by OO languages that lack properties or equivalent machinery. For example, client code can simply use natural idioms such as:

```
some_instance.widget_count += 1
```

rather than being forced into contorted nests of accessors and mutators such as:

```
some_instance.set_widget_count(some_instance.get_widget_count() + 1)
```

If you're ever tempted to code methods whose natural names are something like `get_this` or `set_that`, wrap those methods into properties instead, for clarity.

Properties and inheritance

Inheritance of properties is just like for any other attribute. However, there's a little trap for the unwary: *the methods called upon to access a property are those defined in the class in which the property itself is defined*, without intrinsic use of further overriding that may happen in subclasses. For example:

```
class B(object):
  def f(self): return 23
  g = property(f)
class C(B):
  def f(self): return 42
c = C()
print(c.g)                 # prints: 23, not 42
```

Accessing property `c.g` calls `B.f`, not `C.f` as you might expect. The reason is quite simple: the property constructor receives (directly or via the decorator syntax) the *function object f* (and that happens at the time the `class` statement for `B` executes, so the function object in question is the one also known as `B.f`). The fact that the subclass `C` later redefines *name f* is therefore irrelevant, since the property performs no lookup for that name, but rather uses the function object it was passed at creation time. If you need to work around this issue, you can always do it by adding the extra level of lookup indirection yourself:

```
class B(object):
  def f(self): return 23
  def _f_getter(self): return self.f()
  g = property(_f_getter)
class C(B):
  def f(self): return 42
```

```
c = C()
print(c.g)                    # prints: 42, as expected
```

Here, the function object held by the property is *B._f_getter*, which in turn does perform a lookup for name *f* (since it calls `self.f()`); therefore, the overriding of *f* has the expected effect. After all, as David Wheeler famously put it, "All problems in computer science can be solved by another level of indirection."[1]

__slots__

Normally, each instance object *x* of any class *C* has a dictionary `x.__dict__` that Python uses to let you bind arbitrary attributes on *x*. To save a little memory (at the cost of letting *x* have only a predefined set of attribute names), you can define in class *C* a class attribute named `__slots__`, a sequence (normally a tuple) of strings (normally identifiers). When class *C* has an attribute `__slots__`, a direct instance *x* of class *C* has no `x.__dict__`, and any attempt to bind on *x* any attribute whose name is not in `C.__slots__` raises an exception.

Using `__slots__` lets you reduce memory consumption for small instance objects that can do without the powerful and convenient ability to have arbitrarily named attributes. `__slots__` is worth adding only to classes that can have so many instances that saving a few tens of bytes per instance is important—typically classes that could have millions, not mere thousands, of instances alive at the same time. Unlike most other class attributes, `__slots__` works as we've just described only if an assignment in the class body binds it as a class attribute. Any later alteration, rebinding, or unbinding of `__slots__` has no effect, nor does inheriting `__slots__` from a base class. Here's how to add `__slots__` to the *Rectangle* class defined earlier to get smaller (though less flexible) instances:

```
class OptimizedRectangle(Rectangle):
    __slots__ = 'width', 'height'
```

We do not need to define a slot for the *area* property. `__slots__` does not constrain properties, only ordinary *instance* attributes, which would reside in the instance's `__dict__` if `__slots__` wasn't defined.

__getattribute__

All references to instance attributes go through special method `__getattribute__`. This method comes from `object`, where it implements the details of object attribute reference semantics documented in "Attribute Reference Basics" on page 110. However, you may override `__getattribute__` for special purposes, such as hiding inherited class attributes for a subclass's instances. The following example shows one way to implement a list without `append`:

1 To complete, for once, the usually truncated famous quote: "except of course for the problem of too many indirections."

```
class listNoAppend(list):
    def __getattribute__(self, name):
        if name == 'append': raise AttributeError(name)
        return list.__getattribute__(self, name)
```

An instance *x* of class *listNoAppend* is almost indistinguishable from a built-in list object, except that performance is substantially worse, and any reference to *x*.append raises an exception.

Per-Instance Methods

An instance can have instance-specific bindings for all attributes, including callable attributes (methods). For a method, just like for any other attribute (except those bound to overriding descriptors), an instance-specific binding hides a class-level binding: attribute lookup does not consider the class when it finds a binding directly in the instance. An instance-specific binding for a callable attribute does not perform any of the transformations detailed in "Bound and Unbound Methods" on page 112: the attribute reference returns exactly the same callable object that was earlier bound directly to the instance attribute.

However, this does not work as you might expect for per-instance bindings of the special methods that Python calls implicitly as a result of various operations, as covered in "Special Methods" on page 126. Such implicit uses of special methods always rely on the class-level binding of the special method, if any. For example:

```
def fake_get_item(idx): return idx
class MyClass(object): pass
n = MyClass()
n.__getitem__ = fake_get_item
print(n[23])                      # results in:
# Traceback (most recent call last):
#   File "<stdin>", line 1, in ?
# TypeError: unindexable object
```

Inheritance from Built-in Types

A class can inherit from a built-in type. However, a class may directly or indirectly extend multiple built-in types only if those types are specifically designed to allow this level of mutual compatibility. Python does not support unconstrained inheritance from multiple arbitrary built-in types. Normally, a new-style class only extends at most one substantial built-in type—this means at most one built-in type in addition to `object`, which is the superclass of all built-in types and classes and imposes no constraints on multiple inheritance. For example:

```
class noway(dict, list): pass
```

raises a `TypeError` exception, with a detailed explanation of "multiple bases have instance lay-out conflict." If you ever see such error messages, it means that you're trying to inherit, directly or indirectly, from multiple built-in types that are not specifically designed to cooperate at such a deep level.

Special Methods

A class may define or inherit special methods (i.e., methods whose names begin and end with double underscores, AKA "dunder" or "magic" methods). Each special method relates to a specific operation. Python implicitly calls a special method whenever you perform the related operation on an instance object. In most cases, the method's return value is the operation's result, and attempting an operation when its related method is not present raises an exception.

Throughout this section, we point out the cases in which these general rules do not apply. In the following, *x* is the instance of class *C* on which you perform the operation, and *y* is the other operand, if any. The parameter `self` of each method also refers to the instance object *x*. In the following sections, whenever we mention calls to `x.__whatever__(...)`, keep in mind that the exact call happening is rather, pedantically speaking, `x.__class__.__whatever__(x, ...)`.

General-Purpose Special Methods

Some special methods relate to general-purpose operations. A class that defines or inherits these methods allows its instances to control such operations. These operations can be divided into the following categories:

Initialization and finalization
: A class can control its instances' initialization (a very common requirement) via the special methods `__new__` and `__init__`, and/or their finalization (a rare requirement) via `__del__`.

Representation as string
: A class can control how Python renders its instances as strings via special methods `__repr__`, `__str__`, `__format__`, (v3 only) `__bytes__`, and (v2 only) `__unicode__`.

Comparison, hashing, and use in a Boolean context
: A class can control how its instances compare with other objects (methods `__lt__`, `__le__`, `__gt__`, `__ge__`, `__eq__`, `__ne__`), how dictionaries use them as keys and sets use them as members (`__hash__`), and whether they evaluate to true or false in Boolean contexts (`__nonzero__` in v2, `__bool__` in v3).

Attribute reference, binding, and unbinding
: A class can control access to its instances' attributes (reference, binding, unbinding) via special methods `__getattribute__`, `__getattr__`, `__setattr__`, and `__delattr__`.

Callable instances
: An instance is callable, just like a function object, if its class has the special method `__call__`.

Table 4-1 documents the general-purpose special methods.

Table 4-1. General-purpose special methods

__bytes__

`__bytes__(self)`

In v3, calling `bytes(x)` calls `x.__bytes__()`, if present. If a class supplies both special methods `__bytes__` and `__str__`, the two should return equivalent strings (of bytes and text type, respectively).

__call__

`__call__(self[,args...])`

When you call `x([args...])`, Python translates the operation into a call to `x.__call__([args...])`. The arguments for the call operation correspond to the parameters for the `__call__` method, minus the first. The first parameter, conventionally called `self`, refers to *x*, and Python supplies it implicitly and automatically, just as in any other call to a bound method.

__dir__

`__dir__(self)`

When you call `dir(x)`, Python translates the operation into a call to `x.__dir__()`, which must return a sorted list of *x*'s attributes. If *x*'s class does not have a `__dir__`, then `dir(x)` does its own introspection to return a list of *x*'s attributes, striving to produce relevant, rather than complete, information.

Object-Oriented Python

__del__

`__del__(self)`

Just before *x* disappears because of garbage collection, Python calls `x.__del__()` to let *x* finalize itself. If `__del__` is absent, Python performs no special finalization upon garbage-collecting *x* (this is the usual case: very few classes need to define `__del__`). Python ignores the return value of `__del__` and performs no implicit call to `__del__` methods of class *C*'s superclasses. `C.__del__` must explicitly perform any needed finalization, including, if need be, by delegation. For example, when class *C* has a base class *B* to finalize, the code in `C.__del__` must call `super(C, self).__del__()` (or, in v3, just `super().__del__()`).

Note that the `__del__` method has no direct connection with the `del` statement, as covered in "del Statements" on page 56.

`__del__` is generally not the best approach when you need timely and guaranteed finalization. For such needs, use the `try/finally` statement covered in "try/finally" on page 152 (or, even better, the `with` statement, covered in "The with Statement" on page 82). Instances of classes defining `__del__` cannot participate in cyclic-garbage collection, covered in "Garbage Collection" on page 388. Therefore, you should be particularly careful to avoid reference loops involving such instances, and define `__del__` only when there is no feasible alternative.

__delattr__

`__delattr__(self, name)`

At every request to unbind attribute `x.y` (typically, a `del` statement `del x.y`), Python calls `x.__delattr__('y')`. All the considerations discussed later for `__setattr__` also apply to `__delattr__`. Python ignores the return value of `__delattr__`. If `__delattr__` is absent, Python translates `del x.y` into `del x.__dict__['y']`.

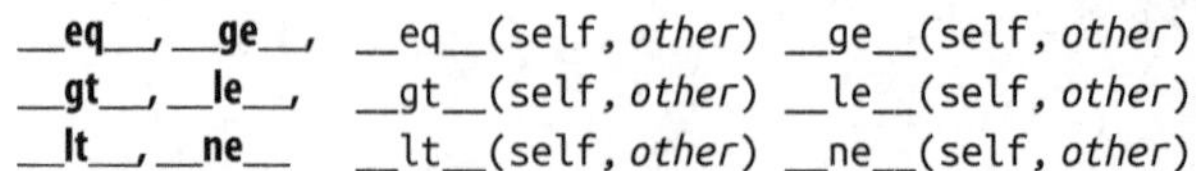

__eq__, __ge__, __gt__, __le__, __lt__, __ne__

`__eq__(self, other) __ge__(self, other)`
`__gt__(self, other) __le__(self, other)`
`__lt__(self, other) __ne__(self, other)`

The comparisons *x==y*, *x>=y*, *x>y*, *x<=y*, *x<y*, and `x!=y`, respectively, call the special methods listed here, which should return `False` or `True`. Each method may return `NotImplemented` to tell Python to handle the comparison in alternative ways (e.g., Python may then try *y>x* in lieu of *x<y*).

Best practice is to define only one inequality comparison method (normally `__lt__`) plus `__eq__`, and decorate the class with `functools.total_ordering` (covered in Table 7-4) to avoid boilerplate, and any risk of logical contradictions in your comparisons.

__getattr__

`__getattr__(self, name)`

When the attribute *x.y* can't be found by the usual steps (i.e., when `AttributeError` would normally be raised), Python calls `x.__getattr__('y')` instead. Python does not call `__getattr__` for attributes found by normal means (i.e., as keys in `x.__dict__`, or via `x.__class__`). If you want Python to call `__getattr__` on every attribute reference, keep the attributes elsewhere (e.g., in another dictionary referenced by an attribute with a private name), or else override `__getattribute__` instead. `__getattr__` should raise `AttributeError` if it cannot find *y*.

__getattribute__

`__getattribute__(self, name)`

At every request to access attribute `x.y`, Python calls `x.__getattribute__('y')`, which must get and return the attribute value or else raise `AttributeError`. The normal semantics of attribute access (using `x.__dict__`, `C.__slots__`, *C*'s class attributes, `x.__getattr__`) are all due to `object.__getattribute__`.

When class *C* overrides `__getattribute__`, it must implement all of the attribute access semantics it wants to offer. Most often, the most convenient way to implement attribute access semantics is by delegating (e.g., calling `object.__getattribute__(self, ...)` as part of the operation of your override of `__getattribute__`).

Overriding __getattribute__ slows attribute access

When a class overrides `__getattribute__`, attribute accesses on instances of the class become slow, since the overriding code executes on every such attribute access.

__hash__

`__hash__(self)`

Calling `hash(x)` calls `x.__hash__()` (and so do other contexts that need to know *x*'s hash value, namely, using *x* as a dictionary key, such as `D[x]` where *D* is a dictionary, or using *x* as a set member). `__hash__` must return an `int` such that *x*==*y* implies `hash(x)==hash(y)`, and must always return the same value for a given object.

When `__hash__` is absent, calling `hash(x)` calls `id(x)` instead, as long as `__eq__` is also absent. Other contexts that need to know *x*'s hash value behave the same way.

Any *x* such that `hash(x)` returns a result, rather than raising an exception, is known as a *hashable object*. When `__hash__` is absent, but `__eq__` is present, calling `hash(x)` raises an exception (and so do other contexts that need to know *x*'s hash value). In this case, *x* is not hashable and therefore cannot be a dictionary key or set member.

You normally define `__hash__` only for immutable objects that also define `__eq__`. Note that if there exists any *y* such that *x*==*y*, even if *y* is of a different type, and both *x* and *y* are hashable, you *must* ensure that `hash(x)==hash(y)`.

Object-Oriented Python

__init__

`__init__(self[,args...])`

When a call `C([args...])` creates instance *x* of class *C*, Python calls `x.__init__([args...])` to let *x* initialize itself. If `__init__` is absent (i.e., it's inherited from `object`), you must call class *C* without arguments, `C()`, and *x* has no instance-specific attributes upon creation. Python performs no implicit call to `__init__` methods of class *C*'s superclasses. `C.__init__` must explicitly perform any needed initialization, including, if need be, by delegation. For example, when class *C* has a base class *B* to initialize without arguments, the code in `C.__init__` must explicitly call `super(C, self).__init__()` (or, in v3, just `super().__init__()`). However, `__init__`'s inheritance works just like for any other method or attribute: that is, if class *C* itself does not override `__init__`, it just inherits it from the first superclass in its `__mro__` to override `__init__`, like for every other attribute.

`__init__` must return `None`; otherwise, calling the class raises a `TypeError`.

__new__

`__new__(cls[,args...])`

When you call *C*(`[`*args*`...]`), Python gets the new instance *x* that you are creating by invoking *C*.__new__(*C*,`[`*args*`...]`). Every class has the class method __new__ (most often simply inheriting it from `object`), which can return any value *x*. In other words, __new__ is not constrained to return a new instance of *C*, although normally it's expected to do so. If, and only if, the value *x* that __new__ returns is indeed an instance of *C* or of any subclass of *C* (whether a new or previously existing one), Python continues after calling __new__ by implicitly calling `__init__` on *x* (with the same `[`*args*`...]` that were originally passed to __new__).

Initialize immutables in __new__, all others in __init__

Since you could perform most kinds of initialization of new instances in either `__init__` or __new__, you may wonder where best to place them. Simple: put the initialization in `__init__` only, unless you have a specific reason to put it in __new__. (If a type is immutable, its instances cannot be changed in `__init__` for initialization purposes, so this is a special case in which __new__ does have to perform all initialization.) This tip makes life simpler, since `__init__` is an instance method, while __new__ is a specialized class method.

__nonzero__

`__nonzero__(self)`

When evaluating *x* as true or false (see "Boolean Values" on page 52)—for example, on a call to `bool(`*x*`)`—v2 calls *x*`.__nonzero__()`, which should return `True` or `False`. When `__nonzero__` is not present, Python calls `__len__` instead, and takes *x* as false when *x*`.__len__()` returns `0` (so, to check if a container is nonempty, avoid coding `if len(`*container*`)>0:`; just code `if` *container*`:` instead). When neither `__nonzero__` nor `__len__` is present, Python always considers *x* true.

In v3, this special method is spelled, more readably, as `__bool__`.

__repr__

`__repr__(self)`

Calling `repr(`*x*`)` (which also happens implicitly in the interactive interpreter when *x* is the result of an expression statement) calls *x*`.__repr__()` to get and return a complete string representation of *x*. If `__repr__` is absent, Python uses a default string representation. `__repr__` should return a string with unambiguous information on *x*. Ideally, when feasible, the string should be an expression such that `eval(repr(`*x*`))==`*x* (but don't go crazy aiming for that goal).

__setattr__ `__setattr__(self, name, value)`

At every request to bind attribute `x.y` (typically, an assignment statement `x.y=value`, but also, for example, `setattr(x, 'y', value)`), Python calls `x.__setattr__('y', value)`. Python always calls `__setattr__` for *any* attribute binding on *x*—a major difference from `__getattr__` (`__setattr__` is closer to `__getattribute__` in this sense). To avoid recursion, when `x.__setattr__` binds *x*'s attributes, it must modify `x.__dict__` directly (e.g., via `x.__dict__[name]=value`); even better, `__setattr__` can delegate the setting to the superclass (by calling `super(C, x).__setattr__('y', value)` or, in v3, just `super().__setattr__('y', value)`). Python ignores the return value of `__setattr__`. If `__setattr__` is absent (i.e., inherited from `object`), and `C.y` is not an overriding descriptor, Python usually translates `x.y=z` into `x.__dict__['y']=z`.

__str__ `__str__(self)`

The `str(x)` built-in type and the `print(x)` function call `x.__str__()` to get an informal, concise string representation of *x*. If `__str__` is absent, Python calls `x.__repr__` instead. `__str__` should return a conveniently human-readable string, even if it entails some approximation.

Object-Oriented Python

__unicode__ `__unicode__(self)`

In v2, calling `unicode(x)` calls `x.__unicode__()`, if present, in preference to `x.__str__()`. If a class supplies both special methods `__unicode__` and `__str__`, the two should return equivalent strings (of Unicode and plain-string type, respectively).

__format__ `__format__(self, format_string='')`

Calling `format(x)` calls `x.__format__()`, and calling `format(x, format_string)` calls `x.__format__(format_string)`. The class is responsible for interpreting the format string (each class may define its own small "language" of format specifications, inspired by those implemented by built-in types as covered in "String Formatting" on page 240). If `__format__` is inherited from `object`, it delegates to `__str__` and does not accept a nonempty format string.

Special Methods for Containers

An instance can be a *container* (a sequence, mapping, or set—mutually exclusive concepts[2]). For maximum usefulness, containers should provide special methods `__getitem__`, `__setitem__`, `__delitem__`, `__len__`, `__contains__`, and `__iter__`, plus nonspecial methods discussed in the following sections. In many cases, suitable

---

2 Third-party extensions can also define types of containers that are not sequences, not mappings, and not sets.

implementations of the nonspecial methods can be had by extending the appropriate *abstract base class*, from module `collections`, such as `Sequence`, `MutableSequence`, and so on, as covered in "Abstract Base Classes" on page 135.

Sequences

In each item-access special method, a sequence that has *L* items should accept any integer *key* such that `-L<=key<L`.[3] For compatibility with built-in sequences, a negative index *key*, `0>key>=-L`, should be equivalent to `key+L`. When *key* has an invalid type, indexing should raise `TypeError`. When *key* is a value of a valid type but out of range, indexing should raise `IndexError`. For sequence classes that do not define `__iter__`, the `for` statement relies on these requirements, as do built-in functions that take iterable arguments. Every item-access special method of a sequence should also, if at all practical, accept as its index argument an instance of the built-in type `slice` whose `start`, `step`, and `stop` attributes are `int`s or `None`; the *slicing* syntax relies on this requirement, as covered in "Container slicing" on page 133.

A sequence should also allow concatenation (with another sequence of the same type) by `+`, and repetition by `*` (multiplication by an integer). A sequence should therefore have special methods `__add__`, `__mul__`, `__radd__`, and `__rmul__`, covered in "Special Methods for Numeric Objects" on page 138; mutable sequences should also have equivalent in-place methods `__iadd__` and `__imul__`. A sequence should be meaningfully comparable to another sequence of the same type, implementing *lexicographic* comparison like lists and tuples do. (Inheriting from ABCs `Sequence` or `MutableSequence`, alas, does not suffice to fulfill these requirements; such inheritance only supplies `__iadd__`.)

Every sequence should have the nonspecial methods covered in "List methods" on page 65: `count` and `index` in any case, and, if mutable, then also `append`, `insert`, `extend`, `pop`, `remove`, `reverse`, and `sort`, with the same signatures and semantics as the corresponding methods of lists. (Inheriting from ABCs `Sequence` or `MutableSequence` does suffice to fulfill these requirements, except for `sort`.)

An immutable sequence should be hashable if, and only if, all of its items are. A sequence type may constrain its items in some ways (for example, accepting only string items), but that is not mandatory.

Mappings

A mapping's item-access special methods should raise `KeyError`, rather than `IndexError`, when they receive an invalid *key* argument value of a valid type. Any mapping should define the nonspecial methods covered in "Dictionary Methods" on page 70: `copy`, `get`, `items`, `keys`, `values`, and, in v2, `iteritems`, `iterkeys`, and `itervalues`. In v2, special method `__iter__` should be equivalent to `iterkeys` (in v3, it

3 Lower-bound included; upper-bound excluded—as always, the norm for Python.

should be equivalent to keys, which, in v3, has the semantics iterkeys has in v2). A mutable mapping should also define methods clear, pop, popitem, setdefault, and update. (Inheriting from ABCs Mapping or MutableMapping does fulfill these requirements, except for copy.)

An immutable mapping should be hashable if all of its items are. A mapping type may constrain its keys in some ways (for example, accepting only hashable keys, or, even more specifically, accepting, say, only string keys), but that is not mandatory. Any mapping should be meaningfully comparable to another mapping of the same type (at least for equality and inequality; not necessarily for ordering comparisons).

Sets

Sets are a peculiar kind of container—containers that are neither sequences nor mappings, and cannot be indexed, but do have a length (number of elements) and are iterable. Sets also support many operators (&, |, ^, -, as well as membership tests and comparisons) and equivalent nonspecial methods (intersection, union, and so on). If you implement a set-like container, it should be polymorphic to Python built-in sets, covered in "Sets" on page 49. (Inheriting from ABCs Set or MutableSet does fulfill these requirements.)

Object-Oriented Python

An immutable set-like type should be hashable if all of its elements are. A set-like type may constrain its elements in some ways (for example, accepting only hashable elements, or, even more specifically, accepting, say, only integer elements), but that is not mandatory.

Container slicing

When you reference, bind, or unbind a slicing such as *x*[*i*:*j*] or *x*[*i*:*j*:*k*] on a container *x* (in practice, this is only used with sequences), Python calls *x*'s applicable item-access special method, passing as *key* an object of a built-in type called a *slice object*. A slice object has the attributes start, stop, and step. Each attribute is None if you omit the corresponding value in the slice syntax. For example, del *x*[:3] calls *x*.__delitem__(*y*), where *y* is a slice object such that *y*.stop is 3, *y*.start is None, and *y*.step is None. It is up to container object *x* to appropriately interpret slice object arguments passed to *x*'s special methods. The method indices of slice objects can help: call it with your container's length as its only argument, and it returns a tuple of three nonnegative indices suitable as start, stop, and step for a loop indexing each item in the slice. A common idiom in a sequence class's __getitem__ special method, to fully support slicing, is, for example:

```
def __getitem__(self, index):
  # Recursively specialcase slicing
  if isinstance(index, slice):
    return self.__class__(self[x]
                          for x in range(*self.indices(len(self))))
  # Check index, dealing with negative indices too
  if not isinstance(index, numbers.Integral): raise TypeError
```

```
    if index < 0: index += len(self)
    if not (0 <= index < len(self)): raise IndexError
    # Index is now a correct integral number, within range(len(self))
    ...rest of __getitem__, dealing with single-item access...
```

This idiom uses generator-expression (genexp) syntax and assumes that your class's `__init__` method can be called with an iterable argument to create a suitable new instance of the class.

Container methods

The special methods `__getitem__`, `__setitem__`, `__delitem__`, `__iter__`, `__len__`, and `__contains__` expose container functionality (see Table 4-2).

Table 4-2. Container methods

__contains__ `__contains__(self,item)`

The Boolean test *y* `in` *x* calls *x*`.__contains__(`*y*`)`. When *x* is a sequence, or set-like, `__contains__` should return `True` when *y* equals the value of an item in *x*. When *x* is a mapping, `__contains__` should return `True` when *y* equals the value of a key in *x*. Otherwise, `__contains__` should return `False`. When `__contains__` is absent, Python performs *y* `in` *x* as follows, taking time proportional to `len(`*x*`)`:

```
for z in x:
    if y==z: return True
return False
```

__delitem__ `__delitem__(self,key)`

For a request to unbind an item or slice of *x* (typically `del` *x*`[`*key*`]`), Python calls *x*`.__delitem__(`*key*`)`. A container *x* should have `__delitem__` only if *x* is mutable so that items (and possibly slices) can be removed.

__getitem__ `__getitem__(self,key)`

When you access *x*`[`*key*`]` (i.e., when you index or slice container *x*), Python calls *x*`.__getitem__(`*key*`)`. All (non-set-like) containers should have `__getitem__`.

__iter__ `__iter__(self)`

For a request to loop on all items of *x* (typically `for` *item* `in` *x*), Python calls *x*`.__iter__()` to get an iterator on *x*. The built-in function `iter(`*x*`)` also calls *x*`.__iter__()`. When `__iter__` is absent, `iter(`*x*`)` synthesizes and returns an iterator object that wraps *x* and yields *x*`[0]`, *x*`[1]`, and so on, until one of these indexings raises `IndexError` to indicate the end of the container. However, it is best to ensure that all of the container classes you code have `__iter__`.

__len__

`__len__(self)`

Calling `len(x)` calls `x.__len__()` (and so do other built-in functions that need to know how many items are in container *x*). `__len__` should return an `int`, the number of items in *x*. Python also calls `x.__len__()` to evaluate *x* in a Boolean context, when `__nonzero__` (`__bool__` in v3) is absent; in this case, a container is taken as false if and only if the container is empty (i.e., the container's length is `0`). All containers should have `__len__`, unless it's just too expensive for the container to determine how many items it contains.

__setitem__

`__setitem__(self,key,value)`

For a request to bind an item or slice of *x* (typically an assignment `x[key]=value`), Python calls `x.__setitem__(key,value)`. A container *x* should have `__setitem__` only if *x* is mutable so that items, and possibly slices, can be added and/or rebound.

Abstract Base Classes

Object-Oriented Python

Abstract base classes (ABCs) are an important pattern in object-oriented (OO) design: they're classes that cannot be directly instantiated, but exist only to be extended by concrete classes (the more usual kind of classes, the ones that can be instantiated).

One recommended approach to OO design is to never extend a concrete class: if two concrete classes have so much in common that you're tempted to have one of them inherit from the other, proceed instead by making an *abstract* base class that subsumes all they do have in common, and have each concrete class extend that ABC. This approach avoids many of the subtle traps and pitfalls of inheritance.

Python offers rich support for ABCs, enough to make them a first-class part of Python's object model.

abc

The standard library module `abc` supplies metaclass `ABCMeta` and, in v3, class `ABC` (subclassing `ABC` makes `ABCMeta` the metaclass, and has no other effect).

When you use `abc.ABCMeta` as the metaclass for any class *C*, this makes *C* an ABC, and supplies the class method `C.register`, callable with a single argument: that argument can be any existing class (or built-in type) *X*.

Calling `C.register(X)` makes *X* a *virtual* subclass of *C*, meaning that `issubclass(X,C)` returns `True`, but *C* does not appear in `X.__mro__`, nor does *X* inherit any of *C*'s methods or other attributes.

Of course, it's also possible to have a new class *Y* inherit from *C* in the normal way, in which case *C* does appear in `Y.__mro__`, and *Y* inherits all of *C*'s methods, as usual in subclassing.

An ABC *C* can also optionally override class method `__subclasshook__`, which `issubclass(X,C)` calls with the single argument *X*, *X* being any class or type. When `C.__subclasshook__(X)` returns `True`, then so does `issubclass(X,C)`; when `C.__subclasshook__(X)` returns `False`, then so does `issubclass(X,C)`; when `C.__subclasshook__(X)` returns `NotImplemented`, then `issubclass(X,C)` proceeds in the usual way.

The module `abc` also supplies the decorator `abstractmethod` (and `abstractproperty`, but the latter is deprecated in v3, where you can just apply both the `abstractmethod` and `property` decorators to get the same effect). Abstract methods and properties can have implementations (available to subclasses via the `super` built-in) —however, the point of making methods and properties abstract is that you can instantiate any nonvirtual subclass *X* of an ABC *C* only if *X* overrides every abstract property and method of *C*.

ABCs in the collections module

`collections` supplies many ABCs. Since Python 3.4, the ABCs are in `collections.abc` (but, for backward compatibility, can still be accessed directly in `collections` itself: the latter access will cease working in some future release of v3).

Some just characterize any class defining or inheriting a specific abstract method, as listed in Table 4-3:

Table 4-3.

Callable	Any class with `__call__`
Container	Any class with `__contains__`
Hashable	Any class with `__hash__`
Iterable	Any class with `__iter__`
Sized	Any class with `__len__`

The other ABCs in `collections` extend one or more of the preceding ones, add more abstract methods, and supply *mixin* methods implemented in terms of the abstract methods (when you extend any ABC in a concrete class, you must override the abstract methods; you can optionally override some or all of the mixin methods, if that helps improve performance, but you don't have to—you can just inherit them, if this results in performance that's sufficient for your purposes).

Here is the set of ABCs directly extending the preceding ones:

ABC	Extends	Abstract methods	Mixin methods
Iterator	`Iterable`	`__next__` (in v2, `next`)	`__iter__`
Mapping	`Container`, `Iterable`, `Sized`	`__getitem__`, `__iter__`, `__len__`	`__contains__`, `__eq__`, `__ne__`, `get`, `items`, `keys`, `values`
MappingView	`Sized`		`__len__`
Sequence	`Container`, `Iterable`, `Sized`	`__getitem__`, `__len__`	`__contains__`, `__iter__`, `__reversed__`, `count`, `index`
Set	`Container`, `Iterable`, `Sized`	`__contains__`, `__iter`, `__len__`	`__and__`, `__eq__`, `__ge__`, `__gt__`, `__le__`, `__lt__`, `__ne__`, `__or__`, `__sub__`, `__xor__`, `isdisjoint`

And lastly, the set of ABCs further extending the previous ones:

ABC	Extends	Abstract methods	Mixin methods
ItemsView	`MappingView`, `Set`		`__contains__`, `__iter__`
KeysView	`MappingView`, `Set`		`__contains__`, `__iter__`
MutableMapping	`Mapping`	`__delitem__`, `__getitem__`, `__iter__`, `__len__`, `__setitem__`	`Mapping`'s methods, plus `clear`, `pop`, `popitem`, `setdefault`, `update`
MutableSequence	`Sequence`	`__delitem__`, `__getitem__`, `__len__`, `__setitem__`, `insert`	`Sequence`'s methods, plus `__iadd__`, `append`, `extend`, `pop`, `remove`, `reverse`
MutableSet	`Set`	`__contains__`, `__iter`, `__len__`, `add`, `discard`	`Set`'s methods, plus `__iand__`, `__ior__`, `__isub__`, `__ixor__`, `clear`, `pop`, `remove`
ValuesView	`MappingView`		`__contains__`, `__iter__`

See the online docs (*https://docs.python.org/2/library/collections.html#collections-abstract-base-classes*) for further details and usage examples.

The numbers module

`numbers` supplies a hierarchy (also known as a *tower*) of ABCs representing various kinds of numbers. `numbers` supplies the following ABCs:

Number	The root of the hierarchy: numbers of *any* kind (need not support any given operation)
Complex	Extends `Number`; must support (via the appropriate special methods) conversions to `complex` and `bool`, +, -, *, /, ==, !=, `abs()`; and, directly, the method `conjugate()` and properties `real` and `imag`
Real	Extends `Complex`; additionally, must support (via the appropriate special methods) conversion to `float`, `math.trunc()`, `round()`, `math.floor()`, `math.ceil()`, `divmod()`, //, %, <, <=, >, >=
Rational	Extends `Real`; additionally, must support the properties `numerator` and `denominator`
Integral	Extends `Rational`; additionally, must support (via the appropriate special methods) conversion to `int`, **, and bitwise operations <<, >>, &, ^, |, ~

See the online docs (*https://docs.python.org/2/library/numbers.html*) for notes on implementing your own numeric types.

Special Methods for Numeric Objects

An instance may support numeric operations by means of many special methods. Some classes that are not numbers also support some of the special methods in Table 4-4 in order to overload operators such as + and *. In particular, sequences should have special methods `__add__`, `__mul__`, `__radd__`, and `__rmul__`, as mentioned in "Sequences" on page 132.

Table 4-4.

__abs__, __invert__, __neg__, __pos__	`__abs__(self) __invert__(self) __neg__(self) __pos__(self)` The unary operators `abs(x)`, ~*x*, -*x*, and +*x*, respectively, call these methods.

__add__, __mod__, __mul__, __sub__	`__add__(self,other) __mod__(self,other)`
	`__mul__(self,other) __sub__(self,other)`
	The operators *x*+*y*, *x*%*y*, *x***y*, and *x*-*y*, and *x*/*y*, respectively, call these methods, usually for arithmetic computations.

__div__, __floordiv__, __truediv__

`__div__(self,other) __floordiv__(self,other) __truediv__(self,other)`

The operators *x*/*y* and *x*//*y* call these methods, usually for arithmetic divisions. In v2, operator / calls `__truediv__`, if present, instead of `__div__`, in situations where division is nontruncating, as covered in "Arithmetic Operations" on page 60. In v3, there is no `__div__`, only `__truediv__` and `__floordiv__`.

__and__, __lshift__, __or__, __rshift__, __xor__

`__and__(self,other) __lshift__(self,other) __or__(self,other) __rshift__(self,other) __xor__(self,other)`

The operators *x*&*y*, *x*<<*y*, *x*|*y*, *x*>>*y*, and *x*^*y*, respectively, call these methods, usually for bitwise operations.

__complex__, __float__, __int__, __long__

`__complex__(self) __float__(self) __int__(self) __long__(self)`

The built-in types `complex(x)`, `float(x)`, `int(x)`, and (in v2 only) `long(x)`, respectively, call these methods.

__divmod__

`__divmod__(self,other)`

The built-in function `divmod(x,y)` calls `x.__divmod__(y)`. `__divmod__` should return a pair `(quotient,remainder)` equal to `(x//y,x%y)`.

__hex__, __oct__

`__hex__(self) __oct__(self)`

In v2 only, the built-in function `hex(x)` calls `x.__hex__()`, and built-in function `oct(x)` calls `x.__oct__()`. Each of these special methods should return a string representing the value of *x*, in base 16 and 8, respectively. In v3, these special methods don't exist: the built-in functions `hex` and `oct` operate directly on the result of calling the special method `__index__` on their operand.

__iadd__, __idiv__, __ifloordiv__, __imod__, __imul__, __isub__, __itruediv__

`__iadd__(self,other) __idiv__(self,other) __ifloordiv__(self,other) __imod__(self,other) __imul__(self,other) __isub__(self,other) __itruediv__(self,other)`

The augmented assignments *x*+=*y*, *x*/=*y*, *x*//=*y*, *x*%=*y*, *x**=*y*, *x*-=*y*, and *x*/=*y*, respectively, call these methods. Each method should modify *x* in place and return `self`. Define these methods when *x* is mutable (i.e., when *x* can change in place).

__iand__, __ilshift__, __ior__, __irshift__, __ixor__

`__iand__(self,other) __ilshift__(self,other) __ior__(self,other) __irshift__(self,other) __ixor__(self,other)`

The augmented assignments *x*&=*y*, *x*<<=*y*, *x*|=*y*, *x*>>=*y*, and *x*^=*y*, respectively, call these methods. Each method should modify *x* in place and return `self`.

__index__

`__index__(self)`

Like `__int__`, but meant to be supplied only by types that are alternative implementations of integers (in other words, all of the type's instances can be exactly mapped into integers). For example, out of all built-in types, only `int` (and, in v2, `long`) supply `__index__`; `float` and `str` don't, although they do supply `__int__`. Sequence indexing and slicing internally use `__index__` to get the needed integer indices.

__ipow__

`__ipow__(self,other)`

The augmented assignment *x***=*y* calls *x*.`__ipow__`(*y*). `__ipow__` should modify *x* in place and return `self`.

__pow__

`__pow__(self,other[,modulo])`

*x****y* and `pow(x,y)` both call *x*.`__pow__`(*y*), while `pow(x,y,z)` calls *x*.`__pow__`(*y*,*z*). *x*.`__pow__`(*y*,*z*) should return a value equal to the expression *x*.`__pow__`(*y*)%*z*.

__radd__, __rdiv__, __rmod__, __rmul__, __rsub__

`__radd__(self,other)` `__rdiv__(self,other)`
`__rmod__(self,other)` `__rmul__(self,other)`
`__rsub__(self,other)`

The operators *y*+*x*, *y*/*x*, *y*%*x*, *y***x*, and *y*-*x*, respectively, call these methods on *x* when *y* doesn't have a needed method `__add__`, `__div__`, and so on, or when that method returns `NotImplemented`.

__rand__, __rlshift__, __ror__, __rrshift__, __rxor__

`__rand__(self,other)` `__rlshift__(self,other)`
`__ror__(self,other)` `__rrshift__(self,other)`
`__rxor__(self,other)`

The operators *y*&*x*, *y*<<*x*, *y*|*x*, *y*>>*x*, and *x*^*y*, respectively, call these methods on *x* when *y* doesn't have a needed method `__and__`, `__lshift__`, and so on, or when that method returns `NotImplemented`.

__rdivmod__

`__rdivmod__(self,other)`

The built-in function `divmod(y,x)` calls *x*.`__rdivmod__`(*y*) when *y* doesn't have `__divmod__`, or when that method returns `NotImplemented`. `__rdivmod__` should return a pair (*remainder*,*quotient*).

__rpow__

`__rpow__(self,other)`

*y****x* and `pow(y,x)` call *x*.`__rpow__`(*y*) when *y* doesn't have `__pow__`, or when that method returns `NotImplemented`. There is no three-argument form in this case.

Decorators

In Python, you often use so-called *higher-order functions*, callables that accept a function as an argument and return a function as their result. For example, descriptor types such as staticmethod and classmethod, covered in "Class-Level Methods" on page 120, can be used, within class bodies, as:

```
def f(cls, ...):
  ...definition of f snipped...
f = classmethod(f)
```

However, having the call to classmethod textually *after* the def statement decreases code readability: while reading *f*'s definition, the reader of the code is not yet aware that *f* is going to become a class method rather than an instance method. The code is more readable if the mention of classmethod comes *before*, not *after*, the def. For this purpose, use the syntax form known as *decoration*:

```
@classmethod
def f(cls, ...):
  ...definition of f snipped...
```

The decorator must be immediately followed by a def statement and means that *f*=classmethod(*f*) executes right after the def statement (for whatever name *f* the def defines). More generally, @*expression* evaluates the expression (which must be a name, possibly qualified, or a call) and binds the result to an internal temporary name (say, *__aux*); any decorator must be immediately followed by a def (or class) statement, and means that *f*=*__aux*(*f*) executes right after the def or class (for whatever name *f* the def or class defines). The object bound to *__aux* is known as a *decorator*, and it's said to *decorate* function or class *f*.

Decorators afford a handy shorthand for some higher-order functions. You may apply decorators to any def or class statement, not just ones occurring in class bodies. You may also code custom decorators, which are just higher-order functions, accepting a function or class object as an argument and returning a function or class object as the result. For example, here is a simple example decorator that does not modify the function it decorates, but rather prints the function's docstring to standard output at function-definition time:

```
def showdoc(f):
    if f.__doc__:
        print('{}: {}'.format(f.__name__, f.__doc__))
    else:
        print('{}: No docstring!'.format(f.__name__))
    return f

@showdoc
def f1(): """a docstring"""
# prints: f1: a docstring

@showdoc
def f2(): pass
# prints: f2: No docstring!
```

The standard library module functools offers a handy decorator, wraps, to enhance decorators built by the common "wrapping" idiom:

```
import functools
def announce(f):
    @functools.wraps(f)
    def wrap(*a, **k):
        print('Calling {}'.format(f.__name__))
        return f(*a, **k)
    return wrap
```

Decorating a function *f* with `@announce` causes a line announcing the call to be printed before each call to *f*. Thanks to the `functools.wraps(f)` decorator, the wrapper function adopts the name and docstring of the wrapped one, which is useful, for example, when calling the built-in `help` on such a decorated function.

Metaclasses

Any object, even a class object, has a type. In Python, types and classes are also first-class objects. The type of a class object is also known as the class's *metaclass*.[4] An object's behavior is mostly determined by the type of the object. This also holds for classes: a class's behavior is mostly determined by the class's metaclass. Metaclasses are an advanced subject, and you may want to skip the rest of this section. However, fully grasping metaclasses can lead you to a deeper understanding of Python, and, very occasionally, it can be useful to define your own custom metaclasses.[5]

How Python v2 Determines a Class's Metaclass

To execute a `class` statement, v2 first collects the base classes into a tuple `t` (an empty one if there are no base classes) and executes the class body, storing the names there defined in a temporary dictionary *d*. Then, Python determines the metaclass `M` to use for the new class object `C` that the `class` statement is creating.

When `'__metaclass__'` is a key in *d*, `M` is *d*`['__metaclass__']`. Thus, you can explicitly control class *C*'s metaclass by binding the attribute `__metaclass__` in *C*'s class body (for clarity, do that as the first statement in the class body, right after the docstring). Otherwise, when `t` is nonempty (i.e., when `C` has one or more base classes), `M` is the *leafmost* metaclass among all of the metaclasses of *C*'s bases (i.e., the metaclass of a base of `C` that `issubclass` of all other metaclasses of bases of *C*; it is an

4 Strictly speaking, the type of a class `C` could be said to be the metaclass only of instances of `C` rather than of `C` itself, but this subtle distinction is rarely, if ever, observed in practice.

5 ***New in 3.6***: while metaclasses work in 3.6 just like in 3.5, 3.6 also offers simpler ways to customize class creation (covered in PEP 487 (*https://www.python.org/dev/peps/pep-0487/*)) that are often a good alternative to using a custom metaclass.

error, and Python raises an exception, if no metaclass of a base of *C* `issubclass` of all others).[6]

This is why inheriting from `object`, in v2, indicates that *C* is a new-style class (rather than a legacy-style class, a concept that exists only for backward compatibility and that this book does not cover). Since `type(object)` is `type`, a class *C* that inherits from `object` (or some other built-in type) gets the same metaclass as `object` (i.e., `type(C)`, *C*'s metaclass, is also `type`). Thus, in v2, "being a new-style class" is synonymous with "having `type` as the metaclass."

When *C* has no base classes, but the current module has a global variable `__metaclass__`, in v2, *M* is the value of that global variable. This lets you make classes without bases default to being new-style classes, rather than legacy classes, throughout a module. Just place the following statement toward the start of the module body, before any `class` statement:

```
__metaclass__ = type
```

When none of these conditions applies (that is, when the metaclass is not explicitly specified, not inherited, and not defined as the module's global variable), *M*, in v2, defaults to `types.ClassType` (making an old-style, legacy class).

How Python v3 Determines a Class's Metaclass

In v3, the `class` statement accepts optional named arguments (after the bases, if any). The most important named argument is `metaclass`, which, if present, identifies the new class's metaclass. Other named arguments are allowed only if a non-`type` metaclass is present, and in this case they are passed on to the `__prepare__` method of the metaclass (it's entirely up to said method `__prepare__` to make use of such named arguments). When the named argument `metaclass` is absent, v3 determines the metaclass by inheritance, exactly like v2, or else, for classes with no explicitly specified bases, defaults to `type`.

In v3, a metaclass has an optional method `__prepare__`, which Python calls as soon as it determines the metaclass, as follows:

```
class MC:
    def __prepare__(classname, *classbases, **kwargs):
        return {}
  ...rest of MC snipped...

class X(onebase, another, metaclass=MC, foo='bar'):
  ...body of X snipped...
```

6 In other, more precise (but fancy) words, if *C*'s bases' metaclasses do not form an inheritance lattice including its lower bound—that is, if there is no leafmost metaclass, no metaclass that `issubclass` of all others—Python raises an exception diagnosing this metatype conflict.

Here, the call is equivalent to `MC.__prepare__('X', onebase, another, foo='bar')`. `__prepare__`, if present, must return a mapping (most often just a dictionary), which Python uses as the *d* in which it executes the class body. If a metaclass wants to retain the order in which names get bound in the class body, its `__prepare__` method can return an instance of `collections.OrderedDict` (covered in "OrderedDict" on page 219); this allows a v3 metaclass to use a class to naturally represent constructs in which the ordering of attributes matters, such as database schemas (a feature that is just not possible in v2).[7] If `__prepare__` is absent, v3 uses a dictionary as *d* (as v2 does in all cases).

How a Metaclass Creates a Class

Having determined *M*, Python calls *M* with three arguments: the class name (a string), the tuple of base classes `t`, and the dictionary (or, in v3, other mapping resulting from `__prepare__`) *d* in which the class body just finished executing. The call returns the class object *C*, which Python then binds to the class name, completing the execution of the `class` statement. Note that this is in fact an instantiation of type *M*, so the call to *M* executes `M.__init__(C, namestring, t, d)`, where *C* is the return value of `M.__new__(M, namestring, t, d)`, just as in any other instantiation of a class.

After Python creates class object *C*, the relationship between class *C* and its type (`type(C)`, normally *M*) is the same as that between any object and its type. For example, when you call the class object *C* (to create an instance of *C*), `M.__call__` executes with class object *C* as the first argument.

Note the benefit, in this context, of the approach described in "Per-Instance Methods" on page 125, whereby special methods are looked up only on the class, not on the instance—the core difference in the "new style" object model versus v2's old "legacy style." Calling *C* to instantiate it must execute the metaclass's `M.__call__`, whether or not *C* has a per-instance attribute (method) `__call__` (i.e., independently of whether *instances* of *C* are or aren't callable). This is simply impossible in an object model like the legacy one, where per-instance methods override per-class ones for implicitly called special methods. The Python object model (specifically the "new-style" one in v2, and the only one existing in v3) avoids having to make the relationship between a class and its metaclass an ad hoc special case. Avoiding ad hoc special cases is a key to Python's power: Python has few, simple, general rules, and applies them consistently.

Defining and using your own metaclasses

It's easy to define custom metaclasses: inherit from `type` and override some of its methods. You can also perform most of these tasks with `__new__`, `__init__`,

7 ***New in 3.6***: it is no longer necessary to use `OrderedDict` here—3.6 guarantees the mapping used here preserves key order.

__getattribute__, and so on, without involving metaclasses. However, a custom metaclass can be faster, since special processing is done only at class creation time, which is a rare operation. A custom metaclass lets you define a whole category of classes in a framework that magically acquire whatever interesting behavior you've coded, quite independently of what special methods the classes themselves may choose to define.

A good alternative, to alter a specific class in an explicit way, is often to use a class decorator, as mentioned in "Decorators" on page 140. However, decorators are not inherited, so the decorator must be explicitly applied to each class of interest. Metaclasses, on the other hand, *are* inherited; in fact, when you define a custom metaclass *M*, it's usual to also define an otherwise-empty class *C* with metaclass *M*, so that other classes requiring metaclass *M* can just inherit from *C*.

Some behavior of class objects can be customized only in metaclasses. The following example shows how to use a metaclass to change the string format of class objects:

```
class MyMeta(type):
    def __str__(cls):
        return 'Beautiful class {!r}'.format(cls.__name__)
class MyClass(metaclass=MyMeta):
    # in v2, remove the `metaclass=`, and use, as the class body:
    # __metaclass__ = MyMeta
x = MyClass()
print(type(x))      # prints: Beautiful class 'MyClass'
```

Object-Oriented Python

A substantial custom metaclass example

Suppose that, programming in Python, we miss C's struct type: an object that is just a bunch of data attributes, in order, with fixed names (collections.namedtuple, covered in "namedtuple" on page 221, comes close, but named tuples are immutable, and we may not want that in some cases). Python lets us easily define a generic *Bunch* class, apart from the fixed order and names:

```
class SimpleBunch(object):
    def __init__(self, **fields):
        self.__dict__ = fields
p = SimpleBunch(x=2.3, y=4.5)
print(p)        # prints: <__main__.SimpleBunch object at 0x00AE8B10>
```

A custom metaclass lets us exploit the fact that the attribute names are fixed at class creation time. The code shown in Example 4-1 defines a metaclass, *MetaBunch*, and a class, *Bunch*, that let us write code like the following:

```
class Point(Bunch):
    """ A point has x and y coordinates, defaulting to 0.0,
        and a color, defaulting to 'gray'—and nothing more,
        except what Python and the metaclass conspire to add,
        such as __init__ and __repr__
    """
    x = 0.0
```

```
        y = 0.0
        color = 'gray'
    # example uses of class Point
    q = Point()
    print(q)                    # prints: Point()
    p = Point(x=1.2, y=3.4)
    print(p)                    # prints: Point(y=3.399999999, x=1.2)
```

In this code, the `print` calls emit readable string representations of our *Point* instances. *Point* instances are quite memory-lean, and their performance is basically the same as for instances of the simple class *SimpleBunch* in the previous example (there is no extra overhead due to implicit calls to special methods). Example 4-1 is quite substantial, and following all its details requires understanding aspects of Python covered later in this book, such as strings (Chapter 8) and module `warnings` ("The warnings Module" on page 476). The identifier *mcl* used in Example 4-1 stands for "metaclass," clearer in this special advanced case than the habitual case of *cls* standing for "class."

The example's code works in both v2 and v3, except that, in v2, a tiny syntax adjustment must be made at the end, in `Bunch`, as shown in that class's docstring.

Example 4-1. The MetaBunch metaclass

```
import collections
import warnings

class MetaBunch(type):
    """
    Metaclass for new and improved "Bunch": implicitly defines
    __slots__, __init__ and __repr__ from variables bound in
    class scope.
    A class statement for an instance of MetaBunch (i.e., for a
    class whose metaclass is MetaBunch) must define only
    class-scope data attributes (and possibly special methods, but
    NOT __init__ and __repr__).  MetaBunch removes the data
    attributes from class scope, snuggles them instead as items in
    a class-scope dict named __dflts__, and puts in the class a
    __slots__ with those attributes' names, an __init__ that takes
    as optional named arguments each of them (using the values in
    __dflts__ as defaults for missing ones), and a __repr__ that
    shows the repr of each attribute that differs from its default
    value (the output of __repr__ can be passed to __eval__ to make
    an equal instance, as per usual convention in the matter, if
    each non-default-valued attribute respects the convention too).

    In v3, the order of data attributes remains the same as in the
    class body; in v2, there is no such guarantee.
    """
    def __prepare__(name, *bases, **kwargs):
        # precious in v3—harmless although useless in v2
```

```
        return collections.OrderedDict()

    def __new__(mcl, classname, bases, classdict):
        """ Everything needs to be done in __new__, since
            type.__new__ is where __slots__ are taken into account.
        """
        # define as local functions the __init__ and __repr__ that
        # we'll use in the new class
        def __init__(self, **kw):
            """ Simplistic __init__: first set all attributes to
                default values, then override those explicitly
                passed in kw.
            """
            for k in self.__dflts__:
                setattr(self, k, self.__dflts__[k])
            for k in kw:
                setattr(self, k, kw[k])
        def __repr__(self):
            """ Clever __repr__: show only attributes that differ
                from default values, for compactness.
            """
            rep = ['{}={!r}'.format(k, getattr(self, k))
                    for k in self.__dflts__
                    if getattr(self, k) != self.__dflts__[k]
                  ]
            return '{}({})'.format(classname, ', '.join(rep))
        # build the newdict that we'll use as class-dict for the
        # new class
        newdict = { '__slots__':[],
            '__dflts__':collections.OrderedDict(),
            '__init__':__init__, '__repr__':__repr__, }
        for k in classdict:
            if k.startswith('__') and k.endswith('__'):
                # dunder methods: copy to newdict, or warn
                # about conflicts
                if k in newdict:
                    warnings.warn(
                        "Can't set attr {!r} in bunch-class {!r}".
                        format(k, classname))
                else:
                    newdict[k] = classdict[k]
            else:
                # class variables, store name in __slots__, and
                # name and value as an item in __dflts__
                newdict['__slots__'].append(k)
                newdict['__dflts__'][k] = classdict[k]
        # finally delegate the rest of the work to type.__new__
        return super(MetaBunch, mcl).__new__(
                     mcl, classname, bases, newdict)

class Bunch(metaclass=MetaBunch):
    """ For convenience: inheriting from Bunch can be used to get
```

```
        the new metaclass (same as defining metaclass= yourself).

        In v2, remove the (metaclass=MetaBunch) above and add
        instead __metaclass__=MetaBunch as the class body.
    """
    pass
```

5
Exceptions

Python uses exceptions to communicate errors and anomalies. An *exception* is an object that indicates an error or anomaly. When Python detects an error, it *raises* an exception—that is, Python signals the occurrence of an anomalous condition by passing an exception object to the exception-propagation mechanism. Your code can explicitly raise an exception by executing a `raise` statement.

Handling an exception means receiving the exception object from the propagation mechanism and performing whatever actions are needed to deal with the anomalous situation. If a program does not handle an exception, the program terminates with an error traceback message. However, a program can handle exceptions and keep running despite errors or other abnormal conditions.

Python also uses exceptions to indicate some special situations that are not errors, and are not even abnormal. For example, as covered in "Iterators" on page 76, calling the `next` built-in on an iterator raises `StopIteration` when the iterator has no more items. This is not an error; it is not even an anomaly, since most iterators run out of items eventually. The optimal strategies for checking and handling errors and other special situations in Python are therefore different from what might be best in other languages, and we cover such considerations in "Error-Checking Strategies" on page 166. This chapter also covers the `logging` module of the Python standard library, in "Logging Errors" on page 169, and the `assert` Python statement, in "The assert Statement" on page 171.

The try Statement

The `try` statement provides Python's exception-handling mechanism. It is a compound statement that can take one of two forms:

- A try clause followed by one or more except clauses (and optionally exactly one else clause)
- A try clause followed by exactly one finally clause

A try statement can also have except clauses (and optionally an else clause) followed by a finally clause, as covered at "The try/except/finally Statement" on page 153.

try/except

Here's the syntax for the try/except form of the try statement:

```
try:
    statement(s)
except [expression [as target]]:
    statement(s)
[else:
    statement(s)]
```

This form of the try statement has one or more except clauses, as well as an optional else clause.

The body of each except clause is known as an *exception handler*. The code executes when the *expression* in the except clause matches an exception object propagating from the try clause. *expression* is a class (or tuple of classes, enclosed in parentheses), and matches any instance of one of those classes or any of their subclasses. The optional *target* is an identifier that names a variable that Python binds to the exception object just before the exception handler executes. A handler can also obtain the current exception object by calling the exc_info function of module sys (covered in Table 7-3).

Here is an example of the try/except form of the try statement:

```
try:
    1/0
except ZeroDivisionError:
    print('caught divide-by-0 attempt')
```

If a try statement has several except clauses, the exception-propagation mechanism tests the except clauses in order; the first except clause whose expression matches the exception object executes as the handler.

Place handlers for specific exceptions before more general ones

Always place exception handlers for specific cases before handlers for more general cases: if you place a general case first, the more specific except clauses that follow never enter the picture.

The last except clause may lack an expression. This clause handles any exception that reaches it during propagation. Such unconditional handling is rare, but it does occur, generally in wrapper functions that must perform some extra task before re-raising an exception, as we'll discuss in "The raise Statement" on page 157.

Avoid writing a "bare except" that doesn't re-raise the exception

Beware of using a "bare except" (an except clause without an expression) unless you're re-raising the exception in it: such sloppy style can make bugs very hard to find, since the bare except is over-broad and can easily mask coding errors and other kinds of bugs.

Exception propagation terminates when it finds a handler whose expression matches the exception object. When a try statement is nested (lexically in the source code, or dynamically within function calls) in the try clause of another try statement, a handler established by the inner try is reached first during propagation, and therefore handles the exception when it matches the expression. This may not be what you want. For example:

```
try:
    try:
        1/0
    except:
        print('caught an exception')
except ZeroDivisionError:
    print('caught divide-by-0 attempt')
# prints: caught an exception
```

Exceptions

In this case, it does not matter that the handler established by the clause `except ZeroDivisionError:` in the outer try clause is more specific and appropriate than the catch-all `except:` in the inner try clause. The outer try does not even enter into the picture, because the exception doesn't propagate out of the inner try. For more on exception propagation, see "Exception Propagation" on page 155.

The optional else clause of try/except executes only when the try clause terminates normally. In other words, the else clause does not execute when an exception propagates from the try clause, or when the try clause exits with a break, continue, or return statement. The handlers established by try/except cover only the try clause, not the else clause. The else clause is useful to avoid accidentally handling unexpected exceptions. For example:

```
print(repr(value), 'is ', end=' ')
try:
    value + 0
except TypeError:
    # not a number, maybe a string...?
    try:
        value + ''
```

```
        except TypeError:
            print('neither a number nor a string')
        else:
            print('some kind of string')
    else:
        print('some kind of number')
```

try/finally

Here's the syntax for the `try/finally` form of the `try` statement:

```
try:
    statement(s)
finally:
    statement(s)
```

This form has exactly one `finally` clause (and cannot have an `else` clause—unless it also has one or more `except` clauses, as covered in "The try/except/finally Statement" on page 153).

The `finally` clause establishes what is known as a *clean-up handler*. The code always executes after the `try` clause terminates in any way. When an exception propagates from the `try` clause, the `try` clause terminates, the clean-up handler executes, and the exception keeps propagating. When no exception occurs, the clean-up handler executes anyway, regardless of whether the `try` clause reaches its end or exits by executing a `break`, `continue`, or `return` statement.

Clean-up handlers established with `try/finally` offer a robust and explicit way to specify finalization code that must always execute, no matter what, to ensure consistency of program state and/or external entities (e.g., files, databases, network connections); such assured finalization, however, is usually best expressed via a *context manager* used in a `with` statement (see "The with Statement" on page 82). Here is an example of the `try/finally` form of the `try` statement:

```
f = open(some_file, 'w')
try:
    do_something_with_file(f)
finally:
    f.close()
```

and here is the corresponding, more concise and readable, example of using `with` for exactly the same purpose:

```
with open(some_file, 'w') as f:
    do_something_with_file(f)
```

Avoid break and return statements in a finally clause

A `finally` clause may not directly contain a `continue` statement, but it's allowed to contain a `break` or `return` statement. Such usage, however, makes your program less clear: exception propagation stops when such a `break` or `return` executes, and most programmers would not expect propagation to be stopped within a `finally` clause. The usage may confuse people who are reading your code, so avoid it.

The try/except/finally Statement

A `try/except/finally` statement, such as:

```
try:
    ...guarded clause...
except ...expression...:
    ...exception handler code...
finally:
    ...clean-up code...
```

is equivalent to the nested statement:

```
try:
    try:
        ...guarded clause...
    except ...expression...:
        ...exception handler code...
finally:
    ...clean-up code...
```

A `try` statement can have multiple `except` clauses, and optionally an `else` clause, before a terminating `finally` clause. In all variations, the effect is always as just shown—that is, just like nesting a `try/except` statement, with all the `except` clauses and the `else` clause if any, into a containing `try/finally` statement.

The with Statement and Context Managers

The `with` statement is a compound statement with the following syntax:

```
with expression [as varname]:
    statement(s)
```

The semantics of `with` are equivalent to:

```
_normal_exit = True
_manager = expression
varname = _manager.__enter__()
try:
    statement(s)
except:
    _normal_exit = False
    if not _manager.__exit__(*sys.exc_info()):
```

```
            raise
        # exception does not propagate if __exit__ returns a true value
    finally:
        if _normal_exit:
            _manager.__exit__(None, None, None)
```

where *_manager* and *_normal_exit* are arbitrary internal names that are not used elsewhere in the current scope. If you omit the optional as *varname* part of the with clause, Python still calls *_manager*.__enter__(), but doesn't bind the result to any name, and still calls *_manager*.__exit__() at block termination. The object returned by the *expression*, with methods __enter__ and __exit__, is known as a *context manager*.

The with statement is the Python embodiment of the well-known C++ idiom "resource acquisition is initialization" (RAII (*https://en.wikipedia.org/wiki/Resource_Acquisition_Is_Initialization*)): you need only write context manager classes—that is, classes with two special methods __enter__ and __exit__ . __enter__ must be callable without arguments. __exit__ must be callable with three arguments: all None if the body completes without propagating exceptions, and otherwise the type, value, and traceback of the exception. This provides the same guaranteed finalization behavior as typical *ctor*/*dtor* pairs have for auto variables in C++, and try/finally statements have in Python or Java. In addition, you gain the ability to finalize differently depending on what exception, if any, propagates, as well as optionally blocking a propagating exception by returning a true value from __exit__.

For example, here is a simple, purely illustrative way to ensure <name> and </name> tags are printed around some other output:

```
class tag(object):
    def __init__(self, tagname):
        self.tagname = tagname
    def __enter__(self):
        print('<{}>'.format(self.tagname), end='')
    def __exit__(self, etyp, einst, etb):
        print('</{}>'.format(self.tagname))
# to be used as:
tt = tag('sometag')
...
with tt:
    ...statements printing output to be enclosed in
      a matched open/close `sometag` pair
```

A simpler way to build context managers is the contextmanager decorator in the contextlib module of the standard Python library, which turns a generator function into a factory of context manager objects. contextlib also offers wrapper function closing (to call some object's close method upon __exit__), and also further, more advanced utilities in v3.

The contextlib way to implement the tag context manager, having imported contextlib earlier, is:

```
@contextlib.contextmanager
def tag(tagname):
    print('<{}>'.format(tagname), end='')
    try:
        yield
    finally:
        print('</{}>'.format(tagname))
# to be used the same way as before
```

Many more examples and detailed discussion can be found in PEP 343 (*https://www.python.org/dev/peps/*).

New in 3.6: contextlib now also has an AbstractContextManager class that can act as a base class for context managers.

Generators and Exceptions

To help generators cooperate with exceptions, yield statements are allowed inside try/finally statements. Moreover, generator objects have two other relevant methods, throw and close. Given a generator object *g*, built by calling a generator function, the throw method's signature is, in v2:

```
g.throw(exc_type, exc_value=None, exc_traceback=None]
```

and, in v3, the simpler:

```
g.throw(exc_value)
```

When the generator's caller calls *g*.throw, the effect is just as if a raise statement with the same arguments executed at the spot of the yield at which generator *g* is suspended.

The generator method close has no arguments; when the generator's caller calls *g*.close(), the effect is just like calling *g*.throw(GeneratorExit()). GeneratorExit is a built-in exception class that inherits directly from BaseException. A generator's close method should re-raise (or propagate) the GeneratorExit exception, after performing whatever clean-up operations the generator may need. Generators also have a finalizer (special method __del__) that is exactly equivalent to the method close.

Exceptions

Exception Propagation

When an exception is raised, the exception-propagation mechanism takes control. The normal control flow of the program stops, and Python looks for a suitable exception handler. Python's try statement establishes exception handlers via its except clauses. The handlers deal with exceptions raised in the body of the try clause, as well as exceptions propagating from functions called by that code, directly or indirectly. If an exception is raised within a try clause that has an applicable except handler, the try clause terminates and the handler executes. When the handler finishes, execution continues with the statement after the try statement.

If the statement raising the exception is not within a try clause that has an applicable handler, the function containing the statement terminates, and the exception propagates "upward" along the stack of function calls to the statement that called the function. If the call to the terminated function is within a try clause that has an applicable handler, that try clause terminates, and the handler executes. Otherwise, the function containing the call terminates, and the propagation process repeats, *unwinding* the stack of function calls until an applicable handler is found.

If Python cannot find any applicable handler, by default the program prints an error message to the standard error stream (file *sys.stderr*). The error message includes a traceback that gives details about functions terminated during propagation. You can change Python's default error-reporting behavior by setting sys.excepthook (covered in Table 7-3). After error reporting, Python goes back to the interactive session, if any, or terminates if no interactive session is active. When the exception class is SystemExit, termination is silent, and ends the interactive session, if any.

Here are some functions to show exception propagation at work:

```
def f():
    print('in f, before 1/0')
    1/0    # raises a ZeroDivisionError exception
    print('in f, after 1/0')

def g():
    print('in g, before f()')
    f()
    print('in g, after f()')

def h():
    print('in h, before g()')
    try:
        g()
        print('in h, after g()')
    except ZeroDivisionError:
        print('ZD exception caught')
    print('function h ends')
```

Calling the h function prints the following:

```
>>> h()
in h, before g()
in g, before f()
in f, before 1/0
ZD exception caught
function h ends
```

That is, none of the "after" print statements execute, since the flow of exception propagation "cuts them off."

The function *h* establishes a `try` statement and calls the function *g* within the `try` clause. *g*, in turn, calls *f*, which performs a division by `0`, raising an exception of the class `ZeroDivisionError`. The exception propagates all the way back to the `except` clause in *h*. The functions *f* and *g* terminate during the exception-propagation phase, which is why neither of their "after" messages is printed. The execution of *h*'s `try` clause also terminates during the exception-propagation phase, so its "after" message isn't printed either. Execution continues after the handler, at the end of *h*'s `try`/`except` block.

The raise Statement

You can use the `raise` statement to raise an exception explicitly. `raise` is a simple statement with the following syntax (acceptable both in v2 and v3):

```
raise [expression]
```

Only an exception handler (or a function that a handler calls, directly or indirectly) can use `raise` without any expression. A plain `raise` statement re-raises the same exception object that the handler received. The handler terminates, and the exception propagation mechanism keeps going up the call stack, searching for other applicable handlers. Using `raise` without any expression is useful when a handler discovers that it is unable to handle an exception it receives, or can handle the exception only partially, so the exception should keep propagating to allow handlers up the call stack to perform their own handling and cleanup.

When *`expression`* is present, it must be an instance of a class inheriting from the built-in class `BaseException`, and Python raises that instance.

In v2 only, *`expression`* could also be a class object, which `raise` instantiated to raise the resulting instance, and another expression could follow to provide the argument for instantiation. We recommend that you ignore these complications, which are not present in v3 nor needed in either version: just instantiate the exception object you want to raise, and `raise` that instance.

Here's an example of a typical use of the `raise` statement:

```
def cross_product(seq1, seq2):
    if not seq1 or not seq2:
        raise ValueError('Sequence arguments must be non-empty')
    return [(x1, x2) for x1 in seq1 for x2 in seq2]
```

This *`cross_product`* example function returns a list of all pairs with one item from each of its sequence arguments, but first it tests both arguments. If either argument is empty, the function raises `ValueError` rather than just returning an empty list as the list comprehension would normally do.

Check only what you need to

There is no need for *cross_product* to check whether *seq1* and *seq2* are iterable: if either isn't, the list comprehension itself raises the appropriate exception, presumably a TypeError.

Once an exception is raised, by Python itself or with an explicit raise statement in your code, it's up to the caller to either handle it (with a suitable try/except statement) or let it propagate further up the call stack.

Don't use raise for duplicate, redundant error checks

Use the raise statement only to raise additional exceptions for cases that would normally be okay but that your specification defines to be errors. Do not use raise to duplicate the same error-checking that Python already, implicitly, does on your behalf.

Exception Objects

Exceptions are instances of subclasses of BaseException. Any exception has attribute args, the tuple of arguments used to create the instance; this error-specific information is useful for diagnostic or recovery purposes. Some exception classes interpret args and conveniently supply them as named attributes.

The Hierarchy of Standard Exceptions

Exceptions are instances of subclasses of BaseException (in v2 only, for backward compatibility, it's possible to treat some other objects as "exceptions," but we do not cover this legacy complication in this book).

The inheritance structure of exception classes is important, as it determines which except clauses handle which exceptions. Most exception classes extend the class Exception; however, the classes KeyboardInterrupt, GeneratorExit, and SystemExit inherit directly from BaseException and are not subclasses of Exception. Thus, a handler clause except Exception as e: does not catch KeyboardInterrupt, GeneratorExit, or SystemExit (we cover exception handlers in "try/except" on page 150). Instances of SystemExit are normally raised via the exit function in module sys (covered in Table 7-3). We cover GeneratorExit in "Generators and Exceptions" on page 155. When the user hits Ctrl-C, Ctrl-Break, or other interrupting keys on their keyboard, that raises KeyboardInterrupt.

v2 only introduces another subclass of Exception: StandardError. Only StopIteration and Warning classes inherit directly from Exception (StopIteration is part of the iteration protocol, covered in "Iterators" on page 76; Warning is covered in "The warnings Module" on page 476)—all other standard exceptions inherit from

StandardError. However, v3 has removed this complication. So, in v2, the inheritance hierarchy from BaseException down is, roughly:

```
BaseException
  Exception
    StandardError
      AssertionError, AttributeError, BufferError, EOFError,
      ImportError, MemoryError, SystemError, TypeError
      ArithmeticError
        FloatingPointError, OverflowError, ZeroDivisionError
      EnvironmentError
        IOError, OSError
      LookupError
        IndexError, KeyError
      NameError
        UnboundLocalError
      RuntimeError
        NotImplementedError
      SyntaxError
        IndentationError
      ValueError
        UnicodeError
          UnicodeDecodeError, UnicodeEncodeError
    StopIteration
    Warning
  GeneratorExit
  KeyboardInterrupt
  SystemExit
```


There are other exception subclasses (in particular, Warning has many), but this is the gist of the hierarchy—in v2. In v3, it's simpler, as StandardError disappears (and all of its direct subclasses become direct subclasses of Exception), and so do EnvironmentError and IOError (the latter becomes a synonym of OSError, which, in v3, directly subclasses Exception), as per the following condensed table:

```
BaseException
  Exception
    AssertionError
    ...
    OSError  # no longer a subclass of EnvironmentError
    RuntimeError
    StopIteration
    SyntaxError
    ValueError
    Warning
  GeneratorExit
  KeyboardInterrupt
  SystemExit
```

Three subclasses of Exception are never instantiated directly. Their only purpose is to make it easier for you to specify except clauses that handle a broad range of related errors. These three "abstract" subclasses of Exception are:

`ArithmeticError`
: The base class for exceptions due to arithmetic errors (i.e., `OverflowError`, `ZeroDivisionError`, `FloatingPointError`)

`EnvironmentError`
: The base class for exceptions due to external causes (i.e., `IOError`, `OSError`, `WindowsError`), in v2 only

`LookupError`
: The base class for exceptions that a container raises when it receives an invalid key or index (i.e., `IndexError`, `KeyError`)

Standard Exception Classes

Common runtime errors raise exceptions of the following classes:

`AssertionError`
: An assert statement failed.

`AttributeError`
: An attribute reference or assignment failed.

`FloatingPointError`
: A floating-point operation failed. Extends `ArithmeticError`.

`IOError`
: An I/O operation failed (e.g., the disk was full, a file was not found, or needed permissions were missing). In v2, extends `EnvironmentError`; in v3, it's a synonym of `OSError`.

`ImportError`
: An `import` statement (covered in "The import Statement" on page 174) couldn't find the module to import or couldn't find a name to be imported from the module.[1]

`IndentationError`
: The parser encountered a syntax error due to incorrect indentation. Extends `SyntaxError`.

`IndexError`
: An integer used to index a sequence is out of range (using a noninteger as a sequence index raises `TypeError`). Extends `LookupError`.

`KeyError`
: A key used to index a mapping is not in the mapping. Extends `LookupError`.

---

1 ***New in 3.6***: `ModuleNotFoundError` is a new, explicit subclass of `ImportError`.

`KeyboardInterrupt`
: The user pressed the interrupt key combination (Ctrl-C, Ctrl-Break, Delete, or others, depending on the platform's handling of the keyboard).

`MemoryError`
: An operation ran out of memory.

`NameError`
: A variable was referenced, but its name was not bound.

`NotImplementedError`
: Raised by abstract base classes to indicate that a concrete subclass must override a method.

`OSError`
: Raised by functions in the module `os` (covered in "The os Module" on page 297 and "Running Other Programs with the os Module" on page 424) to indicate platform-dependent errors. In v2, extends `EnvironmentError`. In v3 only, it has many subclasses, covered at "OSError and subclasses (v3 only)" on page 162.

`OverflowError`
: The result of an operation on an integer is too large to fit into an integer. Extends `ArithmeticError`.

OverflowError still exists only for legacy/compatibility

This error never happens in modern versions of Python: integer results too large to fit into a platform's integers implicitly become long integers, without raising exceptions (indeed, in v3, there's no `long` type, just `int` for all integers). This standard exception remains a built-in for backward compatibility (to support old code that raises or tries to catch it). Do *not* use it in any new code.

`SyntaxError`
: The parser encountered a syntax error.

`SystemError`
: An internal error within Python itself or some extension module. You should report this to the authors and maintainers of Python, or of the extension in question, with all possible details to allow them to reproduce the problem.

`TypeError`
: An operation or function was applied to an object of an inappropriate type.

`UnboundLocalError`
: A reference was made to a local variable, but no value is currently bound to that local variable. Extends `NameError`.

`UnicodeError`
: An error occurred while converting Unicode to a byte string or vice versa.

`ValueError`
: An operation or function was applied to an object that has a correct type but an inappropriate value, and nothing more specific (e.g., `KeyError`) applies.

`WindowsError`
: Raised by functions in the module `os` (covered in "The os Module" on page 297 and "Running Other Programs with the os Module" on page 424) to indicate Windows-specific errors. Extends `OSError`.

`ZeroDivisionError`
: A divisor (the righthand operand of a `/`, `//`, or `%` operator, or the second argument to the built-in function `divmod`) is `0`. Extends `ArithmeticError`.

OSError and subclasses (v3 only)

In v3, `OSError` subsumes many errors that v2 kept separate, such as `IOError` and `socket.error`. To compensate (and more!) in v3, `OSError` has spawned many useful subclasses, which you can catch to handle environment errors much more elegantly —see the online docs (*https://docs.python.org/3/library/exceptions.html#os-exceptions*).

For example, consider this task: try to read and return the contents of a certain file; return a default string if the file does not exist; propagate any other exception that makes the file unreadable (except for the file not existing). A v2/v3 portable version:

```
import errno

def read_or_default(filepath, default):
    try:
        with open(filepath) as f:
            return f.read()
    except IOError as e:
        if e.errno == errno.ENOENT:
           return default
        else:
           raise
```

However, see how much simpler it can be in v3, using an `OSError` subclass:

```
def read_or_default(filepath, default):
    try:
        with open(filepath) as f:
            return f.read()
    except FileNotFoundError:
        return default
```

The `FileNotFoundError` subclass of `OSError`, in v3 only, makes this kind of common task much simpler and more direct for you to express in your code.

Exceptions "wrapping" other exceptions or tracebacks

Sometimes, you incur an exception while trying to handle another. In v2, there's not much you can do about it, except perhaps by coding and specially handling custom exception classes, as shown in the next section. v3 offers much more help. In v3, each exception instance holds its own traceback object; you can make another exception instance with a different traceback with the `with_traceback` method. Moreover, v3 automatically remembers which exception it's handling as the "context" of any one raised during the handling.

For example, consider the deliberately broken code:

```
try: 1/0
except ZeroDivisionError:
    1+'x'
```

In v2, that code displays something like:

```
Traceback (most recent call last):
  File "<stdin>", line 3, in <module>
TypeError: unsupported operand type(s) for +: 'int' and 'str'
```

which hides the zero-division error that was being handled. In v3, by contrast:

```
Traceback (most recent call last):
  File "<stdin>", line 1, in <module>
ZeroDivisionError: division by zero

During handling of the above exception, another exception occurred:

Traceback (most recent call last):
  File "<stdin>", line 3, in <module>
TypeError: unsupported operand type(s) for +: 'int' and 'str'
```

...both exceptions, the original and the intervening one, are clearly displayed.

If this isn't enough, in v3, you can also `raise` *`e`* `from` *`ex`*, with both *e* and *ex* being exception objects: *e* is the one that propagates, and *ex* is its "cause." For all details and motivations, see PEP 3134 (*http://legacy.python.org/dev/peps/pep-3134/*).

Custom Exception Classes

You can extend any of the standard exception classes in order to define your own exception class. Often, such a subclass adds nothing more than a docstring:

```
class InvalidAttribute(AttributeError):
    """Used to indicate attributes that could never be valid"""
```

Any empty class or function should have a docstring, not pass

As covered in "The pass Statement" on page 81, you don't need a pass statement to make up the body of a class. The docstring (which you should always write, to document the class's purpose) is enough to keep Python happy. Best practice for all "empty" classes (regardless of whether they are exception classes), just like for all "empty" functions, is to always have a docstring, and no pass statement.

Given the semantics of try/except, raising a custom exception class such as InvalidAttribute is almost the same as raising its standard exception superclass, AttributeError. Any except clause that can handle AttributeError can handle InvalidAttribute just as well. In addition, client code that knows about your InvalidAttribute custom exception class can handle it specifically, without having to handle all other cases of AttributeError when it is not prepared for those. For example:

```
class SomeFunkyClass(object):
    """much hypothetical functionality snipped"""
    def __getattr__(self, name):
        """only clarifies the kind of attribute error"""
        if name.startswith('_'):
            raise InvalidAttribute, 'Unknown private attribute '+name
        else:
            raise AttributeError, 'Unknown attribute '+name
```

Now client code can be more selective in its handlers. For example:

```
s = SomeFunkyClass()
try:
    value = getattr(s, thename)
except InvalidAttribute, err:
    warnings.warn(str(err))
    value = None
# other cases of AttributeError just propagate, as they're unexpected
```

Define and raise custom exception classes

It's an excellent idea to define, and raise, custom exception classes in your modules, rather than plain standard exceptions: by using custom exceptions, you make it easier for callers of your module's code to handle exceptions that come from your module separately from others.

A special case of custom exception class that you may find useful (at least in v2, which does not directly support an exception wrapping another) is one that wraps another exception and adds information. To gather information about a pending exception, you can use the exc_info function from module sys (covered in Table 7-3). Given this, your custom exception class could be defined as follows:

```
import sys
class CustomException(Exception):
    """Wrap arbitrary pending exception, if any,
       in addition to other info."""
    def __init__(self, *args):
        Exception.__init__(self, *args)
        self.wrapped_exc = sys.exc_info()
```

You would then typically use this class in a wrapper function such as:

```
def call_wrapped(callable, *args, **kwds):
    try:
        return callable(*args, **kwds)
    except:
        raise CustomException('Wrapped function '
                              'propagated exception')
```

Custom Exceptions and Multiple Inheritance

A particularly effective approach to custom exceptions is to multiply inherit exception classes from your module's special custom exception class and a standard exception class, as in the following snippet:

```
class CustomAttributeError(CustomException, AttributeError):
    """An AttributeError which is ALSO a CustomException."""
```

Now, when your code raises an instance of `CustomAttributeError`, that exception can be caught by calling code that's designed to catch all cases of `AttributeError` as well as by code that's designed to catch all exceptions raised only by your module.

Use the multiple inheritance approach for custom exceptions

Whenever you must decide whether to raise a specific standard exception, such as `AttributeError`, or a custom exception class you define in your module, consider this multiple-inheritance approach, which gives you the best of both worlds. Make sure you clearly document this aspect of your module; since the technique is not widely used, users of your module may not expect it unless you clearly and explicitly document what you are doing.

Other Exceptions Used in the Standard Library

Many modules in Python's standard library define their own exception classes, which are equivalent to the custom exception classes that your own modules can define. Typically, all functions in such standard library modules may raise exceptions of such classes, in addition to exceptions in the standard hierarchy covered in "Standard Exception Classes" on page 160. For example, in v2, module `socket` supplies class `socket.error`, which is directly derived from built-in class `Exception`, and several subclasses of `error` named `sslerror`, `timeout`, `gaierror`, and `herror`;

all functions and methods in module `socket`, besides standard exceptions, may raise exceptions of class `socket.error` and subclasses thereof. We cover the main cases of such exception classes throughout the rest of this book, in chapters covering the standard library modules that supply them.

Error-Checking Strategies

Most programming languages that support exceptions raise exceptions only in rare cases. Python's emphasis is different. Python deems exceptions appropriate whenever they make a program simpler and more robust, even if that makes exceptions rather frequent.

LBYL Versus EAFP

A common idiom in other languages, sometimes known as "Look Before You Leap" (LBYL), is to check in advance, before attempting an operation, for anything that might make the operation invalid. This approach is not ideal for several reasons:

- The checks may diminish the readability and clarity of the common, mainstream cases where everything is okay.
- The work needed for checking may duplicate a substantial part of the work done in the operation itself.
- The programmer might easily err by omitting some needed check.
- The situation might change between the moment you perform the checks and the moment you attempt the operation.

The preferred idiom in Python is generally to attempt the operation in a `try` clause and handle the exceptions that may result in `except` clauses. This idiom is known as "it's Easier to Ask Forgiveness than Permission" (EAFP (*https://ep2013.europython.eu/conference/talks/permission-or-forgiveness*)), a motto widely credited to Rear Admiral Grace Murray Hopper, co-inventor of COBOL. EAFP shares none of the defects of LBYL. Here is a function written using the LBYL idiom:

```
def safe_divide_1(x, y):
    if y==0:
        print('Divide-by-0 attempt detected')
        return None
    else:
        return x/y
```

With LBYL, the checks come first, and the mainstream case is somewhat hidden at the end of the function. Here is the equivalent function written using the EAFP idiom:

```
def safe_divide_2(x, y):
    try:
        return x/y
    except ZeroDivisionError:
```

```
        print('Divide-by-0 attempt detected')
        return None
```

With EAFP, the mainstream case is up front in a `try` clause, and the anomalies are handled in an `except` clause that lexically follows.

Proper usage of EAFP

EAFP is a good error-handling strategy, but it is not a panacea. In particular, don't cast too wide a net, catching errors that you did not expect and therefore did not mean to catch. The following is a typical case of such a risk (we cover built-in function `getattr` in Table 7-2):

```
def trycalling(obj, attrib, default, *args, **kwds):
    try:
        return getattr(obj, attrib)(*args, **kwds)
    except AttributeError:
        return default
```

The intention of function *`trycalling`* is to try calling a method named *`attrib`* on object *`obj`*, but to return *`default`* if *`obj`* has no method thus named. However, the function as coded does not do *just* that: it also mistakenly hides any error case where `AttributeError` is raised inside the sought-after method, silently returning `default` in those cases. This may easily hide bugs in other code. To do exactly what's intended, the function must take a little bit more care:

```
def trycalling(obj, attrib, default, *args, **kwds):
    try:
        method = getattr(obj, attrib)
    except AttributeError:
        return default
    else:
        return method(*args, **kwds)
```

This implementation of *`trycalling`* separates the `getattr` call, placed in the `try` clause and therefore guarded by the handler in the `except` clause, from the call of the method, placed in the `else` clause and therefore free to propagate any exceptions. The proper approach to EAFP involves frequent use of the `else` clause on `try/except` statements (which is more explicit, and thus better style, than just placing the nonguarded code after the whole `try/except` statement).

Handling Errors in Large Programs

In large programs, it is especially easy to err by making your `try/except` statements too wide, particularly once you have convinced yourself of the power of EAFP as a general error-checking strategy. A `try/except` combination is too wide when it catches too many different errors, or an error that can occur in too many different places. The latter is a problem when you need to distinguish exactly what went wrong, and where, and the information in the traceback is not sufficient to pinpoint such details (or you discard some or all of the information in the traceback). For effective error handling, you have to keep a clear distinction between errors and anomalies that you expect (and thus know how to handle) and unexpected errors and anomalies that indicate a bug in your program.

Some errors and anomalies are not really erroneous, and perhaps not even all that anomalous: they are just special cases, perhaps somewhat rare but nevertheless quite expected, which you choose to handle via EAFP rather than via LBYL to avoid LBYL's many intrinsic defects. In such cases, you should just handle the anomaly, often without even logging or reporting it.

Keep your try/except constructs narrow

Be very careful to keep `try/except` constructs as narrow as feasible. Use a small `try` clause that contains a small amount of code that doesn't call too many other functions, and use very specific exception-class tuples in the `except` clauses; if need be, further analyze the details of the exception in your handler code, and `raise` again as soon as you know it's not a case this handler can deal with.

Errors and anomalies that depend on user input or other external conditions not under your control are always expected, to some extent, precisely because you have no control over their underlying causes. In such cases, you should concentrate your effort on handling the anomaly gracefully, reporting and logging its exact nature and details, and keeping your program running with undamaged internal and persistent state. The breadth of `try/except` clauses under such circumstances should also be reasonably narrow, although this is not quite as crucial as when you use EAFP to structure your handling of not-really-erroneous special cases.

Lastly, entirely unexpected errors and anomalies indicate bugs in your program's design or coding. In most cases, the best strategy regarding such errors is to avoid `try/except` and just let the program terminate with error and traceback messages. (You might want to log such information and/or display it more suitably with an application-specific hook in `sys.excepthook`, as we'll discuss shortly.) In the unlikely case that your program must keep running at all costs, even under the direst circumstances, `try/except` statements that are quite wide may be appropriate, with the `try` clause guarding function calls that exercise vast swaths of program functionality, and broad `except` clauses.

In the case of a long-running program, make sure to log all details of the anomaly or error to some persistent place for later study (and also report some indication of the problem, so that you know such later study is necessary). The key is making sure that you can revert the program's persistent state to some undamaged, internally consistent point. The techniques that enable long-running programs to survive some of their own bugs, as well as environmental adversities, are known as checkpointing (*http://www.cism.ucl.ac.be/Services/Formations/checkpointing.pdf*) (basically, periodically saving program state, and writing the program so it can reload the saved state and continue from there) and transaction processing (*https://*

en.wikipedia.org/wiki/Transaction_processing), but we do not cover them further in this book.

Logging Errors

When Python propagates an exception all the way to the top of the stack without finding an applicable handler, the interpreter normally prints an error traceback to the standard error stream of the process (`sys.stderr`) before terminating the program. You can rebind `sys.stderr` to any file-like object usable for output in order to divert this information to a destination more suitable for your purposes.

When you want to change the amount and kind of information output on such occasions, rebinding `sys.stderr` is not sufficient. In such cases, you can assign your own function to `sys.excepthook`: Python calls it when terminating the program due to an unhandled exception. In your exception-reporting function, output whatever information you think will help you diagnose and debug the problem and direct that information to whatever destinations you please. For example, you might use module `traceback` (covered in "The traceback Module" on page 472) to help you format stack traces. When your exception-reporting function terminates, so does your program.

The logging package

The Python standard library offers the rich and powerful `logging` package to let you organize the logging of messages from your applications in systematic and flexible ways. You might write a whole hierarchy of `Logger` classes and subclasses. You might couple the loggers with instances of `Handler` (and subclasses thereof). You might also insert instances of class `Filter` to fine-tune criteria determining what messages get logged in which ways. The messages that do get emitted are formatted by instances of the `Formatter` class—indeed, the messages themselves are instances of the `LogRecord` class. The `logging` package even includes a dynamic configuration facility, whereby you may dynamically set logging-configuration files by reading them from disk files, or even by receiving them on a dedicated socket in a specialized thread.

While the `logging` package sports a frighteningly complex and powerful architecture, suitable for implementing highly sophisticated logging strategies and policies that may be needed in vast and complicated programming systems, in most applications you may get away with using a tiny subset of the package through some simple functions supplied by the `logging` module itself. First of all, `import logging`. Then, emit your message by passing it as a string to any of the functions `debug`, `info`, `warning`, `error`, or `critical`, in increasing order of severity. If the string you pass contains format specifiers such as `%s` (as covered in "Legacy String Formatting with %" on page 246) then, after the string, pass as further arguments all the values to be formatted in that string. For example, don't call:

```
logging.debug('foo is %r' % foo)
```

which performs the formatting operation whether it's needed or not; rather, call:

```
logging.debug('foo is %r', foo)
```

which performs formatting if and only if needed (i.e., if and only if calling `debug` is going to result in logging output, depending on the current threshold level).

Unfortunately, the `logging` module does not support the more readable formatting approach covered in "String Formatting" on page 240, but only the antiquated one covered in "Legacy String Formatting with %" on page 246. Fortunately, it's very rare that you'll need any formatting specifier, except the simple `%s` and `%r`, for logging purposes.

By default, the threshold level is `WARNING`, meaning that any of the functions `warning`, `error`, or `critical` results in logging output, but the functions `debug` and `info` don't. To change the threshold level at any time, call `logging.getLogger().setLevel`, passing as the only argument one of the corresponding constants supplied by module `logging`: `DEBUG`, `INFO`, `WARNING`, `ERROR`, or `CRITICAL`. For example, once you call:

```
logging.getLogger().setLevel(logging.DEBUG)
```

all of the logging functions from `debug` to `critical` result in logging output until you change level again; if later you call:

```
logging.getLogger().setLevel(logging.ERROR)
```

then only the functions `error` and `critical` result in logging output (`debug`, `info`, and `warning` won't result in logging output); this condition, too, persists only until you change level again, and so forth.

By default, logging output is to your process's standard error stream (`sys.stderr`, as covered in Table 7-3) and uses a rather simplistic format (for example, it does not include a timestamp on each line it outputs). You can control these settings by instantiating an appropriate handler instance, with a suitable formatter instance, and creating and setting a new logger instance to hold it. In the simple, common case in which you just want to set these logging parameters once and for all, after which they persist throughout the run of your program, the simplest approach is to call the `logging.basicConfig` function, which lets you set up things quite simply via named parameters. Only the very first call to `logging.basicConfig` has any effect, and only if you call it before any of the logging functions (`debug`, `info`, and so on). Therefore, the most common use is to call `logging.basicConfig` at the very start of your program. For example, a common idiom at the start of a program is something like:

```
import logging
logging.basicConfig(
    format='%(asctime)s %(levelname)8s %(message)s',
    filename='/tmp/logfile.txt', filemode='w')
```

This setting emits all logging messages to a file and formats them nicely with a precise human-readable timestamp, followed by the severity level right-aligned in an eight-character field, followed by the message proper.

For excruciatingly large amounts of detailed information on the logging package and all the wonders you can perform with it, be sure to consult Python's *rich online information about it (https://docs.python.org/3/library/logging.html?module-logging)*.

The assert Statement

The `assert` statement allows you to introduce "sanity checks" into a program. `assert` is a simple statement with the following syntax:

```
assert condition[,expression]
```

When you run Python with the optimize flag (`-O`, as covered in "Command-Line Syntax and Options" on page 27), `assert` is a null operation: the compiler generates no code for it. Otherwise, `assert` evaluates *`condition`*. When *`condition`* is satisfied, `assert` does nothing. When *`condition`* is not satisfied, `assert` instantiates `AssertionError` with *`expression`* as the argument (or without arguments, if there is no *`expression`*) and raises the resulting instance.[2]

`assert` statements can be an effective way to document your program. When you want to state that a significant, nonobvious condition *`C`* is known to hold at a certain point in a program's execution (known as an *invariant* of your program), `assert` *`C`* is often better than a comment that just states that *`C`* holds.

The advantage of `assert` is that, when *`C`* does *not* in fact hold, `assert` immediately alerts you to the problem by raising `AssertionError`, if the program is running without the `-O` flag. Once the code is thoroughly debugged, run it with `-O`, turning `assert` into a null operation and incurring no overhead (the `assert` remains in your source code to document the invariant).

Exceptions

Don't overuse assert

Never use `assert` for other purposes besides sanity-checking program invariants. A serious but very common mistake is to use `assert` about the values of inputs or arguments: checking for erroneous arguments or inputs is best done more explicitly, and in particular must not be turned into a null operation by a command-line flag.

2 Some third-party frameworks, such as pytest (*http://docs.pytest.org/en/latest/*), materially improve the usefulness of the `assert` statement.

The __debug__ Built-in Variable

When you run Python without option **-O**, the __debug__ built-in variable is True. When you run Python with option **-O**, __debug__ is False. Also, with option **-O**, the compiler generates no code for any if statement whose condition is __debug__.

To exploit this optimization, surround the definitions of functions that you call only in assert statements with if __debug__:. This technique makes compiled code smaller and faster when Python is run with **-O**, and enhances program clarity by showing that those functions exist only to perform sanity checks.

6 Modules

A typical Python program is made up of several source files. Each source file is a *module*, grouping code and data for reuse. Modules are normally independent of each other, so that other programs can reuse the specific modules they need. Sometimes, to manage complexity, you group together related modules into a *package*—a hierarchical, tree-like structure.

A module explicitly establishes dependencies upon other modules by using `import` or `from` statements. In some programming languages, global variables provide a hidden conduit for coupling between modules. In Python, global variables are not global to all modules, but rather are attributes of a single module object. Thus, Python modules always communicate in explicit and maintainable ways.

Python also supports *extension modules*—modules coded in other languages such as C, C++, Java, or C#—for use in Python. For the Python code importing a module, it does not matter whether the module is pure Python or an extension. You can always start by coding a module in Python. Later, should you need more speed, you refactor and recode some parts of modules in lower-level languages, without changing the client code that uses those modules. Chapter 24 shows how to write extensions in C and Cython.

This chapter discusses module creation and loading. It also covers grouping modules into packages, and using Python's distribution utilities (`distutils` and `setuptools`) to install distributed packages, and to prepare packages for distribution; this latter subject is more thoroughly covered in Chapter 25. This chapter closes with a discussion on how best to manage your Python environment(s).

Module Objects

A module is a Python object with arbitrarily named attributes that you can bind and reference. The Python code for a module named *aname* usually lives in a file named *aname.py*, as covered in "Module Loading" on page 178.

In Python, modules are objects (values), handled like other objects. Thus, you can pass a module as an argument in a call to a function. Similarly, a function can return a module as the result of a call. A module, just like any other object, can be bound to a variable, an item in a container, or an attribute of an object. Modules can be keys or values in a dictionary, and can be members of a set. For example, the `sys.modules` dictionary, covered in "Module Loading" on page 178, holds module objects as its values. The fact that modules can be treated like other values in Python is often expressed by saying that modules are *first-class* objects.

The import Statement

You can use any Python source file as a module by executing an `import` statement in another Python source file. `import` has the following syntax:

```
import modname [as varname][,...]
```

After the `import` keyword comes one or more module specifiers separated by commas. In the simplest, most common case, a module specifier is just *`modname`*, an identifier—a variable that Python binds to the module object when the `import` statement finishes. In this case, Python looks for the module of the same name to satisfy the `import` request. For example:

```
import mymodule
```

looks for the module named `mymodule` and binds the variable named *`mymodule`* in the current scope to the module object. *`modname`* can also be a sequence of identifiers separated by dots (`.`) to name a module in a package, as covered in "Packages" on page 184.

When `as` *`varname`* is part of a module specifier, Python looks for a module named *`modname`* and binds the module object to the variable *`varname`*. For example:

```
import mymodule as alias
```

looks for the module named `mymodule` and binds the module object to variable *`alias`* in the current scope. *`varname`* must always be a simple identifier.

Module body

The body of a module is the sequence of statements in the module's source file. There is no special syntax required to indicate that a source file is a module; any valid Python source file can be used as a module. A module's body executes immediately the first time the module is imported in a given run of a program. During execution of the body, the module object has already been created, and an entry in `sys.modules` is already bound to the module object. The module's (global) namespace is gradually populated as the module's body executes.

Attributes of module objects

An `import` statement creates a new namespace containing all the attributes of the module. To access an attribute in this namespace, use the name or alias of the module as a prefix:

```
import mymodule
a = mymodule.f()
```

or:

```
import mymodule as alias
a = alias.f()
```

Attributes of a module object are normally bound by statements in the module body. When a statement in the module body binds a (global) variable, what gets bound is an attribute of the module object.

A module body exists to bind the module's attributes

The normal purpose of a module body is to create the module's attributes: `def` statements create and bind functions, `class` statements create and bind classes, and assignment statements can bind attributes of any type. For clarity and cleanliness of your code, be wary about doing anything else in the top logical level of the module's body *except* binding the module's attributes.

You can also bind module attributes outside the body (i.e., in other modules), generally using the attribute reference syntax *`M.name`* (where *`M`* is any expression whose value is the module, and identifier *`name`* is the attribute name). For clarity, however, it's usually best to bind module attributes only in the module's own body.

The `import` statement sets some module attributes as soon as it creates the module object, before the module's body executes. The `__dict__` attribute is the `dict` object that the module uses as the namespace for its attributes. Unlike other attributes of the module, `__dict__` is not available to code in the module as a global variable. All other attributes in the module are items in `__dict__` and are available to code in the module as global variables. Attribute `__name__` is the module's name; attribute `__file__` is the filename from which the module was loaded; other dunder-named attributes hold other module metadata (v3 adds yet more dunder-named attributes to all modules).

For any module object *`M`*, any object *`x`*, and any identifier string *`S`* (except `__dict__`), binding *`M.S = x`* is equivalent to binding *`M.__dict__['S'] = x`*. An attribute reference such as *`M.S`* is also substantially equivalent to *`M.__dict__['S']`*. The only difference is that, when *`S`* is not a key in *`M.__dict__`*, accessing *`M.__dict__['S']`* raises

KeyError, while accessing *M.S* raises AttributeError. Module attributes are also available to all code in the module's body as global variables. In other words, within the module body, *S* used as a global variable is equivalent to *M.S* (i.e., *M.__dict__['S']*) for both binding and reference (when *S* is *not* a key in *M.__dict__*, however, referring to *S* as a global variable raises NameError).

Python built-ins

Python supplies several built-in objects (covered in Chapter 7). All built-in objects are attributes of a preloaded module named builtins (in v2, this module's name is __builtin__). When Python loads a module, the module automatically gets an extra attribute named __builtins__, which refers either to the module builtins (in v2, __builtin__) or to its dictionary. Python may choose either, so don't rely on __builtins__. If you need to access the module builtins directly (a rare need), use an import builtins statement (in v2, import __builtin__ as builtins). When you access a variable not found in either the local namespace or the global namespace of the current module, Python looks for the identifier in the current module's __builtins__ before raising NameError.

The lookup is the only mechanism that Python uses to let your code access built-ins. The built-ins' names are not reserved, nor are they hardwired in Python itself. The access mechanism is simple and documented, so your own code can use the mechanism directly (do so in moderation, or your program's clarity and simplicity will suffer). Since Python accesses built-ins only when it cannot resolve a name in the local or module namespace, it is usually sufficient to define a replacement in one of those namespaces. You can, however, add your own built-ins or substitute your functions for the normal built-in ones, in which case all modules see the added or replaced one. The following v3 toy example shows how you can wrap a built-in function with your own function, allowing abs() to take a string argument (and return a rather arbitrary mangling of the string):

```
# abs takes a numeric argument; let's make it accept a string as well
import builtins
_abs = builtins.abs                              # save original built-in
def abs(str_or_num):
    if isinstance(str_or_num, str):              # if arg is a string
        return ''.join(sorted(set(str_or_num)))  # get this instead
    return _abs(str_or_num)                      # call real built-in
builtins.abs = abs                           # override built-in w/wrapper
```

The only change needed to make this example work in v2 is to replace import builtins with import __builtin__ as builtins.

Module documentation strings

If the first statement in the module body is a string literal, Python binds that string as the module's documentation string attribute, named __doc__. Documentation strings are also called *docstrings*; we cover them in "Docstrings" on page 87.

Module-private variables

No variable of a module is truly private. However, by convention, every identifier starting with a single underscore (_), such as `_secret`, is meant to be private. In other words, the leading underscore communicates to client-code programmers that they should not access the identifier directly.

Development environments and other tools rely on the leading-underscore naming convention to discern which attributes of a module are public (i.e., part of the module's interface) and which are private (i.e., to be used only within the module).

Respect the "leading underscore means private" convention

It's important to respect the "leading underscore means private" convention, particularly when you write client code that uses modules written by others. Avoid using any attributes in such modules whose names start with _. Future releases of the modules will presumably maintain their public interface, but are quite likely to change private implementation details, and private attributes are meant exactly for such implementation details.

The from Statement

Python's `from` statement lets you import specific attributes from a module into the current namespace. `from` has two syntax variants:

```
from modname import attrname [as varname][,...]
from modname import *
```

A `from` statement specifies a module name, followed by one or more attribute specifiers separated by commas. In the simplest and most common case, an attribute specifier is just an identifier *`attrname`*, which is a variable that Python binds to the attribute of the same name in the module named *`modname`*. For example:

```
from mymodule import f
```

`modname` can also be a sequence of identifiers separated by dots (`.`) to name a module within a package, as covered in "Packages" on page 184.

When `as` *`varname`* is part of an attribute specifier, Python gets from the module the value of attribute *`attrname`* and binds it to variable *`varname`*. For example:

```
from mymodule import f as foo
```

`attrname` and *`varname`* are always simple identifiers.

You may optionally enclose in parentheses all the attribute specifiers that follow the keyword `import` in a `from` statement. This is sometimes useful when you have many attribute specifiers, in order to split the single logical line of the `from` statement into multiple logical lines more elegantly than by using backslashes (`\`):

```
from some_module_with_a_long_name import (
    another_name, and_another as x, one_more, and_yet_another as y)
```

from ... import *

Code that is directly inside a module body (not in the body of a function or class) may use an asterisk (`*`) in a `from` statement:

```
from mymodule import *
```

The `*` requests that "all" attributes of module *modname* be bound as global variables in the importing module. When module *modname* has an attribute named `__all__`, the attribute's value is the list of the attribute names that are bound by this type of `from` statement. Otherwise, this type of `from` statement binds all attributes of *modname* except those beginning with underscores.

Beware using from M import * in your code

Since `from M import *` may bind an arbitrary set of global variables, it can often have unforeseen and undesired side effects, such as hiding built-ins and rebinding variables you still need. Use the `*` form of `from` very sparingly, if at all, and only to import modules that are explicitly documented as supporting such usage. Your code is most likely better off *never* using this form, meant just as a convenience for occasional use in interactive Python sessions.

from versus import

The `import` statement is often a better choice than the `from` statement. Think of the `from` statement, particularly `from M import *`, as a convenience meant only for occasional use in interactive Python sessions. When you always access module *M* with the statement `import M` and always access *M*'s attributes with explicit syntax `M.A`, your code is slightly less concise but far clearer and more readable. One good use of `from` is to import specific modules from a package, as we discuss in "Packages" on page 184. But, in most other cases, `import` is better than `from`.

Module Loading

Module-loading operations rely on attributes of the built-in sys module (covered in "The sys Module" on page 212) and are implemented in the built-in function `__import__`. Your code could call `__import__` directly, but this is strongly discouraged in modern Python; rather, `import importlib` and call `importlib.import_module` with the module name string as the argument. `import_module` returns the module object or, should the import fail, raises `ImportError`. However, it's best to have a clear understanding of the semantics of `__import__`, because `import_module` and `import` statements both depend on it.

To import a module named *M*, `__import__` first checks dictionary `sys.modules`, using string *M* as the key. When key *M* is in the dictionary, `__import__` returns the corresponding value as the requested module object. Otherwise, `__import__` binds `sys.modules[M]` to a new empty module object with a `__name__` of *M*, then looks for the right way to initialize (load) the module, as covered in "Searching the Filesystem for a Module" on page 179.

Thanks to this mechanism, the relatively slow loading operation takes place only the first time a module is imported in a given run of the program. When a module is imported again, the module is not reloaded, since `__import__` rapidly finds and returns the module's entry in `sys.modules`. Thus, all imports of a given module after the first one are very fast: they're just dictionary lookups. (To *force* a reload, see "Reloading Modules" on page 181.)

Built-in Modules

When a module is loaded, `__import__` first checks whether the module is built-in. The tuple `sys.builtin_module_names` names all built-in modules, but rebinding that tuple does not affect module loading. When Python loads a built-in module, as when it loads any other extension, Python calls the module's initialization function. The search for built-in modules also looks for modules in platform-specific locations, such as the Registry in Windows.

Searching the Filesystem for a Module

If module *M* is not built-in, `__import__` looks for *M*'s code as a file on the filesystem. `__import__` looks at the strings, which are the items of list `sys.path`, in order. Each item is the path of a directory, or the path of an archive file in the popular ZIP format. `sys.path` is initialized at program startup, using the environment variable `PYTHONPATH` (covered in "Environment Variables" on page 26), if present. The first item in `sys.path` is always the directory from which the main program is loaded. An empty string in `sys.path` indicates the current directory.

Your code can mutate or rebind `sys.path`, and such changes affect which directories and ZIP archives `__import__` searches to load modules. Changing `sys.path` does *not* affect modules that are already loaded (and thus already recorded in `sys.modules`) when you change `sys.path`.

If a text file with the extension *.pth* is found in the *PYTHONHOME* directory at startup, the file's contents are added to `sys.path`, one item per line. *.pth* files can contain blank lines and comment lines starting with the character #; Python ignores any such lines. *.pth* files can also contain `import` statements (which Python executes before your program starts to execute), but no other kinds of statements.

When looking for the file for the module *M* in each directory and ZIP archive along `sys.path`, Python considers the following extensions in this order:

1. *.pyd* and *.dll* (Windows) or *.so* (most Unix-like platforms), which indicate Python extension modules. (Some Unix dialects use different extensions; e.g., *.sl* on HP-UX.) On most platforms, extensions cannot be loaded from a ZIP archive—only source or bytecode-compiled Python modules can.
2. *.py*, which indicates Python source modules.
3. *.pyc* (or *.pyo*, in v2, if Python is run with option `-O`), which indicates bytecode-compiled Python modules.
4. If a *.py* file is found, in v3 only, then Python also looks for a directory called *__pycache__*; if such a directory is found, then Python looks in that directory for the extension *.<tag>.pyc*, where *<tag>* is a string specific to the version of Python that is looking for the module.

One last path in which Python looks for the file for module `M` is *M/__init__.py*, meaning a file named *__init__.py* in a directory named *M*, as covered in "Packages" on page 184.

Upon finding source file *M.py*, Python (v3) compiles it to *M.<tag>.pyc*, unless the bytecode file is already present, is newer than *M.py*, and was compiled by the same version of Python. If *M.py* is compiled from a writable directory, Python creates a *__pycache__* directory if necessary and saves the bytecode file to the filesystem in that subdirectory so that future runs won't needlessly recompile. (In v2, *M.py* compiles to *M.pyc* or *M.pyo*, and Python saves the bytecode file in the same directory as `M.py`.) When the bytecode file is newer than the source file (based on an internal timestamp in the bytecode file, not on trusting the date as recorded in the filesystem), Python does not recompile the module.

Once Python has the bytecode, whether just built by compilation or read from the filesystem, Python executes the module body to initialize the module object. If the module is an extension, Python calls the module's initialization function.

The Main Program

Execution of a Python application normally starts with a top-level script (also known as the *main program*), as explained in "The python Program" on page 25. The main program executes like any other module being loaded, except that Python keeps the bytecode in memory without saving it to disk. The module name for the main program is always `'__main__'`, both as the `__name__` global variable (module attribute) and as the key in `sys.modules`.

Don't import the .py file you're using as the main program

You should not import the same *.py* file that is the main program. If you do, the module is loaded again, and the body executes once more from the top in a separate module object with a different `__name__`.

Code in a Python module can test if the module is being used as the main program by checking if global variable `__name__` has the value `'__main__'`. The idiom:

```
if __name__ == '__main__':
```

is often used to guard some code so that it executes only when the module is run as the main program. If a module is meant only to be imported, it should normally execute unit tests when it is run as the main program, as covered in "Unit Testing and System Testing" on page 456.

Reloading Modules

Python loads a module only the first time you import the module during a program run. When you develop interactively, you need to make sure you explicitly *reload* your modules each time you edit them (some development environments provide automatic reloading).

To reload a module, in v3, pass the module object (*not* the module name) as the only argument to the function `reload` from the `importlib` module (in v2, call the built-in function `reload` instead, to the same effect). `importlib.reload(`*`M`*`)` ensures the reloaded version of *`M`* is used by client code that relies on `import` *`M`* and accesses attributes with the syntax *`M.A`*. However, `importlib.reload(`*`M`*`)` has no effect on other existing references bound to previous values of *`M`*'s attributes (e.g., with a `from` statement). In other words, already-bound variables remain bound as they were, unaffected by `reload`. `reload`'s inability to rebind such variables is a further incentive to use `import` rather than `from`.

`reload` is not recursive: when you reload module *`M`*, this does not imply that other modules imported by *`M`* get reloaded in turn. You must arrange to reload, by explicit calls to the `reload` function, each and every module you have modified.

Circular Imports

Python lets you specify circular imports. For example, you can write a module *a.py* that contains `import b`, while module *b.py* contains `import a`.

If you decide to use a circular import for some reason, you need to understand how circular imports work in order to avoid errors in your code.

Avoid circular imports

In practice, you are nearly always better off avoiding circular imports, since circular dependencies are fragile and hard to manage.

Say that the main script executes `import a`. As discussed earlier, this `import` statement creates a new empty module object as `sys.modules['a']` and then the body of module `a` starts executing. When `a` executes `import b`, this creates a new empty module object as `sys.modules['b']`, and then the body of module `b` starts executing. The execution of a's module body cannot proceed until b's module body finishes.

Now, when b executes `import a`, the `import` statement finds `sys.modules['a']` already bound, and therefore binds global variable a in module b to the module object for module a. Since the execution of a's module body is currently blocked, module a is usually only partly populated at this time. Should the code in b's module body immediately try to access some attribute of module a that is not yet bound, an error results.

If you insist on keeping a circular import, you must carefully manage the order in which each module binds its own globals, imports other modules, and accesses globals of other modules. You can have greater control on the sequence in which things happen by grouping your statements into functions, and calling those functions in a controlled order, rather than just relying on sequential execution of top-level statements in module bodies. Usually, removing circular dependencies is easier than ensuring bomb-proof ordering with circular dependencies.

sys.modules Entries

`__import__` never binds anything other than a module object as a value in `sys.modules`. However, if `__import__` finds an entry already in `sys.modules`, it returns that value, whatever type it may be. The `import` and `from` statements internally rely on `__import__`, so they too can end up using objects that are not modules. This lets you set class instances as entries in `sys.modules`, in order to exploit features such as `__getattr__` and `__setattr__` special methods, covered in "General-Purpose Special Methods" on page 126. This rarely needed advanced technique lets you import module-like objects whose attributes you can compute on the fly. Here's a toy-like example:

```
class TT(object):
    def __getattr__(self, name): return 23
import sys
sys.modules[__name__] = TT()
```

The first import of this code as a module overwrites the module's `sys.modules` entry with an instance of class *TT*. Any attribute name you try to get from it then appears to have the integer value 23.

Custom Importers

An advanced, rarely needed functionality that Python offers is the ability to change the semantics of some or all `import` and `from` statements.

Rebinding __import__

You can rebind the `__import__` attribute of the module `builtin` to your own custom importer function—for example, one using the generic built-in-wrapping technique shown in "Python built-ins" on page 176. Such a rebinding affects all `import` and from statements that execute after the rebinding and thus can have undesired global impact. A custom importer built by rebinding `__import__` must implement the same interface and semantics as the built-in `__import__`, and, in particular, it is responsible for supporting the correct use of `sys.modules`.

Beware rebinding builtin __import__

While rebinding `__import__` may initially look like an attractive approach, in most cases where custom importers are necessary, you're better off implementing them via *import hooks* (described next).

Import hooks

Python offers rich support for selectively changing the details of imports. Custom importers are an advanced and rarely needed technique, yet some applications may need them for purposes such as importing code from archives other than ZIP files, databases, network servers, and so on.

The most suitable approach for such highly advanced needs is to record *importer factory* callables as items in the attributes `meta_path` and/or `path_hooks` of the module `sys`, as detailed in PEP 302 (*https://www.python.org/dev/peps/pep-0302/*) (and, for v3, PEP 451 (*https://www.python.org/dev/peps/pep-0451/*)). This is how Python hooks up the standard library module `zipimport` to allow seamless importing of modules from ZIP files, as previously mentioned. A full study of the details of PEP 302 and 451 is indispensable for any substantial use of `sys.path_hooks` and friends, but here's a toy-level example to help understand the possibilities, should you ever need them.

Suppose that, while developing a first outline of some program, you want to be able to use `import` statements for modules that you haven't written yet, getting just messages (and empty modules) as a consequence. You can obtain such functionality (leaving aside the complexities connected with packages, and dealing with simple modules only) by coding a custom importer module as follows:

```
import sys, types

class ImporterAndLoader(object):
     '''importer and loader are often a single class'''
     fake_path = '!dummy!'
     def __init__(self, path):
         # only handle our own fake-path marker
         if path != self.fake_path: raise ImportError
     def find_module(self, fullname):
         # don't even try to handle any qualified module name
         if '.' in fullname: return None
         return self
     def create_module(self, spec):
         # run in v3 only: create module "the default way"
         return None
```

```
        def exec_module(self, mod):
            # run in v3 only: populate the already-initialized module
            # just print a message in this toy example
            print('NOTE: module {!r} not yet written'.format(mod))
        def load_module(self, fullname):
            # run in v2 only: make and populate the module
            if fullname in sys.modules: return sys.modules[fullname]
            # just print a message in this toy example
            print('NOTE: module {!r} not written yet'.format(fullname))
            # make new empty module, put it in sys.modules
            mod = sys.modules[fullname] = types.ModuleType(fullname)
            # minimally initialize new module and return it
            mod.__file__ = 'dummy_{}'.format(fullname)
            mod.__loader__ = self
            return mod
    # add the class to the hook and its fake-path marker to the path
    sys.path_hooks.append(ImporterAndLoader)
    sys.path.append(ImporterAndLoader.fake_path)

    if __name__ == '__main__':          # self-test when run as main script
        import missing_module           # importing a simple missing module
        print(missing_module)           # ...should succeed
        print(sys.modules.get('missing_module'))  # ...should also succeed
```

In v2, we have to implement the method `load_module`, which must also perform some boilerplate tasks such as dealing with `sys.modules` and setting dunder attributes such as `__file__` on the module object. In v3, the system does such boilerplate for us, so we just write trivial versions of `create_module` (which in this case just returns `None`, asking the system to create the module object in the default way) and `exec_module` (which receives the module object already initialized with dunder attributes, and would normally populate it appropriately).

In v3, we could use the powerful new *module spec* concept. However, that requires the standard library module `importlib`, which is mostly missing in v2; moreover, for this toy example we don't need such power. Therefore, we choose instead to implement the method `find_module`, which we do need anyway in v2—and, although now deprecated, it also works in v3 for backward compatibility.

Packages

A *package* is a module containing other modules. Some or all of the modules in a package may be *subpackages*, resulting in a hierarchical tree-like structure. A package named *P* resides in a subdirectory, also called *P*, of some directory in `sys.path`. Packages can also live in ZIP files; in this section, we explain the case in which the package lives on the filesystem, since the case in which a package is in a ZIP file is similar, relying on the hierarchical filesystem structure within the ZIP file.

The module body of *P* is in the file *P/__init__.py*. This file *must* exist (except, in v3, for *namespace packages*, covered in "Namespace Packages (v3 Only)" on page 186), even if it's empty (representing an empty module body), in order to tell Python that directory *P* is indeed a package. The module body of a package is loaded when you first import the package (or any of the package's modules) and behaves in all respects like any other Python module. The other *.py* files in directory *P* are the modules of package *P*. Subdirectories of *P* containing *__init__.py* files are *subpackages* of *P*. Nesting can proceed to any depth.

You can import a module named *M* in package *P* as `P.M`. More dots let you navigate a hierarchical package structure. (A package's module body is always loaded *before* any module in the package is loaded.) If you use the syntax `import P.M`, the variable *P* is bound to the module object of package *P*, and the attribute *M* of object *P* is bound to the module `P.M`. If you use the syntax `import P.M` as *V*, the variable *V* is bound directly to the module `P.M`.

Using `from P import M` to import a specific module *M* from package *P* is a perfectly acceptable, indeed highly recommended practice: the `from` statement is specifically okay in this case. `from P import M as V` is also just fine, and perfectly equivalent to `import P.M as V`.

In v2, by default, when module *M* in package *P* executes `import X`, Python searches for *X* in *M*, before searching in `sys.path`. However, this does not apply in v3: indeed, to avoid the ambiguity of these semantics, we strongly recommend that, in v2, you use `from __future__ import absolute_import` to make v2 behave like v3 in this respect. Module *M* in package *P* can then explicitly import its "sibling" module *X* (also in package *P*) with `from . import X`.

Sharing objects among modules in a package

The simplest, cleanest way to share objects (e.g., functions or constants) among modules in a package *P* is to group the shared objects in a module conventionally named *P/common.py*. That way, you can `from . import common` in every module in the package that needs to access some of the common objects, and then refer to the objects as `common.f`, `common.K`, and so on.

Special Attributes of Package Objects

A package *P*'s `__file__` attribute is the string that is the path of *P*'s module body—that is, the path of the file *P/__init__.py*. *P*'s `__package__` attribute is the name of *P*'s package.

A package *P*'s module body—that is, the Python source that is in the file *P/__init__.py*—can optionally set a global variable named `__all__` (just like any other module can) to control what happens if some other Python code executes the statement `from P import *`. In particular, if `__all__` is not set, `from P import *` does not import *P*'s modules, but only names that are set in *P*'s module body and lack a leading `_`. In any case, this is *not* recommended usage.

A package *P*'s `__path__` attribute is the list of strings that are the paths to the directories from which *P*'s modules and subpackages are loaded. Initially, Python sets `__path__` to a list with a single element: the path of the directory containing the file *__init__.py* that is the module body of the package. Your code can modify this list to affect future searches for modules and subpackages of this package. This advanced technique is rarely necessary, but can be useful when you want to place a package's modules in several disjoint directories. In v3 only, a namespace package, as covered next, is the usual way to accomplish this goal.

Namespace Packages (v3 Only)

In v3 only, on `import foo`, when one or more directories that are immediate children of `sys.path` members are named *foo*, and none of them contains a file named *__init__.py*, Python deduces that `foo` is a *namespace package*. As a result, Python creates (and assigns to `sys.modules['foo']`) a package object `foo` without a `__file__` attribute; `foo.__path__` is the list of all the various directories that make up the package (and, like for a normal package, your code may optionally choose to further alter it). This advanced approach is rarely needed.

Absolute Versus Relative Imports

As mentioned in "Packages" on page 184, an `import` statement normally expects to find its target somewhere on `sys.path`, a behavior known as an *absolute* import (to ensure this reliable behavior in v2, start your module with `from __future__ import absolute_import`). Alternatively, you can explicitly use a *relative* import, meaning an import of an object from within the current package. Relative imports use module or package names beginning with one or more dots, and are only available in the `from` statement. `from . import` *`X`* looks for the module or object named *`X`* in the current package; `from .`*`X`* `import` *`y`* looks in module or subpackage *`X`* within the current package for the module or object named *y*. If your package has subpackages, their code can access higher-up objects in the package by using multiple dots at the start of the module or subpackage name you place between `from` and `import`. Each additional dot ascends the directory hierarchy one level. Getting too fancy with this feature can easily damage your code's clarity, so use it with care, and only when necessary.

Distribution Utilities (distutils) and setuptools

Python modules, extensions, and applications can be packaged and distributed in several forms:

Compressed archive files
: Generally *.zip* or *.tar.gz* (AKA *.tgz*) files—both forms are portable, and many other forms of compressed archives of trees of files and directories exist

Self-unpacking or self-installing executables
: Normally *.exe* for Windows

Self-contained, ready-to-run executables that require no installation
: For example, *.exe* for Windows, ZIP archives with a short script prefix on Unix, *.app* for the Mac, and so on

Platform-specific installers
: For example, *.msi* on Windows, *.rpm* and *.srpm* on many Linux distributions, *.deb* on Debian GNU/Linux and Ubuntu, *.pkg* on macOS

Python Wheels (and Eggs)
: Popular third-party extensions, covered in "Python Wheels (and Eggs)" on page 188

When you distribute a package as a self-installing executable or platform-specific installer, a user installs the package simply by running the installer. How to run such an installer program depends on the platform, but it no longer matters which language the program was written in. We cover building self-contained, runnable executables for various platforms in Chapter 25.

When you distribute a package as an archive file or as an executable that unpacks but does not install itself, it *does* matter that the package was coded in Python. In this case, the user must first unpack the archive file into some appropriate directory, say *C:\Temp\MyPack* on a Windows machine or *~/MyPack* on a Unix-like machine. Among the extracted files there should be a script, conventionally named *setup.py*, which uses the Python facility known as the *distribution utilities* (the standard library package `distutils`) or the more popular and powerful third-party package setuptools (*https://pypi.python.org/pypi/setuptools*). The distributed package is then almost as easy to install as a self-installing executable. The user opens a command prompt window and changes to the directory into which the archive is unpacked. Then the user runs, for example:

```
C:\Temp\MyPack> python setup.py install
```

(`pip` is the preferred way to install packages nowadays, and is briefly discussed in "Python Environments" on page 188.) The *setup.py* script, run with this **`install`** command, installs the package as a part of the user's Python installation, according to the options specified by the package's author in the setup script. Of course, the user needs appropriate permissions to write into the directories of the Python installations, so permission-raising commands such as *sudo* may also be needed, or better yet, you can install into a *virtual environment*, covered in "Python Environments" on page 188. `distutils` and `setuptools`, by default, print information when the user runs *setup.py*. Option **`--quiet`**, right before the **`install`** command, hides most details (the user still sees error messages, if any). The following command gives detailed help on `distutils` or `setuptools`, depending on which toolset the package author used in their *setup.py*:

```
C:\Temp\MyPack> python setup.py --help
```

Recent versions of both v2 and v3 come with the excellent installer `pip` (a recursive acronym for "`pip` installs packages"), copiously documented online (*https://*

pip.pypa.io/en/stable/user_guide/), yet very simple to use in most cases. `pip install` *`package`* finds the online version of *package* (usually on the huge PyPI (*https://pypi.python.org/pypi*) repository, hosting almost 100,000 packages at the time of writing), downloads it, and installs it for you (in a virtual environment, if one is active—see "Python Environments" on page 188). This books' authors have been using that simple, powerful approach for well over 90% of their installs for quite a while now.

Even if you have downloaded the package locally (say to */tmp/mypack*), for whatever reason (maybe it's not on PyPI, or you're trying out an experimental version not yet there), `pip` can still install it for you: just run `pip install --no-index --find-links=/tmp/mypack` and `pip` does the rest.

Python Wheels (and Eggs)

Python *wheels* (like their precursor, *eggs*, still supported but not recommended for future development) are an archive format including structured metadata as well as Python code. Both formats, especially wheels, offer excellent ways to package and distribute your Python packages, and `setuptools` (with the `wheel` extension, easily installed with, of course, `pip install wheel`) works seamlessly with them. Read all about them online (*http://pythonwheels.com/*) and in Chapter 25.

Python Environments

A typical Python programmer works on several projects concurrently, each with its own list of dependencies (typically, third-party libraries and data files). When the dependencies for all projects are installed into the same Python interpreter, it is very difficult to determine which projects use which dependencies, and impossible to handle projects with conflicting versions of certain dependencies.

Early Python interpreters were built on the assumption that each computer system would have "a Python interpreter" installed on it, which would be used to process all Python that ran on that system. Operating system distributions started to include Python in their base installation, but, because Python was being actively developed, users often complained that they would like to use a more up-to-date version of the language than their operating system provided.

Techniques arose to let multiple versions of the language be installed on a system, but installation of third-party software remained nonstandard and intrusive. This problem was eased by the introduction of the *site-packages* directory as the repository for modules added to a Python installation, but it was still not possible to maintain projects with conflicting requirements using the same interpreter.

Programmers accustomed to command-line operations are familiar with the concept of a *shell environment*. A shell program running in a process has a current directory, variables that can be set by shell commands (very similar to a Python namespace), and various other pieces of process-specific state data. Python programs have access to the shell environment through `os.environ`.

Various aspects of the shell environment affect Python's operation, as mentioned in "Environment Variables" on page 26. For example, the interpreter executed in response to **python** and other commands is determined by the `PATH` environment variable. You can think of those aspects of your shell environment that affect Python's operation as your *Python environment*. By modifying it you can determine which Python interpreter runs in response to the **python** command, which packages and modules are available under certain names, and so on.

Leave the system's Python to the system

We recommend taking control of your Python environment. In particular, do not build applications on top of a system's distributed Python. Instead, install another Python distribution independently and adjust your shell environment so that the **python** command runs your locally installed Python rather than the system's Python.

Enter the Virtual Environment

The introduction of the `pip` utility created a simple way to install (and, for the first time, to uninstall) packages and modules in a Python environment. Modifying the system Python's *site-packages* still requires administrative privileges, and hence so does `pip` (although it can optionally install somewhere other than *site-packages*). Installed modules are still visible to all programs.

The missing piece is the ability to make controlled changes to the Python environment, to direct the use of a specific interpreter and a specific set of Python libraries. That is just what *virtual environments* (*virtualenvs*) give you. Creating a virtualenv based on a specific Python interpreter copies or links to components from that interpreter's installation. Critically, though, each one has its own *site-packages* directory, into which you can install the Python resources of your choice.

Creating a virtualenv is *much* simpler than installing Python, and requires far less system resources (a typical newly created virtualenv takes less than 20 MB). You can easily create and activate them on demand, and deactivate and destroy them just as easily. You can activate and deactivate a virtualenv as many times as you like during its lifetime, and if necessary use `pip` to update the installed resources. When you are done with it, removing its directory tree reclaims all storage occupied by the virtualenv. A virtualenv's lifetime can be from minutes to months.

What Is a Virtual Environment?

A virtualenv is essentially a self-contained subset of your Python environment that you can switch in or out on demand. For a Python X.Y interpreter it includes, among other things, a *bin* directory containing a Python X.Y interpreter and a *lib/pythonX.Y/site-packages* directory containing preinstalled versions of `easy-install`, `pip`, `pkg_resources`, and `setuptools`. Maintaining separate copies of these important distribution-related resources lets you update them as necessary rather than forcing reliance on the base Python distribution.

A virtualenv has its own copies of (on Windows), or symbolic links to (on other platforms), Python distribution files. It adjusts the values of `sys.prefix` and `sys.exec_prefix`, from which the interpreter and various installation utilities determine the location of some libraries. This means that `pip` can install dependencies in isolation from other environments, in the virtualenv's *site-packages* directory. In effect the virtualenv redefines which interpreter runs when you run the `python` command and which libraries are available to it, but leaves most aspects of your Python environment (such as the `PYTHONPATH` and `PYTHONHOME` variables) alone. Since its changes affect your shell environment they also affect any subshells in which you run commands.

With separate virtualenvs you can, for example, test two different versions of the same library with a project, or test your project with multiple versions of Python (very useful to check v2/v3 compatibility of your code). You can also add dependencies to your Python projects without needing any special privileges, since you normally create your virtualenvs somewhere you have write permission.

For a long time the only way to create virtual environments was the third-party `virtualenv` (*https://virtualenv.pypa.io/en/stable/*) package, with or without help from `virtualenvwrapper` (*https://virtualenvwrapper.readthedocs.io/en/latest/*), both of which are still available for v2. You can read more about these tools in the Python Packaging User Guide (*https://packaging.python.org/*). They also work with v3, but the 3.3 release added the `venv` module, making virtual environments a native feature of Python for the first time. ***New in 3.6***: use **`python -m venv`** ***`envpath`*** in preference to the **`pyvenv`** command, which is now deprecated.

Creating and Deleting Virtual Environments

In v3 the command **`python -m venv`** ***`envpath`*** creates a virtual environment (in the *envpath* directory, which it also creates if necessary) based on the Python interpreter used to run the command. You can give multiple directory arguments to create with a single command several virtual environments, into which you then install different sets of dependencies. `venv` can take a number of options, as shown in Table 6-1.

Table 6-1. venv options

Option	Purpose
`--clear`	Removes any existing directory content before installing the virtual environment
`--copies`	Installs files by copying on the Unix-like platforms where using symbolic links is the default
`--h` or `--help`	Prints out a command-line summary and a list of available options

Option	Purpose
`--system-site-packages`	Adds the standard system *site-packages* directory to the environment's search path, making modules already installed in the base Python available inside the environment
`--symlinks`	Installs files by using symbolic links on platforms where copying is the system default
`--upgrade`	Installs the running Python in the virtual environment, replacing whichever version the environment was created with
`--without-pip`	Inhibits the usual behavior of calling `ensurepip` to bootstrap the `pip` installer utility into the environment

v2 users must use the `python -m virtualenv` command, which does not accept multiple directory arguments.

The following terminal session shows the creation of a virtualenv and the structure of the directory tree created. The listing of the *bin* subdirectory shows that this particular user by default uses a v3 interpreter installed in */usr/local/bin*.

```
machine:~ user$ python3 -m venv /tmp/tempenv
machine:~ user$ tree -dL 4 /tmp/tempenv
/tmp/tempenv
├── bin
├── include
└── lib
    └── python3.5
        └── site-packages
            ├── __pycache__
            ├── pip
            ├── pip-8.1.1.dist-info
            ├── pkg_resources
            ├── setuptools
            └── setuptools-20.10.1.dist-info

11 directories
machine:~ user$ ls -l /tmp/tempenv/bin/
total 80
-rw-r--r-- 1 sh wheel 2134 Oct 24 15:26 activate
-rw-r--r-- 1 sh wheel 1250 Oct 24 15:26 activate.csh
-rw-r--r-- 1 sh wheel 2388 Oct 24 15:26 activate.fish
-rwxr-xr-x 1 sh wheel  249 Oct 24 15:26 easy_install
-rwxr-xr-x 1 sh wheel  249 Oct 24 15:26 easy_install-3.5
-rwxr-xr-x 1 sh wheel  221 Oct 24 15:26 pip
-rwxr-xr-x 1 sh wheel  221 Oct 24 15:26 pip3
-rwxr-xr-x 1 sh wheel  221 Oct 24 15:26 pip3.5
lrwxr-xr-x 1 sh wheel    7 Oct 24 15:26 python->python3
lrwxr-xr-x 1 sh wheel   22 Oct 24 15:26 python3->/usr/local/bin/python3
```

Deletion of the virtualenv is as simple as removing the directory in which it resides (and all subdirectories and files in the tree: **`rm -rf`** ***`envpath`*** in Unix-like systems). Ease of removal is a helpful aspect of using virtualenvs.

The `venv` module includes features to help the programmed creation of tailored environments (e.g., by preinstalling certain modules in the environment or performing other post-creation steps). It is comprehensively documented online (*https://docs.python.org/3/library/venv.html*), and we therefore do not cover the API further in this book.

Working with Virtual Environments

To use a virtualenv you *activate* it from your normal shell environment. Only one virtualenv can be active at a time—activations don't "stack" like function calls. Activation conditions your Python environment to use the virtualenv's Python interpreter and *site-packages* (along with the interpreter's full standard library). When you want to stop using those dependencies, deactivate the virtualenv and your standard Python environment is once again available. The virtualenv directory tree continues to exist until deleted, so you can activate and deactivate it at will.

Activating a virtualenv in Unix-based environments requires use of the `source` shell command so that the commands in the activation script make changes to the current shell environment. Simply running the script would mean its commands were executed in a subshell, and the changes would be lost when the subshell terminated. For bash and similar shells, you activate an environment located at path *`envpath`* with the command:

```
source envpath/bin/activate
```

Users of other shells are accommodated with *activate.csh* and *activate.fish* scripts located in the same directory. On Windows systems, use *activate.bat*:

```
envpath/Scripts/activate.bat
```

Activation does several things, most importantly:

- Adds the virtualenv's *bin* directory at the beginning of the shell's `PATH` environment variable, so its commands get run in preference to anything of the same name already on the `PATH`
- Defines a `deactivate` command to remove all effects of activation and return the Python environment to its former state
- Modifies the shell prompt to include the virtualenv's name at the start
- Defines a `VIRTUAL_ENV` environment variable as the path to the virtualenv's root directory (scripting can use this to introspect the virtualenv)

As a result of these actions, once a virtualenv is activated the `python` command runs the interpreter associated with that virtualenv. The interpreter sees the libraries (modules and packages) that have been installed in that environment, and `pip`—

now the one from the virtualenv, since installing the module also installed the command in the virtualenv's *bin* directory—by default installs new packages and modules in the environment's *site-packages* directory.

Those new to virtualenvs should understand that a virtualenv is not tied to any project directory. It's perfectly possible to work on several projects, each with its own source tree, using the same virtualenv. Activate it, then move around your filestore as necessary to accomplish your programming tasks, with the same libraries available (because the virtualenv determines the Python environment).

When you want to disable the virtualenv and stop using that set of resources, simply issue the command **`deactivate`**.

This undoes the changes made on activation, removing the virtualenv's *bin* directory from your `PATH`, so the `python` command once again runs your usual interpreter. As long as you don't delete it, the virtualenv remains available for future use by repeating the invocation to activate it.

Managing Dependency Requirements

Since virtualenvs were designed to complement installation with `pip`, it should come as no surprise that `pip` is the preferred way to maintain dependencies in a virtualenv. Because `pip` is already extensively documented, we mention only enough here to demonstrate its advantages in virtual environments. Having created a virtualenv, activated it, and installed dependencies, you can use the `pip freeze` command to learn the exact versions of those dependencies:

```
(tempenv) machine:~ user$ pip freeze
appnope==0.1.0
decorator==4.0.10
ipython==5.1.0
ipython-genutils==0.1.0
pexpect==4.2.1
pickleshare==0.7.4
prompt-toolkit==1.0.8
ptyprocess==0.5.1
Pygments==2.1.3
requests==2.11.1
simplegeneric==0.8.1
six==1.10.0
traitlets==4.3.1
wcwidth==0.1.7
```

If you redirect the output of this command to a file called *filename*, you can recreate the same set of dependencies in a different virtualenv with the command `pip install -r` *`filename`*.

To distribute code for use by others, Python developers conventionally include a *requirements.txt* file listing the necessary dependencies. When you are installing software from the Python Package Index, `pip` installs the packages you request along with any indicated dependencies. When you're developing software it's convenient to have a requirements file, as you can use it to add the necessary dependencies to the active virtualenv (unless they are already installed) with a simple `pip install -r requirements.txt`.

To maintain the same set of dependencies in several virtualenvs, use the same requirements file to add dependencies to each one. This is a convenient way to develop projects to run on multiple Python versions: create virtualenvs based on each of your required versions, then install from the same requirements file in each. While the preceding example uses exactly versioned dependency specifications as produced by `pip freeze`, in practice you can specify dependencies and constrain version requirements in quite complex ways.

Best Practices with virtualenvs

There is remarkably little advice on how best to manage your work with virtualenvs, though there are several sound tutorials: any good search engine gives you access to the most current ones. We can, however, offer a modest amount of advice that we hope will help you to get the most out of them.

When you are working with the same dependencies in multiple Python versions, it is useful to indicate the version in the environment name and use a common prefix. So for project *mutex* you might maintain environments called *mutex_35* and *mutex_27* for v3 and v2 development. When it's obvious which Python is involved (and remember you see the environment name in your shell prompt), there's less chance of testing with the wrong version. You maintain dependencies using common requirements to control resource installation in both.

Keep the requirements file(s) under source control, not the whole environment. Given the requirements file it's easy to re-create a virtualenv, which depends only on the Python release and the requirements. You distribute your project, and let your consumers decide which version(s) of Python to run it on and create the appropriate (hopefully virtual) environment(s).

Keep your virtualenvs outside your project directories. This avoids the need to explicitly force source code control systems to ignore them. It really doesn't matter where you store them—the `virtualenvwrapper` system keeps them all in a central location.

Your Python environment is independent of your process's location in the filesystem. You can activate a virtual environment and then switch branches and move around a change-controlled source tree to use it wherever convenient.

To investigate a new module or package, create and activate a new virtualenv and then `pip install` the resources that interest you. You can play with this new environment to your heart's content, confident in the knowledge that you won't be installing rogue dependencies into other projects.

You may find that experiments in a virtualenv require installation of resources that aren't currently project requirements. Rather than pollute your development environment, fork it: create a new virtualenv from the same requirements plus the testing functionality. Later, to make these changes permanent, use change control to merge your source and requirements changes back in from the fork.

If you are so inclined, you can create virtual environments based on debug builds of Python, giving you access to a wealth of instrumentation information about the performance of your Python code (and, of course, the interpreter).

Developing your virtual environment itself requires change control, and their ease of creation helps here too. Suppose that you recently released version 4.3 of a module, and you want to test your code with new versions of two of its dependencies. You *could*, with sufficient skill, persuade **pip** to replace the existing copies of dependencies in your existing virtualenv.

It's much easier, though, to branch your project, update the requirements, and create an entirely new virtual environment based on the updated requirements. You still have the original virtualenv intact, and you can switch between virtualenvs to investigate specific aspects of any migration issues that might arise. Once you have adjusted your code so that all tests pass with the updated dependencies, you check in your code *and* requirement changes, and merge into version 4.4 to complete the update, advising your colleagues that your code is now ready for the updated versions of the dependencies.

Virtual environments won't solve all of a Python programmer's problems. Tools can always be made more sophisticated, or more general. But, by golly, they work, and we should take all the advantage of those that we can.

7 Core Built-ins and Standard Library Modules

The term *built-in* has more than one meaning in Python. In most contexts, a *built-in* means an object directly accessible to Python code without an `import` statement. "Python built-ins" on page 176 shows the mechanism that Python uses to allow this direct access. Built-in types in Python include numbers, sequences, dictionaries, sets, functions (all covered in Chapter 3), classes (covered in "Python Classes" on page 102), standard exception classes (covered in "Exception Objects" on page 158), and modules (covered in "Module Objects" on page 174). "The io Module" on page 273 covers the (built-in, in v2) `file` type, and "Internal Types" on page 387 covers some other built-in types intrinsic to Python's internal operation. This chapter provides additional coverage of core built-in types (in "Built-in Types" on page 198) and covers built-in functions available in the module `builtins` (named `__builtins__` in v2) in "Built-in Functions" on page 201.

As mentioned in "Python built-ins" on page 176, some modules are known as "built-in" because they are an integral part of the Python standard library (even though it takes an `import` statement to access them), as distinguished from separate, optional add-on modules, also called Python *extensions*. This chapter covers some *core* built-in modules: namely, the modules `sys` in "The sys Module" on page 212, `copy` in "The copy Module" on page 216, `collections` in "The collections Module" on page 217, `functools` in "The functools Module" on page 222, `heapq` in "The heapq Module" on page 224, `argparse` in "The argparse Module" on page 227, and `itertools` in "The itertools Module" on page 228. Chapter 8 covers some string-related core built-in modules (`string` in "The string Module" on page 239, `codecs` in "The codecs Module" on page 251, and `unicodedata` in "The unicodedata Module" on page 252), and Chapter 9 covers `re` in "Regular Expressions and the re Module" on page 253. Parts III and IV of this book cover other Python standard library modules.

Built-in Types

Table 7-1 covers Python's core built-in types, such as `int`, `float`, `dict`, and many others. More details about many of these types, and about operations on their instances, are found throughout Chapter 3. In this section, by "number" we mean, specifically, "noncomplex number."

Table 7-1. Core built-in types

bool	`bool(x=False)` Returns `False` if *x* evaluates as false; returns `True` if *x* evaluates as true. (See "Boolean Values" on page 52.) `bool` extends `int`: built-in names `False` and `True` refer to the only two instances of `bool`. These instances are also `int`s, equal to `0` and `1`, respectively, but `str(True)` is `'True'`, `str(False)` is `'False'`.
bytearray	`bytearray(x=b''[,codec[,errors]])` A mutable sequence of *bytes* (`int`s with values from `0` to `255`), supporting the usual methods of mutable sequences, plus methods of `str` (covered in Table 7-1). When *x* is a `str` in v3, or a `unicode` instance in v2, you must also pass `codec` and may pass `errors`; the result is like calling `bytearray(x.encode(codec,errors))`. When *x* is an `int`, it must be `>=0`: the resulting instance has a length of *x* and each item is initialized to `0`. When *x* conforms to the `buffer` interface, the read-only buffer of bytes from *x* initializes the instance. Otherwise, *x* must be an iterable yielding `int`s `>=0` and `<256`, which initialize the instance. For example, `bytearray([1,2,3,4])==bytearray(b'\x01\x02\x03\x04')`.
bytes	`bytes(x=b''[,codec[,errors]])` In v2, a synonym of `str`. In v3, an immutable sequence of *bytes*, with the same nonmutating methods, and the same initialization behavior, as `bytearray`. *Beware*: `bytes(2)` is `b'\x00\x00'` in v3, but `'2'` in v2!
complex	`complex(real=0,imag=0)` Converts any number, or a suitable string, to a complex number. *`imag`* may be present only when *`real`* is a number, and in that case it is the imaginary part of the resulting complex number. See also "Complex numbers" on page 44.

dict

`dict(x={})`

Returns a new dictionary with the same items as *x*. (Dictionaries are covered in "Dictionaries" on page 50.) When *x* is a `dict`, `dict(x)` returns a shallow copy of *x*, like `x.copy()`. Alternatively, *x* can be an iterable whose items are pairs (iterables with two items each). In this case, `dict(x)` returns a dictionary whose keys are the first items of each pair in *x*, and whose values are the corresponding second items. In other words, when *x* is a sequence, `c = dict(x)` is equivalent to:

```
c = {}
for key, value in x: c[key] = value
```

You can call `dict` with named arguments, in addition to, or instead of, positional argument *x*. Each named argument becomes an item in the dictionary, with the name as the key: it might overwrite an item from *x*.

float

`float(x=0.0)`

Converts any number, or a suitable string, to a floating-point number. See "Floating-point numbers" on page 44.

frozenset

`frozenset(seq=())`

Returns a new frozen (i.e., immutable) set object with the same items as iterable *seq*. When *seq* is a frozen set, `frozenset(seq)` returns *seq* itself, like `seq.copy()`. See "Set Operations" on page 67.

int

`int(x=0,radix=10)`

Converts any number, or a suitable string, to an `int`. When *x* is a number, `int` truncates toward `0`, dropping any fractional part. *radix* may be present only when *x* is a string: then, *radix* is the conversion base, between `2` and `36`, with `10` as the default. *radix* can be explicitly passed as `0`: the base is then `2`, `8`, `10`, or `16`, depending on the form of string *x*, just like for integer literals, as covered in "Integer numbers" on page 44.

list

`list(seq=())`

Returns a new list object with the same items as iterable *seq*, in the same order. When *seq* is a list, `list(seq)` returns a shallow copy of *seq*, like `seq[:]`. See "Lists" on page 49.

memoryview `memoryview(x)`

x must be an object supporting the buffer interface (for example, `bytes` and `bytearray` do; in v3 only, so do `array` instances, covered in "The array Module" on page 446). `memoryview` returns an object *m* "viewing" exactly the same underlying memory as *x*, with items of `m.itemsize` bytes each (always `1`, in v2); `len(m)` is the number of items. *m* can be indexed (returning, in v2, a `str` instance of length `1`; in v3, an `int`) and sliced (returning another instance of `memoryview` "viewing" the appropriate subset of the same underlying memory). *m* is mutable if *x* is (but *m*'s size cannot be changed, so a slice assignment must be from a sequence of the same length as the slice getting assigned).

m supplies several read-only attributes and v3-only methods; see the online docs (*https://docs.python.org/3/library/stdtypes.html#typememoryview*) for details. Two useful methods available in both v2 and 3 are `m.tobytes()` (returns *m*'s data as an instance of `bytes`) and `m.tolist()` (returns *m*'s data as a list of `int`s).

object `object()`

Returns a new instance of `object`, the most fundamental type in Python. Direct instances of type `object` have no functionality: only use of such instances is as "sentinels"—that is, objects comparing `!=` to any distinct object.

set `set(seq=())`

Returns a new mutable set object with the same items as the iterable object *seq*. When *seq* is a set, `set(seq)` returns a shallow copy of *seq*, like `seq.copy()`. See "Sets" on page 49.

slice `slice([start,]stop[,step])`

Returns a slice object with the read-only attributes `start`, `stop`, and `step` bound to the respective argument values, each defaulting to `None` when missing. For positive indices, such a slice signifies the same indices as `range(start,stop,step)`. The slicing syntax `obj[start:stop:step]` passes a slice object as the argument to the `__getitem__`, `__setitem__`, or `__delitem__` method of object *obj*. It is up to *obj*'s class to interpret the slice objects that its methods receive. See also "Container slicing" on page 133.

str `str(obj='')`

Returns a concise, readable string representation of *obj*. If *obj* is a string, `str` returns *obj*. See also `repr` in Table 7-2 and `__str__` in Table 4-1. In v2, synonym of `bytes`; in v3, equivalent to v2's `unicode`.

super `super(cls,obj)`

Returns a super-object of object *obj* (which must be an instance of class *cls* or of any subclass of *cls*), suitable for calling superclass methods. Instantiate this built-in type only within a method's code. See "Cooperative superclass method calling" on page 117. In v3, you can just call `super()`, without arguments, within a method, and Python automatically determines the *cls* and *obj* by introspection.

tuple `tuple(seq=())`

Returns a tuple with the same items as iterable *seq*, in order. When *seq* is a tuple, `tuple` returns *seq* itself, like *seq*[:]. See "Tuples" on page 48.

type `type(obj)`

Returns the type object that is the type of *obj* (i.e., the most-derived, AKA *leafmost*, type of which *obj* is an instance). `type(x)` is the same as `x.__class__` for any *x*. Avoid checking equality or identity of types: see Type checking: avoid it below.

unicode `unicode(string[,codec[,errors]])`

(v2 only.) Returns the Unicode string object built by decoding byte-string *string*, just like `string.decode(codec,errors)`. *codec* names the codec to use. If *codec* is missing, `unicode` uses the default codec (normally `'ascii'`). *errors*, if present, is a string that specifies how to handle decoding errors. See also "Unicode" on page 250, particularly for information about codecs and *errors*, and `__unicode__` in Table 4-1. In v3, Unicode strings are of type `str`.

Type checking: avoid it

Use `isinstance` (covered in Table 7-2), *not* equality comparison of types, to check whether an instance belongs to a particular class, in order to properly support inheritance. Checking `type(x)` for equality or identity to some other type object is known as *type checking*. Type checking is inappropriate in production Python code, as it interferes with polymorphism. Just try to use *x* as if it were of the type you expect, handling any problems with a `try/except` statement, as discussed in "Error-Checking Strategies" on page 166; this is known as *duck typing*.

When you just *have* to type-check, typically for debugging purposes, use `isinstance` instead. `isinstance(x,atype)`, although in a more general sense it, too, is type checking, nevertheless is a lesser evil than `type(x) is atype`, since it accepts an *x* that is an instance of any subclass of *atype*, not just a direct instance of *atype* itself. In particular, `isinstance` is perfectly fine when you're checking specifically for an ABC (abstract base class: see "Abstract Base Classes" on page 135); this newer idiom is known as *goose typing*.

Built-in Functions

Table 7-2 covers Python functions (and some types that in practice are only used as if they were functions) in the module `builtins` (in v2, `__builtins__`), in alphabetical order. Built-ins' names are *not* reserved words. You can bind, in local or global scope, an identifier that's a built-in name (although we recommend you avoid doing so; see the following warning). Names bound in local or global scope override names bound in built-in scope: local and global names *hide* built-in ones. You can also rebind names in built-in scope, as covered in "Python built-ins" on page 176.

Don't hide built-ins

Avoid accidentally hiding built-ins: your code might need them later. It's tempting to use, for your own variables, natural names such as `input`, `list`, or `filter`, but *don't do it*: these are names of built-in Python types or functions. Unless you get into the habit of *never* hiding built-ins' names with your own, sooner or later you'll get mysterious bugs in your code caused by just such hiding occurring accidentally.

Several built-in functions work in slightly different ways in v3 than they do in v2. To remove some differences, start your v2 module with `from future_builtins import *`: this makes the built-ins `ascii`, `filter`, `hex`, `map`, `oct`, and `zip` work the v3 way. (To use the built-in `print` function in v2, however, use `from __future__ import print_function`.)

Most built-ins don't accept named arguments

Most built-in functions and types cannot be called with named arguments, only with positional ones. In the following list, we specifically mention cases in which this limitation does not hold.

Table 7-2.

__import__ `__import__(`*`module_name`*`[,`*`globals`*`[,`*`locals`*`[,`*`fromlist`*`]]])`

Deprecated in modern Python; use, instead, `importlib.import_module`, covered in "Module Loading" on page 178.

abs `abs(`*`x`*`)`

Returns the absolute value of number *x*. When *x* is complex, `abs` returns the square root of *`x`*`.imag**2+`*`x`*`.real**2` (also known as the *magnitude* of the complex number). Otherwise, `abs` returns `-`*`x`* if *x* is `<0`, *x* if *x* is `>=0`. See also `__abs__`, `__invert__`, `__neg__`, `__pos__` in Table 4-4.

all `all(seq)`

seq is any iterable (often a *generator expression*; see "Generator expressions" on page 97). `all` returns `False` when any item of *seq* is false; otherwise (including when *seq* is empty), `all` returns `True`. Like operators `and` and `or`, covered in "Short-Circuiting Operators" on page 59, `all` stops evaluating, and returns a result, as soon as the answer is known; in the case of `all`, this means that evaluation stops as soon as a false item is reached, but proceeds throughout *seq* if all of *seq*'s items are true. Here is a typical toy example of the use of `all`:

```
if all(x>0 for x in the_numbers):
    print('all of the numbers are positive')
else:
    print('some of the numbers are not positive')
```

any `any(seq)`

seq is any iterable (often a *generator expression*; see "Generator expressions" on page 97). `any` returns `True` if any item of *seq* is true; otherwise (including when *seq* is empty), `any` returns `False`. Like operators `and` and `or`, covered in "Short-Circuiting Operators" on page 59, `any` stops evaluating, and returns a result, as soon as the answer is known; in the case of `any`, this means that evaluation stops as soon as a true item is reached, but proceeds throughout *seq* if all of *seq*'s items are false. Here is a typical toy example of the use of `any`:

```
if any(x<0 for x in the_numbers):
    print('some of the numbers are negative')
else:
    print('none of the numbers are negative')
```

ascii `ascii(x)`

v3 only, unless you have `from future_builtins import *` at the start of your v2 module. Like `repr`, but escapes all non-ASCII characters in the string it returns, so the result is quite similar to that of `repr` in v2.

bin `bin(x)`

Returns a binary string representation of integer *x*.

callable `callable(obj)`

Returns `True` if *obj* can be called, and otherwise `False`. An object can be called if it is a function, method, class, type, or an instance of a class with a `__call__` method. See also `__call__` in Table 4-1.

chr `chr(code)`

Returns a string of length `1`, a single character corresponding to integer *code* in Unicode (in v2, `chr` works only for *code* `< 256`; use `unichr` to avoid this limitation, and get a `unicode` instance of length `1`). See also `ord` and `unichr` in this table.

Core Built-ins and Modules

compile `compile(string,filename,kind)`

Compiles a string and returns a code object usable by `exec` or `eval`. `compile` raises `SyntaxError` when *`string`* is not syntactically valid Python. When *`string`* is a multiline compound statement, the last character must be `'\n'`. *`kind`* must be `'eval'` when *`string`* is an expression and the result is meant for `eval`; otherwise, *`kind`* must be `'exec'`. *`filename`* must be a string, used only in error messages (if any error occurs). See also `eval` in this table and "Compile and Code Objects" on page 384.

delattr `delattr(obj,name)`

Removes the attribute *name* from *`obj`*. `delattr(obj,'ident')` is like `del obj.ident`. If *`obj`* has an attribute named *name* just because its class has it (as is normally the case, for example, with methods of *`obj`*), you cannot delete that attribute from *`obj`* itself. You may be able to delete that attribute from the *class*, if the metaclass lets you. If you can delete the class attribute, *`obj`* ceases to have the attribute, and so does every other instance of that class.

dir `dir([obj])`

Called without arguments, `dir` returns a sorted list of all variable names that are bound in the current scope. `dir(obj)` returns a sorted list of names of attributes of *`obj`*, including ones coming from *`obj`*'s type or by inheritance. See also `vars` in this table.

divmod `divmod(dividend,divisor)`

Divides two numbers and returns a pair whose items are the quotient and remainder. See also `__divmod__` in Table 4-4.

enumerate `enumerate(iterable,start=0)`

Returns a new iterator object whose items are pairs. For each such pair, the second item is the corresponding item in *`iterable`*, while the first item is an integer: *`start`*, *`start`*`+1`, *`start`*`+2`.... For example, the following snippet loops on a list `L` of integers, changing `L` in-place by halving every even value:

```
for i, num in enumerate(L):
    if num % 2 == 0:
        L[i] = num // 2
```

eval `eval(expr,[globals[,locals]])`

Returns the result of an expression. *expr* may be a code object ready for evaluation, or a string; if a string, `eval` gets a code object by internally calling `compile(expr, '<string>', 'eval')`. `eval` evaluates the code object as an expression, using the *`globals`* and *`locals`* dictionaries as namespaces. When both arguments are missing, `eval` uses the current namespace. `eval` cannot execute statements; it only evaluates expressions. Nevertheless, `eval` is dangerous unless you know and trust that *expr* comes from a source that you are certain is safe. See also "Expressions" on page 384 and `ast.literal_eval`, covered in "Standard Input" on page 318.

exec `exec(statement,[globals[,locals]])`

In v3, like `eval`, but applies to any statement and returns `None`. In v2, `exec` works similarly, but it's a statement, not a function. In either version, `exec` is dangerous unless you know and trust that *statement* comes from a source that you are certain is safe. See also "Statements" on page 42.

filter `filter(func,seq)`

In v2, returns a list of those items of *seq* for which *func* is true. *func* can be any callable object accepting a single argument, or `None`. *seq* can be any iterable. When *func* is callable, `filter` calls *func* on each item of *seq*, just like the following list comprehension:

```
[item for item in seq if func(item)]
```

In v2, when *seq* is a string or tuple, `filter`'s result is also a string or tuple rather than a list. When *func* is `None`, `filter` tests for true items, just like:

```
[item for item in seq if item]
```

In v3, whatever the type of *seq*, `filter` returns an iterator, rather than a list (or other sequence type) as in v2; therefore, in v3, `filter` is equivalent to a generator expression rather than to a list comprehension.

format `format(x,format_spec='')`

Returns `x.__format__(format_spec)`. See Table 4-1.

getattr `getattr(obj,name[,default])`

Returns *obj*'s attribute named by string *name*. `getattr(obj, 'ident')` is like `obj.ident`. When *default* is present and *name* is not found in *obj*, `getattr` returns *default* instead of raising `AttributeError`. See also "Object attributes and items" on page 53 and "Attribute Reference Basics" on page 110.

globals `globals()`

Returns the `__dict__` of the calling module (i.e., the dictionary used as the global namespace at the point of call). See also `locals` in this table.

hasattr `hasattr(obj,name)`

Returns `False` when *obj* has no attribute *name* (i.e., when `getattr(obj,name)` raises `AttributeError`). Otherwise, `hasattr` returns `True`. See also "Attribute Reference Basics" on page 110.

hash `hash(obj)`

Returns the hash value for *obj*. *obj* can be a dictionary key, or an item in a set, only if *obj* can be hashed. All objects that compare equal must have the same hash value, even if they are of different types. If the type of *obj* does not define equality comparison, `hash(obj)` normally returns `id(obj)`. See also `__hash__` in Table 4-1.

hex `hex(x)`

Returns a hexadecimal string representation of integer *x*. See also __hex__ in Table 4-4.

id `id(obj)`

Returns the integer value that denotes the identity of *obj*. The `id` of *obj* is unique and constant during *obj*'s lifetime (but may be reused at any later time after *obj* is garbage-collected, so, don't rely on storing or checking `id` values). When a type or class does not define equality comparison, Python uses `id` to compare and hash instances. For any objects *x* and *y*, identity check *x* `is` *y* is the same as `id(x)==id(y)`, but more readable and better-performing.

input `input(prompt='')`

In v2, `input(prompt)` is a shortcut for `eval(raw_input(prompt))`. In other words, in v2, `input` prompts the user for a line of input, evaluates the resulting string as an expression, and returns the expression's result. The implicit `eval` may raise `SyntaxError` or other exceptions. `input` is rather user-unfriendly and inappropriate for most programs, but it can sometimes be handy for small experiments and small exploratory scripts. See also `eval` and `raw_input` in this table.

In v3, `input` is equivalent to v2's `raw_input`—that is, it always returns a `str` and does no `eval`.

intern `intern(string)`

Ensures that *string* is held in a table of interned strings and returns *string* itself or a copy. Interned strings may compare for equality slightly faster than other strings because you can use operator `is` instead of operator == for such comparisons. However, garbage collection can never recover the memory used for interned strings, so interning strings can slow down your program by making it take up too much memory. We do not cover interned strings in this book. In v3, function `intern` is not a built-in: rather, it lives, more appropriately, in the module `sys`.

isinstance `isinstance(obj,cls)`

Returns `True` when *obj* is an instance of class *cls* (or of any subclass of *cls*); otherwise, it returns `False`. *cls* can be a tuple whose items are classes: in this case, `isinstance` returns `True` if *obj* is an instance of any of the items of *cls*; otherwise, it returns `False`. See also "Abstract Base Classes" on page 135.

issubclass `issubclass(cls1,cls2)`

Returns `True` when *cls1* is a direct or indirect subclass of *cls2*; otherwise, it returns `False`. *cls1* and *cls2* must be classes. *cls2* can also be a tuple whose items are classes. In this case, `issubclass` returns `True` when *cls1* is a direct or indirect subclass of any of the items of *cls2*; otherwise, it returns `False`. For any class *C*, `issubclass(C,C)` returns `True`.

iter `iter(obj) iter(func,sentinel)`

Creates and returns an *iterator*, an object that you can repeatedly pass to the `next` built-in function to get one item at a time (see "Iterators" on page 76). When called with one argument, `iter(obj)` normally returns `obj.__iter__()`. When `obj` is a sequence without a special method `__iter__`, `iter(obj)` is equivalent to the generator:

```
def iter_sequence(obj):
    i = 0
    while True:
        try: yield obj[i]
        except IndexError: raise StopIteration
        i += 1
```

See also "Sequences" on page 45 and `__iter__` in Table 4-2.

When called with two arguments, the first argument must be callable without arguments, and `iter(func,sentinel)` is equivalent to the generator:

```
def iter_sentinel(func, sentinel):
    while True:
        item = func()
        if item == sentinel: raise StopIteration
        yield item
```

Don't call iter in a for clause

As discussed in "The for Statement" on page 74, the statement `for x in obj` is exactly equivalent to `for x in iter(obj)`; therefore, do *not* call `iter` in such a `for` statement: it would be redundant, and therefore bad Python style, slower, and less readable.

`iter` is *idempotent*. In other words, when *x* is an iterator, `iter(x)` is *x*, as long as *x*'s class supplies an `__iter__` method whose body is just `return self`, as an iterator's class should.

len `len(container)`

Returns the number of items in `container`, which may be a sequence, a mapping, or a set. See also `__len__` in "Container methods" on page 134.

locals `locals()`

Returns a dictionary that represents the current local namespace. Treat the returned dictionary as read-only; trying to modify it may or may not affect the values of local variables, and might raise an exception. See also `globals` and `vars` in this table.

map `map(func,seq,*seqs)`

`map` calls *func* on every item of iterable *seq* and returns the sequence of results. When `map` is called with *n*+1 arguments, the first one, *func*, can be any callable object that accepts *n* arguments; all remaining arguments to `map` must be iterable. `map` repeatedly calls *func* with *n* arguments (one corresponding item from each iterable).

In v3, `map` returns an iterator yielding the results. For example, `map(func, seq)` is just like the generator expression `(func(item) for item in seq)`. When `map`'s iterable arguments have different lengths, in v3, `map` acts as if the longer ones were truncated.

In v2, `map` returns a list of the results. For example, `map(func, seq)` is just like the list comprehension `[func(item) for item in seq]`. When `map`'s iterable arguments have different lengths, in v2, `map` acts as if the shorter ones were padded with `None`. Further, in v2 only, *func* can be `None`: in this case, each result is a tuple with *n* items (one item from each iterable).

max `max(s,*args,key=None[,default=...])`

Returns the largest item in the only positional argument *s* (*s* must then be iterable) or the largest one of multiple arguments. `max` is one of the built-in functions that you can call with named arguments: specifically, you can pass a `key=` argument, with the same semantics covered in "Sorting a list" on page 66. In v3 only, you can also pass a `default=` argument, the value to return if the only positional argument *s* is empty; when you don't pass `default`, and `s` is empty, `max` raises `ValueError`.

min `min(s,*args,key=None[,default=...])`

Returns the smallest item in the only positional argument *s* (*s* must then be iterable) or the smallest one of multiple arguments. `min` is one of the built-in functions that you can call with named arguments: specifically, you can pass a `key=` argument, with the same semantics covered in "Sorting a list" on page 66. In v3 only, you can also pass a `default=` argument, the value to return if the only positional argument *s* is empty; when you don't pass `default`, and `s` is empty, `min` raises `ValueError`.

next `next(it[,default])`

Returns the next item from iterator *it*, which advances to the next item. When *it* has no more items, `next` returns *default*, or, when you don't pass *default*, raises `StopIteration`.

oct `oct(x)`

Converts integer *x* to an octal string representation. See also `__oct__` in Table 4-4.

open `open(filename,mode='r',bufsize=-1)`

Opens or creates a file and returns a new file object. In v3, `open` accepts many optional parameters, and, in v2, you can `from io import open` to override the built-in function `open` with one very similar to v3's. See "The io Module" on page 273.

ord `ord(ch)`

In v2, returns the ASCII/ISO integer code between `0` and `255` (inclusive) for the single-character `str` *ch*. When, in v2, *ch* is of type `unicode` (and always, in v3), `ord` returns an integer code between `0` and `sys.maxunicode` (inclusive). See also `chr` and `unichr` in this table.

pow `pow(x,y[,z])`

When *z* is present, `pow(x,y,z)` returns *x****y*%*z*. When *z* is missing, `pow(x,y)` returns *x****y*. See also __pow__ in Table 4-4.

print `print(value, ..., sep=' ', end='\n', file=sys.stdout, flush=False)`

In v3, formats with `str`, and emits to stream `file`, each *value*, separated by `sep`, with `end` after all of them (then flushes the stream if `flush` is true). In v2, `print` is a statement, unless you start your module with `from __future__ import print_function`, as we *highly* recommend (and which we assume in *every* example in this book), in which case `print` works just as it does in v3.

range `range([start,]stop[,step=1])`

In v2, returns a list of integers in arithmetic progression:

```
[start, start+step, start+2*step, ...]
```

When *start* is missing, it defaults to `0`. When *step* is missing, it defaults to `1`. When *step* is `0`, `range` raises `ValueError`. When *step* is greater than `0`, the last item is the largest *start+i*step* strictly less than *stop*. When *step* is less than `0`, the last item is the smallest *start+i*step* strictly greater than *stop*. The result is an empty list when *start* is greater than or equal to *stop* and *step* is greater than `0`, or when *start* is less than or equal to *stop* and *step* is less than `0`. Otherwise, the first item of the result list is always *start*. See also `xrange` in this table.

In v3, `range` is a built-in type, a compact and efficient representation of the equivalent of a *read-only* list of integers in arithmetic progression; it is equivalent to v2's `range` or `xrange` in most practical uses, but more efficient. If you do need specifically a `list` in arithmetic progression, in v3, call `list(range(...))`.

raw_input `raw_input(prompt='')`

v2 only: writes *prompt* to standard output, reads a line from standard input, and returns the line (without `\n`) as a string. When at end-of-file, `raw_input` raises `EOFError`. See also `input` in this table. In v3, this function is named `input`.

reduce `reduce(func,seq[,init])`

(In v3, function `reduce` is not a built-in: rather, it lives in the module `functools`.) Applies *func* to the items of *seq*, from left to right, to reduce the iterable to a single value. *func* must be callable with two arguments. `reduce` calls *func* on the first two items of *seq*, then on the result of the first call and the third item, and so on. `reduce` returns the result of the last such call. When *init* is present, it is used before *seq*'s first item, if any. When *init* is missing, *seq* must be nonempty. When *init* is missing and *seq* has only one item, `reduce` returns *seq*`[0]`. Similarly, when *init* is present and *seq* is empty, `reduce` returns *init*. `reduce` is thus roughly equivalent to:

```
def reduce_equivalent(func,seq,init=None):
    seq = iter(seq)
    if init is None: init = next(seq)
    for item in seq: init = func(init,item)
    return init
```

An example use of `reduce` is to compute the product of a sequence of numbers:

```
theprod = reduce(operator.mul, seq, 1)
```

reload `reload(module)`

Reloads and reinitializes the module object *module*, and returns *module*. In v3, function `reload` is not a built-in: rather, it lives in module `imp` in early versions of Python 3, `importlib` in current ones, 3.4, and later.

repr `repr(obj)`

Returns a complete and unambiguous string representation of *obj*. When feasible, `repr` returns a string that you can pass to `eval` in order to create a new object with the same value as *obj*. See also `str` in Table 7-1 and `__repr__` in Table 4-1.

reversed `reversed(seq)`

Returns a new iterator object that yields the items of *seq* (which must be specifically a sequence, not just any iterable) in reverse order.

round `round(x,n=0)`

Returns a `float` whose value is number *x* rounded to *n* digits after the decimal point (i.e., the multiple of `10**-`*n* that is closest to *x*). When two such multiples are equally close to *x*, `round`, in v2, returns the one that is farther from `0`; in v3, `round` returns the *even* multiple. Since today's computers represent floating-point numbers in binary, not in decimal, most of `round`'s results are not exact, as the online tutorial (*https://docs.python.org/3/tutorial/floatingpoint.html*) explains in detail. See also "The decimal Module" on page 444.

setattr `setattr(obj,name,value)`

Binds *obj*'s attribute *name* to *value*. `setattr(obj,'ident',val)` is like *obj*`.`*ident*`=`*val*. See also built-in `getattr` covered in this table, "Object attributes and items" on page 53, and "Setting an attribute" on page 112.

sorted `sorted(seq,cmp=None,key=None,reverse=False)`

Returns a list with the same items as iterable *seq*, in sorted order. Same as:

```
def sorted(seq,cmp=None,key=None,reverse=False):
    result = list(seq)
    result.sort(cmp,key,reverse)
    return result
```

Argument `cmp` exists only in v2, not in v3; see `cmp_to_key` in Table 7-4. See "Sorting a list" on page 66 for the meaning of the arguments; `sorted` is one of the built-in functions that's callable with named arguments, specifically so you can optionally pass `key=` and/or `reverse=`.

sum `sum(seq,start=0)`

Returns the sum of the items of iterable *seq* (which should be numbers, and, in particular, cannot be strings) plus the value of *start*. When *seq* is empty, returns *start*. To "sum" (concatenate) an iterable of strings, in order, use `''.join(iterofstrs)`, as covered in Table 8-1 and "Building up a string from pieces" on page 490.

unichr `unichr(code)`

v2 only: returns a Unicode string whose single character corresponds to *code*, where *code* is an integer between `0` and `sys.maxunicode` (inclusive). See also `str` and `ord` in Table 7-1. In v3, use `chr` for this purpose.

vars `vars([obj])`

When called with no argument, `vars` returns a dictionary with all variables that are bound in the current scope (like `locals`, covered in this table). Treat this dictionary as read-only. `vars(obj)` returns a dictionary with all attributes currently bound in *obj*, as covered in `dir` in this table. This dictionary may be modifiable, depending on the type of *obj*.

xrange `xrange([start,]stop[,step=1])`

v2 only: an iterable of integers in arithmetic progression, and otherwise similar to `range`. In v3, `range` plays this role. See `range` in this table.

zip `zip(seq,*seqs)`

In v2, returns a list of tuples, where the *n*th tuple contains the *n*th element from each of the argument sequences. `zip` must be called with at least one argument, and all arguments must be iterable. If the iterables have different lengths, `zip` returns a list as long as the shortest iterable, ignoring trailing items in the other iterable objects. See also `map` in this table and `izip_longest` in Table 7-5. In v3, `zip` returns an iterator, rather than a list, and therefore it's equivalent to a generator expression rather than to a list comprehension.

The sys Module

The attributes of the sys module are bound to data and functions that provide information on the state of the Python interpreter or affect the interpreter directly. Table 7-3 covers the most frequently used attributes of sys, in alphabetical order. Most sys attributes we don't cover are meant specifically for use in debuggers, profilers, and integrated development environments; see the online docs (*https://docs.python.org/3/library/sys.html*) for more information. Platform-specific information is best accessed using the `platform` module, covered online (*https://docs.python.org/3/library/platform.html?highlight=platform%20module#module-platform*), which we do not cover in this book.

Table 7-3.

argv	The list of command-line arguments passed to the main script. `argv[0]` is the name or full path of the main script, or `'-c'` if the command line used the **-c** option. See "The argparse Module" on page 227 for one good way to use `sys.argv`.
byteorder	`'little'` on little-endian platforms, `'big'` on big-endian ones. See Wikipedia (*https://en.wikipedia.org/wiki/Endianness*) for more information on endianness.
builtin_module_names	A tuple of strings, the name of all the modules compiled into this Python interpreter.

displayhook	`displayhook(value)`
	In interactive sessions, the Python interpreter calls `displayhook`, passing it the result of each expression statement you enter. The default `displayhook` does nothing if *value* is None; otherwise, it preserves (in the built-in variable _), and displays via `repr`, *value*:
	`def _default_sys_displayhook(value):`
	`    if value is not None:`
	`        __builtins__._ = value`
	`        print(repr(value))`
	You can rebind `sys.displayhook` in order to change interactive behavior. The original value is available as `sys.__displayhook__`.

dont_write_bytecode	If true, Python does not write a bytecode file (with extension *.pyc* or, in v2, *.pyo*) to disk, when it imports a source file (with extension *.py*). Handy, for example, when importing from a read-only filesystem.

exceptHook

`excepthook(type,value,traceback)`

When an exception is not caught by any handler, propagating all the way up the call stack, Python calls `excepthook`, passing it the exception class, object, and traceback, as covered in "Exception Propagation" on page 155. The default `excepthook` displays the error and traceback. You can rebind `sys.excepthook` to change how uncaught exceptions (just before Python returns to the interactive loop or terminates) are displayed and/or logged. The original value is available as `sys.__excepthook__`.

exc_info

`exc_info()`

If the current thread is handling an exception, `exc_info` returns a tuple with three items: the class, object, and traceback for the exception. If the current thread is not handling an exception, `exc_info` returns `(None,None,None)`. To display information from a traceback, see "The traceback Module" on page 472.

Holding on to a traceback object can make some garbage uncollectable

A traceback object indirectly holds references to all variables on the call stack; if you hold a reference to the traceback (e.g., indirectly, by binding a variable to the tuple that `exc_info` returns), Python must keep in memory data that might otherwise be garbage-collected. Make sure that any binding to the traceback object is of short duration, for example with a `try/finally` statement (discussed in "try/finally" on page 152).

exit

`exit(arg=0)`

Raises a `SystemExit` exception, which normally terminates execution after executing cleanup handlers installed by `try/finally` statements, `with` statements, and the `atexit` module. When *arg* is an `int`, Python uses *arg* as the program's exit code: `0` indicates successful termination, while any other value indicates unsuccessful termination of the program. Most platforms require exit codes to be between `0` and `127`. When *arg* is not an `int`, Python prints *arg* to `sys.stderr`, and the exit code of the program is `1` (a generic "unsuccessful termination" code).

float_info

A read-only object whose attributes hold low-level details about the implementation of the `float` type in this Python interpreter. See the online docs (*https://docs.python.org/3/library/sys.html#sys.float_info*) for details.

getrefcount `getrefcount(object)`

Returns the reference count of *`object`*. Reference counts are covered in "Garbage Collection" on page 388.

getrecursionlimit `getrecursionlimit()`

Returns the current limit on the depth of Python's call stack. See also "Recursion" on page 98 and `setrecursionlimit` in this table.

getsizeof `getsizeof(obj,[default])`

Returns the size in bytes of *`obj`* (not counting any items or attributes *`obj`* may refer to), or *`default`* when *`obj`* does not provide a way to retrieve its size (in the latter case, when *`default`* is absent, `getsizeof` raises `TypeError`).

maxint (v2 only.) The largest `int` in this version of Python (at least `2**31-1`; that is, `2147483647`). Negative `int`s can go down to `-maxint-1`, due to two's complement representation (*https://en.wikipedia.org/wiki/Two%27s_complement*). In v3, an `int` is of unbounded size (like a `long` in v2), so there *is* no "largest" `int`.

maxsize Maximum number of bytes in an object in this version of Python (at least `2**31-1`; that is, `2147483647`).

maxunicode The largest codepoint for a Unicode character in this version of Python (at least `2**16-1`, that is, `65535`). In v3, always `1114111` (`0x10FFFF`).

modules A dictionary whose items are the names and module objects for all loaded modules. See "Module Loading" on page 178 for more information on `sys.modules`.

path A list of strings that specifies the directories and ZIP files that Python searches when looking for a module to load. See "Searching the Filesystem for a Module" on page 179 for more information on `sys.path`.

platform A string that names the platform on which this program is running. Typical values are brief operating system names, such as `'darwin'`, `'linux2'`, and `'win32'`. To check for Linux specifically, use `sys.platform.startswith('linux')`, for portability among Linux versions and between v2 and v3.

ps1, ps2

ps1 and ps2 specify the primary and secondary interpreter prompt strings, initially '>>> ' and '... ', respectively. These attributes exist only in interactive interpreter sessions. If you bind either attribute to a nonstring object *x*, Python prompts by calling str(*x*) on the object each time a prompt is output. This feature allows dynamic prompting: code a class that defines __str__, then assign an instance of that class to sys.ps1 and/or sys.ps2. For example, to get numbered prompts:

```
>>> import sys
>>> class Ps1(object):
...   def __init__(self):
...     self.p = 0
...   def __str__(self):
...     self.p += 1
...     return '[{}]>>> '.format(self.p)
...
>>> class Ps2(object):
...   def __str__(self):
...     return '[{}]... '.format(sys.ps1.p)
...
>>> sys.ps1 = Ps1(); sys.ps2 = Ps2()
[1]>>> (2 +
[1]... 2)
4
[2]>>>
```

setrecursionlimit

setrecursionlimit(*limit*)

Sets the limit on the depth of Python's call stack (the default is 1000). The limit prevents runaway recursion from crashing Python. Raising the limit may be necessary for programs that rely on deep recursion, but most platforms cannot support very large limits on call-stack depth. More usefully, *lowering* the limit may help you check, during testing and debugging, that your program is gracefully degrading, rather than abruptly crashing with a RuntimeError, under situations of almost-runaway recursion. See also "Recursion" on page 98 and getrecursionlimit in this table.

stdin, stdout, stderr

stdin, stdout, and stderr are predefined file-like objects that correspond to Python's standard input, output, and error streams. You can rebind stdout and stderr to file-like objects open for writing (objects that supply a write method accepting a string argument) to redirect the destination of output and error messages. You can rebind stdin to a file-like object open for reading (one that supplies a readline method returning a string) to redirect the source from which built-in functions raw_input (v2 only) and input read. The original values are available as __stdin__, __stdout__, and __stderr__. File objects are covered in "The io Module" on page 273.

tracebacklimit

The maximum number of levels of traceback displayed for unhandled exceptions. By default, this attribute is not set (i.e., there is no limit). When sys.tracebacklimit is <=0, Python prints only the exception type and value, without traceback.

version A string that describes the Python version, build number and date, and C compiler used. `sys.version[:3]` is `'2.7'` for Python 2.7, `'3.5'` for Python 3.5, and so on.

The copy Module

As discussed in "Assignment Statements" on page 53, assignment in Python does not copy the righthand-side object being assigned. Rather, assignment adds a reference to the righthand-side object. When you want a copy of object *x*, you can ask *x* for a copy of itself, or you can ask *x*'s type to make a new instance copied from *x*. If *x* is a list, `list(x)` returns a copy of *x*, as does `x[:]`. If *x* is a dictionary, `dict(x)` and `x.copy()` return a copy of *x*. If *x* is a set, `set(x)` and `x.copy()` return a copy of *x*. In each case, we think it's best to use the uniform and readable idiom of calling the type, but there is no consensus on this style issue in the Python community.

The `copy` module supplies a `copy` function to create and return a copy of many types of objects. Normal copies, such as `list(x)` for a list *x* and `copy.copy(x)`, are known as *shallow* copies: when *x* has references to other objects (either as items or as attributes), a normal (shallow) copy of *x* has distinct references to the same objects. Sometimes, however, you need a *deep* copy, where referenced objects are deep-copied recursively; fortunately, this need is rare, since a deep copy can take a lot of memory and time. The `copy` module supplies a `deepcopy` function to create and return a deep copy.

copy `copy(x)`

Creates and returns a shallow copy of *x*, for *x* of many types (copies of several types, such as modules, classes, files, frames, and other internal types, are, however, not supported). If *x* is immutable, `copy.copy(x)` may return *x* itself as an optimization. A class can customize the way `copy.copy` copies its instances by having a special method `__copy__(self)` that returns a new object, a shallow copy of `self`.

deepcopy `deepcopy(x,[memo])`

Makes a deep copy of *x* and returns it. Deep copying implies a recursive walk (*https://en.wikipedia.org/wiki/Glossary_of_graph_theory#Walks*) over a directed (not necessarily acyclic) graph of references. A special precaution is needed to reproduce the graph's exact shape: when references to the same object are met more than once during the walk, distinct copies must not be made. Rather, references to the same copied object must be used. Consider the following simple example:

```
sublist = [1,2]
original = [sublist, sublist]
thecopy = copy.deepcopy(original)
```

`original[0] is original[1]` is `True` (i.e., the two items of `original` refer to the same object). This is an important property of `original` and anything claiming to "be a copy" must preserve it. The semantics of `copy.deepcopy` ensure that `thecopy[0] is thecopy[1]` is also `True`: the graphs of references of `original` and `thecopy` have the same shape. Avoiding repeated copying has an important beneficial side effect: it prevents infinite loops that would otherwise occur when the graph of references has cycles.

`copy.deepcopy` accepts a second, optional argument *memo*, a `dict` that maps the `id` of objects already copied to the new objects that are their copies. *memo* is passed by all recursive calls of `deepcopy` to itself; you may also explicitly pass it (normally as an originally empty `dict`) if you need to maintain a correspondence map between the identities of originals and copies.

A class can customize the way `copy.deepcopy` copies its instances by having a special method `__deepcopy__(self, memo)` that returns a new object, a deep copy of `self`. When `__deepcopy__` needs to deep copy some referenced object *`subobject`*, it must do so by calling `copy.deepcopy(subobject, memo)`. When a class has no special method `__deepcopy__`, `copy.deepcopy` on an instance of that class also tries calling the special methods `__getinitargs__`, `__getnewargs__`, `__getstate__`, and `__setstate__`, covered in "Pickling instances" on page 345.

The collections Module

The `collections` module supplies useful types that are collections (i.e., containers), as well as the *abstract base classes* (ABCs) covered in "Abstract Base Classes" on page 135. Since Python 3.4, the ABCs are in `collections.abc` (but, for backward compatibility, can still be accessed directly in `collections` itself: the latter access will cease working in some future release of v3).

ChainMap (v3 Only)

`ChainMap` "chains" multiple mappings together; given a `ChainMap` instance *c*, accessing `c[key]` returns the value in the first of the mappings that has that key, while *all* changes to *c* only affect the very first mapping in *c*. In v2, you could approximate this as follows:

```
class ChainMap(collections.MutableMapping):
    def __init__(self, *maps):
        self.maps = list(maps)
        self._keys = set()
        for m in self.maps: self._keys.update(m)
    def __len__(self): return len(self._keys)
    def __iter__(self): return iter(self._keys)
    def __getitem__(self, key):
        if key not in self._keys: raise KeyError(key)
        for m in self.maps:
            try: return m[key]
            except KeyError: pass
    def __setitem__(self, key, value)
        self.maps[0][key] = value
        self._keys.add(key)
    def __delitem__(self, key)
        del self.maps[0][key]
        self._keys = set()
        for m in self.maps: self._keys.update(m)
```

Other methods could be defined for efficiency, but this is the minimum set that `MutableMapping` requires. A stable, production-level backport of `ChainMap` to v2 (and early versions of Python 3) is available on PyPI (*https://pypi.python.org/pypi/chainmap/*) and can therefore be installed like all PyPI modules—for example, by running **`pip install chainmap`**.

See the ChainMap documentation in the online Python docs (*https://docs.python.org/3/library/collections.html?highlight=collections#collections.ChainMap*) for more details and a collection of "recipes" on how to use `ChainMap`.

Counter

`Counter` is a subclass of `dict` with `int` values that are meant to *count* how many times the key has been seen (although values are allowed to be `<=0`); it roughly corresponds to types that other languages call "bag" or "multi-set." A `Counter` instance is normally built from an iterable whose items are hashable: `c = collections.Counter(`*`iterable`*`)`. Then, you can index *c* with any of *`iterable`*'s items, to get the number of times that item appeared. When you index *c* with any missing key, the result is `0` (to remove an entry in *c*, use `del c[`*`entry`*`]`; setting `c[`*`entry`*`] = 0` leaves *`entry`* in *c*, just with a corresponding value of `0`).

c supports all methods of `dict`; in particular, `c.update(`*`otheriterable`*`)` updates all the counts, incrementing them according to occurrences in *`otheriterable`*. So, for example:

```
c = collections.Counter('moo')
c.update('foo')
```

leaves `c['o']` giving 4, and `c['f']` and `c['m']` each giving 1.

In addition to `dict` methods, *c* supports three extra methods:

elements `c.elements()`

Yields, in arbitrary order, keys in *c* with `c[key]>0`, yielding each key as many times as its count.

most_common `c.most_common([n])`

Returns a list of pairs for the *n* keys in *c* with the highest counts (all of them, if you omit *n*) in order of decreasing count ("ties" between keys with the same count are resolved arbitrarily); each pair is of the form `(k, c[k])` where *k* is one of the *n* most common keys in *c*.

subtract `c.subtract(iterable)`

Like `c.update(iterable)` "in reverse"—that is, *subtracting* counts rather than *adding* them. Resulting counts in *c* can be `<=0`.

See the Counter documentation in the online Python docs (*https://docs.python.org/3/library/collections.html?highlight=collections#collections.Counter*) for more details and a collection of useful "recipes" on how to use `Counter`.

OrderedDict

`OrderedDict` is a subclass of `dict` that remembers the order in which keys were originally inserted (assigning a new value for an existing key does not change the order, but removing a key and inserting it again does). Given an `OrderedDict` instance *o*, iterating on *o* yields keys in order of insertion (oldest to newest key), and `o.popitem()` removes and returns the item at the key most recently inserted. Equality tests between two instances of `OrderedDict` are order-sensitive; equality tests between an instance of `OrderedDict` and a `dict` or other mapping are not. See the OrderedDict documentation in the online Python docs (*https://docs.python.org/3/library/collections.html?highlight=collections#ordereddict-objects*) for more details and a collection of "recipes" on how to use `OrderedDict`.

defaultdict

`defaultdict` extends `dict` and adds one per-instance attribute, named `default_factory`. When an instance *d* of `defaultdict` has `None` as the value of `d.default_factory`, *d* behaves exactly like a `dict`. Otherwise, `d.default_factory` must be callable without arguments, and *d* behaves just like a `dict` except when you access *d* with a key *k* that is not `in` *d*. In this specific case, the indexing `d[k]` calls `d.default_factory()`, assigns the result as the value of `d[k]`, and returns the result. In other words, the type `defaultdict` behaves much like the following Python-coded class:

```
class defaultdict(dict):
    def __init__(self, default_factory, *a, **k):
        dict.__init__(self, *a, **k)
```

```
        self.default_factory = default_factory
    def __getitem__(self, key):
        if key not in self and self.default_factory is not None:
            self[key] = self.default_factory()
        return dict.__getitem__(self, key)
```

As this Python equivalent implies, to instantiate `defaultdict` you pass it an extra first argument (before any other arguments, positional and/or named, if any, to be passed on to plain `dict`). That extra first argument becomes the initial value of `default_factory`; you can access and rebind `default_factory` .

All behavior of `defaultdict` is essentially as implied by this Python equivalent (except `str` and `repr`, which return strings different from those they'd return for a `dict`). Named methods, such as `get` and `pop`, are not affected. All behavior related to keys (method `keys`, iteration, membership test via operator `in`, etc.) reflects exactly the keys that are currently in the container (whether you put them there explicitly, or implicitly via an indexing that called `default_factory`).

A typical use of `defaultdict` is to set `default_factory` to `list`, to make a mapping from keys to lists of values:

```
def make_multi_dict(items):
    d = collections.defaultdict(list)
    for key, value in items: d[key].append(value)
    return d
```

Called with any iterable whose items are pairs of the form (*key*,*value*), with all keys being hashable, this *make_multi_dict* function returns a mapping that associates each key to the lists of one or more values that accompanied it in the iterable (if you want a pure `dict` result, change the last statement into `return dict(d)`—this is rarely necessary).

If you don't want duplicates in the result, and every `value` is hashable, use a `collections.defaultdict(set)`, and `add` rather than `append` in the loop.

deque

deque `deque(`*seq*`=(), `*maxlen*`=None)`

`deque` is a sequence type whose instances are "double-ended queues" (additions and removals at either end are fast). A `deque` instance *d* is a mutable sequence and can be indexed and iterated on (however, *d* cannot be sliced, only indexed one item at a time, whether for access, rebinding, or deletion). The initial items of *d* are those of *seq*, in the same order. *d*`.maxlen` is a read-only attribute: when `None`, *d* has no maximum length; when an `int`, it must be `>=0`, and *d*'s length is limited to *d*`.maxlen` (when too many items are added, items are silently dropped from the other side)—a useful data type to maintain "the latest *N* things seen," also known in other languages as a *ring buffer*.

d supplies the following methods:

append `d.append(item)`

Appends *item* at the right (end) of *d*.

appendleft `d.appendleft(item)`

Appends *item* at the left (start) of *d*.

clear `d.clear()`

Removes all items from *d*, leaving it empty.

extend `d.extend(iterable)`

Appends all items of *iterable* at the right (end) of *d*.

extendleft `d.extendleft(item)`

Appends all items of *iterable* at the left (start) of *d* in reverse order.

pop `d.pop()`

Removes and returns the last (rightmost) item from *d*. If *d* is empty, raises `IndexError`.

popleft `d.popleft()`

Removes and returns the first (leftmost) item from *d*. If *d* is empty, raises `IndexError`.

rotate `d.rotate(n=1)`

Rotates *d* *n* steps to the right (if *n*<0, rotates left).

namedtuple

`namedtuple` is a factory function, building and returning a subclass of `tuple` whose instances' items you can access by attribute reference, as well as by index.

namedtuple `namedtuple(typename,fieldnames)`

typename is a string that's a valid identifier (starts with a letter, may continue with letters, digits, and underscores; can't be a reserved word such as `'class'`) and names the new type that `namedtuple` builds and returns. *fieldnames* is a sequence of strings that are valid identifiers and name the new type's attributes, in order (for convenience, *fieldnames* can also be a single string with identifiers separated by spaces or commas). `namedtuple` returns a type: you can bind that type to a name, then use it to make immutable instances initialized with either positional or named arguments. Calling `repr` or `str` on those instances formats them in named-argument style. For example:

```
point = collections.namedtuple('point', 'x,y,z')
p = point(x=1,y=2,z=3)   # can build with named arguments
x, y, z = p               # can unpack like a normal tuple
if p.x < p.y:             # can access items as attributes
    print(p)              # formats with named argument
# prints point(x=1, y=2, z=3)
```

A `namedtuple` such as *point* and its instances such as *p* also supply attributes and methods (whose names start with an underscore only to avoid conflicts with field names, *not* to indicate they are in any way "private"):

_asdict `p._asdict()`

Returns a `dict` whose keys are *p*'s field names, with values from *p*'s corresponding items.

_fields `point._fields`

Returns a tuple of field name strings, here `('x', 'y', 'z')`.

_make `point._make(seq)`

Returns a *point* instance with items initialized from iterable *seq*, in order (`len(seq)` must equal `len(point._fields)`).

_replace `p._replace(**kwargs)`

Returns a copy of *p*, with `0` or more items replaced as per the named arguments.

For more details and advice about using `namedtuple`, see the online docs (*http://bit.ly/2nBbGfK*).

The functools Module

The `functools` module supplies functions and types supporting functional programming in Python, listed in Table 7-4.

Table 7-4.

cmp_to_key `cmp_to_key(func)`

func must be callable with two arguments and return a number: `<0` if the first argument is to be considered "less than" the second one, `>0` if vice versa, `0` if the two arguments are to be considered equal (like the old `cmp` built-in function, deprecated in v2 and removed in v3, and the old `cmp=` named argument to `sort` and `sorted`). `cmp_to_key` returns a callable *k* suitable as the `key=` named argument to functions and methods such as `sort`, `sorted`, `min`, `max`, and so on. This is useful to convert programs using old-style `cmp=`

arguments to new-style key= ones, which is required to use v3 and highly recommended in v2.

lru_cache `lru_cache(max_size=128, typed=False)`

(v3 only; to use in v2, **pip install** Jason Coombs' backport (*https://pypi.python.org/pypi/backports.functools_lru_cache*).) A *memoizing* decorator suitable for decorating a function whose arguments are all hashable, adding to the function a cache storing the last *max_size* results (*max_size* should be a power of 2, or None to have the cache keep all previous results); when the decorated function is called again with arguments that are in the cache, it immediately returns the previously cached result, bypassing the underlying function's body code. When *typed* is true, arguments that compare equal but have different types, such as 23 and 23.0, are cached separately. For more details and examples, see the online docs (*https://docs.python.org/3/library/functools.html#functools.lru_cache*).

partial `partial(func,*a,**k)`

func is any callable. `partial` returns another callable *p* that is just like *func*, but with some positional and/or named parameters already bound to the values given in *a* and *k*. In other words, *p* is a *partial application* of *func*, often also known (with debatable correctness, but colorfully) as a *currying* of *func* to the given arguments (named in honor of mathematician Haskell Curry). For example, say that we have a list of numbers L and want to clip the negative ones to 0; one way to do it is:

```
L = map(functools.partial(max, 0), L)
```

as an alternative to the lambda-using snippet:

```
L = map(lambda x: max(0, x), L)
```

and to the most concise approach, a list comprehension:

```
L = [max(0, x) for x in L]
```

`functools.partial` comes into its own in situations that demand callbacks, such as event-driven programming for GUIs and networking applications (covered in Chapter 18).

`partial` returns a callable with the attributes `func` (the wrapped function), `args` (the `tuple` of prebound positional arguments), and `keywords` (the `dict` of prebound named arguments, or None).

reduce `reduce(func,seq[,init])`

Like the built-in function `reduce`, covered in Table 7-2. In v3, `reduce` is not a built-in, but it's still available in `functools`.

total_ordering A class decorator suitable for decorating classes that supply at least one inequality comparison method, such as `__lt__`, and also supply `__eq__`. Based on the class's existing methods, the class decorator `total_ordering` adds to the class all other inequality comparison methods, removing the need for you to add boilerplate code for them.

wraps `wraps(wrapped)`

A decorator suitable for decorating functions that wrap another function *wrapped* (often nested functions within another decorator). `wraps` copies the `__name__`, `__doc__`, and `__module__` attributes of *wrapped* on the decorated function, thus improving the behavior of the built-in function `help`, and of doctests, covered in "The doctest Module" on page 459.

The heapq Module

The `heapq` module uses *min heap* algorithms to keep a list in "nearly sorted" order as items are inserted and extracted. `heapq`'s operation is faster than calling a list's `sort` method after each insertion, and much faster than `bisect` (covered in the online docs (*https://docs.python.org/3/library/bisect.html*)). For many purposes, such as implementing "priority queues," the nearly sorted order supported by `heapq` is just as good as a fully sorted order, and faster to establish and maintain. The `heapq` module supplies the following functions:

heapify `heapify(alist)`

Permutes *alist* as needed to make it satisfy the (min) *heap condition*:

- for any `i>=0`
  - `alist[i]<=alist[2*i+1]` and
  - `alist[i]<=alist[2*i+2]`
- as long as all the indices in question are < `len(alist)`

If a list satisfies the (min) heap condition, the list's first item is the smallest (or equal-smallest) one. A sorted list satisfies the heap condition, but many other permutations of a list also satisfy the heap condition, without requiring the list to be fully sorted. `heapify` runs in `O(len(alist))` time.

heappop `heappop(alist)`

Removes and returns the smallest (first) item of *alist*, a list that satisfies the heap condition, and permutes some of the remaining items of *alist* to ensure the heap condition is still satisfied after the removal. `heappop` runs in `O(log(len(alist)))` time.

heappush `heappush(alist, item)`

Inserts the *item* in *alist*, a list that satisfies the heap condition, and permutes some items of *alist* to ensure the heap condition is still satisfied after the insertion. `heappush` runs in `O(log(len(alist)))` time.

heappushpop heappushpop(*alist*, *item*)

Logically equivalent to heappush followed by heappop, similar to:

```
def heappushpop(alist, item):
    heappush(alist, item)
    return heappop(alist)
```

heappushpop runs in O(log(len(*alist*))) time and is generally faster than the logically equivalent function just shown. heappushpop can be called on an empty *alist*: in that case, it returns the *item* argument, as it does when *item* is smaller than any existing item of *alist*.

heapreplace heapreplace(*alist*, *item*)

Logically equivalent to heappop followed by heappush, similar to:

```
def heapreplace(alist, item):
    try: return heappop(alist)
    finally: heappush(alist, item)
```

heapreplace runs in O(log(len(*alist*))) time and is generally faster than the logically equivalent function just shown. heapreplace cannot be called on an empty *alist*: heapreplace always returns an item that was already in *alist*, not the *item* being pushed onto it.

merge merge(**iterables*)

Returns an iterator yielding, in sorted order (smallest to largest), the items of the *iterables*, each of which must be smallest-to-largest sorted.

nlargest nlargest(*n*, *seq*, *key*=None)

Returns a reverse-sorted list with the *n* largest items of iterable *seq* (less than *n* if *seq* has fewer than *n* items); like sorted(*seq*, reverse=True)[:*n*] but faster for small values of *n*. You may also specify a key= argument, like you can for sorted.

nsmallest nsmallest(*n*, *seq*, *key*=None)

Returns a sorted list with the *n* smallest items of iterable *seq* (less than *n* if *seq* has fewer than *n* items); like sorted(*seq*)[:*n*] but faster for small values of *n*. You may also specify a key= argument, like you can for sorted.

Core Built-ins and Modules

The Decorate-Sort-Undecorate Idiom

Several functions in the heapq module, although they perform comparisons, do not accept a key= argument to customize the comparisons. This is inevitable, since the functions operate in-place on a plain list of the items: they have nowhere to "stash away" custom comparison keys computed once and for all.

When you need both heap functionality and custom comparisons, you can apply the good old *decorate-sort-undecorate (DSU)* idiom (which used to be crucial to optimize sorting in old versions of Python, before the key= functionality was introduced).

The DSU idiom, as applied to heapq, has the following components:

1. *Decorate*: Build an auxiliary list *A* where each item is a tuple starting with the sort key and ending with the item of the original list *L*.
2. Call heapq functions on *A*, typically starting with heapq.heapify(*A*).
3. *Undecorate*: When you extract an item from *A*, typically by calling heapq.heappop(*A*), return just the last item of the resulting tuple (which corresponds to an item of the original list *L*).

When you add an item to *A* by calling heapq.heappush(*A*, *item*), decorate the actual item you're inserting into a tuple starting with the sort key.

This sequencing is best wrapped up in a class, as in this example:

```
import heapq

class KeyHeap(object):
    def __init__(self, alist, key):
        self.heap = [
            (key(o), i, o)
            for i, o in enumerate(alist)]
        heapq.heapify(self.heap)
        self.key = key
        if alist:
            self.nexti = self.heap[-1][1] + 1
        else:
            self.nexti = 0

    def __len__(self):
        return len(self.heap)

    def push(self, o):
        heapq.heappush(
            self.heap,
            (self.key(o), self.nexti, o))
        self.nexti += 1

    def pop(self):
        return heapq.heappop(self.heap)[-1]
```

In this example, we use an increasing number in the middle of the decorated tuple (after the sort key, before the actual item) to ensure that actual items are never compared directly, even if their sort keys are equal (this semantic guarantee is an important aspect of the *key=* argument's functionality to sort and the like).

The argparse Module

When you write a Python program meant to be run from the command line (or from a "shell script" in Unix-like systems or a "batch file" in Windows), you often want to let the user pass to the program, on the command line, *command-line arguments* (including *command-line options*, which by convention are usually arguments starting with one or two dash characters). In Python, you can access the arguments as `sys.argv`, an attribute of module `sys` holding those arguments as a list of strings (`sys.argv[0]` is the name by which the user started your program; the arguments are in sublist `sys.argv[1:]`). The Python standard library offers three modules to process those arguments; we only cover the newest and most powerful one, `argparse`, and we only cover a small, *core* subset of `argparse`'s rich functionality. See the online reference (*https://docs.python.org/3/library/argparse.html*) and tutorial (*https://docs.python.org/3.4/howto/argparse.html*) for much, much more.

ArgumentParser `ArgumentParser(**kwargs)`

`ArgumentParser` is the class whose instances perform argument parsing. It accepts many named arguments, mostly meant to improve the help message that your program displays if command-line arguments include `-h` or `--help`. One named argument you should pass is `description=`, a string summarizing the purpose of your program.

Given an instance *ap* of `ArgumentParser`, prepare it by one or more calls to *ap*.`add_argument`; then, use it by calling *ap*.`parse_args()` without arguments (so it parses `sys.argv`): the call returns an instance of `argparse.Namespace`, with your program's args and options as attributes.

`add_argument` has a mandatory first argument: either an identifier string, for positional command-line arguments, or a flag name, for command-line options. In the latter case, pass one or more flag names; an option often has both a short name (one dash, then a single character) and a long name (two dashes, then an identifier).

After the positional arguments, pass to `add_argument` zero or more named arguments to control its behavior. Here are the common ones:

Core Built-ins and Modules

action What the parser does with this argument. Default: `'store'`, store the argument's value in the namespace (at the name given by `dest`). Also useful: `'store_true'` and `'store_false'`, making an option into a `bool` one (defaulting to the opposite `bool` if the option is not present); and `'append'`, appending argument values to a list (and thus allowing an option to be repeated).

choices A set of values allowed for the argument (parsing the argument raises an exception if the value is not among these); default, no constraints.

default Value to use if the argument is not present; default, `None`.

dest Name of the attribute to use for this argument; default, same as the first positional argument stripped of dashes.

help A short string mentioning the argument's role, for help messages.

nargs Number of command-line arguments used by this logical argument (by default, `1`, stored as-is in the namespace). Can be an integer >`0` (uses that many arguments and stores them as a list), `'?'` (one, or none in which case `default` is used), `'*'` (`0` or more, stored as a list), `'+'` (`1` or more, stored as a list), or `argparse.REMAINDER` (all remaining arguments, stored as a list).

type A callable accepting a string, often a type such as `int`; used to transform values from strings to something else. Can be an instance of `argparse.FileType` to open the string as a filename (for reading if `FileType('r')`, for writing if `FileType('w')`, and so on).

Here's a simple example of `argparse`—save this code in a file called *greet.py*:

```
import argparse
ap = argparse.ArgumentParser(description='Just an example')
ap.add_argument('who', nargs='?', default='World')
ap.add_argument('--formal', action='store_true')
ns = ap.parse_args()
if ns.formal:
    greet = 'Most felicitous salutations, o {}.'
else:
    greet = 'Hello, {}!'
print(greet.format(ns.who))
```

Now, **`python greet.py`** prints **`Hello, World!`**, while **`python greet.py --formal Cornelia`** prints **`Most felicitous salutations, o Cornelia.`**

The itertools Module

The `itertools` module offers high-performance building blocks to build and manipulate iterators. To handle long processions of items, iterators are often better than lists, thanks to iterators' intrinsic "lazy evaluation" approach: an iterator produces items one at a time, as needed, while all items of a list (or other sequence) must be in memory at the same time. This approach even makes it feasible to build and use unbounded iterators, while lists must always have finite numbers of items (since any machine has a finite amount of memory).

Table 7-5 covers the most frequently used attributes of `itertools`; each of them is an iterator type, which you call to get an instance of the type in question, or a factory function behaving similarly. See the itertools documentation in the online Python docs (*https://docs.python.org/3/library/itertools.html*) for more `itertools` attributes, including *combinatoric* generators for permutations, combinations, and Cartesian products, as well as a useful taxonomy of `itertools` attributes.

The online docs also offer *recipes*, ways to combine and use `itertools` attributes. The recipes assume you have `from itertools import *` at the top of your module; this is *not* recommended use, just an assumption to make the recipes' code more compact. It's best to `import itertools as it`, then use references such as `it.`*`something`* rather than the more verbose `itertools.`*`something`*.

Table 7-5.

chain `chain(*iterables)`

Yields items from the first argument, then items from the second argument, and so on until the end of the last argument, just like the generator expression:

```
(item for iterable in iterables for item
in iterable)
```

chain.from_iterable `chain.from_iterable(iterables)`

Yields items from the iterables in the argument, in order, just like the genexp:

```
(item for iterable in iterables for item
in iterable)
```

compress `compress(data, conditions)`

Yields each item from *`data`* corresponding to a true item in *`conditions`*, just like the generator expression:

```
(item for item, cond in zip(data, conditions)
if cond)
```

count `count(start=0, step=1)`

Yields consecutive integers starting from *`start`*, just like the generator:

```
def count(start=0, step=1):
    while True:
        yield start
        start += step
```

cycle `cycle(iterable)`

Yields each item of *`iterable`*, endlessly repeating items from the beginning each time it reaches the end, just like the generator:

```
def cycle(iterable):
    saved = []
    for item in iterable:
        yield item
        saved.append(item)
    while saved:
        for item in saved: yield item
```

dropwhile

`dropwhile(func,iterable)`

Drops the `0`+ leading items of *`iterable`* for which *`func`* is true, then yields each other item, just like the generator:

```
def dropwhile(func,iterable):
    iterator = iter(iterable)
    for item in iterator:
        if not func(item):
            yield item
            break
    for item in iterator: yield item
```

groupby

`groupby(iterable,key=None)`

`iterable` normally needs to be already sorted according to *`key`* (`None`, as usual, standing for the identity function). `groupby` yields pairs (*`k`*,*`g`*), each pair representing a *group* of adjacent items from *`iterable`* having the same value *k* for *`key`*(*`item`*); each *g* is an iterator yielding the items in the group. When the `groupby` object advances, previous iterators *g* become invalid (so, if a group of items needs to be processed later, store somewhere a `list` "snapshot" of it, `list(`*`g`*`)`).

Another way of looking at the groups `groupby` yields is that each terminates as soon as *`key`*(*`item`*) changes (which is why you normally call `groupby` only on an *`iterable`* that's already sorted by *`key`*).

For example, suppose that, given a `set` of lowercase words, we want a `dict` that maps each initial to the longest word having that initial (with "ties" broken arbitrarily):

```
import itertools as it, operator
def set2dict(aset):
    first = operator.itemgetter(0)
    words = sorted(aset, key=first)
    adict = {}
    for initial,
        group in it.groupby(words, key=first):
        adict[initial] = max(group, key=len)
    return adict
```

ifilter

`ifilter(func,iterable)`

Yields those items of *`iterable`* for which *`func`* is true, just like the genexp:

```
(item for item in iterable if func(item))
```

`func` can be any callable object that accepts a single argument, or `None`. When *`func`* is `None`, `ifilter` yields true items, just like the genexp:

```
(item for item in iterable if item)
```

ifilterfalse

`ifilterfalse(func,iterable)`

Yields those items of *iterable* for which *func* is false, just like the genexp:

```
(item for item in iterable if not func(item))
```

func can be any callable accepting a single argument, or `None`. When *func* is `None`, `ifilterfalse` yields false items, just like the genexp:

```
(item for item in iterable if not item)
```

imap

`imap(func,*iterables)`

Yields the results of *func*, called with one argument from each of the *iterables*; stops when the shortest of the *iterables* is exhausted, just like the generator:

```
def imap(func,*iterables):
    iters = [iter(x) for x in iterables]
    while True: yield func(*(next(x) for x in iters))
```

islice

`islice(iterable[,start],stop[,step])`

Yields items of *iterable*, skipping the first *start* ones (default `0`), until the *stop*th one excluded, advancing by steps of *step* (default `1`) at a time. All arguments must be nonnegative integers (or `None`), and *step* must be `>0`. Apart from checks and optional arguments, it's like the generator:

```
def islice(iterable,start,stop,step=1):
    en = enumerate(iterable)
    n = stop
    for n, item in en:
        if n>=start: break
    while n<stop:
        yield item
        for x in range(step): n, item = next(en)
```

izip

`izip(*iterables)`

Yields tuples with one corresponding item from each of the *iterables*; stops when the shortest of the *iterables* is exhausted. Just like `imap(tuple,*iterables)`. v2 only; in v3, the built-in function `zip`, covered in Table 7-2, has this functionality.

izip_longest

`izip_longest(*iterables,fillvalue=None)`

Yields tuples with one corresponding item from each of the *iterables*; stops when the longest of the *iterables* is exhausted, behaving as if each of the others was "padded" to that same length with references to *fillvalue*.

repeat

`repeat(`*`item`*`[,`*`times`*`])`

Repeatedly yields *`item`*, just like the generator expression:

```
(item for x in range(times))
```

When *`times`* is absent, the iterator is unbounded, yielding a potentially infinite number of items, which are all the object *`item`*. Just like the generator:

```
def repeat_unbounded(item):
    while True: yield item
```

starmap

`starmap(`*`func`*`,`*`iterable`*`)`

Yields `func(*`*`item`*`)` for each *`item`* in *`iterable`* (each *`item`* must be an iterable, normally a tuple), just like the generator:

```
def starmap(func,iterable):
    for item in iterable:
        yield func(*item)
```

takewhile

`takewhile(`*`func`*`,`*`iterable`*`)`

Yields items from *`iterable`* as long as `func(`*`item`*`)` is true, then stops, just like the generator:

```
def takewhile(func,iterable):
    for item in iterable:
        if func(item):
            yield item
        else:
            break
```

tee

`tee(`*`iterable`*`,`*`n=2`*`)`

Returns a tuple of *n* independent iterators, each yielding items that are the same as those of *`iterable`*. The returned iterators are independent from each other, but they are *not* independent from *`iterable`*; avoid altering the object *`iterable`* in any way, as long as you're still using any of the returned iterators.

We have shown equivalent generators and genexps for many attributes of `itertools`, but it's important to remember the sheer speed of `itertools` types. To take a trivial example, consider repeating some action 10 times:

```
for _ in itertools.repeat(0, 10): pass
```

This turns out to be about 10 to 20 percent faster, depending on Python release and platform, than the straightforward alternative:

```
for _ in range(10): pass
```

8
Strings and Things

v3 supplies Unicode text strings as type `str`, with operators, built-in functions, methods, and dedicated modules. It also supplies the somewhat similar `bytes` type, representing arbitrary binary data as a sequence of bytes, also known as a *bytestring* or *byte string*. This is a major difference from v2, where type `str` is a sequence of bytes, while Unicode text strings are of type `unicode`. Many textual operations, in both versions, are possible on objects of either type.

This chapter covers the methods of string objects, in "Methods of String and Bytes Objects" on page 233; string formatting, in "String Formatting" on page 240; and the modules `string` (in "The string Module" on page 239) and `pprint` (in "The pprint Module" on page 249). Issues related specifically to Unicode are also covered, in "Unicode" on page 250. The new (v3.6) formatted string literals are covered in "New in 3.6: Formatted String Literals" on page 246.

Methods of String and Bytes Objects

Unicode `str` and `bytes` objects are immutable sequences, as covered in "Strings" on page 64. All immutable-sequence operations (repetition, concatenation, indexing, and slicing) apply to them, returning an object of the same type. A string or bytes object *s* also supplies several nonmutating methods, as documented in Table 8-1.

Unless otherwise noted, methods are present on objects of either type. In v3, `str` methods return a Unicode string, while methods of `bytes` objects return a bytestring (in v2, type `unicode` stands for a textual string—i.e., Unicode—and type `str` for a bytestring). Terms such as "letters," "whitespace," and so on, refer to the corresponding attributes of the `string` module, covered in "The string Module" on page 239.

In Table 8-1, for conciseness, we use `sys.maxsize` for integer default values meaning, in practice, "any number, no matter how large."

Table 8-1.

capitalize `s.capitalize()`

Returns a copy of *s* where the first character, if a letter, is uppercase, and all other letters, if any, are lowercase.

casefold `s.casefold()`

`str` only, v3 only. Returns a string processed by the algorithm described in section 3.13 of the Unicode standard. This is similar to `s.lower` (described later in this list) but also takes into account broader equivalences, such as that between the German lowercase `'ß'` and `'ss'`, and is thus better suited to case-insensitive matching.

center `s.center(n,fillchar=' ')`

Returns a string of length `max(len(s), n)`, with a copy of *s* in the central part, surrounded by equal numbers of copies of character *fillchar* on both sides (e.g., `'ciao'.center(2)` is `'ciao'` and `'x'.center(4,'_')` is `'_x__'`).

count `s.count(sub,start=0,end=sys.maxsize)`

Returns the number of nonoverlapping occurrences of substring *sub* in `s[start:end]`.

decode `s.decode(encoding='utf-8',errors='strict')`

`bytes` only. Returns a `str` object decoded from the bytes *s* according to the given encoding. *errors* determines how decoding errors are handled. `'strict'` cause errors to raise `UnicodeError` exceptions, `'ignore'` ignores the malformed data, and `'replace'` replaces them with question marks; see "Unicode" on page 250 for details. Other values can be registered via `codec.register_error()`, covered in Table 8-7.

encode `s.encode(encoding=None,errors='strict')`

`str` only. Returns a `bytes` object obtained from *s* with the given encoding and error handling. See "Unicode" on page 250 for more details.

endswith `s.endswith(suffix,start=0,end=sys.maxsize)`

Returns `True` when `s[start:end]` ends with string *suffix*; otherwise, `False`. *suffix* can be a tuple of strings, in which case `endswith` returns `True` when `s[start:end]` ends with any one of them.

expandtabs `s.expandtabs(tabsize=8)`

Returns a copy of *s* where each tab character is changed into one or more spaces, with tab stops every *tabsize* characters.

find `s.find(sub,start=0,end=sys.maxsize)`

Returns the lowest index in *s* where substring *sub* is found, such that *sub* is entirely contained in `s[start:end]`. For example, `'banana'.find('na')` is 2, as is `'banana'.find('na',1)`, while `'banana'.find('na',3)` is 4, as is `'banana'.find('na',-2)`. `find` returns `-1` when *sub* is not found.

format `s.format(*args,**kwargs)`

`str` only. Formats the positional and named arguments according to formatting instructions contained in the string *s*. See "String Formatting" on page 240 for further details.

format_map `s.format_map(mapping)`

`str` only, v3 only. Formats the mapping argument according to formatting instructions contained in the string *s*. Equivalent to `s.format(**mapping)` but uses the mapping directly.

index `s.index(sub,start=0,end=sys.maxsize)`

Like `find`, but raises `ValueError` when *sub* is not found.

isalnum `s.isalnum()`

Returns `True` when `len(s)` is greater than `0` and all characters in *s* are letters or digits. When *s* is empty, or when at least one character of *s* is neither a letter nor a digit, `isalnum` returns `False`.

isalpha `s.isalpha()`

Returns `True` when `len(s)` is greater than `0` and all characters in *s* are letters. When *s* is empty, or when at least one character of *s* is not a letter, `isalpha` returns `False`.

isdecimal `s.isdecimal()`

`str` only, v3 only. Returns `True` when `len(s)` is greater than `0` and all characters in *s* can be used to form decimal-radix numbers. This includes Unicode characters defined as Arabic digits.[a]

isdigit `s.isdigit()`

Returns `True` when `len(s)` is greater than `0` and all characters in *s* are digits. When *s* is empty, or when at least one character of *s* is not a digit, `isdigit` returns `False`.

isidentifier

`s.isidentifier()`

`str` only, v3 only. Returns `True` when *s* is a valid identifier according to the Python language's definition; keywords also satisfy the definition, so, for example, `'class'.isidentifier()` returns `True`.

islower

`s.islower()`

Returns `True` when all letters in *s* are lowercase. When *s* contains no letters, or when at least one letter of *s* is uppercase, `islower` returns `False`.

isnumeric

`s.isnumeric()`

`str` only, v3 only. Similar to `s.isdigit()`, but uses a broader definition of numeric characters that includes all characters defined as numeric in the Unicode standard (such as fractions).

isprintable

`s.isprintable()`

`str` only, v3 only. Returns `True` when all characters in *s* are spaces (`'\x20'`) or are defined in the Unicode standard as printable. Differently from other methods starting with `is`, `''.isprintable()` returns `True`.

isspace

`s.isspace()`

Returns `True` when `len(s)` is greater than `0` and all characters in *s* are whitespace. When *s* is empty, or when at least one character of *s* is not whitespace, `isspace` returns `False`.

istitle

`s.istitle()`

Returns `True` when letters in *s* are *titlecase*: a capital letter at the start of each contiguous sequence of letters, all other letters lowercase (e.g., `'King Lear'.istitle()` is `True`). When *s* contains no letters, or when at least one letter of *s* violates the titlecase condition, `istitle` returns `False` (e.g., `'1900'.istitle()` and `'Troilus and Cressida'.istitle()` return `False`).

isupper

`s.isupper()`

Returns `True` when all letters in *s* are uppercase. When *s* contains no letters, or when at least one letter of *s* is lowercase, `isupper` returns `False`.

join

`s.join(seq)`

Returns the string obtained by concatenating the items of *seq*, which must be an iterable whose items are strings, and interposing a copy of *s* between each pair of items (e.g., `''.join(str(x) for x in range(7))` is `'0123456'` and `'x'.join('aeiou')` is `'axexixoxu'`).

ljust

`s.ljust(n,fillchar=' ')`

Returns a string of length `max(len(s),n)`, with a copy of *s* at the start, followed by zero or more trailing copies of character *fillchar*.

lower `s.lower()`

Returns a copy of *s* with all letters, if any, converted to lowercase.

lstrip `s.lstrip(x=string.whitespace)`

Returns a copy of *s*, removing leading characters that are found in string *x*. For example, `'banana'.lstrip('ab')` returns `'nana'`.

replace `s.replace(old,new,maxsplit=sys.maxsize)`

Returns a copy of *s* with the first *maxsplit* (or fewer, if there are fewer) nonoverlapping occurrences of substring *old* replaced by string *new* (e.g., `'banana'.replace('a', 'e',2)` returns `'benena'`).

rfind `s.rfind(sub,start=0,end=sys.maxsize)`

Returns the highest index in *s* where substring *sub* is found, such that *sub* is entirely contained in `s[start:end]`. `rfind` returns `-1` if *sub* is not found.

rindex `s.rindex(sub,start=0,end=sys.maxsize)`

Like `rfind`, but raises `ValueError` if *sub* is not found.

rjust `s.rjust(n,fillchar=' ')`

Returns a string of length `max(len(s),n)`, with a copy of *s* at the end, preceded by zero or more leading copies of character *fillchar*.

rstrip `s.rstrip(x=string.whitespace)`

Returns a copy of *s*, removing trailing characters that are found in string *x*. For example, `'banana'.rstrip('ab')` returns `'banan'`.

split `s.split(sep=None,maxsplit=sys.maxsize)`

Returns a list *L* of up to *maxsplit*+1 strings. Each item of *L* is a "word" from *s*, where string *sep* separates words. When *s* has more than *maxsplit* words, the last item of *L* is the substring of *s* that follows the first *maxsplit* words. When *sep* is None, any string of whitespace separates words (e.g., `'four score and seven years'.split(None,3)` is `['four','score','and','seven years']`).

Note the difference between splitting on `None` (any string of whitespace is a separator) and splitting on `' '` (each single space character, *not* other whitespace such as tabs and newlines, and *not* strings of spaces, is a separator). For example:

```
>>> x = 'a  b'  # two spaces between a and b
>>> x.split()  # or, equivalently, x.split(None)
['a', 'b']
>>> x.split(' ')
['a', '', 'b']
```

In the first case, the two-spaces string in the middle is a single separator; in the second case, each single space is a separator, so that there is an empty string between the two spaces.

splitlines `s.splitlines(`*keepends*`=False)`

Like `s.split('\n')`. When *keepends* is true, however, the trailing `'\n'` is included in each item of the resulting list.

startswith `s.startswith(`*prefix*`,`*start*`=0,`*end*`=sys.maxsize)`

Returns `True` when `s[`*start*`:`*end*`]` starts with string *prefix*; otherwise, `False`. *prefix* can be a tuple of strings, in which case `startswith` returns `True` when `s[`*start*`:`*end*`]` starts with any one of them.

strip `s.strip(`*x*`=string.whitespace)`

Returns a copy of *s*, removing both leading and trailing characters that are found in string *x*. For example, `'banana'.strip('ab')` is `'nan'`.

swapcase `s.swapcase()`

Returns a copy of *s* with all uppercase letters converted to lowercase and vice versa.

title `s.title()`

Returns a copy of *s* transformed to titlecase: a capital letter at the start of each contiguous sequence of letters, with all other letters (if any) lowercase.

translate `s.translate(`*table*`)`

Returns a copy of *s* where characters found in *table* are translated or deleted. In v3 (and in v2, when *s* is an instance of `unicode`), *table* is a `dict` whose keys are Unicode ordinals; values are Unicode ordinals, Unicode strings, or `None` (to delete the character)—for example (coded to work both in v2 and v3, with the redundant-in-v3 `u` prefix on strings):

```
print(u'banana'.translate({ord('a'):None,ord('n'):u'ze'}))
# prints: 'bzeze'
```

In v2, when *s* is a string of bytes, its `translate` method is quite different—see the online docs (*https://docs.python.org/2/library/string.html#string.translate*). Here are some examples of v2's `translate`:

```
import string
identity = string.maketrans('','')
print('some string'.translate(identity,'aeiou'))
# prints: sm strng
```

The Unicode or v3 equivalent of this would be:

```
no_vowels = dict.fromkeys(ord(x) for x in 'aeiou')
print(u'some string'.translate(no_vowels))
# prints: sm strng
```

Here are v2 examples of turning all vowels into *a*'s and also deleting *s*'s:

```
intoas = string.maketrans('eiou','aaaa')
print('some string'.translate(intoas))
```

```
# prints: sama strang
print('some string'.translate(intoas,'s'))
# prints: ama trang
```

The Unicode or v3 equivalent of this would be:

```
intoas = dict.fromkeys((ord(x) for x in 'eiou'), 'a')
print(u'some string'.translate(intoas))
# prints: sama strang
intoas_nos = dict(intoas, s='None')
print(u'some string'.translate(intoas_nos))
# prints: ama trang
```

upper `s.upper()`

Returns a copy of *s* with all letters, if any, converted to uppercase.

[a] Note that this does not include the punctuation marks used as a radix, such as dot (.) and comma (,).

The string Module

The `string` module supplies several useful string attributes:

`ascii_letters`
The string `ascii_lowercase+ascii_uppercase`

`ascii_lowercase`
The string `'abcdefghijklmnopqrstuvwxyz'`

`ascii_uppercase`
The string `'ABCDEFGHIJKLMNOPQRSTUVWXYZ'`

`digits`
The string `'0123456789'`

`hexdigits`
The string `'0123456789abcdefABCDEF'`

`octdigits`
The string `'01234567'`

`punctuation`
The string `'!"#$%&\'()*+,-./:;<=>?@[\]^_'{|}~'` (i.e., all ASCII characters that are deemed punctuation characters in the `'C'` locale; does not depend on which locale is active)

`printable`
The string of those ASCII characters that are deemed printable (i.e., digits, letters, punctuation, and whitespace)

Strings and Things

`whitespace`
: A string containing all ASCII characters that are deemed whitespace: at least space, tab, linefeed, and carriage return, but more characters (e.g., certain control characters) may be present, depending on the active locale

You should not rebind these attributes; the effects of doing so are undefined, since other parts of the Python library may rely on them.

The module `string` also supplies the class `Formatter`, covered in "String Formatting" on page 240.

String Formatting

v3 has introduced a powerful new string formatting facility, which has also been backported into v2. Unicode strings (but, in v3, *not* bytestrings) provide a `format` method that you call with arguments to interpolate into the format string, in which values to be formatted are indicated by replacement fields enclosed within braces.

The formatting process is best understood as a sequence of operations, each of which is guided by its replacement field. First, each value to be formatted is *selected*; next, it is *converted*, if required; finally, it is *formatted*.

Value Selection

```
'[str]{[selector]}[str]'.format(*args, **kwargs)
```

The `format` selector can handle positional (automatic or numbered) and named arguments. The simplest replacement field is the empty pair of braces ({}). With no indication of which argument is to be interpolated, each such replacement field automatically refers to the value of the next positional argument to `format`:

```
>>> 'First: {} second: {}'.format(1, 'two')
'First: 1 second: two'
```

To repeatedly select an argument, or use it out of order, use the argument's number to specify its position in the list of arguments:

```
>>> 'Second: {1} first: {0}'.format(1, 'two')
'Second: two first: 1'
```

You cannot mix automatic and numbered replacement fields: it's an either-or choice. For named arguments, you can use argument names and mix them with (automatic or numbered) positional arguments:

```
>>> 'a: {a}, 1st: {}, 2nd: {}, a again: {a}'.format(1, 'two', a=3)
'a: 3, 1st: 1, 2nd: two, a again: 3'
>>> 'a: {a} first:{0} second: {1} first: {0}'.format(1, 'two', a=3)
'a: 3 first:1 second: two first: 1'
```

If an argument is a sequence, you can use numeric indexes within it to select a specific element of the argument as the value to be formatted. This applies to both positional (automatic or numbered) and named arguments.

```
>>> 'p0[1]: {[1]} p1[0]: {[0]}'.format(('zero', 'one'),
                                       ('two', 'three'))
'p0[1]: one p1[0]: two'
>>> 'p1[0]: {1[0]} p0[1]: {0[1]}'.format(('zero', 'one'),
                                         ('two', 'three'))
'p1[0]: two p0[1]: one'
>>> '{} {} {a[2]}'.format(1, 2, a=(5, 4, 3))
'1 2 3'
```

If an argument is a composite object, you can select its individual attributes as values to be formatted by applying attribute-access dot notation to the argument selector. Here is an example using complex numbers, which have `real` and `imag` attributes that hold the real and imaginary parts, respectively:

```
>>> 'First r: {.real} Second i: {a.imag}'.format(1+2j, a=3+4j)
'First r: 1.0 Second i: 4.0'
```

Indexing and attribute-selection operations can be used multiple times, if required.

Value Conversion

You may apply a default conversion to the value via one of its methods. You indicate this by following any selector with `!s` to apply the object's `__str__` method, `!r` for its `__repr__` method, or `!a` for the `ascii` built-in (v3 only).

If you apply any conversion, the converted value replaces the originally selected value in the remainder of the formatting process.

Value Formatting

`'{[`*`selector`*`][conversion]:[`*`format_specifier`*`]}'.format(`*`value`*`)`

The formatting of the value (if any further formatting is required) is determined by a final (optional) portion of the replacement field, following a colon (`:`), known as the *format specifier*. The absence of a colon in the replacement field means that the converted value is used with no further formatting. Format specifiers may include one or more of the following: *fill, alignment, sign, #, width, comma, precision, type.*

Alignment, with optional (preceding) fill

If alignment is required the formatted value is filled to the correct field width. The default fill character is the space, but an alternative fill character (which may not be an opening or closing brace) can, if required, precede the alignment indicator. See Table 8-2.

Table 8-2. Alignment indicators

Character	Significance as alignment indicator
'<'	Align value on left of field
'>'	Align value on right of field

Character	Significance as alignment indicator
'^'	Align value in the center of the field
'='	Only for numeric types: add fill characters between the sign and the first digit of the numeric value

When no alignment is specified, most values are left-aligned, except that numeric values are right-aligned. Unless a field width is specified later in the format specifier no fill characters are added, whatever the fill and alignment may be.

Optional sign indication

For numeric values only, you can indicate how positive and negative numbers are differentiated by optionally including a sign indicator. See Table 8-3.

Table 8-3. Sign indicators

Character	Significance as sign indicator
'+'	Insert '+' as sign for positive numbers; '-' as sign for negative numbers
'-'	Insert '-' as sign for negative numbers; do not insert any sign for positive numbers (default behavior if no sign indicator is included)
' '	Insert ' ' as sign for positive numbers; '-' as sign for negative numbers

Radix indicator

For numeric integer formats only, you can include a radix indicator, the `'#'` character. If present, this indicates that the digits of binary-formatted numbers is preceded by `'0b'`, those of octal-formatted numbers by `'0o'`, and those of hexadecimal-formatted numbers by `'0x'`. For example, `'{:x}'.format(23)` is `'17'`, while `'{:#x}'.format(23)` is `'0x17'`.

Field width

You can specify the width of the field to be printed. If the width specified is less than the length of the value, the length of the value is used (no truncation). If alignment is not specified, the value is left-justified (except numbers, which are right-justified):

```
>>> s = 'a string'
>>> '{:^12s}'.format(s)
'  a string  '
>>> '{:.>12s}'.format(s)
'....a string'
```

Comma separation

For numeric values only, only in decimal (default) format type, you can insert a comma to request that each group of three digits in the result be separated by a comma. This behavior ignores system locale; for a locale-aware use of appropriate digit grouping and decimal point character, see format type 'n' in Table 8-4. For example:

```
print('{:,}'.format(12345678))
# prints 12,345,678
```

Precision specification

The precision (e.g., .2) has different meaning for different format types (see the following section), with .6 as the default for most numeric formats. For the f and F format types, it specifies the number of *decimal* digits to which the value should be rounded in formatting; for the g and G format types, it specifies the number of *significant* digits to which the value should be rounded; for nonnumeric values, it specifies *truncation* of the value to its leftmost characters before formatting.

```
>>> s = 'a string'
>>> x = 1.12345
>>> 'as f: {:.4f}'.format(x)
'as f: 1.1235'
>>> 'as g: {:.4g}'.format(x)
'as g: 1.123'
>>> 'as s: {:.6s}'.format(s)
'as s: a stri'
```

Format type

The format specification ends with an optional *format type*, which determines how the value gets represented in the given width and at the given precision. When the format type is omitted, the value being formatted applies a default format type.

The s format type is used to format Unicode strings.

Integer numbers have a range of acceptable format types, listed in Table 8-4.

Table 8-4.

Format type	Formatting description
'b'	Binary format—a series of ones and zeros
'c'	The Unicode character whose ordinal value is the formatted value
'd'	Decimal (the default format type)
'o'	Octal format—a series of octal digits
'x' or 'X'	Hexadecimal format—a series of hexadecimal digits, with the letters, respectively, in lower- or uppercase
'n'	Decimal format, with locale-specific separators (commas in the UK and US) when system locale is set

Floating-point numbers have a different set of format types, shown in Table 8-5.

Table 8-5.

Format type	Formatting description
'e' or 'E'	Exponential format—scientific notation, with an integer part between one and nine, using 'e' or 'E' just before the exponent
'f' or 'F'	Fixed-point format with infinities ('inf') and nonnumbers ('nan') in lower- or uppercase
'g' or 'G'	General format—uses a fixed-point format if possible, and otherwise uses exponential format; uses lower- or uppercase representations for 'e', 'inf', and 'nan', depending on the case of the format type
'n'	Like general format, but uses locale-specific separators, when system locale is set, for groups of three digits and decimal points
'%'	Percentage format—multiplies the value by 100 and formats it as a fixed-point followed by '%'

When no format type is specified, a `float` uses the `'g'` format, with at least one digit after the decimal point and a default precision of 12.

```
>>> n = [3.1415, -42, 1024.0]
>>> for num in n:
...     '{:>+9,.2f}'.format(num)
...
'    +3.14'
'   -42.00'
'+1,024.00'
```

Nested format specifications

In some cases you want to include an argument to `format` to help determine the precise format of another argument. Nested formatting can be used to achieve this. For example, to format a string in a field four characters wider than the string itself, you can pass a value for the width to `format`, as in:

```
>>> s = 'a string'
>>> '{0:>{1}s}'.format(s, len(s)+4)
'    a string'
>>> '{0:_^{1}s}'.format(s, len(s)+4)
'__a string__'
```

With some care, you can use width specification and nested formatting to print a sequence of tuples into well-aligned columns. For example:

```
def print_strings_in_columns(seq_of_strings, widths):
    for cols in seq_of_strings:
        row = ['{c:{w}.{w}s}'.format(c=c, w=w)
               for c, w in zip(cols, widths)]
        print(' '.join(row))
```

(In 3.6, `'{c:{w}.{w}s}'.format(c=c, w=w)` can be simplified to `f'{c:{w}.{w}s}'`, as covered in "New in 3.6: Formatted String Literals" on page 246.) Given this function, the following code:

```
c = [
        'four score and'.split(),
        'seven years ago'.split(),
        'our forefathers brought'.split(),
        'forth on this'.split(),
    ]

print_strings_in_columns(c, (8, 8, 8))
```

prints:

```
four     score    and
seven    years    ago
our      forefath brought
forth    on       this
```

Formatting of user-coded classes

Values are ultimately formatted by a call to their `__format__` method with the format specification as an argument. Built-in types either implement their own method or inherit from `object`, whose `format` method only accepts an empty string as an argument.

```
>>> object().__format__('')
'<object object at 0x110045070>'
>>> math.pi.__format__('18.6')
'           3.14159'
```

You can use this knowledge to implement an entirely different formatting minilanguage of your own, should you choose. The following simple example demonstrates the passing of format specifications and the return of a (constant) formatted string result. Since the format specification is arbitrary, you may choose to implement whatever formatting notation you choose.

```
>>> class S(object):
...     def __format__(self, fstr):
...         print('Format string:', fstr)
...         return '42'
...
>>> my_s = S()
>>> '{:format_string}'.format(s)
Format string: format string
'42'
>>> 'The formatted value is: {:anything you like}'.format(s)
Format string: anything you like
'The formatted value is: 42'
```

The return value of the `__format__` method is substituted for the replacement field in the output of the call to `format`, allowing any desired interpretation of the format string.

In order to control your objects' formatting more easily, the `string` module provides a `Formatter` class with many helpful methods for handling formatting tasks. See the documentation for `Formatter` in the online docs (*https://docs.python.org/3.5/library/string.html#string.Formatter*).

New in 3.6: Formatted String Literals

This new feature helps use the formatting capabilities just described. It uses the same formatting syntax, but lets you specify expression values inline rather than through parameter substitution. Instead of argument specifiers, f-strings use expressions, evaluated and formatted as specified. For example, instead of:

```
>>> name = 'Dawn'
>>> print('{name!r} is {l} characters long'
          .format(name=name, l=len(name)))
'Dawn' is 4 characters long
```

from 3.6 onward you can use the more concise form:

```
>>> print(f'{name!r} is {len(name)} characters long')
'Dawn' is 4 characters long
```

You can use nested braces to specify components of formatting expressions:

```
>>> for width in 8, 11:
...     for precision in 2, 3, 4, 5:
...         print(f'{3.14159:{width}.{precision}}')
...
     3.1
    3.14
   3.142
  3.1416
        3.1
       3.14
      3.142
     3.1416
```

Do remember, though, that these string literals are *not* constants—they evaluate each time a statement containing them runs, potentially implying runtime overhead.

Legacy String Formatting with %

A legacy form of string formatting expression in Python has the syntax:

```
format % values
```

where *`format`* is a string containing format specifiers and *`values`* are the values to format, usually as a tuple (in this book we cover only the subset of this legacy feature, the format specifier, that you must know to properly use the `logging` module, covered in "The logging package" on page 169).

The equivalent use in `logging` would be, for example:

```
logging.info(format, *values)
```

with the *`values`* coming as positional arguments after the first, *`format`* one.

The legacy string-formatting approach has roughly the same set of features as the C language's `printf` and operates in a similar way. Each format specifier is a substring of *`format`* that starts with a percent sign (`%`) and ends with one of the conversion characters shown in Table 8-6.

Table 8-6. String-formatting conversion characters

Character	Output format	Notes
`d`, `i`	Signed decimal integer	Value must be number.
`u`	Unsigned decimal integer	Value must be number.
`o`	Unsigned octal integer	Value must be number.
`x`	Unsigned hexadecimal integer (lowercase letters)	Value must be number.
`X`	Unsigned hexadecimal integer (uppercase letters)	Value must be number.
`e`	Floating-point value in exponential form (lowercase e for exponent)	Value must be number.
`E`	Floating-point value in exponential form (uppercase E for exponent)	Value must be number.
`f`, `F`	Floating-point value in decimal form	Value must be number.
`g`, `G`	Like `e` or `E` when *`exp`* is >=4 or < precision; otherwise, like `f` or `F`	*`exp`* is the exponent of the number being converted.
`c`	Single character	Value can be integer or single-character string.
`r`	String	Converts any value with `repr`.
`s`	String	Converts any value with `str`.
`%`	Literal % character	Consumes no value.

The r, s, and % conversion characters are the ones most often used with the logging module. Between the % and the conversion character, you can specify a number of optional modifiers, as we'll discuss shortly.

What is logged with a formatting expression is *format*, where each format specifier is replaced by the corresponding item of *values* converted to a string according to the specifier. Here are some simple examples:

```
import logging
logging.getLogger().setLevel(logging.INFO)
x = 42
y = 3.14
z = 'george'
logging.info('result = %d', x)          # logs: result = 42
logging.info('answers: %d %f', x, y)  # logs: answers: 42 3.140000
logging.info('hello %s', z)             # logs: hello george
```

Format Specifier Syntax

A format specifier can include modifiers to control how the corresponding item in *values* is converted to a string. The components of a format specifier, in order, are:

1. The mandatory leading % character that marks the start of the specifier
2. Zero or more optional conversion flags:

   #
   : The conversion uses an alternate form (if any exists for its type).

   0
   : The conversion is zero-padded.

   -
   : The conversion is left-justified.

   A space
   : A space is placed before a positive number.

   +
   : A numeric sign (+ or -) is placed before any numeric conversion.

3. An optional minimum width of the conversion: one or more digits, or an asterisk (*), meaning that the width is taken from the next item in *values*
4. An optional precision for the conversion: a dot (.) followed by zero or more digits, or by a *, meaning that the precision is taken from the next item in *values*
5. A mandatory conversion type from Table 8-6

Each format specifier corresponds to an item in *values* by position, and there must be exactly as many *values* as *format* has specifiers (plus one extra for each width or precision given by *). When a width or precision is given by *, the * consumes one item in *values*, which must be an integer and is taken as the number of characters to use as width or precision of that conversion.

When to use %r

Most often, the format specifiers in your *format* string are all `%s`; occasionally, you'll want to ensure horizontal alignment on the output (for example, in a right-justified, possibly truncated space of exactly six characters, in which case you might use `%6.6s`). However, there is an important special case for `%r`.

Always use %r to log possibly erroneous strings
When you're logging a string value that might be erroneous (for example, the name of a file that is not found), don't use `%s`: when the error is that the string has spurious leading or trailing spaces, or contains some nonprinting characters such as `\b`, `%s` might make this hard for you to spot by studying the logs. Use `%r` instead, so that all characters are clearly shown.

Text Wrapping and Filling

The `textwrap` module supplies a class and a few functions to format a string by breaking it into lines of a given maximum length. To fine-tune the filling and wrapping, you can instantiate the `TextWrapper` class supplied by `textwrap` and apply detailed control. Most of the time, however, one of the two main functions exposed by `textwrap` suffices:

wrap `wrap(`*`s`*`,`*`width`*`=70)`

Returns a list of strings (without terminating newlines), each of which is no longer than *`width`* characters, and which (joined back together with spaces) equal *`s`*. `wrap` also supports other named arguments (equivalent to attributes of instances of class `TextWrapper`); for such advanced uses, see the online docs (*https://docs.python.org/2/library/textwrap.html*).

fill `fill(`*`s`*`,`*`width`*`=70)`

Returns a single multiline string equal to `'\n'.join(wrap(`*`s`*`,`*`width`*`))`.

The pprint Module

The `pprint` module pretty-prints complicated data structures, with formatting that strives to be more readable than that supplied by the built-in function `repr` (covered in Table 7-2). To fine-tune the formatting, you can instantiate the `PrettyPrinter` class supplied by `pprint` and apply detailed control, helped by auxiliary functions also supplied by `pprint`. Most of the time, however, one of two functions exposed by `pprint` suffices:

pformat `pformat(obj)`

Returns a string representing the pretty-printing of *obj*.

pprint `pprint(obj,stream=sys.stdout)`

Outputs the pretty-printing of *obj* to open-for-writing file object *stream*, with a terminating newline.

The following statements do exactly the same thing:

```
print(pprint.pformat(x))
pprint.pprint(x)
```

Either of these constructs is roughly the same as `print(x)` in many cases, such as when the string representation of *x* fits within one line. However, with something like `x=list(range(30))`, `print(x)` displays *x* in two lines, breaking at an arbitrary point, while using the module `pprint` displays *x* over 30 lines, one line per item. You can use `pprint` when you prefer the module's specific display effects to the ones of normal string representation.

The reprlib Module

The `reprlib` module (named `repr` in v2) supplies an alternative to the built-in function `repr` (covered in Table 7-2), with limits on length for the representation string. To fine-tune the length limits, you can instantiate or subclass the `Repr` class supplied by the module and apply detailed control. Most of the time, however, the function exposed by the module suffices.

repr `repr(obj)`

Returns a string representing *obj*, with sensible limits on length.

Unicode

To convert bytestrings into Unicode strings, in v2, use the `unicode` built-in or the `decode` method of bytestrings; or, you can let the conversion happen implicitly, when you pass a bytestring to a function that expects Unicode. In v3, the conversion must always be explicit, with the `decode` method of bytestrings.

In either case, the conversion is done by an auxiliary object known as a *codec* (short for *co*der-*dec*oder). A codec can also convert Unicode strings to bytestrings, either explicitly, with the `encode` method of Unicode strings, or, in v2 only, implicitly.

To identify a codec, pass the codec name to `unicode`, `decode`, or `encode`. When you pass no codec name, and for v2 implicit conversion, Python uses a default encoding, normally `'ascii'` in v2 (`'utf8'` in v3).

Every conversion has a parameter *errors*, a string specifying how conversion errors are to be handled. The default is `'strict'`, meaning any error raises an exception.

When *errors* is 'replace', the conversion replaces each character causing errors with '?' in a bytestring result, with u'\ufffd' in a Unicode result. When *errors* is 'ignore', the conversion silently skips characters causing errors. When *errors* is 'xmlcharrefreplace', the conversion replaces each character causing errors with the XML character reference representation of that character in the result. You may code your own function to implement a conversion-error-handling strategy and register it under an appropriate name by calling codecs.register_error, covered in Table 8-7.

The codecs Module

The mapping of codec names to codec objects is handled by the codecs module. This module also lets you develop your own codec objects and register them so that they can be looked up by name, just like built-in codecs. The codecs module also lets you look up any codec explicitly, obtaining the functions the codec uses for encoding and decoding, as well as factory functions to wrap file-like objects. Such advanced facilities of the module codecs are rarely used, and we do not cover them in this book.

The codecs module, together with the encodings package of the standard Python library, supplies built-in codecs useful to Python developers dealing with internationalization issues. Python comes with over 100 codecs; a list of these codecs, with a brief explanation of each, is in the online docs (*https://docs.python.org/3/library/codecs.html#standard-encodings*). It's technically possible to install any supplied codec as the site-wide default in the module sitecustomize, but this is not good practice: rather, the preferred usage is to always specify the codec by name whenever you are converting between byte and Unicode strings. The codec installed by default in v2 is 'ascii', which accepts only characters with codes between 0 and 127, the 7-bit range of the American Standard Code for Information Interchange (ASCII) that is common to almost all encodings. A popular codec in Western Europe is 'latin-1', a fast, built-in implementation of the ISO 8859-1 encoding that offers a one-byte-per-character encoding of special characters found in Western European languages (note that 'latin-1' lacks the Euro currency character '€'; if you need that, use 'iso8859-15').

The codecs module also supplies codecs implemented in Python for most ISO 8859 encodings, with codec names from 'iso8859-1' to 'iso8859-15'. For example, if you use ASCII plus some Greek letters, as is common in scientific papers, you might choose 'iso8859-7'. On Windows systems only, the codec named 'mbcs' wraps the platform's multibyte character set conversion procedures. Many codecs specifically support Asian languages. The codecs module also supplies several standard code pages (codec names from 'cp037' to 'cp1258'), old Mac-specific encodings (codec names from 'mac-cyrillic' to 'mac-turkish'), and Unicode standard encodings 'utf-8' (likely to be most often the best choice, thus recommended, and the default in v3) and 'utf-16' (the latter also has specific big-endian and little-endian variants: 'utf-16-be' and 'utf-16-le'). For use with UTF-16, codecs also supplies attributes `BOM_BE` and `BOM_LE`, byte-order marks for big-endian and little-endian machines, respectively, and `BOM`, the byte-order mark for the current platform.

The `codecs` module also supplies a function to let you register your own conversion-error-handling functions, as described in Table 8-7.

Table 8-7.

register_error `register_error(`*`name`*`,`*`func`*`)`

name must be a string. *func* must be callable with one argument *e* that's an instance of exception `UnicodeDecodeError`, and must return a tuple with two items: the Unicode string to insert in the converted-string result and the index from which to continue the conversion (the latter is normally *e*`.end`). The function's body can use *e*`.encoding`, the name of the codec of this conversion, and *e*`.object[`*e*`.start:`*e*`.end]`, the substring that caused the conversion error.

The `codecs` module also supplies a function to help with files of encoded text:

EncodedFile `EncodedFile(`*`file`*`,`*`datacodec`*`,`*`filecodec`*`=None,`*`errors`*`='strict')`

Wraps the file-like object *file*, returning a file-like object *ef* that implicitly and transparently applies the given encodings to all data read from or written to the file. When you write a bytestring *s* to *ef*, *ef* first decodes *s* with the codec named by *datacodec*, then encodes the result with the codec named by *filecodec* and writes it to *file*. When you read a string, *ef* applies *filecodec* first, then *datacodec*. When *filecodec* is None, *ef* uses *datacodec* for both steps in either direction.

For example, if you want to write bytestrings that are encoded in `latin-1` to `sys.stdout` and have the strings come out in `utf-8`, in v2, use the following:

```
import sys, codecs
sys.stdout = codecs.EncodedFile(sys.stdout,'latin-1',
'utf-8')
```

It's normally sufficient to use, instead, `io.open`, covered in "Creating a "file" Object with io.open" on page 274.

The unicodedata Module

The `unicodedata` module supplies easy access to the Unicode Character Database. Given any Unicode character, you can use functions supplied by `unicodedata` to obtain the character's Unicode category, official name (if any), and other, more exotic information. You can also look up the Unicode character (if any) that corresponds to a given official name. Such advanced facilities are rarely needed, and we do not cover them further in this book.

9 Regular Expressions

Regular expressions let you specify pattern strings and perform searches and substitutions. Regular expressions are not easy to master, but they can be a powerful tool for processing text. Python offers rich regular expression functionality through the built-in `re` module.

Regular Expressions and the re Module

A *regular expression* (RE) is built from a string that represents a pattern. With RE functionality, you can examine any string with the pattern, and see which parts of the string, if any, match the pattern.

The `re` module supplies Python's RE functionality. The `compile` function builds an RE object from a pattern string and optional flags. The methods of an RE object look for matches of the RE in a string or perform substitutions. The `re` module also exposes functions equivalent to an RE object's methods, but with the RE's pattern string as the first argument.

REs can be difficult to master, and this book does not purport to teach them; we cover only the ways in which you can use REs in Python. For general coverage of REs, we recommend the book *Mastering Regular Expressions*, by Jeffrey Friedl (O'Reilly). Friedl's book offers thorough coverage of REs at both tutorial and advanced levels. Many tutorials and references on REs can also be found online, including an excellent, detailed tutorial in the online docs (*https://docs.python.org/3/howto/regex.html*). Sites like Pythex (*http://pythex.org/*) and regex101 (*https://regex101.com/*) let you test your REs interactively.

re and bytes Versus Unicode Strings

In v3, by default, REs work in two ways: when applied to `str` instances, an RE matches accordingly (for example, a Unicode character *c* is deemed to be "a letter" if `'LETTER' in unicodedata.name(c)`); when applied to `bytes` instances, an RE matches in terms of ASCII (for example, a byte character *c* is deemed to be "a letter" if `c in string.ascii_letters`). In v2, REs, by default, match in terms of ASCII, whether applied to `str` or `unicode` instances; you can override this behavior by explicitly specifying optional flags such as `re.U`, covered in "Optional Flags" on page 259. For example, in v3:

```
import re
print(re.findall(r'\w+', 'cittá'))
# prints ['cittá']
```

while, in v2:

```
import re
print(re.findall(r'\w+', u'cittá'))
# prints ['citt']
print(re.findall(r'\w+', u'cittá', re.U))
# prints ['citt\xe1']
```

Pattern-String Syntax

The pattern string representing a regular expression follows a specific syntax:

- Alphabetic and numeric characters stand for themselves. An RE whose pattern is a string of letters and digits matches the same string.
- Many alphanumeric characters acquire special meaning in a pattern when they are preceded by a backslash (\).
- Punctuation works the other way around: self-matching when escaped, special meaning when unescaped.
- The backslash character is matched by a repeated backslash (i.e., pattern \\).

Since RE patterns often contain backslashes, it's best to always specify them using raw-string syntax (covered in "Strings" on page 45). Pattern elements (such as `r'\t'`, equivalent to the nonraw string literal `'\\t'`) do match the corresponding special characters (in this case, the tab character `'\t'`, AKA `chr(9)`); so, you can use raw-string syntax even when you need a literal match for such special characters.

Table 9-1 lists the special elements in RE pattern syntax. The exact meanings of some pattern elements change when you use optional flags, together with the pattern string, to build the RE object. The optional flags are covered in "Optional Flags" on page 259.

Table 9-1. RE pattern syntax

Element	Meaning
.	Matches any single character except \n (if DOTALL, also matches \n)
^	Matches start of string (if MULTILINE, also matches right after \n)
$	Matches end of string (if MULTILINE, also matches right before \n)
*	Matches zero or more cases of the previous RE; greedy (match as many as possible)
+	Matches one or more cases of the previous RE; greedy (match as many as possible)
?	Matches zero or one case of the previous RE; greedy (match one if possible)
*?, +?, ??	Nongreedy versions of *, +, and ?, respectively (match as few as possible)
{*m*, *n*}	Matches between *m* and *n* cases of the previous RE (greedy)
{*m*, *n*}?	Matches between *m* and *n* cases of the previous RE (nongreedy)
[...]	Matches any one of a set of characters contained within the brackets
[^...]	Matches one character *not* contained within the brackets after the caret ^
|	Matches either the preceding RE or the following RE
(...)	Matches the RE within the parentheses and indicates a *group*
(?iLmsux)	Alternate way to set optional flags; no effect on match[a]
(?:...)	Like (...) but does not indicate a group
(?P<*id*>...)	Like (...) but the group also gets the name *id*
(?P=*id*)	Matches whatever was previously matched by group named *id*
(?#...)	Content of parentheses is just a comment; no effect on match
(?=...)	*Lookahead assertion*: matches if RE ... matches what comes next, but does not consume any part of the string
(?!...)	*Negative lookahead assertion*: matches if RE ... does not match what comes next, and does not consume any part of the string

Element	Meaning
(?<=...)	*Lookbehind assertion*: matches if there is a match ending at the current position for RE ... (... must match a fixed length)
(?<!...)	*Negative lookbehind assertion*: matches if there is no match ending at the current position for RE ... (... must match a fixed length)
\ *number*	Matches whatever was previously matched by group numbered *number* (groups are automatically numbered left to right, from 1 to 99)
\A	Matches an empty string, but only at the start of the whole string
\b	Matches an empty string, but only at the start or end of a word (a maximal sequence of alphanumeric characters; see also \w)
\B	Matches an empty string, but not at the start or end of a word
\d	Matches one digit, like the set [0-9] (in Unicode mode, many other Unicode characters also count as "digits" for \d, but not for [0-9])
\D	Matches one nondigit, like the set [^0-9] (in Unicode mode, many other Unicode characters also count as "digits" for \D, but not for [^0-9])
\s	Matches a whitespace character, like the set [\t\n\r\f\v]
\S	Matches a nonwhitespace character, like the set [^\t\n\r\f\v]
\w	Matches one alphanumeric character; unless in Unicode mode, or LOCALE or UNICODE is set, \w is like [a-zA-Z0-9_]
\W	Matches one nonalphanumeric character, the reverse of \w
\Z	Matches an empty string, but only at the end of the whole string
\\	Matches one backslash character

[a] Always place the (?...) construct, if any, at the start of the pattern, for readability; since 3.6, placing it elsewhere causes a DeprecationWarning.

Common Regular Expression Idioms

Always use r'...' syntax for RE pattern literals

Use raw-string syntax for all RE pattern literals, and for them only: this ensures you'll never forget to escape a backslash (\), and improves code readability as it makes your RE pattern literals stand out.

`.*` as a substring of a regular expression's pattern string means "any number of repetitions (zero or more) of any character." In other words, `.*` matches any substring of a target string, including the empty substring. `.+` is similar, but matches only a nonempty substring. For example:

```
r'pre.*post'
```

matches a string containing a substring `'pre'` followed by a later substring `'post'`, even if the latter is adjacent to the former (e.g., it matches both `'prepost'` and `'pre23post'`). On the other hand:

```
r'pre.+post'
```

matches only if `'pre'` and `'post'` are not adjacent (e.g., it matches `'pre23post'` but does not match `'prepost'`). Both patterns also match strings that continue after the `'post'`. To constrain a pattern to match only strings that *end* with `'post'`, end the pattern with `\Z`. For example:

```
r'pre.*post\Z'
```

matches `'prepost'`, but not `'preposterous'`.

All of these examples are *greedy*, meaning that they match the substring beginning with the first occurrence of `'pre'` all the way to the *last* occurrence of `'post'`. When you care about what part of the string you match, you may want to specify *nongreedy* matching, meaning to match the substring beginning with the first occurrence of `'pre'` but only up to the *first* following occurrence of `'post'`.

For example, when the string is `'preposterous and post facto'`, the greedy RE pattern `r'pre.*post'` matches the substring `'preposterous and post'`; the nongreedy variant `r'pre.*?post'` matches just the substring `'prepost'`.

Another frequently used element in RE patterns is `\b`, which matches a word boundary. To match the word `'his'` only as a whole word and not its occurrences as a substring in such words as `'this'` and `'history'`, the RE pattern is:

```
r'\bhis\b'
```

with word boundaries both before and after. To match the beginning of any word starting with `'her'`, such as `'her'` itself and `'hermetic'`, but not words that just contain `'her'` elsewhere, such as `'ether'` or `'there'`, use:

```
r'\bher'
```

with a word boundary before, but not after, the relevant string. To match the end of any word ending with `'its'`, such as `'its'` itself and `'fits'`, but not words that contain `'its'` elsewhere, such as `'itsy'` or `'jujitsu'`, use:

```
r'its\b'
```

with a word boundary after, but not before, the relevant string. To match whole words thus constrained, rather than just their beginning or end, add a pattern element `\w*` to match zero or more word characters. To match any full word starting with `'her'`, use:

```
r'\bher\w*'
```

To match just the first three letters of any word starting with `'her'`, but not the word `'her'` itself, use a negative word boundary `\B`:

```
r'\bher\B'
```

To match any full word ending with `'its'`, including `'its'` itself, use:

```
r'\w*its\b'
```

Sets of Characters

You denote sets of characters in a pattern by listing the characters within brackets (`[]`). In addition to listing characters, you can denote a range by giving the first and last characters of the range separated by a hyphen (`-`). The last character of the range is included in the set, differently from other Python ranges. Within a set, special characters stand for themselves, except `\`, `]`, and `-`, which you must escape (by preceding them with a backslash) when their position is such that, if unescaped, they would form part of the set's syntax. You can denote a class of characters within a set by escaped-letter notation, such as `\d` or `\S`. `\b` in a set means a backspace character (`chr(8)`), not a word boundary. If the first character in the set's pattern, right after the `[`, is a caret (`^`), the set is *complemented*: such a set matches any character *except* those that follow `^` in the set pattern notation.

A frequent use of character sets is to match a word using a definition of which characters can make up a word that differs from `\w`'s default (letters and digits). To match a word of one or more characters, each of which can be a letter, an apostrophe, or a hyphen, but not a digit (e.g., `"Finnegan-O'Hara"`), use:

```
r"[a-zA-Z'\-]+"
```

Escape a hyphen that's part of an RE character set, for readability

It's not strictly necessary to escape the hyphen with a backslash in this case, since its position at the end of the set makes the situation syntactically unambiguous. However, the backslash is advisable because it makes the pattern more readable by visually distinguishing the hyphen that you want to have as a character in the set from those used to denote ranges.

Alternatives

A vertical bar (`|`) in a regular expression pattern, used to specify alternatives, has low syntactic precedence. Unless parentheses change the grouping, `|` applies to the whole pattern on either side, up to the start or end of the pattern, or to another `|`. A pattern can be made up of any number of subpatterns joined by `|`. To match such an RE, the first subpattern is tried, and if it matches, the others are skipped. If the first subpattern doesn't match, the second subpattern is tried, and so on. `|` is neither greedy nor nongreedy: it just doesn't take the length of the match into account.

Given a list *L* of words, an RE pattern that matches any one of the words is:

```
'|'.join(r'\b{}\b'.format(word) for word in L)
```

Escaping strings

If the items of *L* can be more general strings, not just words, you need to escape each of them with the function `re.escape` (covered in Table 9-3), and you may not want the `\b` word boundary markers on either side. In this case, use the following RE pattern:

```
'|'.join(re.escape(s) for s in L)
```

Groups

A regular expression can contain any number of groups, from none to 99 (or even more, but only the first 99 groups are fully supported). Parentheses in a pattern string indicate a group. Element `(?P<id>...)` also indicates a group, and gives the group a name, *id*, that can be any Python identifier. All groups, named and unnamed, are numbered from left to right, 1 to 99; "group 0" means the whole RE.

For any match of the RE with a string, each group matches a substring (possibly an empty one). When the RE uses `|`, some groups may not match any substring, although the RE as a whole does match the string. When a group doesn't match any substring, we say that the group does not *participate* in the match. An empty string (`''`) is used as the matching substring for any group that does not participate in a match, except where otherwise indicated later in this chapter. For example:

```
r'(.+)\1+\Z'
```

matches a string made up of two or more repetitions of any nonempty substring. The `(.+)` part of the pattern matches any nonempty substring (any character, one or more times) and defines a group, thanks to the parentheses. The `\1+` part of the pattern matches one or more repetitions of the group, and `\Z` anchors the match to the end of the string.

Optional Flags

A regular expression pattern element with one or more of the letters `iLmsux` between `(?` and `)` lets you set RE options within the pattern, rather than by the *flags* argument to the compile function of the re module. Options apply to the whole RE, no matter where the options element occurs in the pattern.

For clarity, always place options at the start of an RE's pattern

In particular, placement at the start is mandatory if x is among the options, since x changes the way Python parses the pattern. In 3.6, options not at the start of the pattern produce a deprecation warning.

Using the explicit *flags* argument is more readable than placing an options element within the pattern. The *flags* argument to the function compile is a coded integer built by bitwise ORing (with Python's bitwise OR operator, |) one or more of the following attributes of the module re. Each attribute has both a short name (one uppercase letter), for convenience, and a long name (an uppercase multiletter identifier), which is more readable and thus normally preferable:

I *or* IGNORECASE
: Makes matching case-insensitive

L *or* LOCALE
: Causes \w, \W, \b, and \B matches to depend on what the current locale deems alphanumeric; deprecated in v3

M *or* MULTILINE
: Makes the special characters ^ and $ match at the start and end of each line (i.e., right after/before a newline), as well as at the start and end of the whole string (\A and \Z always match only the start and end of the whole string)

S *or* DOTALL
: Causes the special character . to match any character, including a newline

U *or* UNICODE
: Makes \w, \W, \b, and \B matches depend on what Unicode deems alphanumeric; deprecated in v3

X *or* VERBOSE
: Causes whitespace in the pattern to be ignored, except when escaped or in a character set, and makes a # character in the pattern begin a comment that lasts until the end of the line

For example, here are three ways to define equivalent REs with function compile, covered in Table 9-3. Each of these REs matches the word "hello" in any mix of upper- and lowercase letters:

```
import re
r1 = re.compile(r'(?i)hello')
r2 = re.compile(r'hello', re.I)
r3 = re.compile(r'hello', re.IGNORECASE)
```

The third approach is clearly the most readable, and thus the most maintainable, even though it is slightly more verbose. The raw-string form is not necessary here, since the patterns do not include backslashes; however, using raw strings is innocuous, and we recommend you always do that for RE patterns, to improve clarity and readability.

Option `re.VERBOSE` (or `re.X`) lets you make patterns more readable and understandable by appropriate use of whitespace and comments. Complicated and verbose RE patterns are generally best represented by strings that take up more than one line, and therefore you normally want to use the triple-quoted raw-string format for such pattern strings. For example, to match old-style Python v2 `int` literals:

```
repat_num1 = r'(0[0-7]*|0x[\da-fA-F]+|[1-9]\d*)L?\Z'
repat_num2 = r'''(?x)            # pattern matching int literals
              (0 [0-7]*         | # octal: leading 0, 0+ octal digits
               0x [\da-fA-F]+   | # hex: 0x, then 1+ hex digits
               [1-9] \d*        ) # decimal: leading non-0, 0+ digits
               L?\Z               # optional trailing L, end of string
              '''
```

The two patterns defined in this example are equivalent, but the second one is made more readable and understandable by the comments and the free use of whitespace to visually group portions of the pattern in logical ways.

Match Versus Search

So far, we've been using regular expressions to *match* strings. For example, the RE with pattern `r'box'` matches strings such as `'box'` and `'boxes'`, but not `'inbox'`. In other words, an RE match is implicitly anchored at the start of the target string, as if the RE's pattern started with `\A`.

Often, you're interested in locating possible matches for an RE anywhere in the string, without anchoring (e.g., find the `r'box'` match inside such strings as `'inbox'`, as well as in `'box'` and `'boxes'`). In this case, the Python term for the operation is a *search*, as opposed to a match. For such searches, use the `search` method of an RE object; the `match` method deals with matching only from the start. For example:

```
import re
r1 = re.compile(r'box')
if r1.match('inbox'):
    print('match succeeds')
else:
    print('match fails')          # prints: match fails
if r1.search('inbox'):
    print('search succeeds')      # prints: search succeeds
else:
    print('search fails')
```

Regular Expressions

Anchoring at String Start and End

The pattern elements ensuring that a regular expression search (or match) is anchored at string start and string end are `\A` and `\Z`, respectively. More traditionally, elements `^` for start and `$` for end are also used in similar roles. `^` is the same as `\A`, and `$` is the same as `\Z`, for RE objects that are not multiline (i.e., that do not contain pattern element `(?m)` and are not compiled with the flag `re.M` or `re.MULTILINE`). For a multiline RE, however, `^` anchors at the start of any line (i.e., either at the start of the whole string or at any position right after a newline character `\n`). Similarly, with a multiline RE, `$` anchors at the end of any line (i.e., either at the end of the whole string or at any position right before a `\n`). On the other hand, `\A` and `\Z` anchor at the start and end of the string whether the RE object is multiline or not. For example, here's a way to check whether a file has any lines that end with digits:

```
import re
digatend = re.compile(r'\d$', re.MULTILINE)
with open('afile.txt') as f:
    if digatend.search(f.read()):
        print('some lines end with digits')
    else:
        print('no line ends with digits')
```

A pattern of `r'\d\n'` is almost equivalent, but in that case the search fails if the very last character of the file is a digit not followed by an end-of-line character. With the preceding example, the search succeeds if a digit is at the very end of the file's contents, as well as in the more usual case where a digit is followed by an end-of-line character.

Regular Expression Objects

A regular expression object *r* has the following read-only attributes that detail how *r* was built (by the function `compile` of the module `re`, covered in Table 9-3):

`flags`
: The *`flags`* argument passed to `compile`, or `0` when *`flags`* is omitted (in v2; in v3, the default when *`flags`* is omitted is `re.UNICODE`)

`groupindex`
: A dictionary whose keys are group names as defined by elements `(?P<`*`id`*`>...)`; the corresponding values are the named groups' numbers

`pattern`
: The pattern string from which *r* is compiled

These attributes make it easy to get back from a compiled RE object to its pattern string and flags, so you never have to store those separately.

An RE object *r* also supplies methods to locate matches for *r* within a string, as well as to perform substitutions on such matches (Table 9-2). Matches are generally represented by special objects, covered in "Match Objects" on page 265.

Table 9-2.

findall `r.findall(s)`

When *r* has no groups, `findall` returns a list of strings, each a substring of *s* that is a nonoverlapping match with *r*. For example, to print out all words in a file, one per line:

```
import re
reword = re.compile(r'\w+')
with open('afile.txt') as f:
    for aword in reword.findall(f.read()):
        print(aword)
```

When *r* has one group, `findall` also returns a list of strings, but each is the substring of *s* that matches *r*'s group. For example, to print only words that are followed by whitespace (not the ones followed by punctuation), you need to change only one statement in the example:

```
reword = re.compile('(\w+)\s')
```

When *r* has *n* groups (with *n*>1), `findall` returns a list of tuples, one per nonoverlapping match with *r*. Each tuple has *n* items, one per group of *r*, the substring of *s* matching the group. For example, to print the first and last word of each line that has at least two words:

```
import re
first_last =
  re.compile(r'^\W*(\w+)\b.*\b(\w+)\W*$',re.MULTILINE)
with open('afile.txt') as f:
    for first, last in first_last.findall(f.read()):
        print(first, last)
```

finditer `r.finditer(s)`

`finditer` is like `findall` except that instead of a list of strings (or tuples), it returns an iterator whose items are match objects. In most cases, `finditer` is therefore more flexible and performs better than `findall`.

match `r.match(s,start=0,end=sys.maxsize)`

Returns an appropriate match object when a substring of *s*, starting at index *start* and not reaching as far as index *end*, matches *r*. Otherwise, `match` returns `None`. Note that `match` is implicitly anchored at the starting position *start* in *s*. To search for a match with *r* at any point in *s* from *start* onward, call `r.search`, not `r.match`. For example, here one way to print all lines in a file that start with digits:

```
import re
digs = re.compile(r'\d')
with open('afile.txt') as f:
    for line in f:
        if digs.match(line):
            print(line, end='')
```

search `r.search(s,start=0,end=sys.maxsize)`

Returns an appropriate match object for the leftmost substring of *s*, starting not before index *start* and not reaching as far as index *end*, that matches *r*. When no such substring exists, `search` returns `None`. For example, to print all lines containing digits, one simple approach is as follows:

```
import re
digs = re.compile(r'\d')
with open('afile.txt') as f:
    for line in f:
        if digs.search(line):
            print(line, end='')
```

split `r.split(s,maxsplit=0)`

Returns a list *L* of the *splits* of *s* by *r* (i.e., the substrings of *s* separated by nonoverlapping, nonempty matches with *r*). For example, here's one way to eliminate all occurrences of substring `'hello'` (in any mix of lowercase and uppercase) from a string:

```
import re
rehello = re.compile(r'hello', re.IGNORECASE)
astring = ''.join(rehello.split(astring))
```

When *r* has *n* groups, *n* more items are interleaved in *L* between each pair of splits. Each of the *n* extra items is the substring of *s* that matches *r*'s corresponding group in that match, or `None` if that group did not participate in the match. For example, here's one way to remove whitespace only when it occurs between a colon and a digit:

```
import re
re_col_ws_dig = re.compile(r'(:)\s+(\d)')
astring = ''.join(re_col_ws_dig.split(astring))
```

If *maxsplit* is greater than `0`, at most *maxsplit* splits are in *L*, each followed by *n* items as above, while the trailing substring of *s* after *maxsplit* matches of *r*, if any, is *L*'s last item. For example, to remove only the first occurrence of substring `'hello'` rather than all of them, change the last statement in the first example above to:

```
astring = ''.join(rehello.split(astring, 1))
```

sub `r.sub(repl,s,count=0)`

Returns a copy of *s* where non-overlapping matches with *r* are replaced by *repl*, which can be either a string or a callable object, such as a function. An empty match is replaced only when not adjacent to the previous match. When *count* is greater than `0`, only the first *count* matches of *r* within *s* are replaced. When *count* equals `0`, all matches of *r* within *s* are replaced. For example, here's another, more natural way to remove only the first occurrence of substring `'hello'` in any mix of cases:

```
import re
rehello = re.compile(r'hello', re.IGNORECASE)
astring = rehello.sub('', astring, 1)
```

Without the final `1` argument to `sub`, the example removes all occurrences of `'hello'`.

When *repl* is a callable object, *repl* must accept one argument (a match object) and return a string (or `None`, which is equivalent to returning the empty string `''`) to use as the replacement for the match. In this case, sub calls *repl*, with a suitable match-object argument, for each match with *r* that sub is replacing. For example, here's one way to uppercase all occurrences of words starting with 'h' and ending with 'o' in any mix of cases:

```
import re
h_word = re.compile(r'\bh\w*o\b', re.IGNORECASE)
def up(mo): return mo.group(0).upper()
astring = h_word.sub(up, astring)
```

When *repl* is a string, sub uses *repl* itself as the replacement, except that it expands back references. A *back reference* is a substring of *repl* of the form \g<*id*>, where *id* is the name of a group in *r* (established by syntax (?P<*id*>...) in *r*'s pattern string) or *dd*, where *dd* is one or two digits taken as a group number. Each back reference, named or numbered, is replaced with the substring of *s* that matches the group of *r* that the back reference indicates. For example, here's a way to enclose every word in braces:

```
import re
grouped_word = re.compile('(\w+)')
astring = grouped_word.sub(r'{\1}', astring)
```

subn *r*.subn(*repl*,*s*, *count*=0)

subn is the same as sub, except that subn returns a pair (*new_string*, *n*), where *n* is the number of substitutions that subn has performed. For example, here's one way to count the number of occurrences of substring 'hello' in any mix of cases:

```
import re
rehello = re.compile(r'hello', re.IGNORECASE)
_, count = rehello.subn('', astring)
print('Found', count, 'occurrences of "hello"')
```

Match Objects

Match objects are created and returned by the methods match and search of a regular expression object, and are the items of the iterator returned by the method finditer. They are also implicitly created by the methods sub and subn when the argument *repl* is callable, since in that case the appropriate match object is passed as the argument on each call to *repl*. A match object *m* supplies the following read-only attributes that detail how *m* was created:

pos
: The *start* argument that was passed to search or match (i.e., the index into *s* where the search for a match began)

endpos
: The *end* argument that was passed to search or match (i.e., the index into *s* before which the matching substring of *s* had to end)

lastgroup
: The name of the last-matched group (None if the last-matched group has no name, or if no group participated in the match)

`lastindex`
: The integer index (1 and up) of the last-matched group (`None` if no group participated in the match)

`re`
: The RE object *r* whose method created *m*

`string`
: The string *s* passed to `finditer`, `match`, `search`, `sub`, or `subn`

A match object *m* also supplies several methods, detailed in Table 9-3.

Table 9-3.

end, span, start	*m*`.end(`*groupid*`=0)` *m*`.span(`*groupid*`=0)` *m*`.start(`*groupid*`=0)` These methods return the limit indices, within *m*`.string`, of the substring that matches the group identified by *groupid* (a group number or name; "group `0`", the default value for *groupid*, means "the whole RE"). When the matching substring is *m*`.string[`*i*`:`*j*`]`, *m*`.start` returns *i*, *m*`.end` returns *j*, and *m*`.span` returns `(`*i*`,` *j*`)`. If the group did not participate in the match, *i* and *j* are `-1`.
expand	*m*`.expand(`*s*`)` Returns a copy of *s* where escape sequences and back references are replaced in the same way as for the method *r*`.sub`, covered in Table 9-2.
group	*m*`.group(`*groupid*`=0,*`*groupids*`)` When called with a single argument *groupid* (a group number or name), `group` returns the substring that matches the group identified by *groupid*, or `None` if that group did not participate in the match. The idiom *m*`.group()`, also spelled *m*`.group(0)`, returns the whole matched substring, since group number `0` means the whole RE. When `group` is called with multiple arguments, each argument must be a group number or name. `group` then returns a tuple with one item per argument, the substring matching the corresponding group, or `None` if that group did not participate in the match.
groups	*m*`.groups(`*default*`=None)` Returns a tuple with one item per group in *r*. Each item is the substring that matches the corresponding group, or *default* if that group did not participate in the match.
groupdict	*m*`.groupdict(`*default*`=None)` Returns a dictionary whose keys are the names of all named groups in *r*. The value for each name is the substring that matches the corresponding group, or *default* if that group did not participate in the match.

Functions of the re Module

The re module supplies the attributes listed in "Optional Flags" on page 259. It also provides one function for each method of a regular expression object (findall, finditer, match, search, split, sub, and subn), each with an additional first argument, a pattern string that the function implicitly compiles into an RE object. It's usually better to compile pattern strings into RE objects explicitly and call the RE object's methods, but sometimes, for a one-off use of an RE pattern, calling functions of the module re can be slightly handier. For example, to count the number of occurrences of 'hello' in any mix of cases, one concise, function-based way is:

```
import re
_, count = re.subn(r'(?i)hello', '', astring)
print('Found', count, 'occurrences of "hello"')
```

In such cases, RE options (here, case insensitivity) must be encoded as RE pattern elements (here (?i)): the functions of the re module do not accept a *flags* argument. The re module internally caches RE objects it creates from the patterns passed to functions; to purge the cache and reclaim some memory, call re.purge().

The re module also supplies error, the class of exceptions raised upon errors (generally, errors in the syntax of a pattern string), and two more functions:

compile compile(*pattern*,*flags*=0)

Creates and returns an RE object, parsing string *pattern* as per the syntax covered in "Pattern-String Syntax" on page 254, and using integer *flags*, as covered in "Optional Flags" on page 259.

escape escape(*s*)

Returns a copy of string *s* with each nonalphanumeric character escaped (i.e., preceded by a backslash \); useful to match string *s* literally as part of an RE pattern string.

III

Python Library and Extension Modules

10 File and Text Operations

This chapter covers most of the issues related to dealing with files and filesystems in Python. A *file* is a stream of text or bytes that a program can read and/or write; a *filesystem* is a hierarchical repository of files on a computer system.

Other Chapters That Also Deal with Files

Because files are such a crucial concept in programming, even though this chapter is the largest one in the book, several other chapters also contain material that is relevant when you're handling specific kinds of files. In particular, Chapter 11 deals with many kinds of files related to persistence and database functionality (JSON files in "The json Module" on page 338, pickle files in "The pickle and cPickle Modules" on page 341, shelve files in "The shelve Module" on page 347, DBM and DBM-like files in "The v3 dbm Package" on page 348, and SQLite database files in "SQLite" on page 358), Chapter 22 deals with files and other streams in HTML format, and Chapter 23 deals with files and other streams in XML format.

Organization of This Chapter

Files and streams come in many flavors: their contents can be arbitrary bytes or text (with various encodings, if the underlying storage or channel deals only with bytes, as most do); they may be suitable for reading, writing, or both; they may or may not be *buffered*; they may or may not allow "random access," going back and forth in the file (a stream whose underlying channel is an Internet socket, for example, only allows sequential, "going forward" access—there's no "going back and forth").

Traditionally, old-style Python coalesced most of this diverse functionality into the built-in `file` object, working in different ways depending on how the built-in function `open` created it. These built-ins are still in v2, for backward compatibility.

In both v2 and v3, however; input/output (I/O) is more logically structured, within the standard library's `io` module. In v3, the built-in function `open` is, in fact, simply an alias for the function `io.open`. In v2, the built-in `open` still works the old-fashioned way, creating and returning an old-fashioned built-in `file` object (a type that does not exist anymore in v3). However, you can `from io import open` to use, instead, the new and better structured `io.open`: the file-like objects it returns operate quite similarly to the old-fashioned built-in `file` objects in most simple cases, and you can call the new function in a similar way to old-fashioned built-in function `open`, too. (Alternatively, of course, in both v2 and v3, you can practice the excellent principle "explicit is better than implicit" by doing `import io` and then explicitly using `io.open`.)

If you have to maintain old code using built-in file objects in complicated ways, and don't want to port that code to the newer approach, use the online docs (*https://docs.python.org/2.7/library/stdtypes.html#file-objects*) as a reference to the details of old-fashioned built-in `file` objects. This book (and, specifically, the start of this chapter) does not cover old-fashioned built-in `file` objects, just `io.open` and the various classes from the `io` module.

Immediately after that, this chapter covers the polymorphic concept of file-like objects (objects that are not actually files but behave to some extent like files) in "File-Like Objects and Polymorphism" on page 278.

The chapter next covers modules that deal with temporary files and file-like objects (`tempfile` in "The tempfile Module" on page 279, and `io.StringIO` and `io.BytesIO` in "In-Memory "Files": io.StringIO and io.BytesIO" on page 286).

Next comes the coverage of modules that help you access the contents of text and binary files (`fileinput` in "The fileinput Module" on page 281, `linecache` in "The linecache Module" on page 283, and `struct` in "The struct Module" on page 284) and support compressed files and other data archives (`gzip` in "The gzip Module" on page 287, `bz2` in "The bz2 Module" on page 289, `tarfile` in "The tarfile Module" on page 290, `zipfile` in "The zipfile Module" on page 292, and `zlib` in "The zlib Module" on page 297). v3 also supports LZMA compression, as used, for example, by the `xz` program: we don't cover that issue in this book, but see the online docs (*https://docs.python.org/3/library/lzma.html*) and PyPI (*https://pypi.python.org/pypi/backports.lzma*) for a backport to v2.

In Python, the `os` module supplies many of the functions that operate on the filesystem, so this chapter continues by introducing the `os` module in "The os Module" on page 297. The chapter then covers, in "Filesystem Operations" on page 299, operations on the filesystem (comparing, copying, and deleting directories and files; working with file paths; and accessing low-level file descriptors) offered by `os` (in "File and Directory Functions of the os Module" on page 300), `os.path` (in "The os.path Module" on page 305), and other modules (`dircache` under `listdir` in Table 10-3, `stat` in "The stat Module" on page 308, `filecmp` in "The filecmp Module" on page 309, `fnmatch` in "The fnmatch Module" on page 311, `glob` in "The glob

Module" on page 312, and `shutil` in "The shutil Module" on page 313). We do not cover the module `pathlib`, supplying an object-oriented approach to filesystem paths, since, as of this writing, it has been included in the standard library only on a *provisional* basis, meaning it can undergo backward-incompatible changes, up to and including removal of the module; if you nevertheless want to try it out, see the online docs (*https://docs.python.org/3/library/pathlib.html*), and PyPI (*https://pypi.python.org/pypi/pathlib/*) for a v2 backport.

While most modern programs rely on a graphical user interface (GUI), often via a browser or a smartphone app, text-based, nongraphical "command-line" user interfaces are still useful, since they're simple, fast to program, and lightweight. This chapter concludes with material about text input and output in Python in "Text Input and Output" on page 317, richer text I/O in "Richer-Text I/O" on page 319, interactive command-line sessions in "Interactive Command Sessions" on page 325, and, finally, a subject generally known as *internationalization* (often abbreviated *i18n*). Building software that processes text understandable to different users, across languages and cultures, is described in "Internationalization" on page 329.

The io Module

As mentioned in "Organization of This Chapter" on page 271, `io` is a standard library module in Python and provides the most common ways for your Python programs to read or write files. Use `io.open` to make a Python "file" object—which, depending on what parameters you pass to `io.open`, can in fact be an instance of `io.TextIOWrapper` if textual, or, if binary, `io.BufferedReader`, `io.BufferedWriter`, or `io.BufferedRandom`, depending on whether it's read-only, write-only, or read-write—to read and/or write data to a file as seen by the underlying operating system. We refer to these as "file" objects, in quotes, to distinguish them from the old-fashioned built-in `file` type still present in v2.

In v3, the built-in function `open` is a synonym for `io.open`. In v2, use `from io import open` to get the same effect. We use `io.open` explicitly (assuming a previous `import io` has executed, of course), for clarity and to avoid ambiguity.

This section covers such "file" objects, as well as the important issue of making and using *temporary* files (on disk, or even in memory).

Python reacts to any I/O error related to a "file" object by raising an instance of built-in exception class `IOError` (in v3, that's a synonym for `OSError`, but many useful subclasses exist, and are covered in "OSError and subclasses (v3 only)" on page 162). Errors that cause this exception include `open` failing to open a file, calls to a method on a "file" to which that method doesn't apply (e.g., calling `write` on a read-only "file," or calling `seek` on a nonseekable file)—which could also cause `ValueError` or `AttributeError`—and I/O errors diagnosed by a "file" object's methods.

The `io` module also provides the underlying web of classes, both abstract and concrete, that, by inheritance and by composition (also known as *wrapping*), make up the "file" objects (instances of classes mentioned in the first paragraph of this section) that your program generally uses. We do not cover these advanced topics in this book. If you have access to unusual channels for data, or nonfilesystem data storage, and want to provide a "file" interface to those channels or storage, you can ease your task, by appropriate subclassing and wrapping, using other classes in the module `io`. For such advanced tasks, consult the online docs (*https://docs.python.org/3/library/io.html*).

Creating a "file" Object with io.open

To create a Python "file" object, call `io.open` with the following syntax:

```
open(file, mode='r', buffering=-1, encoding=None, errors='strict',
     newline=None, closefd=True, opener=os.open)
```

`file` can be a string, in which case it's any path to a file as seen by the underlying OS, or it can be an integer, in which case it's an OS-level *file descriptor* as returned by `os.open` (or, in v3 only, whatever function you pass as the *`opener`* argument—*`opener`* is not supported in v2). When *`file`* is a string, `open` opens the file thus named (possibly creating it, depending on *`mode`*—despite its name, `open` is not just for opening existing files: it can also create new ones); when *`file`* is an integer, the underlying OS file must already be open (via `os.open` or whatever).

Opening a file Pythonically

`open` is a context manager: use `with io.open(...) as f:`, *not* `f = io.open(...)`, to ensure the "file" *f* gets closed as soon as the `with` statement's body is done.

`open` creates and returns an instance *f* of the appropriate class of the module `io`, depending on mode and buffering—we refer to all such instances as "file" objects; they all are reasonably polymorphic with respect to each other.

mode

`mode` is a string indicating how the file is to be opened (or created). `mode` can be:

`'r'`
: The file must already exist, and it is opened in read-only mode.

`'w'`
: The file is opened in write-only mode. The file is truncated to zero length and overwritten if it already exists, or created if it does not exist.

`'a'`
: The file is opened in write-only mode. The file is kept intact if it already exists, and the data you write is appended to what's already in the file. The file is created if it does not exist. Calling `f.seek` on the file changes the result of the method `f.tell`, but does not change the write position in the file.

`'r+'`
: The file must already exist and is opened for both reading and writing, so all methods of *f* can be called.

`'w+'`
: The file is opened for both reading and writing, so all methods of *f* can be called. The file is truncated and overwritten if it already exists, or created if it does not exist.

`'a+'`
: The file is opened for both reading and writing, so all methods of *f* can be called. The file is kept intact if it already exists, and the data you write is appended to what's already in the file. The file is created if it does not exist. Calling `f.seek` on the file, depending on the underlying operating system, may have no effect when the next I/O operation on *f* *writes* data, but does work normally when the next I/O operation on *f* *reads* data.

Binary and text modes

The *`mode`* string may have any of the values just explained, followed by a `b` or `t`. `b` means a binary file, while `t` means a text one. When *`mode`* has neither `b` nor `t`, the default is text (i.e., `'r'` is like `'rt'`, `'w'` is like `'wt'`, and so on).

Binary files let you read and/or write strings of type `bytes`; text ones let you read and/or write Unicode text strings (`str` in v3, `unicode` in v2). For text files, when the underlying channel or storage system deals in bytes (as most do), *`encoding`* (the name of an encoding known to Python) and *`errors`* (an error-handler name such as `'strict'`, `'replace'`, and so on, as covered under `decode` in Table 8-6) matter, as they specify how to translate between text and bytes, and what to do on encoding and decoding errors.

Buffering

`buffering` is an integer that denotes the buffering you're requesting for the file. When *`buffering`* is less than `0`, a default is used. Normally, this default is line buffering for files that correspond to interactive consoles, and a buffer of `io.DEFAULT_BUFFER_SIZE` bytes for other files. When *`buffering`* is `0`, the file is unbuffered; the effect is as if the file's buffer were flushed every time you write anything to the file. When *`buffering`* equals `1`, the file (which must be text mode) is line-buffered, which means the file's buffer is flushed every time you write `\n` to the file. When *`buffering`* is greater than `1`, the file uses a buffer of about *`buffering`* bytes, rounded up to some reasonable amount.

Sequential and nonsequential ("random") access

A "file" object *f* is inherently sequential (a stream of bytes or text). When you read, you get bytes or text in the sequential order in which they're present. When you write, the bytes or text you write are added in the order in which you write them.

To allow nonsequential access (also known as "random access"), a "file" object whose underlying storage allows this keeps track of its current position (the position in the underlying file where the next read or write operation starts transferring data). `f.seekable()` returns `True` when *f* supports nonsequential access.

When you open a file, the initial position is at the start of the file. Any call to `f.write` on a "file" object *f* opened with a *mode* of `'a'` or `'a+'` always sets *f*'s position to the end of the file before writing data to *f*. When you write or read *n* bytes to/from "file" object *f*, *f*'s position advances by *n*. You can query the current position by calling `f.tell` and change the position by calling `f.seek`, both covered in the next section.

`f.tell` and `f.seek` also work on a text-mode *f*, but in this case the offset you pass to `f.seek` must be `0` (to position *f* at the start or end, depending on `f.seek`'s second parameter), or the opaque result previously returned by a call to `f.tell`, to position *f* back to a position you had thus "bookmarked" before.

Attributes and Methods of "file" Objects

A "file" object *f* supplies the attributes and methods documented in this section.

close `f.close()`

Closes the file. You can call no other method on *f* after `f.close`. Multiple calls to `f.close` are allowed and innocuous.

closed `closed`

`f.closed` is a read-only attribute that is `True` when `f.close()` has been called; otherwise, `False`.

encoding `encoding`

`f.encoding` is a read-only attribute, a string naming the encoding (as covered in "Unicode" on page 250). The attribute does not exist on binary "files."

flush `f.flush()`

Requests that *f*'s buffer be written out to the operating system, so that the file as seen by the system has the exact contents that Python's code has written. Depending on the platform and the nature of *f*'s underlying file, `f.flush` may not be able to ensure the desired effect.

isatty `f.isatty()`

`True` when *f*'s underlying file is an interactive terminal; otherwise, `False`.

fileno `f.fileno()`

Returns an integer, the file descriptor of *f*'s file at operating-system level. File descriptors are covered in "File and Directory Functions of the os Module" on page 300.

mode `mode`

`f.mode` is a read-only attribute that is the value of the *`mode`* string used in the `io.open` call that created *f*.

name `name`

`f.name` is a read-only attribute that is the value of the *`file`* string or `int` used in the `io.open` call that created *f*.

read `f.read(size=-1)`

In v2, or in v3 when *f* is open in binary mode, `read` reads up to *`size`* bytes from *f*'s file and returns them as a bytestring. `read` reads and returns less than *`size`* bytes if the file ends before *`size`* bytes are read. When *`size`* is less than `0`, `read` reads and returns all bytes up to the end of the file. `read` returns an empty string when the file's current position is at the end of the file or when *`size`* equals `0`. In v3, when *f* is open in text mode, *`size`* is a number of characters, not bytes, and `read` returns a text string.

readline `f.readline(size=-1)`

Reads and returns one line from *f*'s file, up to the end of line (`\n`), included. When *`size`* is greater than or equal to `0`, `readline` reads no more than *`size`* bytes. In that case, the returned string might not end with `\n`. `\n` might also be absent when `readline` reads up to the end of the file without finding `\n`. `readline` returns an empty string when the file's current position is at the end of the file or when *`size`* equals `0`.

readlines `f.readlines(size=-1)`

Reads and returns a list of all lines in *f*'s file, each a string ending in `\n`. If *`size`*`>0`, `readlines` stops and returns the list after collecting data for a total of about *`size`* bytes rather than reading all the way to the end of the file; in that case, the last string in the list might not end in `\n`.

seek `f.seek(pos, how=io.SEEK_SET)`

Sets *f*'s current position to the signed integer byte offset *`pos`* away from a reference point. *`how`* indicates the reference point. The `io` module has attributes named `SEEK_SET`, `SEEK_CUR`, and `SEEK_END`, to specify that the reference point is, respectively, the file's beginning, current position, or end.

When *f* is opened in text mode, `f.seek` must have a *`pos`* of `0`, or, for `io.SEEK_SET` only, a *`pos`* that is the result of a previous call to `f.tell`.

When *f* is opened in mode `'a'` or `'a+'`, on some but not all platforms, data written to *f* is appended to the data that is already in *f*, regardless of calls to `f.seek`.

tell `f.tell()`

Returns *f*'s current position: for a binary file, that's an integer offset in bytes from the start of the file; for a text file, an opaque value usable in future calls to `f.seek` to position *f* back to the position that is now current.

truncate `f.truncate([size])`

Truncates *f*'s file, which must be open for writing. When *size* is present, truncates the file to be at most *size* bytes. When *size* is absent, uses `f.tell()` as the file's new size.

write `f.write(s)`

Writes the bytes of string *s* (binary or text, depending on *f*'s mode) to the file.

writelines `f.writelines(lst)`

Like:

```
for line in lst: f.write(line)
```

It does not matter whether the strings in iterable *lst* are lines: despite its name, the method `writelines` just writes each of the strings to the file, one after the other. In particular, `writelines` does not add line-ending markers: such markers must, if required, already be present in the items of *lst*.

Iteration on "File" Objects

A "file" object *f*, open for text-mode reading, is also an iterator whose items are the file's lines. Thus, the loop:

```
for line in f:
```

iterates on each line of the file. Due to buffering issues, interrupting such a loop prematurely (e.g., with `break`), or calling `next(f)` instead of `f.readline()`, leaves the file's position set to an arbitrary value. If you want to switch from using *f* as an iterator to calling other reading methods on *f*, be sure to set the file's position to a known value by appropriately calling `f.seek`. On the plus side, a loop directly on *f* has very good performance, since these specifications allow the loop to use internal buffering to minimize I/O without taking up excessive amounts of memory even for huge files.

File-Like Objects and Polymorphism

An object *x* is file-like when it behaves *polymorphically* to a "file" object as returned by `io.open`, meaning that we can use *x* "as if" *x* were a "file." Code using such an object (known as *client code* of the object) usually gets the object as an argument, or by calling a factory function that returns the object as the result. For example, if the only method that client code calls on *x* is `x.read()`, without arguments, then all *x* needs to supply in order to be file-like for that code is a method `read` that is callable without arguments and returns a string. Other client code may need *x* to implement a larger subset of file methods. File-like objects and polymorphism are not absolute concepts: they are relative to demands placed on an object by some specific client code.

Polymorphism is a powerful aspect of object-oriented programming, and file-like objects are a good example of polymorphism. A client-code module that writes to or reads from files can automatically be reused for data residing elsewhere, as long as the module does not break polymorphism by the dubious practice of type checking. When we discussed built-ins `type` and `isinstance` in Table 7-1, we mentioned that type checking is often best avoided, as it blocks the normal polymorphism that Python otherwise supplies. Most often, to support polymorphism in your client code, all you have to do is avoid type checking.

You can implement a file-like object by coding your own class (as covered in Chapter 4) and defining the specific methods needed by client code, such as `read`. A file-like object *fl* need not implement all the attributes and methods of a true "file" object *f*. If you can determine which methods the client code calls on *fl*, you can choose to implement only that subset. For example, when *fl* is only going to be written, *fl* doesn't need "reading" methods, such as `read`, `readline`, and `readlines`.

If the main reason you want a file-like object instead of a real file object is to keep the data in memory, use the `io` module's classes `StringIO` and `BytesIO`, covered in "In-Memory "Files": io.StringIO and io.BytesIO" on page 286. These classes supply "file" objects that hold data in memory and largely behave polymorphically to other "file" objects.

The tempfile Module

The `tempfile` module lets you create temporary files and directories in the most secure manner afforded by your platform. Temporary files are often a good solution when you're dealing with an amount of data that might not comfortably fit in memory, or when your program must write data that another process later uses.

The order of the parameters for the functions in this module is a bit confusing: to make your code more readable, always call these functions with named-argument syntax. The `tempfile` module exposes the functions and classes outlined in Table 10-1.

Table 10-1.

mkdtemp

`mkdtemp(`*`suffix`*`=None,` *`prefix`*`=None,` *`dir`*`=None)`

Securely creates a new temporary directory that is readable, writable, and searchable only by the current user, and returns the absolute path to the temporary directory. The optional arguments *`suffix`*, *`prefix`*, and *`dir`* are like for function `mkstemp`. Ensuring that the temporary directory is removed when you're done using it is your program's responsibility. Here is a typical usage example that creates a temporary directory, passes its path to another function, and finally ensures the directory is removed together with all of its contents:

```
import tempfile, shutil
path = tempfile.mkdtemp()
try:
    use_dirpath(path)
finally:
    shutil.rmtree(path)
```

mkstemp

`mkstemp(`*`suffix`*`=None,` *`prefix`*`=None,` *`dir`*`=None,` *`text`*`=False)`

Securely creates a new temporary file, readable and writable only by the current user, not executable, not inherited by subprocesses; returns a pair `(`*`fd`*`,` *`path`*`)`, where *`fd`* is the file descriptor of the temporary file (as returned by `os.open`, covered in Table 10-5) and string *`path`* is the absolute path to the temporary file. You can optionally pass arguments to specify strings to use as the start (*`prefix`*) and end (*`suffix`*) of the temporary file's filename, and the path to the directory in which the temporary file is created (*`dir`*); if you want the temporary file to be a text file, explicitly pass the argument *`text`*`=True`.

Ensuring that the temporary file is removed when you're done using it is up to you: `mkstemp` is not a context manager, so you can't use a `with` statement—you'll generally use `try/finally` instead. Here is a typical usage example that creates a temporary text file, closes it, passes its path to another function, and finally ensures the file is removed:

```
import tempfile, os
fd, path =
  tempfile.mkstemp(suffix='.txt', text=True)
try:
    os.close(fd)
    use_filepath(path)
finally:
    os.unlink(path)
```

SpooledTemporaryFile `SpooledTemporaryFile(`*`mode`*`='w+b',`*`bufsize`*`=-1,` *`suffix`*`=None,`*`prefix`*`=None,`*`dir`*`=None)`

Just like `TemporaryFile`, covered next, except that the "file" object `SpooledTemporaryFile` returns can stay in memory, if space permits, until you call its `fileno` method (or the `rollover` method, which ensures the file gets materialized on disk); as a result, performance can be better with `SpooledTemporaryFile`, as long as you have enough memory that's not otherwise in use.

TemporaryFile `TemporaryFile(`*`mode`*`='w+b',`*`bufsize`*`=-1,`*`suffix`*`=None,` *`prefix`*`=None,`*`dir`*`=None)`

Creates a temporary file with `mkstemp` (passing to `mkstemp` the optional arguments *`suffix`*, *`prefix`*, and *`dir`*), makes a "file" object from it with `os.fdopen` as covered in Table 10-5 (passing to `fdopen` the optional arguments *`mode`* and *`bufsize`*), and returns the "file" object. The temporary file is removed as soon as the file object is closed (implicitly or explicitly). For greater security, the temporary file has no name on the filesystem, if your platform allows that (Unix-like platforms do; Windows doesn't). The returned "file" object from `TemporaryFile` is a context manager, so you can use a `with` statement to ensure it's closed when you're done with it.

NamedTemporaryFile `NamedTemporaryFile(`*`mode`*`='w+b',` *`bufsize`*`=-1,`*`suffix`*`=None,` *`prefix`*`=None,` *`dir`*`=None)`

Like `TemporaryFile`, except that the temporary file does have a name on the filesystem. Use the `name` attribute of the "file" object to access that name. Some platforms, mainly Windows, do not allow the file to be opened again; therefore, the usefulness of the name is limited if you want to ensure that your program works cross-platform. If you need to pass the temporary file's name to another program that opens the file, you can use function `mkstemp`, instead of `NamedTemporaryFile`, to guarantee correct cross-platform behavior. Of course, when you choose to use `mkstemp`, you do have to take care to ensure the file is removed when you're done with it. The returned "file" object from `NamedTemporaryFile` is a context manager, so you can use a `with` statement.

Auxiliary Modules for File I/O

"File" objects supply the minimal functionality needed for file I/O. Some auxiliary Python library modules, however, offer convenient supplementary functionality, making I/O even easier and handier in several important cases.

The fileinput Module

The `fileinput` module lets you loop over all the lines in a list of text files. Performance is good, comparable to the performance of direct iteration on each file, since buffering is used to minimize I/O. You can therefore use module `fileinput` for line-oriented file input whenever you find the module's rich functionality convenient, with no worry about performance. The `input` function is the key function of module `fileinput`; the module also supplies a `FileInput` class whose methods support the same functionality as the module's functions. The module contents are listed here:

close `close()`

Closes the whole sequence so that iteration stops and no file remains open.

FileInput `class FileInput(`*files*`=None,` *inplace*`=False,` *backup*`='',` *bufsize*`=0,` *openhook*`=None)`

Creates and returns an instance *f* of class `FileInput`. Arguments are the same as for `fileinput.input`, and methods of *f* have the same names, arguments, and semantics, as functions of module `fileinput`. *f* also supplies a method `readline`, which reads and returns the next line. You can use class `FileInput` explicitly when you want to nest or mix loops that read lines from more than one sequence of files.

filelineno `filelineno()`

Returns the number of lines read so far from the file now being read. For example, returns `1` if the first line has just been read from the current file.

filename `filename()`

Returns the name of the file being read, or `None` if no line has been read yet.

input `input(`*files*`=None,` *inplace*`=False,` *backup*`='',` *bufsize*`=0,` *openhook*`=None)`

Returns the sequence of lines in the files, suitable for use in a `for` loop. *files* is a sequence of filenames to open and read one after the other, in order. Filename `'-'` means standard input (`sys.stdin`). When *files* is a string, it's a single filename to open and read. When *files* is `None`, `input` uses `sys.argv[1:]` as the list of filenames. When the sequence of filenames is empty, `input` reads `sys.stdin`.

The sequence object that `input` returns is an instance of the class `FileInput`; that instance is also the global state of the module `input`, so all other functions of the `fileinput` module operate on the same shared state. Each function of the `fileinput` module corresponds directly to a method of the class `FileInput`.

When *inplace* is `False` (the default), `input` just reads the files. When *inplace* is `True`, `input` moves each file being read (except standard input) to a backup file and redirects standard output (`sys.stdout`) to write to a new file with the same path as the original one of the file being read. This way, you can simulate overwriting files in-place. If *backup* is a string that starts with a dot, `input` uses *backup* as the extension of the backup files and does not remove the backup files. If *backup* is an empty string (the default), `input` uses *.bak* and deletes each backup file as the input files are closed.

bufsize is the size of the internal buffer that `input` uses to read lines from the input files. When *bufsize* is `0`, `input` uses a buffer of 8,192 bytes.

You can optionally pass an *openhook* function to use as an alternative to `io.open`. A popular one: `openhook=fileinput.hook_compressed`, which transparently decompresses any input file with extension *.gz* or *.bzip* (not compatible with `inplace=True`).

isfirstline `isfirstline()`

Returns `True` or `False`, just like `filelineno()==1`.

isstdin `isstdin()`

Returns `True` when the current file being read is `sys.stdin`; otherwise, `False`.

lineno `lineno()`

Returns the total number of lines read since the call to `input`.

nextfile `nextfile()`

Closes the file being read: the next line to read is the first one of the next file.

Here's a typical example of using `fileinput` for a "multifile search and replace," changing one string into another throughout the text files whose name were passed as command-line arguments to the script:

```
import fileinput
for line in fileinput.input(inplace=True):
    print(line.replace('foo', 'bar'), end='')
```

In such cases it's important to have the `end=''` argument to `print`, since each *`line`* has its line-end character `\n` at the end, and you need to ensure that `print` doesn't add another (or else each file would end up "double-spaced").

The linecache Module

The `linecache` module lets you read a given line (specified by number) from a file with a given name, keeping an internal cache so that, when you read several lines from a file, it's faster than opening and examining the file each time. The `linecache` module exposes the following functions:

checkcache `checkcache()`

Ensures that the module's cache holds no stale data and reflects what's on the filesystem. Call `checkcache` when the files you're reading may have changed on the filesystem, to ensure that further calls to `getline` return updated information.

clearcache `clearcache()`

Drops the module's cache so that the memory can be reused for other purposes. Call `clearcache` when you know you don't need to perform any reading for a while.

getline `getline(`*`filename, lineno`*`)`

Reads and returns the *`lineno`* line (the first line is `1`, not `0` as is usual in Python) from the text file named *`filename`*, including the trailing `\n`. For any error, `getline` does not raise exceptions but rather returns the empty string `''`. If *`filename`* is not found, `getline` looks for the file in the directories listed in `sys.path` (ignoring ZIP files, if any, in `sys.path`).

getlines `getlines(`*`filename`*`)`

Reads and returns all lines from the text file named *`filename`* as a list of strings, each including the trailing `\n`. For any error, `getlines` does not raise exceptions but rather returns the empty list `[]`. If *`filename`* is not found, `getlines` looks for the file in the directories listed in `sys.path`.

The struct Module

The `struct` module lets you pack binary data into a bytestring, and unpack the bytes of such a bytestring back into the data they represent. Such operations are useful for many kinds of low-level programming. Most often, you use `struct` to interpret data records from binary files that have some specified format, or to prepare records to write to such binary files. The module's name comes from C's keyword `struct`, which is usable for related purposes. On any error, functions of the module `struct` raise exceptions that are instances of the exception class `struct.error`, the only class the module supplies.

The `struct` module relies on *struct format strings* following a specific syntax. The first character of a format string gives byte order, size, and alignment of packed data:

@

Native byte order, native data sizes, and native alignment for the current platform; this is the default if the first character is none of the characters listed here (note that format `P` in Table 10-2 is available only for this kind of `struct` format string). Look at string `sys.byteorder` when you need to check your system's byte order (`'little'` or `'big'`).

=

Native byte order for the current platform, but standard size and alignment.

<

Little-endian byte order (like Intel platforms); standard size and alignment.

>, !

Big-endian byte order (network standard); standard size and alignment.

Table 10-2. Format characters for struct

Character	C type	Python type	Standard size
B	unsigned char	int	1 byte
b	signed char	int	1 byte
c	char	bytes (length 1)	1 byte
d	double	float	8 bytes
f	float	float	4 bytes
H	unsigned short	int	2 bytes
h	signed short	int	2 bytes
I	unsigned int	long	4 bytes
i	signed int	int	4 bytes
L	unsigned long	long	4 bytes
l	signed long	int	4 bytes
P	void*	int	N/A
p	char[]	bytes	N/A
s	char[]	bytes	N/A
x	padding byte	no value	1 byte

Standard sizes are indicated in Table 10-2. Standard alignment means no forced alignment, with explicit padding bytes used if needed. Native sizes and alignment are whatever the platform's C compiler uses. Native byte order can put the most significant byte at either the lowest (big-endian) or highest (little-endian) address, depending on the platform.

After the optional first character, a format string is made up of one or more format characters, each optionally preceded by a count (an integer represented by decimal digits). (The format characters are shown in Table 10-2.) For most format characters, the count means repetition (e.g., `'3h'` is exactly the same as `'hhh'`). When the format character is `s` or `p`—that is, a bytestring—the count is not a repetition: it's the total number of bytes in the string. Whitespace can be freely used between formats, but not between a count and its format character.

Format `s` means a fixed-length bytestring as long as its count (the Python string is truncated, or padded with copies of the null byte `b'\0'`, if needed). The format `p` means a "Pascal-like" bytestring: the first byte is the number of significant bytes that follow, and the actual contents start from the second byte. The count is the total number of bytes, *including* the length byte.

The `struct` module supplies the following functions:

calcsize `calcsize(`*`fmt`*`)`

Returns the size in bytes corresponding to format string *`fmt`*.

pack `pack(`*`fmt, *values`*`)`

Packs the values per format string *`fmt`*, returns the resulting bytestring. *`values`* must match in number and type the values required by *`fmt`*.

pack_into `pack_into(`*`fmt,buffer,offset,*values`*`)`

Packs the values per format string *`fmt`* into writeable *buffer* *`buffer`* (usually an instance of `bytearray`) starting at index *`offset`* in it. *`values`* must match in number and type the values required by *`fmt`*. `len(buffer[offset:])` must be `>= struct.calcsize(fmt)`.

unpack `unpack(`*`fmt, s`*`)`

Unpacks bytestring *`s`* per format string *`fmt`*, returns a tuple of values (if just one value, a one-item tuple). `len(`*`s`*`)` must equal `struct.calcsize(`*`fmt`*`)`.

unpack_from `unpack_from(`*`fmt,s,offset`*`)`

Unpacks bytestring (or other readable *buffer*) *`s`*, starting from offset *`offset`*, per format string *`fmt`*, returning a tuple of values (if just one value, a 1-item tuple). `len(`*`s`*`[`*`offset`*`:])` must be `>= struct.calcsize(`*`fmt`*`)`.

In-Memory "Files": io.StringIO and io.BytesIO

You can implement file-like objects by writing Python classes that supply the methods you need. If all you want is for data to reside in memory, rather than on a file as seen by the operating system, use the class `StringIO` or `BytesIO` of the `io` module. The difference between them is that instances of `StringIO` are text-mode "files," so reads and writes consume or produce Unicode strings, while instances of `BytesIO` are binary "files," so reads and writes consume or produce bytestrings.

When you instantiate either class you can optionally pass a string argument, respectively Unicode or bytes, to use as the initial content of the "file." An instance `f` of either class, in addition to "file" methods, supplies one extra method:

getvalue `f.getvalue()`

Returns the current data contents of *f* as a string (text or bytes). You cannot call `f.getvalue` after you call `f.close`: `close` frees the buffer that *f* internally keeps, and `getvalue` needs to return the buffer as its result.

File and Text Operations

Compressed Files

Storage space and transmission bandwidth are increasingly cheap and abundant, but in many cases you can save such resources, at the expense of some extra computational effort, by using compression. Computational power grows cheaper and more abundant even faster than some other resources, such as bandwidth, so compression's popularity keeps growing. Python makes it easy for your programs to support compression, since the Python standard library contains several modules dedicated to compression.

Since Python offers so many ways to deal with compression, some guidance may be helpful. Files containing data compressed with the `zlib` module are not automatically interchangeable with other programs, except for those files built with the `zipfile` module, which respects the standard format of ZIP file archives. You can write custom programs, with any language able to use InfoZip's free *zlib* compression library, to read files produced by Python programs using the `zlib` module. However, if you need to interchange compressed data with programs coded in other languages but have a choice of compression methods, we suggest you use the modules `bzip2` (best), `gzip`, or `zipfile` instead. The `zlib` module, however, may be useful when you want to compress some parts of datafiles that are in some proprietary format of your own and need not be interchanged with any other program except those that make up your application.

In v3 only, you can also use the newer module `lzma` for even (marginally) better compression and compatibility with the newer `xz` utility. We do not cover `lzma` in this book; see the online docs (*https://docs.python.org/3/library/lzma.html?highlight=lzma#module-lzma*), and, for use in v2, the v2 backport (*https://pypi.python.org/pypi/backports.lzma*).

The gzip Module

The `gzip` module lets you read and write files compatible with those handled by the powerful GNU compression programs `gzip` and `gunzip`. The GNU programs support many compression formats, but the module `gzip` supports only the *gzip* format, often denoted by appending the extension *.gz* to a filename. The `gzip` module supplies the `GzipFile` class and an `open` factory function:

GzipFile `class GzipFile(filename=None, mode=None, compresslevel=9, fileobj=None)`

Creates and returns a file-like object *f* wrapping the "file" or file-like object *fileobj*. When *fileobj* is None, *filename* must be a string that names a file; GzipFile opens that file with the *mode* (by default, 'rb'), and *f* wraps the resulting file object.

mode should be 'ab', 'rb', 'wb', or None. When *mode* is None, *f* uses the mode of *fileobj* if it can discover that mode; otherwise, it uses 'rb'. When *filename* is None, *f* uses the filename of *fileobj* if it can discover that name; otherwise, it uses ''. *compresslevel* is an integer between 1 and 9: 1 requests modest compression but fast operation; 9 requests the best compression at the cost of more computation.

The file-like object *f* delegates most methods to the underlying file-like object *fileobj*, transparently accounting for compression as needed. However, *f* does not allow nonsequential access, so *f* does not supply methods seek and tell. Calling *f*.close does *not* close *fileobj* if *f* was created with a not-None *fileobj*. This matters especially when *fileobj* is an instance of io.BytesIO: you can call *fileobj*.getvalue after *f*.close to get the compressed data string. So, you always have to call *fileobj*.close (explicitly, or implicitly by using a with statement) after *f*.close.

open `open(filename, mode='rb', compresslevel=9)`

Like GzipFile(*filename*, *mode*, *compresslevel*), but *filename* is mandatory and there is no provision for passing an already opened *fileobj*. In v3 only, *filename* can be an already-opened "file" object; also, in v3, mode can be a text one (for example 'rt'), in which case open wraps an io.TextIOWrapper around the "file" it returns.

A gzip example

Say that you have some function f(*x*) that writes Unicode text to a text file object *x* passed in as an argument, by calling *x*.write and/or *x*.writelines. To make *f* write text to a *gzip*-compressed file instead:

```
import gzip, io
with io.open('x.txt.gz', 'wb') as underlying:
    with gzip.GzipFile(fileobj=underlying, mode='wb') as wrapper:
        f(io.TextIOWrapper(wrapper, 'utf8'))
```

This example opens the underlying binary file *x.txt.gz* and explicitly wraps it with gzip.GzipFile; thus, we need two nested with statements. This separation is not strictly necessary: we could pass the filename directly to gzip.GzipFile (or gzip.open); in v3 only, with gzip.open, we could even ask for mode='wt' and have the TextIOWrapper transparently provided for us. However, the example is coded to be maximally explicit, and portable between v2 and v3.

Reading back a compressed text file—for example, to display it on standard output—uses a pretty similar structure of code:

```
import gzip, io
with io.open('x.txt.gz', 'rb') as underlying:
    with gzip.GzipFile(fileobj=underlying, mode='rb') as wrapper:
        for line in wrapper:
            print(line.decode('utf8'), end='')
```

Here, we can't just use an `io.TextIOWrapper`, since, in v2, it would not be iterable by line, given the characteristics of the underlying (decompressing) wrapper. However, the explicit `decode` of each line works fine in both v2 and v3.

The bz2 Module

The `bz2` module lets you read and write files compatible with those handled by the compression programs `bzip2` and `bunzip2`, which often achieve even better compression than `gzip` and `gunzip`. Module `bz2` supplies the `BZ2File` class, for transparent file compression and decompression, and functions `compress` and `decompress` to compress and decompress data strings in memory. It also provides objects to compress and decompress data incrementally, enabling you to work with data streams that are too large to comfortably fit in memory at once. For the latter, advanced functionality, consult the Python standard library's online docs (*https://docs.python.org/3.5/library/bz2.html#incremental-de-compression*).

For richer functionality in v2, consider the third-party module bz2file (*https://pypi.python.org/pypi/bz2file*), with more complete features, matching v3's standard library module's ones as listed here:

BZ2File `class BZ2File(`*`filename`*`=None,` *`mode`*`='r',` *`buffering`*`=0,` *`compresslevel`*`=9)`

Creates and returns a file-like object *f*, corresponding to the `bzip2`-compressed file named by *`filename`*, which must be a string denoting a file's path (in v3 only, *`filename`* can also be an open file object). *`mode`* can be `'r'`, for reading, or `'w'`, for writing (in v3 only, `'a'` for appending, and `'x'` for exclusive-open—like `'w'`, but raising an exception when the file already exists—are also OK; and so is appending a `'b'` to the mode string, since the resulting file-like object *f* is binary).

`buffering` is deprecated; don't pass it. *`compresslevel`* is an integer between 1 and 9: 1 requests modest compression but fast operation; 9 requests the best compression at the cost of more computation.

f supplies all methods of "file" objects, including `seek` and `tell`. Thus, *f* is seekable; however, the `seek` operation is emulated, and, while guaranteed to be semantically correct, may in some cases be very slow.

compress `compress(`*`s`*`,` *`level`*`=9)`

Compresses string *s* and returns the string of compressed data. *`level`* is an integer between 1 and 9: 1 requests modest compression but fast operation; 9 requests the best compression at the cost of more computation.

decompress `decompress(s)`

Decompresses the compressed data string *s* and returns the string of uncompressed data.

The tarfile Module

The `tarfile` module lets you read and write TAR files (archive files compatible with those handled by popular archiving programs such as `tar`), optionally with either `gzip` or `bzip2` compression (and, in v3 only, `lzma` too). In v3 only, **`python -m tarfile`** offers a useful command-line interface to the module's functionality: run it without further arguments to get a brief help message.

When handling invalid TAR files, functions of `tarfile` raise instances of `tarfile.TarError`. The `tarfile` module supplies the following classes and functions:

is_tarfile `is_tarfile(filename)`

Returns `True` when the file named by string *filename* appears to be a valid TAR file (possibly with compression), judging by the first few bytes; otherwise, returns `False`.

TarInfo `class TarInfo(name='')`

The methods `getmember` and `getmembers` of `TarFile` instances return instances of `TarInfo`, supplying information about members of the archive. You can also build a `TarInfo` instance with a `TarFile` instance's method `gettarinfo`. The most useful attributes supplied by a `TarInfo` instance *t* are:

`linkname`

A string, the target file's name, when `t.type` is `LNKTYPE` or `SYMTYPE`

`mode`

Permission and other mode bits of the file identified by *t*

`mtime`

Time of last modification of the file identified by *t*

`name`

Name in the archive of the file identified by *t*

`size`

Size in bytes (uncompressed) of the file identified by *t*

`type`

File type, one of many constants that are attributes of module `tarfile` (`SYMTYPE` for symbolic links, `REGTYPE` for regular files, `DIRTYPE` for directories, and so on)

To check the type of *t*, rather than testing `t.type`, you can call *t*'s methods. The most frequently used methods of *t* are:

`t.isdir()`

Returns `True` if the file is a directory

`t.isfile()`

Returns `True` if the file is a regular file

`t.issym()`

Returns `True` if the file is a symbolic link

open `open(filename, mode='r', fileobj=None, bufsize=10240, **kwargs)`

Creates and returns a `TarFile` instance *f* to read or create a TAR file through file-like object *fileobj*. When *fileobj* is `None`, *filename* must be a string naming a file; `open` opens the file with the given *mode* (by default, `'r'`), and *f* wraps the resulting file object. Calling `f.close` does *not* close *fileobj* if *f* was opened with a *fileobj* that is not `None`. This behavior of `f.close` is important when *fileobj* is an instance of `io.BytesIO`: you can call `fileobj.getvalue` after `f.close` to get the archived and possibly compressed data as a string. This behavior also means that you have to call `fileobj.close` explicitly after calling `f.close`.

mode can be `'r'`, to read an existing TAR file, with whatever compression it has (if any); `'w'`, to write a new TAR file, or truncate and rewrite an existing one, without compression; or `'a'`, to append to an existing TAR file, without compression. Appending to compressed TAR files is not supported. To write a new TAR file with compression, *mode* can be `'w:gz'` for `gzip` compression, or `'w:bz2'` for `bzip2` compression. Special mode strings `'r:'` or `'w:'` can be used to read or write uncompressed, nonseekable TAR files using a buffer of *bufsize* bytes, and `'r:gz'` and `'r:bz2'` can be used to read such files with compression. In v3 only, you can also use `'r:xz'` and `'w:xz'` to specify LZMA compression.

In the mode strings specifying compression, you can use a vertical bar `|` instead of a colon `:` in order to force sequential processing and fixed-size blocks (precious if you're ever handling a tape device).

A `TarFile` instance *f* supplies the following methods.

add `f.add(filepath, arcname=None, recursive=True)`

Adds to archive *f* the file named by *filepath* (can be a regular file, a directory, or a symbolic link). When *arcname* is not `None`, it's used as the archive member name in lieu of *filepath*. When *filepath* is a directory, `add` recursively adds the whole filesystem subtree rooted in that directory, unless you pass *recursive* as `False`.

addfile `f.addfile(tarinfo, fileobj=None)`

Adds to archive *f* a member identified by *tarinfo*, a `TarInfo` instance (if *fileobj* is not `None`, the data is the first `tarinfo.size` bytes of file-like object *fileobj*).

close `f.close()`

Closes archive *f*. You must call `close`, or else an incomplete, unusable TAR file might be left on disk. Such mandatory finalization is best performed with a `try/finally`, as covered in "try/finally" on page 152, or, even better, a `with` statement, covered in "The with Statement and Context Managers" on page 153.

extract `f.extract(member, path='.')`

Extracts the archive member identified by *`member`* (a name or a `TarInfo` instance) into a corresponding file in the directory named by *`path`* (the current directory by default).

extractfile `f.extractfile(member)`

Extracts the archive member identified by *`member`* (a name or a `TarInfo` instance) and returns a read-only file-like object with the methods `read`, `readline`, `readlines`, `seek`, and `tell`.

getmember `f.getmember(name)`

Returns a `TarInfo` instance with information about the archive member named by the string *name*.

getmembers `f.getmembers()`

Returns a list of `TarInfo` instances, one for each member in archive *f*, in the same order as the entries in the archive itself.

getnames `f.getnames()`

Returns a list of strings, the names of each member in archive *f*, in the same order as the entries in the archive itself.

gettarinfo `f.gettarinfo(name=None, arcname=None,fileobj=None)`

Returns a `TarInfo` instance with information about the open "file" object *`fileobj`*, when not `None`, or else the existing file whose path is string *name*. When *`arcname`* is not `None`, it's used as the `name` attribute of the resulting `TarInfo` instance.

list `f.list(verbose=True)`

Outputs a directory of the archive *f* to *sys.stdout*. If the optional argument *`verbose`* is `False`, outputs only the names of the archive's members.

The zipfile Module

The `zipfile` module can read and write ZIP files (i.e., archive files compatible with those handled by popular compression programs such as `zip` and `unzip`, `pkzip` and `pkunzip`, `WinZip`, and so on). **`python -m zipfile`** offers a useful command-line interface to the module's functionality: run it without further arguments to get a brief help message.

Detailed information about ZIP files is at the pkware (*https://pkware.cachefly.net/webdocs/casestudies/APPNOTE.TXT*) and info-zip (*http://www.info-zip.org/pub/infozip/*) web pages. You need to study that detailed information to perform advanced ZIP file handling with `zipfile`. If you do not specifically need to interoperate with other programs using the ZIP file standard, the modules `gzip` and `bz2` are often better ways to deal with file compression.

The `zipfile` module can't handle multidisk ZIP files, and cannot create encrypted archives (however, it can decrypt them, albeit rather slowly). The module also cannot handle archive members using compression types besides the usual ones, known as *stored* (a file copied to the archive without compression) and *deflated* (a file compressed using the ZIP format's default algorithm). (In v3 only, `zipfile` also handles compression types *bzip2* and *lzma*, but beware: not all tools, including v2's `zipfile`, can handle those, so if you use them you're sacrificing some portability to get better compression.) For errors related to invalid *.zip* files, functions of `zipfile` raise exceptions that are instances of the exception class `zipfile.error`.

The `zipfile` module supplies the following classes and functions:

is_zipfile `is_zipfile(`*`file`*`)`

Returns `True` when the file named by string *`file`* (or, the file-like object *`file`*) seems to be a valid ZIP file, judging by the first few and last bytes of the file; otherwise, returns `False`.

ZipInfo `class ZipInfo(`*`file`*`='NoName', `*`date_time`*`=(1980, 1, 1))`

The methods `getinfo` and `infolist` of `ZipFile` instances return instances of `ZipInfo` to supply information about members of the archive. The most useful attributes supplied by a `ZipInfo` instance *z* are:

`comment`

A string that is a comment on the archive member

`compress_size`

Size in bytes of the compressed data for the archive member

`compress_type`

An integer code recording the type of compression of the archive member

`date_time`

A tuple of six integers with the time of the last modification to the file: the items are year, month, day (`1` and up), hour, minute, second (`0` and up)

`file_size`

Size in bytes of the uncompressed data for the archive member

`filename`

Name of the file in the archive

ZipFile

```
class ZipFile(file, mode='r', compression=zipfile.ZIP_STORED,
allowZip64=True)
```

Opens a ZIP file named by string *file* (or, the file-like object *file*). *mode* can be 'r', to read an existing ZIP file; 'w', to write a new ZIP file or truncate and rewrite an existing one; or 'a', to append to an existing file. (In v3 only, it can also be 'x', which is like 'w' but raises an exception if the ZIP file already existed—here, 'x' stands for "exclusive.")

When *mode* is 'a', *filename* can name either an existing ZIP file (in which case new members are added to the existing archive) or an existing non-ZIP file. In the latter case, a new ZIP file–like archive is created and appended to the existing file. The main purpose of this latter case is to let you build a self-unpacking executable file that unpacks itself when run. The existing file must then be a pristine copy of a self-unpacking executable prefix, as supplied by *www.info-zip.org* and by other purveyors of ZIP file compression tools.

compression is an integer code that can be either of two attributes of the module zipfile. zipfile.ZIP_STORED requests that the archive use no compression; zipfile.ZIP_DEFLATED requests that the archive use the *deflation* mode of compression (i.e., the most usual and effective compression approach used in *.zip* files). In v3 only, it can also be zipfile.ZIP_BZIP2 or zipfile.ZIP_LZMA (sacrificing portability for more compression).

When *allowZip64* is true, the ZipFile instance is allowed to use the ZIP64 extensions to produce an archive larger than 4 GB; otherwise, any attempt to produce such a large archive raises exception LargeZipFile. The default is True in v3, but False in v2.

A ZipFile instance *z* has the attributes compression and mode, corresponding to the arguments with which *z* was instantiated; fp and filename, the file-like object *z* works on and its filename if known; comment, the possibly empty string that is the archive's comment; and filelist, the list of ZipInfo instances in the archive.

In addition, *z* has a writable attribute called debug, an int from 0 to 3 that you can assign to control how much debugging output to emit to sys.stdout—from nothing, when *z*.debug is 0, to the maximum amount of information available, when *z*.debug is 3.

ZipFile is a context manager; thus, you can use it in a with statement to ensure the underlying file gets closed when you're done with it. For example:

```
with ZipFile('archive.zip') as z:
    data = z.read('data.txt')
```

A ZipFile instance *z* supplies the following methods:

close

```
z.close()
```

Closes archive file *z*. Make sure the close method gets called, or else an incomplete and unusable ZIP file might be left on disk. Such mandatory finalization is generally best performed with a try/finally statement, as covered in "try/finally" on page 152, or—even better—a with statement.

extract

`z.extract(member, path=None, pwd=None)`

Extract an archive member to disk, to the directory *path*, or, by default, to the current working directory; *member* is the member's full name, or an instance of `ZipInfo` identifying the member. `extract` normalizes path info within *member*, turning absolute paths into relative ones, removing any component that's `'..'`, and, on Windows, turning characters that are illegal in filenames into underscores (_). *pwd*, if present, is the password to use to decrypt an encrypted member.

Returns the path to the file it has created (or overwritten if it already existed), or to the directory it has created (or left alone if it already existed).

extractall

`z.extractall(path=None, members=None, pwd=None)`

Extract archive members to disk (by default, all of them), to directory *path*, or, by default, to the current working directory; *members* optionally limits which members to extract, and must be a subset of the list of strings returned by `z.namelist()`. `extractall` normalizes path info within members it extracts, turning absolute paths into relative ones, removing any component that's `'..'`, and, on Windows, turning characters that are illegal in filenames into underscores (_). *pwd*, if present, is the password to use to decrypt an encrypted member.

getinfo

`z.getinfo(name)`

Returns a `ZipInfo` instance that supplies information about the archive member named by the string *name*.

infolist

`z.infolist()`

Returns a list of `ZipInfo` instances, one for each member in archive *z*, in the same order as the entries in the archive.

namelist

`z.namelist()`

Returns a list of strings, the name of each member in archive *z*, in the same order as the entries in the archive.

open

`z.open(name, mode='r', pwd=None)`

Extracts and returns the archive member identified by *name* (a member name string or `ZipInfo` instance) as a read-only file-like object. mode should be `'r'`: in v2 and early v3 versions it could also be `'U'` or `'rU'` to get "universal newlines" mode, but that's now deprecated. *pwd*, if present, is the password to use to decrypt an encrypted member.

printdir

`z.printdir()`

Outputs a textual directory of the archive *z* to file *sys.stdout*.

read

`z.read(name, pwd)`

Extracts the archive member identified by *name* (a member name string or `ZipInfo` instance) and returns the bytestring of its contents. *pwd*, if present, is the password to use to decrypt an encrypted member.

setpassword `z.setpassword(pwd)`

Sets string *pwd* as the default password to use to decrypt encrypted files.

testzip `z.testzip()`

Reads and checks the files in archive *z*. Returns a string with the name of the first archive member that is damaged, or `None` if the archive is intact.

write `z.write(filename, arcname=None, compress_type=None)`

Writes the file named by string *filename* to archive *z*, with archive member name *arcname*. When *arcname* is `None`, `write` uses *filename* as the archive member name. When *compress_type* is `None`, `write` uses *z*'s compression type; otherwise, *compress_type* specifies how to compress the file. *z* must be opened for `'w'` or `'a'`.

writestr `z.writestr(zinfo, bytes)`

zinfo must be a `ZipInfo` instance specifying at least *filename* and *date_time*, or a string (in which case it's used as the archive member name, and the date and time are set to the current moment). *bytes* is a string of bytes. `writestr` adds a member to archive *z* using the metadata specified by *zinfo* and the data in *bytes*. *z* must be opened for `'w'` or `'a'`. When you have data in memory and need to write the data to the ZIP file archive *z*, it's simpler and faster to use `z.writestr` rather than `z.write`: the latter would require you to write the data to disk first and later remove the useless disk file. The following example shows both approaches, encapsulated into functions polymorphic to each other:

```
import zipfile

def data_to_zip_direct(z, data, name):
    import time
    zinfo = zipfile.ZipInfo(name, time.localtime()[:6])
    zinfo.compress_type = zipfile.ZIP_DEFLATED
    z.writestr(zinfo, data)

def data_to_zip_indirect(z, data, name):
    import os
    flob = open(name, 'wb')
    flob.write(data)
    flob.close()
    z.write(name)
    os.unlink(name)

with zipfile.ZipFile('z.zip', 'w',
zipfile.ZIP_DEFLATED) as zz:
    data = 'four score\nand seven\nyears ago\n'
    data_to_zip_direct(zz, data, 'direct.txt')
    data_to_zip_indirect(zz, data, 'indirect.txt')
```

Besides being faster and more concise, `data_to_zip_direct` is handier, since it works in memory and doesn't require the current working directory to be writable, as `data_to_zip_indirect` does. Of course, `write` has its uses, when the data is in a file on disk and you just want to add the file to the archive.

File and Text Operations

Here's how you can print a list of all files contained in the ZIP file archive created by the previous example, followed by each file's name and contents:

```
import zipfile
zz = zipfile.ZipFile('z.zip')
zz.printdir()
for name in zz.namelist():
    print('{}: {!r}'.format(name, zz.read(name)))
zz.close()
```

The zlib Module

The `zlib` module lets Python programs use the free InfoZip *zlib* compression library (*http://www.info-zip.org/pub/infozip/*) version 1.1.4 or later. `zlib` is used by the modules `gzip` and `zipfile`, but is also available directly for any special compression needs. The most commonly used functions supplied by `zlib` are:

compress `compress(s, level=6)`

Compresses string *s* and returns the string of compressed data. *level* is an integer between 1 and 9; 1 requests modest compression but fast operation, and 9 requests best compression, requiring more computation.

decompress `decompress(s)`

Decompresses the compressed bytestring *s* and returns the bytestring of uncompressed data (also accepts optional arguments for pretty advanced uses—see the online docs (*https://docs.python.org/3/library/zlib.html?highlight=zlib#zlib.decompress*)).

The `zlib` module also supplies functions to compute Cyclic-Redundancy Check (CRC), which allows detection of damage in compressed data, as well as objects to compress and decompress data incrementally to allow working with data streams too large to fit in memory at once. For such advanced functionality, consult the Python library's online docs (*https://docs.python.org/3/library/zlib.html*).

The os Module

`os` is an umbrella module presenting a reasonably uniform cross-platform view of the capabilities of various operating systems. It supplies low-level ways to create and handle files and directories, and to create, manage, and destroy processes. This section covers filesystem-related functions of `os`; "Running Other Programs with the os Module" on page 424 covers process-related functions.

The `os` module supplies a `name` attribute, a string that identifies the kind of platform on which Python is being run. Common values for `name` are `'posix'` (all kinds of Unix-like platforms, including Linux and macOS), `'nt'` (all kinds of 32-bit Windows platforms), and `'java'` (Jython). You can exploit some unique capabilities of a platform through functions supplied by `os`. However, this book deals with cross-platform programming, not with platform-specific functionality, so we do not cover parts of `os` that exist only on one platform, nor platform-specific modules. Functionality covered in this book is available at least on `'posix'` and `'nt'` platforms. We do, though, cover some of the differences among the ways in which a given functionality is provided on various platforms.

OSError Exceptions

When a request to the operating system fails, `os` raises an exception, an instance of `OSError`. `os` also exposes built-in exception class `OSError` with the synonym `os.error`. Instances of `OSError` expose three useful attributes:

`errno`
: The numeric error code of the operating system error

`strerror`
: A string that summarily describes the error

`filename`
: The name of the file on which the operation failed (file-related functions only)

In v3 only, `OSError` has many subclasses that specify more precisely what problem was encountered, as covered in "OSError and subclasses (v3 only)" on page 162.

`os` functions can also raise other standard exceptions, such as `TypeError` or `ValueError`, when the cause of the error is that you have called them with invalid argument types or values, so that the underlying operating system functionality has not even been attempted.

The errno Module

The `errno` module supplies dozens of symbolic names for error code numbers. To handle possible system errors selectively, based on error codes, use `errno` to enhance your program's portability and readability. For example, here's how you might handle "file not found" errors, while propagating all other kinds of errors (when you want your code to work as well in v2 as in v3):

```
try: os.some_os_function_or_other()
except OSError as err:
    import errno
    # check for "file not found" errors, re-raise other cases
    if err.errno != errno.ENOENT: raise
    # proceed with the specific case you can handle
    print('Warning: file', err.filename, 'not found—continuing')
```

If you're coding for v3 only, however, you can make an equivalent snippet much simpler and clearer, by catching just the applicable `OSError` subclass:

```
try: os.some_os_function_or_other()
except FileNotFoundError as err:
    print('Warning: file', err.filename, 'not found—continuing')
```

errno also supplies a dictionary named errorcode: the keys are error code numbers, and the corresponding names are the error names, which are strings such as 'ENOENT'. Displaying errno.errorcode[err.errno], as part of your diagnosis of some OSError instance err, can often make the diagnosis clearer and more understandable to readers who specialize in the specific platform.

Filesystem Operations

Using the os module, you can manipulate the filesystem in a variety of ways: creating, copying, and deleting files and directories; comparing files; and examining filesystem information about files and directories. This section documents the attributes and methods of the os module that you use for these purposes, and covers some related modules that operate on the filesystem.

Path-String Attributes of the os Module

A file or directory is identified by a string, known as its *path*, whose syntax depends on the platform. On both Unix-like and Windows platforms, Python accepts Unix syntax for paths, with a slash (/) as the directory separator. On non-Unix-like platforms, Python also accepts platform-specific path syntax. On Windows, in particular, you may use a backslash (\) as the separator. However, you then need to double-up each backslash as \\ in string literals, or use raw-string syntax as covered in "Literals" on page 42; you needlessly lose portability. Unix path syntax is handier and usable everywhere, so we strongly recommend that you *always* use it. In the rest of this chapter, we assume Unix path syntax in both explanations and examples.

The os module supplies attributes that provide details about path strings on the current platform. You should typically use the higher-level path manipulation operations covered in "The os.path Module" on page 305 rather than lower-level string operations based on these attributes. However, the attributes may be useful at times.

curdir
: The string that denotes the current directory ('.' on Unix and Windows)

defpath
: The default search path for programs, used if the environment lacks a PATH environment variable

linesep
: The string that terminates text lines ('\n' on Unix; '\r\n' on Windows)

extsep
: The string that separates the extension part of a file's name from the rest of the name ('.' on Unix and Windows)

pardir
: The string that denotes the parent directory ('..' on Unix and Windows)

`pathsep`
: The separator between paths in lists of paths, such as those used for the environment variable `PATH` (`':'` on Unix; `';'` on Windows)

`sep`
: The separator of path components (`'/'` on Unix; `'\\'` on Windows)

Permissions

Unix-like platforms associate nine bits with each file or directory: three each for the file's owner, its group, and anybody else (AKA "the world"), indicating whether the file or directory can be read, written, and executed by the given subject. These nine bits are known as the file's *permission bits*, and are part of the file's *mode* (a bit string that includes other bits that describe the file). These bits are often displayed in octal notation, since that groups three bits per digit. For example, mode `0o664` indicates a file that can be read and written by its owner and group, and read—but not written—by anybody else. When any process on a Unix-like system creates a file or directory, the operating system applies to the specified mode a bit mask known as the process's *umask*, which can remove some of the permission bits.

Non-Unix-like platforms handle file and directory permissions in very different ways. However, the `os` functions that deal with file permissions accept a *`mode`* argument according to the Unix-like approach described in the previous paragraph. Each platform maps the nine permission bits in a way appropriate for it. For example, on versions of Windows that distinguish only between read-only and read/write files and do not distinguish file ownership, a file's permission bits show up as either `0o666` (read/write) or `0o444` (read-only). On such a platform, when creating a file, the implementation looks only at bit `0o200`, making the file read/write when that bit is `1`, read-only when `0`.

File and Directory Functions of the os Module

The `os` module supplies several functions to query and set file and directory status. In all versions and platforms, the argument *`path`* to any of these functions can be a string giving the path of the file or directory involved. In v3 only, on some Unix platforms, some of the functions also support as argument *`path`* a *file descriptor* (AKA *fd*), an `int` denoting a file (as returned, for example, by `os.open`). In this case, the module attribute `os.supports_fd` is the set of functions of the `os` module that do support a file descriptor as argument *`path`* (the module attribute is missing in v2, and in v3 on platforms lacking such support).

In v3 only, on some Unix platforms, some functions support the optional, keyword-only argument *`follow_symlinks`*, defaulting to `True`. When true, and always in v2, if *`path`* indicates a symbolic link, the function follows it to reach an actual file or directory; when false, the function operates on the symbolic link itself. The module attribute `os.supports_follow_symlinks`, if present, is the set of functions of the `os` module that do support this argument.

File and Text Operations

In v3 only, on some Unix platforms, some functions support the optional, keyword-only argument *dir_fd*, defaulting to None. When present, *path* (if relative) is taken as being relative to the directory open at that file descriptor; when missing, and always in v2, *path* (if relative) is taken as relative to the current working directory. The module attribute os.supports_dir_fd, if present, is the set of functions of the os module that do support this argument.

Table 10-3. os module functions

access access(*path*, *mode*)

Returns True when the file *path* has all of the permissions encoded in integer *mode*; otherwise, False. *mode* can be os.F_OK to test for file existence, or one or more of the constant integers named os.R_OK, os.W_OK, and os.X_OK (with the bitwise-OR operator | joining them, if more than one) to test permissions to read, write, and execute the file.

access does not use the standard interpretation for its *mode* argument, covered in "Permissions" on page 300. Rather, access tests only if this specific process's real user and group identifiers have the requested permissions on the file. If you need to study a file's permission bits in more detail, see the function stat, covered in Table 10-4.

In v3 only, access supports an optional, keyword-only argument *effective_ids*, defaulting to False. When this argument is passed as true, access uses effective rather than real user and group identifiers.

chdir chdir(*path*)

Sets the current working directory of the process to *path*.

chmod chmod(*path*, *mode*)

Changes the permissions of the file *path*, as encoded in integer *mode*. *mode* can be zero or more of os.R_OK, os.W_OK, and os.X_OK (with the bitwise-OR operator | joining them, if more than one) for read, write, and execute (respectively). On Unix-like platforms, *mode* can be a richer bit pattern (as covered in "Permissions" on page 300) to specify different permissions for user, group, and other, as well as other special bits defined in the module stat and listed in the online docs (*https://docs.python.org/3/library/os.html?#os.chmod*).

getcwd getcwd()

Returns a str, the path of the current working directory. In v3, getcwdb returns the same value as bytes; in v2, getcwdu returns the same value as unicode.

link link(*src*,*dst*)

Create a hard link named *dst*, pointing to *src*. In v2, this is only available on Unix platforms; in v3, it's also available on Windows.

listdir `listdir(`*`path`*`)`

Returns a list whose items are the names of all files and subdirectories in the directory *`path`*. The list is in arbitrary order and does *not* include the special directory names `'.'` (current directory) and `'..'` (parent directory). See also the v3-only alternative function `scandir`, covered later in this table, which can offer performance improvements in some cases.

The v2-only `dircache` module also supplies a function named `listdir`, which works like `os.listdir`, with two enhancements. `dircache.listdir` returns a sorted list; and `dircache` caches the list, so that repeated requests for the same directory are faster if the directory's contents don't change. `dircache` automatically detects changes: when you call `dircache.listdir`, you get a list of the directory's contents at that time.

makedirs, mkdir `makedirs(`*`path`*`, `*`mode`*`=0777) mkdir(`*`path`*`, `*`mode`*`=0777)`

`makedirs` creates all directories that are part of *`path`* and do not yet exist. `mkdir` creates only the rightmost directory of *`path`* and raises `OSError` if any of the previous directories in *`path`* do not exist. Both functions use *`mode`* as permission bits of directories they create. Both raise `OSError` when creation fails, or when a file or directory named *`path`* already exists.

remove, unlink `remove(`*`path`*`) unlink(`*`path`*`)`

Removes the file named *`path`* (see `rmdir` in this table to remove a directory). `unlink` is a synonym of `remove`.

removedirs `removedirs(`*`path`*`)`

Loops from right to left over the directories that are part of *`path`*, removing each one. The loop ends when a removal attempt raises an exception, generally because a directory is not empty. `removedirs` does not propagate the exception, as long as it has removed at least one directory.

rename `rename(`*`source`*`, `*`dest`*`)`

Renames (i.e., moves) the file or directory named *`source`* to *`dest`*. If *`dest`* already exists, `rename` may either replace *`dest`*, or raise an exception; in v3 only, to guarantee replacement rather than exception, call, instead, the function `os.replace`.

renames `renames(`*`source`*`, `*`dest`*`)`

Like `rename`, except that `renames` tries to create all intermediate directories needed for *`dest`*. Also, after renaming, `renames` tries to remove empty directories from the path *`source`* using `removedirs`. It does not propagate any resulting exception; it's not an error if the starting directory of *`source`* does not become empty after the renaming.

rmdir `rmdir(`*`path`*`)`

Removes the empty directory named *`path`* (raises `OSError` if the removal fails, and, in particular, if the directory is not empty).

scandir `scandir(path)` *v3 only*

Returns an iterator over `os.DirEntry` instances representing each item in the path; using `scandir`, and calling each resulting instance's methods to determine its characteristics, can offer performance improvements compared to using `listdir` and `stat`, depending on the underlying platform.

`class DirEntry`

An instance *d* of class `DirEntry` supplies string attributes `name` and `path`, holding the item's base name and full path, respectively; and several methods, of which the most frequently used are the no-arguments, bool-returning methods `is_dir`, `is_file`, and `is_symlink`—`is_dir` and `is_file` by default follow symbolic links: pass named-only argument `follow_symlinks=False` to avoid this behavior. For more complete information, see the online docs (*https://docs.python.org/3/library/os.html#os.scandir*). *d* avoids system calls as much as feasible, and, when it needs one, it caches the results; if you need information that's guaranteed to be up to date, call `os.stat(d.path)` and use the `stat_result` instance it returns (however, this sacrifices `scandir`'s potential performance improvements).

stat `stat(path)`

Returns a value *x* of type `stat_result`, which provides 10 items of information about the file or subdirectory *path*. Accessing those items by their numeric indices is possible but generally not advisable, because the resulting code is not very readable; use the corresponding attribute names instead. Table 10-4 lists the attributes of a `stat_result` instance and the meaning of corresponding items.

Table 10-4. Items (attributes) of a stat_result instance

Item index	Attribute name	Meaning
0	`st_mode`	Protection and other mode bits
1	`st_ino`	Inode number
2	`st_dev`	Device ID
3	`st_nlink`	Number of hard links
4	`st_uid`	User ID of owner
5	`st_gid`	Group ID of owner
6	`st_size`	Size in bytes

Item index	Attribute name	Meaning
7	`st_atime`	Time of last access
8	`st_mtime`	Time of last modification
9	`st_ctime`	Time of last status change

For example, to print the size in bytes of file *path*, you can use any of:

```
import os
print(os.path.getsize(path))
print(os.stat(path)[6])
print(os.stat(path).st_size)
```

Time values are in seconds since the epoch, as covered in Chapter 12 (`int` on most platforms). Platforms unable to give a meaningful value for an item use a dummy value.

tempnam, tmpnam

`tempnam(`*`dir`*`=None, `*`prefix`*`=None) tmpnam( )`

Returns an absolute path usable as the name of a new temporary file.

Note: `tempnam` and `tmpnam` are weaknesses in your program's security. Avoid these functions and use instead the standard library module `tempfile`, covered in "The tempfile Module" on page 279.

utime

`utime(`*`path`*`, `*`times`*`=None)`

Sets the accessed and modified times of file or directory *path*. If *times* is None, `utime` uses the current time. Otherwise, *times* must be a pair of numbers (in seconds since the epoch, as covered in Chapter 12) in the order (*accessed*, *modified*).

walk

`walk(`*`top`*`, `*`topdown`*`=True, `*`onerror`*`=None, `*`followlinks`*`=False)`

A generator yielding an item for each directory in the tree whose root is directory *top*. When *topdown* is `True`, the default, `walk` visits directories from the tree's root downward; when *topdown* is `False`, `walk` visits directories from the tree's leaves upward. When *onerror* is `None`, `walk` catches and ignores any `OSError` exception raised during the tree-walk. Otherwise, *onerror* must be a function; `walk` catches any `OSError` exception raised during the tree-walk and passes it as the only argument in a call to *onerror*, which may process it, ignore it, or `raise` it to terminate the tree-walk and propagate the exception.

Each item `walk` yields is a tuple of three subitems: *dirpath*, a string that is the directory's path; *dirnames*, a list of names of subdirectories that are immediate children of the directory (special directories '.' and '..' are *not* included); and *filenames*, a list of names of files that are directly in the directory. If *topdown* is `True`, you can alter list *dirnames* in-place, removing some items and/or reordering others, to affect the tree-walk of the subtree rooted at *dirpath*; `walk` iterates only on subdirectories left in *dirnames*, in the order in which they're left. Such alterations have no effect if *topdown* is `False` (in this case, `walk` has already visited all subdirectories by the time it visits the current directory and yields its item).

By default, `walk` does not walk down symbolic links that resolve to directories. To get such extra walking, pass *`followlinks`* as true, but beware: this can cause infinite looping if a symbolic link resolves to a directory that is its ancestor—`walk` doesn't take precautions against this anomaly.

The os.path Module

The `os.path` module supplies functions to analyze and transform path strings. To use this module, you can `import os.path`; however, even if you just `import os`, you can also access the `os.path` module and all of its attributes. The most commonly useful functions from the module are listed here:

abspath `abspath(`*`path`*`)`

Returns a normalized absolute path string equivalent to *`path`*, just like:

```
os.path.normpath(os.path.join(os.getcwd(), path))
```

For example, `os.path.abspath(os.curdir)` is the same as `os.getcwd()`.

basename `basename(`*`path`*`)`

Returns the base name part of *`path`*, just like `os.path.split(`*`path`*`)[1]`. For example, `os.path.basename('b/c/d.e')` returns `'d.e'`.

commonprefix `commonprefix(`*`list`*`)`

Accepts a list of strings and returns the longest string that is a prefix of all items in the list. Unlike all other functions in `os.path`, `commonprefix` works on arbitrary strings, not just on paths. For example, `os.path.commonprefix('foobar', 'foolish')` returns `'foo'`.

In v3 only, function `os.path.commonpath` works similarly, but returns, specifically, only common prefix *paths*, not arbitrary *string* prefixes.

dirname `dirname(`*`path`*`)`

Returns the directory part of *`path`*, just like `os.path.split(`*`path`*`)[0]`. For example, `os.path.dirname('b/c/d.e')` returns `'b/c'`.

exists, lexists `exists(`*`path`*`) lexists(`*`path`*`)`

Returns `True` when *`path`* names an existing file or directory; otherwise, `False`. In other words, `os.path.exists(`*`x`*`)` is the same as `os.access(`*`x`*`, os.F_OK)`. `lexists` is the same, but also returns `True` when *`path`* names a symbolic link that indicates a nonexisting file or directory (sometimes known as a *broken symlink*), while `exists` returns `False` in such cases.

expandvars, expanduser

`expandvars(path) expanduser(path)`

Returns a copy of string *path*, where each substring of the form `$name` or `${name}` is replaced with the value of environment variable `name`. For example, if environment variable `HOME` is set to `/u/alex`, the following code:

```
import os
print(os.path.expandvars('$HOME/foo/'))
```

emits `/u/alex/foo/`.

`os.path.expanduser` expands a leading ~ to the path of the home directory of the current user.

getatime, getmtime, getctime, getsize

`getatime(path) getmtime(path) getctime(path) getsize(path)`

Each of these functions returns an attribute from the result of `os.stat(path)`: respectively, `st_atime`, `st_mtime`, `st_ctime`, and `st_size`. See Table 10-4 for more details about these attributes.

isabs

`isabs(path)`

Returns `True` when *path* is absolute. (A path is absolute when it starts with a slash (/), or, on some non-Unix-like platforms, with a drive designator followed by `os.sep`.) When *path* is not absolute, `isabs` returns `False`.

isfile

`isfile(path)`

Returns `True` when *path* names an existing regular file (however, `isfile` also follows symbolic links); otherwise, `False`.

isdir

`isdir(path)`

Returns `True` when *path* names an existing directory (however, `isdir` also follows symbolic links); otherwise, `False`.

islink

`islink(path)`

Returns `True` when *path* names a symbolic link; otherwise, `False`.

ismount

`ismount(path)`

Returns `True` when *path* names a mount point; otherwise, `False`.

join

`join(path, *paths)`

Returns a string that joins the argument strings with the appropriate path separator for the current platform. For example, on Unix, exactly one slash character / separates adjacent path components. If any argument is an absolute path, `join` ignores previous components. For example:

```
print(os.path.join('a/b', 'c/d', 'e/f'))
# on Unix prints: a/b/c/d/e/f
print(os.path.join('a/b', '/c/d', 'e/f'))
# on Unix prints: /c/d/e/f
```

The second call to `os.path.join` ignores its first argument `'a/b'`, since its second argument `'/c/d'` is an absolute path.

normcase

`normcase(path)`

Returns a copy of *path* with case normalized for the current platform. On case-sensitive filesystems (as is typical in Unix-like systems), *path* is returned unchanged. On case-insensitive filesystems (as is typical in Windows), all letters in the returned string are lowercase. On Windows, `normcase` also converts each / to a \.

normpath

`normpath(path)`

Returns a normalized pathname equivalent to *path*, removing redundant separators and path-navigation aspects. For example, on Unix, `normpath` returns `'a/b'` when *path* is any of `'a//b'`, `'a/./b'`, or `'a/c/../b'`. `normpath` makes path separators appropriate for the current platform. For example, on Windows, separators become \.

realpath

`realpath(path)`

Returns the actual path of the specified file or directory, resolving symlinks along the way.

relpath

`relpath(path, start=os.curdir)`

Returns a relative path to the specified file or directory, relative to directory *start* (by default, the process's current working directory).

samefile

`samefile(path1, path2)`

Returns `True` if both arguments refer to the same file or directory.

sameopenfile

`sameopenfile(fd1, fd2)`

Returns `True` if both file descriptor arguments refer to the same open file or directory.

samestat

`samestat(stat1, stat2)`

Returns `True` if both arguments, instances of `os.stat_result` (typically, results of `os.stat` calls), refer to the same file or directory.

split `split(path)`

Returns a pair of strings `(dir, base)` such that `join(dir, base)` equals *path*. *base* is the last component and never contains a path separator. If *path* ends in a separator, *base* is `''`. *dir* is the leading part of *path*, up to the last separator, shorn of trailing separators. For example, `os.path.split('a/b/c/d')` returns `('a/b/c', 'd')`.

splitdrive `splitdrive(path)`

Returns a pair of strings `(drv,pth)` such that *drv+pth* equals *path*. *drv* is either a drive specification, or `''`—always `''` on platforms not supporting drive specifications, such as Unix-like systems. On Windows, `os.path.splitdrive('c:d/e')` returns `('c:', 'd/e')`.

splitext `splitext(path)`

Returns a pair `(root, ext)` such that *root+ext* equals *path*. *ext* is either `''` or starts with a `'.'` and has no other `'.'` or path separator. For example, `os.path.splitext('a.a/b.c.d')` returns the pair `('a.a/b.c', '.d')`.

walk `walk(path, func, arg)`

(v2 only) Calls `func(arg, dirpath, namelist)` for each directory in the tree whose root is the directory *path*, starting with *path* itself. This function is hard to use and obsolete; use, instead, generator `os.walk`, covered in Table 10-4, on both v2 and v3.

The stat Module

The function `os.stat` (covered in Table 10-4) returns instances of `stat_result`, whose item indices, attribute names, and meaning are also covered there. The `stat` module supplies attributes with names like those of `stat_result`'s attributes, turned into uppercase, and corresponding values that are the corresponding item indices.

The more interesting contents of the `stat` module are functions to examine the `st_mode` attribute of a `stat_result` instance and determine the kind of file. `os.path` also supplies functions for such tasks, which operate directly on the file's *path*. The functions supplied by `stat` shown in the following list are faster when you perform several tests on the same file: they require only one `os.stat` call at the start of a series of tests, while the functions in `os.path` implicitly ask the operating system for the same information at each test. Each function returns `True` when *mode* denotes a file of the given kind; otherwise, `False`.

`S_ISDIR(mode)`
: Is the file a directory?

`S_ISCHR(mode)`
: Is the file a special device-file of the character kind?

`S_ISBLK(`*`mode`*`)`
: Is the file a special device-file of the block kind?

`S_ISREG(`*`mode`*`)`
: Is the file a normal file (not a directory, special device-file, and so on)?

`S_ISFIFO(`*`mode`*`)`
: Is the file a FIFO (also known as a "named pipe")?

`S_ISLNK(`*`mode`*`)`
: Is the file a symbolic link?

`S_ISSOCK(`*`mode`*`)`
: Is the file a Unix-domain socket?

Several of these functions are meaningful only on Unix-like systems, since other platforms do not keep special files such as devices and sockets in the namespace for regular files, as Unix-like systems do.

The `stat` module supplies two more functions that extract relevant parts of a file's *mode* (*x*`.st_mode`, for some result *x* of function `os.stat`):

S_IFMT `S_IFMT(`*`mode`*`)`

Returns those bits of *mode* that describe the kind of file (i.e., those bits that are examined by functions `S_ISDIR`, `S_ISREG`, etc.).

S_IMODE `S_IMODE(`*`mode`*`)`

Returns those bits of *mode* that can be set by the function `os.chmod` (i.e., the permission bits and, on Unix-like platforms, a few other special bits such as the `set-user-id` flag).

The filecmp Module

The `filecmp` module supplies the following functions to compare files and directories:

cmp `cmp(`*`f1`*`, `*`f2`*`, `*`shallow`*`=True)`

Compares the files named by path strings *f1* and *f2*. If the files are deemed to be equal, `cmp` returns `True`; otherwise, `False`. If *shallow* is true, files are deemed to be equal if their `stat` tuples are. When *shallow* is `False`, `cmp` reads and compares the contents of files whose `stat` tuples are equal.

File and Text Operations

cmpfiles `cmpfiles(dir1, dir2, common, shallow=True)`

Loops on the sequence *common*. Each item of *common* is a string that names a file present in both directories *dir1* and *dir2*. `cmpfiles` returns a tuple whose items are three lists of strings: `(equal, diff, errs)`. *equal* is the list of names of files that are equal in both directories, *diff* is the list of names of files that differ between directories, and *errs* is the list of names of files that could not be compared (because they do not exist in both directories, or there is no permission to read them). The argument *shallow* is the same as for `cmp`.

dircmp `class dircmp(dir1, dir2, ignore=('RCS', 'CVS', 'tags'), hide=('.', '..'))`

Creates a new directory-comparison instance object, comparing directories named *dir1* and *dir2*, ignoring names listed in *ignore*, and hiding names listed in *hide*. (In v3, the default value for *ignore* lists more files, and is supplied by attribute `DEFAULT_IGNORE` of module `filecmp`; at the time of this writing, `['RCS', 'CVS', 'tags', '.git', '.hg', '.bzr', '_darcs', '__pycache__']`.)

A `dircmp` instance *d* supplies three methods:

d.`report()`

Outputs to `sys.stdout` a comparison between *dir1* and *dir2*

d.`report_partial_closure()`

Outputs to `sys.stdout` a comparison between *dir1* and *dir2* and their common immediate subdirectories

d.`report_full_closure()`

Outputs to `sys.stdout` a comparison between *dir1* and *dir2* and all their common subdirectories, recursively

In addition, *d* supplies several attributes, covered in the next section.

dircmp instance attributes

A `dircmp` instance *d* supplies several attributes, computed "just in time" (i.e., only if and when needed, thanks to a `__getattr__` special method) so that using a `dircmp` instance suffers no unnecessary overhead:

d.`common`
: Files and subdirectories that are in both *dir1* and *dir2*

d.`common_dirs`
: Subdirectories that are in both *dir1* and *dir2*

d.`common_files`
: Files that are in both *dir1* and *dir2*

`d.common_funny`
: Names that are in both *dir1* and *dir2* for which `os.stat` reports an error or returns different kinds for the versions in the two directories

`d.diff_files`
: Files that are in both *dir1* and *dir2* but with different contents

`d.funny_files`
: Files that are in both *dir1* and *dir2* but could not be compared

`d.left_list`
: Files and subdirectories that are in *dir1*

`d.left_only`
: Files and subdirectories that are in *dir1* and not in *dir2*

`d.right_list`
: Files and subdirectories that are in *dir2*

`d.right_only`
: Files and subdirectories that are in *dir2* and not in *dir1*

`d.same_files`
: Files that are in both *dir1* and *dir2* with the same contents

`d.subdirs`
: A dictionary whose keys are the strings in `common_dirs`; the corresponding values are instances of `dircmp` for each subdirectory

The fnmatch Module

The `fnmatch` module (an abbreviation for *filename match*) matches filename strings with patterns that resemble the ones used by Unix shells:

`*`
: Matches any sequence of characters

`?`
: Matches any single character

[chars]
: Matches any one of the characters in *chars*

[!chars]
: Matches any one character not among those in *chars*

`fnmatch` does *not* follow other conventions of Unix shells' pattern matching, such as treating a slash `/` or a leading dot `.` specially. It also does not allow escaping special characters: rather, to literally match a special character, enclose it in brackets. For example, to match a filename that's a single closed bracket, use the pattern `'[]]'`.

The `fnmatch` module supplies the following functions:

filter `filter(names,pattern)`

Returns the list of items of *names* (a sequence of strings) that match *pattern*.

fnmatch `fnmatch(filename,pattern)`

Returns `True` when string *filename* matches *pattern*; otherwise, `False`. The match is case-sensitive when the platform is, for example, any Unix-like system, and otherwise (for example, on Windows) case-insensitive; beware of that, if you're dealing with a filesystem whose case-sensitivity doesn't match your platform (for example, macOS is Unix-like, however, its typical filesystems are case-insensitive).

fnmatchcase `fnmatchcase(filename,pattern)`

Returns `True` when string *filename* matches *pattern*; otherwise, `False`. The match is always case-sensitive on any platform.

translate `translate(pattern)`

Returns the *regular expression* pattern (as covered in "Pattern-String Syntax" on page 254) equivalent to the `fnmatch` pattern *pattern*. This can be quite useful, for example, to perform matches that are always case-insensitive on any platform—a functionality `fnmatch` doesn't supply:

```
import fnmatch, re

def fnmatchnocase(filename, pattern):
    re_pat = fnmatch.translate(pattern)
    return re.match(re_pat, filename, re.IGNORECASE)
```

The glob Module

The `glob` module lists (in arbitrary order) the path names of files that match a path *pattern* using the same rules as `fnmatch`; in addition, it does treat a leading dot `.` specially, like Unix shells do.

glob `glob(pathname)`

Returns the list of path names of files that match pattern *pathname*. In v3 only, you can also optionally pass named argument *recursive*=`True` to have path component `**` recursively match zero or more levels of subdirectories.

iglob `iglob(pathname)`

Like `glob`, but returns an iterator yielding one relevant path name at a time.

The shutil Module

The `shutil` module (an abbreviation for *shell utilities*) supplies the following functions to copy and move files, and to remove an entire directory tree. In v3 only, on some Unix platforms, most of the functions support optional, keyword-only argument *`follow_symlinks`*, defaulting to `True`. When true, and always in v2, if a path indicates a symbolic link, the function follows it to reach an actual file or directory; when false, the function operates on the symbolic link itself.

copy `copy(`*`src, dst`*`)`

Copies the contents of the file *`src`*, creating or overwriting the file *`dst`*. If *`dst`* is a directory, the target is a file with the same base name as *`src`*, but located in *`dst`*. `copy` also copies permission bits, but not last-access and modification times. In v3 only, returns the path to the destination file it has copied to (in v2, less usefully, `copy` returns `None`).

copy2 `copy2(`*`src, dst`*`)`

Like `copy`, but also copies times of last access and modification.

copyfile `copyfile(`*`src, dst`*`)`

Copies just the contents (not permission bits, nor last-access and modification times) of the file *`src`*, creating or overwriting the file *`dst`*.

copyfileobj `copyfileobj(`*`fsrc, fdst, bufsize`*`=16384)`

Copies all bytes from the "file" object *`fsrc`*, which must be open for reading, to "file" object *`fdst`*, which must be open for writing. Copies no more than *`bufsize`* bytes at a time if *`bufsize`* is greater than `0`. "File" objects are covered in "The io Module" on page 273.

copymode `copymode(`*`src, dst`*`)`

Copies permission bits of the file or directory *`src`* to file or directory *`dst`*. Both *`src`* and *`dst`* must exist. Does not change *`dst`*'s contents, nor its status as being a file or a directory.

copystat `copystat(`*`src, dst`*`)`

Copies permission bits and times of last access and modification of the file or directory *`src`* to the file or directory *`dst`*. Both *`src`* and *`dst`* must exist. Does not change *`dst`*'s contents, nor its status as being a file or a directory.

copytree `copytree(src, dst, symlinks=False, ignore=None)`

Copies the directory tree rooted at *src* into the destination directory named by *dst*. *dst* must not already exist: `copytree` creates it (as well as creating any missing parent directory). `copytree` copies each file by using function `copy2` (in v3 only, you can optionally pass a different file-copy function as named argument *copy_function*).

When *symlinks* is true, `copytree` creates symbolic links in the new tree when it finds symbolic links in the source tree. When *symlinks* is false, `copytree` follows each symbolic link it finds and copies the linked-to file with the link's name. On platforms that do not have the concept of a symbolic link, `copytree` ignores argument *symlinks*.

When *ignore* is not `None`, it must be a callable accepting two arguments (a directory path and a list of the directory's immediate children) and returning a list of such children to be ignored in the copy process. If present, *ignore* is usually the result of a call to `shutil.ignore_patterns`; for example:

```
import shutil
ignore = shutil.ignore_patterns('.*', '*.bak')
shutil.copytree('src', 'dst', ignore=ignore)
```

copies the tree rooted at directory `src` into a new tree rooted at directory `dst`, ignoring any file or subdirectory whose name starts with a dot, and any file or subdirectory whose name ends with `'.bak'`.

ignore_patterns `ignore_patterns(*patterns)`

Returns a callable picking out files and subdirectories matching *patterns*, like those used in the `fnmatch` module (see "The fnmatch Module" on page 311). The result is suitable for passing as the *ignore* argument to function `copytree`.

move `move(src, dst)`

Moves the file or directory *src* to *dst*. First tries `os.rename`. Then, if that fails (because *src* and *dst* are on separate filesystems, or because *dst* already exists), copies *src* to *dst* (`copy2` for a file, `copytree` for a directory; in v3 only, you can optionally pass a file-copy function other than `copy2` as named argument *copy_function*), then removes *src* (`os.unlink` for a file, `rmtree` for a directory).

rmtree `rmtree(path, ignore_errors=False, onerror=None)`

Removes directory tree rooted at *path*. When *ignore_errors* is `True`, `rmtree` ignores errors. When *ignore_errors* is `False` and *onerror* is `None`, errors raise exceptions. When *onerror* is not `None`, it must be callable with three parameters: *func*, *path*, and *ex*. *func* is the function raising the exception (`os.remove` or `os.rmdir`), *path* is the path passed to *func*, and *ex* the tuple of information `sys.exc_info()` returns. When *onerror* raises an exception, `rmtree` terminates, and the exception propagates.

Beyond offering functions that are directly useful, the source file *shutil.py* in the standard Python library is an excellent example of how to use many `os` functions.

File Descriptor Operations

The os module supplies, among many others, many functions to handle *file descriptors*, integers the operating system uses as opaque handles to refer to open files. Python "file" objects (covered in "The io Module" on page 273) are usually better for I/O tasks, but sometimes working at file-descriptor level lets you perform some operation faster, or (sacrificing portability) in ways not directly available with `io.open`. "File" objects and file descriptors are not interchangeable.

To get the file descriptor *n* of a Python "file" object *f*, call *n*=*f*.`fileno()`. To wrap a new Python "file" object *f* around an open file descriptor *fd*, call *f*=`os.fdopen(`*fd*`)`, or pass *fd* as the first argument of `io.open`. On Unix-like and Windows platforms, some file descriptors are pre-allocated when a process starts: `0` is the file descriptor for the process's standard input, `1` for the process's standard output, and `2` for the process's standard error.

`os` provides many functions dealing with file descriptors; the most often used ones are listed in Table 10-5.

Table 10-5.

close `close(`*fd*`)`

Closes file descriptor *fd*.

closerange `closerange(`*fd_low*`, `*fd_high*`)`

Closes all file descriptors from *fd_low*, included, to *fd_high*, excluded, ignoring any errors that may occur.

dup `dup(`*fd*`)`

Returns a file descriptor that duplicates file descriptor *fd*.

dup2 `dup2(`*fd*`, `*fd2*`)`

Duplicates file descriptor *fd* to file descriptor *fd2*. When file descriptor *fd2* is already open, `dup2` first closes *fd2*.

fdopen `fdopen(`*fd*`, *`*a*`, **`*k*`)`

Like `io.open`, except that *fd must* be an `int` that's an open file descriptor.

fstat `fstat(`*fd*`)`

Returns a `stat_result` instance *x*, with info about the file open on file descriptor *fd*. Table 10-4 covers *x*'s contents.

lseek `lseek(fd, pos, how)`

Sets the current position of file descriptor *fd* to the signed integer byte offset *pos* and returns the resulting byte offset from the start of the file. *how* indicates the reference (point `0`). When *how* is `os.SEEK_SET`, the reference is the start of the file; when `os.SEEK_CUR`, the current position; when `os.SEEK_END`, the end of the file. In particular, `lseek(fd, 0, os.SEEK_CUR)` returns the current position's byte offset from the start of the file without affecting the current position. Normal disk files support seeking; calling `lseek` on a file that does not support seeking (e.g., a file open for output to a terminal) raises an exception.

open `open(file, flags, mode=0o777)`

Returns a file descriptor, opening or creating a file named by string *file*. If `open` creates the file, it uses *mode* as the file's permission bits. *flags* is an `int`, normally the bitwise OR (with operator |) of one or more of the following attributes of `os`:

`O_RDONLY O_WRONLY O_RDWR`

Opens *file* for read-only, write-only, or read/write, respectively (mutually exclusive: exactly one of these attributes must be in *flags*)

`O_NDELAY O_NONBLOCK`

Opens *file* in nonblocking (no-delay) mode if the platform supports this

`O_APPEND`

Appends any new data to *file*'s previous contents

`O_DSYNC O_RSYNC O_SYNC O_NOCTTY`

Sets synchronization mode accordingly if the platform supports this

`O_CREAT`

Creates *file* if *file* does not already exist

`O_EXCL`

Raises an exception if *file* already exists

`O_TRUNC`

Throws away previous contents of *file* (incompatible with `O_RDONLY`)

`O_BINARY`

Opens *file* in binary rather than text mode on non-Unix platforms (innocuous and without effect on Unix-like platforms)

pipe `pipe()`

Creates a pipe and returns a pair of file descriptors `(r, w)`, respectively open for reading and writing.

read

`read(fd, n)`

Reads up to *n* bytes from file descriptor *fd* and returns them as a bytestring. Reads and returns *m*<*n* bytes when only *m* more bytes are currently available for reading from the file. In particular, returns the empty string when no more bytes are currently available from the file, typically because the file is finished.

write

`write(fd, s)`

Writes all bytes from bytestring *s* to file descriptor *fd* and returns the number of bytes written (i.e., `len(s)`).

Text Input and Output

Python presents non-GUI text input and output channels to your programs as "file" objects, so you can use the methods of "file" objects (covered in "Attributes and Methods of "file" Objects" on page 276) to operate on these channels.

Standard Output and Standard Error

The `sys` module (covered in "The sys Module" on page 212) has the attributes `stdout` and `stderr`, writeable "file" objects. Unless you are using shell redirection or pipes, these streams connect to the "terminal" running your script. Nowadays, actual terminals are very rare: a so-called "terminal" is generally a screen window that supports text I/O (e.g., a command prompt console on Windows or an `xterm` window on Unix).

The distinction between `sys.stdout` and `sys.stderr` is a matter of convention. `sys.stdout`, known as *standard output*, is where your program emits results. `sys.stderr`, known as *standard error*, is where error messages go. Separating results from error messages helps you use shell redirection effectively. Python respects this convention, using `sys.stderr` for errors and warnings.

The print Function

Programs that output results to standard output often need to write to `sys.stdout`. Python's `print` function (covered in Table 7-2) can be a rich, convenient alternative to `sys.stdout.write`. (In v2, start your module with `from __future__ import print_function` to make `print` a *function*—otherwise, for backward compatibility, it's a less-convenient *statement*.)

`print` is fine for the informal output used during development to help you debug your code. For production output, you may need more control of formatting than `print` affords. You may need to control spacing, field widths, number of decimals for floating-point, and so on. If so, prepare the output as a string with string-formatting method `format` (covered in "String Formatting" on page 240), then output the string, usually with the `write` method of the appropriate "file" object. (You can pass formatted strings to `print`, but `print` may add spaces and newlines; the write method adds nothing at all, so it's easier for you to control what exactly gets output.)

To direct the output from print calls to a certain file, as an alternative to repeated use of file=*destination* on each print, you can temporarily change the value of sys.stdout. The following example is a general-purpose redirection function usable for such a temporary change; in the presence of asynchronous operations, make sure to also add a lock in order to avoid any contention:

```
def redirect(func, *args, **kwds):
    """redirect(func, ...) -> (string result, func's return value)
    func must be a callable and may emit results to standard output.
    redirect captures those results as a string and returns a pair,
    with the output string as the first item and func's return value
    as the second one.
    """
    import sys, io
    save_out = sys.stdout
    sys.stdout = io.StringIO()
    try:
        retval = func(*args, **kwds)
        return sys.stdout.getvalue(), retval
    finally:
        sys.stdout.close()
        sys.stdout = save_out
```

To output a few text values to a file object *f* that isn't the current sys.stdout, avoid such manipulations. For such simple purposes, just calling *f*.write is often best, and print(file=*f*,...) is, even more often, a handy alternative.

Standard Input

The sys module provides the stdin attribute, which is a readable "file" object. When you need a line of text from the user, you can call built-in function input (covered in Table 7-2; in v2, it's named raw_input), optionally with a string argument to use as a prompt.

When the input you need is not a string (for example, when you need a number), use input to obtain a string from the user, then other built-ins, such as int, float, or ast.literal_eval (covered below), to turn the string into the number you need.

You could, in theory, also use eval (normally preceded by compile, for better control of error diagnostics), so as to let the user input any expression, as long as you totally trust the user. A nasty user can exploit eval to breach security and cause damage (a well-meaning but careless user can also unfortunately cause just about as much damage). There is no effective defense—just avoid eval (and exec!) on any input from sources you do not fully trust.

One advanced alternative we do recommend is to use the function literal_eval from the standard library module ast (as covered in the online docs (*https://*

docs.python.org/3/library/ast.html#ast.literal_eval)). `ast.literal_eval(`*astring*`)` returns a valid Python value for the given literal *astring* when it can, or else raises a `SyntaxError` or `ValueError`; it never has any side effect. However, to ensure complete safety, *astring* in this case cannot use any operator, nor any nonkeyword identifier. For example:

```
import ast
print(ast.literal_eval('23'))    # prints 23
print(ast.literal_eval('[2,3]')) # prints [2, 3]
print(ast.literal_eval('2+3'))   # raises ValueError
print(ast.literal_eval('2+'))    # raises SyntaxError
```

The getpass Module

Very occasionally, you may want the user to input a line of text in such a way that somebody looking at the screen cannot see what the user is typing. This may occur when you're asking the user for a password. The `getpass` module provides the following functions:

getpass `getpass(`*prompt*`='Password: ')`

Like `input`, except that the text the user inputs is not echoed to the screen as the user is typing. `getpass`'s default *prompt* is different from `input`'s.

getuser `getuser()`

Returns the current user's username. `getuser` tries to get the username as the value of one of the environment variables `LOGNAME`, `USER`, `LNAME`, and `USERNAME`, in order. If none of these variables are in `os.environ`, `getuser` asks the operating system.

Richer-Text I/O

The tools covered so far supply the minimal subset of text I/O functionality on all platforms. Most platforms offer richer-text I/O, such as responding to single keypresses (not just entire lines) and showing text in any spot on the terminal.

Python extensions and core Python modules let you access platform-specific functionality. Unfortunately, various platforms expose this functionality in very different ways. To develop cross-platform Python programs with rich-text I/O functionality, you may need to wrap different modules uniformly, importing platform-specific modules conditionally (usually with the `try/except` idiom covered in "try/except" on page 150).

The readline Module

The `readline` module wraps the GNU Readline Library. Readline lets the user edit text lines during interactive input, and recall previous lines for editing and reentry. Readline comes pre-installed on many Unix-like platforms, and it's available online (*http://tiswww.case.edu/php/chet/readline/rltop.html*). On Windows, you can install and use the third-party module pyreadline (*https://pypi.python.org/pypi/pyreadline/2.0*).

When `readline` is available, Python uses it for all line-oriented input, such as `input`. The interactive Python interpreter always tries to load `readline` to enable line editing and recall for interactive sessions. Some `readline` functions control advanced functionality, particularly *history*, for recalling lines entered in previous sessions, and *completion*, for context-sensitive completion of the word being entered. (See the GNU Readline docs (*http://tiswww.case.edu/php/chet/readline/rltop.html#Documentation*) for details on configuration commands.) You can access the module's functionality using the following functions:

add_history `add_history(`*`s`*`)`

Adds string *`s`* as a line at the end of the history buffer.

clear_history `clear_history(`*`s`*`)`

Clears the history buffer.

get_completer `get_completer()`

Returns the current completer function (as last set by `set_completer`), or `None` if no completer function is set.

get_history_length `get_history_length()`

Returns the number of lines of history to be saved to the history file. When the result is less than `0`, all lines in the history are to be saved.

parse_and_bind `parse_and_bind(`*`readline_cmd`*`)`

Gives Readline a configuration command. To let the user hit Tab to request completion, call `parse_and_bind('tab: complete')`. See the Readline documentation for other useful values of string *`readline_cmd`*.

A good completion function is in the module `rlcompleter`. In the interactive interpreter (or in the startup file executed at the start of interactive sessions, covered in "Environment Variables" on page 26), enter:

```
import readline, rlcompleter
readline.parse_and_bind('tab: complete')
```

For the rest of this interactive session, you can hit Tab during line editing and get completion for global names and object attributes.

read_history_file `read_history_file(`*`filename`*`='~/.history')`

Loads history lines from the text file at path *`filename`*.

read_init_file `read_init_file(`*`filename`*`=None)`

Makes Readline load a text file: each line is a configuration command. When *`filename`* is `None`, loads the same file as last time.

set_completer `set_completer(`*`f`*`=None)`

Sets the completion function. When *f* is `None`, Readline disables completion. Otherwise, when the user types a partial word *`start`*, then Tab, Readline calls *`f(start, i)`*, with *`i`* initially `0`. *f* returns the *`i`*th possible word starting with *`start`*, or `None` when there are no more. Readline loops calling *f*, with *`i`* set to `0`, `1`, `2`, etc., until *f* returns `None`.

set_history_length `set_history_length(`*`x`*`)`

Sets the number of lines of history that are to be saved to the history file. When *x* is less than `0`, all lines in the history are to be saved.

write_history_file `write_history_file(`*`filename`*`='~/.history')`

Saves history lines to the text file whose name or path is *`filename`*.

Console I/O

"Terminals" today are usually text windows on a graphical screen. You may also, in theory, use a true terminal, or (perhaps a tad less theoretical, but, these days, not by much) the console (main screen) of a personal computer in text mode. All such "terminals" in use today offer advanced text I/O functionality, accessed in platform-dependent ways. The `curses` package works on Unix-like platforms; for a cross-platform (Windows, Unix, Mac) solution, you may use third-party package UniCurses (*https://pypi.python.org/pypi/UniCurses*). The `msvcrt` module, on the contrary, exists only on Windows.

The curses package

The classic Unix approach to advanced terminal I/O is named *curses*, for obscure historical reasons.[1] The Python package `curses` affords reasonably simple use, but still lets you exert detailed control if required. We cover a small subset of `curses`, just enough to let you write programs with rich-text I/O functionality. (See Eric Raymond's tutorial Curses Programming with Python (*https://docs.python.org/2/howto/curses.html#curses-howto*) for more). Whenever we mention "the screen" in this section, we mean the screen of the terminal (usually, these days, that's the text window of a terminal-emulator program).

1 "Curses" does describe well the typical utterances of programmers faced with this rich, complicated approach.

The simplest and most effective way to use `curses` is through the `curses.wrapper` function:

wrapper `wrapper(`*`func`*`, *`*`args`*`)`

When you call `wrapper` you must pass as its first argument a function, *`func`*. `wrapper` initializes the `curses` system, creating a top-level `curses.window` object *w*, and then calls *`func`* with *w* as its first argument and the remaining arguments to `wrapper` as further arguments to *`func`*. When *`func`* returns, the `wrapper` function returns the terminal to normal functionality and itself terminates by returning the return value of *`func`*. Performs `curses` initialization, calls *`func`*`(`*`w`*`, *`*`args`*`)`, performs `curses` finalization (setting the terminal back to normal behavior), and finally returns *`func`*'s result (or re-raises whatever exception *`func`* may have propagated). The key factor is that `wrapper` sets the terminal back to normal behavior, whether *`func`* terminates normally or propagates an exception.

`func` should be a function that performs all tasks in your program that may need `curses` functionality. In other words, *`func`* normally contains (or calls, directly or indirectly, functions containing) all of your program's functionality, save perhaps for some noninteractive initialization and/or finalization tasks.

`curses` models text and background colors as *character attributes*. Colors available on the terminal are numbered from `0` to `curses.COLORS`. The function `color_content` takes a color number *n* as its argument and returns a tuple `(`*`r`*`, `*`g`*`, `*`b`*`)` of integers between `0` and `1000` giving the amount of each primary color in *n*. The function `color_pair` takes a color number *n* as its argument and returns an attribute code that you can pass to various methods of a `curses.Window` object in order to display text in that color.

`curses` lets you create multiple instances of type `curses.Window`, each corresponding to a rectangle on the screen. You can also create exotic variants, such as instances of `Panel`, polymorphic with `Window` but not tied to a fixed screen rectangle. You do not need such advanced functionality in simple `curses` programs: just use the `Window` object `stdscr` that `curses.wrapper` gives you. Call *`w`*`.refresh()` to ensure that changes made to any `Window` instance *w*, including `stdscr`, show up on screen. `curses` can buffer the changes until you call `refresh`.

An instance *w* of `Window` supplies, among many others, the following frequently used methods:

addstr *`w`*`.addstr([`*`y`*`, `*`x`*`, ]`*`s`*`[, `*`attr`*`])`

Puts the characters in the string *s*, with the attribute *`attr`*, on *w* at the given coordinates `(`*`x`*`, `*`y`*`)`, overwriting any previous contents. All `curses` functions and methods accept coordinate arguments in reverse order, with *y* (the row number) before *x* (the column number). If you omit *y* and *x*, `addstr` uses *w*'s current cursor coordinates. If you omit *`attr`*, `addstr` uses *w*'s current default attribute. In any case, `addstr`, when done adding the string, sets *w*'s current cursor coordinates to the end of the string it has added.

clrtobot, clrtoeol

`w.clrtobot() w.clrtoeol()`

`clrtoeol` writes blanks from *w*'s current cursor coordinates to the end of the line. `clrtobot`, in addition, also blanks all lines lower down on the screen.

delch

`w.delch([y, x])`

Deletes one character from *w* at coordinates `(x, y)`. If you omit the *y* and *x* arguments, `delch` uses *w*'s current cursor coordinates. In any case, `delch` does not change *w*'s current cursor coordinates. All the following characters in line *y*, if any, shift left by one.

deleteln

`w.deleteln()`

Deletes from *w* the entire line at *w*'s current cursor coordinates, and scrolls up by one line all lines lower down on the screen.

erase

`w.erase()`

Writes spaces to the entire terminal screen.

getch

`w.getch()`

Returns an integer *c* corresponding to a user keystroke. A value between `0` and `255` represents an ordinary character, while a value greater than `255` represents a special key. `curses` supplies names for special keys, so you can test *c* for equality with readable constants such as `curses.KEY_HOME` (the *Home* special key), `curses.KEY_LEFT` (the left-arrow special key), and so on. (The list of all of `curses` many special-key names is in Python's online docs (*https://docs.python.org/3.5/library/curses.html?highlight=curses#constants*).)

If you have set window *w* to no-delay mode by calling `w.nodelay(True)`, `w.getch` raises an exception when no keystroke is ready. By default, `w.getch` waits until the user hits a key.

getyx

`w.getyx()`

Returns *w*'s current cursor coordinates as a tuple `(y, x)`.

insstr

`w.insstr([y, x, ]s[, attr])`

Inserts the characters in string *s*, with attribute *attr*, on *w* at coordinates `(x, y)`, shifting the rest of line rightward. Any characters shifted beyond line end are lost. If you omit *y* and *x*, `insstr` uses *w*'s current cursor coordinates. If you omit *attr*, `insstr` uses *w*'s current default attribute. In any case, when done inserting the string, `insstr` sets *w*'s current cursor coordinates to the first character of the string it has inserted.

move

`w.move(y, x)`

Moves *w*'s cursor to the given coordinates `(x, y)`.

nodelay

`w.nodelay(flag)`

Sets *w* to no-delay mode when *flag* is true; resets *w* back to normal mode when *flag* is false. No-delay mode affects the method `w.getch`.

refresh `w.refresh()`

Updates window *w* on screen with all changes the program has effected on *w*.

The `curses.textpad` module supplies the `Textpad` class, which lets you support advanced input and text editing.

Textpad `class Textpad(window)`

Creates and returns an instance *t* of class `Textpad` that wraps the `curses` window instance *window*. Instance *t* has one frequently used method:

`t.edit()`

Lets the user perform interactive editing on the contents of the window instance that *t* wraps. The editing session supports simple Emacs-like key bindings: normal characters overwrite the window's previous contents, arrow keys move the cursor, and Ctrl-H deletes the character to the cursor's left. When the user hits Ctrl-G, the editing session ends, and `edit` returns the window's contents as a single string, with newlines as line separators.

The msvcrt Module

The `msvcrt` module, available only on Windows, supplies functions that let Python programs access a few proprietary extras supplied by the Microsoft Visual C++'s runtime library *msvcrt.dll*. Some `msvcrt` functions let you read user input character by character rather than reading a full line at a time, as listed here:

getch, getche `getch() getche()`

Reads and returns one character from keyboard input, and waits if no character is yet available for reading. `getche` also echoes the character to screen (if printable), while `getch` doesn't. When the user presses a special key (arrows, function keys, etc.), it's seen as two characters: first a `chr(0)` or `chr(224)`, then a second character that, together with the first one, defines the special key the user pressed. To find out what `getch` returns for any key, run the following small script on a Windows machine:

```
import msvcrt
print("press z to exit, or any other key
       to see the key's code:")
while True:
    c = msvcrt.getch()
    if c == 'z': break
    print('{} ({!r})'.format(ord(c), c))
```

kbhit `kbhit()`

Returns `True` when a character is available for reading (`getch`, when called, returns immediately); otherwise, `False` (`getch`, when called, waits).

ungetch `ungetch(c)`

"Ungets" character *c*; the next call to `getch` or `getche` returns *c*. It's an error to call `ungetch` twice without intervening calls to `getch` or `getche`.

Interactive Command Sessions

The `cmd` module offers a simple way to handle interactive sessions of commands. Each command is a line of text. The first word of each command is a verb defining the requested action. The rest of the line is passed as an argument to the method that implements the verb's action.

The `cmd` module supplies the class `Cmd` to use as a base class, and you define your own subclass of `cmd.Cmd`. Your subclass supplies methods with names starting with `do_` and `help_`, and may optionally override some of `Cmd`'s methods. When the user enters a command line such as *`verb and the rest`*, as long as your subclass defines a method named `do_`*`verb`*, `Cmd.onecmd` calls:

```
self.do_verb('and the rest')
```

Similarly, as long as your subclass defines a method named `help_`*`verb`*, `Cmd.do_help` calls the method when the command line starts with `'help verb'` or `'?verb'`. `Cmd` shows suitable error messages if the user tries to use, or asks for help about, a verb for which the needed method is not defined.

Initializing a Cmd Instance

Your subclass of `cmd.Cmd`, if it defines its own `__init__` special method, must call the base class's `__init__`, whose signature is as follows:

__init__ `Cmd.__init__(self, completekey='Tab', stdin=sys.stdin, stdout=sys.stdout)`

Initializes the instance `self` with specified or default values for *`completekey`* (name of the key to use for command completion with the `readline` module; pass `None` to disable command completion), *`stdin`* (file object to get input from), and *`stdout`* (file object to emit output to).

If your subclass does not define `__init__`, then it just inherits the one from the base class `cmd.Cmd` that we just covered. In this case, to instantiate your subclass, call it, with the optional parameters *`completekey`*, *`stdin`*, and *`stdout`*, as documented in the previous paragraph.

Methods of Cmd Instances

An instance *c* of a subclass of the class `Cmd` supplies the following methods (many of these methods are "hooks" meant to be optionally overridden by the subclass):

cmdloop `c.cmdloop(intro=None)`

Performs an interactive session of line-oriented commands. `cmdloop` starts by calling `c.preloop()`, and then emits string *`intro`* (`c.intro` if *`intro`* is None). Then `c.cmdloop` enters a loop. In each iteration of the loop, `cmdloop` reads line *s* with `s=input(c.prompt)`. When standard input reaches end-of-file, `cmdloop` sets `s='EOF'`. If *s* is not `'EOF'`, `cmdloop` preprocesses string *s* with `s=c.precmd(s)`, and then calls `flag=c.onecmd(s)`. When `onecmd` returns a true value, this is a tentative request to terminate the command loop. Whatever the value of *`flag`*, `cmdloop` calls `flag=c.postcmd(flag, s)` to check whether the loop should terminate. If *`flag`* is now true, the loop terminates; otherwise, the loop repeats again. When the loop terminates, `cmdloop` calls `c.postloop()`, and then terminates. This structure of `cmdloop` that we just described is easiest to understand by looking at equivalent Python code:

```
def cmdloop(self, intro=None):
    self.preloop()
    if intro is None: intro = self.intro
    print(intro)
    finis_flag = False
    while not finis_flag:
        try: s = raw_input(self.prompt)
        except EOFError: s = 'EOF'
        else: s = self.precmd(s)
        finis_flag = self.onecmd(s)
        finis_flag = self.postcmd(finis_flag, s)
    self.postloop()
```

`cmdloop` is a good example of the classic design pattern known as *Template Method*. Such a method performs little substantial work itself; rather, it structures and organizes calls to other methods, known as *hook* methods. Subclasses may override some or all of the hook methods to define the details of class behavior within the overall framework thus established. When you inherit from `Cmd`, you almost never override the method `cmdloop`, since `cmdloop`'s structure is the main thing you get by subclassing `Cmd`.

default `c.default(s)`

`c.onecmd` calls `c.default(s)` when there is no method `c.do_verb` for the first word *`verb`* of line *s*. Subclasses often override `default`. The base-class method `Cmd.default` prints an error message.

do_help `c.do_help(verb)`

`c.onecmd` calls `c.do_help(verb)` when the command-line *s* starts with `'help verb'` or `'?verb'`. Subclasses rarely override `do_help`. The `Cmd.do_help` method calls the method `help_verb` if the subclass supplies it; otherwise, it displays the docstring of the method `do_verb` if the subclass supplies that method with a nonempty docstring. If the subclass does not supply either source of help, `Cmd.do_help` outputs a message to inform the user that no help is available on *`verb`*.

emptyline `c.emptyline()`

`c.onecmd` calls `c.emptyline( )` when command-line *s* is empty or blank. Unless a subclass overrides this method, the base-class method `Cmd.emptyline` reexecutes the last nonblank command line seen, stored in the attribute `c.lastcmd` of *c*.

onecmd `c.onecmd(s)`

`c.cmdloop` calls `c.onecmd(s)` for each command-line *s* that the user inputs. You can also call `onecmd` directly if you have otherwise obtained a line *s* to process as a command. Normally, subclasses do not override `onecmd`. `Cmd.onecmd` sets `c.lastcmd=s`. Then `onecmd` calls `do_verb` when *s* starts with the word *verb* and the subclass supplies such a method; otherwise, it calls `emptyline` or `default`, as explained earlier. In any case, `Cmd.onecmd` returns the result of whatever other method it calls to be interpreted by `postcmd` as a termination-request flag.

postcmd `c.postcmd(flag, s)`

`c.cmdloop` calls `c.postcmd(flag, s)` for each command-line *s* after `c.onecmd(s)` has returned value *flag*. If *flag* is true, the command just executed is posing a tentative request to terminate the command loop. If `postcmd` returns a true value, `cmdloop`'s loop terminates. Unless your subclass overrides this method, the base-class method `Cmd.postcmd` is called and returns *flag* itself as the method's result.

postloop `c.postloop()`

`c.cmdloop` calls `c.postloop( )` when `cmdloop`'s loop terminates. Your subclass may override this method; the base-class method `Cmd.postloop` does nothing.

precmd `c.precmd(s)`

`c.cmdloop` calls `s=c.precmd(s)` to preprocess each command-line *s*. The current leg of the loop bases all further processing on the string that `precmd` returns. Your subclass may override this method; the base-class method `Cmd.precmd` just returns *s* itself as the method's result.

preloop `c.preloop()`

`c.cmdloop` calls `c.preloop()` before `cmdloop`'s loop begins. Your subclass may override this method; the base-class method `Cmd.preloop` does nothing.

Attributes of Cmd Instances

An instance *c* of a subclass of the class `Cmd` supplies the following attributes:

`identchars`
: A string whose characters are all those that can be part of a verb; by default, `c.identchars` contains letters, digits, and an underscore (_).

`intro`
: The message that `cmdloop` outputs first, when called with no argument.

`lastcmd`
: The last nonblank command line seen by `onecmd`.

`prompt`
: The string that `cmdloop` uses to prompt the user for interactive input. You almost always bind `c.prompt` explicitly, or override `prompt` as a class attribute of your subclass; the default `Cmd.prompt` is just `'(Cmd) '`.

`use_rawinput`
: When false (default is true), `cmdloop` prompts and inputs via calls to methods of `sys.stdout` and `sys.stdin`, rather than via `input`.

Other attributes of `Cmd` instances, which we do not cover here, let you exert fine-grained control on many formatting details of help messages.

A Cmd Example

The following example shows how to use `cmd.Cmd` to supply the verbs `print` (to output the rest of the line) and `stop` (to end the loop):

```
import cmd

class X(cmd.Cmd):
    def do_print(self, rest):
        print(rest)
    def help_print(self):
        print('print (any string): outputs (any string)')
    def do_stop(self, rest):
        return True
    def help_stop(self):
        print('stop: terminates the command loop')

if __name__ == '__main__':
    X().cmdloop()
```

A session using this example might proceed as follows:

```
C:\>python examples/chapter10/cmdex.py
(Cmd) help
Documented commands (type help <topic>):
= == == == == == == == == == == == == == == == == == == =
print          stop
Undocumented commands:
= == == == == == == == == == == =
help
(Cmd) help print
print (any string): outputs (any string)
(Cmd) print hi there
hi there
(Cmd) stop
```

Internationalization

Most programs present some information to users as text. Such text should be understandable and acceptable to the user. For example, in some countries and cultures, the date "March 7" can be concisely expressed as "3/7." Elsewhere, "3/7" indicates "July 3," and the string that means "March 7" is "7/3." In Python, such cultural conventions are handled with the help of the standard module `locale`.

Similarly, a greeting can be expressed in one natural language by the string "Benvenuti," while in another language the string to use is "Welcome." In Python, such translations are handled with the help of standard module `gettext`.

Both kinds of issues are commonly called *internationalization* (often abbreviated *i18n*, as there are 18 letters between *i* and *n* in the full spelling)—a misnomer, since the same issues apply to different languages or cultures within a single nation.

The locale Module

Python's support for cultural conventions imitates that of C, slightly simplified. A program operates in an environment of cultural conventions known as a *locale*. The locale setting permeates the program and is typically set at program startup. The locale is not thread-specific, and the `locale` module is not thread-safe. In a multithreaded program, set the program's locale before starting secondary threads.

locale is only useful for process-wide settings

If your application needs to handle multiple locales at the same time in a single process—whether that's in threads or asynchronously—`locale` is not the answer, due to its process-wide nature. Consider alternatives such as PyICU, mentioned in "More Internationalization Resources" on page 335.

If a program does not call `locale.setlocale`, the locale is a neutral one known as the *C locale*. The C locale is named from this architecture's origins in the C language; it's similar, but not identical, to the U.S. English locale. Alternatively, a program can find out and accept the user's default locale. In this case, the `locale` module interacts with the operating system (via the environment or in other system-dependent ways) to find the user's preferred locale. Finally, a program can set a specific locale, presumably determining which locale to set on the basis of user interaction or via persistent configuration settings.

Locale setting is normally performed across the board for all relevant categories of cultural conventions. This wide-spectrum setting is denoted by the constant attribute `LC_ALL` of module `locale`. However, the cultural conventions handled by `locale` are grouped into categories, and, in some cases, a program can choose to mix and match categories to build up a synthetic composite locale. The categories are identified by the following constant attributes of the `locale` module:

`LC_COLLATE`
: String sorting; affects functions `strcoll` and `strxfrm` in `locale`

`LC_CTYPE`
: Character types; affects aspects of the module `string` (and string methods) that have to do with lowercase and uppercase letters

`LC_MESSAGES`
: Messages; may affect messages displayed by the operating system—for example, the function `os.strerror` and module `gettext`

`LC_MONETARY`
: Formatting of currency values; affects function `locale.localeconv`

`LC_NUMERIC`
: Formatting of numbers; affects the functions `atoi`, `atof`, `format`, `localeconv`, and `str` in `locale`

`LC_TIME`
: Formatting of times and dates; affects the function `time.strftime`

The settings of some categories (denoted by `LC_CTYPE`, `LC_TIME`, and `LC_MESSAGES`) affect behavior in other modules (`string`, `time`, `os`, and `gettext`, as indicated). Other categories (denoted by `LC_COLLATE`, `LC_MONETARY`, and `LC_NUMERIC`) affect only some functions of `locale` itself.

The `locale` module supplies the following functions to query, change, and manipulate locales, as well as functions that implement the cultural conventions of locale categories `LC_COLLATE`, `LC_MONETARY`, and `LC_NUMERIC`:

atof

`atof(`*`s`*`)`

Converts string *s* to a floating-point number using the current `LC_NUMERIC` setting.

atoi

`atoi(`*`s`*`)`

Converts string *s* to an integer number using the `LC_NUMERIC` setting.

format

`format(`*`fmt`*`, `*`num`*`, `*`grouping`*`=False)`

Returns the string obtained by formatting number *num* according to the format string *fmt* and the `LC_NUMERIC` setting. Except for cultural convention issues, the result is like *fmt%num*. If *grouping* is true, `format` also groups digits in the result string according to the `LC_NUMERIC` setting. For example:

```
>>> locale.setlocale(locale.LC_NUMERIC, 'en')
'English_United States.1252'
>>> locale.format('%s', 1000*1000)
'1000000'
>>> locale.format('%s', 1000*1000, grouping=True)
'1,000,000'
```

When the numeric locale is U.S. English and argument *grouping* is true, `format` groups digits by threes with commas.

getdefaultlocale `getdefaultlocale(envvars=('LANGUAGE', 'LC_ALL', 'LC_TYPE', 'LANG'))`

Checks the environment variables whose names are specified by *envvars*, in order. The first one found in the environment determines the default locale. `getdefaultlocale` returns a pair of strings `(lang, encoding)` compliant with RFC 1766 (except for the `'C'` locale), such as `('en_US', 'ISO8859-1')`. Each item of the pair may be `None` if `gedefaultlocale` is unable to discover what value the item should have.

getlocale `getlocale(category=LC_CTYPE)`

Returns a pair of strings `(lang, encoding)` with the current setting for the given *category*. The category cannot be `LC_ALL`.

localeconv `localeconv()`

Returns a dict *d* with the cultural conventions specified by categories `LC_NUMERIC` and `LC_MONETARY` of the current locale. While `LC_NUMERIC` is best used indirectly, via other functions of module `locale`, the details of `LC_MONETARY` are accessible only through *d*. Currency formatting is different for local and international use. The U.S. currency symbol, for example, is `'$'` for local use only. `'$'` is ambiguous in international use, since the same symbol is also used for other currencies called "dollars" (Canadian, Australian, Hong Kong, etc.). In international use, therefore, the U.S. currency symbol is the unambiguous string `'USD'`. The keys into *d* to use for currency formatting are the following strings:

`'currency_symbol'`
: Currency symbol to use locally.

`'frac_digits'`
: Number of fractional digits to use locally.

`'int_curr_symbol'`
: Currency symbol to use internationally.

`'int_frac_digits'`
: Number of fractional digits to use internationally.

`'mon_decimal_point'`
: String to use as the "decimal point" (AKA *radix*) for monetary values.

`'mon_grouping'`
: List of digit-grouping numbers for monetary values.

`'mon_thousands_sep'`
: String to use as digit-groups separator for monetary values.

'negative_sign' 'positive_sign'

Strings to use as the sign symbol for negative (positive) monetary values.

'n_cs_precedes' 'p_cs_precedes'

True if the currency symbol comes before negative (positive) monetary values.

'n_sep_by_space' 'p_sep_by_space'

True if a space goes between sign and negative (positive) monetary values.

'n_sign_posn' 'p_sign_posn'

Numeric codes to use to format negative (positive) monetary values:

0 The value and the currency symbol are placed inside parentheses.

1 The sign is placed before the value and the currency symbol.

2 The sign is placed after the value and the currency symbol.

3 The sign is placed immediately before the value.

4 The sign is placed immediately after the value.

CHAR_MAX

The current locale does not specify any convention for this formatting.

d['mon_grouping'] is a list of numbers of digits to group when formatting a monetary value. When *d*['mon_grouping'][-1] is 0, there is no further grouping beyond the indicated numbers of digits. When *d*['mon_grouping'][-1] is locale.CHAR_MAX, grouping continues indefinitely, as if *d*['mon_grouping'][-2] were endlessly repeated. locale.CHAR_MAX is a constant used as the value for all entries in *d* for which the current locale does not specify any convention.

normalize

normalize(*localename*)

Returns a string, suitable as an argument to setlocale, that is the normalized equivalent to *localename*. If normalize cannot normalize string *localename*, then normalize returns *localename* unchanged.

resetlocale

resetlocale(*category*=LC_ALL)

Sets the locale for *category* to the default given by getdefaultlocale.

setlocale `setlocale(category, locale=None)`

Sets the locale for *category* to *locale*, if not None; returns the setting (the existing one when *locale* is None; otherwise, the new one). *locale* can be a string, or a pair (*lang*, *encoding*). *lang* is normally a language code based on ISO 639 two-letter codes ('en' is English, 'nl' is Dutch, and so on). When *locale* is the empty string '', setlocale sets the user's default locale.

str `str(num)`

Like locale.format('%f', *num*).

strcoll `strcoll(str1, str2)`

Like cmp(*str1*, *str2*), but per the LC_COLLATE setting.

strxfrm `strxfrm(s)`

Returns a string *sx* such that Python's built-in comparisons of strings so transformed is equivalent to calling locale.strcoll on the original strings. strxfrm lets you use the key= argument for sorts that involve locale-conformant string comparisons. For example:

```
def locale_sort(list_of_strings):
    list_of_strings.sort(key=locale.strxfrm)
```

The gettext Module

A key issue in internationalization is the ability to use text in different natural languages, a task known as *localization*. Python supports localization via the module gettext, inspired by GNU *gettext*. The gettext module is optionally able to use the latter's infrastructure and APIs, but also offers a simpler, higher-level approach, so you don't need to install or study GNU *gettext* to use Python's gettext effectively.

For full coverage of gettext from a different perspective, see the online docs (*https://docs.python.org/3/library/gettext.html*).

Using gettext for localization

gettext does not deal with automatic translation between natural languages. Rather, it helps you extract, organize, and access the text messages that your program uses. Pass each string literal subject to translation, also known as a *message*, to a function named _ (underscore) rather than using it directly. gettext normally installs a function named _ in the __builtin__ module. To ensure that your program runs with or without gettext, conditionally define a do-nothing function, named _, that just returns its argument unchanged. Then you can safely use _('*message*') wherever you would normally use a literal '*message*' that should be translated if feasible. The following example shows how to start a module for conditional use of gettext:

```
try:
    _
except NameError:
    def _(s): return s

def greet():
    print(_('Hello world'))
```

If some other module has installed `gettext` before you run this example code, the function `greet` outputs a properly localized greeting. Otherwise, `greet` outputs the string `'Hello world'` unchanged.

Edit your source, decorating message literals with function _. Then use any of various tools to extract messages into a text file (normally named *messages.pot*) and distribute the file to the people who translate messages into the various natural languages your application must support. Python supplies a script *pygettext.py* (in directory *Tools/i18n* in the Python source distribution) to perform message extraction on your Python sources.

Each translator edits *messages.pot* to produce a text file of translated messages with extension *.po*. Compile the *.po* files into binary files with extension *.mo*, suitable for fast searching, using any of various tools. Python supplies script *Tools/i18n/msgfmt.py* for this purpose. Finally, install each *.mo* file with a suitable name in a suitable directory.

Conventions about which directories and names are suitable differ among platforms and applications. `gettext`'s default is subdirectory *share/locale/<lang>/LC_MESSAGES/* of directory *sys.prefix*, where *<lang>* is the language's code (two letters). Each file is named *<name>.mo*, where *<name>* is the name of your application or package.

Once you have prepared and installed your *.mo* files, you normally execute, at the time your application starts up, some code such as the following:

```
import os, gettext
os.environ.setdefault('LANG', 'en')    # application-default language
gettext.install('your_application_name')
```

This ensures that calls such as `_('message')` return the appropriate translated strings. You can choose different ways to access `gettext` functionality in your program—for example, if you also need to localize C-coded extensions, or to switch between languages during a run. Another important consideration is whether you're localizing a whole application, or just a package that is distributed separately.

Essential gettext functions

`gettext` supplies many functions; the most often used ones are:

install `install(domain, localedir=None, unicode=False)`

Installs in Python's built-in namespace a function named _ to perform translations given in the file *<lang>/LC_MESSAGES/<domain>.mo* in the directory `localedir`, with language code *<lang>* as per `getdefaultlocale`. When `localedir` is None, `install` uses the directory `os.path.join(sys.prefix, 'share', 'locale')`. When *unicode* is true, function _ accepts and returns Unicode strings, not bytestrings.

translation `translation(domain, localedir=None, languages=None)`

Searches for a *.mo* file similarly to function `install`. When `languages` is None, `translation` looks in the environment for the *lang* to use, like *install*. It examines, in order, environment variables LANGUAGE, LC_ALL, LC_MESSAGES, LANG; the first nonempty one is split on `':'` to give a list of language names (for example, `'de:en'` is split into `['de', 'en']`). When not None, `languages` must be a list of one or more language names (for example, `['de', 'en']`). Translation uses the first language name in the list for which it finds a *.mo* file. The function `translation` returns an instance object that supplies methods `gettext` (to translate a bytestring), `ugettext` (to translate a Unicode string), and `install` (to install `gettext` or `ugettext` under name _ in Python's built-in namespace).

`translation` offers more detailed control than `install`, which is like `translation(domain, localedir).install(unicode)`. With `translation`, you can localize a single package without affecting the built-in namespace, by binding name _ on a per-module basis—for example, with:

```
_ = translation(domain).ugettext
```

`translation` also lets you switch globally between several languages, since you can pass an explicit `languages` argument, keep the resulting instance, and call the `install` method of the appropriate language as needed:

```
import gettext
trans = {}
def switch_to_language(lang, domain='my_app',
use_unicode=True):
    if lang not in translators:
        trans[lang] = gettext.translation(domain,
languages=[lang])
    trans[lang].install(use_unicode)
```

More Internationalization Resources

Internationalization is a very large topic. For a general introduction, see Wikipedia (*https://en.wikipedia.org/wiki/Internationalization_and_localization*). One of the best packages of code and information for internationalization is ICU (*http://site.icu-project.org/*), which also embeds the Unicode Consortium's excellent Common Locale Data Repository (CLDR) database of locale conventions, and code to access the CLDR. To use ICU in Python, install the third-party package PyICU (*https://pypi.python.org/pypi/PyICU/*).

11 Persistence and Databases

Python supports several ways of persisting data. One way, *serialization*, views data as a collection of Python objects. These objects can be *serialized* (saved) to a byte stream, and later *deserialized* (loaded and re-created) back from the byte stream. *Object persistence* lives on top of serialization, adding features such as object naming. This chapter covers the Python modules that support serialization and object persistence.

Another way to make data persistent is to store it in a database (DB). One simple category of DBs are just file formats that use *keyed access* to enable selective reading and updating of relevant parts of the data. This chapter covers Python standard library modules that support several variations of such a file format, known as *DBM*.

A *relational DB management system* (RDBMS), such as PostgreSQL or Oracle, offers a more powerful approach to storing, searching, and retrieving persistent data. Relational DBs rely on dialects of *Structured Query Language* (SQL) to create and alter a DB's schema, insert and update data in the DB, and query the DB with search criteria. (This book does not provide reference material on SQL. We recommend *SQL in a Nutshell*, by Kevin Kline [O'Reilly].) Unfortunately, despite the existence of SQL standards, no two RDBMSes implement exactly the same SQL dialect.

The Python standard library does not come with an RDBMS interface. However, many third-party modules let your Python programs access a specific RDBMS. Such modules mostly follow the Python Database API 2.0 (*https://www.python.org/dev/peps/pep-0249/*) standard, also known as the *DBAPI*. This chapter covers the DBAPI standard and mentions a few of the most popular third-party modules that implement it.

A DBAPI module that is particularly handy—because it comes with every standard installation of Python—is sqlite3 (*https://docs.python.org/3/library/sqlite3.html*), which wraps SQLite (*https://www.sqlite.org/*), "a self-contained, server-less, zero-configuration, transactional SQL DB engine," which is the most widely deployed relational DB engine in the world. We cover `sqlite3` in "SQLite" on page 358.

Besides relational DBs, and the simpler approaches covered in this chapter, there exist Python-specific object DBs such as ZODB (*http://www.zodb.org/en/latest/*), as well as many NoSQL (*http://nosql-database.org/*) DBs, each with Python interfaces. We do not cover advanced nonrelational DBs in this book.

Serialization

Python supplies several modules to *serialize* (save) Python objects to various kinds of byte streams and *deserialize* (load and re-create) Python objects back from streams. Serialization is also known as *marshaling*, or as "formatting for *data interchange*."

Serialization approaches span the range from (by now) language-independent JSON to (low-level, Python-version-specific) `marshal`, both limited to elementary data types, through richer but Python-specific `pickle` in addition to rich cross-language formats such as XML, YAML (*http://yaml.org/*), protocol buffers (*https://developers.google.com/protocol-buffers/*), and MessagePack (*http://msgpack.org/*).

In this section, we cover JSON and `pickle`. We cover XML in Chapter 23. `marshal` is too low-level to use in applications; should you need to maintain old code using it, refer to the online docs (*https://docs.python.org/3/library/marshal.html*). As for protocol buffers, MessagePack, YAML, and other data-interchange/serialization approaches (each with specific advantages and weaknesses), we cannot cover everything in this book; we recommend studying them via the resources available on the web (*https://en.wikipedia.org/wiki/Serialization*).

The json Module

The standard library's `json` module supplies four key functions:

dump `dump(value,fileobj,skipkeys=False,ensure_ascii=True, check_circular=True,allow_nan=True,cls=JSONEncoder,indent=None, separators=(', ', ': '),encoding='utf-8',default=None, sort_keys=False,**kw)`

`dump` writes the JSON serialization of object *`value`* to file-like object *`fileobj`*, which must be opened for writing in text mode, via calls to *`fileobj`*`.write`. In v3, each call to *`fileobj`*`.write` passes as argument a text (Unicode) string; in v2, it passes a plain (byte) string obtained with encoding *`encoding`*. Argument *`encoding`* is only allowed in v2: in v3, `dump` does not perform any text encoding.

When *`skipkeys`* is `True` (by default, it's `False`), `dict` keys that are not scalars (i.e., are not of types `bool`, `float`, `int`, `str`, or `None`; in v2, also `long` and `unicode`) are silently skipped, instead of raising an exception. In any case, keys that *are* scalars are turned into strings (e.g., `None` becomes `"null"`): JSON only allows strings as keys in its mappings.

When *ensure_ascii* is True (as it is by default), all non-ASCII characters in the output are escaped; when it's False, they're output as is.

When *check_circular* is True (as it is by default), containers in *value* are checked for circular references, raising a ValueError exception if circular references are found; when it's False, the check is skipped, and many different exceptions can get raised as a result (even a crash is possible).

When *allow_nan* is True (as it is by default), float scalars nan, inf, and -inf are output as their respective JavaScript equivalents, NaN, Infinity, -Infinity; when it's False, the presence of such scalars raises a ValueError.

You can optionally pass *cls* in order to use a customized subclass of JSONEncoder (such advanced customization is rarely needed and we don't cover it in this book); in this case, ***kw* gets passed in the call to *cls* which instantiates it. By default, encoding uses the JSONEncoder class directly.

When *indent* is an int>0, dump "pretty-prints" the output by prepending that many spaces to each array element and object member; when an int<=0, dump just inserts \n characters; when None, which is the default, dump uses the most compact representation. In v3 only, *indent* can be a str—for example, '\t'—and in that case dump uses that string for indenting.

separators must be a pair (a tuple with two items), respectively the strings used to separate items, and keys from values. You can explicitly pass separators=(',',':') to ensure dump inserts no whitespace.

You can optionally pass *default* in order to transform some otherwise nonserializable objects into serializable ones; *default* is a function, called with a single argument that's a nonserializable object, and must return a serializable object or else raise ValueError (by default, the presence of nonserializable objects raises ValueError).

When *sort_keys* is True (by default, it's False), mappings are output in sorted order of their keys; when it's False, they're output in whatever is their natural order of iteration (essentially random for dicts, but you could use a collections.OrderedDict to control iteration order).

dumps dumps(*value*,*skipkeys*=False,*ensure_ascii*=True,*check_circular*=True, *allow_nan*=True,*cls*=JSONEncoder,*indent*=None,*separators*=(', ', ': '), *encoding*='utf-8',*default*=None,*sort_keys*=False,***kw*)

dumps returns the string that's the JSON serialization of object *value*—that is, the string that dump would write to its file-object argument. All arguments to dumps have exactly the same meaning as the arguments to dump.

load

JSON serializes just one object per file

JSON is not what is known as a *framed format*: this means it is *not* possible to call dump more than once in order to serialize multiple objects into the same file, nor later call load more than once to deserialize the objects, as would be possible with pickle. So, technically, JSON serializes just one object per file. However, you can make that one object be a list, or dict, which in turn can contain as many items as you wish.

`load(`*`fileobj`*`,`*`encoding`*`='utf-8',`*`cls`*`=JSONDecoder,`*`object_hook`*`=None,` *`parse_float`*`=float,`*`parse_int`*`=int,`*`parse_constant`*`=None,` *`object_pairs_hook`*`=None,**`*`kw`*`)`

`load` creates and returns the object *v* previously serialized into file-like object *`fileobj`*, which must be opened for reading in text mode, getting *`fileobj`*'s contents via a call to *`fileobj`*`.read`. In v3, the call to *`fileobj`*`.read` must return a text (Unicode) string; in v2, it can alternatively return a plain (byte) string that gets decoded with encoding *`encoding`*. The argument *`encoding`* is only allowed in v2: in v3, `load` does not perform any text decoding.

The functions `load` and `dump` are complementary. In other words, a single call to `load(`*`f`*`)` deserializes the same value previously serialized when *f*'s contents were created by a single call to `dump(`*`v`*`,`*`f`*`)` (possibly with some alterations: e.g., all dictionary keys are turned into strings).

You can optionally pass *`cls`* in order to use a customized subclass of `JSONDecoder` (such advanced customization is rarely needed and we don't cover it in this book); in this case, `**`*`kw`* gets passed in the call to *`cls`*, which instantiates it. By default, decoding uses the `JSONDecoder` class directly.

You can optionally pass *`object_hook`* or *`object_pairs_hook`* (if you pass both, *`object_hook`* is ignored and only *`object_pairs_hook`* is used), a function that lets you implement custom decoders. When you pass *`object_hook`* but not *`object_pairs_hook`*, then, each time an object is decoded into a `dict`, `load` calls *`object_hook`* with the `dict` as the only argument, and uses *`object_hook`*'s return value instead of that `dict`. When you pass *`object_pairs_hook`*, then, each time an object is decoded, `load` calls *`object_pairs_hook`* with, as the only argument, a list of the pairs of `(`*`key`*`, `*`value`*`)` items of the object, in the order in which they are present in the input, and uses *`object_pairs_hook`*'s return value; this lets you perform specialized decoding that potentially depends on the order of `(`*`key`*`, `*`value`*`)` pairs in the input.

`parse_float`, *`parse_int`*, and *`parse_constant`* are functions called with a single argument that's a `str` representing a `float`, an `int`, or one of the three special constants `'NaN'`, `'Infinity'`, `'-Infinity'`; `load` calls the appropriate function each time it identifies in the input a `str` representing a number, and uses the function's return value. By default, *`parse_float`* is `float`, *`parse_int`* is `int`, and *`parse_constant`* returns one of the three special float scalars `nan`, `inf`, `-inf`, as appropriate. For example, you could pass `parse_float=decimal.Decimal` to ensure that all numbers in the result that would normally be `float`s are instead decimals (covered in "The decimal Module" on page 444).

loads `loads(`*`s`*`,`*`encoding`*`='utf-8',`*`cls`*`=JSONDecoder,`*`object_hook`*`=None,` *`parse_float`*`=float,`*`parse_int`*`=int,`*`parse_constant`*`=None,` *`object_pairs_hook`*`=None,**`*`kw`*`)`

`loads` creates and returns the object *v* previously serialized into the string *s*. All argument to `loads` have exactly the same meaning as the arguments to `load`.

A JSON example

Say you need to read several text files, whose names are given as your program's arguments, recording where each distinct word appears in the files. What you need to record for each word is a list of `(`*`filename`*`, `*`linenumber`*`)` pairs. The following example uses json to encode lists of (*filename, linenumber*) pairs as strings and store them in a DBM-like file (as covered in "DBM Modules" on page 348). Since these lists contain tuples, each containing a string and a number, they are within json's abilities to serialize.

```
import collections, fileinput, json, dbm
word_pos = collections.defaultdict(list)
for line in fileinput.input():
    pos = fileinput.filename(), fileinput.filelineno()
    for word in line.split():
        word_pos[word].append(pos)
dbm_out = dbm.open('indexfilem', 'n')
for word in word_pos:
    dbm_out[word] = json.dumps(word_pos[word])
dbm_out.close()
```

(In v3 only, dbm.open is a context manager, so we could indent the second for loop as the body of a statement with dbm.open('indexfilem', 'n') as dbm_out: and omit the dbm_out.close(); however, the example, as coded, works in both v2 and v3, except that in v2, to ensure the example works across platforms, you'd import and use the module anydbm instead of the package dbm, and that also applies to the following example.) We also need json to deserialize the data stored in the DBM-like file *indexfilem*, as shown in the following example:

```
import sys, json, dbm, linecache
dbm_in = dbm.open('indexfilem')
for word in sys.argv[1:]:
    if word not in dbm_in:
         print('Word {!r} not found in index file'.format(word),
               file=sys.stderr)
         continue
    places = json.loads(dbm_in[word])
    for fname, lineno in places:
        print('Word {!r} occurs in line {} of file {}:'.format(
               word,lineno,fname))
        print(linecache.getline(fname, lineno), end='')
```

The pickle and cPickle Modules

The pickle and, in v2, cPickle modules supply factory functions, named Pickler and Unpickler, to generate objects that wrap file-like objects and supply Python-specific serialization mechanisms. Serializing and deserializing via these modules is also known as *pickling* and *unpickling*.

In v2 only, the difference between the modules is that, in pickle, Pickler and Unpickler are classes, so you can inherit from these classes to create customized serializer objects, overriding methods as needed. In cPickle, on the other hand, Pickler and Unpickler are factory functions that generate instances of non-subclassable types, not classes. Performance is much better with cPickle, but inheritance is not feasible. In the rest of this section, we'll be talking about the module pickle, but everything applies to cPickle too. v3 only supplies pickle, which is quite fast and supplies Pickler and Unpickler as classes.

Serialization shares some of the issues of deep copying, covered in "The copy Module" on page 216. The pickle module deals with these issues in much the same way as the copy module does. Serialization, like deep copying, implies a recursive walk over a directed graph of references. pickle preserves the graph's shape: when the same object is encountered more than once, the object is serialized only the first time, and other occurrences of the same object serialize references to that single value. pickle also correctly serializes graphs with reference cycles. However, this means that if a mutable object o is serialized more than once to the same Pickler instance p, any changes to o after the first serialization of o to p are not saved.

Don't alter objects while their serialization is in progress

For clarity, correctness, and simplicity, don't alter objects that are being serialized while serialization to a Pickler instance is in progress.

pickle can serialize with a legacy ASCII protocol or with one of a few compact binary ones. In v2, the ASCII protocol 0 is the default, for backward compatibility, but you should normally explicitly request binary protocol 2, the v2-supported protocol that's most parsimonious of time and storage space. In v3, protocols range from 0 to 4, included; the default is 3, which is usually a reasonable choice, but you may explicitly specify protocol 2 (to ensure that your saved pickles can be loaded by v2 programs), or protocol 4, incompatible with earlier versions but with performance advantages for very large objects.

Always pickle with protocol 2 or higher

Always specify at least protocol 2. The size and speed savings can be substantial, and binary format has basically no downside except loss of compatibility of resulting pickles with truly ancient versions of Python.

When you reload objects, pickle transparently recognizes and uses any protocol that the Python version you're currently using supports.

pickle serializes classes and functions by name, not by value. pickle can therefore deserialize a class or function only by importing it from the same module where the class or function was found when pickle serialized it. In particular, pickle can normally serialize and deserialize classes and functions only if they are top-level names for their module (i.e., attributes of their module). For example, consider the following:

```
def adder(augend):
    def inner(addend, augend=augend): return addend+augend
    return inner
plus5 = adder(5)
```

This code binds a closure to name `plus5` (as covered in "Nested functions and nested scopes" on page 93)—a nested function `inner` plus an appropriate outer scope. Therefore, trying to pickle `plus5` raises a `pickle.PicklingError` exception (in v2; just `AttributeError` in v3): a function can be pickled only when it is top-level, and the function `inner`, whose closure is bound to the name `plus5` in this code, is not top-level but rather nested inside the function `adder`. Similar issues apply to pickling nested functions and nested classes (i.e., classes that are not top-level).

Functions and classes of pickle and cPickle

The `pickle` module (and, in v2 only, the module `cPickle`) exposes the following functions and classes:

dump, dumps

`dump(`*`value`*`,`*`fileobj`*`,`*`protocol`*`=None,`*`bin`*`=None)`
`dumps(`*`value`*`,`*`protocol`*`=None,`*`bin`*`=None)`

`dumps` returns a bytestring representing object *`value`*. `dump` writes the same string to the file-like object *`fileobj`*, which must be opened for writing. `dump(`*`v`*`,`*`f`*`)` is like *`f`*`.write(dumps(`*`v`*`))`. Do not pass the *`bin`* parameter, which exists only for compatibility with old versions of Python. The *`protocol`* parameter can be `0` (the default in v2, for compatibility reasons; ASCII output, slowest and bulkiest), `1` (binary output that's compatible with very old versions of Python), or `2` (fastest and leanest in v2); in v3, it can also be `3` or `4`. We recommend that, in v2, you always pass the value `2`; in v3, pass `2` if you need the result to be compatible with v2, otherwise `3` (the v3 default) or `4`. Unless *`protocol`* is `0` or (in v2) absent, implying ASCII output, the *`fileobj`* parameter to `dump` must be open for binary writing.

load, loads

`load(`*`fileobj`*`)` `loads(`*`s`*`)` in v2; in v3, `loads(`*`s`*`,*,fix_imports=True, encoding="ASCII", errors="strict")`

The functions `load` and `dump` are complementary. In other words, a sequence of calls to `load(`*`f`*`)` deserializes the same values previously serialized when *f*'s contents were created by a sequence of calls to `dump(`*`v`*`,`*`f`*`)`. `load` reads the right number of bytes from file-like object *`fileobj`* and creates and returns the object *v* represented by those bytes. `load` and `loads` transparently support pickles performed in any binary or ASCII protocol. If data is pickled in any binary format, the file must be open as binary for both `dump` and `load`. `load(`*`f`*`)` is like `Unpickler(`*`f`*`).load()`.

`loads` creates and returns the object *v* represented by byte string *s*, so that for any object *v* of a supported type, *v*`==loads(dumps(`*`v`*`))`. If *s* is longer than `dumps(`*`v`*`)`, `loads` ignores the extra bytes. Optional v3-only arguments `fix_imports`, `encoding`, and `errors`, are provided for handling v2-generated streams. See pickle.loads v3 docs (*https://docs.python.org/3/library/pickle.html#pickle.loads*).

Don't unpickle untrusted data

Unpickling from an untrusted data source is a security risk; an attacker could exploit this vulnerability to execute arbitrary code.

Pickler `Pickler(`*`fileobj`*`,`*`protocol`*`=None,`*`bin`*`=None)`

Creates and returns an object *p* such that calling *p*`.dump` is equivalent to calling the function `dump` with the *`fileobj`*, *`protocol`*, and *`bin`* arguments passed to `Pickler`. To serialize many objects to a file, `Pickler` is more convenient and faster than repeated calls to `dump`. You can subclass `pickle.Pickler` to override `Pickler` methods (particularly the method `persistent_id`) and create your own persistence framework. However, this is an advanced issue and is not covered further in this book.

Unpickler `Unpickler(`*`fileobj`*`)`

Creates and returns an object *u* such that calling the *u*`.load` is equivalent to calling function `load` with the *`fileobj`* argument passed to `Unpickler`. To deserialize many objects from a file, `Unpickler` is more convenient and faster than repeated calls to the function `load`. You can subclass `pickle.Unpickler` to override `Unpickler` methods (particularly method `persistent_load`) and create your own persistence framework. However, this is an advanced issue and is not covered further in this book.

A pickling example

The following example handles the same task as the `json` example shown earlier, but uses `pickle` instead of `json` to serialize lists of `(`*`filename`*`, `*`linenumber`*`)` pairs as strings:

```
import collections, fileinput, pickle, dbm
word_pos = collections.defaultdict(list)
for line in fileinput.input():
    pos = fileinput.filename(), fileinput.filelineno()
    for word in line.split():
        word_pos[word].append(pos)
dbm_out = dbm.open('indexfilep','n')
for word in word_pos:
    dbm_out[word] = pickle.dumps(word_pos[word],2)
dbm_out.close()
```

We can then use `pickle` to read back the data stored to the DBM-like file *indexfilep*, as shown in the following example:

```
import sys, pickle, dbm, linecache
dbm_in = dbm.open('indexfilep')
for word in sys.argv[1:]:
    if word not in dbm_in:
         print('Word {!r} not found in index file'.format(word),
               file=sys.stderr)
         continue
```

```
        places = pickle.loads(dbm_in[word])
        for fname, lineno in places:
            print('Word {!r} occurs in line {} of file {}:'.format(
                   word,lineno,fname))
            print(linecache.getline(fname, lineno), end='')
```

In v2, in both examples, to ensure the code works across platforms, you'd import and use the module `anydbm` instead of the package `dbm`.

Pickling instances

In order for `pickle` to reload an instance *x*, `pickle` must be able to import *x*'s class from the same module in which the class was defined when `pickle` saved the instance. Here is how `pickle` saves the state of instance object *x* of class *T* and later reloads the saved state into a new instance *y* of *T* (the first step of the reloading is always to make a new empty instance *y* of *T*, except where we explicitly say otherwise in the following):

- When *T* supplies the method `__getstate__`, `pickle` saves the result *d* of calling `T.__getstate__(x)`.
- When *T* supplies the method `__setstate__`, *d* can be of any type, and `pickle` reloads the saved state by calling `T.__setstate__(y, d)`.
- Otherwise, *d* must be a dictionary, and `pickle` just sets `y.__dict__ = d`.
- Otherwise, when *T* supplies the method `__getnewargs__`, and `pickle` is pickling with protocol 2 or higher, `pickle` saves the result *t* of calling `T.__getnewargs__(x)`; *t* must be a tuple.
- `pickle`, in this one case, does not start with an empty *y*, but rather creates *y* by executing `y = T.__new__(T, *t)`, which concludes the reloading.
- Otherwise, by default, `pickle` saves as *d* the dictionary `x.__dict__`.
- When *T* supplies the method `__setstate__`, `pickle` reloads the saved state by calling `T.__setstate__ (y, d)`.
- Otherwise, `pickle` just sets `y.__dict__ = d`.

All the items in the *d* or *t* object that `pickle` saves and reloads (normally a dictionary or tuple) must in turn be instances of types suitable for pickling and unpickling (AKA *pickleable* objects), and the procedure just outlined may be repeated recursively, if necessary, until `pickle` reaches primitive pickleable built-in types (dictionaries, tuples, lists, sets, numbers, strings, etc.).

As mentioned in "The copy Module" on page 216, the special methods `__getnewargs__`, `__getstate__`, and `__setstate__` also control the way instance objects are copied and deep-copied. If a class defines `__slots__`, and therefore its instances do not have a `__dict__`, `pickle` does its best to save and restore a dictionary equivalent to the names and values of the slots. However, such a class should define `__get` state__ and __setstate__; otherwise, its instances may not be correctly pickleable and copy-able through such best-effort endeavors.

Pickling customization with the copy_reg module

You can control how `pickle` serializes and deserializes objects of an arbitrary type by registering factory and reduction functions with the module `copy_reg`. This is particularly, though not exclusively, useful when you define a type in a C-coded Python extension. The `copy_reg` module supplies the following functions:

constructor `constructor(`*`fcon`*`)`

Adds *fcon* to the table of constructors, which lists all factory functions that `pickle` may call. *fcon* must be callable and is normally a function.

pickle `pickle(`*`type`*`,`*`fred`*`,`*`fcon`*`=None)`

Registers function *fred* as the *reduction function* for type *type*, where *type* must be a type object. To save an object *o* of type *type*, the module `pickle` calls *fred*(*o*) and saves the result. *fred*(*o*) must return a tuple (*fcon*,*t*) or (*fcon*,*t*,*d*), where *fcon* is a constructor and *t* is a tuple. To reload *o*, `pickle` uses *o*=*fcon*(**t*). Then, when *fred* also returned a *d*, `pickle` uses *d* to restore *o*'s state (when *o* supplies `__setstate__`, *o*.`__setstate__`(*d*); otherwise, *o*.`__dict__.update`(*d*)), as in "Pickling instances" on page 345. If *fcon* is not None, `pickle` also calls `constructor`(*fcon*) to register *fcon* as a constructor.

`pickle` does not support pickling of code objects, but `marshal` does. Here's how you could customize pickling to support code objects by delegating the work to `marshal` thanks to `copy_reg`:

```
>>> import pickle, copy_reg, marshal
>>> def marsh(x): return marshal.loads, (marshal.dumps(x),)
...
>>> c=compile('2+2','','eval')
>>> copy_reg.pickle(type(c), marsh)
>>> s=pickle.dumps(c, 2)
>>> cc=pickle.loads(s)
>>> print eval(cc)
4
```

Using marshal makes your code Python-version-dependent

Beware using `marshal` in your code, as the preceding example does: `marshal`'s serialization can vary with every version of Python, so using `marshal` means you may be unable to load objects serialized with one Python version, with other versions.

The shelve Module

The shelve module orchestrates the modules pickle (or cPickle, in v2, when available), io (in v3; in v2, cStringIO when available, and otherwise StringIO), and dbm (and its underlying modules for access to DBM-like archive files, as discussed in "DBM Modules" on page 348; that's in v3—anydbm in v2) in order to provide a simple, lightweight persistence mechanism.

Persistence and Databases

shelve supplies a function open that is polymorphic to anydbm.open. The mapping *s* returned by shelve.open is less limited than the mapping *a* returned by anydbm.open. *a*'s keys and values must be strings. *s*'s keys must also be strings, but *s*'s values may be of any pickleable types. pickle customizations (copy_reg, __getnewargs__, __getstate__, and __setstate__) also apply to shelve, as shelve delegates serialization to pickle.

Beware of a subtle trap when you use shelve with mutable objects: when you operate on a mutable object held in a shelf, the changes don't "take" unless you assign the changed object back to the same index. For example:

```
import shelve
s = shelve.open('data')
s['akey'] = list(range(4))
print(s['akey'])              # prints: [0, 1, 2, 3]
s['akey'].append(9)           # trying direct mutation
print(s['akey'])              # doesn't "take"; prints: [0, 1, 2, 3]

x = s['akey']                 # fetch the object
x.append(9)                   # perform mutation
s['akey'] = x                 # key step: store the object back!
print(s['akey'])              # now it "takes", prints: [0, 1, 2, 3, 9]
```

You can finesse this issue by passing the named argument writeback=True when you call shelve.open, but beware: if you do pass that argument, you may seriously impair the performance of your program.

A shelving example

The following example handles the same task as the earlier json and pickle examples, but uses shelve to persist lists of (*filename*, *linenumber*) pairs:

```
import collections, fileinput, shelve
word_pos = collections.defaultdict(list)
for line in fileinput.input():
    pos = fileinput.filename(), fileinput.filelineno()
    for word in line.split():
        word_pos[word].append(pos)
sh_out = shelve.open('indexfiles','n')
sh_out.update(word_pos)
sh_out.close()
```

We must use shelve to read back the data stored to the DBM-like file *indexfiles*, as shown in the following example:

```
import sys, shelve, linecache
sh_in = shelve.open('indexfiles')

for word in sys.argv[1:]:
    if word not in sh_in:
         print('Word {!r} not found in index file'.format(word),
               file=sys.stderr)
         continue
    places = sh_in[word]
    for fname, lineno in places:
        print('Word {!r} occurs in line {} of file {}:'.format(
               word,lineno,fname))
        print(linecache.getline(fname, lineno), end='')
```

These two examples are the simplest and most direct of the various equivalent pairs of examples shown throughout this section. This reflects the fact that the module shelve is higher-level than the modules used in previous examples.

DBM Modules

DBM (*https://en.wikipedia.org/wiki/Dbm*), a long-time Unix tradition, is a family of libraries supporting data files with pairs of strings (*key*,*data*), with fast fetching and storing of the data given a key, a usage pattern known as *keyed access*. Keyed access, while nowhere as powerful as the data-access functionality of relational DBs, imposes less overhead, yet may suffice for a given program's needs. If DBM-like files are sufficient, you may end up with a program that is smaller and faster than one using a relational DB.

v3 organizes DBM support in Python's standard library in a clean and elegant way: the package dbm exposes two general functions, and within the same package live other modules supplying specific implementations. v2's support, while functionally equivalent, evolved over time in a less organized fashion, thus ending up in a less elegant arrangement, as a collection of top-level modules not organized into a package. This section briefly presents v3's organization first, and then v2's, with references from the latter back to the former to show equivalent functionality.

The v3 dbm Package

v3's dbm package supplies the following two top-level functions:

open `open(filepath,flag='r',mode=0o666)`

Opens or creates the DBM file named by *filepath* (any path to a file) and returns a mapping object corresponding to the DBM file. When the DBM file already exists, `open` uses the function `whichdb` to determine which DBM submodule can handle the file. When `open` creates a new DBM file, it chooses the first available `dbm` submodule in the following order of preference: `gnu`, `ndbm`, `dumb`.

flag is a one-character string that tells `open` how to open the file and whether to create it, as shown in Table 11-1. *mode* is an integer that `open` uses as the file's permission bits if `open` creates the file, as covered in "Creating a "file" Object with io.open" on page 274.

Table 11-1. Flag values for anydbm.open

Flag	Read-only?	If file exists	If file does not exist
'r'	Yes	open opens the file.	open raises error.
'w'	No	open opens the file.	open raises error.
'c'	No	open opens the file.	open creates the file.
'n'	No	open truncates the file.	open creates the file.

`dbm.open` returns a mapping object *m* with a subset of the functionality of dictionaries (covered in "Dictionary Operations" on page 69). *m* only accepts strings as keys and values, and the only non-special mapping methods *m* supplies are `m.get`, `m.keys`, and `m.setdefault`. You can bind, rebind, access, and unbind items in *m* with the same indexing syntax `m[key]` that you would use if *m* were a dictionary. If *flag* is `'r'`, *m* is read-only, so that you can only access *m*'s items, not bind, rebind, or unbind them. You can check if a string *s* is a key in *m* with the usual expression `s in m`; you cannot iterate directly on *m*, but you can, equivalently, iterate on `m.keys()`.

One extra method that *m* supplies is `m.close`, with the same semantics as the `close` method of a "file" object. Just like for "file" objects, you should ensure `m.close()` is called when you're done using *m*. The `try/finally` statement (covered in "try/finally" on page 152) is a good way to ensure finalization, but the `with` statement, covered in "The with Statement" on page 82, is even better than `try/finally` (you can use `with`, since *m* is a context manager).

whichdb `whichdb(filename)`

Opens and reads the file specified by *filename* to discover which `dbm` submodule created the file. `whichdb` returns `None` when the file does not exist or cannot be opened and read. `whichdb` returns `''` when the file exists and can be opened and read, but it is not possible to determine which `dbm` submodule created the file (typically, this means that the file is not a DBM file). If it can find out which module can read the DBM-like file, `whichdb` returns a string that names a `dbm` submodule, such as `'dbm.ndbm'`, `'dbm.dumbdbm'`, or `'dbm.gdbm'`.

In addition to these two top-level functions, the v3 package `dbm` contains specific modules, such as `ndbm`, `gnu`, and `dumb`, which provide various implementations of

DBM functionality, which you normally access only via the two top-level functions of the package `dbm`. Third-party packages can install further implementation modules in `dbm`.

The only implementation module of the `dbm` package that's guaranteed to exist on all platforms is `dumb`. The `dumb` submodule of `dbm` has minimal DBM functionality and mediocre performance. `dumb`'s only advantage is that you can use it anywhere, since `dumb` does not rely on any library. You don't normally `import dbm.dumb`: rather, `import dbm`, and let `dbm.open` supply the best DBM module available, defaulting to `dumb` if nothing else is available on the current Python installation. The only case in which you import `dumb` directly is the rare one in which you need to create a DBM-like file guaranteed to be readable from any Python installation. The `dumb` module supplies an `open` function polymorphic to `dbm`'s.

v2's dbm modules

v2's `anydbm` module is a generic interface to any other DBM module. `anydbm` supplies a single factory function `open`, equivalent to v3's `dbm.open`.

v2's `whichdb` module supplies a single function, `whichdb`, equivalent to v3's `dbm.whichdb`.

DBM implementation modules, in v2, are top-level ones, named `dbm`, `gdbm`, `dumbdbm`, and so forth, and otherwise paralleling v3 `dbm` submodules.

Examples of DBM-Like File Use

DBM's keyed access is suitable when your program needs to record persistently the equivalent of a Python dictionary, with strings as both keys and values. For example, suppose you need to analyze several text files, whose names are given as your program's arguments, and record where each word appears in those files. In this case, the keys are words and, therefore, intrinsically strings. The data you need to record for each word is a list of (*filename*, *linenumber*) pairs. However, you can encode the data as a string in several ways—for example, by exploiting the fact that the path separator string `os.pathsep` (covered in "Path-String Attributes of the os Module" on page 299) does not normally appear in filenames. (More solid, general, and reliable approaches to the issue of encoding data as strings are covered with the same example in "Serialization" on page 338.) With this simplification, the program that records word positions in files might be as follows, in v3:

```
import collections, fileinput, os, dbm
word_pos = collections.defaultdict(list)
for line in fileinput.input():
    pos = '{}{}{}'.format(
        fileinput.filename(), os.pathsep, fileinput.filelineno())
    for word in line.split():
        word_pos[word].append(pos)
sep2 = os.pathsep * 2
with dbm.open('indexfile','n') as dbm_out:
```

```
        for word in word_pos:
            dbm_out[word] = sep2.join(word_pos[word])
```

We can read back the data stored to the DBM-like file *indexfile* in several ways. The following example accepts words as command-line arguments and prints the lines where the requested words appear, in v3:


```
import sys, os, dbm, linecache
dbm_in = dbm.open('indexfile')
sep = os.pathsep
sep2 = sep * 2
for word in sys.argv[1:]:
    if word not in dbm_in:
         print('Word {!r} not found in index file'.format(word),
               file=sys.stderr)
         continue
    places = dbm_in[word].split(sep2)
    for place in places:
        fname, lineno = place.split(sep)
        print('Word {!r} occurs in line {} of file {}:'.format(
              word,lineno,fname))
        print(linecache.getline(fname, lineno), end='')
```

In v2, in both examples, import and use the module `anydbm` instead of the package `dbm`.

Berkeley DB Interfacing

v2 comes with the `bsddb` package, which wraps the Berkeley Database (also known as BSD DB) library if that library is installed on your system and your Python installation is built to support it. However, `bsddb` is deprecated in v2, and not present in v3, so we cannot recommend it. If you do need to interface to a BSD DB archive, we recommend instead the excellent third-party package bsddb3 (*https://pypi.python.org/pypi/bsddb3*).

The Python Database API (DBAPI) 2.0

As we mentioned earlier, the Python standard library does not come with an RDBMS interface (except for `sqlite3`, covered in "SQLite" on page 358, which is a rich implementation, not just an interface). Many third-party modules let your Python programs access specific DBs. Such modules mostly follow the Python Database API 2.0 standard, also known as the DBAPI, as specified in PEP 249 (*https://www.python.org/dev/peps/pep-0249/*).

After importing any DBAPI-compliant module, call the module's `connect` function with DB-specific parameters. `connect` returns *x*, an instance of `Connection`, which represents a connection to the DB. *x* supplies `commit` and `rollback` methods to deal with transactions, a `close` method to call as soon as you're done with the DB, and a `cursor` method to return *c*, an instance of `Cursor`. *c* supplies the methods and attributes used for DB operations. A DBAPI-compliant module also supplies exception classes, descriptive attributes, factory functions, and type-description attributes.

Exception Classes

A DBAPI-compliant module supplies the exception classes `Warning`, `Error`, and several subclasses of `Error`. `Warning` indicates anomalies such as data truncation on insertion. `Error`'s subclasses indicate various kinds of errors that your program can encounter when dealing with the DB and the DBAPI-compliant module that interfaces to it. Generally, your code uses a statement of the form:

```
try:
    ...
except module.Error as err:
    ...
```

to trap all DB-related errors that you need to handle without terminating.

Thread Safety

When a DBAPI-compliant module has a `threadsafety` attribute greater than `0`, the module is asserting some level of thread safety for DB interfacing. Rather than relying on this, it's usually safer, and always more portable, to ensure that a single thread has exclusive access to any given external resource, such as a DB, as outlined in "Threaded Program Architecture" on page 420.

Parameter Style

A DBAPI-compliant module has an attribute called `paramstyle` to identify the style of markers used as placeholders for parameters. Insert such markers in SQL statement strings that you pass to methods of `Cursor` instances, such as the method `execute`, to use runtime-determined parameter values. Say, for example, that you need to fetch the rows of DB table *`ATABLE`* where field *`AFIELD`* equals the current value of Python variable `x`. Assuming the cursor instance is named `c`, you *could* theoretically (but ill-advisedly) perform this task with Python's string formatting:

```
c.execute('SELECT * FROM ATABLE WHERE AFIELD={!r}'.format(x))
```

Avoid SQL query string formatting: use parameter substitution

String formatting is *not* the recommended approach. It generates a different string for each value of x, requiring statements to be parsed and prepared anew each time; it also opens up the possibility of security weaknesses such as SQL injection (*https://en.wikipedia.org/wiki/SQL_injection*) vulnerabilities. With parameter substitution, you pass to `execute` a single statement string, with a placeholder instead of the parameter value. This lets `execute` parse and prepare the statement just once, for better performance; more importantly, parameter substitution improves solidity and security.

For example, when a module's `paramstyle` attribute (described next) is `'qmark'`, express the preceding query as:

```
c.execute('SELECT * FROM ATABLE WHERE AFIELD=?', (some_value,))
```

The read-only string attribute `paramstyle` tells your program how it should use parameter substitution with that module. The possible values of `paramstyle` are:

`format`
: The marker is `%s`, as in old-style string formatting (always with `s`: never use other type indicator letters, whatever the data's type). A query looks like:

```
c.execute('SELECT * FROM ATABLE WHERE AFIELD=%s', (some_value,))
```

`named`
: The marker is `:`*`name`*, and parameters are named. A query looks like:

```
c.execute('SELECT * FROM ATABLE WHERE AFIELD=:x', {'x':some_value})
```

`numeric`
: The marker is `:n`, giving the parameter's number, `1` and up. A query looks like:

```
c.execute('SELECT * FROM ATABLE WHERE AFIELD=:1', (some_value,))
```

`pyformat`
: The marker is `%(`*`name`*`)s`, and parameters are named. Always use `s`: never use other type indicator letters, whatever the data's type. A query looks like:

```
c.execute('SELECT * FROM ATABLE WHERE AFIELD=%(x)s', {'x':some_value})
```

`qmark`
: The marker is ?. A query looks like:

```
c.execute('SELECT * FROM ATABLE WHERE AFIELD=?', (x,))
```

When parameters are named (i.e., when `paramstyle` is `'pyformat'` or `'named'`), the second argument of the `execute` method is a mapping. Otherwise, the second argument is a sequence.

format and pyformat only accept type indicator s

The *only* valid type indicator letter for `format` or `pyformat` is `s`; neither accepts any other type indicator—for example, never use `%d` nor `%(`*`name`*`)d`. Use `%s` or `%(`*`name`*`)s` for all parameter substitutions, regardless of the type of the data.

Factory Functions

Parameters passed to the DB via placeholders must typically be of the right type: this means Python numbers (integers or floating-point values), strings (bytes or Unicode), and `None` to represent SQL `NULL`. There is no type universally used to represent dates, times, and binary large objects (BLOBs). A DBAPI-compliant module supplies factory functions to build such objects. The types used for this purpose by most DBAPI-compliant modules are those supplied by the modules `datetime` or `mxDateTime` (covered in Chapter 12), and strings or buffer types for BLOBs. The factory functions specified by the DBAPI are as follows:

Binary `Binary(`*`string`*`)`

Returns an object representing the given *`string`* of bytes as a BLOB.

Date `Date(`*`year,month,day`*`)`

Returns an object representing the specified date.

DateFromTicks `DateFromTicks(`*`s`*`)`

Returns an object representing the date *s* seconds after the epoch of module `time`, covered in Chapter 12. For example, `DateFromTicks(time.time())` means "today."

Time `Time(`*`hour,minute,second`*`)`

Returns an object representing the specified time.

TimeFromTicks `TimeFromTicks(`*`s`*`)`

Returns an object representing the time *s* seconds after the epoch of module `time`, covered in Chapter 12. For example, `TimeFromTicks(time.time())` means "the current time of day."

Timestamp `Timestamp(`*`year,month,day,hour,minute,second`*`)`

Returns an object representing the specified date and time.

TimestampFromTicks `TimestampFromTicks(`*`s`*`)`

Returns an object representing the date and time *s* seconds after the epoch of module `time`, covered in Chapter 12. For example, `TimestampFromTicks( time.time())` is the current date and time.

Type Description Attributes

A `Cursor` instance's attribute `description` describes the types and other characteristics of each column of the `SELECT` query you last `executed` on that cursor. Each column's *type* (the second item of the tuple describing the column) equals one of the following attributes of the DBAPI-compliant module:

`BINARY`	Describes columns containing BLOBs
`DATETIME`	Describes columns containing dates, times, or both
`NUMBER`	Describes columns containing numbers of any kind
`ROWID`	Describes columns containing a row-identification number
`STRING`	Describes columns containing text of any kind

A cursor's description, and in particular each column's type, is mostly useful for introspection about the DB your program is working with. Such introspection can help you write general modules and work with tables using different schemas, including schemas that may not be known at the time you are writing your code.

The connect Function

A DBAPI-compliant module's `connect` function accepts arguments that depend on the kind of DB and the specific module involved. The DBAPI standard recommends that `connect` accept named arguments. In particular, `connect` should at least accept optional arguments with the following names:

`database`	Name of the specific database to connect
`dsn`	Data-source name to use for the connection
`host`	Hostname on which the database is running
`password`	Password to use for the connection
`user`	Username for the connection

Connection Objects

A DBAPI-compliant module's `connect` function returns an object *x* that is an instance of the class `Connection`. *x* supplies the following methods:

close `x.close()`

Terminates the DB connection and releases all related resources. Call `close` as soon as you're done with the DB. Keeping DB connections open needlessly can be a serious resource drain on the system.

commit `x.commit()`

Commits the current transaction in the DB. If the DB does not support transactions, `x.commit()` is an innocuous no-op.

cursor `x.cursor()`

Returns a new instance of the class `Cursor`, covered in "Cursor Objects" on page 356.

rollback `x.rollback()`

Rolls back the current transaction in the DB. If the DB does not support transactions, `x.rollback()` raises an exception. The DBAPI recommends that, for DBs that do not support transactions, the class `Connection` supplies no `rollback` method, so that `x.rollback()` raises `AttributeError`: you can test whether transactions are supported with `hasattr(x,'rollback')`.

Cursor Objects

A `Connection` instance provides a `cursor` method that returns an object *c* that is an instance of the class `Cursor`. A SQL cursor represents the set of results of a query and lets you work with the records in that set, in sequence, one at a time. A cursor as modeled by the DBAPI is a richer concept, since it's the only way your program executes SQL queries in the first place. On the other hand, a DBAPI cursor allows you only to advance in the sequence of results (some relational DBs, but not all, also provide higher-functionality cursors that are able to go backward as well as forward), and does not support the SQL clause `WHERE CURRENT OF CURSOR`. These limitations of DBAPI cursors enable DBAPI-compliant modules to easily provide DBAPI cursors even on RDBMSes that provide no real SQL cursors at all. An instance of the class `Cursor` *c* supplies many attributes and methods; the most frequently used ones are the following:

close `c.close()`

Closes the cursor and releases all related resources.

description A read-only attribute that is a sequence of seven-item tuples, one per column in the last query executed:

```
name, typecode, displaysize, internalsize, precision,
scale, nullable
```

`c.description` is None if the last operation on *c* was not a `SELECT` query or returned no usable description of the columns involved. A cursor's description is mostly useful for introspection about the DB your program is working with. Such introspection can help you write general modules that are able to work with tables using different schemas, including schemas that may not be fully known at the time you are writing your code.

execute `c.execute(statement,parameters=None)`

Executes a SQL *statement* string on the DB with the given *parameters*. *parameters* is a sequence when the module's `paramstyle` is `'format'`, `'numeric'`, or `'qmark'`, and a mapping when `paramstyle` is `'named'` or `'pyformat'`. Some DBAPI modules require the sequences to be specifically tuples.

executemany `c.executemany(statement,*parameters)`

Executes a SQL *statement* on the DB, once for each item of the given *parameters*. *parameters* is a sequence of sequences when the module's `paramstyle` is `'format'`, `'numeric'`, or `'qmark'`, and a sequence of mappings when `paramstyle` is `'named'` or `'pyformat'`. For example, the statement:

```
c.executemany('UPDATE atable SET x=? '
              'WHERE y=?',(12,23),(23,34))
```

when `paramstyle` is `'qmark'`, is equivalent to—but faster than—the two statements:

```
c.execute('UPDATE atable SET x=12 WHERE y=23')

c.execute('UPDATE atable SET x=23 WHERE y=34')
```

fetchall `c.fetchall()`

Returns all remaining result rows from the last query as a sequence of tuples. Raises an exception if the last operation was not a `SELECT` query.

fetchmany `c.fetchmany(n)`

Returns up to `n` remaining result rows from the last query as a sequence of tuples. Raises an exception if the last operation was not a `SELECT` query.

fetchone `c.fetchone()`

Returns the next result row from the last query as a tuple. Raises an exception if the last operation was not a `SELECT` query.

rowcount A read-only attribute that specifies the number of rows fetched or affected by the last operation, or `-1` if the module is unable to determine this value.

DBAPI-Compliant Modules

Whatever relational DB you want to use, there's at least one (often more than one) Python DBAPI-compliant module downloadable from the Internet. There are so many DBs and modules, and the set of possibilities is so constantly shifting, that we couldn't possibly list them all, nor (importantly) could we maintain the list over time. Rather, we recommend you start from the community-maintained wiki page (*https://wiki.python.org/moin/DatabaseInterfaces*), which has at least a fighting chance to be complete and up-to-date at any time.

What follows is therefore only a very short, time-specific list of a very few DBAPI-compliant modules that, at the time of writing, are very popular themselves, and interface to very popular open source DBs.

ODBC
: Open DataBase Connectivity (ODBC) is a standard way to connect to many different DBs, including a few not supported by other DBAPI-compliant modules. For an ODBC-compliant DBAPI-compliant module with a liberal open source license, use pyodbc (*https://pypi.python.org/pypi/pyodbc/*); for a commercially supported one, mxODBC (*http://www.egenix.com/products/python/mxODBC/*).

MySQL
: MySQL is a popular open source RDBMS, currently owned by Oracle. Oracle's own "official" DBAPI-compliant interface to it is MySQL Connector/Python (*https://pypi.python.org/pypi/mysql-connector-python/2.0.4*).

PostgreSQL
: PostgreSQL is an excellent open source RDBMS. The most popular DBAPI-compliant interface to it is psycopg2 (*https://pypi.python.org/pypi/psycopg2*).

SQLite

SQLite (*http://www.sqlite.org*) is "a self-contained, server-less, zero-configuration, transactional SQL database engine," which is the most widely deployed DB engine in the world—it's a C-coded library that implements a DB within a single file, or even in memory for sufficiently small and transient cases. Python's standard library supplies the package `sqlite3`, which is a DBAPI-compliant interface to `SQLite`.

`SQLite` has rich advanced functionality, with many options you can choose; `sqlite3` offers access to much of that functionality, plus further possibilities to make interoperation between your Python code and the underlying DB even smoother and more natural. In this book, we don't cover every nook and cranny of these two powerful software systems; we focus on the subset that is most commonly used and most useful. For a great level of detail, including examples and tips about best practices, see SQLite's documentation (*https://www.sqlite.org/docs.html*) and sqlite3's online documentation (*https://docs.python.org/3/library/sqlite3.html*). If you want a book on the subject, we recommend O'Reilly's *Using SQLite.*

Package `sqlite3` supplies the following functions:

connect

`connect(`*`filepath`*`, `*`timeout`*`=5.0, `*`detect_types`*`=0, `*`isolation_level`*`='', `*`check_same_thread`*`=True, `*`factory`*`=Connection, `*`cached_statements`*`=100, `*`uri`*`=False)`

`connect` connects to the `SQLite` DB in the file named by *`filepath`* (creating it if necessary) and returns an instance of the `Connection` class (or subclass thereof passed as *factory*). To create an in-memory DB, pass `':memory:'` as the first argument, *filepath*.

The *uri* argument can be passed only in v3; if `True`, it activates SQLite's URI (*http://www.sqlite.org/uri.html*) functionality, allowing a few extra options to be passed, along with the file path, via the *filepath* argument.

timeout is the number of seconds to wait, before raising an exception, if another connection is keeping the DB locked in a transaction.

`sqlite3` directly supports only the SQLite native types: `BLOB`, `INTEGER`, `NULL`, `REAL`, and `TEXT` (any other type name is treated as `TEXT` unless properly detected and passed through a converter registered with the function `register_converter`, covered later in this section), converting as follows:

SQLite type	Python type
`BLOB`	`buffer` in v2, `bytes` in v3
`INTEGER`	`int` (or, in v2, `long` for very large values)
`NULL`	`None`
`REAL`	`float`
`TEXT`	depends on the `text_factory` attribute of the `Connection` instance, covered later in this section; by default, `unicode` in v2, `str` in v3

To allow type name detection, pass as *detect_types* either of the constants `PARSE_COLNAMES` and `PARSE_DECLTYPES`, supplied by the `sqlite3` package (or both, joining them with the `|` bitwise-or operator).

When you pass `detect_types=sqlite3.PARSE_COLNAMES`, the type name is taken from the name of the column in the SELECT SQL statement that retrieves the column; for example, a column retrieved as *foo* `AS [`*foo* `CHAR(10)]` has a type name of `CHAR`.

When you pass `detect_types=sqlite3.PARSE_DECLTYPES`, the type name is taken from the declaration of the column in the original `CREATE TABLE` or `ALTER TABLE` SQL statement that added the column; for example, a column declared as *foo* `CHAR(10)` has a type name of `CHAR`.

When you pass `detect_types=sqlite3.PARSE_COLNAMES|sqlite3.PARSE_DECLTYPES`, both mechanisms are used, with precedence given to the column name when it has at least two words (the second word gives the type name in this case), falling back to the type that was given for that column at declaration (the first word of the declaration type gives the type name in this case).

isolation_level lets you exercise some control over how SQLite processes transactions; it can be `''` (the default), `None` (to use *autocommit* mode), or one of the three strings `'DEFERRED'`, `'EXCLUSIVE'`, and `'IMMEDIATE'`. The SQLite online docs cover the details of types of transactions (*https://www.sqlite.org/lang_transaction.html*) and their relation to the various levels of file locking (*https://www.sqlite.org/lockingv3.html*) that SQLite intrinsically performs.

By default, a connection object can be used only in the Python thread that created it, to avoid accidents that could easily corrupt the DB due to minor bugs in your program; minor bugs are common in multithreaded programming. If you're entirely confident about your threads' use of locks and other synchronization mechanisms, and do need to reuse a connection object among multiple threads, you can pass `check_same_thread=False`: then, `sqlite3` performs no checks, trusting your assertion that you know what you're doing and that your multithreading architecture is 100% bug-free—good luck!

cached_statements is the number of SQL statements that `sqlite3` caches in a parsed and prepared state, to avoid the overhead of parsing them repeatedly. You can pass in a value lower than the default `100` to save a little memory, or a larger one if your application uses a dazzling variety of SQL statements.

register_adapter `register_adapter(`*type*`,`*callable*`)`

`register_adapter` registers *callable* as the adapter, from any object of Python type *type*, to a corresponding value of one of the few Python types that `sqlite3` handles directly—`int`, `float`, `str` (in v3, also `bytes`; in v2, also `buffer`, `long`, `unicode`—also note that, in v2, a `str` must be encoded in `'utf-8'`). *callable* must accept a single argument, the value to adapt, and return a value of a type that `sqlite3` handles directly.

register_converter `register_converter(`*typename*`,`*callable*`)`

`register_converter` registers *callable* as the converter, from any value identified in SQL as being of a type named *typename* (see parameter *detect_types* to function `connect` for an explanation of how the type name is identified), to a corresponding Python object. *callable* must accept a single argument, the string form of the value obtained from SQL, and return the corresponding Python object. The *typename* matching is case-sensitive.

In addition, `sqlite3` supplies the classes `Connection`, `Cursor`, and `Row`. Each can be subclassed for further customization; however, this is an advanced issue that we do not cover further in this book. The `Cursor` class is a standard DBAPI cursor class, except for an extra convenience method `executescript` accepting a single argument, a string of multiple statements separated by `;` (no parameters). The other two classes are covered in the following sections.

class sqlite3.Connection

In addition to the methods common to all `Connection` classes of DBAPI-compliant modules, covered in "Connection Objects" on page 355, `sqlite3.Connection` supplies the following methods and other attributes:

Persistence and Databases

create_aggregate `create_aggregate(`*`name`*`,`*`num_params`*`,`*`aggregate_class`*`)`

`aggregate_class` must be a class supplying two instance methods: `step`, accepting exactly *`num_param`* arguments, and *`finalize`*, accepting no arguments and returning the final result of the aggregate, a value of a type natively supported by `sqlite3`. The aggregate function can be used in SQL statements by the given *`name`*.

create_collation `create_collation(`*`name`*`,`*`callable`*`)`

`callable` must accept two bytestring arguments (encoded in `'utf-8'`), and return `-1` if the first must be considered "less than" the second, `1` if it must be considered "greater than," and `0` if it must be considered "equal," for the purposes of this comparison. Such a collation can be named by the given *`name`* in a SQL `ORDER BY` clause in a `SELECT` statement.

create_function `create_function(`*`name`*`,`*`num_params`*`,`*`func`*`)`

`func` must accept exactly *`num_params`* arguments and return a value of a type natively supported by `sqlite3`; such a user-defined function can be used in SQL statements by the given *`name`*.

interrupt `interrupt()`

Call from any other thread to abort all queries executing on this connection (raising an exception in the thread using the connection).

isolation_level A read-only attribute that's the value given as *`isolation_level`* parameter to the `connect` function.

iterdump `iterdump()`

Returns an iterator that yields strings: the SQL statements that build the current DB from scratch, including both schema and contents. Useful, for example, to persist an in-memory DB to one on disk for future reuse.

row_factory A callable that accepts the cursor and the original row as a tuple, and returns an object to use as the real result row. A common idiom is *`x`*`.row_factory=sqlite3.Row`, to use the highly optimized `Row` class covered in "class sqlite3.Row" on page 362, supplying both index-based and case-insensitive name-based access to columns with negligible overhead.

text_factory A callable that accepts a single bytestring parameter and returns the object to use for that TEXT column value—by default, `str` in v3, `unicode` in v2, but you can set it to any similar callable.

total_changes	The total number of rows that have been modified, inserted, or deleted since the connection was created.

class sqlite3.Row

`sqlite3` supplies the class `Row`, which is mostly like a `tuple` but also supplies the method `keys()`, returning a list of column names, and supports indexing by a column name as an extra alternative to indexing by column number.

A sqlite3 example

The following example handles the same task as the examples shown earlier in the chapter, but uses `sqlite3` for persistence, without creating the index in memory:

```
import fileinput, sqlite3
connect = sqlite3.connect('database.db')
cursor = connect.cursor()
cursor.execute('CREATE TABLE IF NOT EXISTS Words '
               '(Word TEXT, File TEXT, Line INT)')
for line in fileinput.input():
    f, l = fileinput.filename(), fileinput.filelineno()
    cursor.executemany('INSERT INTO Words VALUES (:w, :f, :l)',
        [{'w':w, 'f':f, 'l':l} for w in line.split()])
connect.commit()
connect.close()
```

We can then use `sqlite3` to read back the data stored in the DB file *database.db*, as shown in the following example:

```
import sys, sqlite3, linecache
connect = sqlite3.connect('database.db')
cursor = connect.cursor()
for word in sys.argv[1:]:
    cursor.execute('SELECT File, Line FROM Words '
                   'WHERE Word=?', [word])
    places = cursor.fetchall()
    if not places:
         print('Word {!r} not found in index file'.format(word),
               file=sys.stderr)
         continue
    for fname, lineno in places:
        print('Word {!r} occurs in line {} of file {}:'.format(
              word,lineno,fname))
        print(linecache.getline(fname, lineno), end='')
```

12
Time Operations

A Python program can handle time in several ways. Time intervals are floating-point numbers in units of seconds (a fraction of a second is the fractional part of the interval): all standard library functions accepting an argument that expresses a time interval in seconds accept a float as the value of that argument. Instants in time are expressed in seconds since a reference instant, known as the *epoch*. (Midnight, UTC, of January 1, 1970, is a popular epoch used on both Unix and Windows platforms.) Time instants often also need to be expressed as a mixture of units of measurement (e.g., years, months, days, hours, minutes, and seconds), particularly for I/O purposes. I/O, of course, also requires the ability to format times and dates into human-readable strings, and parse them back from string formats.

This chapter covers the `time` module, which supplies Python's core time-handling functionality. The `time` module is somewhat dependent on the underlying system's C library. The chapter also presents the `datetime`, `sched`, and `calendar` modules from the standard Python library, and the third-party modules `dateutil` and `pytz`.

The time Module

The underlying C library determines the range of dates that the `time` module can handle. On Unix systems, years 1970 and 2038 are typical cut-off points, a limitation that `datetime` avoids. Time instants are normally specified in UTC (Coordinated Universal Time, once known as GMT, or Greenwich Mean Time). The `time` module also supports local time zones and daylight saving time (DST), but only to the extent the underlying C system library does.

As an alternative to seconds since the epoch, a time instant can be represented by a tuple of nine integers, called a *timetuple*. (Timetuples are covered in Table 12-1.) All items are integers: timetuples don't keep track of fractions of a second. A timetuple is an instance of `struct_time`. You can use it as a tuple, and you can also access the items as the read-only attributes `x.tm_year`, `x.tm_mon`, and so on, with the attribute names listed in Table 12-1. Wherever a function requires a timetuple argument, you can pass an instance of `struct_time` or any other sequence whose items are nine integers in the right ranges (all ranges in the table include both lower and upper bounds).

Table 12-1. Tuple form of time representation

Item	Meaning	Field name	Range	Notes
0	Year	`tm_year`	1970–2038	Wider on some platforms.
1	Month	`tm_mon`	1–12	`1` is January; `12` is December.
2	Day	`tm_mday`	1–31	
3	Hour	`tm_hour`	0–23	`0` is midnight; `12` is noon.
4	Minute	`tm_min`	0–59	
5	Second	`tm_sec`	0–61	`60` and `61` for leap seconds.
6	Weekday	`tm_wday`	0–6	`0` is Monday; `6` is Sunday.
7	Year day	`tm_yday`	1–366	Day number within the year.
8	DST flag	`tm_isdst`	−1 to 1	`-1` means library determines DST.

To translate a time instant from a "seconds since the epoch" floating-point value into a timetuple, pass the floating-point value to a function (e.g., `localtime`) that returns a timetuple with all nine items valid. When you convert in the other direction, `mktime` ignores redundant items six (`tm_wday`) and seven (`tm_yday`) of the tuple. In this case, you normally set item eight (`tm_isdst`) to `-1` so that `mktime` itself determines whether to apply DST.

`time` supplies the functions and attributes listed in Table 12-2.

Table 12-2.

asctime `asctime([tupletime])`

Accepts a timetuple and returns a readable 24-character string such as `'Sun Jan 8 14:41:06 2017'`. `asctime()` without arguments is like `asctime(localtime(time()))` (formats current time in local time).

clock `clock()`

Returns the current CPU time as a floating-point number of seconds, but is platform dependent. Deprecated in v3. To measure computational costs of different approaches, use the standard library module `timeit`, covered in "The timeit module" on page 489 instead. To implement a timeout or schedule events, in v3, use `perf_counter()` or `process_time()` instead. See also the `sched` module for multithreading safe event scheduling.

ctime `ctime([`*`secs`*`])`

Like `asctime(localtime(`*`secs`*`))`, accepts an instant expressed in seconds since the epoch and returns a readable 24-character string form of that instant, in local time. `ctime()` without arguments is like `asctime()` (formats the current time instant in local time).

gmtime `gmtime([`*`secs`*`])`

Accepts an instant expressed in seconds since the epoch and returns a timetuple *`t`* with the UTC time (*`t`*`.tm_isdst` is always `0`). `gmtime()` without arguments is like `gmtime(time())` (returns the timetuple for the current time instant).

localtime `localtime([`*`secs`*`])`

Accepts an instant expressed in seconds since the epoch and returns a timetuple *`t`* with the local time (*`t`*`.tm_isdst` is `0` or `1`, depending on whether DST applies to instant *`secs`* by local rules). `localtime()` without arguments is like `localtime(time())` (returns the timetuple for the current time instant).

mktime `mktime(`*`tupletime`*`)`

Accepts an instant expressed as a timetuple in local time and returns a floating-point value with the instant expressed in seconds since the epoch.[a] DST, the last item in *`tupletime`*, is meaningful: set it to `0` to get solar time, to `1` to get DST, or to `-1` to let `mktime` compute whether DST is in effect at the given instant.

monotonic `monotonic()`

v3 only. Like `time()`, returns the current time instant, a `float` with seconds since the epoch. Guaranteed to never go backward between calls, even when the system clock is adjusted (e.g., due to leap seconds).

perf_counter `perf_counter()`

v3 only. Returns the value in fractional seconds using the highest-resolution clock available to get accuracy for short durations. It is system-wide and *includes* time elapsed during `sleep`. Use only the difference between successive calls, as there is no defined reference point.

process_time `process_time()`

v3 only. Returns the value in fractional seconds using the highest-resolution clock available to get accuracy for short durations. It is process-wide and *doesn't* include time elapsed during `sleep`. Use only the difference between successive calls, as there is no defined reference point.

sleep `sleep(secs)`

Suspends the calling thread for *`secs`* seconds. The calling thread may start executing again before *`secs`* seconds (when it's the main thread and some signal wakes it up) or after a longer suspension (depending on system scheduling of processes and threads). You can call sleep with `secs=0` to offer other threads a chance to run, incurring no significant delay if the current thread is the only one ready to run.

strftime `strftime(fmt[,tupletime])`

Accepts an instant expressed as a timetuple in local time and returns a string representing the instant as specified by string *`fmt`*. If you omit *`tupletime`*, `strftime` uses `localtime(time())` (formats the current time instant). The syntax of string *`format`* is similar to the one covered in "Legacy String Formatting with %" on page 246. Conversion characters are different, as shown in Table 12-3. Refer to the time instant specified by *`tupletime`*; the format can't specify width and precision.

Table 12-3. Conversion characters for strftime

Type char	Meaning	Special notes
a	Weekday name, abbreviated	Depends on locale
A	Weekday name, full	Depends on locale
b	Month name, abbreviated	Depends on locale
B	Month name, full	Depends on locale
c	Complete date and time representation	Depends on locale
d	Day of the month	Between 1 and 31
G	***New in 3.6***: ISO 8601:2000 standard week-based year number	
H	Hour (24-hour clock)	Between 0 and 23
I	Hour (12-hour clock)	Between 1 and 12
j	Day of the year	Between 1 and 366

Type char	Meaning	Special notes
m	Month number	Between 1 and 12
M	Minute number	Between 0 and 59
p	A.M. or P.M. equivalent	Depends on locale
S	Second number	Between 0 and 61
u	***New in 3.6***: day of week	Numbered from Monday == 1
U	Week number (Sunday first weekday)	Between 0 and 53
V	***New in 3.6***: ISO 8601:2000 standard week-based week number	
w	Weekday number	0 is Sunday, up to 6
W	Week number (Monday first weekday)	Between 0 and 53
x	Complete date representation	Depends on locale
X	Complete time representation	Depends on locale
y	Year number within century	Between 0 and 99
Y	Year number	1970 to 2038, or wider
Z	Name of time zone	Empty if no time zone exists
%	A literal % character	Encoded as %%

For example, you can obtain dates just as formatted by `asctime` (e.g., `'Tue Dec 10 18:07:14 2002'`) with the format string:

```
'%a %b %d %H:%M:%S %Y'
```

You can obtain dates compliant with RFC 822 (e.g., `'Tue, 10 Dec 2002 18:07:14 EST'`) with the format string:

```
'%a, %d %b %Y %H:%M:%S %Z'
```

strptime `strptime(`*`str`*`,[`*`fmt`*`='%a %b %d %H:%M:%S %Y'])`

Parses *`str`* according to format string *`fmt`* and returns the instant as a timetuple. The format string's syntax is as covered in `strftime` earlier.

time `time()`

Returns the current time instant, a `float` with seconds since the epoch. On some (mostly, older) platforms, the precision of this time is as low as one second. May return a lower value in a subsequent call if the system clock is adjusted backward between calls (e.g., due to leap seconds).

timezone `timezone`

The offset in seconds of the local time zone (without DST) from UTC (`>0` in the Americas; `<=0` in most of Europe, Asia, and Africa).

tzname `tzname`

A pair of locale-dependent strings, which are the names of the local time zone without and with DST, respectively.

[a] `mktime`'s result's fractional part is always 0, since its timetuple argument does not account for fractions of a second.

The datetime Module

`datetime` provides classes for modeling date and time objects, which can be either *aware* of time zones or *naive* (the default). The class `tzinfo`, whose instances model a time zone, is abstract: the module `datetime` supplies no implementation (for all the gory details, see the online docs (*https://docs.python.org/3/library/datetime.html#tzinfo-objects*)). See the module `pytz`, in "The pytz Module" on page 374, for a good, simple implementation of `tzinfo`, which lets you easily create time zone-aware `datetime` objects. All types in `datetime` have immutable instances: attributes are read-only, and instances can be keys in a `dict` or items in a `set`.

The date Class

Instances of the `date` class represent a date (no time of day in particular within that date), are always naive, and assume the Gregorian calendar was always in effect. `date` instances have three read-only integer attributes: `year`, `month`, and `day`:

date `date(year,month,day)`

The `date` class supplies class methods usable as alternative constructors:

fromordinal `date.fromordinal(ordinal)`

Returns a `date` object corresponding to the proleptic Gregorian ordinal (*https://en.wikipedia.org/wiki/Proleptic_Gregorian_calendar*) `ordinal`, where a value of `1` corresponds to the first day of year 1 CE.

fromtimestamp `date.fromtimestamp(timestamp)`

Returns a `date` object corresponding to the instant *timestamp* expressed in seconds since the epoch.

today `date.today()`

Returns a `date` object representing today's date.

Time Operations

Instances of the `date` class support some arithmetic: the difference between `date` instances is a `timedelta` instance; you can add or subtract a `timedelta` to/from a `date` instance to make another `date` instance. You can compare any two instances of the `date` class (the later one is greater).

An instance *d* of the class `date` supplies the following methods:

ctime `d.ctime()`

Returns a string representing the date *d* in the same 24-character format as `time.ctime` (with the time of day set to 00:00:00, midnight).

isocalendar `d.isocalendar()`

Returns a tuple with three integers (ISO year, ISO week number, and ISO weekday). See the ISO 8601 standard (*https://en.wikipedia.org/?title=ISO_8601*) for more details about the ISO (International Standards Organization) calendar.

isoformat `d.isoformat()`

Returns a string representing date *d* in the format `'YYYY-MM-DD'`; same as `str(d)`.

isoweekday `d.isoweekday()`

Returns the day of the week of date *d* as an integer, `1` for Monday through `7` for Sunday; like `d.weekday() + 1`.

replace `d.replace(year=None,month=None,day=None)`

Returns a new `date` object, like *d* except for those attributes explicitly specified as arguments, which get replaced. For example:

```
date(x,y,z).replace(month=m) == date(x,m,z)
```

strftime `d.strftime()`

Returns a string representing date *d* as specified by string *fmt*, like:

```
time.strftime(fmt, d.timetuple())
```

timetuple `d.timetuple()`

Returns a time tuple corresponding to date *d* at time 00:00:00 (midnight).

toordinal `d.toordinal()`

Returns the proleptic Gregorian ordinal for date *d*. For example:

```
date(1,1,1).toordinal() == 1
```

weekday `d.weekday()`

Returns the day of the week of date *d* as an integer, 0 for Monday through 6 for Sunday; like `d.isoweekday() - 1`.

The time Class

Instances of the `time` class represent a time of day (of no particular date), may be naive or aware regarding time zones, and always ignore leap seconds. They have five attributes: four read-only integers (`hour`, `minute`, `second`, and `microsecond`) and an optional `tzinfo` (`None` for naive instances).

time `time(hour=0,minute=0,second=0,microsecond=0,tzinfo=None)`

Instances of the class `time` do not support arithmetic. You can compare two instances of `time` (the one that's later in the day is greater), but only if they are either both aware or both naive.

An instance *t* of the class `time` supplies the following methods:

isoformat `t.isoformat()`

Returns a string representing time *t* in the format `'HH:MM:SS'`; same as `str(t)`. If `t.microsecond!=0`, the resulting string is longer: `'HH:MM:SS.mmmmmm'`. If *t* is aware, six more characters, `'+HH:MM'`, are added at the end to represent the time zone's offset from UTC. In other words, this formatting operation follows the ISO 8601 standard (*https://en.wikipedia.org/wiki/ISO_8601*).

replace `t.replace(hour=None,minute=None,second=None,microsecond=None[, tzinfo])`

Returns a new `time` object, like *t* except for those attributes explicitly specified as arguments, which get replaced. For example:

```
time(x,y,z).replace(minute=m) == time(x,m,z)
```

strftime `t.strftime()`

Returns a string representing time *t* as specified by the string *fmt*.

An instance *t* of the class `time` also supplies methods `dst`, `tzname`, and `utcoffset`, which accept no arguments and delegate to `t.tzinfo`, returning None when `t.tzinfo` is None.

Time Operations

The datetime Class

Instances of the `datetime` class represent an instant (a date, with a specific time of day within that date), may be naive or aware of time zones, and always ignore leap seconds. `datetime` extends `date` and adds `time`'s attributes; its instances have read-only integers `year`, `month`, `day`, `hour`, `minute`, `second`, and `microsecond`, and an optional `tzinfo` (`None` for naive instances).

Instances of `datetime` support some arithmetic: the difference between `datetime` instances (both aware, or both naive) is a `timedelta` instance, and you can add or subtract a `timedelta` instance to/from a `datetime` instance to construct another `datetime` instance. You can compare two instances of the `datetime` class (the later one is greater) as long as they're both aware or both naive.

datetime `datetime(year,month,day,hour=0,minute=0,second=0, microsecond=0,tzinfo=None)`

The class `datetime` also supplies some class methods usable as alternative constructors.

combine `datetime.combine(date,time)`

Returns a `datetime` object with the date attributes taken from *date* and the time attributes (including `tzinfo`) taken from *time*. `datetime.combine(d,t)` is like:

```
datetime(d.year, d.month, d.day,
         t.hour, t.minute, t.second,
         t.microsecond, t.tzinfo)
```

fromordinal `datetime.fromordinal(ordinal)`

Returns a `datetime` object for the date given proleptic Gregorian ordinal *ordinal*, where a value of 1 means the first day of year 1 CE, at midnight.

fromtimestamp `datetime.fromtimestamp(timestamp,tz=None)`

Returns a `datetime` object corresponding to the instant *timestamp* expressed in seconds since the epoch, in local time. When *tz* is not `None`, returns an aware `datetime` object with the given `tzinfo` instance *tz*.

now `datetime.now(tz=None)`

Returns a `datetime` object for the current local date and time. When *tz* is not `None`, returns an aware `datetime` object with the given `tzinfo` instance *tz*.

strptime `datetime.strptime(str,fmt='%a %b %d %H:%M:%S %Y %z')`

Returns a `datetime` representing *str* as specified by string *fmt*. In v3 only, when `%z` is specified, the resulting `datetime` object is time zone-aware.

today `datetime.today()`

Returns a naive `datetime` object representing the current local date and time, same as the now class method (but not accepting optional argument *tz*).

utcfromtimestamp `datetime.utcfromtimestamp(timestamp)`

Returns a naive `datetime` object corresponding to the instant *timestamp* expressed in seconds since the epoch, in UTC.

utcnow `datetime.utcnow()`

Returns a naive `datetime` object representing the current date and time, in UTC.

An instance *d* of `datetime` also supplies the following methods:

astimezone `d.astimezone(tz)`

Returns a new aware `datetime` object, like *d* (which must also be aware), except that the time zone is converted to the one in `tzinfo` object *tz*. Note that `d.astimezone(tz)` is quite different from `d.replace(tzinfo=tz)`: the latter does no time zone conversion, but rather just copies all of *d*'s attributes except for `d.tzinfo`.

ctime `d.ctime()`

Returns a string representing date and time *d* in the same 24-character format as `time.ctime`.

date `d.date()`

Returns a date object representing the same date as *d*.

isocalendar `d.isocalendar()`

Returns a tuple with three integers (ISO year, ISO week number, and ISO weekday) for *d*'s date.

isoformat `d.isoformat(sep='T')`

Returns a string representing *d* in the format `'YYYY-MM-DDxHH:MM:SS'`, where *x* is the value of argument *sep* (must be a string of length 1). If `d.microsecond!=0`, seven characters, `'.mmmmmm'`, are added after the `'SS'` part of the string. If *t* is aware, six more characters, `'+HH:MM'`, are added at the end to represent the time zone's offset from UTC. In other words, this formatting operation follows the ISO 8601 standard. `str(d)` is the same as `d.isoformat(' ')`.

isoweekday `d.isoweekday()`

Returns the day of the week of *d*'s date as an integer; 1 for Monday through 7 for Sunday.

replace `d.replace(year=None,month=None,day=None,hour=None,minute=None, second=None,microsecond=None[,tzinfo])`

Returns a new `datetime` object, like *d* except for those attributes specified as arguments, which get replaced. For example:

```
datetime(x,y,z).replace(month=m) == datetime(x,m,z)
```

strftime `d.strftime(fmt)`

Returns a string representing *d* as specified by the format string *fmt*.

time `d.time()`

Returns a naive time object representing the same time of day as *d*.

timestamp `d.timestamp()`

Returns a float with the seconds since the epoch (v3 only). Naive instances are assumed to be in the local time zone.

timetz `d.timetz()`

Returns a `time` object representing the same time of day as *d*, with the same `tzinfo`.

timetuple `d.timetuple()`

Returns a timetuple corresponding to instant *d*.

toordinal `d.toordinal()`

Returns the proleptic Gregorian ordinal for *d*'s date. For example:

```
datetime(1,1,1).toordinal() == 1
```

utctimetuple *d*.utctimetuple()

Returns a timetuple corresponding to instant *d*, normalized to UTC if *d* is aware.

weekday *d*.weekday()

Returns the day of the week of *d*'s date as an integer; 0 for Monday through 6 for Sunday.

An instance *d* of the class datetime also supplies the methods dst, tzname, and utcoffset, which accept no arguments and delegate to *d*.tzinfo, returning None when *d*.tzinfo is None.

The timedelta Class

Instances of the timedelta class represent time intervals with three read-only integer attributes: days, seconds, and microseconds.

timedelta timedelta(*days*=0, *seconds*=0, *microseconds*=0, *milliseconds*=0, *minutes*=0, *hours*=0, *weeks*=0)

Converts all units with the obvious factors (a week is 7 days, an hour is 3,600 seconds, and so on) and normalizes everything to the three integer attributes, ensuring that 0<=seconds<3600*24 and 0<=microseconds<1000000. For example:

```
print(repr(timedelta(minutes=0.5)))
# prints: datetime.timedelta(0, 30)
print(repr(timedelta(minutes=-0.5)))
# prints: datetime.timedelta(-1, 86370)
```

Instances of timedelta support arithmetic (+ and - between themselves and with instances of the classes date and datetime; * and / with integers) and comparisons between themselves. v3 also supports division between timedelta instances (floor division, true division, divmod, %). The instance method total_seconds returns the total seconds in a timedelta instance.

The pytz Module

The third-party pytz module offers the best, simplest ways to create tzinfo instances to make time zone–aware instances of the classes time and datetime. (pytz is based on the Olson library of time zones (*http://www.twinsun.com/tz/tz-link.htm*). pytz, like just about every third-party Python package, is available from PyPI (*https://pypi.python.org/pypi*): just **pip install pytz**.)

Dealing with time zones

The best way to program around the traps and pitfalls of time zones is to always use the UTC time zone internally, converting from other time zones on input, and to other time zones only for display purposes.

pytz supplies the attributes common_timezones, a list of over 400 strings that name the most common time zones you might want to use (mostly of the form *continent/city*, with some synonyms like 'UTC' and 'US/Pacific') and all_timezones, a list of over 500 strings that also supply other synonyms for the time zones. For example, to specify the time zone of Lisbon, Portugal, by Olson library standards, the canonical way is 'Europe/Lisbon', and that is what you find in common_timezones; however, you may also use 'Portugal', which you find only in all_timezones. pytz also supplies the attributes utc and UTC, two names for the same object: a tzinfo instance representing Coordinated Universal Time (UTC).

pytz also supplies two functions:

country_timezones country_timezones(*code*)

Returns a list of time zone names corresponding to the country whose two-letter ISO code is *code*. For example, pytz.country_timezones('US') returns a list of 22 strings, from 'America/New_York' to 'Pacific/Honolulu'.

timezone timezone(*name*)

Returns an instance of tzinfo corresponding to the time zone named *name*.

For example, to print the Honolulu equivalent of midnight, December 31, 2005, in New York:

```
dt = datetime.datetime(2005,12,31,
tzinfo=pytz.timezone('America/New_York'))
print(dt.astimezone(
  pytz.timezone('Pacific/Honolulu')))
# prints: 2005-12-30 19:00:00-10:00
```

The dateutil Module

The third-party package dateutil (*http://labix.org/python-dateutil*) (which you can install with **pip install python-dateutil**) offers modules to manipulate dates in many ways: time deltas, recurrence, time zones, Easter dates, and fuzzy parsing. (See the package's website (*https://labix.org/python-dateutil*) for complete documentation of its rich functionality.) dateutil's main modules are:

easter easter.easter(*year*)

Returns the datetime.date object for Easter of the given *year*. For example:

```
from dateutil import easter
print(easter.easter(2006))
```

prints **2006-04-16**.

parser `parser.parse(s)`

Returns the `datetime.datetime` object denoted by string *s*, with very permissive (AKA "fuzzy") parsing rules. For example:

```
from dateutil import parser
print(parser.parse('Saturday, January 28, 2006,
                    at 11:15pm'))
```

prints **2006-01-28 23:15:00**.

relativedelta `relativedelta.relativedelta(...)`

You can call `relativedelta` with two instances of `datetime.datetime`: the resulting `relativedelta` instance captures the relative difference between the two arguments. Alternatively, you can call `relativedelta` with a named argument representing absolute information (*year*, *month*, *day*, *hour*, *minute*, *second*, *microsecond*); relative information (*years*, *months*, *weeks*, *days*, *hours*, *minutes*, *seconds*, *microseconds*), which may have positive or negative values; or the special named argument *weekday*, which can be a number from 0 (Monday) to 6 (Sunday), or one of the module attributes `MO`, `TU`,..., `SU`, which can also be called with a numeric argument *n* to specify the nth weekday. In any case, the resulting `relativedelta` instance captures the information in the call. For example, after:

```
from dateutil import relativedelta
r = relativedelta.relativedelta(weekday=relativedelta.MO(1))
```

r means "next Monday." You can add a `relativedelta` instance to a `datetime.datetime` instance to get a new `datetime.datetime` instance at the stated relative delta from the other:

```
print(datetime.datetime(2006,1,29)+r)

# prints: 2006-01-30

print(datetime.datetime(2006,1,30)+r)

# prints: 2006-01-30

print(datetime.datetime(2006,1,31)+r)

# prints: 2006-02-06
```

Note that "next Monday," by `relativedelta`'s interpretation, is the very same date, if that day is already a Monday (so, a more detailed name might be "the first date, on or following the given date, which falls on a Monday"). `dateutil`'s site (*https://labix.org/python-dateutil*) has detailed explanations of the rules defining the inevitably complicated behavior of `relativedelta` instances.

rrule `rrule.rrule(freq, ...)`

Module `rrule` implements RFC2445 (*https://www.ietf.org/rfc/rfc2445.txt*) (also known as the `iCalendar` RFC), in all the glory of its 140+ pages. *`freq`* must be one of the constant attributes of module `rrule`: `YEARLY`, `MONTHLY`, `WEEKLY`, `DAILY`, `HOURLY`, `MINUTELY`, or `SECONDLY`. After mandatory argument *`freq`* may optionally come some of many possible named arguments, such as `interval=2`, to specify that the recurrence is only on alternate occurrences of the specified frequency (for example, `rrule.rrule(rrule.YEARLY)` repeats every year, while `rrule.rrule(rrule.YEARLY, interval=7)` repeats only every seven years, as a typical academic sabbatical year (*https://en.wikipedia.org/wiki/Sabbatical*) would).

An instance *r* of the type `rrule.rrule` supplies several methods:

after `r.after(d, inc=False)`

Returns the earliest `datetime.datetime` instance that's an occurrence of recurrence rule *r* and happens after date *d* (when *`inc`* is true, an occurrence happening on the date *d* itself is also acceptable).

before `r.before(d, inc=False)`

Returns the latest `datetime.datetime` instance that's an occurrence of recurrence rule *r* and happens before date *d* (when *`inc`* is true, an occurrence happening on date *d* itself is also acceptable).

between `r.between(start, finish, inc=False)`

Returns all `datetime.datetime` instances that are occurrences of recurrence rule *r* and happen between the dates *`start`* and *`finish`* (when *`inc`* is true, occurrences on the dates *`start`* and *`finish`* themselves are also acceptable).

For example, to say "once a week throughout January 2018," the snippet:

```
start=datetime.datetime(2018,1,1)
r=rrule.rrule(rrule.WEEKLY, dtstart=start)
for d in r.between(start,datetime.datetime(2018,2,1),True):
    print(d.date(),end=' ')
```

prints: **2018-01-01 2018-01-08 2018-01-15 2018-01-22 2018-01-29**

count `r.count()`

Returns the number of occurrences of recurrence rule *r* (may loop forever when *r* has an unbounded number of occurrences).

The sched Module

The sched module implements an event scheduler, letting you easily deal, along a single thread of execution or in multithreaded environments, with events that may be scheduled in either a "real" or a "simulated" time scale. `sched` supplies a `scheduler` class:

scheduler `class scheduler([`*`timefunc`*`],[`*`delayfunc`*`])`

The arguments *`timefunc`* and *`delayfunc`* are mandatory in v2, and optional in v3 (where they default to `time.monotonic` and `time.sleep`, respectively).

`timefunc` must be callable without arguments to get the current time instant (in any unit of measure); for example, you can pass `time.time` (or, in v3 only, `time.monotonic`). *`delayfunc`* is callable with one argument (a time duration, in the same units as *`timefunc`*) to delay the current thread for that time; for example, you can pass `time.sleep`. `scheduler` calls *`delayfunc`*`(0)` after each event to give other threads a chance; this is compatible with `time.sleep`. By taking functions as arguments, `scheduler` lets you use whatever "simulated time" or "pseudotime" fits your application's needs (a great example of the dependency injection (*https://en.wikipedia.org/wiki/Dependency_injection*) design pattern for purposes not necessarily related to testing).

If monotonic time (time cannot go backward, even if the system clock is adjusted backward between calls, e.g., due to leap seconds) is important to your application, use v3 `time.monotonic` for your scheduler. A `scheduler` instance *s* supplies the following methods:

cancel *`s`*`.cancel(`*`event_token`*`)`

Removes an event from *s*'s queue. *`event_token`* must be the result of a previous call to *`s`*`.enter` or *`s`*`.enterabs`, and the event must not yet have happened; otherwise, `cancel` raises `RuntimeError`.

empty *`s`*`.empty()`

Returns `True` when *s*'s queue is currently empty; otherwise, `False`.

enterabs *`s`*`.enterabs(`*`when,priority,func,args=(),kwargs={}`*`)`

Schedules a future event (a callback to *`func`*`(`*`args, kwargs`*`)`) at time *`when`*. This is the v3 signature; in v2, sequence *`args`* is mandatory, and mapping *`kwargs`* is not allowed.

`when` is in the units used by the time functions of *s*. Should several events be scheduled for the same time, *s* executes them in increasing order of *`priority`*. `enterabs` returns an event token *t*, which you may pass to *`s`*`.cancel` to cancel this event.

enter `s.enter(delay,priority,func,args=(),kwargs={})`

Like `enterabs`, except that *`delay`* is a relative time (a positive difference forward from the current instant), while `enterabs`'s argument *`when`* is an absolute time (a future instant). In v3, *`args`* is optional and *`kwargs`* is added.

To schedule an event for *repeated* execution, use a little wrapper function; for example:

```
def enter_repeat(s, first_delay, period, priority, func, args):
    def repeating_wrapper():
        s.enter(period, priority, repeating_wrapper, ())
        func(*args)
    s.enter(first_delay, priority, repeating_wrapper, ())
```

run `s.run(blocking=True)`

Runs scheduled events. In v2, or if *`blocking`* is true (v3 only), `s.run` loops until `s.empty()`, using the *`delayfunc`* passed on *s*'s initialization to wait for each scheduled event. If *`blocking`* is false (v3 only), executes any soon-to-expire events, then returns the next event's deadline (if any). When a callback *`func`* raises an exception, *`s`* propagates it, but *`s`* keeps its own state, removing the event from the schedule. If a callback *`func`* runs longer than the time available before the next scheduled event, *`s`* falls behind but keeps executing scheduled events in order, never dropping any. Call `s.cancel` to drop an event explicitly if that event is no longer of interest.

The calendar Module

The `calendar` module supplies calendar-related functions, including functions to print a text calendar for a given month or year. By default, `calendar` takes Monday as the first day of the week and Sunday as the last one. To change this, call `calendar.setfirstweekday`. `calendar` handles years in module `time`'s range, typically (at least) 1970 to 2038.

`python -m calendar` offers a useful command-line interface to the module's functionality: run **`python -m calendar -h`** to get a brief help message.

The `calendar` module supplies the following functions:

calendar `calendar(year,w=2,l=1,c=6)`

Returns a multiline string with a calendar for year *`year`* formatted into three columns separated by *`c`* spaces. *`w`* is the width in characters of each date; each line has length `21*w+18+2*c`. *`l`* is the number of lines for each week.

firstweekday `firstweekday()`

Returns the current setting for the weekday that starts each week. By default, when `calendar` is first imported, this is `0`, meaning Monday.

isleap `isleap(year)`

Returns `True` if *year* is a leap year; otherwise, `False`.

leapdays `leapdays(y1,y2)`

Returns the total number of leap days in the years within `range(y1,y2)` (remember, this means that *y2* is excluded).

month `month(year,month,w=2,l=1)`

Returns a multiline string with a calendar for month *month* of year *year*, one line per week plus two header lines. *w* is the width in characters of each date; each line has length `7*w+6`. *l* is the number of lines for each week.

monthcalendar `monthcalendar(year,month)`

Returns a list of lists of `int`s. Each sublist denotes a week. Days outside month *month* of year *year* are set to `0`; days within the month are set to their day-of-month, `1` and up.

monthrange `monthrange(year,month)`

Returns two integers. The first one is the code of the weekday for the first day of the month *month* in year *year*; the second one is the number of days in the month. Weekday codes are `0` (Monday) to `6` (Sunday); month numbers are `1` to `12`.

prcal `prcal(year,w=2,l=1,c=6)`

Like `print(calendar.calendar(year,w,l,c))`.

prmonth `prmonth(year,month,w=2,l=1)`

Like `print(calendar.month(year,month,w,l))`.

setfirstweekday `setfirstweekday(weekday)`

Sets the first day of each week to weekday code *weekday*. Weekday codes are `0` (Monday) to `6` (Sunday). `calendar` supplies the attributes `MONDAY`, `TUESDAY`, `WEDNESDAY`, `THURSDAY`, `FRIDAY`, `SATURDAY`, and `SUNDAY`, whose values are the integers `0` to `6`. Use these attributes when you mean weekdays (e.g., `calendar.FRIDAY` instead of `4`) to make your code clearer and more readable.

timegm `timegm(tupletime)`

The inverse of `time.gmtime`: accepts a time instant in timetuple form and returns that instant as a `float` num of seconds since the epoch.

weekday `weekday(year,month,day)`

Returns the weekday code for the given date. Weekday codes are `0` (Monday) to `6` (Sunday); month numbers are `1` (Jan) to `12` (Dec).

13 Controlling Execution

Python directly exposes, supports, and documents many of its internal mechanisms. This may help you understand Python at an advanced level, and lets you hook your own code into such Python mechanisms, controlling them to some extent. For example, "Python built-ins" on page 176 covers the way Python arranges for built-ins to be visible. This chapter covers some other advanced Python techniques; Chapter 16 covers issues specific to testing, debugging, and profiling. Other issues related to controlling execution are about using multiple threads and processes, covered in Chapter 14, and about asynchronous processing, covered in Chapter 18.

Site and User Customization

Python provides a specific "hook" to let each site customize some aspects of Python's behavior at the start of each run. Customization by each single user is not enabled by default, but Python specifies how programs that want to run user-provided code at startup can explicitly support such customization (a rarely used facility).

The site and sitecustomize Modules

Python loads the standard module `site` just before the main script. If Python is run with option `-S`, Python does not load `site`. `-S` allows faster startup but saddles the main script with initialization chores. `site`'s tasks are:

- Putting `sys.path` in standard form (absolute paths, no duplicates).
- Interpreting each *.pth* file found in the Python home directory, adding entries to `sys.path`, and/or importing modules, as each *.pth* file indicates.
- Adding built-ins used to print information in interactive sessions (`exit`, `copyright`, `credits`, `license`, and `quit`).

- In v2 only, setting the default Unicode encoding to `'ascii'` (in v3, the default encoding is built-in as `'utf-8'`). v2's `site` source code includes two blocks, each guarded by `if 0:`, one to set the default encoding to be locale-dependent, and the other to completely disable any default encoding between Unicode and plain strings. You may optionally edit *site.py* to select either block, but this is *not* a good idea, even though a comment in *site.py* says "if you're willing to experiment, you can change this."
- In v2 only, trying to import `sitecustomize` (should `import sitecustomize` raise an `ImportError` exception, `site` catches and ignores it). `sitecustomize` is the module that each site's installation can optionally use for further site-specific customization beyond `site`'s tasks. It is best not to edit *site.py*, since any Python upgrade or reinstallation would overwrite customizations.
- After `sitecustomize` is done, removing the attribute `sys.setdefaultencoding` from the `sys` module, so that the default encoding can't be changed.

User Customization

Each interactive Python interpreter session starts by running the script named by the environment variable `PYTHONSTARTUP`. Outside of interactive interpreter sessions, there is no automatic per-user customization. To request per-user customization, a Python (v2 only) main script can explicitly `import user`. The v2 standard library module `user`, when loaded, first determines the user's home directory, as indicated by the environment variable `HOME` (or, failing that, `HOMEPATH`, possibly preceded by `HOMEDRIVE` on Windows systems only). If the environment does not indicate a home directory, `user` uses the current directory. If the `user` module finds a file named *.pythonrc.py* in the indicated directory, `user` executes that file, with the built-in Python v2 function `execfile`, in `user`'s own global namespace.

Scripts that don't import `user` do not run *.pythonrc.py*; no Python v3 script does, either, since the `user` module is not defined in v3. Of course, any given script is free to arrange other specific ways to run whatever user-specific startup module it requires. Such application-specific arrangements, even in v2, are more common than importing `user`. A generic *.pythonrc.py*, as loaded via `import user`, needs to be usable with any application that loads it. Specialized, application-specific startup files only need to follow whatever convention a specific application documents.

For example, your application *MyApp.py* could document that it looks for a file named *.myapprc.py* in the user's home directory, as indicated by the environment variable `HOME`, and loads it in the application's main script's global namespace. You could then have the following code in your main script:

```
import os
homedir = os.environ.get('HOME')
if homedir is not None:
    userscript = os.path.join(homedir, '.myapprc.py')
    if os.path.isfile(userscript):
```

```
    with open(userscript) as f:
        exec(f.read())
```

In this case, the *.myapprc.py* user customization script, if present, has to deal only with `MyApp`-specific user customization tasks. This approach is better than relying on the `user` module, and works just as well in v3 as it does in v2.

Termination Functions

The `atexit` module lets you register termination functions (i.e., functions to be called at program termination, "last in, first out"). Termination functions are similar to clean-up handlers established by `try/finally` or `with`. However, termination functions are globally registered and get called at the end of the whole program, while clean-up handlers are established lexically and get called at the end of a specific `try` clause or `with` statement. Termination functions and clean-up handlers are called whether the program terminates normally or abnormally, but not when the program ends by calling `os._exit` (which is why you normally call `sys.exit` instead). The `atexit` module supplies a function called `register`:

Control Execution

register `register(`*`func`*`,*`*`args`*`,**`*`kwds`*`)`

Ensures that *`func`*`(*`*`args`*`,**`*`kwds`*`)` is called at program termination time.

Dynamic Execution and exec

Python's `exec` statement (built-in function, in v3) can execute code that you read, generate, or otherwise obtain during a program's run. `exec` dynamically executes a statement or a suite of statements. In v2, `exec` is a simple keyword statement with the following syntax:

```
exec code[ in globals[,locals]]
```

code can be a string, an open file-like object, or a code object. *`globals`* and *`locals`* are mappings. In v3, `exec` is a built-in function with the syntax:

```
exec(code, globals=None, locals=None)
```

code can be a string, bytes, or code object. *`globals`* is a dict; *`locals`*, any mapping.

If both *`globals`* are *`locals`* are present, they are the global and local namespaces in which *code* runs. If only *`globals`* is present, `exec` uses *`globals`* as both namespaces. If neither is present, *code* runs in the current scope.

Never run exec in the current scope

Running `exec` in the current scope is a very bad idea: it can bind, rebind, or unbind any global name. To keep things under control, use `exec`, if at all, only with specific, explicit dictionaries.

Avoiding exec

A frequently asked question about Python is "How do I set a variable whose name I just read or built?" Literally, for a *global* variable, exec allows this, but it's a bad idea. For example, if the name of the variable is in *varname*, you might think to use:

```
exec(varname + '= 23')
```

Don't do this. An exec like this in current scope makes you lose control of your namespace, leading to bugs that are extremely hard to find, and making your program unfathomably difficult to understand. Keep the "variables" that you need to set, not as variables, but as entries in a dictionary, say *mydict*. You could then use:

```
exec(varname+'=23', mydict)
```

While this is not quite as terrible as the previous example, it is *still* a bad idea. Keeping such "variables" as dictionary entries means that you don't have any need to use exec to set them. Just code:

```
mydict[varname] = 23
```

This way, your program is clearer, direct, elegant, and faster. There *are* some valid uses of exec, but they are extremely rare: just use explicit dictionaries instead.

Strive to avoid exec

Use exec only when it's really indispensable, which is *extremely* rare. Most often, it's best to avoid exec and choose more specific, well-controlled mechanisms: exec weakens your control of your code's namespace, can damage your program's performance, and exposes you to numerous hard-to-find bugs and huge security risks.

Expressions

exec can execute an expression, because any expression is also a valid statement (called an *expression statement*). However, Python ignores the value returned by an expression statement. To evaluate an expression and obtain the expression's value, see the built-in function eval, covered in Table 7-2.

Compile and Code Objects

To make a code object to use with exec, call the built-in function compile with the last argument set to 'exec' (as covered in Table 7-2).

A code object *c* exposes many interesting read-only attributes whose names all start with 'co_', such as:

co_argcount
: Number of parameters of the function of which *c* is the code (0 when *c* is not the code object of a function, but rather is built directly by compile)

co_code
: A bytestring with *c*'s bytecode

co_consts
: The tuple of constants used in *c*

co_filename
: The name of the file *c* was compiled from (the string that is the second argument to compile, when *c* was built that way)

co_firstlinenumber
: The initial line number (within the file named by co_filename) of the source code that was compiled to produce *c*, if *c* was built by compiling from a file

co_name
: The name of the function of which *c* is the code ('<module>' when *c* is not the code object of a function but rather is built directly by compile)

co_names
: The tuple of all identifiers used within *c*

co_varnames
: The tuple of local variables' identifiers in *c*, starting with parameter names

Control Execution

Most of these attributes are useful only for debugging purposes, but some may help advanced introspection, as exemplified later in this section.

If you start with a string that holds some statements, first use compile on the string, then call exec on the resulting code object—that's better than giving exec the string to compile and execute. This separation lets you check for syntax errors separately from execution-time errors. You can often arrange things so that the string is compiled once and the code object executes repeatedly, which speeds things up. eval can also benefit from such separation. Moreover, the compile step is intrinsically safe (both exec and eval are extremely risky if you execute them on code that you don't trust), and you may be able to perform some checks on the code object, before it executes, to lessen the risk (though never truly down to zero).

A code object has a read-only attribute co_names, which is the tuple of the names used in the code. For example, say that you want the user to enter an expression that contains only literal constants and operators—no function calls or other names. Before evaluating the expression, you can check that the string the user entered satisfies these constraints:

```
def safer_eval(s):
    code = compile(s, '<user-entered string>', 'eval')
    if code.co_names:
        raise ValueError('No names {!r} allowed in expression {!r}'
                         .format(code.co_names, s))
    return eval(code)
```

This function safer_eval evaluates the expression passed in as argument *s* only when the string is a syntactically valid expression (otherwise, compile raises SyntaxError) and contains no names at all (otherwise, safer_eval explicitly raises ValueError). (This is similar to the standard library function ast.literal_eval, covered in "Standard Input" on page 318, but a bit more powerful, since it does allow the use of operators.)

Knowing what names the code is about to access may sometimes help you optimize the preparation of the dictionary that you need to pass to exec or eval as the namespace. Since you need to provide values only for those names, you may save work by not preparing other entries. For example, say that your application dynamically accepts code from the user with the convention that variable names starting with *data_* refer to files residing in the subdirectory *data* that user-written code doesn't need to read explicitly. User-written code may in turn compute and leave results in global variables with names starting with *result_*, which your application writes back as files in subdirectory *data*. Thanks to this convention, you may later move the data elsewhere (e.g., to BLOBs in a database instead of files in a subdirectory), and user-written code won't be affected. Here's how you might implement these conventions efficiently (in v3; in v2, use exec user_code in datadict instead of exec(user_code, datadict)):

```
def exec_with_data(user_code_string):
    user_code = compile(user_code_string, '<user code>', 'exec')
    datadict = {}
    for name in user_code.co_names:
        if name.startswith('data_'):
            with open('data/{}'.format(name[5:]), 'rb') as datafile:
                datadict[name] = datafile.read()
    exec(user_code, datadict)
    for name in datadict:
        if name.startswith('result_'):
            with open('data/{}'.format(name[7:]), 'wb') as datafile:
                datafile.write(datadict[name])
```

Never exec or eval Untrusted Code

Old versions of Python tried to supply tools to ameliorate the risks of using exec and eval, under the heading of "restricted execution," but those tools were never entirely secure against the ingenuity of able hackers, and current versions of Python have therefore dropped them. If you need to ward against such attacks, take advantage of your operating system's protection mechanisms: run untrusted code in a separate process, with privileges as restricted as you can possibly make them (study the mechanisms that your OS supplies for the purpose, such as chroot, setuid, and jail), or run untrusted code in a separate, highly constrained virtual machine. To guard against "denial of service" attacks, have the main process monitor the separate one and terminate the latter if and when resource consumption becomes excessive. Processes are covered in "Running Other Programs" on page 424.

exec and eval are unsafe with untrusted code

The function `exec_with_data` is not at all safe against untrusted code: if you pass it, as the argument *`user_code_string`*, some string obtained in a way that you cannot *entirely* trust, there is essentially no limit to the amount of damage it might do. This is unfortunately true of just about any use of both `exec` and `eval`, except for those rare cases in which you can set very strict and checkable limits on the code to execute or evaluate, as was the case for the function `safer_eval`.

Internal Types

Some of the internal Python objects in this section are hard to use. Using such objects correctly and to good effect requires some study of your Python implementation's own C (or Java, or C#) sources. Such black magic is rarely needed, except to build general-purpose development tools, and similar wizardly tasks. Once you do understand things in depth, Python empowers you to exert control if and when needed. Since Python exposes many kinds of internal objects to your Python code, you can exert that control by coding in Python, even when an understanding of C (or Java, or C#) is needed to read Python's sources to understand what's going on.

Type Objects

The built-in type named `type` acts as a callable factory, returning objects that are types. Type objects don't have to support any special operations except equality comparison and representation as strings. However, most type objects are callable and return new instances of the type when called. In particular, built-in types such as `int`, `float`, `list`, `str`, `tuple`, `set`, and `dict` all work this way; specifically, when called without arguments, they return a new empty instance or, for numbers, one that equals `0`. The attributes of the `types` module are the built-in types, each with one or more names. For example, in v2, `types.DictType` and `types.DictionaryType` both refer to `type({})`, also known as `dict`. In v3, `types` only supplies names for built-in types that don't already have a built-in name, as covered in Chapter 7. Besides being callable to generate instances, many type objects are also useful because you can inherit from them, as covered in "Classes and Instances" on page 102.

The Code Object Type

Besides using the built-in function `compile`, you can get a code object via the `__code__` attribute of a function or method object. (For the attributes of code objects, see "Compile and Code Objects" on page 384.) Code objects are not callable, but you can rebind the `__code__` attribute of a function object with the right number of parameters in order to wrap a code object into callable form. For example:

```
def g(x): print('g', x)
code_object = g.__code__
def f(x): pass
f.__code__ = code_object
f(23)      # prints: g 23
```

Code objects that have no parameters can also be used with `exec` or `eval`. To create a new object, call the type object you want to instantiate. However, directly creating code objects requires many parameters; see Stack Overflow's nonofficial docs (*http://stackoverflow.com/questions/16064409/how-to-create-a-code-object-in-python*) on how to do it, but, almost always, you're better off calling `compile` instead.

The frame Type

The function `_getframe` in the module `sys` returns a frame object from Python's call stack. A frame object has attributes giving information about the code executing in the frame and the execution state. The modules `traceback` and `inspect` help you access and display such information, particularly when an exception is being handled. Chapter 16 provides more information about frames and tracebacks, and covers the module `inspect`, which is the best way to perform such introspection.

Garbage Collection

Python's garbage collection normally proceeds transparently and automatically, but you can choose to exert some direct control. The general principle is that Python collects each object *x* at some time after *x* becomes unreachable—that is, when no chain of references can reach *x* by starting from a local variable of a function instance that is executing, nor from a global variable of a loaded module. Normally, an object *x* becomes unreachable when there are no references at all to *x*. In addition, a group of objects can be unreachable when they reference each other but no global or local variables reference any of them, even indirectly (such a situation is known as a *mutual reference loop*).

Classic Python keeps with each object *x* a count, known as a *reference count*, of how many references to *x* are outstanding. When *x*'s reference count drops to `0`, CPython immediately collects *x*. The function `getrefcount` of the module `sys` accepts any object and returns its reference count (at least `1`, since `getrefcount` itself has a reference to the object it's examining). Other versions of Python, such as Jython or IronPython, rely on other garbage-collection mechanisms supplied by the platform they run on (e.g., the JVM or the MSCLR). The modules `gc` and `weakref` therefore apply only to CPython.

When Python garbage-collects *x* and there are no references at all to *x*, Python then finalizes *x* (i.e., calls `x.__del__()`) and makes the memory that *x* occupied available for other uses. If *x* held any references to other objects, Python removes the references, which in turn may make other objects collectable by leaving them unreachable.

The gc Module

The gc module exposes the functionality of Python's garbage collector. gc deals only with unreachable objects that are part of mutual reference loops. In such a loop, each object in the loop refers to others, keeping the reference counts of all objects positive. However, no outside references to any one of the set of mutually referencing objects exist any longer. Therefore, the whole group, also known as *cyclic garbage*, is unreachable, and therefore garbage-collectable. Looking for such cyclic garbage loops takes time, which is why the module gc exists: to help you control whether and when your program spends that time. The functionality of "cyclic garbage collection," by default, is enabled with some reasonable default parameters: however, by importing the gc module and calling its functions, you may choose to disable the functionality, change its parameters, and/or find out exactly what's going on in this respect.

gc exposes functions you can use to help you keep cyclic garbage-collection times under control. These functions can sometimes let you track down a memory leak—objects that are not getting collected even though there *should* be no more references to them—by helping you discover what other objects are in fact holding on to references to them:

Control Execution

collect `collect()`

Forces a full cyclic garbage collection run to happen immediately.

disable `disable()`

Suspends automatic, periodic cyclic garbage collection.

enable `enable()`

Reenables periodic cyclic garbage collection previously suspended with `disable`.

garbage A read-only attribute that lists the unreachable but uncollectable objects. This happens when any object in a cyclic garbage loop has a `__del__` special method, as there may be no demonstrably safe order for Python to finalize such objects.

get_debug `get_debug()`

Returns an `int` bit string, the garbage-collection debug flags set with `set_debug`.

get_objects `get_objects()`

Returns a list of all objects currently tracked by the cyclic garbage collector.

get_referrers `get_referrers(*objs)`

Returns a list of all container objects, currently tracked by the cyclic garbage collector, that refer to any one or more of the arguments.

get_threshold `get_threshold()`

Returns a three-item tuple `(`*`thresh0`*`, `*`thresh1`*`, `*`thresh2`*`)`, the garbage-collection thresholds set with `set_threshold`.

isenabled `isenabled()`

Returns `True` when cyclic garbage collection is currently enabled. Returns `False` when collection is currently disabled.

set_debug `set_debug(`*`flags`*`)`

Sets debugging flags for garbage collection. *`flags`* is an `int`, interpreted as a bit string, built by ORing (with the bitwise-OR operator `|`) zero or more constants supplied by the module `gc`:

`DEBUG_COLLECTABLE`

> Prints information on collectable objects found during collection

`DEBUG_INSTANCES`

> If `DEBUG_COLLECTABLE` or `DEBUG_UNCOLLECTABLE` is also set, prints information on objects found during collection that are instances of old-style classes (v2 only)

`DEBUG_LEAK`

> The set of debugging flags that make the garbage collector print all information that can help you diagnose memory leaks; same as the bitwise-OR of all other constants (except `DEBUG_STATS`, which serves a different purpose)

`DEBUG_OBJECTS`

> If `DEBUG_COLLECTABLE` or `DEBUG_UNCOLLECTABLE` is also set, prints information on objects found during collection that are not instances of old-style classes (v2 only)

`DEBUG_SAVEALL`

> Saves all collectable objects to the list `gc.garbage` (where uncollectable ones are also always saved) to help you diagnose leaks

`DEBUG_STATS`

> Prints statistics during collection to help you tune the thresholds

`DEBUG_UNCOLLECTABLE`

> Prints information on uncollectable objects found during collection

set_threshold `set_threshold(thresh0[,thresh1[,thresh2]])`

Sets thresholds that control how often cyclic garbage-collection cycles run. A *thresh0* of 0 disables garbage collection. Garbage collection is an advanced, specialized topic, and the details of the generational garbage-collection approach used in Python (and consequently the detailed meanings of these thresholds) are beyond the scope of this book; see the online docs (*https://docs.python.org/3/library/gc.html#gc.set_threshold*) for some details.

When you know there are no cyclic garbage loops in your program, or when you can't afford the delay of cyclic garbage collection at some crucial time, suspend automatic garbage collection by calling `gc.disable()`. You can enable collection again later by calling `gc.enable()`. You can test whether automatic collection is currently enabled by calling `gc.isenabled()`, which returns `True` or `False`. To control *when* time is spent collecting, you can call `gc.collect()` to force a full cyclic collection run to happen immediately. To wrap some time-critical code:

```
import gc
gc_was_enabled = gc.isenabled()
if gc_was_enabled:
    gc.collect()
    gc.disable()
# insert some time-critical code here
if gc_was_enabled:
    gc.enable()
```

Other functionality in the module `gc` is more advanced and rarely used, and can be grouped into two areas. The functions `get_threshold` and `set_threshold` and debug flag `DEBUG_STATS` help you fine-tune garbage collection to optimize your program's performance. The rest of `gc`'s functionality can help you diagnose memory leaks in your program. While `gc` itself can automatically fix many leaks (as long as you avoid defining `__del__` in your classes, since the existence of `__del__` can block cyclic garbage collection), your program runs faster if it avoids creating cyclic garbage in the first place.

The weakref Module

Careful design can often avoid reference loops. However, at times you need objects to know about each other, and avoiding mutual references would distort and complicate your design. For example, a container has references to its items, yet it can often be useful for an object to know about a container holding it. The result is a reference loop: due to the mutual references, the container and items keep each other alive, even when all other objects forget about them. Weak references solve this problem by allowing objects to reference others without keeping them alive.

A *weak reference* is a special object *w* that refers to some other object *x* without incrementing *x*'s reference count. When *x*'s reference count goes down to `0`, Python finalizes and collects *x*, then informs *w* of *x*'s demise. Weak reference *w* can now either disappear or get marked as invalid in a controlled way. At any time, a given *w* refers to either the same object *x* as when *w* was created, or to nothing at all; a weak reference is never retargeted. Not all types of objects support being the target *x* of a weak reference *w*, but classes, instances, and functions do.

The `weakref` module exposes functions and types to create and manage weak references:

getweakrefcount `getweakrefcount(x)`

Returns `len(getweakrefs(x))`.

getweakrefs `getweakrefs(x)`

Returns a list of all weak references and proxies whose target is *x*.

proxy `proxy(x[,f])`

Returns a weak proxy *p* of type `ProxyType` (`CallableProxyType` when *x* is callable) with object *x* as the target. In most contexts, using *p* is just like using *x*, except that when you use *p* after *x* has been deleted, Python raises `ReferenceError`. *p* is not hashable (thus, you cannot use *p* as a dictionary key), even when *x* is. When *f* is present, it must be callable with one argument and is the finalization callback for *p* (i.e., right before finalizing *x*, Python calls `f(p)`). *f* executes right *after* *x* is no longer reachable from *p*.

ref `ref(x[,f])`

Returns a weak reference *w* of type `ReferenceType` with object *x* as the target. *w* is callable without arguments: calling `w()` returns *x* when *x* is still alive; otherwise, `w()` returns `None`. *w* is hashable when *x* is hashable. You can compare weak references for equality (==, !=), but not for order (<, >, <=, >=). Two weak references *x* and *y* are equal when their targets are alive and equal, or when `x is y`. When *f* is present, it must be callable with one argument and is the finalization callback for *w* (i.e., right before finalizing *x*, Python calls `f(w)`). *f* executes right *after* *x* is no longer reachable from *w*.

WeakKeyDictionary `class WeakKeyDictionary(adict={})`

A `WeakKeyDictionary` *d* is a mapping weakly referencing its keys. When the reference count of a key *k* in *d* goes to `0`, item `d[k]` disappears. *adict* is used to initialize the mapping.

WeakValueDictionary `class WeakValueDictionary(adict={})`

A `WeakValueDictionary` *d* is a mapping weakly referencing its values. When the reference count of a value *v* in *d* goes to `0`, all items of *d* such that `d[k] is v` disappear. *adict* is used to initialize the mapping.

`WeakKeyDictionary` lets you noninvasively associate additional data with some hashable objects, with no change to the objects. `WeakValueDictionary` lets you noninvasively record transient associations between objects, and build caches. In each case, use a weak mapping, rather than a `dict`, to ensure that an object that is otherwise garbage-collectable is not kept alive just by being used in a mapping.

A typical example is a class that keeps track of its instances, but does not keep them alive just in order to keep track of them:

```
import weakref
class Tracking(object):
    _instances_dict = weakref.WeakValueDictionary()
    def __init__(self):
        Tracking._instances_dict[id(self)] = self
    @classmethod
    def instances(cls): return cls._instances_dict.values()
```

14
Threads and Processes

A *thread* is a flow of control that shares global state (memory) with other threads; all threads appear to execute simultaneously, although they are usually "taking turns" on a single processor/core. Threads are not easy to master, and multithreaded programs are often hard to test, and to debug; however, as covered in "Use Threading, Multiprocessing, or async Programming?" on page 396, when used appropriately, multithreading may sometimes improve program performance in comparison to traditional "single-threaded" programming. This chapter covers the facilities that Python provides for dealing with threads, including the `threading`, `queue`, and `concurrent` modules.

A *process* is an instance of a running program. The operating system protects processes from one another. Processes that want to communicate must explicitly arrange to do so via *inter-process communication* (IPC) mechanisms. Processes may communicate via files (covered in Chapter 10) and databases (covered in Chapter 11). The general way in which processes communicate using data storage mechanisms, such as files and databases, is that one process writes data, and another process later reads that data back. This chapter covers the Python standard library modules `subprocess` and `multiprocessing`; the process-related parts of the module `os`, including simple IPC by means of *pipes*; and a cross-platform IPC mechanism known as *memory-mapped files*, which is supplied to Python programs by the module `mmap`.

Network mechanisms are well suited for IPC, as they work between processes that run on different nodes of a network, not just between ones that run on the same node. `multiprocessing` supplies some mechanisms that are suitable for IPC over a network; Chapter 17 covers low-level network mechanisms that provide a basis for IPC. Other, higher-level mechanisms, known as *distributed computing*, such as

CORBA, DCOM/COM+, EJB, SOAP, XML-RPC, and .NET, can make IPC easier, whether locally or remotely. We do not cover distributed computing in this book.

Use Threading, Multiprocessing, or async Programming?

In many cases, the best answer is "none of the above." Each of these approaches can just, at best, be an optimization, and (as covered in "Optimization" on page 479) optimization is often unneeded or premature. Each approach can be prone to bugs, hard to test, hard to debug; if you can, stick with single-threading.

When you do need optimization and your program is *I/O bound* (meaning that it spends much time doing I/O), *async* programming (covered in Chapter 18) is fastest, as long as you can make your I/O operations *nonblocking* ones. When your I/O absolutely *has* to be blocking, the `threading` module can help an I/O bound program's performance.

When your program is *CPU bound* (meaning that it spends much time performing computations), then, in CPython, `threading` usually does not help performance. This is because CPython uses a *Global Interpreter Lock* (GIL), so that only one Python-coded thread at a time executes; this also applies to PyPy. Jython, and IronPython, however, don't use a GIL. A C-coded extension can "drop the GIL" while it's doing a time-consuming operation; in particular, NumPy (covered in "NumPy" on page 449) does so for array operations. As a consequence, if your program is CPU bound via calls to lengthy CPU operations in NumPy, or other similarly optimized C-coded extension, the `threading` module may help your program's performance on a multi-processor or multicore computer.

When your program is CPU bound via pure Python code, and you use CPython or PyPy on a multiprocessor or multicore computer, the `multiprocessing` module may help performance. This is particularly true when you can arrange to run your program in parallel on multiple computers, ideally ones connected by very fast networking; however, in this case, you're better off using approaches and packages discussed on the Python wiki (*https://wiki.python.org/moin/ParallelProcessing*), which we don't cover in this book.

Threads in Python

Python offers multithreading on platforms that support threads, such as Win32, Linux, and other variants of Unix. An action is known as *atomic* when it's guaranteed that no thread switching occurs between the start and the end of the action. In practice, in CPython, operations that *look* atomic (e.g., simple assignments and accesses) mostly *are* atomic, when executed on built-in types (augmented and multiple assignments, however, aren't atomic). Mostly, though, it's *not* a good idea to rely on atomicity. You might be dealing with an instance of a user-coded class rather than of a built-in type, so there might be implicit calls to Python code, making assumptions of atomicity unwarranted. Relying on implementation-dependent atomicity may lock your code into a specific implementation, hampering future upgrades. You're better off using the synchronization facilities covered in the rest of this chapter, rather than relying on atomicity assumptions.

Python offers multithreading in two flavors. An older and lower-level module, `_thread` (named `thread` in v2), has low-level functionality and is not recommended for direct use in your code; we do not cover `_thread` in this book. The higher-level module `threading`, built on top of `_thread`, is the recommended one. The key design issue in multithreading systems is how best to coordinate multiple threads. `threading` supplies several synchronization objects. Alternatively, the `queue` module is very useful for thread synchronization, as it supplies synchronized, thread-safe queue types, handy for communication and coordination between threads. The package `concurrent`, covered after `multiprocessing`, supplies a unified interface for communication and coordination that can be implemented by pools of either threads or processes.

The threading Module

The `threading` module supplies multithreading functionality. The approach of `threading` is similar to Java's, but locks and conditions are modeled as separate objects (in Java, such functionality is part of every object), and threads cannot be directly controlled from the outside (thus, no priorities, groups, destruction, or stopping). All methods of objects supplied by `threading` are atomic.

`threading` supplies classes dealing with threads: `Thread`, `Condition`, `Event`, `Lock`, `RLock`, `Semaphore`, `BoundedSemaphore`, and `Timer` (and, in v3 only, `Barrier`). `threading` also supplies functions, including:

active_count `active_count()`

Returns an `int`, the number of `Thread` objects currently alive (not ones that have terminated or not yet started).

current_thread `current_thread()`

Returns a `Thread` object for the calling thread. If the calling thread was not created by `threading`, `current_thread` creates and returns a semi-dummy `Thread` object with limited functionality.

enumerate `enumerate()`

Returns a `list` of all `Thread` objects currently alive (not ones that have terminated or not yet started).

stack_size `stack_size([size])`

Returns the stack size, in bytes, used for new threads; `0` means "the system's default." When you pass *`size`*, that's what going to be used for new threads created afterward (on platforms that allow setting threads' stack size); acceptable values for *`size`* are subject to platform-specific constraints, such as being at least `32768` (or an even higher minimum, on some platforms) and (on some platforms) being a multiple of `4096`. Passing *`size`* as `0` is always acceptable and means "use the system's default." When you pass a value for *`size`* that is not acceptable on the current platform, `stack_size` raises a `ValueError` exception.

Thread Objects

A `Thread` instance *t* models a thread. You can pass a function to be used as *t*'s main function as an argument when you create *t*, or you can subclass `Thread` and override the `run` method (you may also override `__init__` but should not override other methods). *t* is not yet ready to run when you create it; to make *t* ready (active), call `t.start()`. Once *t* is active, it terminates when its main function ends, either normally or by propagating an exception. A `Thread` *t* can be a *daemon*, meaning that Python can terminate even if *t* is still active, while a normal (nondaemon) thread keeps Python alive until the thread terminates. The `Thread` class supplies the following constructor, properties, and methods:

Thread `class Thread(name=None,target=None,args=(),kwargs={})`

Always call `Thread` with named arguments: the number and order of parameters may change in the future, but the parameter names are guaranteed to stay. When you instantiate the class `Thread` itself, pass *`target`*: `t.run` calls *`target(*args,**kwargs)`*. When you extend `Thread` and override `run`, don't pass *`target`*. In either case, execution doesn't begin until you call `t.start()`. *name* is *t*'s name. If *name* is None, `Thread` generates a unique name for *t*. If a subclass *T* of `Thread` overrides `__init__`, *T*`.__init__` *must* call `Thread.__init__` on `self` before any other `Thread` method.

daemon `t.daemon`

`daemon` is a property, `True` when *t* is a daemon (i.e., the process can terminate even when *t* is still active; such a termination also ends *t*); otherwise, `daemon` is `False`. Initially, *t* is a daemon if and only if the thread that creates *t* is a daemon. You can assign to `t.daemon` only before `t.start`; assigning to `t.daemon` sets *t* to be a daemon if, and only if, you assign a true value.

is_alive `t.is_alive()`

Returns `True` when *t* is active (i.e., when `t.start` has executed and `t.run` has not yet terminated). Otherwise, `is_alive` returns `False`.

name `t.name`

`name` is a property returning *t*'s name; assigning `name` rebinds *t*'s name (`name` exists to help you debug; `name` need not be unique among threads).

join `t.join(timeout=None)`

Suspends the calling thread (which must not be *t*) until *t* terminates (when *t* is already terminated, the calling thread does not suspend). *`timeout`* is covered in "Timeout parameters" on page 399. You can call `t.join` only after `t.start`. It's OK to call `join` more than once.

run `t.run()`

`run` is the method that executes *t*'s main function. Subclasses of `Thread` can override `run`. Unless overridden, `run` calls the *`target`* callable passed on *t*'s creation. Do *not* call `t.run` directly; calling `t.run` is the job of `t.start`!

start `t.start()`

`start` makes *t* active and arranges for `t.run` to execute in a separate thread. You must call `t.start` only once for any given thread object *t*; if you call it again, it raises an exception.

Thread Synchronization Objects

The `threading` module supplies several synchronization primitives, types that let threads communicate and coordinate. Each primitive type has specialized uses.

You may not need thread synchronization primitives

As long as you avoid having nonqueue global variables that change, and which several threads access, `queue` (covered in "The queue Module" on page 406) can often provide all the coordination you need, and so can `concurrent` (covered in "The concurrent.futures Module" on page 417). "Threaded Program Architecture" on page 420 shows how to use `Queue` objects to give your multithreaded programs simple and effective architectures, often without needing any explicit use of synchronization primitives.

Timeout parameters

The synchronization primitives `Condition` and `Event` supply `wait` methods that accept an optional *`timeout`* argument. A `Thread` object's `join` method also accepts an optional *`timeout`* argument, as do the `acquire` methods of locks. A *`timeout`* argument can be `None` (the default) to obtain normal blocking behavior (the calling thread suspends and waits until the desired condition is met). When it is not `None`, a *`timeout`* argument is a floating-point value that indicates an interval of time in seconds (*`timeout`* can have a fractional part, so it can indicate any time interval, even a very short one). If *`timeout`* seconds elapse, the calling thread becomes ready again, even if the desired condition has not been met; in this case, the waiting method returns `False` (otherwise, the method returns `True`). *`timeout`* lets you design systems that are able to overcome occasional anomalies in a few threads, and thus are more robust. However, using *`timeout`* may slow your program down: when that matters, be sure to measure your code's speed accurately.

Lock and RLock objects

`Lock` and `RLock` objects supply the same three methods. Here are the signatures and the semantics for an instance *`L`* of `Lock`:

acquire *`L`*`.acquire(`*`blocking`*`=True)`

When *`blocking`* is `True`, `acquire` locks *`L`*. When *`L`* is already locked, the calling thread suspends and waits until *`L`* is unlocked, then locks *`L`*. Even when the calling thread was the one that last locked *`L`*, it still suspends and waits until another thread releases *`L`*. When *`blocking`* is `False` and *`L`* is unlocked, `acquire` locks *`L`* and returns `True`. When *`blocking`* is `False` and *`L`* is locked, `acquire` does not affect *`L`* and returns `False`.

locked *`L`*`.locked()`

Returns `True` when *`L`* is locked; otherwise, returns `False`.

release *`L`*`.release()`

Unlocks *`L`*, which must be locked. When *`L`* is locked, any thread may call *`L`*`.release`, not just the thread that locked *`L`*. When more than one thread is blocked on *`L`* (i.e., has called *`L`*`.acquire`, found *`L`* locked, and is waiting for *`L`* to be unlocked), `release` wakes up an arbitrary waiting thread. The thread calling `release` does not suspend: it stays ready and continues to execute.

The semantics of an `RLock` object *`r`* are often more convenient (except in peculiar architectures where you need other threads to be able to release locks that a different thread has acquired). `RLock` is a *re-entrant* lock, meaning that, when *`r`* is locked, it keeps track of the *owning* thread (i.e., the thread that locked it—which, for an `RLock`, is also the only thread that can release it). The owning thread can call *`r`*`.acquire` again without blocking; *`r`* then just increments an internal count. In a similar situation involving a `Lock` object, the thread would block until some other thread releases the lock. For example, consider the following code snippet:

```
lock = threading.RLock()
global_state = []
def recursive_function(some, args):
    with lock:  # acquires lock, guarantees release at end
        ...modify global_state...
        if more_changes_needed(global_state):
            recursive_function(other, args)
```

If *`lock`* was an instance of `threading.Lock`, *`recursive_function`* would block its calling thread when it calls itself recursively: the `with` statement, finding that the lock has already been acquired (even though that was done by the same thread), would block and wait...and wait... With a `threading.RLock`, no such problem occurs: in this case, since the lock has already been acquired *by the same thread*, on getting acquired again it just increments its internal count and proceeds.

An `RLock` object *r* is unlocked only when it's been released as many times as it has been acquired. An `RLock` is useful to ensure exclusive access to an object when the object's methods call each other; each method can acquire at the start, and release at the end, the same `RLock` instance. `try/finally` (covered in "try/finally" on page 152) is one way to ensure that a lock is indeed released. A `with` statement, covered in "The with Statement" on page 82, is usually better: all locks, conditions, and semaphores are context managers, so an instance of any of these types can be used directly in a `with` clause to `acquire` it (implicitly with blocking) and ensure it's `released` at the end of the `with` block.

Condition objects

A `Condition` object *c* wraps a `Lock` or `RLock` object *L*. The class `Condition` exposes the following constructor and methods:

Condition `class Condition(lock=None)`

Creates and returns a new `Condition` object *c* with the lock *L* set to *lock*. If *lock* is None, *L* is set to a newly created `RLock` object.

acquire, release `c.acquire(blocking=1) c.release()`

These methods just call *L*'s corresponding methods. A thread must never call any other method on *c* unless the thread holds lock *L*.

notify, notify_all `c.notify() c.notify_all()`

`notify` wakes up one of the threads waiting on *c*. The calling thread must hold *L* before it calls `c.notify()`, and `notify` does not release *L*. The woken-up thread does not become ready until it can acquire *L* again. Therefore, the calling thread normally calls `release` after calling `notify`. `notify_all` is like `notify` but wakes up all waiting threads, not just one.

wait `c.wait(timeout=None)`

`wait` releases *L*, and then suspends the calling thread until some other thread calls `notify` or `notify_all` on *c*. The calling thread must hold *L* before it calls `c.wait()`. *`timeout`* is covered in "Timeout parameters" on page 399. After a thread wakes up, either by notification or timeout, the thread becomes ready when it acquires *L* again. When `wait` returns `True` (meaning it has exited normally, not by timeout), the calling thread always holds *L* again.

Usually, a `Condition` object *c* regulates access to some global state *s* shared among threads. When a thread must wait for *s* to change, the thread loops:

```
with c:
    while not is_ok_state(s):
        c.wait()
    do_some_work_using_state(s)
```

Meanwhile, each thread that modifies *s* calls `notify` (or `notify_all` if it needs to wake up all waiting threads, not just one) each time *s* changes:

```
with c:
    do_something_that_modifies_state(s)
    c.notify()    # or, c.notify_all()
# no need to call c.release(), exiting `with` intrinsically does
```

You always need to acquire and release *c* around each use of *c*'s methods: doing so via a `with` statement makes using `Condition` instances less error-prone.

Event objects

Event objects let any number of threads suspend and wait. All threads waiting on `Event` object *e* become ready when any other thread calls `e.set()`. *e* has a flag that records whether the event happened; it is initially `False` when *e* is created. `Event` is thus a bit like a simplified `Condition`. Event objects are useful to signal one-shot changes, but brittle for more general use; in particular, relying on calls to `e.clear()` is error-prone. The `Event` class exposes the following methods:

Event `class Event()`

Creates and returns a new `Event` object *e*, with *e*'s flag set to `False`.

clear `e.clear()`

Sets *e*'s flag to `False`.

is_set `e.is_set()`

Returns the value of *e*'s flag, `True` or `False`.

set `e.set()`

Sets *e*'s flag to `True`. All threads waiting on *e*, if any, become ready to run.

wait `e.wait(timeout=None)`

If *e*'s flag is `True`, `wait` returns immediately. Otherwise, `wait` suspends the calling thread until some other thread calls `set`. *`timeout`* is covered in "Timeout parameters" on page 399.

Semaphore objects

Semaphores (also known as *counting semaphores*) are a generalization of locks. The state of a `Lock` can be seen as `True` or `False`; the state of a `Semaphore` *s* is a number between `0` and some *n* set when *s* is created (both bounds included). Semaphores can be useful to manage a fixed pool of resources (e.g., 4 printers or 20 sockets), although it's often more robust to use `Queues` for such purposes. The class `BoundedSemaphore` is very similar, but raises `ValueError` if the state ever becomes higher than the initial value: in many cases, such behavior can be a useful indicator of a coding bug.

Semaphore
BoundedSemaphore

`class Semaphore(`*`n`*`=1) class BoundedSemaphore(`*`n`*`=1)`

`Semaphore` creates and returns a semaphore object *s* with the state set to *n*; `BoundedSemaphore` is very similar, except that *s*`.release()` raises `ValueError` if the state becomes higher than *n*. A semaphore object *s* exposes the following methods:

acquire *s*`.acquire(`*`blocking`*`=True)`

When *s*'s state is >`0`, `acquire` decrements the state by `1` and returns `True`. When *s*'s state is `0` and *`blocking`* is `True`, `acquire` suspends the calling thread and waits until some other thread calls *s*`.release`. When *s*'s state is `0` and *`blocking`* is `False`, `acquire` immediately returns `False`.

release *s*`.release()`

When *s*'s state is >`0`, or when the state is `0` but no thread is waiting on *s*, `release` increments the state by `1`. When *s*'s state is `0` and some threads are waiting on *s*, `release` leaves *s*'s state at `0` and wakes up an arbitrary one of the waiting threads. The thread that calls `release` does not suspend; it remains ready and continues to execute normally.

Threads and Processes

Timer objects

A `Timer` object calls a specified callable, in a newly made thread, after a given delay. The class `Timer` exposes the following constructor and methods:

Timer `class Timer(`*`interval,callable,args=(),kwargs={}`*`)`

Makes an object *t*, which calls *`callable`*, *`interval`* seconds after starting (*`interval`* is a floating-point number and can include a fractional part).

cancel `cancel()`

t`.cancel()` stops the timer and cancels the execution of its action, as long as *t* is still waiting (hasn't called its callable yet) when you call `cancel`.

start `start()`

t`.start()` starts *t*.

Timer extends Thread and adds the attributes function, interval, args, and kwargs.

A Timer is "one-shot"—*t* calls its callable only once. To call *callable* periodically, every *interval* seconds, here's a simple recipe:

```
class Periodic(threading.Timer):
  def __init__(self, interval, callable, args=(), kwargs={}):
    self.callable = callable
    threading.Timer.__init__(self, interval, self._f, args, kwargs)

  def _f(self, *args, **kwargs):
    Periodic(self.interval, self.callable, args, kwargs).start()
    self.callable(*args, **kwargs)
```

Barrier objects (v3 only)

A Barrier is a synchronization primitive allowing a certain number of threads to wait until they've all reached a certain point in their execution, before all of them resume. Specifically, when a thread calls *b*.wait(), it blocks until the specified number of threads have done the same call on *b*; at that time, all the threads blocked on *b* are released.

The class Barrier exposes the following constructor, methods, and properties:

Barrier `class Barrier(num_threads, action=None, timeout=None)`

action is callable without arguments: if you pass this argument, it executes on any single one of the blocked threads when they are all unblocked. *timeout* is covered in "Timeout parameters" on page 399.

abort `abort()`

b.abort() puts Barrier *b* in the *broken state*, meaning that any thread currently waiting resumes with a threading.BrokenBarrierException (the same exception also gets raised on any subsequent call to *b*.wait()). This is an emergency action typically used when a waiting thread is suffering some abnormal termination, to avoid deadlocking the whole program.

broken `broken`

True when *b* is in the broken state; otherwise, False.

n_waiting `n_waiting`

Number of threads currently waiting on *b*.

parties `parties`

The value passed as *num_threads* in the constructor of *b*.

reset `reset()`

Returns *b* to the initial, empty, nonbroken state; any thread currently waiting on *b*, however, resumes with a `threading.BrokenBarrierException`.

wait `wait()`

The first `b.parties-1` threads calling `b.wait()` block; when the number of threads blocked on *b* is `b.parties-1` and one more thread calls `b.wait()`, all the threads blocked on *b* resume. `b.wait()` returns an `int` to each resuming thread, all distinct and in `range(b.parties)`, in unspecified order; threads can use this return value to determine which one should do what next (though passing *`action`* in the `Barrier`'s constructor is simpler and often sufficient).

`threading.Barrier` exists only in v3; in v2, you could implement it yourself, as shown, for example, on Stack Overflow (*http://stackoverflow.com/questions/26622745/implementing-barrier-in-python2-7*).

Thread Local Storage

The `threading` module supplies the class `local`, which a thread can use to obtain *thread-local storage* (TLS), also known as *per-thread data*. An instance *`L`* of `local` has arbitrary named attributes that you can set and get, and stores them in a dictionary *`L`*`.__dict__` that you can also access. *`L`* is fully thread-safe, meaning there is no problem if multiple threads simultaneously set and get attributes on *`L`*. Most important, each thread that accesses *`L`* sees a disjoint set of attributes, and any changes made in one thread have no effect in other threads. For example:

```
import threading
L = threading.local()
print('in main thread, setting zop to 42')
L.zop = 42
def targ():
  print('in subthread, setting zop to 23')
  L.zop = 23
  print('in subthread, zop is now', L.zop)
t = threading.Thread(target=targ)
t.start()
t.join()
print('in main thread, zop is now', L.zop)
# prints:
# in main thread, setting zop to 42
# in subthread, setting zop to 23
# in subthread, zop is now 23
# in main thread, zop is now 42
```

TLS makes it easier to write code meant to run in multiple threads, since you can use the same namespace (an instance of `threading.local`) in multiple threads without the separate threads interfering with each other.

Threads and Processes

The queue Module

The queue module (named `Queue` in v2) supplies queue types supporting multi-thread access, with one main class, two subclasses, and two exception classes:

Queue

`class Queue(maxsize=0)`

`Queue`, the main class for module `queue`, implements a *First-In, First-Out* (*FIFO*) queue (the item retrieved each time is the one that was added earliest), and is covered in "Methods of Queue Instances" on page 406.

When *maxsize* is `>0`, the new `Queue` instance *q* is considered full when *q* has *maxsize* items. A thread inserting an item with the *block* option, when *q* is full, suspends until another thread extracts an item. When *maxsize* is `<=0`, *q* is never considered full, and is limited in size only by available memory, like normal Python containers.

LifoQueue

`class LifoQueue(maxsize=0)`

`LifoQueue` is a subclass of `Queue`; the only difference is that `LifoQueue` is *Last-In, First-Out* (*LIFO*), which means the item retrieved each time is the one that was added most recently.

PriorityQueue

`class PriorityQueue(maxsize=0)`

`PriorityQueue` is a subclass of `Queue`; the only difference is that `PriorityQueue` implements a *priority* queue—the item retrieved each time is the smallest one currently in the queue. As there's no *key=* argument, you generally use, as queue items, pairs `(priority, payload)`, with low values of *priority* meaning earlier retrieval.

Empty

`Empty` is the exception that `q.get(False)` raises when *q* is empty.

Full

`Full` is the exception that `q.put(x,False)` raises when *q* is full.

Methods of Queue Instances

An instance *q* of the class `Queue` (or either of its subclasses) supplies the following methods, all thread-safe and guaranteed to be atomic:

empty

`q.empty()`

Returns `True` if *q* is empty; otherwise, `False`.

full

`q.full()`

Returns `True` if *q* is full; otherwise, `False`.

get, get_nowait

`q.get(block=True, timeout=None)`

When *block* is `False`, `get` removes and returns an item from *q* if one is available; otherwise, `get` raises `Empty`. When *block* is `True` and *timeout* is `None`, `get` removes and returns an item from *q*, suspending the calling thread, if need be, until an item is available. When *block* is `True` and *timeout* is not `None`, *timeout* must be a number `>=0` (which may include a fractional part to specify a fraction of a second), and `get` waits for no longer than *timeout* seconds (if no item is yet available by then, `get` raises `Empty`). `q.get_nowait()` is like `q.get(False)`, which is also like `q.get(timeout=0.0)`. `get` removes and returns items in the same order as `put` inserted them (FIFO), if *q* is a direct instance of `Queue` itself; LIFO, if *q* is an instance of `LifoQueue`; smallest-first, if *q* is an instance of `PriorityQueue`.

put, put_nowait

`q.put(item,block=True, timeout=None)`

When *block* is `False`, `put` adds *item* to *q* if *q* is not full; otherwise, `put` raises `Full`. When *block* is `True` and *timeout* is `None`, `put` adds *item* to *q*, suspending the calling thread, if need be, until *q* is not full. When *block* is `True` and *timeout* is not `None`, *timeout* must be a number `>=0` (which may include a fractional part to specify a fraction of a second), and `put` waits for no longer than *timeout* seconds (if *q* is still full by then, `put` raises `Full`). `q.put_nowait(item)` is like `q.put(item,False)`, also like `q.put(item,timeout=0.0)`.

qsize

`q.qsize()`

Returns the number of items that are currently in *q*.

Threads and Processes

Moreover, *q* maintains an internal, hidden count of *unfinished tasks*, which starts at zero. Each call to `get` increments the count by one. To decrement the count by one, when a worker thread has finished processing a task, it calls `q.task_done()`. To synchronize on "all tasks done," call `q.join()`: `join` continues the calling thread when the count of unfinished tasks is zero; when the count is nonzero, `q.join()` blocks the calling thread, and unblocks later, when the count goes to zero.

You don't have to use `join` and `task_done` if you prefer to coordinate threads in other ways, but `join` and `task_done` do provide a simple, useful approach to coordinate systems of threads using a `Queue`.

`Queue` offers a good example of the idiom "It's easier to ask forgiveness than permission" (EAFP), covered in "Error-Checking Strategies" on page 166. Due to multithreading, each nonmutating method of *q* (`empty`, `full`, `qsize`) can only be advisory. When some other thread executes and mutates *q*, things can change between the instant a thread gets the information from a nonmutating method and the very next moment, when the thread acts on the information. Relying on the "look before you leap" (LBYL) idiom is therefore futile, and fiddling with locks to try to fix things is a substantial waste of effort. Just avoid fragile LBYL code, such as:

```
if q.empty():
    print('no work to perform')
else:
    x = q.get_nowait()
    work_on(x)
```

and instead use the simpler and more robust EAFP approach:

```
try:
    x = q.get_nowait()
except queue.Empty:
    print('no work to perform')
else:
    work_on(x)
```

The multiprocessing Module

The `multiprocessing` module supplies functions and classes you can use to code pretty much as you would for multithreading, but distributing work across processes, rather than across threads: the class `Process` (similar to `threading.Thread`) and classes for synchronization primitives (`BoundedSemaphore`, `Condition`, `Event`, `Lock`, `RLock`, `Semaphore`, and, in v3 only, `Barrier`—each similar to the class with the same names in module `threading`; also, `Queue`, and `JoinableQueue`, both similar to `queue.Queue`). These classes make it easy to take code written to use `threading`, and make a version that uses `multiprocessing` instead; you just need to pay attention to the differences we cover in "Differences Between Multiprocessing and Threading" on page 409.

It's usually best to avoid sharing state among processes: use queues, instead, to explicitly pass messages among them. However, for those occasions in which you do need to share some state, `multiprocessing` supplies classes to access shared memory (`Value` and `Array`), and—more flexibly (including coordination among different computers on a network) though with more overhead—a `Process` subclass, `Manager`, designed to hold arbitrary data and let other processes manipulate that data via *proxy* objects. We cover state sharing in "Sharing State: Classes Value, Array, and Manager" on page 410.

When you're writing new multiprocessing code, rather than porting code originally written to use `threading`, you can often use different approaches supplied by `multiprocessing`. The `Pool` class, in particular, can often simplify your code. We cover `Pool` in "Multiprocessing Pool" on page 414.

Other advanced approaches, based on `Connection` objects built by the `Pipe` factory function or wrapped in `Client` and `Listener` objects, are, on the other hand, more flexible, but potentially more complex; we do not cover them further in this book. For more thorough coverage of `multiprocessing`, refer to the online docs (*https://docs.python.org/3/library/multiprocessing.html*) and to good third-party online tutorials (*https://pymotw.com/2/multiprocessing/index.html*).

Differences Between Multiprocessing and Threading

You can port code written to use `threading` into a variant using `multiprocessing` instead—however, there are differences you must consider.

Structural differences

All objects that you exchange between processes (for example, via a queue, or an argument to a `Process`'s *`target`* function) are serialized via `pickle`, covered in "The pickle and cPickle Modules" on page 341. Therefore, you can exchange only objects that can be thus serialized. Moreover, the serialized bytestring cannot exceed about 32 MB (depending on the platform), or else an exception gets raised; therefore, there are limits to the size of objects you can exchange.

Especially in Windows, child processes *must* be able to import as a module the main script that's spawning them. Therefore, be sure to guard all top-level code in the main script (meaning code that must not be executed again by child processes) with the usual `if __name__ == '__main__'` idiom, covered in "The Main Program" on page 180.

If a process is abruptly killed (for example, via a signal) while using a queue, or holding a synchronization primitive, it won't be able to perform proper cleanup on that queue or primitive. As a result, that queue or primitive may get corrupted, causing errors in all other processes trying to use it.

The Process class The class `multiprocessing.Process` is very similar to `threading.Thread`, but, in addition to all of `Thread`'s attributes and methods, it supplies a few more:

authkey `authkey`

The process's authorization key, a bytestring: initialized to random bytes supplied by `os.urandom()`, but you can reassign it later if you wish. Used in the authorization handshake for advanced uses we do not cover in this book.

exitcode `exitcode`

None when the process has not exited yet; otherwise, the process's exit code: an `int`, `0` for success, `>0` for failure, `<0` when the process was killed.

pid `pid`

None when the process has not started yet; otherwise, the process's identifier as set by the operating system.

terminate `terminate()`

Kills the process (without giving it a chance to execute termination code, such as cleanup of queues and synchronization primitives; beware of the likelihood of causing errors when the process is using a queue or holding a primitive).

Differences in queues

The class `multiprocessing.Queue` is very similar to `queue.Queue`, except that an instance *q* of `multiprocessing.Queue` does *not* supply the methods `join` and `task_done`. When methods of *q* raise exceptions due to time-outs, they raise instances of `queue.Empty` or `queue.Full`. `multiprocessing` has no equivalents to `queue`'s `LifoQueue` and `PriorityQueue` classes.

The class `multiprocessing.JoinableQueue` does supply the methods `join` and `task_done`, but with a semantic difference compared to `queue.Queue`: with an instance *q* of `multiprocessing.JoinableQueue`, the process that calls *q*`.get` *must* call *q*`.task_done` when it's done processing that unit of work (it's not optional, as it would be when using `queue.Queue`).

All objects you `put` in multiprocessing queues must be serializable by `pickle`. There may be a small delay between the time you execute `q.put` and the time the object is available from `q.get`. Lastly, remember that an abrupt exit (crash or signal) of a process using *q* may leave *q* unusable for any other process.

Differences in synchronization primitives

In the `multiprocessing` module, the `acquire` method of the synchronization primitive classes `BoundedSemaphore`, `Lock`, `RLock`, and `Semaphore` has the signature `acquire(`*block*`=True,` *timeout*`=None)`; `timeout`'s semantics are covered in "Timeout parameters" on page 399.

Sharing State: Classes Value, Array, and Manager

To use shared memory to hold a single primitive value in common among two or more processes, `multiprocessing` supplies the class `Value`; for a fixed-length array of primitive values, the class `Array`. For more flexibility (including nonprimitive values, and "sharing" among different systems joined by a network but sharing no memory) at the cost of higher overhead, `multiprocessing` supplies the class `Manager`, which is a subclass of `Process`.

The Value class

The constructor for the class `Value` has the signature:

Value `Value(*typecode*, **args*, lock=True)`

typecode is a string defining the primitive type of the value, just like for module `array`, as covered in Table 15-3. (Alternatively, *typecode* can be a type from the module `ctypes`, mentioned in "ctypes" on page 682, but this is rarely necessary.) *args* is passed on to the type's constructor: therefore, *args* is either absent (in which case the primitive is initialized as per its default, typically `0`) or a single value, which is used to initialize the primitive.

When `lock` is `True` (the default), `Value` makes and uses a new lock to guard the instance. Alternatively, you can pass as `lock` an existing `Lock` or `RLock` instance. You can even pass `lock=False`, but that is rarely advisable: when you do, the instance is not guarded (thus, it is not synchronized among processes) and is missing the method `get_lock`. If you do pass `lock`, you *must* pass it as a named argument, using `lock=*something*`.

An instance *v* of the class `Value` supplies the following attributes and methods:

get_lock `get_lock()`

Returns (but neither acquires nor releases) the lock guarding *v*.

value `value`

A read/write attribute, used to set and get *v*'s underlying primitive value.

To ensure atomicity of operations on *v*'s underlying primitive value, guard the operation in a `with *v*.get_lock():` statement. A typical example of such usage might be for augmented assignment, as in:

```
with v.get_lock():
    v.value += 1
```

If any other process does an unguarded operation on that same primitive value, however, even an atomic one such as a simple assignment like `*v*.value = *x*`, "all bets are off": the guarded operation and the unguarded one can get your system into a *race condition*. Play it safe: if any operation at all on `*v*.value` is not atomic (and thus needs to be guarded by being within a `with *v*.get_lock():` block), guard *all* operations on `*v*.value` by placing them within such blocks.

The Array class

The constructor for the class `Array` has the signature:

Array `Array(typecode, size_or_initializer, lock=True)`

A fixed-length array of primitive values (all items being of the same primitive type).

typecode is a string defining the primitive type of the value, just like for the module `array`, as covered in Table 15-3. (Alternatively, *typecode* can be a type from the module `ctypes`, mentioned in "ctypes" on page 682, but this is rarely necessary.) *size_or_initializer* can be an iterable, used to initialize the array; alternatively, it can be an integer, used as the length of the array (in this case, each item of the array is initialized to `0`).

When `lock` is `True` (the default), `Array` makes and uses a new lock to guard the instance. Alternatively, you can pass as `lock` an existing `Lock` or `RLock` instance. You can even pass `lock=False`, but that is rarely advisable: when you do, the instance is not guarded (thus it is not synchronized among processes) and is missing the method `get_lock`. If you do pass `lock`, you *must* pass it as a named argument, using `lock=something`.

An instance *a* of the class `Array` supplies the following method:

get_lock `get_lock()`

Returns (but neither acquires nor releases) the lock guarding *a*.

a is accessed by indexing and slicing, and modified by assigning to an indexing or to a slice. *a* is fixed-length: therefore, when you assign to a slice, you must assign an iterable of the same length as the slice you're assigning to. *a* is also iterable.

In the special case where *a* was built with *typecode* `'c'`, you can also access `a.value` to get *a*'s contents as a bytestring, and you can assign to `a.value` any bytestring no longer than `len(a)`. When *s* is a bytestring with `len(s)<len(a)`, `a.value = s` means `a[:len(s)+1] = s+b'\0'`; this mirrors the representation of `char` strings in the C language, terminated with a `0` byte. For example:

```
a = multiprocessing.Array('c', b'four score and seven')
a.value = b'five'
print(a.value)   # prints b'five'
print(a[:])      # prints b'five\x00score and seven'
```

The Manager class

`multiprocessing.Manager` is a subclass of `multiprocessing.Process`, with the same methods and attributes. In addition, it supplies methods to build an instance of any of the multiprocessing synchronization primitives, plus `Queue`, `dict`, `list`, and `Namespace`, the latter being a class that just lets you set and get arbitrary named attributes. Each of the methods has the name of the class whose instances it builds, and returns a *proxy* to such an instance, which any process can use to call methods (including special methods, such as indexing of instances of `dict` or `list`) on the instance held in the manager process.

Proxy objects pass most operators, and accesses to methods and attributes, on to the instance they proxy for; however, they don't pass on *comparison* operators—if you need a comparison, you need to take a local copy of the proxied object. For example:

```
p = some_manager.list()
p[:] = [1, 2, 3]
print(p == [1, 2, 3])        # prints False, as it compares with p
print(list(p) == [1, 2, 3])  # prints True, as it compares with copy
```

The constructor of `Manager` takes no arguments. There are advanced ways to customize `Manager` subclasses to allow connections from unrelated processes (including ones on different computers connected via a network) and to supply a different set of building methods, but we do not cover them in this book. Rather, one simple, often-sufficient approach to using `Manager` is to explicitly transfer to other processes the proxies it produces, typically via queues, or as arguments to a `Process`'s *`target`* function.

For example, suppose there's a long-running, CPU-bound function *f* that, given a string as an argument, eventually returns a corresponding result; given a `set` of strings, we want to produce a `dict` with the strings as keys and the corresponding results as values. To be able to follow on which processes *f* runs, we also `print` the process ID just before calling *f*. Here's one way to do it:

Threads and Processes

Example 14-1.

```
import multiprocessing as mp

def f(s):
    """Run a long time, and eventually return a result."""
    import time, random
    time.sleep(random.random()*2)  # simulate slowness
    return s+s  # some computation or other

def runner(s, d):
    print(os.getpid())
    d[s] = f(s)

def make_dict(set_of_strings):
    mgr = mp.Manager()
    d = mgr.dict()
    workers = []
    for s in set_of_strings:
        p = mp.Process(target=runner, args=(s, d))
        p.start()
        workers.append(p)
```

```
    for p in workers:
        p.join()
    return dict(d)
```

Multiprocessing Pool

In real life, beware of creating an unbounded number of worker processes, as we just did in Example 14-1. Performance benefits accrue only up to the number of cores in your machine (available by calling `multiprocessing.cpu_count()`), or a number just below or just above this, depending on such minutiae as your platform and other load on your computer. Making more worker processes than such an optimal number incurs substantial extra overhead to no good purpose.

As a consequence, it's a common design pattern to start a *pool* with a limited number of worker processes, and farm out work to them. The class `multiprocessing.Pool` handles the orchestration of this design pattern on your behalf.

The Pool class

The constructor for the class `Pool` has the signature:

Pool `Pool(`*`processes`*`=None,` *`initializer`*`=None,` *`initargs`*`=(),` *`maxtasksperchild`*`=None)`

Builds and returns an instance *p* of `Pool`. *`processes`* is the number of processes in the pool; it defaults to the value returned by `cpu_count()`. When *`initializer`* is not `None`, it's a function, called at the start of each process in the pool, with *`initargs`* as arguments, like *`initializer`*`(*`*`initargs`*`)`.

When *`maxtasksperchild`* is not `None`, it's the maximum number of tasks executed in each process in the pool. When a process in the pool has executed that many tasks, it terminates, and a new process starts and joins the pool. When *`maxtasksperchild`* is `None` (the default), processes live as long as the pool.

An instance *p* of the class `Pool` supplies the following methods (all of them must be called only in the process that built instance *p*):

apply `apply(`*`func`*`,` *`args`*`=(),` *`kwds`*`={})`

In an arbitrary one of the worker processes, runs *`func`*`(*`*`args`*`, **`*`kwds`*`)`, waits for it to finish, and returns *func*'s result.

apply_async `apply_async(func, args=(), kwds={}, callback=None)`

In an arbitrary one of the worker processes, starts running `func(*args, **kwds)`, and, without waiting for it to finish, immediately returns an `AsyncResult` (see "The AsyncResult class" on page 416) instance, which eventually gives *func*'s result, when that result is ready. When *callback* is not `None`, it's a function called (in a separate thread in the process that calls `apply_async`), with *func*'s result as the only argument, when that result is ready; *callback* should execute rapidly, or otherwise it blocks the process. *callback* may mutate its argument if that argument is mutable; *callback*'s return value is irrelevant.

close `close()`

No more tasks can be submitted to the pool. Worker processes terminate when they're done with all outstanding tasks.

imap `imap(func, iterable, chunksize=1)`

Returns an iterator calling *func* on each item of *iterable*, in order. *chunksize* determines how many consecutive items are sent to each process; on a very long *iterable*, a large *chunksize* can improve performance. When *chunksize* is `1` (the default), the returned iterator has a method `next` (even on v3, where the canonical name of the iterator's method is `__next__`), which optionally accepts a *timeout* argument (a floating-point value in seconds), and raises `multiprocessing.TimeoutError` should the result not yet be ready after *timeout* seconds.

imap_unordered `imap_unordered(func, iterable, chunksize=1)`

Same as `imap`, but the ordering of the results is arbitrary (this can sometimes improve performance, when you don't care about the order the results are iterated on).

join `join()`

Waits for all worker processes to exit. You must call `close` or `terminate` before you call `join`.

map `map(func, iterable, chunksize=1)`

Calls *func* on each item of *iterable*, in order, in worker processes in the pool; waits for them all to finish, and returns the list of results. *chunksize* determines how many consecutive items are sent to each process; on a very long *iterable*, a large *chunksize* can improve performance.

map_async `map_async(func, iterable, chunksize=1, callback=None)`

Arranges for *func* to be called on each item of *iterable* in worker processes in the pool; without waiting for any of this to finish, immediately returns an `AsyncResult` (see "The AsyncResult class" on page 416) instance, which eventually gives the list of *func*'s results, when that list is ready.

When *callback* is not `None`, it's a function and gets called (in a separate thread in the process that calls `map_async`) with the list of *func*'s results, in order, as the only argument, when that list is ready; *callback* should execute rapidly, or otherwise it blocks the process. *callback* may mutate its list argument; *callback*'s return value is irrelevant.

terminate `terminate()`

Terminates all worker processes immediately, without waiting for them to complete work.

For example, here's a `Pool`-based approach to perform the same task as in Example 14-1:

```
import multiprocessing as mp

def f(s):
    """Run a long time, and eventually return a result."""
    import time, random
    time.sleep(random.random()*2)  # simulate slowness
    return s+s  # some computation or other

def runner(s):
    print(os.getpid())
    return s, f(s)

def make_dict(set_of_strings):
    with mp.Pool() as pool:
        d = dict(pool.imap_unordered(runner, set_of_strings))
        return d
```

The AsyncResult class

The methods `apply_async` and `map_async` of the class `Pool` return an instance of the class `AsyncResult`. An instance *r* of the class `AsyncResult` supplies the following methods:

get `get(timeout=None)`

Blocks and returns the result when ready, or re-raises the exception raised while computing the result. When *timeout* is not `None`, it's a floating-point value in seconds; `get` raises `multiprocessing.TimeoutError` should the result not yet be ready after *timeout* seconds.

ready `ready()`

Does not block; returns `True` if the result is ready; otherwise, returns `False`.

successful `successful()`

Does not block: returns `True` if the result is ready and the computation did not raise an exception; returns `False` if the computation raised an exception. If the result is not yet ready, `successful` raises `AssertionError`.

wait `wait(`*`timeout`*`=None)`

Blocks and waits until the result is ready. When *`timeout`* is not None, it's a `float` in seconds: `wait` raises `multiprocessing.TimeoutError` should the result not yet be ready after *`timeout`* seconds.

The concurrent.futures Module

The `concurrent` package supplies a single module, `futures`. `concurrent.futures` is in the standard library only in v3; to use it in v2, download and install the backport (*https://pypi.python.org/pypi/futures*) with **`pip2 install futures`** (or, equivalently, **`python2 -m pip install futures`**).

Threads and Processes

`concurrent.futures` supplies two classes, `ThreadPoolExecutor` (using threads as workers) and `ProcessPoolExecutor` (using processes as workers), which implement the same abstract interface, `Executor`. Instantiate either kind of pool by calling the class with one argument, *`max_workers`*, specifying how many threads or processes the pool should contain. You can omit *`max_workers`* to let the system pick the number of workers (except that you have to explicitly specify *`max_workers`* to instantiate `ThreadPoolExecutor` for the v2 backport, only).

An instance *`e`* of an `Executor` class supports the following methods:

map `map(`*`func, *iterables, timeout`*`=None)`

Returns an iterator *`it`* whose items are the results of *`func`* called with one argument from each of the *`iterables`*, in order (using multiple worker threads or processes to execute *`func`* in parallel). When *`timeout`* is not None, it's a `float` number of seconds: should `next(`*`it`*`)` not produce any result in *`timeout`* seconds, raises `concurrent.futures.TimeoutError`.

In v3 only, you may specify (by name) argument *`chunksize`*: ignored for a `ThreadPoolExecutor`, for a `ProcessPoolExecutor` it sets how many items of each iterable in *`iterables`* are passed to each worker process.

shutdown `shutdown(`*`wait`*`=True)`

No more calls to `map` or `submit` allowed. When *`wait`* is `True`, `shutdown` blocks until all pending futures are done; when `False`, *`shutdown`* returns immediately. In either case, the process does not terminate until all pending futures are done.

submit `submit(func, *a, **k)`

Ensures *func(*a, **k)* executes on an arbitrary one of the pool's processes or threads. Does not block, but rather returns a `Future` instance.

Any instance of an `Executor` is also a context manager, and therefore suitable for use on a `with` statement (`__exit__` being like `shutdown(wait=True)`).

For example, here's a `concurrent`-based approach to perform the same task as in Example 14-1:

```
import concurrent.futures as cf

def f(s):
    """run a long time and eventually return a result"""
    ...

def runner(s):
    return s, f(s)

def make_dict(set_of_strings):
    with cf.ProcessPoolExecutor() as e:
        d = dict(e.map(runner, set_of_strings))
    return d
```

The `submit` method of an `Executor` returns a `Future` instance. A `Future` instance *f* supplies the methods described in Table 14-1.

Table 14-1.

add_done_callback	`add_done_callback(func)` Add callable *func* to *f*; *func* is called, with *f* as the only argument, when *f* completes (i.e., is cancelled or finishes).
cancel	`cancel()` Tries cancelling the call; returns `False` when the call is being executed and cannot be cancelled; otherwise, returns `True`.
cancelled	`cancelled()` Returns `True` when the call was successfully cancelled; otherwise, returns `False`.
done	`done()` Returns True when the call is completed (i.e., is finished or succesfully cancelled).

exception `exception(timeout=None)`

Returns the exception raised by the call, or None if the call raised no exception. When *timeout* is not None, it's a float number of seconds to wait; if the call hasn't completed after *timeout* seconds, raises concurrent.futures.TimeoutError; if the call is cancelled, raises concurrent.futures.CancelledError.

result `result(timeout=None)`

Returns the call's result. When *timeout* is not None, it's a float number of seconds; if the call hasn't completed after *timeout* seconds, raises concurrent.futures.TimeoutError; if the call is cancelled, raises concurrent.futures.CancelledError.

running `running()`

Returns True when the call is executing and cannot be cancelled.

The concurrent.futures module also supplies two functions:

as_completed `as_completed(fs, timeout=None)`

Returns an iterator *it* over the Future instances that are the items of iterator *fs*. If there are duplicates in *fs*, each is only yielded once. *it* yields one completed future at a time, as they complete; if *timeout* is not None, it's a float number of seconds, and—should it ever happen that no new future can be yielded after *timeout* seconds from the previous one—as_completed raises concurrent.futures.Timeout.

wait `wait(fs, timeout=None, return_when=ALL_COMPLETED)`

Waits for the Future instances that are the items of iterator *fs*. Returns a named 2-tuple of sets: the first set, named done, contains the futures that completed (meaning that they either finished or were cancelled) before wait returned. The second set, named not_done, contains yet-uncompleted futures.

timeout, if not None, is a float number of seconds, the maximum time wait lets elapse before returning (when *timeout* is None, wait returns only when *return_when* is satisfied, no matter the elapsed time before that happens).

return_when controls when, exactly, wait returns; it must be one of three constants supplied by module concurrent.futures:

ALL_COMPLETED

Return when all futures finish or are cancelled

FIRST_COMPLETED

Return when any future finishes or is cancelled

FIRST_EXCEPTION

Return when any future raises an exception; should no future raise an exception, becomes equivalent to ALL_COMPLETED

Threaded Program Architecture

A threaded program should always try to arrange for a *single* thread to deal with any given object or subsystem that is external to the program (such as a file, a database, a GUI, or a network connection). Having multiple threads that deal with the same external object is possible, but can often cause gnarly problems.

When your threaded program must deal with some external object, devote a thread to such dealings, using a Queue object from which the external-interfacing thread gets work requests that other threads post. The external-interfacing thread can return results by putting them on one or more other Queue objects. The following example shows how to package this architecture into a general, reusable class, assuming that each unit of work on the external subsystem can be represented by a callable object. (In examples, remember: in v2, the module queue is spelled Queue; the class Queue in that module is spelled with an uppercase Q in both v2 and v3).

```
import threading, queue
class ExternalInterfacing(threading.Thread):
    def __init__(self, external_callable, **kwds):
        threading.Thread.__init__(self, **kwds)  # could use `super`
        self.daemon = True
        self.external_callable = external_callable
        self.work_request_queue = queue.Queue()
        self.result_queue = queue.Queue()
        self.start()
    def request(self, *args, **kwds):
        """called by other threads as external_callable would be"""
        self.work_request_queue.put((args,kwds))
        return self.result_queue.get()
    def run(self):
        while True:
            a, k = self.work_request_queue.get()
            self.result_queue.put(self.external_callable(*a, **k))
```

Once some ExternalInterfacing object *ei* is instantiated, any other thread may call *ei*.request just as it would call *external_callable* without such a mechanism (with or without arguments as appropriate). The advantage of the ExternalInterfacing mechanism is that all calls upon *external_callable* are serialized. This means they are performed by just one thread (the thread object bound to *ei*) in some defined sequential order, without overlap, race conditions (hard-to-debug errors that depend on which thread happens to get there first), or other anomalies that might otherwise result.

If several callables need to be serialized together, you can pass the callable as part of the work request, rather than passing it at the initialization of the class ExternalIn terfacing, for greater generality. The following example shows this more general approach:

```
import threading, queue
class Serializer(threading.Thread):
    def __init__(self, **kwds):
        threading.Thread.__init__(self, **kwds)  # could use `super`
        self.daemon = True
        self.work_request_queue = queue.Queue()
        self.result_queue = queue.Queue()
        self.start()
    def apply(self, callable, *args, **kwds):
        """called by other threads as callable would be"""
        self.work_request_queue.put((callable, args, kwds))
        return self.result_queue.get()
    def run(self):
        while True:
            callable, args, kwds = self.work_request_queue.get()
            self.result_queue.put(callable(*args, **kwds))
```

Once a Serializer object *ser* has been instantiated, any other thread may call *ser*.apply(*external_callable*) just as it would call *external_callable* without such a mechanism (with or without further arguments as appropriate). The Serial izer mechanism has the same advantages as ExternalInterfacing, except that all calls to the same or different callables wrapped by a single *ser* instance are now serialized.

The user interface of the whole program is an external subsystem, and thus should be dealt with by a single thread—specifically, the main thread of the program (this is mandatory for some user interface toolkits, and advisable even when not mandatory). A Serializer thread is therefore inappropriate. Rather, the program's main thread should deal only with user-interface issues, and farm out actual work to worker threads that accept work requests on a Queue object and return results on another. A set of worker threads is generally known as a *thread pool*. As shown in the following example, all worker threads should share a single queue of requests and a single queue of results, since the main thread is the only one to post work requests and harvest results:

```
import threading
class Worker(threading.Thread):
    IDlock = threading.Lock()
    request_ID = 0
    def __init__(self, requests_queue, results_queue, **kwds):
        threading.Thread.__init__(self, **kwds)
        self.daemon = True
        self.work_request_queue = requests_queue
        self.result_queue = results_queue
        self.start()
    def perform_work(self, callable, *args, **kwds):
```

Threads and Processes

```
        """called by main thread as callable would be, but w/o return"""
        with self.IDlock:
            Worker.request_ID += 1
            self.work_request_queue.put(
                (Worker.request_ID, callable, args, kwds))
            return Worker.request_ID
    def run(self):
        while True:
            request_ID, callable, a, k = self.work_request_queue.get()
            self.result_queue.put((request_ID, callable(*a, **k)))
```

The main thread creates the two queues, and then instantiates worker threads as follows:

```
import queue
requests_queue = queue.Queue()
results_queue = queue.Queue()
for i in range(number_of_workers):
    worker = Worker(requests_queue, results_queue)
```

Whenever the main thread needs to farm out work (execute some callable object that may take substantial elapsed time to produce results), the main thread calls *`worker`*`.perform_work(`*`callable`*`)` , much as it would call *`callable`* without such a mechanism (with or without further arguments as appropriate). However, `perform_work` does not return the result of the call. Instead of the results, the main thread gets an *`id`* that identifies the work request. If the main thread needs the results, it can keep track of that *`id`*, since the request's results are tagged with that *`id`* when they appear. The advantage of this mechanism is that the main thread does not block waiting for the callable's lengthy execution to complete, but rather becomes ready again at once and can immediately return to its main business of dealing with the user interface.

The main thread must arrange to check the `results_queue`, since the result of each work request eventually appears there, tagged with the request's *`id`*, when the worker thread that took that request from the queue finishes computing the result. How the main thread arranges to check for both user interface events and the results coming back from worker threads onto the results queue depends on what user interface toolkit is used or—if the user interface is text-based—on the platform on which the program runs.

A widely applicable, though not always optimal, general strategy is for the main thread to *poll* (check the state of the results queue periodically). On most Unix-like platforms, the function `alarm` of the module `signal` allows polling. The `Tkinter` GUI toolkit supplies method `after`, which is usable for polling. Some toolkits and platforms afford more effective strategies (letting a worker thread alert the main thread when it places some result on the results queue), but there is no generally available, cross-platform, cross-toolkit way to arrange for this. Therefore, the following artificial example ignores user interface events and just simulates work by evaluating random expressions, with random delays, on several worker threads, thus completing the previous example:

```
import random, time
def make_work():
    return '{} {} {}'.format(random.randrange(2,10),
        random.choice(('+', '-', '*', '/', '%', '**')),
        random.randrange(2,10))
def slow_evaluate(expression_string):
    time.sleep(random.randrange(1,5))
    return eval(expression_string)
workRequests = {}
def showResults():
    while True:
        try: id, results = results_queue.get_nowait()
        except queue.Empty: return
        print('Result {}: {} -> {}'.format(
            id, work_requests[id], results))
        del work_requests[id]
for i in range(10):
    expression_string = make_work()
    id = worker.perform_work(slow_evaluate, expression_string)
    work_requests[id] = expression_string
    print('Submitted request {}: {}'.format(id, expression_string))
    time.sleep(1)
    showResults()
while work_requests:
    time.sleep(1)
    showResults()
```

Threads and Processes

Process Environment

The operating system supplies each process *P* with an *environment*, a set of variables whose names are strings (most often, by convention, uppercase identifiers) and whose contents are strings. In "Environment Variables" on page 26, we cover environment variables that affect Python's operations. Operating system shells offer ways to examine and modify the environment via shell commands and other means mentioned in "Environment Variables" on page 26.

Process environments are self-contained

The environment of any process *P* is determined when *P* starts. After startup, only *P* itself can change *P*'s environment. Changes to *P*'s environment affect only *P* itself: the environment is *not* a means of inter-process communication (IPC). Nothing that *P* does affects the environment of *P*'s parent process (the process that started *P*), nor of those of child processes *previously* started from *P* and now running, nor of processes unrelated to *P*. Child processes of *P* normally get a copy of *P*'s environment as their starting environment. In this narrow sense, changes to *P*'s environment do affect child processes that *P* starts *after* such changes.

The module os supplies the attribute environ, a mapping that represents the current process's environment. os.environ is initialized from the process environment when Python starts. Changes to os.environ update the current process's environment if the platform supports such updates. Keys and values in os.environ must be strings. On Windows (but not on Unix-like platforms), keys into os.environ are implicitly uppercased. For example, here's how to try to determine which shell or command processor you're running under:

```
import os
shell = os.environ.get('COMSPEC')
if shell is None: shell = os.environ.get('SHELL')
if shell is None: shell = 'an unknown command processor'
print('Running under', shell)
```

When a Python program changes its environment (e.g., via os.environ['X']='Y'), this does not affect the environment of the shell or command processor that started the program. As already explained—and for all programming languages including Python—changes to a process's environment affect only the process itself, not other processes that are currently running.

Running Other Programs

You can run other programs via functions in the os module or (at a higher and usually preferable level of abstraction) with the subprocess module.

Running Other Programs with the os Module

The best way for your program to run other processes is usually with the subprocess module, covered in "The Subprocess Module" on page 426. However, the os module also offers several ways to do this, which, in some rare cases, may be simpler.

The simplest way to run another program is through the function os.system, although this offers no way to control the external program. The os module also provides a number of functions whose names start with exec. These functions offer fine-grained control. A program run by one of the exec functions replaces the current program (i.e., the Python interpreter) in the same process. In practice, therefore, you use the exec functions mostly on platforms that let a process duplicate itself by fork (i.e., Unix-like platforms). os functions whose names start with spawn and popen offer intermediate simplicity and power: they are cross-platform and not quite as simple as system, but simple and usable enough for many purposes.

The exec and spawn functions run a given executable file, given the executable file's path, arguments to pass to it, and optionally an environment mapping. The system and popen functions execute a command, which is a string passed to a new instance of the platform's default shell (typically */bin/sh* on Unix, *cmd.exe* on Windows). A *command* is a more general concept than an *executable file*, as it can include shell functionality (pipes, redirection, built-in shell commands) using the shell syntax specific to the current platform. os provides the following functions:

execl, execle, execlp, execv, execve, execvp, execvpe

`execl(`*`path`*`,*`*`args`*`) execle(`*`path`*`,*`*`args`*`) execlp(`*`path`*`,*`*`args`*`) execv(`*`path`*`,`*`args`*`) execve(`*`path`*`,`*`args`*`,`*`env`*`) execvp(`*`path`*`,`*`args`*`) execvpe(`*`path`*`,`*`args`*`,`*`env`*`)`

These functions run the executable file (program) indicated by string *path*, replacing the current program (i.e., the Python interpreter) in the current process. The distinctions encoded in the function names (after the prefix exec) control three aspects of how the new program is found and run:

- Does *path* have to be a complete path to the program's executable file, or can the function accept a name as the *path* argument and search for the executable in several directories, as operating system shells do? `execlp`, `execvp`, and `execvpe` can accept a *path* argument that is just a filename rather than a complete path. In this case, the functions search for an executable file of that name along the directories listed in `os.environ['PATH']`. The other functions require *path* to be a complete path to the executable file for the new program.
- Are arguments for the new program accepted as a single sequence argument *args* to the function or as separate arguments to the function? Functions whose names start with `execv` take a single argument *args* that is the sequence of the arguments to use for the new program. Functions whose names start with `execl` take the new program's arguments as separate arguments (`execle`, in particular, uses its last argument as the environment for the new program).
- Is the new program's environment accepted as an explicit mapping argument *env* to the function, or is `os.environ` implicitly used? `execle`, `execve`, and `execvpe` take an argument *env* that is a mapping to use as the new program's environment (keys and values must be strings), while the other functions use `os.environ` for this purpose.

Each `exec` function uses the first item in *args* as the name under which the new program is told it's running (for example, `argv[0]` in a C program's `main`); only *args*`[1:]` are arguments proper to the new program.

popen

`popen(`*`cmd`*`,`*`mode`*`='r',`*`buffering`*`=-1)`

Runs the string command *cmd* in a new process *P* and returns a file-like object *f* that wraps a pipe to *P*'s standard input or from *P*'s standard output (depending on *mode*). *mode* and *buffering* have the same meaning as for Python's open function, covered in "Creating a "file" Object with io.open" on page 274. When *mode* is `'r'` (the default), *f* is read-only and wraps *P*'s standard output. When mode is `'w'`, *f* is write-only and wraps *P*'s standard input.

The key difference of *f* with respect to other file-like objects is the behavior of method *f*`.close`. *f*`.close()` waits for *P* to terminate and returns None, as `close` methods of file-like objects normally do, when *P*'s termination is successful. However, if the operating system associates an integer error code *c* with *P*'s termination, indicating that *P*'s termination was unsuccessful, *f*.close() returns *c*. On Windows systems, c is a signed integer return code from the child process.

spawnv, spawnve spawnv(*mode*,*path*,*args*) spawnve(*mode*,*path*,*args*,*env*)

These functions run the program indicated by *path* in a new process *P*, with the arguments passed as sequence *args*. spawnve uses mapping *env* as *P*'s environment (both keys and values must be strings), while spawnv uses os.environ for this purpose. On Unix-like platforms only, there are other variations of os.spawn, corresponding to variations of os.exec, but spawnv and spawnve are the only two that also exist on Windows.

mode must be one of two attributes supplied by the os module: os.P_WAIT indicates that the calling process waits until the new process terminates, while os.P_NOWAIT indicates that the calling process continues executing simultaneously with the new process. When *mode* is os.P_WAIT, the function returns the termination code *c* of *P*: 0 indicates successful termination, *c* less than 0 indicates *P* was killed by a *signal*, and *c* greater than 0 indicates normal but unsuccessful termination. When *mode* is os.P_NOWAIT, the function returns *P*'s process ID (or on Windows, *P*'s process handle). There is no cross-platform way to use *P*'s ID or handle; platform-specific ways (not covered further in this book) include the function os.waitpid on Unix-like platforms and third-party extension package PyWin32 (*https://pypi.python.org/pypi/pywin32*) on Windows.

For example, your interactive program can give the user a chance to edit a text file that your program is about to read and use. You must have previously determined the full path to the user's favorite text editor, such as *c:\\windows\\notepad.exe* on Windows or */usr/bin/vim* on a Unix-like platform. Say that this path string is bound to variable *editor* and the path of the text file you want to let the user edit is bound to *textfile*:

```
import os
os.spawnv(os.P_WAIT, editor, [editor, textfile])
```

The first item of the argument *args* is passed to the program being spawned as "the name under which the program is being invoked." Most programs don't look at this, so you can usually place just about any string here. Just in case the editor program does look at this special first argument, passing the same string *editor* that is used as the second argument to os.spawnv is the simplest and most effective approach.

system system(*cmd*)

Runs the string command *cmd* in a new process and returns 0 when the new process terminates successfully. When the new process terminates unsuccessfully, system returns an integer error code not equal to 0. (Exactly what error codes may be returned depends on the command you're running: there's no widely accepted standard for this.)

Note that popen is deprecated in v2 (although it was never removed), then reimplemented in v3 as a simple wrapper over subprocess.Popen.

The Subprocess Module

The subprocess module supplies one very broad class: Popen, which supports many diverse ways for your program to run another program.

Popen `class Popen(args, bufsize=0, executable=None, stdin=None, stdout=None, stderr=None, preexec_fn=None, close_fds=False, shell=False, cwd=None, env=None, universal_newlines=False, startupinfo=None, creationflags=0)`

Popen starts a subprocess to run a distinct program, and creates and returns an object *p*, representing that subprocess. The *args* mandatory argument and the many optional named arguments control details of how the subprocess is to run.

When any exception occurs during the subprocess creation (before the distinct program starts), `Popen` re-raises that exception in the calling process with the addition of an attribute named `child_traceback`, which is the Python traceback object for the subprocess. Such an exception would normally be an instance of `OSError` (or possibly `TypeError` or `ValueError` to indicate that you've passed to `Popen` an argument that's invalid in type or value).

What to run, and how: args, executable, shell

args is a sequence (normally a list) of strings: the first item is the path to the program to execute, and the following items, if any, are arguments to pass to the program (*args* can also be just a string, when you don't need to pass arguments). *executable*, when not `None`, overrides *args* in determining which program to execute. When *shell* is true, *executable* specifies which shell to use to run the subprocess; when *shell* is true and *executable* is `None`, the shell used is */bin/sh* on Unix-like systems (on Windows, it's `os.environ['COMSPEC']`).

Threads and Processes

Subprocess files: stdin, stdout, stderr, bufsize, universal_newlines, close_fds

stdin, *stdout*, and *stderr* specify the subprocess's standard input, output, and error files, respectively. Each may be `PIPE`, which creates a new pipe to/from the subprocess; `None`, meaning that the subprocess is to use the same file as this ("parent") process; or a file object (or file descriptor) that's already suitably open (for reading, for the standard input; for writing, for the standard output and standard error). *stderr* may also be `STDOUT`, meaning that the subprocess's standard error must use the same file as its standard output. *bufsize* controls the buffering of these files (unless they're already open), with the same semantics as the same argument to the `open` function covered in "Creating a "file" Object with io.open" on page 274 (the default, `0`, means "unbuffered"). When *universal_newlines* is true, *stdout* and *stderr* (unless they're already open) are opened in "universal newlines" (`'rU'`) mode, covered in "mode" on page 274. When *close_fds* is true, all other files (apart from standard input, output, and error) are closed in the subprocess before the subprocess's program or shell is executed.

Other arguments: preexec_fn, cwd, env, startupinfo, creationflags

When *preexec_fn* is not `None`, it must be a function or other callable object, and gets called in the subprocess before the subprocess's program or shell is executed (only on Unix-like system, where the call happens after `fork` and before `exec`).

When *cwd* is not `None`, it must be a string that gives the path to an existing directory; the current directory gets changed to *cwd* in the subprocess before the subprocess's program or shell is executed.

When *env* is not `None`, it must be a mapping (normally a dictionary) with strings as both keys and values, and fully defines the environment for the new process.

startupinfo and *creationflags* are Windows-only arguments passed to the `CreateProcess` Win32 API call used to create the subprocess, for Windows-specific purposes (they are not covered further in this book, which focuses on cross-platform uses of Python).

Attributes of subprocess.Popen instances

An instance *p* of class `Popen` supplies the following attributes:

`args`
: (v3 only) `Popen`'s *args* argument (string or sequence of strings).

`pid`
: The process ID of the subprocess.

`returncode`
: `None` to indicate that the subprocess has not yet exited; otherwise, an integer: `0` for successful termination, `>0` for termination with an error code, or `<0` if the subprocess was killed by a signal.

`stderr`, `stdin`, `stdout`
: When the corresponding argument to `Popen` was `subprocess.PIPE`, each of these attributes is a file object wrapping the corresponding pipe; otherwise, each of these attributes is `None`. Use the `communicate` method of *p*, not reading and writing to/from these file objects, to avoid possible deadlocks.

Methods of subprocess.Popen instances

An instance *p* of class `Popen` supplies the following methods.

communicate `p.communicate(input=None)`

Sends the string *input* as the subprocess's standard input (when *input* is not `None`), then reads the subprocess's standard output and error files into in-memory strings *so* and *se* until both files are finished, and finally waits for the subprocess to terminate and returns a pair (two-item tuple) `(so, se)`. In v3, also accepts an optional *timeout* argument.

poll `p.poll()`

Checks if the subprocess has terminated, then returns `p.returncode`.

wait `p.wait()`

Waits for the subprocess to terminate, then returns `p.returncode`. In v3, also accepts an optional *`timeout`* argument.

The mmap Module

The `mmap` module supplies memory-mapped file objects. An `mmap` object behaves similarly to a bytestring, so you can often pass an `mmap` object where a bytestring is expected. However, there are differences:

- An `mmap` object does not supply the methods of a string object.
- An `mmap` object is mutable, while string objects are immutable.
- An `mmap` object also corresponds to an open file and behaves polymorphically to a Python file object (as covered in "File-Like Objects and Polymorphism" on page 278).

An `mmap` object *`m`* can be indexed or sliced, yielding bytestrings. Since *`m`* is mutable, you can also assign to an indexing or slicing of *`m`*. However, when you assign to a slice of *`m`*, the righthand side of the assignment statement must be a bytestring of exactly the same length as the slice you're assigning to. Therefore, many of the useful tricks available with list slice assignment (covered in "Modifying a list" on page 64) do not apply to `mmap` slice assignment.

The `mmap` module supplies a factory function that is slightly different on Unix-like systems and on Windows:

Threads and Processes

mmap `mmap(filedesc,length,tagname='', access=None, offset=None)` *Windows*

`mmap(filedesc,length,flags=MAP_SHARED,`
`prot=PROT_READ | PROT_WRITE,`
`access=None, offset=0)` *Unix*

Creates and returns an `mmap` object *`m`* that maps into memory the first *`length`* bytes of the file indicated by file descriptor *`filedesc`*. *`filedesc`* must normally be a file descriptor opened for both reading and writing (except, on Unix-like platforms, when the argument *`prot`* requests only reading or only writing). (File descriptors are covered in "File Descriptor Operations" on page 315.) To get an `mmap` object *`m`* for a Python file object *`f`*, use `m=mmap.mmap(f.fileno(),length)`. *`filedesc`* can be `-1` to map anonymous memory.

On Windows, all memory mappings are readable and writable, and shared among processes, so that all processes with a memory mapping on a file can see changes made by other such processes. On Windows only, you can pass a string *`tagname`* to give an explicit tag name for the memory mapping. This tag name lets you have several memory mappings on the same file, but this is rarely necessary. Calling `mmap` with only two arguments has the advantage of keeping your code portable between Windows and Unix-like platforms.

On Unix-like platforms only, you can pass `mmap.MAP_PRIVATE` as *`flags`* to get a mapping that is private to your process and copy-on-write. `mmap.MAP_SHARED`, the default, gets a mapping that is shared with other processes so that all processes mapping the file can see changes made by one process (same as on Windows). You can pass `mmap.PROT_READ` as the *`prot`* argument to get a mapping that you can only read, not write. Passing `mmap.PROT_WRITE` gets a mapping that you can only write, not read. The bitwise-OR `mmap.PROT_READ|mmap.PROT_WRITE` gets a mapping you can both read and write.

You can pass named argument *`access`*, instead of *`flags`* and *`prot`* (it's an error to pass both *`access`* and either or both of the other two arguments). The value for *`access`* can be one of `ACCESS_READ` (read-only), `ACCESS_WRITE` (write-through, the default on Windows), or `ACCESS_COPY` (copy-on-write).

You can pass named argument *`offset`* to start the mapping after the beginning of the file; offset must be an `int`, `>=0`, multiple of `ALLOCATIONGRANULARITY` (or, on Unix, of `PAGESIZE`).

Methods of mmap Objects

An `mmap` object *`m`* supplies the following methods:

close `m.close()`

Closes the file of *m*.

find `m.find(sub,start=0, end=None)`

Returns the lowest `i>=start` such that `sub==m[i:i+len(sub)]` (and `i+len(sub)-1<=end`, ng when you pass *end*). If no such *i* exists, `m.find` returns `-1`. This is the same behavior as the `find` method of string objects, covered in Table 8-1.

flush `m.flush([offset,n])`

Ensures that all changes made to *m* also exist on *m*'s file. Until you call `m.flush`, it's uncertain whether the file reflects the current state of *m*. You can pass a starting byte offset *`offset`* and a byte count *n* to limit the flushing effect's guarantee to a slice of *m*. Pass both arguments, or neither: it is an error to call `m.flush` with exactly one argument.

move `m.move(dstoff,srcoff,n)`

Like the slice assignment `m[dstoff:dstoff+n]=m[srcoff:srcoff+n]`, but potentially faster. The source and destination slices can overlap. Apart from such potential overlap, `move` does not affect the source slice (i.e., the `move` method *copies* bytes but does not *move* them, despite the method's name).

read `m.read(n)`

Reads and returns a string *s* containing up to *n* bytes starting from *m*'s file pointer, then advances *m*'s file pointer by `len(s)`. If there are fewer than *n* bytes between *m*'s file pointer and *m*'s length, returns the bytes available. In particular, if *m*'s file pointer is at the end of *m*, returns the empty string `''`.

read_byte `m.read_byte()`

Returns a byte string of length `1` containing the byte at *m*'s file pointer, then advances *m*'s file pointer by `1`. `m.read_byte()` is similar to `m.read(1)`. However, if *m*'s file pointer is at the end of *m*, `m.read(1)` returns the empty string `''`, while `m.read_byte()` raises a `ValueError` exception.

readline `m.readline()`

Reads and returns one line from the file of *m*, from *m*'s current file pointer up to the next `'\n'`, included (or up to the end of *m* if there is no `'\n'`), then advances *m*'s file pointer to point just past the bytes just read. If *m*'s file pointer is at the end of *m*, `readline` returns the empty string `''`.

resize `m.resize(n)`

Changes the length of *m* so that `len(m)` becomes *n*. Does not affect the size of *m*'s file. *m*'s length and the file's size are independent. To set *m*'s length to be equal to the file's size, call `m.resize(m.size())`. If *m*'s length is larger than the file's size, *m* is padded with null bytes (`\x00`).

rfind `rfind(sub, start=0, end=None)`

Returns the highest `i>=start` such that `sub==m[i:i+len(sub)]` (and `i+len(sub)-1<=end`, when you pass *end*). If no such `i` exists, `m.rfind` returns `-1`. This is the same behavior as the `rfind` method of string objects, covered in Table 8-1.

seek `m.seek(pos,how=0)`

Sets the file pointer of *m* to the integer byte offset `pos`. *how* indicates the reference point (point `0`): when *how* is `0`, the reference point is the start of the file; when `1`, *m*'s current file pointer; when `2`, the end of *m*. A `seek` that tries to set *m*'s file pointer to a negative byte offset, or to a positive offset beyond *m*'s length, raises a `ValueError` exception.

size `m.size()`

Returns the length (number of bytes) of the file of *m*, not the length of *m* itself. To get the length of *m*, use `len(m)`.

tell `m.tell()`

Returns the current position of the file pointer of *m* as a byte offset from the start of *m*'s file.

write `m.write(str)`

Writes the bytes in `str` into *m* at the current position of *m*'s file pointer, overwriting the bytes that were there, and then advances *m*'s file pointer by `len(str)`. If there aren't at least `len(str)` bytes between *m*'s file pointer and the length of *m*, `write` raises a `ValueError` exception.

write_byte `m.write_byte(byte)`

Writes *byte*, which must be an int in v3, a single-character bytestring in v2, into mapping *m* at the current position of *m*'s file pointer, overwriting the byte that was there, and then advances *m*'s file pointer by 1. When *x* is a single-character bytestring in v2, `m.write_byte(x)` is similar to `m.write(x)`. However, if *m*'s file pointer is at the end of *m*, `m.write_byte(x)` silently does nothing, while `m.write(x)` raises a `ValueError` exception. Note that this is the reverse of the relationship between `read` and `read_byte` at end-of-file: `write` and `read_byte` raise `ValueError`, while `read` and `write_byte` don't.

Using mmap Objects for IPC

The way in which processes communicate using `mmap` is similar to how IPC uses files: one process writes data and another process later reads the same data back. Since an `mmap` object rests on an underlying file, you can also have some processes doing I/O directly on the file (as covered in "The io Module" on page 273), while others use `mmap` to access the same file. You can choose between `mmap` and I/O on file objects on the basis of convenience: the functionality is the same, and performance is roughly equivalent. For example, here is a simple program that uses file I/O to make the contents of a file equal to the last line interactively typed by the user:

```
fileob = open('xxx','w')
while True:
    data = input('Enter some text:')
    fileob.seek(0)
    fileob.write(data)
    fileob.truncate()
    fileob.flush()
```

And here is another simple program that, when run in the same directory as the former, uses `mmap` (and the `time.sleep` function, covered in Table 12-2) to check every second for changes to the file and print out the file's new contents:

```
import mmap, os, time
mx = mmap.mmap(os.open('xxx',os.O_RDWR), 1)
last = None
while True:
    mx.resize(mx.size())
    data = mx[:]
    if data != last:
        print(data)
        last = data
    time.sleep(1)
```

15
Numeric Processing

You can perform some numeric computations with operators (covered in "Numeric Operations" on page 59) and built-in functions (covered in "Built-in Functions" on page 201). Python also provides modules that support additional numeric computations, covered in this chapter: `math` and `cmath` in "The math and cmath Modules" on page 433, `operator` in "The operator Module" on page 438, `random` in "The random Module" on page 441, `fractions` in "The fractions Module" on page 443, and `decimal` in "The decimal Module" on page 444. "The gmpy2 Module" on page 445 also mentions the third-party module `gmpy2`, which further extends Python's numeric computation abilities. Numeric processing often requires, more specifically, the processing of *arrays* of numbers, covered in "Array Processing" on page 446, focusing on the standard library module `array` and popular third-party extension NumPy.

The math and cmath Modules

The `math` module supplies mathematical functions on floating-point numbers; the `cmath` module supplies equivalent functions on complex numbers. For example, `math.sqrt(-1)` raises an exception, but `cmath.sqrt(-1)` returns `1j`.

Just like for any other module, the cleanest, most readable way to use these is to have, for example, `import math` at the top of your code, and explicitly call, say, `math.sqrt` afterward. However, if your code includes many calls to the modules' well-known mathematical functions, it's permissible, as an exception to the general guideline, to use at the top of your code `from math import *`, and afterward just call `sqrt`.

Each module exposes two `float` attributes bound to the values of fundamental mathematical constants, `e` and `pi`, and a variety of functions, including those shown in Table 15-1.

Table 15-1.

acos, asin, atan, cos, sin, tan	`acos(x)` Returns the arccosine, arcsine, arctangent, cosine, sine, or tangent of *x*, respectively, in radians.	math and cmath
acosh, asinh, atanh, cosh, sinh, tanh	`acosh(x)` Returns the arc hyperbolic cosine, arc hyperbolic sine, arc hyperbolic tangent, hyperbolic cosine, hyperbolic sine, or hyperbolic tangent of *x* , respectively, in radians.	math and cmath

atan2	`atan2(y,x)`
	Like `atan(y/x)`, except that `atan2` properly takes into account the signs of both arguments. For example:
	`>>> import math`
	`>>> math.atan(-1./-1.)`
	`0.78539816339744828`
	`>>> math.atan2(-1., -1.)`
	`-2.3561944901923448`
	When *x* equals `0`, `atan2` returns `pi/2`, while dividing by *x* would raise `ZeroDivisionError`.
		math only

ceil	`ceil(x)` Returns `float(i)`, where *i* is the lowest integer such that *i*>=*x*.	math only
e	The mathematical constant *e* (2.718281828459045).	math and cmath
exp	`exp(x)` Returns `e**x`.	math and cmath
erf	`erf(x)` Returns the error function of *x* as used in statistical calculations.	math only

fabs `fabs(x)` — math only

Returns the absolute value of *x*.

factorial `factorial(x)` — math only

Returns the factorial of *x*. Raises `ValueError` when *x* is negative or not integral.

floor `floor(x)` — math only

Returns `float(i)`, where *i* is the lowest integer such that *i*<=*x*.

fmod `fmod(x,y)` — math only

Returns the float *r*, with the same sign as *x*, such that *r*==*x*-*n***y* for some integer *n*, and `abs(r)<abs(y)`. Like *x*%*y*, except that, when *x* and *y* differ in sign, *x*%*y* has the same sign as *y*, not the same sign as *x*.

fsum `fsum(iterable)` — math only

Returns the floating-point sum of the values in *iterable* to greater precision than `sum`.

frexp `frexp(x)` — math only

Returns a pair `(m,e)` with the "mantissa" (pedantically speaking, the *significand*) and exponent of *x*. *m* is a floating-point number, and *e* is an integer such that *x*==*m**(2**e) and `0.5<=abs(m)<1`, except that `frexp(0)` returns `(0.0,0)`.

gcd `gcd(x,y)` — math only, v3 only

Returns the greatest common divisor of *x* and *y*. When *x* and *y* are both zero, returns `0`.

hypot `hypot(x,y)` — math only

Returns `sqrt(x*x+y*y)`.

inf `inf` — math only

A floating-point positive infinity, like `float('inf')`.

Numeric Processing

isclose `isclose(x, y, rel_tol=1e-09, abs_tol=0.0)` math and cmath, v3 only

Returns `True` when *x* and *y* are approximately equal, within relative tolerance `rel_tol`, with minimum absolute tolerance of `abs_tol` ; otherwise, returns `False`. Default is `rel_tol` within 9 decimal digits. `rel_tol` must be greater than `0`. `abs_tol` is used for comparisons near zero: it must be at least `0.0`. `NaN` is not considered close to any value (including `NaN` itself); each of `-inf` and `inf` is only considered close to itself. Except for behavior at +/- `inf`, `isclose` is like:

```
abs(x-y) <= max(rel_tol * max(abs(x), abs(y)),
abs_tol)
```

Don't use == between floating-point numbers

Given the approximate nature of floating-point arithmetic, it rarely makes sense to check whether two `floats` *x* and *y* are equal: tiny variations in how each was computed can easily result in accidental, minuscule, irrelevant differences. Avoid *x==y*; use `math.isclose(x, y)`.

isfinite `isfinite(x)` math and cmath, v3 only

Returns `True` when *x* (in `cmath`, both the real and imaginary part of *x*) is neither infinity nor `NaN`; otherwise, returns `False`.

isinf `isinf(x)` math and cmath

Returns `True` when *x* (in `cmath`, either the real or imaginary part of *x*) is positive or negative infinity; otherwise, returns `False`.

isnan `isnan(x)` math and cmath

Returns `True` when *x* (in `cmath`, either the real or imaginary part of *x*) is `NaN`; otherwise, returns `False`.

ldexp `ldexp(x,i)` math only

Returns `x*(2**i)` (*i* must be an `int`; when *i* is a `float`, `ldexp` raises `TypeError`).

log `log(x)` math and cmath

Returns the natural logarithm of *x*.

log10 `log10(x)` math and cmath

Returns the base-10 logarithm of *x*. Also, `log2(x)` (`math` only, v3 only) returns the base-2 logarithm of *x*.

modf	`modf(x)` Returns a pair `(f,i)` with fractional and integer parts of *x*, meaning two `floats` with the same sign as *x* such that `i==int(i)` and *x*==*f*+*i*.	math only
nan	`nan` A floating-point "Not a Number" (`NaN`) value, like `float('nan')`.	math only
pi	The mathematical constant *π*, 3.141592653589793.	math and cmath
phase	`phase(x)` Returns the phase of *x*, as a float in the range (-*π*, *π*). Like `math.atan2(x.imag, x.real)`. See "Conversions to and from polar coordinates" (*https://docs.python.org/3/library/cmath.html#conversions-to-and-from-polar-coordinates*) in the Python online docs.	cmath only
polar	`polar(x)` Returns the polar coordinate representation of *x*, as a pair `(r, phi)` where `r` is the modulus of *x* and `phi` is the phase of *x*. Like `(abs(x), cmath.phase(x))`. See "Conversions to and from polar coordinates" (*https://docs.python.org/3/library/cmath.html#conversions-to-and-from-polar-coordinates*) in the Python online docs.	cmath only
pow	`pow(x,y)` Returns *x****y*.	math only
sqrt	`sqrt(x)` Returns the square root of *x*.	math and cmath
trunc	`trunc(x)` Returns *x* truncated to an `int`.	math only

Always keep in mind that `floats` are not entirely precise, due to their internal representation in the computer. The following example shows this, and also shows why the new function `isclose` may be useful:

```
>>> f = 1.1 + 2.2 - 3.3  # f is intuitively equal to 0
>>> f==0
False
>>> f
4.440892098500626e-16
>>> math.isclose(0,f,abs_tol=1e-15)  # abs_tol for near-0 comparison
True
>>> g = f-1
```

```
>>> g
-0.9999999999999996  # almost -1 but not quite
>>> math.isclose(-1,g)  # default is fine for this comparison
True
>>> isclose(-1,g,rel_tol=1e-15)  # but you can set the tolerances
True
>>> isclose(-1,g,rel_tol=1e-16)  # including higher precision
False
```

The operator Module

The `operator` module supplies functions that are equivalent to Python's operators. These functions are handy in cases where callables must be stored, passed as arguments, or returned as function results. The functions in `operator` have the same names as the corresponding special methods (covered in "Special Methods" on page 126). Each function is available with two names, with and without "dunder" (leading and trailing double underscores): for example, both `operator.add(`*a*`,`*b*`)` and `operator.__add__(`*a*`,`*b*`)` return *a+b*. Matrix multiplication support has been added for the infix operator `@`, in v3,[1] but you must (as of this writing) implement it by defining your own `__matmul__()` (*https://docs.python.org/3/reference/datamodel.html#object.__matmul__*), `__rmatmul__()` (*https://docs.python.org/3/reference/datamodel.html#object.__rmatmul__*), and/or `__imatmul__()` (*https://docs.python.org/3/reference/datamodel.html#object.__imatmul__*); NumPy, however, does support `@` (but not yet `@=`) for matrix multiplication.

Table 15-2 lists some of the functions supplied by the `operator` module.

Table 15-2. Functions supplied by the operator module

Method	Signature	Behaves like
`abs`	`abs(` *a* `)`	`abs(` *a* `)`
`add`	`add(` *a* `,` *b* `)`	*a* + *b*
`and_`	`and_(` *a* `,` *b* `)`	*a* & *b*
`concat`	`concat(` *a* `,` *b* `)`	*a* + *b*
`contains`	`contains(` *a* `,` *b* `)`	*b* in *a*
`countOf`	`countOf(` *a* `,` *b* `)`	*a* `.count(` *b* `)`
`delitem`	`delitem(` *a* `,` *b* `)`	`del` *a*`[`*b*`]`

1 Specifically in Python 3.5

Method	Signature	Behaves like
delslice	delslice(*a* , *b* , *c*)	del *a*[*b*:*c*]
div	div(*a* , *b*)	*a* / *b*
eq	eq(*a* , *b*)	*a* == *b*
floordiv	floordiv(*a* , *b*)	*a* // *b*
ge	ge(*a* , *b*)	*a* >= *b*
getitem	getitem(*a* , *b*)	*a* [*b*]
getslice	getslice(*a* , *b* , *c*)	*a* [*b* : *c*]
gt	gt(*a* , *b*)	*a* > *b*
indexOf	indexOf(*a* , *b*)	*a* .index(*b*)
invert, inv	*invert(a)*, inv*(a)*	~ *a*
is	*is(a , b)*	*a* is *b*
is_not	*is_not(a , b)*	*a* is not *b*
le	*le(a , b)*	*a* <= *b*
lshift	lshift(*a* , *b*)	*a* << *b*
lt	lt(*a* , *b*)	*a* < *b*
matmul	matmul(*m1*, *m2*)	*m1* @ *m2*
mod	mod(*a* , *b*)	*a* % *b*
mul	mul(*a* , *b*)	*a* * *b*
ne	ne(*a* , *b*)	*a* != *b*
neg	neg(*a*)	- *a*
not_	not_(*a*)	not *a*
or_	or_(*a* , *b*)	*a* | *b*

Method	Signature	Behaves like
`pos`	`pos(` *a* `)`	`+` *a*
`repeat`	`repeat(` *a* `,` *b* `)`	*a* `*` *b*
`rshift`	`rshift(` *a* `,` *b* `)`	*a* `>>` *b*
`setitem`	`setitem(` *a* `,` *b* `,` *c* `)`	*a* `[` *b* `]=` *c*
`setslice`	`setslice(` *a* `,` *b* `,` *c* `,` *d* `)`	*a* `[` *b* `:` *c* `]=` *d*
`sub`	`sub(` *a* `,` *b* `)`	*a* `-` *b*
`truediv`	`truediv(` *a* `,` *b* `)`	*a*`/`*b*`# "true" div -> no truncation`
`truth`	`truth(` *a* `)`	`not not` *a*`, bool(`*a*`)`
`xor`	`xor(` *a* `,` *b* `)`	*a* `^` *b*

The `operator` module also supplies two higher-order functions whose results are functions suitable for passing as named argument *key=* to the `sort` method of lists, the `sorted` built-in function, `itertools.groupby()`, and other built-in functions such as `min` and `max`.

attrgetter `attrgetter(`*attr*`)`

Returns a callable *f* such that `f(`*o*`)` is the same as `getattr(`*o*`,`*attr*`)`. The *attr* string can include dots (`.`), in which case the callable result of `attrgetter` calls `getattr` repeatedly. For example, `operator.attrgetter('a.b')` is equivalent to `lambda o: getattr(getattr(o, 'a'), 'b')`.

`attrgetter(*`*attrs*`)`

When you call `attrgetter` with multiple arguments, the resulting callable extracts each attribute thus named and returns the resulting tuple of values.

itemgetter `itemgetter(`*key*`)`

Returns a callable *f* such that `f(`*o*`)` is the same as `getitem(`*o*`,`*key*`)`.

`itemgetter(*`*keys*`)`

When you call `itemgetter` with multiple arguments, the resulting callable extracts each item thus keyed and returns the resulting tuple of values.

For example, say that `L` is a list of lists, with each sublist at least three items long: you want to sort `L`, in-place, based on the third item of each sublist; with sublists having equal third items sorted by their first items. The simplest way:

```
import operator
L.sort(key=operator.itemgetter(2, 0))
```

Random and Pseudorandom Numbers

The `random` module of the standard library generates pseudorandom numbers with various distributions. The underlying uniform pseudorandom generator uses the Mersenne Twister algorithm, with a period of length `2**19937-1`.

Physically Random and Cryptographically Strong Random Numbers

Pseudorandom numbers provided by the `random` module, while very good, are not of cryptographic quality. If you want higher-quality random numbers, you can call `os.urandom` (from the module `os`, *not* `random`), or instantiate the class `SystemRandom` from `random` (which calls `os.urandom` for you).

urandom `urandom(n)`

Returns *n* random bytes, read from physical sources of random bits such as */dev/urandom* on older Linux releases. In v3 only, uses the `getrandom()` syscall on Linux 3.17 and above. (On OpenBSD 5.6 and newer, the C `getrandom()` function is now used.) Uses cryptographical-strength sources such as the `CryptGenRandom` API on Windows. If no suitable source exists on the current system, `urandom` raises `NotImplementedError`.

An alternative source of physically random numbers: *http://www.fourmilab.ch/hotbits*.

The random Module

All functions of the `random` module are methods of one hidden global instance of the class `random.Random`. You can instantiate `Random` explicitly to get multiple generators that do not share state. Explicit instantiation is advisable if you require random numbers in multiple threads (threads are covered in Chapter 14). Alternatively, instantiate `SystemRandom` if you require higher-quality random numbers. (See "Physically Random and Cryptographically Strong Random Numbers" on page 441.) This section documents the most frequently used functions exposed by module `random`:

choice `choice(seq)`

Returns a random item from nonempty sequence *seq*.

getrandbits `getrandbits(k)`

Returns an `int` >=0 with *k* random bits, like `randrange(2**k)` (but faster, and with no problems for large *k*).

Numeric Processing

getstate `getstate()`

Returns a hashable and pickleable object *S* representing the current state of the generator. You can later pass *S* to function `setstate` to restore the generator's state.

jumpahead `jumpahead(n)`

Advances the generator state as if *n* random numbers had been generated. This is faster than generating and ignoring *n* random numbers.

randint `randint(start, stop)`

Returns a random `int` *i* from a uniform distribution such that *start*<=*i*<=*stop*. Both endpoints are included: this is quite unnatural in Python, so `randrange` is usually preferred.

random `random()`

Returns a random `float` *r* from a uniform distribution, `0`<=*r*<`1`.

randrange `randrange([start,]stop[,step])`

Like `choice(range(start,stop,step))`, but much faster.

sample `sample(seq,k)`

Returns a new list whose *k* items are unique items randomly drawn from *seq*. The list is in random order, so that any slice of it is an equally valid random sample. *seq* may contain duplicate items. In this case, each occurrence of an item is a candidate for selection in the sample, and the sample may also contain such duplicates.

seed `seed(x=None)`

Initializes the generator state. *x* can be any hashable object. When *x* is `None`, and when the module `random` is first loaded, `seed` uses the current system time (or some platform-specific source of randomness, if any) to get a seed. *x* is normally an integer up to `27814431486575`. Larger *x* values are accepted, but may produce the same generator state as smaller ones.

setstate `setstate(S)`

Restores the generator state. *S* must be the result of a previous call to `getstate` (such a call may have occurred in another program, or in a previous run of this program, as long as object *S* has correctly been transmitted, or saved and restored).

shuffle `shuffle(alist)`

Shuffles, in place, mutable sequence *alist*.

uniform `uniform(a,b)`

Returns a random floating-point number *r* from a uniform distribution such that *a*<=*r*<*b*.

The random module also supplies several other functions that generate pseudorandom floating-point numbers from other probability distributions (Beta, Gamma, exponential, Gauss, Pareto, etc.) by internally calling random.random as their source of randomness.

The fractions Module

The fractions module supplies a rational number class called Fraction whose instances can be constructed from a pair of integers, another rational number, or a string. You can pass a pair of (optionally signed) integers: the *numerator* and *denominator*. When the denominator is 0, a ZeroDivisionError is raised. A string can be of the form '3.14', or can include an optionally signed numerator, a slash (/), and a denominator, such as '-22/7'. Fraction also supports construction from decimal.Decimal instances, and from floats (although the latter may not provide the result you'd expect, given floats' bounded precision). Fraction class instances have the properties numerator and denominator.

Reduced to lowest terms

Fraction reduces the fraction to the lowest terms—for example, f = Fraction(226, 452) builds an instance f equal to one built by Fraction(1, 2). The numerator and denominator originally passed to Fraction are not recoverable from the built instance.

```
from fractions import Fraction
>>> Fraction(1,10)
Fraction(1, 10)
>>> Fraction(Decimal('0.1'))
Fraction(1, 10)
>>> Fraction('0.1')
Fraction(1, 10)
>>> Fraction('1/10')
Fraction(1, 10)
>>> Fraction(0.1)
Fraction(3602879701896397, 36028797018963968)
>>> Fraction(-1, 10)
Fraction(-1, 10)
>>> Fraction(-1,-10)
Fraction(1, 10)
```

Fraction also supplies several methods, including limit_denominator, which allows you to create a rational approximation of a float—for example, Fraction(0.0999).limit_denominator(10) returns Fraction(1, 10). Fraction instances are immutable and can be keys in dictionaries and members of sets, as well as being used in arithmetic operations with other numbers. See the fractions docs (*https://docs.python.org/3/library/fractions.html*) for more complete coverage.

The fractions module, in both v2 and v3, also supplies a function called gcd that works just like math.gcd (which exists in v3 only), covered in Table 15-1.

The decimal Module

A Python float is a binary floating-point number, normally in accordance with the standard known as IEEE 754 and implemented in hardware in modern computers. A concise, practical introduction to floating-point arithmetic and its issues can be found in David Goldberg's essay What Every Computer Scientist Should Know about Floating-Point Arithmetic (*https://docs.oracle.com/cd/E19957-01/806-3568/ncg_goldberg.html*). A Python-focused essay on the same issues is part of the online tutorial (*https://docs.python.org/3/tutorial/floatingpoint.html*); another excellent summary is also online (*http://www.lahey.com/float.htm*).

Often, particularly for money-related computations, you may prefer to use *decimal* floating-point numbers; Python supplies an implementation of the standard known as IEEE 854, for base 10, in the standard library module decimal. The module has excellent documentation for both v2 (*https://docs.python.org/2.7/library/decimal.html*) and v3 (*https://docs.python.org/3/library/decimal.html?highlight=decimal#module-decimal*): there you can find complete reference documentation, pointers to the applicable standards, a tutorial, and advocacy for decimal. Here, we cover only a small subset of decimal's functionality that corresponds to the most frequently used parts of the module.

The decimal module supplies a Decimal class (whose immutable instances are decimal numbers), exception classes, and classes and functions to deal with the *arithmetic context*, which specifies such things as precision, rounding, and which computational anomalies (such as division by zero, overflow, underflow, and so on) raise exceptions when they occur. In the default context, precision is 28 decimal digits, rounding is "half-even" (round results to the closest representable decimal number; when a result is exactly halfway between two such numbers, round to the one whose last digit is even), and the anomalies that raise exceptions are: invalid operation, division by zero, and overflow.

To build a decimal number, call Decimal with one argument: an integer, float, string, or tuple. If you start with a float, it is converted losslessly to the exact decimal equivalent (which may require 53 digits or more of precision):

```
from decimal import Decimal
df = Decimal(0.1)
df
Decimal('0.1000000000000000055511151231257827021181583404541015625')
```

If this is not the behavior you want, you can pass the float as a string; for example:

```
ds = Decimal(str(0.1))  # or, directly, Decimal('0.1')
ds
Decimal('0.1')
```

If you wish, you can easily write a factory function for ease of experimentation, particularly interactive experimentation, with `decimal`:

```
def dfs(x):
    return Decimal(str(x))
```

Now *dfs*(0.1) is just the same thing as `Decimal(str(0.1))`, or `Decimal('0.1')`, but more concise and handier to write.

Alternatively, you may use the `quantize` method of `Decimal` to construct a new decimal by rounding a float to the number of significant digits you specify:

```
dq = Decimal(0.1).quantize(Decimal('.00'))
dq
Decimal('0.10')
```

If you start with a tuple, you need to provide three arguments: the sign (0 for positive, 1 for negative), a tuple of digits, and the integer exponent:

```
pidigits = (3, 1, 4, 1, 5)
Decimal((1, pidigits, -4))
Decimal('-3.1415')
```

Once you have instances of `Decimal`, you can compare them, including comparison with `float`s (use `math.isclose` for this); pickle and unpickle them; and use them as keys in dictionaries and as members of sets. You may also perform arithmetic among them, and with integers, but not with `float`s (to avoid unexpected loss of precision in the results), as demonstrated here:

```
>>> a = 1.1
>>> d = Decimal('1.1')
>>> a == d
False
>>> math.isclose(a, d)
True
>>> a + d
Traceback (most recent call last):
  File "<stdin>", line 1, in <module>
TypeError: unsupported operand type(s) for +:
  'decimal.Decimal' and 'float'
>>> d + Decimal(a) # new decimal constructed from a
Decimal('2.200000000000000088817841970') # whoops
>>> d + Decimal(str(a)) # convert a to decimal with str(a)
Decimal('2.20')
```

The online docs include useful recipes (*https://docs.python.org/2.7/library/decimal.html#recipes*) for monetary formatting, some trigonometric functions, and a list of Frequently Asked Questions (FAQ).

The gmpy2 Module

The `gmpy2` module is a C-coded extension that supports the GMP, MPFR, and MPC libraries, to extend and accelerate Python's abilities for multiple-precision arithmetic

(arithmetic in which the precision of the numbers involved is bounded only by the amount of memory available). The main development branch of `gmpy2` supports thread-safe contexts. You can download and install `gmpy2` from PyPI (*https://pypi.python.org/pypi/gmpy2*).

Array Processing

You can represent arrays with lists (covered in "Lists" on page 49), as well as with the `array` standard library module (covered in "The array Module" on page 446). You can manipulate arrays with loops; indexing and slicing; list comprehensions; iterators; generators; genexps (all covered in Chapter 3); built-ins such as `map`, `reduce`, and `filter` (all covered in "Built-in Functions" on page 201); and standard library modules such as `itertools` (covered in "The itertools Module" on page 228). If you only need a lightweight, one-dimensional array, stick with `array`. However, to process large arrays of numbers, such functions may be slower and less convenient than third-party extensions such as NumPy and SciPy (covered in "Extensions for Numeric Array Computation" on page 448). When you're doing data analysis and modeling, pandas, which is built on top of NumPy, might be most suitable.

The array Module

The `array` module supplies a type, also called `array`, whose instances are mutable sequences, like lists. An `array` *a* is a one-dimensional sequence whose items can be only characters, or only numbers of one specific numeric type, fixed when you create *a*.

`array.array`'s advantage is that, compared to a list, it can save memory to hold objects all of the same (numeric or character) type. An `array` object *a* has a one-character, read-only attribute *a*`.typecode`, set on creation: the type code of *a*'s items. Table 15-3 shows the possible type codes for `array`.

Table 15-3. Type codes for the array module

typecode	C type	Python type	Minimum size
`'c'`	`char`	`str (length 1)`	1 byte (v2 only)
`'b'`	`char`	`int`	1 byte
`'B'`	`unsigned char`	`int`	1 byte
`'u'`	`unicode char`	`unicode (length 1)`	2 bytes (4 if this Python is a "wide build")

typecode	C type	Python type	Minimum size
'h'	short	int	2 bytes
'H'	unsigned short	int	2 bytes
'i'	int	int	2 bytes
'I'	unsigned int	int	2 bytes
'l'	long	int	4 bytes
'L'	unsigned long	int	4 bytes
'q'	long long	int	8 bytes (v3 only)
'Q'	unsigned long long	int	8 bytes (v3 only)
'f'	float	float	4 bytes
'd'	double	float	8 bytes

Note: `'c'` is v2 only. `'u'` is in both v2 and v3, with an item size of 2 if this Python is a "narrow build," and 4 if a "wide build." `q` and `Q` (v3 only) are available only if the platform supports C's `long long` (or, on Windows, `__int64`) type.

Numeric Processing

The size in bytes of each item may be larger than the minimum, depending on the machine's architecture, and is available as the read-only attribute `a.itemsize`. The module `array` supplies just the type object called `array`:

array `array(`*`typecode`*`,`*`init`*`='')`

Creates and returns an `array` object *a* with the given *`typecode`*. *`init`* can be a string (a bytestring, except for *`typecode`* `'u'`) whose length is a multiple of `itemsize`: the string's bytes, interpreted as machine values, directly initialize *a*'s items. Alternatively, *`init`* can be an iterable (of chars when *`typecode`* is `'c'` or `'u'`, otherwise of numbers): each item of the iterable initializes one item of *a*.

Array objects expose all methods and operations of mutable sequences (as covered in "Sequence Operations" on page 61), except `sort`. Concatenation with + or +=, and slice assignment, require both operands to be arrays with the same typecode; in contrast, the argument to `a.extend` can be any iterable with items acceptable to *a*.

In addition to the methods of mutable sequences, an array object *a* exposes the following methods.[2]

byteswap `a.byteswap()`

Swaps the byte order of each item of *a*.

fromfile `a.fromfile(f,n)`

Reads *n* items, taken as machine values, from file object *f* and appends the items to *a*. Note that *f* should be open for reading in binary mode—for example, with mode `'rb'`. When fewer than *n* items are available in *f*, `fromfile` raises `EOFError` after appending the items that are available.

fromlist `a.fromlist(L)`

Appends to *a* all items of list *L*.

fromstring, frombytes `a.fromstring(s) a.frombytes(s)`

`fromstring` (v2 only) appends to *a* the bytes, interpreted as machine values, of string *s*. `len(s)` must be an exact multiple of `a.itemsize`. `frombytes` (v3 only) is identical (reading *s* as bytes).

tofile `a.tofile(f)`

Writes all items of *a*, taken as machine values, to file object *f*. Note that *f* should be open for writing in binary mode—for example, with mode `'wb'`.

tolist `a.tolist()`

Creates and returns a list object with the same items as *a*, like `list(a)`.

tostring, tobytes `a.tostring() a.tobytes()`

`tostring` (v2 only) returns the string with the bytes from all items of *a*, taken as machine values. For any *a*, `len(a.tostring())== len(a)*a.itemsize`. `f.write(a.tostring())` is the same as `a.tofile(f)`. `tobytes` (v3 only), similarly, returns the bytes representation of the array items.

Extensions for Numeric Array Computation

As you've seen, Python has great support for numeric processing. However, third-party library SciPy and packages such as NumPy, Matplotlib, Sympy, IPython/Jupyter, and pandas provide even more tools. We introduce NumPy here, then pro-

2 Note that `fromstring` and `tostring`, in v2, are renamed to `frombytes` and `tobytes` in v3 for clarity—`str` in v2 was bytes; in v3, `str` is Unicode.

vide a brief description of SciPy and other packages (see "SciPy" on page 454), with pointers to their documentation.

NumPy

If you need a lightweight one-dimensional array of numbers, the standard library's `array` module may often suffice. If you are doing scientific computing, advanced image handling, multidimensional arrays, linear algebra, or other applications involving large amounts of data, the popular third-party NumPy package meets your needs. Extensive documentation is available online (*https://docs.scipy.org/doc/*); a free PDF of Travis Oliphant's Guide to NumPy (*http://web.mit.edu/dvp/Public/numpybook.pdf*) book is also available.

NumPy or numpy?

The docs variously refer to the package as NumPy or Numpy; however, in coding, the package is called `numpy` and you usually import it with `import numpy as np`. In this section, we use all of these monikers.

`NumPy` provides class `ndarray`, which you can subclass (*https://docs.scipy.org/doc/numpy/user/basics.subclassing.html*) to add functionality for your particular needs. An `ndarray` object has *n* dimensions of homogenous items (items can include containers of heterogenous types). An `ndarray` object *a* has a number of dimensions (AKA *axes*) known as its *rank*. A *scalar* (i.e., a single number) has rank `0`, a *vector* has rank `1`, a *matrix* has rank `2`, and so forth. An `ndarray` object also has a *shape*, which can be accessed as property `shape`. For example, for a matrix *m* with 2 columns and 3 rows, *m*`.shape` is `(3,2)`.

`NumPy` supports a wider range of numeric types (*https://docs.scipy.org/doc/numpy/user/basics.types.html*) (instances of `dtype`) than Python; however, the default numerical types are: `bool_`, one byte; `int_`, either *int64* or *int32* (depending on your platform); `float_`, short for *float64*; and `complex_`, short for *complex128*.

Creating a NumPy Array

There are several ways to create an array in `NumPy`; among the most common are:

- with the factory function `np.array`, from a sequence (often a nested one), with *type inference* or by explicitly specifying *dtype*
- with factory functions `zeros`, `ones`, `empty`, which default to *dtype* `float64`, and `indices`, which defaults to `int64`
- with factory function `arange` (with the usual *start*, *stop*, *stride*), or with factory function `linspace` (*start*, *stop*, *quantity*) for better floating-point behavior
- reading data from files with other `np` functions (e.g., CSV with `genfromtxt`)

Here are examples of creating an array, as just listed:

```
import numpy as np

np.array([1, 2, 3, 4])  # from a Python list
array([1, 2, 3, 4])

np.array(5, 6, 7)  # a common error: passing items separately (they
                   # must be passed as a sequence, e.g. a list)
Traceback (most recent call last):
  File "<stdin>", line 1, in <module>
ValueError: only 2 non-keyword arguments accepted

s = 'alph', 'abet'  # a tuple of two strings
np.array(s)
array(['alph', 'abet'], dtype='<U4')

t = [(1,2), (3,4), (0,1)]  # a list of tuples
np.array(t, dtype='float64')  # explicit type designation
array([[ 1.,  2.],
       [ 3.,  4.],
       [ 0.,  1.]]

x = np.array(1.2, dtype=np.float16)  # a scalar
x.shape
()
x.max()
1.2002

np.zeros(3)  # shape defaults to a vector
array([ 0.,  0.,  0.])

np.ones((2,2))  # with shape specified
array([[ 1.,  1.],
       [ 1.,  1.]])

np.empty(9)  # arbitrary float64s
array([  4.94065646e-324,   9.88131292e-324,   1.48219694e-323,
         1.97626258e-323,   2.47032823e-323,   2.96439388e-323,
         3.45845952e-323,   3.95252517e-323,   4.44659081e-323])

np.indices((3,3))
array([[[0, 0, 0],
        [1, 1, 1],
        [2, 2, 2]],

       [[0, 1, 2],
        [0, 1, 2],
        [0, 1, 2]]])

np.arange(0, 10, 2)  # upper bound excluded
array([0, 2, 4, 6, 8])
```

```
np.linspace(0, 1, 5)  # default: endpoint included
array([ 0.  ,  0.25,  0.5 ,  0.75,  1.  ])

np.linspace(0, 1, 5, endpoint=False)  # endpoint not included
array([ 0. ,  0.2,  0.4,  0.6,  0.8])

import io
np.genfromtxt(io.BytesIO(b'1 2 3\n4 5 6'))  # using a pseudo-file
array([[ 1.,  2.,  3.],
       [ 4.,  5.,  6.]])

with io.open('x.csv', 'wb') as f:
    f.write(b'2,4,6\n1,3,5')
np.genfromtxt('x.csv', delimiter=',')  # using an actual CSV file
array([[ 2.,  4.,  6.],
       [ 1.,  3.,  5.]])
```

Shape, Indexing, and Slicing

Each `ndarray` object *a* has an attribute *a*`.shape`, which is a tuple of `int`s. `len(`*a*`.shape)` is *a*'s rank; for example, a one-dimensional array of numbers (also known as a *vector*) has rank `1`, and *a*`.shape` has just one item. More generally, each item of *a*`.shape` is the length of the corresponding dimension of *a*. *a*'s number of elements, known as its *size*, is the product of all items of *a*`.shape` (also available as property *a*`.size`). Each dimension of *a* is also known as an *axis*. Axis indices are from `0` and up, as usual in Python. Negative axis indices are allowed and count from the right, so `-1` is the last (rightmost) axis.

Each array *a* (except a scalar, meaning an array of rank-`0`) is a Python sequence. Each item *a*`[`*i*`]` of *a* is a subarray of *a*, meaning it is an array with a rank one less than *a*'s: *a*`[`*i*`].shape==`*a*`.shape[1:]`. For example, if *a* is a two-dimensional matrix (*a* is of rank 2), *a*`[`*i*`]`, for any valid index *i*, is a one-dimensional subarray of *a* that corresponds to a row of the matrix. When *a*'s rank is `1` or `0`, *a*'s items are *a*'s elements (just one element, for rank-`0` arrays). Since *a* is a sequence, you can index *a* with normal indexing syntax to access or change *a*'s items. Note that *a*'s items are *a*'s subarrays; only for an array of rank `1` or `0` are the array's *items* the same thing as the array's *elements*.

As for any other sequence, you can also *slice a*: after *b*=*a*`[`*i*`:`*j*`]`, *b* has the same rank as *a*, and *b*`.shape` equals *a*`.shape` except that *b*`.shape[0]` is the length of the slice *i*`:`*j* (*j*`-`*i* when *a*`.shape[0]>`*j*`>=`*i*`>=0`, and so on).

Once you have an array *a*, you can call *a*`.reshape` (or, equivalently, `np.reshape` with *a* as the first argument). The resulting shape must match *a*`.size`: when *a*`.size` is `12`, you can call *a*`.reshape(3,4)` or *a*`.reshape(2,6)`, but *a*`.reshape(2,5)` raises `ValueError`. Note that `reshape` does not work in place: you must explicitly bind or rebind the array—that is, *a* `=` *a*`.reshape(`*i*`,`*j*`)` or *b* `=` *a*`.reshape(`*i*`,`*j*`)`.

You can also loop on (nonscalar) *a* in a `for`, just as you can with any other sequence. For example:

```
for x in a:
    process(x)
```

means the same thing as:

```
for _ in range(len(a)):
    x = a[_]
    process(x)
```

In these examples, each item *x* of *a* in the `for` loop is a subarray of *a*. For example, if *a* is a two-dimensional matrix, each *x* in either of these loops is a one-dimensional subarray of *a* that corresponds to a row of the matrix.

You can also index or slice *a* by a tuple. For example, when *a*'s rank is `>=2`, you can write `a[i][j]` as `a[i,j]`, for any valid `i` and `j`, for rebinding as well as for access; tuple indexing is faster and more convenient. Do not put parentheses inside the brackets to indicate that you are indexing *a* by a tuple: just write the indices one after the other, separated by commas. `a[i,j]` means the same thing as `a[(i,j)]`, but the form without parentheses is more readable.

An indexing is a slicing when one or more of the tuple's items are slices, or (at most once per slicing) the special form `...` (also available, in v3 only, as Python built-in `Ellipsis`). `...` expands into as many all-axis slices (`:`) as needed to "fill" the rank of the array you're slicing. For example, `a[1,...,2]` is like `a[1,:,:,2]` when *a*'s rank is 4, but like `a[1,:,:,:,:,2]` when *a*'s rank is 6.

The following snippets show looping, indexing, and slicing:

```
a = np.arange(8)
a
array([0, 1, 2, 3, 4, 5, 6, 7])

a = a.reshape(2,4)
a
array([[0, 1, 2, 3],
       [4, 5, 6, 7]])

print(a[1,2])
6

a[:,:2]
array([[0, 1],
       [4, 5]])

for row in a:
    print(row)
[0 1 2 3]
[4 5 6 7]
```

```
for row in a:
    for col in row[:2]:  # first two items in each row
        print(col)
0
1
4
5
```

Matrix Operations in NumPy

As mentioned in "The operator Module" on page 438, NumPy implements the new[3] operator `@` for matrix multiplication of arrays. `a1 @ a2` is like `np.matmul(a1,a2)`. When both matrices are two-dimensional, they're treated as conventional matrices. When one argument is a vector, you promote it to a two-dimensional array, by temporarily appending or prepending a 1, as needed, to its shape. Do not use `@` with a scalar; use `*` instead (see the following example). Matrices also allow addition (using `+`) with a scalar (see example), as well as with vectors and other matrices (shapes must be compatible). Dot product is also available for matrices, using `np.dot(a1, a2)`. A few simple examples of these operators follow:

```
a = np.arange(6).reshape(2,3)  # a 2-d matrix
b = np.arange(3)               # a vector

a
array([[0, 1, 2],
       [3, 4, 5]])

a + 1    # adding a scalar
array([[1, 2, 3],
       [4, 5, 6]])

a + b    # adding a vector
array([[0, 2, 4],
       [3, 5, 7]])

a * 2    # multiplying by a scalar
array([[ 0,  2,  4],
       [ 6,  8, 10]])

a * b    # multiplying by a vector
array([[ 0,  1,  4],
       [ 0,  4, 10]])

a @ b    # matrix-multiplying by vector
array([ 5, 14])

c = (a*2).reshape(3,2)  # using scalar multiplication to create
```

3 Since Python 3.5

```
c                          # another matrix
array([[ 0,  2],
       [ 4,  6],
       [ 8, 10]])

a @ c    # matrix multiplying two 2-d matrices
array([[20, 26],
       [56, 80]])
```

NumPy is rich enough to warrant books of its own; we have only touched on a few details. See the NumPy documentation (*https://docs.scipy.org/doc/numpy-1.10.0/index.html*) for extensive coverage of its many features.

SciPy

NumPy contains classes and methods for handling arrays; the SciPy library supports more advanced numeric computation. For example, while NumPy provides a few linear algebra methods, SciPy provides many more functions, including advanced decomposition methods, and also more advanced functions, such as allowing a second matrix argument for solving generalized eigenvalue problems. In general, when you are doing advanced numerical computation, it's a good idea to install both SciPy and NumPy.

SciPy.org (*http://www.scipy.org/index.html*)also hosts the documentation (*http://www.scipy.org/docs.html*) for a number of other packages, which are integrated with SciPy and NumPy: Matplotlib, which provides 2D plotting support; Sympy, which supports symbolic mathematics; IPython, a powerful interactive console shell and web-application kernel (the latter now blossoming as the Jupyter (*http://jupyter.org/*) project); and pandas, which supports data analysis and modeling (you can find the pandas tutorials here (*http://pandas.pydata.org/pandas-docs/stable/tutorials.html*), and many books and other materials here (*https://ssearch.oreilly.com/?q=pandas&x=0&y=0*)). Finally, if you're interested in Deep Learning, consider using the open source TensorFlow, which has a Python API (*https://www.tensorflow.org/api_docs/python/*).

16 Testing, Debugging, and Optimizing

You're not finished with a programming task when you're done writing the code; you're finished when the code runs correctly, with acceptable performance. *Testing* (covered in "Testing" on page 456) means verifying that code runs correctly, by automatically exercising the code under known conditions and checking that results are as expected. *Debugging* (covered in "Debugging" on page 467) means discovering causes of incorrect behavior and repairing them (repair is often easy, once you figure out the causes).

Optimizing (covered in "Optimization" on page 479) is often used as an umbrella term for activities meant to ensure acceptable performance. Optimizing breaks down into *benchmarking* (measuring performance for given tasks to check that it's within acceptable bounds), *profiling* (*instrumenting* the program with extra code to identify performance bottlenecks), and optimizing proper (removing bottlenecks to make overall program performance acceptable). Clearly, you can't remove performance bottlenecks until you've found out where they are (using profiling), which in turn requires knowing that there *are* performance problems (using benchmarking).

This chapter covers the subjects in the natural order in which they occur in development: testing first and foremost, debugging next, and optimizing last. Most programmers' enthusiasm focuses on optimization: testing and debugging are often (wrongly, in our opinion) perceived as being chores, while optimization is seen as being fun. Thus, were you to read only one section of the chapter, we might suggest that section be "Developing a Fast-Enough Python Application" on page 480, which summarizes the Pythonic approach to optimization—close to Jackson's classic "Rules of Optimization (*http://wiki.c2.com/?RulesOfOptimization*): Rule 1: Don't do it. Rule 2 (for experts only): Don't do it *yet*."

All of these tasks are large and important, and each could fill at least a book by itself. This chapter does not even come close to exploring every related technique and implication; it focuses on Python-specific techniques, approaches, and tools.

Testing

In this chapter, we distinguish between two different kinds of testing: unit testing and system testing. Testing is a rich, important field: many more distinctions could be drawn, but we focus on the issues of most importance to software developers. Many developers are reluctant to spend time on testing, seeing it as time stolen from "real" development, but this is short-sighted: defects are easier to fix the earlier you find out about them—an hour spent developing tests can amply pay for itself when you find defects ASAP, saving you many hours of debugging that would otherwise have been needed in later phases of the software development cycle.

Unit Testing and System Testing

Unit testing means writing and running tests to exercise a single module, or an even smaller unit, such as a class or function. *System testing* (also known as *functional* or *integration* or *end-to-end* testing) involves running an entire program with known inputs. Some classic books on testing also draw the distinction between *white-box testing*, done with knowledge of a program's internals, and *black-box testing*, done without such knowledge. This classic viewpoint parallels, but does not exactly duplicate, the modern one of unit versus system testing.

Unit and system testing serve different goals. Unit testing proceeds apace with development; you can and should test each unit as you're developing it. One relatively modern approach (first proposed in 1971 in Weinberg's immortal classic *The Psychology of Computer Programming* (*http://www.geraldmweinberg.com/Site/Programming_Psychology.html*)) is known as *test-driven development* (TDD): for each feature that your program must have, you first write unit tests, and only then do you proceed to write code that implements the feature and makes the tests pass. TDD may seem upside-down, but it has advantages; for example, it ensures that you won't omit unit tests for some feature. Developing test-first is helpful because it urges you to focus first on what tasks a certain function, class, or method should accomplish, dealing only afterward with *how* to implement that function, class, or method. An innovation along the lines of TDD is behavior-driven development (*http://behavior-driven.org/*).

In order to test a unit—which may depend on other units not yet fully developed—you often have to write *stubs*, also known as *mocks*[1]—fake implementations of various units' interfaces giving known, correct responses in cases needed to test other

1 Terminology in this area is confused and confusing: terms like dummies, fakes, spies, mocks, stubs, and "test doubles" are used by different authors with different distinctions. For an authoritative approach (though not the exact one we use), see Martin Fowler's essay (*http://martinfowler.com/articles/mocksArentStubs.html*).

units. The `mock` module (part of v3's standard library (*https://docs.python.org/3/library/unittest.mock.html*), in the package `unittest`; backport available for v2, from PyPI (*https://pypi.python.org/pypi/mock*)) helps you implement such stubs.

System testing comes later, as it requires the system to exist, with at least some subset of system functionality believed (based on unit testing) to be working. System testing offers a sanity check: each module in the program works properly (passes unit tests), but does the *whole* program work? If each unit is okay but the system is not, there's a problem in the integration between units—the way the units cooperate. For this reason, system testing is also known as *integration* testing.

System testing is similar to running the system in production use, except that you fix inputs in advance so that any problems you may find are easy to reproduce. The cost of failures in system testing is lower than in production use, since outputs from system testing are not used to make decisions, serve customers, control external systems, and so on. Rather, outputs from system testing are systematically compared with the outputs that the system *should* produce given the known inputs. The purpose is to find, in cheap and reproducible ways, discrepancies between what the program *should* do and what the program actually *does*.

Failures discovered by system testing (just like system failures in production use) may reveal some defects in unit tests, as well as defects in the code. Unit testing may have been insufficient: a module's unit tests may have failed to exercise all needed functionality of the module. In that case, the unit tests need to be beefed up. Do that *before* you change your code to fix the problem, then run the newly enhanced unit tests to confirm that they now show the problem. Then, fix the problem, and run unit tests again to confirm they show no problem anymore. Finally, rerun the system tests to confirm that the problem has indeed gone away.

Bug-fixing best practice

This best practice is a specific application of test-driven design that we recommend without reservation: never fix a bug before having added unit tests that would have revealed the bug (this practice is excellent, cheap insurance against software regression bugs (*https://en.wikipedia.org/wiki/Software_regression*)).

Often, failures in system testing reveal communication problems within the development team[2]: a module correctly implements a certain functionality, but another module expects different functionality. This kind of problem (an integration problem in the strict sense) is hard to pinpoint in unit testing. In good development practice, unit tests must run often, so it is crucial that they run fast. It's therefore

2 That's partly because the structure of the system tends to mirror the structure of the organization, per Conway's Law (*http://www.melconway.com/Home/Conways_Law.html*).

essential, in the unit-testing phase, that each unit can assume other units are working correctly and as expected.

Unit tests run in reasonably late stages of development can reveal integration problems if the system architecture is hierarchical, a common and reasonable organization. In such an architecture, low-level modules depend on no others (except library modules, which you can assume to be correct), so the unit tests of such low-level modules, if complete, suffice to assure correctness. High-level modules depend on low-level ones, and thus also depend on correct understanding about what functionality each module expects and supplies. Running complete unit tests on high-level modules (using true low-level modules, not stubs) exercises interfaces between modules, as well as the high-level modules' own code.

Unit tests for high-level modules are thus run in two ways. You run the tests with stubs for the low levels during the early stages of development, when the low-level modules are not yet ready or, later, when you only need to check the correctness of the high levels. During later stages of development, you also regularly run the high-level modules' unit tests using the true low-level modules. In this way, you check the correctness of the whole subsystem, from the high levels downward. Even in this favorable case, you *still* need to run system tests to ensure the system's functionality is exercised and checked, and no interface between modules is neglected.

System testing is similar to running the program in normal ways. You need special support only to ensure that known inputs are supplied and that outputs are captured for comparison with expected outputs. This is easy for programs that perform I/O (input/output) on files, and hard for programs whose I/O relies on a GUI, network, or other communication with external entities. To simulate such external entities and make them predictable and entirely observable, you generally need platform-dependent infrastructure. Another useful piece of supporting infrastructure for system testing is a *testing framework* to automate the running of system tests, including logging of successes and failures. Such a framework can also help testers prepare sets of known inputs and corresponding expected outputs.

Both free and commercial programs for these purposes exist, but they are not dependent on which programming languages are used in the system under test. System testing is a close kin to what was classically known as black-box testing, or testing that is independent from the implementation of the system under test (and therefore, in particular, independent from the programming languages used for implementation). Instead, testing frameworks usually depend on the operating system platform on which they run, since the tasks they perform are platform-dependent: running programs with given inputs, capturing their outputs, and particularly simulating and capturing GUI, network, and other interprocess communication I/O. Since frameworks for system testing depend on the platform and not on programming languages, we do not cover them further in this book. For a thorough list of Python testing tools, see the Python wiki (*https://wiki.python.org/moin/PythonTestingToolsTaxonomy*).

The doctest Module

The doctest module exists to let you create good examples in your code's docstrings, by checking that the examples do in fact produce the results that your docstrings show for them. doctest recognizes such examples by looking within the docstring for the interactive Python prompt '>>> ', followed on the same line by a Python statement, and the statement's expected output on the next line(s).

As you develop a module, keep the docstrings up to date and enrich them with examples. Each time a part of the module (e.g., a function) is ready, or partially ready, make it a habit to add examples to its docstring. Import the module into an interactive session, and use the parts you just developed in order to provide examples with a mix of typical cases, limit cases, and failing cases. For this specific purpose only, use `from module import *` so that your examples don't prefix *module.* to each name the module supplies. Copy and paste the interactive session into the docstring in an editor, adjust any glitches, and you're almost done.

Your documentation is now enriched with examples, and readers have an easier time following it, assuming you choose a good mix of examples, wisely seasoned with nonexample text. Make sure you have docstrings, with examples, for the module as a whole, and for each function, class, and method the module exports. You may choose to skip functions, classes, and methods whose names start with _, since (as their names indicate) they're meant to be private implementation details; doctest by default ignores them, and so should readers of your module.

Match reality

Examples that don't match the way your code works are worse than useless. Documentation and comments are useful only if they match reality; docs and comments that lie can be seriously damaging.

Docstrings and comments often get out of date as code changes, and thus become misinformation, hampering, rather than helping, any reader of the source. Better to have no comments and docstrings at all, poor as such a choice would be, than to have ones that lie. doctest can help you through the examples in your docstrings. A failing doctest run should prompt you to review the docstring that contains the failing examples, thus reminding you to keep the whole docstring updated.

At the end of your module's source, insert the following snippet:

```
if __name__ == '__main__':
    import doctest
    doctest.testmod()
```

This code calls the function testmod of the module doctest when you run your module as the main program. testmod examines docstrings (the module docstring, and docstrings of all public functions, classes, and methods thereof). In each docstring, testmod finds all examples (by looking for occurrences of the interpreter prompt '>>> ', possibly preceded by whitespace) and runs each example. `testmod` checks that each example's results match the output given in the docstring right after the example. In case of exceptions, `testmod` ignores the traceback, and just checks that the expected and observed error messages are equal.

When everything goes right, `testmod` terminates silently. Otherwise, it outputs detailed messages about examples that failed, showing expected and actual output. Example 16-1 shows a typical example of `doctest` at work on a module *mod.py*.

Example 16-1. Using doctest

```
"""
This module supplies a single function reverse_words that reverses
a string by words.

>>> reverse_words('four score and seven years')
'years seven and score four'
>>> reverse_words('justoneword')
'justoneword'
>>> reverse_words('')
''

You must call reverse_words with one argument, a string:

>>> reverse_words()
Traceback (most recent call last):
    ...
TypeError: reverse_words() takes exactly 1 argument (0 given)
>>> reverse_words('one', 'another')
Traceback (most recent call last):
    ...
TypeError: reverse_words( ) takes exactly 1 argument (2 given)
>>> reverse_words(1)
Traceback (most recent call last):
    ...
AttributeError: 'int' object has no attribute 'split'
>>> reverse_words(u'however, unicode is all right too')  # v2 check
u'too right all is unicode however,'

As a side effect, reverse_words eliminates any redundant spacing:

>>> reverse_words('with   redundant   spacing')
'spacing redundant with'

"""
def reverseWords(astring):
    words = astring.split()
    words.reverse()
    return ' '.join(words)

if __name__=='__main__':
```

```
import doctest
doctest.testmod()
```

In this module's docstring, we snipped the tracebacks from the docstring and replaced them with ellipses (`...`): this is good practice, since `doctest` ignores tracebacks, which add nothing to the explanatory value of a failing case. Apart from this snipping, the docstring is the copy and paste of an interactive session, plus some explanatory text and empty lines for readability. Save this source as *mod.py*, and then run it with **`python mod.py`**. It produces no output, meaning that all examples work right. Try **`python mod.py -v`** to get an account of all tests tried and a verbose summary at the end. Finally, alter the example results in the module docstring, making them incorrect, to see the messages `doctest` provides for errant examples.

While `doctest` is not meant for general-purpose unit testing, it can be tempting to use it for that purpose. The recommended way to do unit testing in Python is with the module `unittest`, covered in "The unittest Module" on page 462. However, unit testing with `doctest` can be easier and faster to set up, since that requires little more than copying and pasting from an interactive session. If you need to maintain a module that lacks unit tests, retrofitting such tests into the module with `doctest` is a reasonable compromise (although you should plan to eventually upgrade to full-fledged tests with `unittest`). It's better to have `doctest`-based unit tests than not to have any unit tests at all, as might otherwise happen should you decide that setting up tests properly with `unittest` from the start would take you too long.[3]

If you do decide to use `doctest` for unit testing, don't cram extra tests into your module's docstrings. This would damage the docstrings by making them too long and hard to read. Keep in the docstrings the right amount and kind of examples, strictly for explanatory purposes, just as if unit testing were not in the picture. Instead, put the extra tests into a global variable of your module, a dictionary named `__test__`. The keys in `__test__` are strings used as arbitrary test names, and the corresponding values are strings that `doctest` picks up and uses in just the same way as it uses docstrings. The values in `__test__` may also be function and class objects, in which case `doctest` examines their docstrings for tests to run. This latter feature is a convenient way to run `doctest` on objects with private names, which `doctest` skips by default.

The `doctest` module also supplies two functions that return instances of the `unittest.TestSuite` class based on doctests so that you can integrate such tests into testing frameworks based on `unittest`. The documentation for this advanced functionality is online (*https://docs.python.org/2/library/doctest.html#unittest-api*).

3 However, be sure you know exactly what you're using doctest for in any given case: to quote Peter Norvig, writing precisely on this subject: "know what you're aiming for; if you aim at two targets at once you usually miss them both."

The unittest Module

The `unittest` module is the Python version of a unit-testing framework originally developed by Kent Beck for Smalltalk. Similar, widespread versions of the framework also exist for many other programming languages (e.g., the `JUnit` package for Java) and are often collectively referred to as `xUnit`.

To use `unittest`, don't put your testing code in the same source file as the tested module: write a separate test module for each module to test. A popular convention is to name the test module like the module being tested, with a prefix such as `'test_'`, and put it in a subdirectory of the source's directory named *test*. For example, the test module for *mod.py* can be *test/test_mod.py*. A simple, consistent naming convention makes it easy for you to write and maintain auxiliary scripts that find and run all unit tests for a package.

Separation between a module's source code and its unit-testing code lets you refactor the module more easily, including possibly recoding its functionality in C, without perturbing unit-testing code. Knowing that *test_mod.py* stays intact, whatever changes you make to *mod.py*, enhances your confidence that passing the tests in *test_mod.py* indicates that *mod.py* still works correctly after the changes.

A unit-testing module defines one or more subclasses of `unittest`'s `TestCase` class. Each subclass specifies one or more test cases by defining *test-case methods*, methods that are callable without arguments and whose names start with `test`.

The subclass may override `setUp`, which the framework calls to prepare a new instance just before each test case, and `tearDown`, which the framework calls to clean things up right after each test case; this setup-teardown arrangement is known as a *test fixture*.

Have setUp use addCleanup when needed

When `setUp` propagates an exception, `tearDown` does not execute. So, if `setUp` prepares several things needing cleanup, and some preparation steps might cause uncaught exceptions, `setUp` must not rely on `tearDown` for the clean-up work; rather, right after each preparation step succeeds, call `self.addCleanup(`*f*`, *`*a*`, **`*k*`)`, passing a clean-up callable *f* (and optionally positional and named arguments for *f*). In this case, *f*`(*`*a*`, **`*k*`)` does get called after the test case (after `tearDown` when `setUp` propagates no exception, but unconditionally even when `setUp` does propagate), so the needed clean-up code always executes.

Each test case calls, on `self`, methods of the class `TestCase` whose names start with `assert` to express the conditions that the test must meet. `unittest` runs the test-case methods within a `TestCase` subclass in arbitrary order, each on a new instance of the subclass, running `setUp` just before each test case and `tearDown` just after each test case.

unittest provides other facilities, such as grouping test cases into test suites, per-class and per-module fixtures, test discovery, and other, even more advanced functionality. You do not need such extras unless you're defining a custom unit-testing framework or, at the very least, structuring complex testing procedures for equally complex packages. In most cases, the concepts and details covered in this section are enough to perform effective and systematic unit testing. Example 16-2 shows how to use unittest to provide unit tests for the module *mod.py* of Example 16-1. This example uses unittest to perform exactly the same tests that Example 16-1 uses as examples in docstrings using doctest.

Example 16-2. Using unittest

```
""" This module tests function reverseWords
provided by module mod.py. """
import unittest
import mod

class ModTest(unittest.TestCase):

    def testNormalCaseWorks(self):
        self.assertEqual(
            mod.reverse_words('four score and seven years'),
            'years seven and score four')

    def testSingleWordIsNoop(self):
        self.assertEqual(
            mod.reverse_words('justoneword'),
            'justoneword')

    def testEmptyWorks(self):
        self.assertEqual(mod.reverse_words(''), '')

    def testRedundantSpacingGetsRemoved(self):
        self.assertEqual(
            mod.reverse_words('with   redundant   spacing'),
            'spacing redundant with')

    def testUnicodeWorks(self):
        self.assertEqual(
            mod.reverse_words(u'unicode is all right too'),
            u'too right all is unicode')

    def testExactlyOneArgumentIsEnforced(self):
        self.assertRaises(TypeError, mod.reverse_words)
        with self.assertRaises(TypeError):
            mod.reverse_words('one', 'another')

    def testArgumentMustBeString(self):
        with self.assertRaises((AttributeError,TypeError)):
            mod.reverse_words(1)
```

```
if __name__=='__main__':
    unittest.main()
```

Running this script with **python test/test_mod.py** (or, equivalently, **python -m test.test_mod**) is a bit more verbose than using **python mod.py** to run doctest, as in Example 16-1. *test_mod.py* outputs a . (dot) for each test case it runs, then a separator line of dashes, and finally a summary line, such as "Ran 7 tests in 0.110s," and a final line of "OK" if every test passed.

Each test-case method makes one or more calls to methods whose names start with assert. Here, the method testExactlyOneArgumentIsEnforced is the only one with two such calls. In more complicated cases, multiple calls to assert methods from a single test-case method are quite common.

Even in a case as simple as this, one minor aspect shows that, for unit testing, unittest is more powerful and flexible than doctest. In the method testArgumentMustBeString, we pass as the argument to assertRaises a pair of exception classes, meaning we accept either kind of exception. *test_mod.py* therefore accepts as valid multiple implementations of *mod.py*. It accepts the implementation in Example 16-1, which tries calling the method split on its argument, and therefore raises AttributeError when called with an argument that is not a string. However, it also accepts a different hypothetical implementation, one that raises TypeError instead when called with an argument of the wrong type. It's possible to code such functionality with doctest, but it would be awkward and nonobvious, while unittest makes it simple and natural.

This kind of flexibility is crucial for real-life unit tests, which to some extent are executable specifications for their modules. You could, pessimistically, view the need for test flexibility as meaning the interface of the code you're testing is not well defined. However, it's best to view the interface as being defined with a useful amount of flexibility for the implementer: under circumstance *X* (argument of invalid type passed to function reverseWords, in this example), either of two things (raising AttributeError or TypeError) is allowed to happen.

Thus, implementations with either of the two behaviors are correct, and the implementer can choose between them on the basis of such considerations as performance and clarity. By viewing unit tests as executable specifications for their modules (the modern view, and the basis of test-driven development), rather than as white-box tests strictly constrained to a specific implementation (as in some traditional taxonomies of testing), you'll find that the tests become an even more vital component of the software development process.

The TestCase class

With unittest, you write test cases by extending TestCase, adding methods, callable without arguments, whose names start with test. Such test-case methods, in turn, call methods that your class inherits from `TestCase`, whose names start with `assert`, to indicate conditions that must hold for the test to succeed.

The `TestCase` class also defines two methods that your class can optionally override to group actions to perform right before and after each test-case method runs. This doesn't exhaust `TestCase`'s functionality, but you won't need the rest unless you're developing testing frameworks or performing other advanced tasks. The frequently called methods in a `TestCase` instance *t* are the following:

assertAlmostEqual

`t.assertAlmostEqual(first,second,places=7,msg=None)`

Fails and outputs *msg* when *first*!=*second* to within *places* decimal digits; otherwise, does nothing. Almost always, this method is preferable to `assertEqual` when what you are comparing are `floats`, because, due to floating-point computation vagaries, equality in that realm is usually approximate, not 100% exact.

assertEqual

`t.assertEqual(first,second,msg=None)`

Fails and outputs *msg* when *first*!=*second*; otherwise, does nothing.

assertFalse

`t.assertFalse(condition, msg=None)`

Fails and outputs *msg* when *condition* is true; otherwise, does nothing.

assertNotAlmostEqual

`t.assertNotAlmostEqual(first,second,places=7,msg=None)`

Fails and outputs *msg* when *first*==*second* to within *places* decimal digits; otherwise, does nothing.

assertNotEqual

`t.assertNotEqual(first,second,msg=None)`

Fails and outputs *msg* when *first*==*second*; otherwise, does nothing.

assertRaises

`t.assertRaises(exceptionSpec,callable,*args,**kwargs)`

Calls *callable*(**args*,***kwargs*). Fails when the call doesn't raise any exception. When the call raises an exception that does not meet *exceptionSpec*, `assertRaises` propagates the exception. When the call raises an exception that meets *exceptionSpec*, `assertRaises` does nothing. *exceptionSpec* can be an exception class or a tuple of classes, just like the first argument of the `except` clause in a `try/except` statement.

An alternative, and usually preferable, way to use `assertRaises` is as a *context manager*—that is, in a `with` statement:

```
with self.assertRaises(exceptionSpec):
    ...a block of code...
```

Here, the "block of code" indented within the `with` statement executes, rather than just the *callable* being called with certain arguments. The expectation (which avoids the construct failing) is that the block of code raises an exception

Test, Debug, Optimize

meeting the given exception specification (an exception class or a tuple of classes). This alternative approach is more general, natural, and readable.

assertTrue `t.assertTrue`*`condition`*`,`*`msg`*`=None)`

Fails and outputs *msg* when *condition* is false; otherwise, does nothing. Do not use this method when you can use a more specific one, such as `assertEqual`: specific methods provide clearer messages.

fail `t.fail(`*`msg`*`=None)`

Fails unconditionally and outputs *msg*. An example snippet might be:

```
if not complex_check_if_its_ok(some, thing):
    self.fail('Complex checks failed on {}, {}'
    .format(some, thing))
```

setUp `t.setUp()`

The framework calls `t.setUp()` just before calling a test-case method. `setUp` in `TestCase` does nothing. `setUp` exists only to let your class override the method when your class needs to perform some preparation for each test.

tearDown `t.tearDown()`

The framework calls `t.tearDown()` just after a test-case method. `tearDown` in `TestCase` does nothing. `tearDown` exists only to let your class override the method when your class needs to perform some cleanup after each test.

In addition, a `TestCase` instance maintains a last-in, first-out list (*LIFO* stack) of *clean-up functions*. When code in one of your tests (or in `setUp`) does something that requires cleanup, call `addCleanup`, passing a clean-up callable `f` and optionally positional and named arguments for `f`. To perform the stacked-up cleanups, you may call `doCleanups`; however, the framework itself calls `doCleanups` after `tearDown`. Here are the signatures of the two cleanup methods:

addCleanup `t.addCleanup(`*`func`*`, *`*`a`*`, **`*`k`*`)`

Appends (*func*, *a*, *k*) at the end of the cleanups' list.

doCleanups `t.doCleanups()`

Perform all cleanups, if any is stacked. Substantially equivalent to:

```
while self.list_of_cleanups:
    func, a, k = self.list_of_cleanups.pop()
    func(*a, **k)
```

for a hypothetical stack *`self.list_of_cleanups`*, plus, of course, error-checking and reporting.

Unit tests dealing with large amounts of data

Unit tests must be fast: run them often as you develop. So, unit-test each aspect of your modules on small amounts of data, when feasible. This makes unit tests faster, and lets you embed the data in the test's source code. When you test a function that reads from or writes to a file object, use an instance of the class `io.TextIO` for a text—that is, Unicode file (`io.BytesIO` for a byte, i.e., binary file, as covered in "In-Memory "Files": io.StringIO and io.BytesIO" on page 286)—to get a "file" with the data in memory: faster than writing to disk, and no clean-up chore (removing disk files after the tests).

In rare cases, it may be impossible to exercise a module's functionality without supplying and/or comparing data in quantities larger than can be reasonably embedded in a test's source code. In such cases, your unit test must rely on auxiliary, external data files to hold the data to supply to the module it tests and/or the data it needs to compare to the output. Even then, you're generally better off using instances of the above-mentioned `io` classes, rather than directing the tested module to perform actual disk I/O. Even more important, we strongly suggest that you generally use stubs to unit-test modules that interact with external entities, such as databases, GUIs, or other programs over a network. It's easier to control all aspects of the test when using stubs rather than real external entities. Also, to reiterate, the speed at which you can run unit tests is important, and it's faster to perform simulated operations in stubs, rather than real operations.

To test, make randomness reproducible by supplying a seed

If your code uses pseudorandom numbers (e.g., as covered in "The random Module" on page 441), you can make it easier to test by ensuring its "random" behavior is *reproducible*: specifically, ensure that it's easy for your tests to have `random.seed` called with a known argument, so that the ensuing pseudorandom numbers become fully predictable. This also applies when you're using pseudorandom numbers to set up your tests by generating random inputs: such generation should default to a known seed, to be used in most testing, keeping the extra flexibility of changing seeds for specific techniques such as fuzzing (*https://en.wikipedia.org/wiki/Fuzzing*).

Test, Debug, Optimize

Debugging

Since Python's development cycle is fast, the most effective way to debug is often to edit your code to output relevant information at key points. Python has many ways to let your code explore its own state in order to extract information that may be relevant for debugging. The `inspect` and `traceback` modules specifically support such exploration, which is also known as reflection or introspection.

Once you have debugging-relevant information, `print` is often the way to display it (`pprint`, covered in "The pprint Module" on page 249, is also often a good choice). Better, log debugging information to files. Logging is useful for programs that run unattended (e.g., server programs). Displaying debugging information is just like displaying other information, as covered in Chapter 10. Logging such information is like writing to files (covered in Chapter 10); however, to help with the frequent task of logging, Python's standard library supplies a `logging` module, covered in "The logging package" on page 169. As covered in Table 7-3, rebinding `excepthook` in the module `sys` lets your program log error info just before terminating with a propagating exception.

Python also offers hooks to enable interactive debugging. The `pdb` module supplies a simple text-mode interactive debugger. Other, powerful interactive debuggers for Python are part of integrated development environments (IDEs), such as IDLE and various commercial offerings, as mentioned in "Python Development Environments" on page 30; we do not cover these debuggers further.

Before You Debug

Before you embark on lengthy debugging explorations, make sure you have thoroughly checked your Python sources with the tools mentioned in Chapter 2. Such tools catch only a subset of the bugs in your code, but they're much faster than interactive debugging: their use amply repays itself.

Moreover, again before starting a debugging session, make sure that all the code involved is well covered by unit tests, covered in "The unittest Module" on page 462. As mentioned earlier in the chapter, once you have found a bug, *before* you fix it, add to your suite of unit tests (or, if need be, to the suite of system tests) a test or two that would have found the bug had they been present from the start, and run the tests again to confirm that they now reveal and isolate the bug; only once that is done should you proceed to fix the bug. By regularly following this procedure, you get a much better suite of tests; learn to write better, more thorough tests; and gain much sounder assurance about the overall, *enduring* correctness of your code.

Remember, even with all the facilities offered by Python, its standard library, and whatever IDEs you fancy, debugging is still *hard*. Take this into account even before you start designing and coding: write and run plenty of unit tests, and keep your design and code *simple*, to reduce to the minimum the amount of debugging you will need! Classic advice about this, by Brian Kernighan: "Debugging is twice as hard as writing the code in the first place. Therefore, if you write the code as cleverly as you can, you are, by definition, not smart enough to debug it." This is part of why "clever" is not a positive word when used to describe Python code, or a coder…

The inspect Module

The `inspect` module supplies functions to get information about all kinds of objects, including the Python call stack (which records all function calls currently executing) and source files. The most frequently used functions of `inspect` are as follows:

getargspec, formatargspec

`getargspec(f)`

Deprecated in v3: still works in Python 3.5 and 3.6, but will be removed in some future version. To introspect callables in v3, use `inspect.signature(f)` and the resulting instance of class `inspect.Signature`, covered in "Introspecting callables in v3" on page 471.

f is a function object. `getargspec` returns a named tuple with four items: `(args, varargs, keywords, defaults)`. *args* is the sequence of names of *f*'s parameters. *varargs* is the name of the special parameter of the form `*a`, or `None` when *f* has no such parameter. *keywords* is the name of the special parameter of the form `**k`, or `None` when *f* has no such parameter. *defaults* is the tuple of default values for *f*'s arguments. You can deduce other details of *f*'s signature from `getargspec`'s results: *f* has `len(args)-len(defaults)` mandatory positional arguments, and the names of *f*'s optional arguments are the strings that are the items of the list slice `args[-len(defaults):]`.

`formatargspec` accepts one to four arguments, same as the items of the named tuple that `getargspec` returns, and returns a string with this information. Thus, `formatargspec(*getargspec(f))` returns a string with *f*'s parameters (also known as *f*'s *signature*) in parentheses, as in the `def` statement that created *f*. For example:

```
import inspect
def f(a,b=23,**c): pass
print(inspect.formatargspec(*inspect.getargspec(f)))
# prints: (a, b=23, **c)
```

getargvalues, formatargvalues

`getargvalues(f)`

Deprecated in v3: still works in Python 3.5 and 3.6, but will be removed in some future version. To introspect callables in v3, use `inspect.signature(f)` and the resulting instance of class `inspect.Signature`, covered in "Introspecting callables in v3" on page 471.

f is a frame object—for example, the result of a call to the function `_getframe` in module `sys` (covered in "The frame Type" on page 388) or to function `currentframe` in module `inspect`. `getargvalues` returns a named tuple with four items: `(args, varargs, keywords, locals)`. *args* is the sequence of names of *f*'s function's parameters. *varargs* is the name of the special parameter of form `*a`, or `None` when *f*'s function has no such parameter. *keywords* is the name of the special parameter of form `**k`, or `None` when *f*'s function has no such parameter. *locals* is the dictionary of local variables for *f*. Since arguments, in particular, are local variables, the value of each argument can be obtained from *locals* by indexing the *locals* dictionary with the argument's corresponding parameter name.

`formatargvalues` accepts one to four arguments that are the same as the items of the named tuple that `getargvalues` returns, and returns a string with this information. `formatargvalues(*getargvalues(f))` returns a string with *f*'s arguments in parentheses, in named form, as used in the call statement that created *f*. For example:

Test, Debug, Optimize

```
def f(x=23): return inspect.currentframe()
print(inspect.formatargvalues(
  *inspect.getargvalues(f())))
# prints: (x=23)
```

currentframe

`currentframe()`

Returns the frame object for the current function (the caller of `currentframe`). `formatargvalues(*getargvalues(currentframe()))`, for example, returns a string with the arguments of the calling function.

getdoc

`getdoc(`*`obj`*`)`

Returns the docstring for *`obj`*, a multiline string with tabs expanded to spaces and redundant whitespace stripped from each line.

getfile, getsourcefile

`getfile(`*`obj`*`)`

Returns the name of the file that defined *`obj`*; raises `TypeError` when unable to determine the file. For example, `getfile` raises `TypeError` when *`obj`* is built-in. `getfile` returns the name of a binary or source file. `getsourcefile` returns the name of a source file and raises `TypeError` when all it can find is a binary file, not the corresponding source file.

getmembers

`getmembers(`*`obj`*`, `*`filter`*`=None)`

Returns all attributes (members), both data and methods (including special methods) of *`obj`*, a sorted list of `(`*`name`*`,`*`value`*`)` pairs. When *`filter`* is not `None`, returns only attributes for which callable *`filter`* is true when called on the attribute's *`value`*, like:

```
sorted((n, v) for n, v in getmembers(obj) if filter(v))
```

getmodule

`getmodule(`*`obj`*`)`

Returns the module object that defined *`obj`*, or `None` when it is unable to determine it.

getmro

`getmro(`*`c`*`)`

Returns a tuple of bases and ancestors of class *`c`* in method resolution order. *`c`* is the first item in the tuple. Each class appears only once in the tuple. For example:

```
class newA(object): pass
class newB(newA): pass
class newC(newA): pass
class newD(newB, newC): pass
for c in inspect.getmro(newD): print(c.__name__, end=' ')
newD newB newC newA object
```

getsource, getsourcelines

`getsource(`*`obj`*`)`

Returns a multiline string that is the source code for *`obj`*; raises `IOError` if it is unable to determine or fetch it. `getsourcelines` returns a pair: the first item is the source code for *`obj`* (a list of lines), and the second item is the line number of first line within its file.

isbuiltin, isclass, iscode, isframe, isfunction, ismethod, ismodule, isroutine

`isbuiltin(obj)`

Each of these functions accepts a single argument *obj* and returns `True` when *obj* is of the kind indicated in the function name. Accepted objects are, respectively: built-in (C-coded) functions, class objects, code objects, frame objects, Python-coded functions (including `lambda` expressions), methods, modules, and—for `isroutine`—all methods or functions, either C-coded or Python-coded. These functions are often used as the *filter* argument to `getmembers`.

stack

`stack(context=1)`

Returns a list of six-item tuples. The first tuple is about `stack`'s caller, the second about the caller's caller, and so on. Each tuple's items, are: frame object, filename, line number, function name, list of *context* source lines around the current line, index of current line within the list.

Introspecting callables in v3

In v3, to introspect a callable's signature, it's best not to use deprecated functions like `inspect.getargspect(f)`, which are scheduled for removal in some future Python version. Rather, call `inspect.signature(f)`, which returns an instance *s* of class `inspect.Signature`.

`s.parameters` is an `OrderedDict` mapping parameter names to `inspect.Parameter` instances. Call `s.bind(*a, **k)` to bind all parameters to the given positional and named arguments, or `s.bind_partial(*a, **k)` to bind a subset of them: each returns an instance *b* of `inspect.BoundArguments`.

For detailed information and examples on how to introspect callables' signatures through these classes and their methods, see PEP 362 (*https://www.python.org/dev/peps/pep-0362/*).

An example of using inspect

Suppose that somewhere in your program you execute a statement such as:

```
x.f()
```

and unexpectedly receive an `AttributeError` informing you that object *x* has no attribute named *f*. This means that object *x* is not as you expected, so you want to determine more about *x* as a preliminary to ascertaining why *x* is that way and what you should do about it. Change the statement to:

```
try: x.f()
except AttributeError:
    import sys, inspect
    print('x is type {}, ({!r})'.format(type(x), x), file=sys.stderr)
    print("x's methods are:", file=sys.stderr, end='')
    for n, v in inspect.getmembers(x, callable):
        print(n, file=sys.stderr, end='')
```

```
        print(file=sys.stderr)
        raise
```

This example uses `sys.stderr` (covered in Table 7-3), since it displays information related to an error, not program results. The function `getmembers` of the module `inspect` obtains the name of all the methods available on *x* in order to display them. If you need this kind of diagnostic functionality often, package it up into a separate function, such as:

```
import sys, inspect
def show_obj_methods(obj, name, show=sys.stderr.write):
    show('{} is type {}({!r})\n'.format(name,obj,type(obj)))
    show("{}'s methods are: ".format(name))
    for n, v in inspect.getmembers(obj, callable):
       show('{} '.format(n))
    show('\n')
```

And then the example becomes just:

```
try: x.f()
except AttributeError:
    show_obj_methods(x, 'x')
    raise
```

Good program structure and organization are just as necessary in code intended for diagnostic and debugging purposes as they are in code that implements your program's functionality. See also "The __debug__ Built-in Variable" on page 172 for a good technique to use when defining diagnostic and debugging functions.

The traceback Module

The `traceback` module lets you extract, format, and output information about tracebacks as normally produced by uncaught exceptions. By default, the `traceback` module reproduces the formatting Python uses for tracebacks. However, the `traceback` module also lets you exert fine-grained control. The module supplies many functions, but in typical use you need only one of them:

print_exc `print_exc(`*`limit`*`=None,` *`file`*`=sys.stderr)`

Call `print_exc` from an exception handler or a function called, directly or indirectly, by an exception handler. `print_exc` outputs to file-like object *`file`* the traceback that Python outputs to `stderr` for uncaught exceptions. When *`limit`* is an integer, `print_exc` outputs only *`limit`* traceback nesting levels. For example, when, in an exception handler, you want to cause a diagnostic message just as if the exception propagated, but stop the exception from propagating further (so that your program keeps running and no further handlers are involved), call `traceback.print_exc()`.

The pdb Module

The pdb module uses the Python interpreter's debugging and tracing hooks to implement a simple command-line interactive debugger. pdb lets you set breakpoints, single-step on source code, examine stack frames, and so on.

To run code under pdb's control, import pdb, then call pdb.run, passing as the single argument a string of code to execute. To use pdb for post-mortem debugging (debugging of code that just terminated by propagating an exception at an interactive prompt), call pdb.pm() without arguments. To trigger pdb directly from your application code, import pdb, then call pdb.set_trace().

When pdb starts, it first reads text files named *.pdbrc* in your home directory and in the current directory. Such files can contain any pdb commands, but most often you put in them alias commands in order to define useful synonyms and abbreviations for other commands that you use often.

When pdb is in control, it prompts with the string '(Pdb) ', and you can enter pdb commands. The command help (which you can enter in the abbreviated form h) lists available commands. Call help with an argument (separated by a space) to get help about any specific command. You can abbreviate most commands to the first one or two letters, but you must always enter commands in lowercase: pdb, like Python itself, is case-sensitive. Entering an empty line repeats the previous command. The most frequently used pdb commands are listed in Table 16-1.

Table 16-1.

!

! *statement*

Executes Python statement *statement* in the currently debugged context.

alias, unalias

alias [*name* [*command*]]

alias with no arguments lists currently defined aliases. alias *name* outputs the current definition of alias *name*. In the full form, *command* is any pdb command, with arguments, and may contain %1, %2, and so on to refer to specific arguments passed to the new alias *name* being defined, or %* to refer to all such arguments. Command unalias *name* removes an alias.

args, a

args

Lists all arguments passed to the function you are currently debugging.

break, b `break [ location[ ,condition] ]`

`break` with no arguments lists currently defined breakpoints and the number of times each breakpoint has triggered. With an argument, `break` sets a breakpoint at the given *`location`*. *`location`* can be a line number or a function name, optionally preceded by *`filename`*`:` to set a breakpoint in a file that is not the current one or at the start of a function whose name is ambiguous (i.e., a function that exists in more than one file). When *`condition`* is present, it is an expression to evaluate (in the debugged context) each time the given line or function is about to execute; execution breaks only when the expression returns a true value. When setting a new breakpoint, `break` returns a breakpoint number, which you can then use to refer to the new breakpoint in any other breakpoint-related `pdb` command.

clear, cl `clear [ breakpoint-numbers ]`

Clears (removes) one or more breakpoints. `clear` with no arguments removes all breakpoints after asking for confirmation. To deactivate a breakpoint without removing it, see `disable`, covered below.

condition `condition breakpoint-number [ expression ]`

`condition` *`n expression`* sets or changes the condition on breakpoint *n*. `condition` *n*, without *`expression`*, makes breakpoint *n* unconditional.

continue, c, cont `continue`

Continues execution of the code being debugged, up to a breakpoint, if any.

disable `disable [ breakpoint-numbers ]`

Disables one or more breakpoints. `disable` without arguments disables all breakpoints (after asking for confirmation). This differs from `clear` in that the debugger remembers the breakpoint, and you can reactivate it via `enable`.

down, d `down`

Moves down one frame in the stack (i.e., toward the most recent function call). Normally, the current position in the stack is at the bottom (i.e., at the function that was called most recently and is now being debugged), so command `down` can't go further down. However, command `down` is useful if you have previously executed command `up`, which moves the current position upward.

enable `enable [ breakpoint-numbers ]`

Enables one or more breakpoints. `enable` without arguments enables all breakpoints after asking for confirmation.

ignore `ignore breakpoint-number [ count ]`

Sets the breakpoint's ignore count (to `0` if *`count`* is omitted). Triggering a breakpoint whose ignore count is greater than `0` just decrements the count. Execution stops, presenting you with an interactive `pdb` prompt, when you trigger a breakpoint whose ignore count is `0`. For example, say that module *fob.py* contains the following code:

```
def f():
    for i in range(1000):
        g(i)
def g(i):
    pass
```

Now consider the following interactive pdb session (minor formatting details may change depending on the Python version you're running):

```
>>> import pdb
>>> import fob
>>> pdb.run('fob.f()')
> <string>(1)?()
(Pdb) break fob.g
Breakpoint 1 at C:\mydir\fob.py:5
(Pdb) ignore 1 500
Will ignore next 500 crossings of breakpoint 1.
(Pdb) continue
> C:\mydir\fob.py(5)g()
-> pass
(Pdb) print(i)
500
```

The `ignore` command, as pdb says, tells pdb to ignore the next `500` hits on breakpoint `1`, which we set at *`fob.g`* in the previous `break` statement. Therefore, when execution finally stops, function g has already been called `500` times, as we show by printing its argument `i`, which indeed is now `500`. The ignore count of breakpoint `1` is now `0`; if we give another `continue` and `print i`, `i` shows as `501`. In other words, once the ignore count decrements to `0`, execution stops every time the breakpoint is hit. If we want to skip some more hits, we must give pdb another `ignore` command, setting the ignore count of breakpoint `1` at some value greater than `0` yet again.

list, l

`list [`*`first`*`[ , `*`last`*`] ]`

`list` without arguments lists `11` (eleven) lines centered on the current one, or the next `11` lines if the previous command was also a `list`. Arguments to the `list` command can optionally specify the first and last lines to list within the current file. The `list` command lists physical lines, including comments and empty lines, not logical lines.

next, n

`next`

Executes the current line, without "stepping into" any function called from the current line. However, hitting breakpoints in functions called directly or indirectly from the current line does stop execution.

print, p

`p` *`expression`* or `print(`*`expression`*`)`

Evaluates *`expression`* in the current context and displays the result.

quit, q

`quit`

Immediately terminates both pdb and the program being debugged.

return, r `return`

Executes the rest of the current function, stopping only at breakpoints, if any.

step, s `step`

Executes the current line, stepping into any function called from the current line.

tbreak `tbreak [ *location* [ ,*condition* ] ]`

Like `break`, but the breakpoint is temporary (i.e., `pdb` automatically removes the breakpoint as soon as the breakpoint is triggered).

up, u `up`

Moves up one frame in the stack (i.e., away from the most recent function call and toward the calling function).

where, w `where`

Shows the stack of frames and indicates the current one (i.e., in which frame's context command `!` executes statements, command `args` shows arguments, command *`print`* evaluates expressions, etc.).

The warnings Module

Warnings are messages about errors or anomalies that aren't serious enough to disrupt the program's control flow (as would happen by raising an exception). The `warnings` module affords fine-grained control over which warnings are output and what happens to them. You can conditionally output a warning by calling the function `warn` in the `warnings` module. Other functions in the module let you control how warnings are formatted, set their destinations, and conditionally suppress some warnings or transform some warnings into exceptions.

Classes

Exception classes that represent warnings are not supplied by `warnings`: rather, they are built-ins. The class `Warning` subclasses `Exception` and is the base class for all warnings. You may define your own warning classes; they must subclass `Warning`, either directly or via one of its other existing subclasses, which include:

`DeprecationWarning`
: Use of deprecated features supplied only for backward compatibility

`RuntimeWarning`
: Use of features whose semantics are error-prone

`SyntaxWarning`
: Use of features whose syntax is error-prone

`UserWarning`
: Other user-defined warnings that don't fit any of the above cases

Objects

Python supplies no concrete warning objects. A warning is made up of a *`message`* (a string), a *`category`* (a subclass of `Warning`), and two pieces of information to identify where the warning was raised from: *`module`* (name of the module that raised the warning) and *`lineno`* (line number of the source code line raising the warning). Conceptually, you may think of these as attributes of a warning object *`w`*: we use attribute notation later for clarity, but no specific object *`w`* actually exists.

Filters

At any time, the `warnings` module keeps a list of active filters for warnings. When you import `warnings` for the first time in a run, the module examines `sys.warnoptions` to determine the initial set of filters. You can run Python with the option `-W` to set `sys.warnoptions` for a given run. Do not rely on the initial set of filters being held specifically in `sys.warnoptions`, as this is an implementation aspect that may change in future versions of Python.

As each warning *`w`* occurs, `warnings` tests *`w`* against each filter until a filter matches. The first matching filter determines what happens to *`w`*. Each filter is a tuple of five items. The first item, *`action`*, is a string that defines what happens on a match. The other four items, *`message`*, *`category`*, *`module`*, and *`lineno`*, control what it means for *`w`* to match the filter, and all conditions must be satisfied for a match. Here are the meanings of these items (using attribute notation to indicate conceptual attributes of *`w`*):

`message`
: A regular expression pattern string; the match condition is `re.match(`*`message`*`,`*`w`*`.message, re.I)` (the match is case-insensitive).

`category`
: `Warning` or a subclass of `Warning`; the match condition is `issubclass(`*`w`*`.category,`*`category`*`)`.

`module`
: A regular expression pattern string; the match condition is `re.match(`*`module`*`,`*`w`*`.module)` (the match is case-sensitive).

`lineno`
: An `int`; the match condition is *`lineno`* `in (0,`*`w`*`.lineno)`: that is, either *`lineno`* is `0`, meaning *`w`*`.lineno` does not matter, or *`w`*`.lineno` must exactly equal *`lineno`*.

Upon a match, the first field of the filter, the *`action`*, determines what happens:

`'always'`
: `w.message` is output whether or not *w* has already occurred.

`'default'`
: `w.message` is output if, and only if, this is the first time *w* occurs from this specific location (i.e., this specific `w.module`, `w.location` pair).

`'error'`
: `w.category(w.message)` is raised as an exception.

`'ignore'`
: *w* is ignored.

`'module'`
: `w.message` is output if, and only if, this is the first time *w* occurs from `w.module`.

`'once'`
: `w.message` is output if, and only if, this is the first time *w* occurs from any location.

__warningsgregistry__

When a module issues a warning, `warnings` adds to that module's global variables a `dict` named `__warningsgregistry__`, if that `dict` is not already present. Each key in the `dict` is a pair (*`message`*`,` *`category`*), or a tuple with three items (*`message`*`,` *`category`*`,` *`lineno`*); the corresponding value is `True` when further occurrences of that message are to be suppressed. Thus, for example, you can reset the suppression state of all warnings from a module *m* by executing *`m`*`.__warningsregistry__.clear()`: when you do that, all messages get output again (once) even if, for example, they've previously triggered a filter with an *`action`* of `'module'`.

Functions

The `warnings` module supplies the following functions:

filterwarnings `filterwarnings(`*`action`*`,`*`message`*`='.*',`*`category`*`=Warning,` *`module`*`='.*',`*`lineno`*`=0,` *`append`*`=False)`

Adds a filter to the list of active filters. When *append* is true, `filterwarnings` adds the filter after all other existing filters (i.e., appends the filter to the list of existing filters); otherwise, `filterwarnings` inserts the filter before any other existing filter. All components, save *`action`*, have default values that mean "match everything." As detailed above, *`message`* and *`module`* are pattern strings for regular expressions, *`category`* is some subclass of `Warning`, *`lineno`* is an integer, and *`action`* is a string that determines what happens when a message matches this filter.

formatwarning `formatwarning(message,category,filename,lineno)`

Returns a string that represents the given warning with standard formatting.

resetwarnings `resetwarnings()`

Removes all filters from the list of filters. `resetwarnings` also discards any filters originally added with the `-W` command-line option.

showwarning `showwarning(message,category,filename, lineno, file=sys.stderr)`

Outputs the given warning to the given file object. Filter actions that output warnings call `showwarning`, letting the argument *`file`* default to `sys.stderr`. To change what happens when filter actions output warnings, code your own function with this signature and bind it to `warnings.showwarning`, thus overriding the default implementation.

warn `warn(message,category=UserWarning,stacklevel=1)`

Sends a warning so that the filters examine and possibly output it. The location of the warning is the current function (caller of `warn`) if *`stacklevel`* is 1, or the caller of the current function if *`stacklevel`* is 2. Thus, passing 2 as the value of *`stacklevel`* lets you write functions that send warnings on their caller's behalf, such as:

```
def toUnicode(bytestr):
    try:
        return bytestr.decode()
    except UnicodeError:
        warnings.warn(
               'Invalid characters in {}'.format(bytestr),
               stacklevel=2)
        return bytestr.decode(errors='ignore')
```

Thanks to the parameter *`stacklevel`*`=2`, the warning appears to come from the caller of `toUnicode`, rather than from `toUnicode` itself. This is very important when the *`action`* of the filter that matches this warning is *`default`* or *`module`*, since these actions output a warning only the first time the warning occurs from a given location or module.

Optimization

"First make it work. Then make it right. Then make it fast." This quotation, often with slight variations, is widely known as "the golden rule of programming." As far as we've been able to ascertain, the quotation is by Kent Beck, who credits his father with it. This principle is often quoted, but too rarely followed. A negative form, slightly exaggerated for emphasis, is in a quotation by Don Knuth (who credits Hoare with it): "Premature optimization is the root of all evil in programming."

Optimization is premature if your code is not working yet, or if you're not sure what, precisely, your code should be doing (since then you cannot be sure if it's working). First make it work: ensure that your code is correctly performing exactly the tasks it is *meant* to perform.

Optimization is also premature if your code is working but you are not satisfied with the overall architecture and design. Remedy structural flaws before worrying about optimization: first make it work, then make it right. These steps are not optional; working, well-architected code is *always* a must.

In contrast, you don't always need to make it fast. Benchmarks may show that your code's performance is already acceptable after the first two steps. When performance is not acceptable, profiling often shows that all performance issues are in a small part of the code, perhaps 10 to 20 percent of the code where your program spends 80 or 90 percent of the time. Such performance-crucial regions of your code are known as *bottlenecks*, or *hot spots*. It's a waste of effort to optimize large portions of code that account for, say, 10 percent of your program's running time. Even if you made that part run 10 times as fast (a rare feat), your program's overall runtime would only decrease by 9 percent, a speedup no user would even notice. If optimization is needed, focus your efforts where they matter: on bottlenecks. You can optimize bottlenecks while keeping your code 100 percent pure Python, thus not preventing future porting to other Python implementations. In some cases, you can resort to recoding some computational bottlenecks as Python extensions (as covered in Chapter 24), potentially gaining even better performance (possibly at the expense of some potential future portability).

Developing a Fast-Enough Python Application

Start by designing, coding, and testing your application in Python, using available extension modules if they save you work. This takes much less time than it would with a classic compiled language. Then benchmark the application to find out if the resulting code is fast enough. Often it is, and you're done—congratulations! Ship it!

Since much of Python itself is coded in highly optimized C (as are many of its standard library and extension modules), your application may even turn out to already be faster than typical C code. However, if the application is too slow, you need, first and foremost, to rethink your algorithms and data structures. Check for bottlenecks due to application architecture, network traffic, database access, and operating system interactions. For typical applications, each of these factors is more likely than language choice to cause slowdowns. Tinkering with large-scale architectural aspects can often dramatically speed up an application, and Python is an excellent medium for such experimentation.

If your program is still too slow, profile it to find out where the time is going. Applications often exhibit computational bottlenecks: small areas of the source code—often 20% or less of it—account for 80% or more of the running time. Optimize the bottlenecks, applying the techniques suggested in the rest of this chapter.

If normal Python-level optimizations still leave some outstanding computational bottlenecks, you can recode those as Python extension modules, as covered in Chapter 24. In the end, your application runs at roughly the same speed as if you had coded it all in C, C++, or Fortran—or faster, when large-scale experimentation has let you find a better architecture. Your overall programming productivity with this process is not much less than if you coded everything in Python. Future changes and maintenance are easy, since you use Python to express the overall structure of the program, and lower-level, harder-to-maintain languages for only a few specific computational bottlenecks.

As you build applications in a given area following this process, you accumulate a library of reusable Python extension modules. You therefore become more and more productive at developing other fast-running Python applications in the same field.

Even if external constraints eventually force you to recode the whole application in a lower-level language, you're still better off for having started in Python. Rapid prototyping has long been acknowledged as the best way to get software architecture just right. A working prototype lets you check that you have identified the right problems and taken a good path to their solution. A prototype also affords the kind of large-scale architectural experiments that can make a real difference in performance. Starting your prototype with Python allows a gradual migration to other languages by way of extension modules, if need be. The application remains fully functional and testable at each stage. This ensures against the risk of compromising a design's architectural integrity in the coding stage. The resulting software is faster and more robust than if all of the coding had been lower-level from the start, and your productivity—while not quite as good as with a pure Python application—is still better than if you had been coding at a lower level throughout.

Benchmarking

Benchmarking (also known as *load testing*) is similar to system testing: both activities are much like running the program for production purposes. In both cases, you need to have at least some subset of the program's intended functionality working, and you need to use known, reproducible inputs. For benchmarking, you don't need to capture and check your program's output: since you make it work and make it right before you make it fast, you're already fully confident about your program's correctness by the time you load-test it. You do need inputs that are representative of typical system operations, ideally ones that may be most challenging for your program's performance. If your program performs several kinds of operations, make sure you run some benchmarks for each different kind of operation.

Elapsed time as measured by your wristwatch is probably precise enough to benchmark most programs. Programs with hard real-time constraints are another matter, but they have needs very different from those of normal programs in most respects. A 5 or 10 percent difference in performance, except in programs with very peculiar constraints, makes no practical difference to a program's real-life usability.

When you benchmark "toy" programs or snippets in order to help you choose an algorithm or data structure, you may need more precision: the `timeit` module of Python's standard library (covered in "The timeit module" on page 489) is quite suitable for such tasks. The benchmarking discussed in this section is of a different kind: it is an approximation of real-life program operation for the sole purpose of checking whether the program's performance at each task is acceptable, before embarking on profiling and other optimization activities. For such "system" benchmarking, a situation that approximates the program's normal operating conditions is best, and high accuracy in timing is not all that important.

Large-Scale Optimization

The aspects of your program that are most important for performance are large-scale ones: your choice of overall architecture, algorithms, and data structures.

The performance issues that you must often take into account are those connected with the traditional big-O notation of computer science. Informally, if you call `N` the input size of an algorithm, big-O notation expresses algorithm performance, for large values of `N`, as proportional to some function of `N`. (In precise computer science lingo, this should be called big-Theta, but in real life, programmers call this big-O, perhaps because an uppercase Theta looks like an O with a dot in the center!)

An `O(1)` algorithm (also known as "constant time") is one that takes a time not growing with `N`. An `O(N)` algorithm (also known as "linear time") is one where, for large enough `N`, handling twice as much data takes about twice as much time, three times as much data three times as much time, and so on, proportionally to `N`. An $O(N^2)$ algorithm (also known as a "quadratic time" algorithm) is one where, for large enough `N`, handling twice as much data takes about four times as much time, three times as much data nine times as much time, and so on, growing proportionally to `N` squared. Identical concepts and notation are used to describe a program's consumption of memory ("space") rather than of time.

To find more information on big-O notation, and about algorithms and their complexity, any good book about algorithms and data structures can help; we recommend Magnus Lie Hetland's excellent book *Python Algorithms: Mastering Basic Algorithms in the Python Language* (*http://www.apress.com/us/book/9781484200568*), 2nd edition (Apress, 2014).

To understand the practical importance of big-O considerations in your programs, consider two different ways to accept all items from an input iterable and accumulate them into a list in reverse order:

```
def slow(it):
    result = []
    for item in it: result.insert(0, item)
    return result

def fast(it):
    result = []
    for item in it: result.append(item)
    result.reverse()
    return result
```

We could express each of these functions more concisely, but the key difference is best appreciated by presenting the functions in these elementary terms. The function `slow` builds the result list by inserting each input item before all previously received ones. The function `fast` appends each input item after all previously received ones, then reverses the result list at the end. Intuitively, one might think that the final reversing represents extra work, and therefore `slow` should be faster than `fast`. But that's not the way things work out.

Each call to `result.append` takes roughly the same amount of time, independent of how many items are already in the list `result`, since there is (nearly) always a free slot for an extra item at the end of the list (in pedantic terms, `append` is *amortized* `O(1)`, but we don't cover amortization in this book). The `for` loop in the function `fast` executes `N` times to receive `N` items. Since each iteration of the loop takes a constant time, overall loop time is `O(N)`. `result.reverse` also takes time `O(N)`, as it is directly proportional to the total number of items. Thus, the total running time of `fast` is `O(N)`. (If you don't understand why a sum of two quantities, each `O(N)`, is also `O(N)`, consider that the sum of any two linear functions of `N` is also a linear function of `N`—and "being `O(N)`" has exactly the same meaning as "consuming an amount of time that is a linear function of `N`.")

On the other hand, each call to `result.insert` makes space at slot `0` for the new item to insert, moving all items that are already in list `result` forward one slot. This takes time proportional to the number of items already in the list. The overall amount of time to receive `N` items is therefore proportional to `1+2+3+...N-1`, a sum whose value is $O(N^2)$. Therefore, total running time of `slow` is $O(N^2)$.

It's almost always worth replacing an $O(N^2)$ solution with an `O(N)` one, unless you can somehow assign rigorous small limits to input size `N`. If `N` can grow without very strict bounds, the $O(N^2)$ solution turns out to be disastrously slower than the `O(N)` one for large values of `N`, no matter what the proportionality constants in each case may be (and, no matter what profiling tells you). Unless you have other $O(N^2)$ or even worse bottlenecks elsewhere that you can't eliminate, a part of the program that is $O(N^2)$ turns into the program's bottleneck, dominating runtime for large values of `N`. Do yourself a favor and watch out for the big O: all other performance issues, in comparison, are usually almost insignificant.

Incidentally, you can make the function `fast` even faster by expressing it in more idiomatic Python. Just replace the first two lines with the following single statement:

```
result = list(it)
```

This change does not affect `fast`'s big-O character (`fast` is still `O(N)` after the change), but does speed things up by a large constant factor.

Simple is better than complex, and usually faster!

More often than not, in Python, the simplest, clearest, most direct and idiomatic way to express something is also the fastest.

Test, Debug, Optimize

Choosing algorithms with good big-O is roughly the same task in Python as in any other language. You just need a few hints about the big-O performance of Python's elementary building blocks, and we provide them in the following sections.

List operations

Python lists are internally implemented as *vectors* (also known as *dynamic arrays*), not as "linked lists." This implementation choice determines just about all performance characteristics of Python lists, in big-O terms.

Chaining two lists `L1` and `L2`, of length `N1` and `N2` (i.e., `L1+L2`) is `O(N1+N2)`. Multiplying a list `L` of length `N` by integer `M` (i.e., `L*M`) is `O(N*M)`. Accessing or rebinding any list item is `O(1)`. `len()` on a list is also `O(1)`. Accessing any slice of length `M` is `O(M)`. Rebinding a slice of length `M` with one of identical length is also `O(M)`. Rebinding a slice of length `M1` with one of different length `M2` is `O(M1+M2+N1)`, where `N1` is the number of items *after* the slice in the target list (in other words, such length-changing slice rebindings are relatively cheap when they occur at the *end* of a list, more costly when they occur at the *beginning* or around the middle of a long list). If you need first-in, first-out (FIFO) operations, a list is probably not the fastest data structure for the purpose: instead, try the type `collections.deque`, covered in "deque" on page 220.

Most list methods, as shown in Table 3-3, are equivalent to slice rebindings and have equivalent big-O performance. The methods `count`, `index`, `remove`, and `reverse`, and the operator `in`, are `O(N)`. The method `sort` is generally `O(N*log(N))`, but is highly optimized to be `O(N)` in some important special cases, such as when the list is already sorted or reverse-sorted except for a few items. `range(a,b,c)` in v2 is `O((b-a)/c)`. `xrange(a,b,c)` in v2, and `range` in v3, is `O(1)`, but looping on all items of the result is `O((b-a)/c)`.

String operations

Most methods on a string of length `N` (be it bytes or Unicode) are `O(N)`. `len(astring)` is `O(1)`. The fastest way to produce a copy of a string with transliterations and/or removal of specified characters is the string's method `translate`. The single most practically important big-O consideration involving strings is covered in "Building up a string from pieces" on page 490.

Dictionary operations

Python `dicts` are implemented with hash tables. This implementation choice determines all performance characteristics of Python dictionaries, in big-O terms.

Accessing, rebinding, adding, or removing a dictionary item is `O(1)`, as are the methods `has_key`, `get`, `setdefault`, and `popitem`, and operator `in`. `d1.update(d2)` is `O(len(d2))`. `len(adict)` is `O(1)`. The methods `keys`, `items`, and `values` are `O(N)` in v2. The same methods in v3, and the methods `iterkeys`, `iteritems`, and `itervalues` in v2, are `O(1)`, but looping on all items of the iterators those methods return is

O(N), and looping directly on a dict has the same big-O performance as v2's iterkeys.

Never code if x in d.keys():

Never test if x in d.keys():! That's O(N), while the equivalent test if x in d: is O(1) (if d.has_key(x): is also O(1), but is slower than if x in d:, has no compensating advantage, and is deprecated—so, never use it either).

When the keys in a dictionary are instances of classes that define __hash__ and equality comparison methods, dictionary performance is of course affected by those methods. The performance indications presented in this section hold when hashing and equality comparison are O(1).

Set operations

Python sets, like dicts, are implemented with hash tables. All performance characteristics of sets are, in big-O terms, the same as for dictionaries.

Adding or removing a set item is O(1), as is operator in. len(*aset*) is O(1). Looping on a set is O(N). When the items in a set are instances of classes that define __hash__ and equality comparison methods, set performance is of course affected by those methods. The performance hints presented in this section hold when hashing and equality comparison are O(1).

Summary of big-O times for operations on Python built-in types

Let *L* be any list, *T* any string (plain/bytes or Unicode), *D* any dict, *S* any set, with (say) numbers as items (just for the purpose of ensuring O(1) hashing and comparison), and *x* any number (ditto):

O(1)
: len(*L*), len(T), len(*D*), len(S), *L*[i], *T*[i], *D*[i], del D[i], if *x* in D, if *x* in *S*, *S*.add(*x*), *S*.remove(*x*), appends or removals to/from the very right end of *L*

O(N)
: Loops on *L*, *T*, *D*, *S*, general appends or removals to/from *L* (except at the very right end), all methods on *T*, if *x* in *L*, if *x* in *T*, most methods on *L*, all shallow copies

O(N log N)
: *L*.sort, mostly (but O(N) if *L* is already nearly sorted or reverse-sorted)

Profiling

Most programs have hot spots (i.e., relatively small regions of source code that account for most of the time elapsed during a program run). Don't try to guess where your program's hot spots are: a programmer's intuition is notoriously unreliable in this field. Instead, use the module `profile` to collect profile data over one or more runs of your program, with known inputs. Then use the module `pstats` to collate, interpret, and display that profile data.

To gain accuracy, you can calibrate the Python profiler for your machine (i.e., determine what overhead profiling incurs on your machine). The `profile` module can then subtract this overhead from the times it measures so that the profile data you collect is closer to reality. The standard library module `cProfile` has similar functionality to `profile`; `cProfile` is preferable, since it's faster, which imposes less overhead. Yet another profiling module in Python's standard library (v2 only) is `hotshot` (*https://docs.python.org/2/library/hotshot.html*); unfortunately, `hotshot` does not support threads, nor v3.

The profile module

The `profile` module supplies one often-used function:

run `run(`*`code`*`,`*`filename`*`=None)`

`code` is a string that is usable with `exec`, normally a call to the main function of the program you're profiling. *`filename`* is the path of a file that `run` creates or rewrites with profile data. Usually, you call `run` a few times, specifying different filenames, and different arguments to your program's main function, in order to exercise various program parts in proportion to what you expect to be their use "in real life." Then, you use module `pstats` to display collated results across the various runs.

You may call `run` without a *`filename`* to get a summary report, similar to the one the `pstats` module could give you, on standard output. However, this approach gives no control over the output format, nor any way to consolidate several runs into one report. In practice, you should rarely use this feature: it's best to collect profile data into files.

The `profile` module also supplies the class `Profile` (mentioned in the next section). By instantiating `Profile` directly, you can access advanced functionality, such as the ability to run a command in specified local and global dictionaries. We do not cover such advanced functionality of the class `profile.Profile` further in this book.

Calibration

To calibrate `profile` for your machine, you need to use the class `Profile`, which `profile` supplies and internally uses in the function `run`. An instance *p* of `Profile` supplies one method you use for calibration:

calibrate `p.calibrate(N)`

Loops *N* times, then returns a number that is the profiling overhead per call on your machine. *N* must be large if your machine is fast. Call `p.calibrate(10000)` a few times and check that the various numbers it returns are close to each other, then pick the smallest one of them. If the numbers vary a lot, try again with larger values of *N*.

The calibration procedure can be time-consuming. However, you need to perform it only once, repeating it only when you make changes that could alter your machine's characteristics, such as applying patches to your operating system, adding memory, or changing Python version. Once you know your machine's overhead, you can tell `profile` about it each time you import it, right before using `profile.run`. The simplest way to do this is as follows:

```
import profile
profile.Profile.bias = ...the overhead you measured...
profile.run('main()', 'somefile')
```

The pstats module

The `pstats` module supplies a single class, `Stats`, to analyze, consolidate, and report on the profile data contained in one or more files written by the function `profile.run`:

Stats `class Stats(filename,*filenames)`

Instantiates `Stats` with one or more filenames of files of profile data written by function `profile.run`.

An instance *s* of the class `Stats` provides methods to add profile data and sort and output results. Each method returns *s*, so you can chain several calls in the same expression. *s*'s main methods are described in Table 16-2.

Table 16-2.

add `s.add(filename)`

Adds another file of profile data to the set that *s* is holding for analysis.

print_callees, print_callers `s.print_callees(*restrictions)`

Outputs the list of functions in *s*'s profile data, sorted according to the latest call to `s.sort_stats` and subject to given restrictions, if any. You can call each printing method with zero or more *`restrictions`*, to be applied one after the other, in order, to reduce the number of output lines. A restriction that is an `int` *n* limits the output to the first *n* lines. A restriction that is a `float` *f* between `0.0` and `1.0` limits the output to a fraction *f* of the lines. A restriction that is a string is compiled as a regular expression pattern (covered in "Regular Expressions and the re Module" on page 253); only lines that satisfy a `search` method call on the regular expression are output. Restrictions are cumulative. For example,

Test, Debug, Optimize

`s.print_callees(10,0.5)` outputs the first 5 lines (half of 10). Restrictions apply only after the summary and header lines: the summary and header are output unconditionally.

Each function *f* that is output is accompanied by the list of *f*'s callers (the functions that called *f*) or *f*'s callees (the functions that *f* called) according to the name of the method.

print_stats `s.print_stats(*restrictions)`

Outputs statistics about *s*'s profile data, sorted according to the latest call to `s.sort_stats` and subject to given restrictions, if any, as covered in **print_callees, print_callers**, above. After a few summary lines (date and time on which profile data was collected, number of function calls, and sort criteria used), the output—absent restrictions—is one line per function, with six fields per line, labeled in a header line. For each function *f*, `print_stats` outputs six fields:

- Total number of calls to *f*
- Total time spent in *f*, exclusive of other functions that *f* called
- Total time per call to *f* (i.e., field 2 divided by field 1)
- Cumulative time spent in *f*, and all functions directly or indirectly called from *f*
- Cumulative time per call to *f* (i.e., field 4 divided by field 1)
- The name of function *f*

sort_stats `s.sort_stats(key, *keys)`

Gives one or more keys on which to sort future output, in priority order. Each key is a string. The sort is descending for keys that indicate times or numbers, and alphabetical for key `'nfl'`. The most frequently used keys when calling `sort_stats` are:

`'calls'`

Number of calls to the function (like field 1 covered in **print_stats**, above)

`'cumulative'`

Cumulative time spent in the function and all functions it called (like field 4 covered in **print_stats**, above)

`'nfl'`

Name of the function, its module, and the line number of the function in its file (like field 6 covered in **print_stats**, above)

`'time'`

Total time spent in the function itself, exclusive of functions it called (like field 2 covered in **print_stats**, above)

strip_dirs `s.strip_dirs()`

Alters *s* by stripping directory names from all module names to make future output more compact. *s* is unsorted after `s.strip_dirs()`, and therefore you normally call `s.sort_stats` right after calling `s.strip_dirs`.

Small-Scale Optimization

Fine-tuning of program operations is rarely important. Tuning may make a small but meaningful difference in some particularly hot spot, but it is hardly ever a decisive factor. And yet, fine-tuning—in the pursuit of mostly irrelevant micro-efficiencies—is where a programmer's instincts are likely to lead. It is in good part because of this that most optimization is premature and best avoided. The most that can be said in favor of fine-tuning is that, if one idiom is *always* speedier than another when the difference is measurable, then it's worth your while to get into the habit of always using the speedier way.

Most often, in Python, if you do what comes naturally, choosing simplicity and elegance, you end up with code that has good performance as well as clarity and maintainability. In other words, "let Python do the work": when Python provides a simple, direct way to do a task, chances are that it's also the fastest way to perform that task. In a few cases, an approach that may not be intuitively preferable still offers performance advantages, as discussed in the rest of this section.

The simplest optimization is to run your Python programs using **`python -O`** or **`-OO`**. **`-OO`** makes little difference to performance compared to **`-O`**, but may save memory, as it removes docstrings from the bytecode, and memory is sometimes (indirectly) a performance bottleneck. The optimizer is not powerful in current releases of Python, but it may gain you performance advantages on the order of 5 percent, sometimes as large as 10 percent (potentially larger if you make use of `assert` statements and `if __debug__:` guards, as suggested in "The assert Statement" on page 171). The best aspect of **`-O`** is that it costs nothing—as long as your optimization isn't premature, of course (don't bother using **`-O`** on a program you're still developing).

The timeit module

The standard library module `timeit` is handy for measuring the precise performance of specific snippets of code. You can import `timeit` to use `timeit`'s functionality in your programs, but the simplest and most normal use is from the command line:

```
python -m timeit -s'setup statement(s)' 'statement(s) to be timed'
```

The "setup statement" is executed only once, to set things up; the "statements to be timed" are executed repeatedly, to carefully measure the average time they take.

For example, say you're wondering about the performance of `x=x+1` versus `x+=1`, where *x* is an `int`. At a command prompt, you can easily try:

```
$ python -m timeit -s 'x=0' 'x=x+1'
1000000 loops, best of 3: 0.0416 usec per loop
$ python -m timeit -s 'x=0' 'x+=1'
1000000 loops, best of 3: 0.0406 usec per loop
```

and find out that performance is, to all intents and purposes, the same in both cases.

Building up a string from pieces

The single Python "anti-idiom" that's likeliest to kill your program's performance, to the point that you should *never* use it, is to build up a large string from pieces by looping on string concatenation statements such as `big_string+=piece`. Python strings are immutable, so each such concatenation means that Python must free the `M` bytes previously allocated for `big_string`, and allocate and fill `M+K` bytes for the new version. Doing this repeatedly in a loop, you end up with roughly $O(N^2)$ performance, where `N` is the total number of characters. More often than not, $O(N^2)$ performance where `O(N)` is available is a disaster—even though Python bends over backward to help with this specific, terrible but common, anti-pattern. On some platforms, things may be even bleaker due to memory fragmentation effects caused by freeing many areas of progressively larger sizes.

To achieve `O(N)` performance, accumulate intermediate pieces in a list, rather than build up the string piece by piece. Lists, unlike strings, are mutable, so appending to a list is `O(1)` (amortized). Change each occurrence of `big_string+=piece` into `temp_list.append(piece)`. Then, when you're done accumulating, use the following code to build your desired string result in `O(N)` time:

```
big_string = ''.join(temp_list)
```

Using a list comprehension, generator expression, or other direct means (such as a call to `map`, or use of the standard library module `itertools`) to build `temp_list` may often offer further (substantial, but not big-O) optimization over repeated calls to `temp_list.append`. Other `O(N)` ways to build up big strings, which some Python programmers find more readable, are to concatenate the pieces to an instance of `array.array('u')` with the array's `extend` method, use a `bytearray`, or write the pieces to an instance of `io.TextIO` or `io.BytesIO`.

In the special case where you want to output the resulting string, you may gain a further small slice of performance by using `writelines` on `temp_list` (never building `big_string` in memory). When feasible (i.e., when you have the output file object open and available in the loop, and the file is buffered), it's just as effective to perform a `write` call for each `piece`, without any accumulation.

Although not nearly as crucial as += on a big string in a loop, another case where removing string concatenation may give a slight performance improvement is when you're concatenating several values in an expression:

```
oneway = str(x)+' eggs and '+str(y)+' slices of '+k+' ham'
another = '{} eggs and {} slices of {} ham'.format(x, y, k)
```

Using the `format` method to format strings is often a good performance choice, as well as being more idiomatic and thereby clearer than concatenation approaches.

Searching and sorting

The operator `in`, the most natural tool for searching, is `O(1)` when the righthand side operand is a `set` or `dict`, but `O(N)` when the righthand side operand is a string, list, or tuple. If you must perform many searches on a container, you're much better off using a `set` or `dict`, rather than a list or tuple, as the container. Python `sets` and `dicts` are highly optimized for searching and fetching items by key. Building the `set` or `dict` from other containers, however, is `O(N)`, so, for this crucial optimization to be worthwhile, you must be able to hold on to the `set` or `dict` over several searches, possibly altering it apace as the underlying sequence changes.

The method `sort` of Python lists is also a highly optimized and sophisticated tool. You can rely on `sort`'s performance. Performance dramatically degrades, however, if, in v2, you pass `sort` a custom callable to perform comparisons (in order to sort a list based on custom comparisons). Most functions and methods that perform comparisons accept a `key=` argument to determine how, exactly, to compare items. If you only have a function suitable as a `cmp` argument, you can use `functools.cmp_to_key`, covered in Table 7-4, to build from it a function suitable as the `key` argument, and pass the new function thus built as the `key=` argument, instead of passing the original function as the `cmp=` argument.

However, most functions in the module `heapq`, covered in "The heapq Module" on page 224, do not accept a `key=` argument. In such cases, you can use the *decorate-sort-undecorate (DSU)* idiom, covered in "The Decorate-Sort-Undecorate Idiom" on page 225. (Heaps are well worth keeping in mind, since in some cases they can save you from having to perform sorting on all of your data.)

The `operator` module supplies the functions `attrgetter` and `itemgetter` that are particularly suitable to support the `key` approach, avoiding slow `lambdas`.

Avoid exec and from ... import *

Code in a function runs faster than code at the top level in a module, because access to a function's local variables is very fast. If a function contains an `exec` without explicit dictionaries, however, the function slows down. The presence of such an `exec` forces the Python compiler to avoid the modest but important optimization it normally performs regarding access to local variables, since the `exec` might alter the function's namespace. A `from` statement of the form:

```
from MyModule import *
```

wastes performance, too, since it also can alter a function's namespace unpredictably, and therefore inhibits Python's local-variable optimizations.

`exec` itself is also quite slow, and even more so if you apply it to a string of source code rather than to a code object. By far the best approach—for performance, for correctness, and for clarity—is to avoid exec altogether. It's most often possible to find better (faster, more robust, and clearer) solutions. If you *must* use exec, *always* use it with explicit dicts. If you need to exec a dynamically obtained string more than once, compile the string just once and then repeatedly exec the resulting code object. But avoiding exec altogether is *far* better, if at all feasible.

eval works on expressions, not on statements; therefore, while still slow, it avoids some of the worst performance impacts of exec. With eval, too, you're best advised to use explicit dicts. If you need several evaluations of the same dynamically obtained string, compile the string once and then repeatedly eval the resulting code object. Avoiding eval altogether is even better.

See "Dynamic Execution and exec" on page 383 for more details and advice about exec, eval, and compile.

Optimizing loops

Most of your program's bottlenecks will be in loops, particularly nested loops, because loop bodies execute repeatedly. Python does not implicitly perform any *code hoisting*: if you have any code inside a loop that you could execute just once by hoisting it out of the loop, and the loop is a bottleneck, hoist the code out yourself. Sometimes the presence of code to hoist may not be immediately obvious:

```
def slower(anobject, ahugenumber):
    for i in range(ahugenumber): anobject.amethod(i)
def faster(anobject, ahugenumber):
    themethod = anobject.amethod
    for i in range(ahugenumber): themethod(i)
```

In this case, the code that faster hoists out of the loop is the attribute lookup anobject.amethod. slower repeats the lookup every time, while faster performs it just once. The two functions are not 100 percent equivalent: it is (barely) conceivable that executing amethod might cause such changes on anobject that the next lookup for the same named attribute fetches a different method object. This is part of why Python doesn't perform such optimizations itself. In practice, such subtle, obscure, and tricky cases happen very rarely; you're safe in performing such optimizations to squeeze the last drop of performance out of some bottleneck.

Python is faster with local variables than with global ones. If a loop repeatedly accesses a global whose value does not change between iterations, cache the value in a local variable, and access the local instead. This also applies to built-ins:

```
def slightly_slower(asequence, adict):
    for x in asequence: adict[x] = hex(x)
def slightly_faster(asequence, adict):
    myhex = hex
    for x in asequence: adict[x] = myhex(x)
```

Here, the speedup is very modest, on the order of 5 percent or so.

Do not cache None. None is a keyword, so no further optimization is needed.

List comprehensions and generator expressions can be faster than loops, and, sometimes, so can `map` and `filter`. For optimization purposes, try changing loops into list comprehensions, generator expressions, or perhaps `map` and `filter` calls, where feasible. The performance advantage of `map` and `filter` is nullified, and worse, if you have to use a `lambda` or an extra level of function call. Only when you pass to `map` or `filter` a built-in function, or a function you'd have to call anyway even from an explicit loop, list comprehension, or generator expression, do you stand to gain some tiny speed-up.

The loops that you can replace most naturally with list comprehensions, or `map` and `filter` calls, are ones that build up a list by repeatedly calling `append` on the list. The following example shows this optimization in a micro-performance benchmark script (of course, we could use the module `timeit` instead of coding our own time measurement, but the example is meant to show how to do the latter):

```
import time, operator

def slow(asequence):
    result = []
    for x in asequence: result.append(-x)
    return result

def middling(asequence):
    return list(map(operator.neg, asequence))

def fast(asequence):
    return [-x for x in asequence]

biggie = range(500*1000)
tentimes = [None]*10
def timit(afunc):
    lobi = biggie
    start = time.clock()
    for x in tentimes: afunc(lobi)
    stend = time.clock()
    return '{:<10}: {:.2f}'.format(afunc.__name__, stend-start)

for afunc in slow, middling, fast, fast, middling, slow:
    print(timit(afunc))
```

Running this example in v2 on an old laptop shows that `fast` takes about 0.36 seconds, `middling` 0.43 seconds, and `slow` 0.77 seconds. In other words, on that machine, `slow` (the loop of `append` method calls) is about 80 percent slower than `middling` (the single `map` call), and `middling`, in turn, is about 20 percent slower than `fast` (the list comprehension).

The list comprehension is the most direct way to express the task being microbenchmarked in this example, so, not surprisingly, it's also fastest—about two times faster than the loop of `append` method calls.

Optimizing I/O

If your program does substantial amounts of I/O, it's likely that performance bottlenecks are due to I/O, not to computation. Such programs are said to be *I/O-bound*, rather than *CPU-bound*. Your operating system tries to optimize I/O performance, but you can help it in a couple of ways. One such way is to perform your I/O in chunks of a size that is optimal for performance, rather than simply convenient for your program's operations. Another way is to use threading. Often the very best way is to "go asynchronous," as covered in Chapter 18.

From the point of view of a program's convenience and simplicity, the ideal amount of data to read or write at a time is often small (one character or one line) or very large (an entire file at a time). That's often okay: Python and your operating system work behind the scenes to let your program use convenient logical chunks for I/O, while arranging for physical I/O operations to use chunk sizes more attuned to performance. Reading and writing a whole file at a time is quite likely to be okay for performance as long as the file is not *very* large. Specifically, file-at-a-time I/O is fine as long as the file's data fits very comfortably in physical RAM, leaving ample memory available for your program and operating system to perform whatever other tasks they're doing at the same time. The hard problems of I/O-bound performance tend to come with huge files.

If performance is an issue, *never* use a file's `readline` method, which is limited in the amount of chunking and buffering it can perform. (Using `writelines`, on the other hand, gives no performance problem when that method is convenient for your program.) When reading a text file, loop directly on the file object to get one line at a time with best performance. If the file isn't too huge, and so can conveniently fit in memory, time two versions of your program—one looping directly on the file object, the other reading the whole file into memory. Either may prove faster by a little.

For binary files, particularly large binary files whose contents you need just a part of on each given run of your program, the module `mmap` (covered in "The mmap Module" on page 429) can sometimes give you both good performance and program simplicity.

Making an I/O-bound program multithreaded sometimes affords substantial performance gains, if you can arrange your architecture accordingly. Start a few worker threads devoted to I/O, have the computational threads request I/O operations from the I/O threads via `Queue` instances, and post the request for each input operation as soon as you know you'll eventually need that data. Performance increases only if there are other tasks your computational threads can perform while I/O threads are blocked waiting for data. You get better performance this way only if you can manage to overlap computation and waiting for data by having different threads do the computing and the waiting. (See "Threads in Python" on page 396 for detailed coverage of Python threading and a suggested architecture.)

On the other hand, a possibly even faster and more scalable approach is to eschew threads in favor of asynchronous (event-driven) architectures, as covered in Chapter 18.

IV

Network and Web Programming

17 Networking Basics

Modern distributed computer systems make extensive use of networking. Understanding network communications is an essential part of building such systems, since such communications underlie the use of any network-based service. A *protocol* is an agreed "language" that two parties (often, nowadays, computer programs) use to communicate with each other. There are two basic flavors of networking, connection-oriented and connectionless, which we cover in "Networking Principles" on page 500, each with its own protocols. Both flavors can operate over a wide range of transport mechanisms thanks to the ubiquity of the TCP/IP stack and the *socket* interface, first devised to support networking in BSD Unix.

The overall task of communication splits networking into *protocol layers*, to separate different functions. Data can be carried between systems in many different ways—over an Ethernet, across a serial link, and so on—and it would needlessly complicate application code to have to handle all the differences. The ISO (International Standards Organization) defined a seven-layer model, but this has proved in practice to be unnecessarily complex; TCP/IP uses a four-layer model.

The application code implements the *process* or *application* layer, concerned with exchanging messages between two processes potentially running on different computers (although TCP/IP works just as well between local processes). This layer passes messages to the *host-to-host* or *transport* layer, concerned with end-to-end communication of messages. The transport layer breaks up longer messages into segments that it passes to the *network* or *Internet* layer, responsible for routing the segments (split into chunks known as *datagrams*) across the required sequence of inter-system "hops." This layer in turn uses a *link* or *subnetwork* layer to pass datagrams between individual systems along the way from source to destination.

To send data, the application passes a chunk of data to the transport layer. This in turn passes the data as segment-sized chunks to the network layer, which uses its knowledge of local network structure to determine which link to use to send the data on its first hop and the size of datagram to split the segments into. Using the appropriate driver, the network layer transmits datagrams as packets across the chosen link. Each intermediate system unwraps network-layer datagrams from link layer packets, and routes them to the next system wrapped in the new link layer protocol for its next hop. Finally, each datagram arrives at its ultimate destination, where the network layer passes it up to the transport layer, which reassembles segments and finally delivers the resulting message to its destination application process.

This chapter covers networking principles, the `socket` module, and a core subset of the `ssl` module: enough to let you write some simple networking clients and servers, and, more importantly, properly use networking modules at higher levels of abstraction, covered in Chapter 19, and asynchronous architectures, covered in Chapter 18.

Networking Principles

Connection-oriented protocols are like making a telephone call. You request a connection to a particular *network endpoint* (equivalent to dialing somebody's phone number), and your party either answers or doesn't. If they do, you can talk to them and hear them talking back (simultaneously, if necessary), so you know that nothing is getting lost. At the end of the conversation you both say goodbye and hang up, so it's obvious something has gone wrong if that finale doesn't occur (for example, if you just suddenly stop hearing the other party). TCP is the main connection-oriented transport protocol of the Internet, used by web browsers, secure shells, email, and many other applications.

Connectionless or *datagram* protocols are more like communicating by sending postcards. Mostly, the messages get through, but if anything goes wrong you have to be prepared to cope with the consequences—the protocol doesn't notify you whether your messages have been received, and messages can arrive out of order. To exchange short messages and get answers, a datagram protocol has less overhead than a connection-oriented one, as long as the overall service can cope with occasional disruptions, like a Domain Name Service (DNS) server failing to respond, for example: most DNS communication is connectionless. UDP is the main connectionless transport protocol for Internet communications.

Nowadays, security is increasingly important: understanding the underlying basis of secure communications helps you ensure that your communications are as secure as they need to be. If this summary dissuades you from trying to implement such technology yourself without a thorough understanding of the issues and risks, it will have served a worthwhile purpose.

All communications across network interfaces exchange strings of bytes (also known as *octets* in networking parlance). To communicate text, for example, the sender must encode it to bytes, which the receiver must decode.

The Berkeley Socket Interface

Most networking nowadays hinges on *sockets*. Sockets give access to pipelines between independent endpoints, using a *transport layer* to move information between the endpoints. The socket concept is general enough that the endpoints can be on the same machine, or on separate computers networked together locally or via a wide-area network. There is no difference in the programming required for these destinations.

The most typical transport layers are UDP (the User Datagram Protocol, for connectionless networking) and TCP (the Transmission Control Protocol, for connection-oriented networking) over a common IP (Internet Protocol) network layer. This combination of protocols, along with the many application protocols that run over them, is collectively known as *TCP/IP*. The Unix operating system also offers its own flavor of sockets for use between different processes on the same machine; such *Unix sockets* can be used for either type of networking.

The socket interface was first implemented in the BSD Unix system, and proved to be a very useful mechanism for network interactions, standardizing the structure of networking programs. Sockets are the basis of Python network programming, so it's important to understand how they work. A good introduction appears in the now somewhat venerable *Socket Programming How-To (https://docs.python.org/3/howto/sockets.html)* online overview.

The two most common kinds of socket (also known as socket *families*) are *Internet sockets* based on TCP/IP communications (available in two flavors to accommodate the modern IPv6 and the more traditional IPv4), and *Unix sockets*, though other families are also available. Internet sockets allow communication between any two computers that can transmit IP datagrams between them; Unix sockets can only communicate between processes on the same Unix machine.

To support many concurrent Internet sockets, the TCP/IP protocol stack uses endpoints identified by an IP address, a *port number* and a protocol. The port numbers allow the protocol-handling software to distinguish between different endpoints at the same IP address using the same protocol. A connected socket also associates with a *remote endpoint*, the *counter-party* socket to which it is connected and with which it can communicate.

Most Unix sockets are associated with names in the Unix filesystem. On Linux platforms, sockets whose names begin with a zero byte live in a name pool maintained by the kernel. These are useful for communicating with a chroot-jail process (*http://unix.stackexchange.com/questions/105/chroot-jail-what-is-it-and-how-do-i-use-it*), for example, where no filesystem is shared between two processes.

Both Internet and Unix sockets support connectionless and connection-oriented networking, so if you write your programs carefully they can work over either socket family. It is beyond the scope of this book to discuss other socket families, though we should mention that *raw sockets*, a subtype of the Internet socket family, let you send and receive link-layer packets (for example, Ethernet packets) directly.

This is useful for experimental applications, but some operating systems of the Windows family do their best to inhibit access to raw sockets by programmers, on the somewhat specious grounds that doing so discourages "hackers."

After creating an Internet socket, you can associate (*bind*) a specific port number with the socket (as long as that port number is not in use by some other socket). This is the strategy many servers use, offering service on so-called *well-known port numbers* defined by Internet standards as being in the range 1–1,023 (on Unix systems, root privileges are required to gain access to these ports). A typical client is unconcerned with the port number it uses, and so it typically requests an *ephemeral port*, assigned, and guaranteed to be unique, by the protocol driver. There is no need to bind ephemeral ports.

Imagine two processes on the same computer, both acting as clients to the same remote server. The full association for each socket is `(local_IP_address, local_port_number, protocol, remote_IP_address, remote_port_number)`. When traffic arrives at the server, the destination IP address, destination port number, protocol, and source IP address are exactly equal for both clients. The guarantee of uniqueness for ephemeral port numbers, however, makes it possible for the server to distinguish between traffic from the two clients. This is how TCP/IP *protocol multiplexing* works, allowing multiple conversations to take place unambiguously between the same two IP addresses.

Socket Addresses

The different types of sockets use different address formats.

Unix socket addresses are strings naming a node in the filesystem (on Linux platforms, strings starting with `b'\0'` correspond to names in a kernel table).

IPv4 socket addresses are pairs `(`*`address, port`*`)`. The first item is an IPv4 address, the second a port number in the range 1–65,535.

IPv6 socket addresses are four-item `(`*`address, port, flowinfo, scopeid`*`)` tuples. When providing an address as an argument, the *`flowinfo`* and *`scopeid`* items can be omitted, though this can sometimes cause problems.

Client-Server Computing

The pattern we discuss hereafter is usually referred to as *client-server* networking, where a *server* listens for traffic on a specific endpoint from *clients* who require the service. We do not cover *peer-to-peer* networking, which, lacking any central server, has to include the ability for peers to discover each other. This is often, ironically, achieved by contacting a central server, although discovery protocols such as SSDP (*https://en.wikipedia.org/wiki/Simple_Service_Discovery_Protocol*) allow complete independence from any central authority.

Most, though by no means all, network communication is performed using client-server techniques. The server listens for incoming traffic at a predetermined or advertised network endpoint. In the absence of such input it does nothing, simply sitting there waiting for input from clients. Communication is somewhat different between connectionless and connection-oriented endpoints.

In connectionless networking such as UDP, requests arrive at a server randomly and are dealt with immediately: a response is dispatched to the requester without delay. Each message is handled on its own, usually without reference to any communications that may previously have occurred between the two parties. Connectionless networking is thus well-suited to short-term, stateless interactions such as those required by DNS or network booting.

In connection-oriented networking, the client engages in an initial exchange with the server that effectively establishes a connection across a network pipeline between two processes (sometimes referred to as a *virtual circuit*), across which the processes can communicate until both have indicated their willingness to end the connection. Serving under these conditions requires the use of parallelism using a concurrency mechanism (such as threads or processes, covered in Chapter 14, or asynchronous programming, covered in Chapter 18) to handle each incoming connection asynchronously or simultaneously. Without such parallelism, the server would be unable to handle new incoming connections before earlier ones had terminated, since calls to socket methods normally *block* (meaning they pause the thread calling them until they terminate or time-out). Connections are the best way to handle lengthy interactions such as mail exchanges, command-line shell interactions, or the transmission of web content, and offer automatic error detection and correction when TCP is used.

Connectionless client and server structures

The broad logic flow of a connectionless server is as follows:

1. Create a socket of type `socket.SOCK_DGRAM` by calling `socket.socket`.
2. Associate the socket with the service endpoint by calling the socket's `bind` method.
3. Repeat the following steps *ad infinitum*:
    a. Request an incoming service datagram from a client by calling the socket's `recvfrom` method; this call blocks until a datagram is received.
    b. Compute the result.
    c. Send the result back to the client by calling the socket's `sendto` method.

The server spends most of its time in step 3a, awaiting input from clients.

A connectionless client's interaction with the server proceeds as follows:

1. Create a socket of type `socket.SOCK_DGRAM` by calling `socket.socket`.
2. Optionally, associate the socket with a specific endpoint by calling the socket's `bind` method.

3. Send a request to the server's endpoint by calling the socket's `sendto` method.
4. Await the server's reply by calling the socket's `recvfrom` method; this call blocks until the response is received. It is always necessary to apply a *timeout* to this call, to handle the case where a datagram goes missing, and either retry or abort the attempt: connectionless sockets do not guarantee delivery.
5. Use the result in the remainder of the client program's logic.

A single client program can perform several interactions with the same or multiple servers, depending on the services it needs to use. Many such interactions are hidden from the application programmer inside library code. A typical example is the resolution of a hostname to the appropriate network address, which commonly uses the `gethostbyname` library function (implemented in Python's `socket` module). Connectionless interactions normally involve sending a single packet to the server and receiving a single packet in response. The main exception involves *streaming* protocols, such as RTP, typically layered on top of UDP to minimize latency and delays: in streaming, many datagrams are sent and received.

Connection-oriented client and server structures

The broad flow of logic of a connection-oriented server is as follows:

1. Create a socket of type `socket.SOCK_STREAM` by calling `socket.socket`.
2. Associate the socket with the appropriate server endpoint by calling the socket's `bind` method.
3. Start the endpoint listening for connection requests by calling the socket's `listen` method.
4. Repeat the following steps *ad infinitum*:
   a. Await an incoming client connection by calling the socket's `accept` method; the server process blocks until an incoming connection request is received. When such a request arrives, a new socket object is created whose other endpoint is the client program.
   b. Create an asynchronous control thread to handle this specific connection, passing it the newly created socket; after which, the main thread continues by looping back to step 4a.
   c. In the new control thread, interact with the client using the new socket's `recv` and `send` methods, respectively, to read data from the client and send data to it. The `recv` method blocks until data is available from the client (or the client indicates it wishes to close the connection, in which case `recv` returns an empty result). The `send` method only blocks when the network software has so much data buffered that communication has to pause until the transport layer has emptied some of its buffer memory. When the server

wishes to close the connection, it can do so by calling the socket's `close` method, optionally calling its `shutdown` method first.

The server spends most of its time in step 4a, awaiting connection requests from clients.

A connection-oriented client's overall logic is as follows:

1. Create a socket of type `socket.SOCK_STREAM` by calling `socket.socket`.
2. Optionally, associate the socket with a specific endpoint by calling the socket's `bind` method.
3. Establish a connection to the server by calling the socket's `connect` method.
4. Interact with the server using the socket's `recv` and `send` methods, respectively, to read data from the server and send data to it. The `recv` method blocks until data is available from the server (or the server indicates it wishes to close the connection, in which case the `recv` call returns an empty result). The `send` method only blocks when the network software has so much data buffered that communications have to pause until the transport layer has emptied some of its buffer memory. When the client wishes to close the connection, it can do so by calling the socket's `close` method, optionally calling its `shutdown` method first.

Connection-oriented interactions tend to be more complex than connectionless ones. Specifically, determining when to read and write data is more complex because inputs must be parsed to determine when a transmission from the other end of the socket is complete. The protocols used in connection-oriented networking have to accommodate this determination; sometimes this is done by indicating the data length as a part of the content, sometimes by more complex methods.

The socket Module

Python's `socket` module handles networking with the socket interface. There are minor differences between platforms, but the module hides most of them, making it relatively easy to write portable networking applications.

The module defines four exceptions: their base class `socket.error`, which in v2 is a subclass of `exceptions.IOError`; in v3 it is a (deprecated) alias for `exceptions.OSError`, and three exception subclasses as follows:

herror `socket.herror` is raised for hostname-resolution errors—that is, when a name cannot be converted to a network address by the `socket.gethostbyname` function, or no hostname can be found for a network address by the `socket.gethostbyaddr` function. The accompanying value is a two-element tuple (*`h_errno, string`*) where *`h_errno`* is the integer error number returned by the operating system and *`string`* is a description of the error.

gaierror `socket.gaierror` is raised for addressing errors encountered in the `getaddrinfo` or `getnameinfo` functions.

timeout `socket.timeout` is raised when an operation takes longer than the timeout limit (established by the module's `setdefaulttimeout` function, overridable on a per-socket basis).

The module also defines a large set of constants. The most important of these are the address families (`AF_*`) and the socket types (`SOCK_*`) listed next. In v2 these constants are integers, while in v3 they are members of `IntEnum` collections. This difference can be disregarded, but, to debug your code, it's more helpful to see, for example, `<SocketKind.SOCK_STREAM: 1>` than a simple `1`. The module defines many other constants, used to set socket options, but the documentation does not define them fully: to use them you must be familiar with the low-level documentation for the C sockets libraries and system calls.

AF_INET Used to create sockets of the IPv4 address family.

AF_INET6 Used to create sockets of the IPv6 address family.

AF_UNIX Used to create sockets of the Unix address family. This constant is only defined on platforms that make Unix sockets available, and so is unavailable to, for example, Windows users.

AF_CAN Used (v3 only) to create sockets for the Controller Area Network (CAN) address family, not further described in this book, but widely used in automation, automotive, and embedded device applications.

SOCK_STREAM Used to create connection-oriented sockets, which provide full error detection and correction facilities.

SOCK_DGRAM Used to create connectionless sockets, which provide best-effort message delivery without connection capabilities or error detection.

SOCK_RAW Used to create sockets that give direct access to the link-layer drivers, typically used to implement lower-level network features outside the scope of this book.

SOCK_RDM Used to create reliable connectionless message sockets used in the TIPC protocol, which is outside the scope of this book.

SOCK_SEQPACKET Used to create reliable connection-oriented message sockets used in the TIPC protocol, which is outside the scope of this book.

The module defines a number of functions to create sockets, manipulate address information, and assist with representing data in a standard way. We do not cover all possibilities in this book, as the socket module documentation (*https://docs.python.org/3/library/socket.html*) is comprehensive; we deal with the ones that are most essential in writing networked applications.

Miscellaneous socket module functions

The `socket` module contains many functions, but most of them are only useful in specific situations. When communication takes place between network endpoints, the computers at either end might have architectural differences and therefore represent the same data in different ways, and so there are functions to handle translation of a limited number of data types to and from a network-neutral form, for example. Here are a few of the more generally applicable functions:

Table 17-1. Generally useful socket module functions

getaddrinfo	`socket.getaddrinfo(`*`host, port, family=0, type=0, proto=0, flags=0`*`)` Takes a *`host`* and *`port`*, returns a list of five-item tuples of the form `(`*`family, type, proto, canonical_name, socket`*`)` that can be used to create a socket connection to a specific service. In v2 all arguments are positional, but named arguments are accepted in v3. The *`canonical_name`* item is an empty string unless the `socket.AI_CANONNAME` bit is set in the *`flags`* argument. When you pass a hostname, rather than an IP address, the function returns a list of tuples, one for each IP address associated with the name.
getdefaulttimeout	`socket.getdefaulttimeout()` Returns the default timeout value in seconds for socket operations, or `None` if no value has yet been set. Some functions also let you specify an explicit timeout.
getfqdn	`socket.getfqdn(`*`[host]`*`)` Returns the fully qualified domain name associated with a hostname or network address (by default, that of the computer on which you call it).
gethostbyaddr	`socket.gethostbyaddr(`*`ip_address`*`)` Takes a string containing an IPv4 or IPv6 address and returns a three-item tuple of the form `(`*`hostname, aliaslist, ipaddrlist`*`)`. *`hostname`* is the canonical name for the IP, *`aliaslist`* a list of alternative names, and *`ipaddrlist`* a list of IPv4 and IPv6 addresses.
gethostbyname	`socket.gethostbyname(hostname)` Returns a string containing the IPv4 address associated with the given hostname. If called with an IP address, returns that address. This function does not support IPv6: use `getaddrinfo` for IPv6.
getnameinfo	`socket.getnameinfo(`*`sock_addr, flags=0`*`)` Takes a socket address and returns a `(`*`host, port`*`)` pair. Without *`flags`*, *`host`* is an IP address and *`port`* is an `int`.
setdefaulttimeout	`socket.setdefaulttimeout(`*`timeout`*`)` Sets sockets' timeout as a value in floating-point seconds. Newly created sockets operate in the mode determined by the *`timeout`* value, as discussed in the next section. Pass *`timeout`* as `None` to cancel the use of timeouts on subsequently created sockets.

Socket Objects

The socket object is the primary means of network communication in Python. A new socket is also created when a SOCK_STREAM socket accepts a connection, each such socket being used to communicate with the relevant client.

Socket objects and with statements

Every socket object is a context manager, so you can use any socket object in a `with` statement initial clause to ensure proper termination of the socket at exit from the `with` statement's body.

There are a number of ways you can create a socket, as detailed in the next section. The socket can operate in different modes, determined by its timeout value, established in one of three ways:

- By providing the timeout value on creation
- By calling the socket object's `settimeout` method
- According to the `socket` module's default timeout value as returned by the `socket.getdefaulttimeout` function

The timeout values to establish each mode are as follows:

`None`	Sets *blocking* mode. Each operation suspends the process (*blocks*) until the operation completes, unless the operating system causes an exception to be raised.
`0`	Sets *nonblocking* mode. Each operation raises an exception when it cannot be completed immediately, or when an error occurs. Use the `selectors` module, covered in "The selectors Module" on page 544, to find whether an operation can be completed immediately.
`>0.0`	Sets *timeout* mode. Each operation blocks until complete, or the timeout elapses (then, a `socket.timeout` exception is raised), or an error occurs.

Socket creation functions

Socket objects represent network endpoints. There are a number of different functions supplied by the `socket` module to create a socket:

create_connection `create_connection([address, [timeout, [source_address]]])`

Creates a socket connected to a TCP endpoint at an address (a `(host, port)` pair). *host* can either be a numeric network address or a DNS hostname; in the latter case, name resolution is attempted for both `AF_INET` and `AF_INET6`, and then a connection is attempted to each returned address in turn—a convenient way to create client programs using either IPv6 or IPv4 as appropriate.

The *timeout* argument, if given, specifies the connection timeout in seconds and thereby sets the socket's mode; when not present, the socket.getdefaulttimeout function is called to determine the value. The *source_address* argument, if given, must also be a pair (*host*, *port*) that the remote socket gets passed as the connecting endpoint. When *host* is '' or *port* is 0, the default OS behavior is used.

socket

socket(*family*=AF_INET, *type*=SOCK_STREAM, *proto*=0, *fileno*=None)

Creates and returns a socket of the appropriate address family and type (by default, a TCP socket on IPv4). The protocol number *proto* is only used with CAN sockets. When you pass the *fileno* argument, other arguments are ignored: the function returns the socket already associated with the given file descriptor.

The socket does not get inherited by child processes.

socketpair

socketpair([*family*[, *type*[, *proto*]]])

Returns a connected pair of sockets of the given address family, socket type, and (CAN sockets only) protocol. When *family* is not specified, the sockets are of family AF_UNIX on platforms where the family is available, and otherwise of family AF_INET. When *type* is not specified, it defaults to SOCK_STREAM.

A socket object *s* provides the following methods (out of which, those dealing with connections or requiring a connected sockets work only for SOCK_STREAM sockets, while the others work with both SOCK_STREAM and SOCK_DGRAM sockets). In the following table, the exact set of flags available depends on your specific platform; the *flags* values available are documented on the appropriate Unix manual page (*http://man7.org/linux/man-pages/man2/recv.2.html*) for recv(2) or manual page (*http://man7.org/linux/man-pages/man2/send.2.html*) for send(2):

accept

accept()

Blocks until a client establishes a connection to *s*, which must have been bound to an address (with a call to *s*.bind) and set to listening (with a call to *s*.listen). Returns a *new* socket object, which can be used to communicate with the other endpoint of the connection.

bind

bind(*address*)

Binds *s* to a specific address. The form of the *address* argument depends on the socket's address family (see "Socket Addresses" on page 502).

close `close()`

Marks the socket as closed. It does not necessarily close the connection immediately, depending on whether other references to the socket exist. If immediate closure is required, call the `s.shutdown` method first. The simplest way to ensure a socket is closed in a timely fashion is to use it in a `with` statement, since sockets are context managers.

connect `connect(`*`address`*`)`

Connects to a remote socket at *`address`*. The form of the *`address`* argument depends on the address family (see "Socket Addresses" on page 502).

detach `detach()`

Puts the socket into closed mode, but allows the socket object to be reused for further connections.

dup `dup()`

Returns a duplicate of the socket, not inheritable by child processes.

fileno `fileno()`

Returns the socket's file descriptor.

get_inheritable `get_inheritable()` (v3 only)

Returns `True` when the socket is going to be inherited by child processes. Otherwise, returns `False`.

getpeername `getpeername()`

Returns the address of the remote endpoint to which this socket is connected.

getsockname `getsockname()`

Returns the address being used by this socket.

gettimeout `gettimeout()`

Returns the timeout associated with this socket.

listen `listen(`*`[backlog]`*`)`

Starts the socket listening for traffic on its associated endpoint. If given, the integer *`backlog`* argument determines how many unaccepted connections the operating system allows to queue up before starting to refuse connections.

makefile `makefile(`*`mode, [bufsize]`*`)` (v2)

`makefile(`*`mode, buffering=None, *, encoding=None, newline=None`*`)` (v3)

Returns a file object allowing the socket to be used with file-like operations such as `read` and `write`. The mode can be `'r'` or `'w'`, to which `'b'` can be added for binary transmissions. The socket must be in blocking mode; if a timeout value is set, unexpected results may be observed if a timeout occurs. Libraries intending to support both v2 and v3 are advised to omit the remaining arguments, which are not well documented and differ between versions.

recv `recv(`*`bufsiz, [flags]`*`)`

Receive a maximum of *`bufsiz`* bytes of data on the socket. Returns the received data.

recvfrom `recvfrom(`*`bufsiz, [flags]`*`)`

Receive a maximum of *`bufsiz`* bytes of data from `s`. Returns a pair `(`*`bytes, address`*`)` where *`bytes`* is the received data, and *`address`* the address of the counter-party socket that sent the data.

recvfrom_into `recvfrom_into(`*`buffer, [nbytes, [flags]]`*`)`

Receive a maximum of *`nbytes`* bytes of data from `s`, writing it into the given *`buffer`* object. Returns a two-element tuple `(`*`nbytes, address`*`)` where *`nbytes`* is the number of bytes received and *`address`* is the address of the socket that sent the data.

recv_into `recv_into(`*`buffer, [nbytes, [flags]]`*`)`

Receive a maximum of *`nbytes`* bytes of data from `s`, writing it into the given *`buffer`* object. Returns the number of bytes received.

recvmsg `recvmsg(`*`bufsiz, [ancbufsiz, [flags]]`*`)`

Receive a maximum of *`bufsiz`* bytes of data on the socket and a maximum of *`ancbufsiz`* of ancillary ("out-of-band") data. Returns a four-item tuple `(`*`data, ancdata, msg_flags, address`*`)`, where *`bytes`* is the received data, *`ancdata`* is a list of three-item `(`*`cmsg_level, cmsg_type, cmsg_data`*`)` tuples representing the received ancillary data, *`msg_flags`* holds any flags received with the message, and *`address`* is the address of the counter-party socket that sent the data (if the socket is connected, this value is undefined, but the sender can be determined from the socket).

send `send(`*`bytes, [flags]]`*`)`

Send the given data *`bytes`* over the socket, which must already be connected to a remote endpoint. Returns the number of bytes sent, which should be verified: the call may not transmit all data, in which case transmission of the remainder will have to be separately requested.

sendall `sendall(bytes, [flags])`

Send all the given data *bytes* over the socket, which must already be connected to a remote endpoint. The socket's timeout value applies to the transmission of all the data, even if multiple transmissions are needed.

sendto `sendto(bytes, address)` or

`sendto(bytes, flags, address)`

Transmit the *bytes* (*s* must not be connected) to the given socket address.

sendmsg `sendmsg(buffers, [ancdata, [flags, [address]]])`

Send normal and ancillary (out-of-band) data to the connected endpoint. *buffers* should be an iterable of bytes-like objects. The *ancdata* argument should be an iterable of `(data, ancdata, msg_flags, address)` tuples representing the ancillary data, and *msg_flags* are flags values documented on the Unix manual page for the `send(2)` system call. *address* should only be provided for an unconnected socket, and determines the endpoint to which the data is sent.

sendfile `sendfile(file, offset=0, count=None)`

Send the contents of file object *file* (which must be open in binary mode) to the connected endpoint. On platforms where `os.sendfile` is available, it's used; otherwise, the `send` call is used. If provided, *offset* determines the starting byte position in the file from which transmission begins, and *count* sets the maximum number of bytes to be transmitted. Returns the total number of bytes transmitted.

set_inheritable `set_inheritable(flag)` (v3 only)

Determines whether the socket gets inherited by child processes, according to the Boolean value of *flag*.

setblocking `setblocking(flag)`

Determines whether *s* operates in blocking mode (see "Socket Objects" on page 508) according to the Boolean value of *flag*. `s.setblocking(True)` is equivalent to `s.settimeout(None)` and `s.set_blocking(False)` is equivalent to `s.settimeout(0.0)`.

settimeout `settimeout(timeout)`

Establishes the mode of `s` (see "Socket Objects" on page 508) according to the value of *timeout*.

shutdown `shutdown(how)`

Shuts down one or both halves of a socket connection according to the value of the *how* argument, as detailed here:

socket.SHUT_RD	No further receive operations can be performed on *s*.
socket.SHUT_WR	No further send operations can be performed on *s*.
socket.SHUT_RDWR	No further receive or send operations can be performed on *s*.

A socket object *s* also has the following attributes:

family An attribute that is *s*'s socket family

type An attribute that is *s*'s socket type

A Connectionless Socket Client

Consider a simplistic packet-echo service. Text encoded in UTF-8 (the assumed encoding of most Python source files) is sent to a server, which sends the same information back to the client originating it. In a connectionless service, all the client has to do is send each chunk of data to the defined server endpoint.

The following client works equally well on either v2 or v3 (printing slightly different output to stdout in each case. In v2, Unicode text strings are marked as `u'...'` while bytestrings are not marked; in v3, Unicode text strings are not marked, while bytestrings are marked as `b'...'`):

```
# coding: utf-8
from __future__ import print_function
import socket

UDP_IP = '127.0.0.1'
UDP_PORT = 8883
MESSAGE = u"""\
This is a bunch of lines, each
of which will be sent in a single
UDP datagram. No error detection
or correction will occur.
Crazy bananas! £€ should go through."""

sock = socket.socket(socket.AF_INET,  # Internet
                     socket.SOCK_DGRAM)  # UDP
server = UDP_IP, UDP_PORT
for line in MESSAGE.splitlines():
```

Networking Basics

```
    data = line.encode('utf-8')
    sock.sendto(data, server)
    print('Sent', repr(data), 'to', server)
    response, address = sock.recvfrom(1024)  # buffer size: 1024
    print('Recv', repr(response.decode('utf-8')), 'from', address)
```

Note that the server is only expected to perform a byte-oriented echo function. The client therefore encodes its Unicode data into specific bytestrings, and decodes the bytestring responses received from the server back into Unicode text.

A Connectionless Socket Server

A server for this service is also quite simple. It binds to its endpoint, receives packets (datagrams) at that endpoint, and returns a packet to the client sending each datagram, with exactly the same data. The server treats all clients equally and does not need to use any kind of concurrency (though this handy characteristic might not hold for a service where request handling takes more time).

The following server works equally well on v2 or v3 (with slightly different output in each version, as explained previously for the client):

```
from __future__ import print_function
import socket

UDP_IP = '127.0.0.1'
UDP_PORT = 8883

sock = socket.socket(socket.AF_INET,  # Internet
                     socket.SOCK_DGRAM)  # UDP
sock.bind((UDP_IP, UDP_PORT))
print('Serving at', UDP_IP, UDP_PORT)

while True:
    data, addr = sock.recvfrom(1024)  # buffer size is 1024 bytes
    print('Recv', repr(data), 'from', addr)
    sock.sendto(data, addr)
    print('Sent', repr(data), 'to', addr)
```

This code offers no way to terminate the service other than by interrupting it (typically from the keyboard, with Ctrl-C or Ctrl-Break).

A Connection-Oriented Socket Client

Consider a simplistic connection-oriented "echo-like" protocol: a server lets clients connect to its listening socket, receives arbitrary bytes from them, and sends back to each client the same bytes that client sent to the server, until the client closes the connection. Here's an example of an elementary test client (fully coded to run equally well in v2 and v3)[1]:

```
# coding: utf-8
from __future__ import print_function
import socket

with socket.socket(socket.AF_INET, socket.SOCK_STREAM) as sock:
    sock.connect(('localhost', 8881))
    print('Connected to server')
    data = u"""A few lines of text
including non-ASCII characters: €£
to test the operation
of both server
and client."""
    for line in data.splitlines():
        sock.sendall(line.encode('utf-8'))
        print('Sent:', line)
        response = sock.recv(1024)
        print('Recv:', response.decode('utf-8'))
print('Disconnected from server')
```

Note that the data is text, so it must be encoded with a suitable representation, for which we chose the usual suspect—UTF-8. The server works in terms of bytes (since it is bytes, AKA octets, that travel on the network); the received bytes object gets decoded with UTF-8 back into Unicode text before printing. Any other suitable codec could be used: the key point is that text must be encoded before transmission and decoded after reception. The server, working in terms of bytes, does not even need to know which encoding is being used, except maybe for logging purposes.

A Connection-Oriented Socket Server

Here is a simplistic server corresponding to the testing client shown in "A Connection-Oriented Socket Client" on page 514, using multithreading via `concurrent.futures`, covered in "The concurrent.futures Module" on page 417, also fully coded to run equally well in v3 and v2 (as long as you've installed the `concurrent` backport—see "The concurrent.futures Module" on page 417):

```
from __future__ import print_function
from concurrent import futures as cf
import socket

def handle(new_sock, address):
    print('Connected from', address)
    while True:
        received = new_sock.recv(1024)
        if not received: break
```

Networking Basics

1 Note this client example isn't secure; see "Transport Layer Security (TLS, AKA SSL)" on page 516 for an introduction to making it secure.

```
            s = received.decode('utf-8', errors='replace')
            print('Recv:', s)
            new_sock.sendall(received)
            print('Echo:', s)
        new_sock.close()
        print('Disconnected from', address)

    servsock = socket.socket(socket.AF_INET, socket.SOCK_STREAM)
    servsock.bind(('localhost', 8881))
    servsock.listen(5)
    print('Serving at', servsock.getsockname())

    with cf.ThreadPoolExecutor(20) as e:
        try:
            while True:
                new_sock, address = servsock.accept()
                e.submit(handle, new_sock, address)
        except KeyboardInterrupt:
            pass
        finally:
            servsock.close()
```

This server has its limits. In particular, it runs only 20 threads, so it cannot be simultaneously serving more than 20 clients; any further client trying to connect while 20 are being served waits in *servsock*'s listening queue, and (should that queue fill up with 5 clients waiting to be accepted) further clients attempting connection get rejected outright. This server is intended just as an elementary example for demonstration purposes, not as a solid, scalable, or secure system.

Transport Layer Security (TLS, AKA SSL)

The Transport Layer Security (TLS) is often also known as the Secure Sockets Layer (SSL), which was in fact the name of its predecessor protocol. TLS provides privacy and data integrity over TCP/IP, helping you defend against server impersonation, eavesdropping on the bytes being exchanged, and malicious alteration of those bytes. For an introduction to TLS, we recommend the extensive Wikipedia (*https://en.wikipedia.org/wiki/Transport_Layer_Security*) entry.

In Python, you can use TLS via the `ssl` module of the standard library, documented in detail online (*https://docs.python.org/3/library/ssl.html*). To use `ssl` well, you need `ssl`'s rich online docs (*https://docs.python.org/3/library/ssl.html*), as well as a deep and broad understanding of TLS itself (the Wikipedia article, excellent and vast as it is, can only begin to cover this large, difficult subject). In particular, the security considerations (*https://docs.python.org/3/library/ssl.html#ssl-security*) section of the online docs must be entirely learned and completely understood, as must the materials at the many links helpfully offered in that section.

If these considerations make it look like perfect implementation of security precautions is a daunting task, that's because it *is*. In security, you're pitting your wits and skills against those of sophisticated attackers who may be more familiar with all the nooks and crannies of the problems involved, since they specialize in finding workarounds and breaking in, while (usually) your focus can't be exclusively on such issues—rather, you're trying to provide useful services in your code, and it's quite risky to see security as an afterthought, a secondary point…it *has* to be front-and-center throughout, to win said battle of skills and wits.

That said, we strongly recommend undertaking the above-outlined study of TLS to all readers—the better all developers understand security considerations, the better off we all are (except, we guess, for "black-hat" security-breaker wannabes).

Unless you have acquired a really deep and broad understanding of TLS and Python's `ssl` module (in which case, you'll know what exactly to do—better than we possibly could!), we recommend using an `SSLContext` instance to hold all details of your use of TLS. Build that instance with the `ssl.create_default_context` function, add your certificate if needed (it *is* needed if you're writing a secure server), then use the instance's `wrap_socket` method to wrap (almost[2]) every `socket.socket` instance you make into an instance of `ssl.SSLSocket`—behaving almost identically to the socket object it wraps, but nearly transparently adding security checks and validation "on the side."

The default TLS contexts strike a good compromise between security and broad usability, and we recommend you stick by them (unless you're knowledgeable enough to further fine-tune and tighten security for special needs). If you need to support outdated counterparts, ones unable to use the most recent, most secure implementations of TLS, you may feel tempted to learn just enough to relax your security demands; do that at your own risk—we most definitely *don't* recommend wandering into such "HC SVNT DRACONES" (here be dragons) lands!

In the following sections, we cover the minimal subset of `ssl` you need if you just want to follow our recommendations. But, remember, even if that is the case, please also read up on TLS and `ssl`, just to gain some background knowledge about the intricate issues involved. It may stand you in good stead one day!

SSLContext

The `ssl` module supplies an `ssl.SSLContext` class, whose instances hold information about TLS configuration (including certificates and private keys) and offer many methods to set, change, check, and use that information. If you know exactly what you're doing, you can manually instantiate, set up, and use your own `SSLContext` instances for your own specialized purposes.

However, we recommend instead that you instantiate an `SSLContext` using the well-tuned function named `ssl.create_default_context` with a single argument: `ssl.Purpose.CLIENT_AUTH` if your code is a server (and thus may need to authenti-

2 We say "almost" because, when you code a server, you don't wrap the socket you bind, listen on, and accept connections from.

cate clients), or `ssl.Purpose.SERVER_AUTH` if your code is a client (and thus definitely needs to authenticate servers). If your code is both a client to some servers and a server to other clients (as, for example, some Internet *proxies* are), then you'll need two instances of `SSLContext`, one for each purpose.

For most client-side uses, your `SSLContext` is ready. If you're coding a server, or a client for one of the rare servers that require TLS authentication of the clients, you need to have a certificate file and a key file, and add them to the `SSLContext` instance (so that counter-parties can verify your identify) with code such as, for example:

```
ctx = ssl.create_default_context(ssl.Purpose.CLIENT_AUTH)
ctx.load_cert_chain(certfile='mycert.pem', keyfile='mykey.key')
```

passing the paths to the certificate and key files to the `load_cert_chain` method. (See the online docs (*https://docs.python.org/3/library/ssl.html#certificates*) to learn how to obtain key and certificate files.)

Once your context instance *`ctx`* is ready, if you're coding a client, just call *`ctx`*`.wrap_socket` to wrap any socket you're about to connect to a server, and use the wrapped result (an instance of `ssl.SSLSocket`) instead of the socket you just wrapped. For example:

```
sock = socket.socket(socket.AF_INET)
sock = ctx.wrap_socket(sock, server_hostname='www.example.com')
sock.connect(('www.example.com', 443))
# just use `sock` normally from here onwards
```

Note that, in the client case, you should also pass `wrap_socket` a `server_hostname` argument corresponding to the server you're about to connect to; this way, the connection can verify that the identity of the server you end up connecting to is indeed correct, one absolutely crucial step to any Internet security.

Server-side, *don't* wrap the socket that you are binding to an address, listening on, or accepting connections on; just bind the new socket to `accept` returns. For example:

```
sock = socket.socket(socket.AF_INET)
sock.bind(('www.example.com', 443))
sock.listen(5)
while True:
    newsock, fromaddr = sock.accept()
    newsock = ctx.wrap_socket(newsock, server_side=True)
    # deal with `newsock` as usual, shutdown and close it when done
```

In this case, what you need to pass to `wrap_socket` is an argument `server_side=True`, so it knows that you're on the server side of things.

Again, we recommend the online docs, and particularly the examples (*https://docs.python.org/3/library/ssl.html#examples*), for better understanding of even this simple subset of `ssl` operations.

ds). Python's standard library's direct support for callbacks-based async rchitectures is not particularly strong nor up-to-date, and we do not recom- nend it nor cover it further in this book; if you're keen to use such an architec- ure, we recommend third-party frameworks Twisted (*https:// wistedmatrix.com/trac/*) (or alternatively, Tornado (*http://www.tornado veb.org/en/stable/*)—more specialized, especially for web tasks, but supports coroutines as mentioned in the next section).

The third, most modern alternative category is *coroutine-based* async architec- tures, covered in the next section.

his chapter, after explaining the general concepts of coroutine-based async itectures, we cover the v3-only module `asyncio`, which lets you implement such itectures as well as callback-based ones, and the lower-level module `selectors` the standard library in v3, but also available as a third-party backport download v2), which lets you implement multiplexed architectures.

routine-Based Async Architectures

frequent problem with both multiplexed and callback-based architectures is that de that would, with blocking I/O, be a single, rather linear function gets fragmen- d into pieces without an immediately clear connection to each other; this can ake the code harder to develop and debug.

o avoid this problem, we need functions able to suspend their execution, hand ontrol over to a framework while preserving their internal state, and later resume, rom right after the suspension point, when the framework gives them the go- head. Such functions are known as *coroutines*.

Coroutine functions and coroutine objects

The term *coroutine* is used to describe two different but related entities: the function defining the coroutine (e.g., in 3.5, one starting with `async def`), more precisely known as a *coroutine function* when disambiguation is needed; and the object returned by a coroutine function, representing some combination of I/O and computation that eventually termi- nates. The latter is more precisely known as a *coroutine object* when disambiguation is needed.

You can think of a coroutine function as a factory for corou- tine objects; more directly, remember that calling a coroutine function does not cause any user-written code to execute, but rather just builds and returns a coroutine object. Coroutine objects are not callable: rather, you schedule them for execu- tion via appropriate calls in a framework such as `asyncio`, or `await` them in the body of another coroutine object.

Asynchronous

For *I/O bound* code (meaning code that spends a lot of time do
the best-performing architectures are usually *asynchronous* (AK
long as the I/O operations can be made *nonblocking*, meaning th
initiate an operation, go on doing other things while that operatic
and then find out when the operation is finished.

Async architectures are also sometimes known as *event-driven* ones,
pletion of I/O operations (new data becoming available on an input
output channel becoming ready to accept new data) can be mode
external to your code, to which your code responds appropriately.

Asynchronous architectures can be classified into three broad categori

- In what is sometimes known as a *multiplexed* async architectur keeps track of the I/O channels on which operations may be pe you can do no more until one or more of the pending I/O oper pletes, the thread running your code goes into a blocking wait (this usually referred to as "your code *blocks*"), specifically waiting for a tion on the relevant set of channels. When a completion wakes up th wait, your code deals with the specifics of that completion (such "dea may include initiating more I/O operations), then, usually, goes ba blocking wait. Python offers several low-level modules supporting mu async architectures, but the best one to use is the higher-level `selecto` ule, covered in "The selectors Module" on page 544.
- In a *callback-based* async architecture, your code associates with each e event a *callback*—a function or other callable that the asynchronous fran calls when the event occurs. The association can be explicit (passing a fu in order to request that it get called back when appropriate), or implicit ir ous ways (for example, extending a base class and overriding appropriate r

v2's stdlib offers no coroutine-based async architecture support; v3, on the other hand, has strong support for coroutine-based async architectures, through the `asyncio` module.

To write coroutine-based async libraries that work with v2 as well as v3, specifically for web uses, consider the third-party framework Tornado (*http://www.tornadoweb.org/en/stable/*), an async web server with a bundled web application framework.

To write an application, target a specific Python version

When you write an application, rather than a library, always pick a specific Python version (we strongly recommend v3), thus freeing yourself of any worry about cross-compatibility concerns, and leaving you free to write the best code for the specific task at hand.

To make writing and using coroutines clearer and faster, the v3 release that's most recent at the time of this writing (Python 3.5) introduces two new keywords, `async` and `await`, covered in "async and await" on page 523. You should use them instead of making coroutines via `yield from` as mentioned in "yield from (v3-only)" on page 97, "The asyncio Module (v3 Only)" on page 521 and "asyncio coroutines" on page 522, as you had to in 3.4 and earlier: using `async` and `await` keeps full interoperability with `yield from`-based coroutines, but makes your code more explicit and readable, avoids certain kinds of errors, and also helps with performance. `tornado` now also supports `async`/`await`-based coroutines.

One thing all async architectures have is an *event loop*—code (either within the framework or explicit at the application level) that loops waiting for *events* (changes of state on I/O channels being watched or—depending on the nature of the application—other external occurrences such as user interactions on a user interface). Coroutine objects can only run when the event loop is running.

Lastly, all kinds of async architectures can also usefully support objects known as *futures* (or sometimes as *promises* or *deferreds*), analogous to the ones covered in Table 14-1 (although the latter rely on a pool of threads or processes, while async futures reflect the completion of some nonblocking I/O operation). Futures wrapping a coroutine object can only run when the event loop is running.

The asyncio Module (v3 Only)

The `asyncio` module is at the core of v3's modern approach to asynchronous programming, especially for network-related tasks. `asyncio` as supplied by the standard library focuses on providing infrastructure and components at a relatively low level of abstraction. However, you can find higher-abstraction modules at this wiki page (*https://github.com/python/asyncio/wiki/ThirdParty*)—building blocks such as aiohttp (*https://pypi.python.org/pypi/aiohttp*) (supporting HTTP servers and clients, including WebSocket (*https://en.wikipedia.org/wiki/WebSocket*)), web frameworks (some working on top of `aiohttp` , some standalone), AsyncSSH (*http://*

asyncssh.readthedocs.io/en/latest/) (supporting SSH servers and clients), and so forth.

Contribute to the asyncio ecosystem

If you find yourself coding a higher-abstraction module for some task or protocol not yet well covered in modules listed at the wiki page, but maybe of general interest, we strongly recommend you make your module high-quality via tests and docs (that serves you well in any case!), package it up and upload it to PyPI as covered in Chapter 25, and then edit the wiki page to add a pointer to it. Fame as an open source code author awaits, and so does help from other programmers in improving your module!

When you write Python code based on `asyncio` (ideally also using add-on modules from *asyncio.org*), you'll usually be writing *coroutine functions*. Up to Python 3.4 included, such functions are generators using the `yield from` statement covered in "yield from (v3-only)" on page 97, decorated with `@asyncio.coroutine`, covered in "asyncio coroutines" on page 522; since Python 3.5, although you could still use the `yield from` (+ decorator) approach for backward compatibility with previous releases, it's better to use the new `async def` statement covered in "async and await" on page 523. In the rest of this chapter, we tag as *coroutine* those functions or methods supplied by `asyncio` that are, indeed, coroutine functions, thus nonblocking and returning coroutine objects (they internally use `async def` in 3.5 and later, and, compatibly, `@asyncio.coroutine` and `yield from` in the body in 3.4 and earlier).

Coroutines in asyncio

For backward compatibility with Python 3.4, v3 (by which, as always, we mean Python 3.5) lets you implement coroutines in either of two different ways: as appropriately decorated generators using the `yield from` statement; or as *native* coroutines, using the new keywords `async` and `await`.

asyncio coroutines

As mentioned in "Coroutine-Based Async Architectures" on page 520, the core concept used in `asyncio` is that of a *coroutine*—a function able to suspend its execution, preserving its internal state; explicitly hand control back to the framework that's orchestrating it (in `asyncio`'s case, that's the event loop, covered in "asyncio's Event Loop" on page 524); and resume execution from the point at which it had suspended, when the framework tells it to resume.

Just as a generator function immediately executes, runs no user code, and returns a generator object, a coroutine function immediately executes, runs no user code, and returns a coroutine object. In fact, up to Python 3.4, a coroutine function was just a specific kind of generator function: a generator function is any function containing one or more occurrences of the `yield` keyword, and a coroutine function was one specifically containing one or more occurrences of the expression `yield from` *`iterable`*...although such a statement could also occur in a generator function not intended for use as a coroutine function, as covered in "yield from (v3-only)" on page 97 (the resulting ambiguity, although marginal, was suboptimal, whence the introduction in Python 3.5 of `async` and `await`, which remove any ambiguity). To mark such a `yield from`–based coroutine function explicitly as being a coroutine, and ensure it was usable in `asyncio`, you decorated it with `@asyncio.coroutine`. For example, here's a coroutine that sleeps for *`delay`* seconds, then returns a *`result`*:

```
@asyncio.coroutine
def delayed_result(delay, result):
  yield from asyncio.sleep(delay)
  return result
```

Calling, for example, *`delayed_result`*`(1.5, 23)`, gives you a generator object (specifically a coroutine object) poised to wait a second and a half, then return `23`. Note that the generator object in question won't execute until it's properly connected to an event loop, covered in "asyncio's Event Loop" on page 524, and the event loop runs; for example,

```
loop = asyncio.get_event_loop()
x = loop.run_until_complete(delayed_result(1.5, 23))
```

sets *x* to `23` after a delay of a second and a half.

Mostly for debugging purposes, you can check whether some object *f* is a coroutine function with `asyncio.iscoroutinefunction(`*`f`*`)`; you can check whether some object *x* is a coroutine object with `asyncio.iscoroutine(`*`x`*`)`.

async and await

To allow more explicit and readable code, Python 3.5 introduces the keywords `async` and `await`.[1] Use `async` to create coroutines (with `async def`), to create asynchronous context managers (with `async with`), and for asynchronous iteration (with `async for`).

When you use `async def` instead of `def`, and `await` instead of `yield from`,[2] the function becomes an explicit coroutine function, with no need for decoration (and without being a generator function as a side effect). For example:

```
async def new_way(delay, result):
  await asyncio.sleep(delay)
  return result
```

1 Pseudokeywords, currently: for backward compatibility, you can also still use `async` and `await` as normal identifiers—but don't do that, as it makes your code less readable and in some future version it will become a syntax error.

2 However, you can't `await` an arbitrary iterable object—only an awaitable object, such as a coroutine object or an `asyncio.Future` instance.

gives you a coroutine function *new_way* that's fully equivalent to the *delayed_result* in the previous example (you could decorate *new_way* with @asyncio.coroutine, but this is not required nor recommended usage). In this way, you can also write a coroutine function that never awaits anything. (It may seem peculiar to need that, but it comes in handy in prototyping, testing, and refactoring.) An async def coroutine function cannot contain any yield; conversely, you can use await only within an async def coroutine function.

Within a native coroutine function (meaning one defined with async def) only, you can also use two useful new constructs: async with and async for.

async with The async with statement is just like the with statement, except that the context manager (the object that's the result of the expression just after the keyword with) must be an *asynchronous* context manager, implementing the special methods __aenter__ and __aexit__, corresponding to __enter__ and __exit__ in a plain context manager (a class might conceivably choose to implement all four special methods, making its instances usable in both plain with and async with statements). __aenter__ and __aexit__ must return awaitable objects (each is typically a coroutine function defined with async def, thus intrinsically returning a coroutine object, which is of course awaitable); async with *x*: implicitly uses await *x*.__aenter__() at entry and await *x*.__aexit__(*type*, *value*, *tb*) at exit, elegantly achieving seamless async context-manager behavior.

async for The async for statement is just like the for statement, except that the iterable (the object that's the result of the expression just after the keyword for) must be an *asynchronous* iterable, implementing the special method __aiter__,[3] corresponding to __iter__ in a plain iterable (a class might conceivably choose to implement both special methods, making its instances usable in both plain for and async for statements). __aiter__ must return an asynchronous iterator (implementing the special method __anext__, corresponding to __next__ in a plain iterator, but returning an awaitable object); async for *x*: implicitly uses *x*.__aiter__() at entry and await *y*.__anext__() on the eventually returned asynchronous iterator *y*, elegantly achieving seamless async looping behavior.

asyncio's Event Loop

asyncio supplies an explicit *event loop* interface, and some basic implementations of that interface, as by far the largest component of the framework.

The event loop interface is a very broad and rich interface supplying several categories of methods; the interface is embodied in the asyncio.BaseEventLoop class. asyncio offers a few alternative implementations of event loops, depending on your

---

3 Note that __aiter__ must *not* be a coroutine, while all the other dunder methods in these sections with names starting with __a must be coroutines.

platform, and third-party add-on packages let you add still more, for example, to integrate with specific user interface frameworks such as `Qt`. The core idea is that all event loop implementations implement the same interface.

In theory, your application can have multiple event loops and manage them through multiple, explicit *event loop policies*; in practice, such complexity is rarely needed, and you can get away with a single event loop, normally in your main thread, managed by a single, implicit global policy. The main exception to this state of things occurs when you want to run `asyncio` code on multiple threads of your program; in that case, while you may still get away with a single policy, you need multiple event loops—a separate one per each thread calling event-loop methods other than `call_soon_threadsafe`, covered in Table 18-1. Each thread can only call methods on a loop instantiated and running in that thread.[4]

In the rest of this chapter, we assume (except when we explicitly state otherwise) that you're using a single event loop, usually the default one obtained by calling *`loop`* `= asyncio.get_event_loop()` near the start of your code. Sometimes, you force a specific implementation, by first instantiating *`loop`* explicitly as your specific platform or third-party framework may require, then immediately calling `asyncio.set_event_loop(`*`loop`*`)`; ignoring platform-specific or framework-specific semantic peculiarities, which we don't cover in this book, the material in the rest of this chapter applies equally well in this second, somewhat-rarer use case.

The following sections cover nine categories of methods supplied by an `asyncio.BaseEventLoop` instance *`loop`*, and a few closely related functions and classes supplied by `asyncio`.

Loop state and debugging mode

`loop` can be in one of three states: *stopped* (that's the state *`loop`* is when just created: nothing yet runs on *`loop`*), *running* (all functionality runs on *`loop`*), or *closed* (*`loop`* is irreversibly terminated, and cannot be started again). Independently, *`loop`* can be in *debug* mode (checking sanity of operations, and giving ample information to help you develop code) or not (faster and quieter operation; that's the normal mode to use "in production," as opposed to development, debugging, and testing), as covered in "asyncio developing and debugging" on page 527. Regarding state and mode, *`loop`* supplies the following methods:

4 For some subtleties regarding event loops on Windows and event-loop backward compatibility with old releases of macOS, see the event loops page of the online docs; there are no such subtleties on other platforms.

close `close()`

Sets *loop* to closed state; loses pending callbacks, flushes queues, asks *loop*'s executor to shut down. You can call *loop*`.close()` only when *loop*`.is_running()` is `False`. After *loop*`.close()`, call no further methods on *loop*, except *loop*`.is_closed()` or *loop*`.is_closing()` (both return `True` in this case) and *loop*`.close()` (which does nothing in this case).

get_debug `get_debug()`

Returns `True` when *loop* is in debug mode; otherwise, returns `False`. The initial value is `True` when the environment variable PYTHONASYNCIODEBUG is a nonempty string; otherwise, `False`.

is_closed `is_closed()`

Returns `True` when *loop* is closed; otherwise, returns `False`.

is_closing `is_closing()`

Returns `True` when *loop* is closing or already closed; otherwise, returns `False`.

is_running `is_running()`

Returns `True` when *loop* is running; otherwise, returns `False`.

run_forever `run_forever()`

Runs *loop* until *loop*`.stop()` is called. Returns, eventually, after a call to `stop` has placed *loop* in stopped mode.

run_until_complete `run_until_complete(`*future*`)`

Runs until *future* (an instance of `asyncio.Future`, covered in "Futures" on page 535) completes; if *future* is a coroutine object or other awaitable, it's wrapped with `asyncio.ensure_future`, covered in "Tasks" on page 531. When *future* is done, `run_until_complete` returns *future*'s result or raises its exception.

set_debug `set_debug(`*debug*`)`

Sets *loop*'s debug mode to `bool(`*debug*`)`.

stop `stop()`

If called when *loop* is stopped, `stop` polls the I/O selector once, with a *`timeout`* of zero; runs all callbacks scheduled (previously, or in response to I/O events that occurred in that one-off poll of the I/O selector); then exits and leaves *loop* in the stopped state.

If called when *loop* is running (e.g., in `run_forever`), `stop` runs the currently scheduled callbacks, then exits and leaves *loop* in the stopped state (in this case, callbacks newly scheduled by other callbacks don't execute; they remain queued, to execute when `run_forever` is called again). After this, the `run_forever` that had put *loop* in running mode returns to its caller.

asyncio developing and debugging When you develop code using `asyncio`, sanity checking and logging help a lot.

Besides calling *`loop`*`.set_debug(True)` (or setting the environment variable `PYTHONASYNCIODEBUG` to a nonempty string), set logging to `DEBUG` level: for example, call `logging.basicConfig(level=logging.DEBUG)` at startup.

In debug mode, you get useful `ResourceWarning` warnings when transports and event loops are not explicitly closed (frequently a symptom of a bug in your code): enable warnings, as covered in "The warnings Module" on page 476—for example, use the command-line option **`-Wdefault`** (with no space between `-W` and `default`) when you start Python, as mentioned in Table 2-1.

For more tips and advice on developing and debugging with `asyncio`, see the appropriate section (*https://docs.python.org/3/library/asyncio-dev.html*) in the online docs.

Calls, time, and sleep

A key functionality of the `asyncio` event loop is to schedule calls to functions (see Table 18-1)—either "as soon as convenient" or with specified delays. For the latter purpose, *loop* maintains its own internal clock (in seconds and fractions), not necessarily coincident with the system clock covered in Chapter 12.

Use functools.partial when you need to pass named arguments in calls

loop's methods to schedule calls don't directly support passing named arguments. If you do need to pass named arguments, wrap the function to be called in `functools.partial`, covered in Table 7-4. This is the best way to achieve this goal (superior to alternatives such as using `lambda` or closures), because debuggers (including `asyncio`'s debug mode) introspect such wrapped functions to supply more and clearer information than they could with alternative approaches.

Table 18-1.

call_at	`call_at(`*`when, callback, *args`*`)` Schedules *`callback(*args)`* to be called when *`loop`*`.time()` equals *`when`* (or, as soon as feasible after that, should something else be running at that precise time). Returns an instance of `asyncio.Handle`, on which you can call the method `cancel()` to cancel the callback (innocuous if the call has already occurred).
call_later	`call_later(`*`delay, callback, *args`*`)` Schedules *`callback(*args)`* to be called *`delay`* seconds from now (*`delay`* can include a fractional part) (or, as soon as feasible after that, should something else be running at that precise time). Returns an instance of `asyncio.Handle`, on which you can call method `cancel()` to cancel the callback (innocuous if the call has already occurred).
call_soon	`call_soon(`*`callback, *args`*`)` Schedules *`callback(*args)`* to be called as soon as possible (in first-in, first-out order with regard to other scheduled callbacks). Returns an instance of `asyncio.Handle`, on which you can call method `cancel()` to cancel the callback (innocuous if the call has already occurred).
call_soon_threadsafe	`call_soon_threadsafe(`*`callback, *args`*`)` Like `call_soon`, but safe to call from a thread different from the one *`loop`* is running in (*`loop`* should normally run in the main thread, to allow signal handling and access from other processes).
time	`time()` Returns a `float` that is *`loop`*'s current internal time.

Besides *`loop`*'s own methods, the current event loop's internal time is also used by one module-level function (i.e., a function supplied directly by the module `asyncio`):

sleep *`coroutine`* `sleep(`*`delay, result`*`=None)`

A coroutine function to build and return a coroutine object that completes after *`delay`* seconds and returns *`result`* (*`delay`* can include a fractional part).

Connections and server

loop can have open communication channels of several kinds: connections that reach out to other systems' listening sockets (stream or datagram or—on Unix—unix sockets), ones that listen for incoming connections (grouped in instances of the Server class), and ones built on pipes to/from subprocesses. Here are the methods *loop* supplies to create the various kinds of connections:

create_connection

coroutine create_connection(*protocol_factory*, *host*=None, *port*=None, *, *ssl*=None, *family*=0, *proto*=0, *flags*=0, *sock*=None, *local_addr*=None, *server_hostname*=None)

protocol_factory, the one argument that's always required, is a callable taking no arguments and returning a protocol instance. *create_connection* is a coroutine function: its resulting coroutine object, as *loop* runs it, creates the connection if required, wraps it into a transport instance, creates a protocol instance, ties the protocol instance to the transport instance with the protocol's connection_made method, and finally—once all is done—returns a pair (*transport*, *protocol*) as covered in "Transports and protocols" on page 538.

When you have an already-connected stream socket that you just want to wrap into a transport and protocol, pass it as the named argument *sock*, and avoid passing any of *host*, *port*, *family*, *proto*, *flags*, *local_addr*; otherwise, create_connection creates and connects a new stream socket for you (family AF_INET or AF_INET6 depending on *host*, or *family* if explicitly specified; type SOCK_STREAM), and you need to pass some or all of those arguments to specify the details of the socket to connect.

Optional arguments must be passed as named arguments, if at all.

ssl, when true, requests an SSL/TLS transport (in particular, when it's an instance of ssl.SSLContext, as covered in "SSLContext" on page 517, that instance is used to create the transport); in this case, you may optionally pass *server_hostname* as the hostname to match the server's certificate against (or an empty string, disabling hostname matching, but that's a serious security risk). When you specify *host*, you may omit *server_hostname*; in this case, *host* is the hostname that must match the certificate.

All other optional named-only arguments can be passed only if *sock* is not passed. *family*, *proto*, and *flags* are passed through to getaddrinfo to resolve the *host*; *local_addr* is a (*local_host*, *local_port*) pair passed through to getaddrinfo to resolve the local address to which to bind the socket being created.

create_datagram_endpoint *coroutine* `create_datagram_endpoint(`*protocol_factory*`,` *local_addr*`=None,` *remote_addr*`=None, *,` *family*`=0,` *proto*`=0,` *flags*`=0,` *reuse_address*`=True,` *reuse_port*`=None,` *allow_broadcast*`=None,` *sock*`=None)`

Much like `create_connection`, except that the connection is a datagram rather than stream one (i.e., socket type is SOCK_DGRAM). *remote_addr* can be optionally be passed as a (*remote_host*, *remote_port*) pair. *reuse_address*, when true (the default), means to reuse a local socket without waiting for its natural timeout to expire. *reuse_port*, when true, on some Unix-like systems, allows multiple datagram connections to be bound to the same port. *allow_broadcast*, when true, allows this connection to send datagrams to the broadcast address.

create_server *coroutine* `create_server(`*protocol_factory*`,` *host*`=None,` *port*`=None, *,` *family*`=socket.AF_UNSPEC,` *flags*`=socket.AI_PASSIVE,` *sock*`=None,` *backlog*`=100,` *ssl*`=None,` *reuse_address*`=None,` *reuse_port*`=None)`

Like `create_connection`, except that it creates or wraps a *listening* socket and returns an instance of the class `asyncio.Server` (with the attribute `sockets`, the list of `socket` objects the server is listening to; the method `close()` to close all sockets asynchronously; and the coroutine method `wait_closed()` to wait until all sockets are closed).

host can be a string, or a sequence of strings in order to bind multiple hosts; when None, it binds all interfaces. *backlog* is the maximum number of queued connections (passed on to the underlying socket's *listen* method). *reuse_address*, when true, means to reuse a local socket without waiting for its natural timeout to expire. *reuse_port*, when true, on some Unix-like systems, allows multiple listening connections to be bound to the same port.

create_unix_connection *coroutine* `create_unix_connection(`*protocol_factory*`,` *path*`, *,` *ssl*`=None,` *sock*`=None,` *server_hostname*`=None)`

Like `create_connection`, except that the connection is on a Unix socket (socket family AF_UNIX, socket type SOCK_STREAM) on the given *path*. Unix sockets allow very fast, secure communication, but only between processes on a single Unix-like computer.

create_unix_server *coroutine* create_unix_server(*protocol_factory*, *path*=None, *, *sock*=None, *backlog*=100, *ssl*=None)

Same as create_server, but for Unix-socket connections on the given *path*.

Besides sockets, event loops can connect subprocess pipes, using these methods:

connect_read_pipe *coroutine* connect_read_pipe(*protocol_factory*, *pipe*)

Returns a (*transport*, *protocol*) pair wrapping read-mode, nonblocking file-like object *pipe*.

connect_write_pipe *coroutine* connect_write_pipe(*protocol_factory*, *pipe*)

Returns a (*transport*, *protocol*) pair wrapping write-mode, nonblocking file-like object *pipe*.

Tasks

An asyncio task (asyncio.Task, covered in "Tasks" on page 536, is a subclass of asyncio.Future, covered in "Futures" on page 535) wraps a coroutine object and orchestrates its execution. *loop* offers a method to create a task:

create_task create_task(*coro*)

Creates and returns a Future (usually, a Task) wrapping the coroutine object *coro*.

You can also customize the factory *loop* uses to create tasks, but that is rarely needed except to write custom implementations of event loops, so we don't cover it.

Another roughly equivalent way to create a task is to call asyncio.ensure_future with a single argument that is a coroutine object or other awaitable; the function in this case creates and returns a Task instance wrapping the coroutine object. (If you call asyncio.ensure_future with an argument that's a Future instance, it returns the argument unchanged.)

Create tasks with loop.create_task

We recommend using more explicit and readable loop.create_task instead of the roughly equivalent asyncio.ensure_future.

Watching file descriptors

You can choose to use *loop* at a somewhat-low abstraction level, watching for file descriptors to become ready for reading or writing, and calling callback functions when they do. (On Windows, with the default `SelectorEventLoop` implementation of *loop*, you can use these methods only on file descriptors representing sockets; with the alternative `ProactorEventLoop` implementation that you can choose to explicitly instantiate, you cannot use these methods at all.) *loop* supplies the following methods related to watching file descriptors:

add_reader `add_reader(`*`fd, callback, *args`*`)`

When *fd* becomes available for reading, call *callback(*args)*.

add_writer `add_writer(`*`fd, callback, *args`*`)`

When *fd* becomes available for writing, call *callback(*args)*.

remove_reader `remove_reader(`*`fd`*`)`

Stop watching for *fd* to become available for reading.

remove_writer `remove_writer(`*`fd`*`)`

Stop watching for *fd* to become available for writing.

socket operations; hostnames

Also at a low level of abstraction, *loop* supplies four coroutine-function methods corresponding to methods on socket objects covered in Chapter 17:

sock_accept *coroutine* `sock_accept(`*`sock`*`)`

sock must be nonblocking, bound to an address, and listening for connections. `sock_accept` returns a coroutine object that, when done, returns a pair (*conn, address*), where *conn* is a new socket object to send and receive data on the connection and *address* is the address bound to the socket of the counterpart.

sock_connect *coroutine* `sock_connect(`*`sock, address`*`)`

sock must be nonblocking and not already connected. *address* must be the result of a `getaddrinfo` call, so that `sock_connect` doesn't have to use DNS itself (for example, for network sockets, *address* must include an IP address, not a hostname). `sock_connect` returns a coroutine object that, when done, returns `None` and leaves *sock* appropriately connected as requested.

sock_recv *coroutine* `sock_recv(`*`sock, nbytes`*`)`

sock must be nonblocking and connected. *nbytes* is an `int`, the maximum number of bytes to receive. `sock_recv` returns a coroutine object that, when done, returns a `bytes` object with the data received on the socket (or raises an exception if a network error occurs).

sock_sendall *coroutine* `sock_sendall(`*sock*`,` *data*`)`

sock must be nonblocking and connected. `sock_sendall` returns a coroutine object that, when done, returns `None`, having sent all the bytes in *data* on the socket. (In case of a network error, an exception is raised; there is no way to determine how many bytes, if any, were sent to the counterpart before the network error occurred.)

It's often necessary to perform DNS lookups. *loop* supplies two coroutine-function methods that work like the same-name functions covered in Table 17-1, but in an async, nonblocking way:

getaddrinfo *coroutine* `getaddrinfo(`*host*`,` *port*`, *,` *family*`=0,` *type*`=0,` *proto*`=0,` *flags*`=0)`

Returns a coroutine object that, when done, returns a five-items tuple `(`*family*`,` *type*`,` *proto*`,` *canonname*`,` *sockaddr*`)`, like `socket.getaddrinfo`.

getnameinfo *coroutine* `getnameinfo(`*sockaddr*`,` *flags*`=0)`

Returns a coroutine object that, when done, returns a pair `(host, port)`, like `socket.getnameinfo`.

Unix signals

On Unix-like platforms, *loop* (when run on the main thread) supplies two methods to add and remove handlers for *signals* (a Unix-specific, limited form of interprocess communication, well covered on Wikipedia (*https://en.wikipedia.org/wiki/Unix_signal*)) the process may receive:

add_signal_handler `add_signal_handler(`*signum*`,` *callback*`, *`*args*`)`

Sets the handler for signal number *signum* to call `callback(*`*args*`)`.

remove_signal_handler `remove_signal_handler(signum)`

Removes the handler for signal number *signum*, if any. Returns `True` when it removes a handler, and `False` when there was no handler to remove (in either case, *signum* now has no handler).

Executor

loop can arrange for a function to run in an *executor*, a pool of threads or processes as covered in "The concurrent.futures Module" on page 417: that's useful when you must do some blocking I/O, or CPU-intensive operations (in the latter case, use as executor an instance of `concurrent.futures.ProcessPoolExecutor`). The two relevant methods are:

run_in_executor *coroutine* run_in_executor(*executor*, *func*, **args*)

Returns a coroutine object that runs *func*(**args*) in *executor* and, when done, returns *func*'s result. *executor* must be an Executor instance, or None, to use *loop*'s current default executor.

set_default_executor set_default_executor(*executor*)

Sets *loop*'s executor to *executor*, which must be an Executor instance, or None, to use the default (thread pool) executor.

Error handling

You can customize exception handling in the event loop; *loop* supplies four methods for this purpose:

call_exception_handler call_exception_handler(*context*)

Call *loop*'s current exception handler.

default_exception_handler default_exception_handler(*context*)

The exception handler supplied by *loop*'s class; it's called when an exception occurs and no handler is set, and may be called by a handler to defer a case to the default behavior.

get_exception_handler get_exception_handler()

Gets and returns *loop*'s current exception handler, a callable accepting two arguments, *loop* and *context*.

set_exception_handler set_exception_handler(*handler*)

Sets *loop*'s current exception handler to *handler*, a callable accepting two arguments, *loop* and *context*.

context is a dict with the following contents (more keys may be added in future releases). All keys, except message, are optional; use *context*.get(*key*) to avoid a KeyError on accessing some key in the context:

exception
: Exception instance

future
: asyncio.Future instance

handle
: asyncio.Handle instance

message
    `str` instance, the error message

protocol
    `asyncio.Protocol` instance

socket
    `socket.socket` instance

transport
    `asyncio.Transport` instance

The following sections cover three more concepts you need in order to use `asyncio`, and functionality supplied by `asyncio` for each of these concepts.

Futures

The `asyncio.Future` class is almost compatible with the `Future` class supplied by the module `concurrent.futures` and covered in Table 14-1 (in some future version of Python, the intention is to fully unify the two `Future` interfaces, but this goal cannot be guaranteed). The main differences between an instance *`af`* of `asyncio.Future` and an instance *`cf`* of `concurrent.futures.Future` are:

- *`af`* is not thread-safe
- *`af`* can't be passed to functions `wait` and `as_completed` of module `concurrent.futures`
- Methods *`af`*`.result` and *`af`*`.exception` don't take a *`timeout`* argument, and can only be called when *`af`*`.done()` is `True`
- There is no method *`af`*`.running()`

For thread-safety, callbacks added with *`af`*`.add_done_callback` get scheduled, once *`af`* is done, via *`loop`*`.call_soon_threadsafe`.

`af` also supplies three extra methods over and above those of *`cf`*:

remove_done_callback `remove_done_callback(`*`func`*`)`

Removes all instances of *`func`* from the list of *`af`*'s callbacks; returns the number of instances it removed.

set_exception `set_exception(`*`exception`*`)`

Marks *`af`* done, and set its exception to *`exception`*. If *`af`* is already done, `set_exception` raises an exception.

Async Alternatives

set_result `set_result(`*`value`*`)`

Marks *af* done, and sets its result to *value*. If *af* is already done, `set_result` raises an exception.

(In fact, *cf* has methods `set_exception` and `set_result`, too, but in *cf*'s case they're meant to be called strictly and exclusively by unit tests and `Executor` implementations; *af*'s identical methods do not have such constraints.)

The best way to create a `Future` in `asyncio` is with *loop*'s `create_future` method, which takes no arguments; at worst, *loop*`.create_future()` just performs exactly the same as `return futures.Future(`*`loop`*`)`, but, this way, alternative loop implementations get a chance to override the method and provide a better implementation of futures.

Tasks

`asyncio.Task` is a subclass of `asyncio.Future`: an instance *at* of `asyncio.Task` wraps a coroutine object and schedules its execution in *loop*.

The class defines two class methods: `all_tasks()`, which returns the `set` of all tasks defined on *loop*; and `current_task()`, which returns the task currently executing (`None` if no task is executing).

at`.cancel()` has slightly different semantics from the `cancel` method of other futures: it does not guarantee the cancellation of the task, but rather raises a `CancelledError` inside the wrapped coroutine—the latter may intercept the exception (intended to enable clean-up work, but also makes it possible for the coroutine to refuse cancellation). *at*`.cancelled()` returns `True` only when the wrapped coroutine has propagated (or spontaneously raised) `CancelledError`.

`asyncio` supplies several functions to ease working with tasks and other futures. All accept an optional (named-only) argument `loop=None` to use an event loop different from the current default one (`None` means to use the current default event loop); for all, arguments that are futures can also be coroutine objects (which get automatically wrapped into instances of `asyncio.Task`). The functions are:

as_completed `as_completed(`*`futures`*`, *, loop=None, timeout=None)`

Returns an iterator whose values are `Future` instances (yielded approximately in order of completion). When `timeout` is not `None`, it's a value in seconds (which may have a fractional part), and in that case `as_completed` raises `asyncio.TimeOuterror` after `timeout` seconds unless all futures have completed by then.

gather `gather(*futures, *, loop>=None, return_exceptions=False)`

Returns a single future *f* whose result is a list of the results of the *futures* arguments, in the same order, when all have completed (all must be futures in the same event loop). When `return_exceptions` is false, any exception raised in a contained future immediately propagates through *f*; when `return_exceptions` is true, contained-future exceptions are put in *f*'s result list, just like contained-future results.

f`.cancel()` cancels any contained future that's not yet done. If any contained future is separately cancelled, that's just as if it had raised a `CancelledError` (therefore, this does not cancel *f*, as long as `return_exceptions` is true).

run_coroutine_threadsafe `run_coroutine_threadsafe(coro, loop)`

Submits coroutine object *coro* to event loop *loop*, returns a `concurrent.futures.Future` instance to access the result. This function is meant to allow other threads to safely submit coroutine objects to *loop*.

shield `shield(f, *, loop=None)`

Waits for `Future` instance *f*, shielding *f* against cancellation if the coroutine doing `await asyncio.shield(f)` (or `yield from asyncio.shield(f)`) is cancelled.

timeout `timeout(timeout, *, loop=None)`

Returns a context manager that raises an `asyncio.TimeoutError` if a block has not completed after *timeout* seconds (*timeout* may have a fractional part). For example:

```
try:
    with asyncio.timeout(0.5):
        await first()
        await second()
except asyncio.TimeoutError:
    print('Alas, too slow!')
else:
    print('Made it!')
```

This snippet prints **`Made it!`** when the two awaitables *first*`()` and *second*`()`, in sequence, both complete within half a second; otherwise, it prints **`Alas, too slow!`**

wait

`coroutine wait(futures, *, loop=None, timeout=None, return_when=ALL_COMPLETED)`

This coroutine function returns a coroutine object that waits for the futures in nonempty iterable *futures*, and returns a tuple of two sets of futures, (*done*, *still_pending*). return_when must be one of three constants defined in module *concurrent.futures*: ALL_COMPLETED, the default, returns when all futures are done (so the returned *still_pending* set is empty); FIRST_COMPLETED returns as soon as any of the futures is done; FIRST_EXCEPTION is like ALL_COMPLETED but also returns if and when any future raises an exception (in which case *still_pending* may be nonempty).

wait_for

`coroutine wait_for(f, timeout, *, loop=None)`

This coroutine function returns a coroutine object that waits for future *f* for up to *timeout* seconds (*timeout* may have a fractional part, or may be None, meaning to wait indefinitely) and returns *f*'s result (or raises *f*'s exception, or asyncio.TimeoutError if a timeout occurs).

Transports and protocols

For details about transports and protocols, see the section about them in the online docs (*https://docs.python.org/3/library/asyncio-protocol.html*). In this section, we're offering just the conceptual basis, some core details about working with them, and two examples. The core idea is that a *transport* does all that's needed to ensure that a stream (or datagram) of "raw," uninterpreted bytes is pushed to an external system, or pulled from an external system; a *protocol* translates those bytes to and from semantically meaningful messages.

A *transport* class is a class supplied by asyncio to abstract any one of various kinds of communication channels (TCP, UDP, SSL, pipes, etc.). You don't directly instantiate a transport class: rather, you call *loop* methods that create the transport instance and the underlying channel, and provide the transport instance when done.

A *protocol* class is one supplied by asyncio to abstract various kinds of protocols (streaming, datagram-based, subprocess-pipes). Extend the appropriate one of those base classes, overriding the callback methods in which you want to perform some action (the base classes supply empty default implementations for such methods, so just don't override methods for events you don't care about). Then, pass your class as the *protocol_factory* argument to *loop* methods.

A protocol instance *p* always has an associated transport instance *t*, in 1-to-1 correspondence. As soon as the connection is established, *loop* calls *p*.connection_made(*t*): *p* must save *t* as an attribute of self, and may perform some initialization-setting method calls on *t*.

When the connection is lost or closed, *loop* calls p.connection_lost(*exc*), where *exc* is None to indicate a regular closing (typically via end-of-file, EOF), or else an Exception instance recording what error caused the connection to be lost.

Each of connection_made and connection_lost gets called exactly once on each protocol instance *p*. All other callbacks to *p*'s methods happen between those two calls; during such other callbacks, *p* gets informed by *t* about data or EOF being received, and/or asks *t* to send data out. All interactions between *p* and *t* occur via callbacks by each other on the other one's methods.

Protocol-based examples: echo client and server Here is a protocol-based implementation of a client for the same simple echo protocol shown in "A Connection-Oriented Socket Client" on page 514. (Since asyncio exists only in v3, we have not bothered maintaining any compatibility with v2 in this example's code.)

```
import asyncio

data = """A few lines of text
including non-ASCII characters: €£
to test the operation
of both server
and client."""

class EchoClient(asyncio.Protocol):

  def __init__(self):
      self.data_iter = iter(data.splitlines())

  def write_one(self):
      chunk = next(self.data_iter, None)
      if chunk is None:
          self.transport.write_eof()
      else:
          line = chunk.encode()
          self.transport.write(line)
          print('Sent:', chunk)

  def connection_made(self, transport):
      self.transport = transport
      print('Connected to server')
      self.write_one()

  def connection_lost(self, exc):
      loop.stop()
      print('Disconnected from server')

  def data_received(self, data):
      print('Recv:', data.decode())
      self.write_one()
```

```
loop = asyncio.get_event_loop()
echo = loop.create_connection(EchoClient, 'localhost', 8881)
transport, protocol = loop.run_until_complete(echo)
loop.run_forever()
loop.close()
```

You wouldn't normally bother using `asyncio` for such a simplistic client, one that is doing nothing beyond sending data to the server, receiving replies, and using `print` to show what's happening. However, the purpose of the example is to show how to use `asyncio` (and, specifically, `asyncio`'s protocols) in a client (which would be handy if a client had to communicate with multiple servers and/or perform other nonblocking I/O operations simultaneously).

Nevertheless, this example, for conciseness, takes shortcuts (such as calling `loop.stop` when connection is lost) that would not be acceptable in high-quality production code. For a critique of simplistic echo examples, and a thoroughly productionized counterexample, see Łukasz Langa's aioecho (*https://github.com/ambv/aioecho*).

Similarly, here is a v3-only protocol-based server for the same (deliberately simplistic) echo functionality:

```
import asyncio

class EchoServer(asyncio.Protocol):

  def connection_made(self, transport):
      self.transport = transport
      self.peer = transport.get_extra_info('peername')
      print('Connected from', self.peer)

  def connection_lost(self, exc):
      print('Disconnected from', self.peer)

  def data_received(self, data):
      print('Recv:', data.decode())
      self.transport.write(data)
      print('Echo:', data.decode())

loop = asyncio.get_event_loop()
echo = loop.create_server(EchoServer, 'localhost', 8881)
server = loop.run_until_complete(echo)
print('Serving at', server.sockets[0].getsockname())
loop.run_forever()
```

This server code has no intrinsic limits on how many clients at a time it can be serving, and the transport deals with any network fragmentation.

asyncio streams Fundamental operations of transports and protocols, as outlined in the previous section, rely on a callback paradigm. As mentioned in "Coroutine-Based Async Architectures" on page 520, this may make development harder when you need to fragment what could be a linear stream of code into multiple functions and methods; with `asyncio`, you may partly finesse that by using coroutines, futures, and tasks for implementation—but there is no intrinsic connection between protocol instances and such tools, so you'd essentially be building your own. It's reasonable to wish for a higher level of abstraction, focused directly on coroutines, for the same networking purposes you could use transports, protocols, and their callbacks for.

`asyncio` comes to the rescue by supplying coroutine-based *streams*, as documented online (*https://docs.python.org/3/library/asyncio-stream.html*). Four convenience coroutine functions based on streams are directly supplied by `asyncio`: `open_connection`, `open_unix_connection`, `start_server`, and `start_unix_server`. While usable on their own, they're mostly supplied as examples of how to best create streams, and the docs explicitly invite you to copy them into your code and edit them as necessary. You can easily find the source code, for example on GitHub (*http://bit.ly/2oc4QPs*). The same logic applies, and is explicitly documented in source code comments, to the stream classes themselves—`StreamReader` and `StreamWriter`; the classes wrap transports and protocols and supply coroutine methods where appropriate.

Here is a streams-based implementation of a client for the same simple echo protocol shown in "A Connection-Oriented Socket Client" on page 514, coded using the legacy (pre–Python 3.5) approach to coroutines:

```
import asyncio

data = """A few lines of data
including non-ASCII characters: €£
to test the operation
of both server
and client."""

@asyncio.coroutine
def echo_client(data):
    reader, writer = yield from asyncio.open_connection(
        'localhost', 8881)
    print('Connected to server')
    for line in data:
        writer.write(line.encode())
        print('Sent:', line)
        response = yield from reader.read(1024)
        print('Recv:', response.decode())
    writer.close()
    print('Disconnected from server')

loop = asyncio.get_event_loop()
loop.run_until_complete(echo_client(data.splitlines()))
loop.close()
```

asyncio.open_connection eventually (via its coroutine-object immediate result, which yield from waits for) returns a pair of streams, *reader* and *writer*, and the rest is easy (with another yield from to get the eventual result of reader.read). The modern native (Python 3.5) kind of coroutine is no harder:

```
import asyncio

data = """A few lines of data
including non-ASCII characters: €£
to test the operation
of both server
and client."""

async def echo_client(data):
    reader, writer = await asyncio.open_connection(
        'localhost', 8881)
    print('Connected to server')
    for line in data:
        writer.write(line.encode())
        print('Sent:', line)
        response = await reader.read(1024)
        print('Recv:', response.decode())
    writer.close()
    print('Disconnected from server')

loop = asyncio.get_event_loop()
loop.run_until_complete(echo_client(data.splitlines()))
loop.close()
```

The transformation needed in this case is purely mechanical: remove the decorator, change def to async def, and change yield from to await.

Similarly for streams-based servers—here's one that uses legacy coroutines:

```
import asyncio

@asyncio.coroutine
def handle(reader, writer):
    address = writer.get_extra_info('peername')
    print('Connected from', address)

    while True:
        data = yield from reader.read(1024)
        if not data: break
        s = data.decode()
        print('Recv:', s)
        writer.write(data)
        yield from writer.drain()
        print('Echo:', s)

    writer.close()
    print('Disconnected from', address)
```

```
loop = asyncio.get_event_loop()
echo = asyncio.start_server(handle, 'localhost', 8881)
server = loop.run_until_complete(echo)

print('Serving on {}'.format(server.sockets[0].getsockname()))
try:
    loop.run_forever()
except KeyboardInterrupt:
    pass
server.close()
loop.run_until_complete(server.wait_closed())
loop.close()
```

And here's the equivalent using modern native coroutines, again with the same mechanical transformation:

```
import asyncio

async def handle(reader, writer):
    address = writer.get_extra_info('peername')
    print('Connected from', address)

    while True:
        data = await reader.read(1024)
        if not data: break
        s = data.decode()
        print('Recv:', s)
        writer.write(data)
        await writer.drain()
        print('Echo:', s)

    writer.close()
    print('Disconnected from', address)

loop = asyncio.get_event_loop()
echo = asyncio.start_server(handle, 'localhost', 8881)
server = loop.run_until_complete(echo)

print('Serving on {}'.format(server.sockets[0].getsockname()))
try:
    loop.run_forever()
except KeyboardInterrupt:
    pass
server.close()
loop.run_until_complete(server.wait_closed())
loop.close()
```

The same considerations as in the previous section apply to these client and server examples: each client, as it stands, may be considered "overkill" for the very simple task it performs (but is useful to suggest how asyncio-based clients for more complex tasks would proceed); each server is intrinsically unbounded in the number of clients it can serve, and immune to any data fragmentation that might have occurred during network transmission.

Synchronization and Queues

`asyncio` offers classes (to synchronize coroutines) that are very similar to the ones that the `threading` module offers (to synchronize threads), as covered in "Thread Synchronization Objects" on page 399, and queues similar to the thread-safe queues covered in "The queue Module" on page 406. This section documents the small differences between the synchronization and queue classes supplied by `asyncio`, and the classes with the same names covered in Chapter 14.

Asyncio synchronization primitives

`asyncio` supplies the classes `BoundedSemaphore`, `Condition`, `Event`, `Loop`, and `Semaphore`, very similar to the classes of the same names covered in "Thread Synchronization Objects" on page 399, except of course that the classes in `asyncio` synchronize coroutines, not threads. The `asyncio` synchronization classes and their methods do not accept a *`timeout`* argument (use `asyncio.wait_for` instead to apply a timeout to a coroutine or `asyncio` future).

Several methods of `asyncio` synchronization classes (all that deal with acquiring or waiting for a synchronization class's instance, and therefore could possibly block) are coroutine methods returning coroutine objects. Specifically, this applies to `BoundedSemaphore.acquire`, `Condition.acquire`, `Condition.wait`, `Condition.wait_for`, `Event.wait`, `Loop.acquire`, and `Semaphore.acquire`.

Asyncio queues

`asyncio` supplies the class `Queue`, and its subclasses `LifoQueue` and `PriorityQueue`, very similar to the classes of the same names covered in "The queue Module" on page 406, except of course that the classes in `asyncio` queue data between coroutines, not between threads. The `asyncio` queue classes and their methods do not accept a *`timeout`* argument (use `asyncio.wait_for` instead to apply a timeout to a coroutine or `asyncio` future).

Several methods of `asyncio` queue classes (all that could possibly block) are coroutine methods, returning coroutine objects. Specifically, this applies to the methods `get`, `join`, and `put`, of the class `Queue` and of both subclasses.

The selectors Module

`selectors` is in Python's standard library only in v3. However, you can install a v2 backport via **`pip2 install selectors34`**, then, for portability, code your import as:

```
try:
    import selectors
```

```
except ImportError:
    import selectors34 as selectors
```

selectors supports I/O multiplexing by picking whatever mechanism is best on your platform from a lower-level module, select; you do not need to know the low-level details of select, and therefore we do not cover select in this book.

The kind of files that selectors can handle depend on your platform. Sockets (covered in Chapter 17) are supported on all platforms; on Windows, no other kinds of files are supported. On Unix-like systems, other kinds may be supported (to open a file in nonblocking mode, use the low-level call os.open, with the flag os.O_NONBLOCK, covered in Table 10-5).

selectors Events

selectors provides two constants, EVENT_READ (meaning that a file is available for reading) and EVENT_WRITE (meaning that a file is available for writing). To indicate both events together, use the "bitwise or" operator |, as in:

```
selectors.EVENT_READ | selectors.EVENT_WRITE
```

The SelectorKey Class

Methods of selector classes return instances of the class SelectorKey, a named tuple that supplies four attributes:

data
: Data associated with the file object when you registered it with the selector

event
: Either of the constants covered in "selectors Events" on page 545, or their "bitwise or"

fd
: The file descriptor on which the event occurred

fileobj
: The file object registered with the selector class: can either be an int (in which case it's equal to *fd*) or an object with a fileno() method (in which case *fd* equals *fileobj*.fileno()).

The BaseSelector Class

Call selectors.DefaultSelector() to get an instance of the concrete subclass of the BaseSelector abstract class that's optimal on your platform. (Don't worry about what specific concrete subclass you're getting; they all implement the same functionality.) Each such class is a context manager, and therefore suitable for use in a with statement to ensure that the selector is closed when you're done with it:

```
with selectors.DefaultSelector() as sel:
    # use sel within this block, or in functions called within it
    ...
# here, after the block's done, sel is properly closed
```

A selector instance *s* supplies the following methods:

close `close()`

Frees all of *s*'s resources. You can't use *s* after calling `s.close()`.

get_key `get_key(fileobj)`

Returns the `SelectorKey` associated with *`fileobj`*, or raises `KeyError` when *`fileobj`* is not registered.

get_map `get_map()`

Returns a mapping with files as keys, and `SelectorKey` instances as values.

modify `modify(fileobj, events, data=None)`

Like `s.unregister(fileobj)` followed by `s.register(fileobj, events, data)`, but faster. Returns the `SelectorKey` associated with *`fileobj`*, or raises `KeyError` when *`fileobj`* is not registered.

register `register(fileobj, events, data=None)`

Registers a file object for selection, monitoring the requested events, and associating with it an arbitrary item of data. *`fileobj`* is either an `int` (a file descriptor) or any object with a `.fileno()` method returning a file descriptor. *`events`* is `EVENT_READ`, `EVENT_WRITE`, or their "bitwise or." `data` is any arbitrary object; a frequently used idiom is to pass, as `data`, a function to call when the monitored events occur.

Returns a new `SelectorKey` instance, or raises `KeyError` when *`fileobj`* is already registered, and `ValueError` when *`fileobj`* and/or *`events`* are invalid.

select `select(timeout=None)`

Returns a list of pairs `(sk, events)` for file objects that have become ready for reading and/or writing. Returns an empty list if the waiting times out (or, depending on Python versions, if the waiting is interrupted by a signal). *`sk`* is a `SelectorKey` instance; *`events`* is `EVENT_READ`, `EVENT_WRITE`, or their "bitwise or" if both events are being monitored and both have occurred.

When `timeout>0`, `select` won't wait for more than that number of seconds (optionally including a fractional part), possibly returning an empty list.

unregister `unregister(fileobj)`

Deregisters file object *`fileobj`* from monitoring; `s.unregister` a file before you close that file. Returns the `SelectorKey` associated with *`fileobj`*, or raises `KeyError` when *`fileobj`* was not registered.

When to Use selectors

`selectors` is quite low-level, but can sometimes come in handy when performance is key, particularly when the task to perform on the sockets is simple.

selectors echo server example

Here is a `selectors`-based example server for the simplistic echo protocol shown in "A Connection-Oriented Socket Client" on page 514. This example is fully coded to run equally well in v2 (as long as you've installed the `selectors34` backport; see "The concurrent.futures Module" on page 417) and v3; it provides more informational `prints` than example "A Connection-Oriented Socket Server" on page 515, to better show the low-level mechanisms involved in communication with multiple clients "at once," in byte chunks of whatever size optimizes all I/O operations:

```
from __future__ import print_function
import socket
try:
    import selectors
except ImportError:
    import selectors34 as selectors
ALL = selectors.EVENT_READ | selectors.EVENT_WRITE

# mapping socket -> bytes to send on that socket when feasible
data = {}

# set of sockets to be closed and unregistered when feasible
socks_to_close = set()

def accept(sel, data, servsock, unused_events):
    # accept a new connection, register it with the selector
    sock, address = servsock.accept()
    print('Connected from', address)
    sel.register(sock, ALL, handle)

def finish(sel, data, sock):
    # sock needs to be closed & unregistered if it's in the selector
    if sock in sel.get_map():
        ad = sock.getpeername()
        print('Disconnected from {}'.format(ad))
        sel.unregister(sock)
        sock.close()
    data.pop(sock, None)

def handle(sel, data, sock, events):
    # a client socket just became ready to write and/or read
    ad = sock.getpeername()
    if events & selectors.EVENT_WRITE:
        tosend = data.get(sock)
        if tosend:
            # send as much as the client's ready to receive
```

```
                nsent = sock.send(tosend)
                s = tosend.decode('utf-8', errors='replace')
                print(u'{} bytes sent to {} ({})'.format(nsent, ad, s))
                # bytes to be sent later, if any
                tosend = tosend[nsent:]
            if tosend:
                # more bytes to send later, keep track of them
                print('{} bytes remain for {}'.format(len(tosend), ad))
                data[sock] = tosend
            else:
                # no more bytes to send -> ignore EVENT_WRITE for now
                print('No bytes remain for {}'.format(ad))
                data.pop(sock, None)
                sel.modify(sock, selectors.EVENT_READ, handle)
        if events & selectors.EVENT_READ:
            # receive up to 1024 bytes at a time
            newdata = sock.recv(1024)
            if newdata:
                # add new data received as needing to be sent back
                s = newdata.decode('utf-8', errors='replace')
                print(u'Got {} bytes from {} ({})'.format(
                      len(newdata), ad, s))
                data[sock] = data.get(sock, b'') + newdata
                sel.modify(sock, ALL, handle)
            else:
                # recv empty string means client disconnected
                socks_to_close.add(sock)

    try:
        servsock = socket.socket(socket.AF_INET, socket.SOCK_STREAM)
        servsock.bind(('', 8881))
        servsock.listen(5)
        print('Serving at', servsock.getsockname())
        with selectors.DefaultSelector() as sel:
            sel.register(servsock, selectors.EVENT_READ, accept)
            while True:
                for sk, events in sel.select():
                    sk.data(sel, data, sk.fileobj, events)
                while socks_to_close:
                    sock = socks_to_close.pop()
                    finish(sel, data, sock)
    except KeyboardInterrupt:
        pass
    finally:
        servsock.close()
```

`selectors` does not supply an event loop; the event loop needed in async programming, in the preceding example, is the simple loop using `while True:`.

The low-level approach, as shown in this example, makes us write a lot of code compared to the simplicity of the task, a task that is made especially simple by the fact that the server does not need to examine or process incoming bytes (for most network jobs, incoming streams or chunks of bytes *do* need to be parsed into semantically meaningful messages). The payback comes in the high performance one can attain, with such a no-overhead approach, consuming minimal resources.

Moreover, it's worth noticing (as is emphasized by the detailed informational `prints`) that this example does not share the limitations of "A Connection-Oriented Socket Server" on page 515: the code, as presented, can handle any number of clients, up to the limits of available memory, as well as arbitrary network fragmentation of data along the arbitrarily high number of simultaneous connections.

19
Client-Side Network Protocol Modules

Python's standard library supplies several modules to simplify the use of Internet protocols, particularly on the client side (or for some simple servers). These days, the Python Package Index (*https://pypi.python.org/pypi*) (PyPI) offers many more such packages. These third-party packages support a wider array of protocols, and several offer better APIs than the standard library's equivalents. When you need to use a protocol that's missing from the standard library, or covered by the standard library in a way you think is not satisfactory, be sure to search PyPI (*https://pypi.python.org/pypi*)—you're likely to find better solutions there.

In this chapter, we cover some standard library packages that may prove satisfactory for some uses of network protocols, especially simple ones: when you can code without requiring third-party packages, your application or library is easier to install on other machines. We also mention a few third-party packages covering important network protocols not included in the standard library. This chapter does not cover third-party packages using an asynchronous programming approach: for that kind of package, see "The asyncio Module (v3 Only)" on page 521.

For the specific, very frequent use case of HTTP[1] clients and other network resources (such as anonymous FTP sites) best accessed via URLs,[2] the standard library offers only complex, incompatible (between v2 and v3) support. For that case, therefore, we have chosen to cover and recommend the splendid third-party package

1 HTTP, the Hypertext Transfer Protocol, is the core protocol of the World Wide Web: every web server and browser uses it, and it has become the dominant application-level protocol on the Internet today.

2 Uniform Resource Locators

`requests` (*http://docs.python-requests.org/*), with its well-designed API and v2/v3 compatibility, instead of any standard library modules.

Email Protocols

Most email today is *sent* via servers implementing the Simple Mail Transport Protocol (SMTP) and *received* via servers and clients implementing the Post Office Protocol version 3 (POP3) and/or the IMAP4 one (either in the original version, specified in RFC 1730 (*http://bit.ly/2nhMOq2*), or the IMAP4rev1 one, specified in RFC 2060 (*http://bit.ly/2oifQrd*)). These protocols, client-side, are supported by the Python standard library modules `smtplib`, `poplib`, and `imaplib`.

If you need to write a client that can connect via either POP3 or IMAP4, a standard recommendation would be to pick IMAP4, since it is definitely more powerful, and —according to Python's own online docs—often more accurately implemented on the server side. Unfortunately, the standard library module for IMAP4, `imaplib`, is also inordinately complicated, and far too vast to cover in this book. If you do choose to go that route, use the online docs, inevitably complemented by voluminous RFCs 1730 or 2060, and possibly other related RFCs, such as 5161 and 6855 for capabilities, and 2342 for namespaces. Using the RFCs, in addition to the online docs for the standard library module, can't be avoided: many of the arguments passed to call `imaplib` functions and methods, and results from such calls, are strings with formats that are only documented in the RFCs, not in Python's own online docs. Therefore, we don't cover `imaplib` in this book; in the following sections, we only cover `poplib` and `stmplib`.

If you do want to use the rich and powerful IMAP4 protocol, we highly recommend that you do so, not directly via the standard library's `imaplib`, but rather by leveraging the simpler, higher-abstraction-level third-party package IMAPClient (*https://pypi.python.org/pypi/IMAPClient*), available with a **`pip install`** for both v2 and v3, and well-documented online (*http://imapclient.readthedocs.io/en/stable/*).

The poplib Module

The `poplib` module supplies a class `POP3` to access a POP mailbox. The specifications of the POP protocol are in RFC 1939 (*http://www.ietf.org/rfc/rfc1939.txt*).

POP3 `class POP3(`*`host`*`,`*`port`*`=110)`

Returns an instance *p* of class `POP3` connected to *`host`* and *`port`*.

Sister class `POP3_SSL` behaves just the same, but connects to the host (by default on port 995) over a more secure TLS channel; it's needed to connect to email servers that demand some minimum security, such as `'pop.gmail.com'`.[a]

[a] To connect to a Gmail account in particular, you also need to configure that account to enaple POP, "Allow less secure apps," and avoid two-step verification—actions that in general we can't recommend, since they weaken your email's security.

Instance *p* supplies many methods, of which the most frequently used are the following (in each case, *msgnum*, the identifying number of a message, can be a string or an `int`):

dele `p.dele(msgnum)`

Marks message *msgnum* for deletion and returns the server response string. The server queues such deletion requests, and executes them later when you terminate this connection by calling `p.quit`.

list `p.list(msgnum=None)`

Returns a tuple `(response, messages, octets)`, where *response* is the server response string; *messages* a list of bytestrings, each of two words `b'msgnum bytes'`, giving message number and length in bytes of each message in the mailbox; and *octets* is the length in bytes of the total response. When `msgnum` is not `None`, `list` returns just a string, the server response for the given `msgnum` instead of a tuple.

pass_ `p.pass_(password)`

Sends the password to the server. Must be called after `p.user`. The trailing underscore in the name is needed because `pass` is a Python keyword. Returns the server response string.

quit `p.quit()`

Ends the session and tells the server to perform deletions that were requested by calls to `p.dele`. Returns the server response string.

retr `p.retr(msgnum)`

Returns a three-item tuple `(response,lines,bytes)`, where *response* is the server response string, *lines* the list of all lines in message *msgnum* as bytestrings, and *bytes* the total number of bytes in the message.

set_debuglevel `p.set_debuglevel(debug_level)`

Sets debug level to `int` *debug_level*: `0`, default, for no debugging; `1` for a modest amount of debugging output; and `2` or more for a complete output trace of all control information exchanged with the server.

stat `p.stat()`

Returns pair `(num_msgs,bytes)`, where *num_msgs* is the number of messages in the mailbox, *bytes* the total number of bytes.

top `p.top(msgnum,maxlines)`

Like `retr`, but returns at most *maxlines* lines from the message's body (in addition to returning all the lines from the headers, just like `retr` does). Can be useful for peeking at the start of long messages.

user `p.user(username)`

Sends the server the username; followed up by a call to `p.pass_`.

The smtplib Module

The `smtplib` module supplies a class `SMTP` to send mail to an SMTP server. The specifications of the SMTP protocol are in RFC 2821 (*http://www.ietf.org/rfc/rfc2821.txt*).

SMTP `class SMTP([host,port=25])`

Returns an instance *s* of the class `SMTP`. When *host* (and optionally `port`) is given, implicitly calls `s.connect(host,port)`.

The sister class `SMTP_SSL` behaves just the same, but connects to the host (by default on port 465) over a more secure TLS channel; it's needed to connect to email servers that demand some minimum security, such as `'smtp.gmail.com'`.

The instance *s* supplies many methods, of which the most frequently used are the following:

connect `s.connect(host=127.0.0.1,port=25)`

Connects to an SMTP server on the given `host` (by default, the local host) and `port` (port `25` is the default port for the SMTP service; `465` is the default port for the more-secure "SMTP over TLS").

login `s.login(user,password)`

Logs into the server with the given *user* and *password*. Needed only if the SMTP server requires authentication (nowadays, just about all do).

quit `s.quit()`

Terminates the SMTP session.

sendmail `s.sendmail(from_addr,to_addrs,msg_string)`

Sends mail message *msg_string* from the sender whose address is in string *from_addr* to each of the recipients whose addresses are the items of list *to_addrs*. *msg_string* must be a complete RFC 822 message in a single multiline bytestring: the headers, an empty line for separation, then the body. *from_addr* and *to_addrs* only direct the mail transport, and don't add or change headers in *msg_string*. To prepare RFC 822–compliant messages, use the package `email`, covered in "MIME and Email Format Handling" on page 595.

HTTP and URL Clients

Most of the time, your code uses HTTP and FTP protocols through the higher-abstraction URL layer, supported by the modules and packages covered in the following sections. Python's standard library also offers lower-level, protocol-specific modules that are less often used: for FTP clients, `ftplib` (*https://docs.python.org/3/library/ftplib.html*); for HTTP clients, in v3, `http.client` (*https://docs.python.org/3/library/http.client.html*), and in v2, `httplib` (*https://docs.python.org/2.7/library/httplib.html*) (we cover HTTP servers in Chapter 20). If you need to write an FTP server, look at the third-party module `pyftpdlib` (*https://pypi.python.org/pypi/pyftpdlib/*). Implementations of the brand-new HTTP/2 (*https://http2.github.io/*) protocol are still at very early stages, but your best bet as of this writing is the third-party module `hyper` (*https://pypi.python.org/pypi/hyper*). (Third-party modules, as usual, can be installed from the PyPI (*https://pypi.python.org/pypi*) repository with the highly recommended tool `pip`.) We do not cover any of these lower-level modules in this book, but rather focus on higher-abstraction, URL-level access throughout the following sections.

URL Access

A URL is a type of URI (Uniform Resource Identifier). A URI is a string that *identifies* a resource (but does not necessarily locate it), while a URL *locates* a resource on the Internet. A URL is a string composed of several optional parts, called *components*: *scheme*, *location*, *path*, *query*, and *fragment*. (The second component is sometimes also known as a *net location*, or *netloc* for short.) A URL with all its parts looks like:

```
scheme://lo.ca.ti.on/pa/th?qu=ery#fragment
```

In *https://www.python.org/community/awards/psf-awards/#october-2016*, for example, the scheme is *http*, the location is *www.python.org*, the path is */community/awards/psf-awards/*, there is no query, and the fragment is *#october-2016*. (Most schemes default to a "well-known port" when the port is not explicitly specified; for example, 80 is the "well-known port" for the HTTP scheme.) Some punctuation is part of one of the components it separates; other punctuation characters are just separators, not part of any component. Omitting punctuation implies missing components. For example, in *mailto:me@you.com*, the scheme is *mailto*, the path is *me@you.com*, and there is no location, query, or fragment. The missing // means the URI has no location, the missing ? means it has no query, and the missing # means it has no fragment.

If the location ends with a colon followed by a number, this denotes a TCP port for the endpoint. Otherwise, the connection uses the "well-known port" associated with the scheme (e.g., port 80 for HTTP).

The urllib.parse (v3) / urlparse (v2) modules

The `urllib.parse` (in v3; `urlparse` in v2) module supplies functions for analyzing and synthesizing URL strings. The most frequently used of these functions are `urljoin`, `urlsplit`, and `urlunsplit`:

urljoin `urljoin(`*`base_url_string`*`,`*`relative_url_string`*`)`

Returns a URL string *u*, obtained by joining *`relative_url_string`*, which may be relative, with *`base_url_string`*. The joining procedure that `urljoin` performs to obtain its result *u* may be summarized as follows:

- When either of the argument strings is empty, *u* is the other argument.
- When *`relative_url_string`* explicitly specifies a scheme that is different from that of *`base_url_string`*, *u* is *`relative_url_string`*. Otherwise, *u*'s scheme is that of *`base_url_string`*.
- When the scheme does not allow relative URLs (e.g., `mailto`) or *`relative_url_string`* explicitly specifies a location (even when it is the same as the location of *`base_url_string`*), all other components of *u* are those of *`relative_url_string`*. Otherwise, *u*'s location is that of *`base_url_string`*.
- *u*'s path is obtained by joining the paths of *`base_url_string`* and *`relative_url_string`* according to standard syntax for absolute and relative URL paths, as per RFC 1808 (*https://tools.ietf.org/html/rfc1808*). For example:

```
from urllib import parse as urlparse  # in v3
# in v2 it would be: import urlparse
urlparse.urljoin(
  'http://somehost.com/some/path/here','../other/path')
# Result is: 'http://somehost.com/some/other/path'
```

urlsplit `urlsplit(`*`url_string`*`,default_scheme='',allow_fragments=True)`

Analyzes *`url_string`* and returns a tuple (actually an instance of `SplitResult`, which you can treat as a tuple or use with named attributes) with five string items: *`scheme`*, *`netloc`*, *`path`*, *`query`*, and *`fragment`*. *`default_scheme`* is the first item when the *`url_string`* lacks an explicit scheme. When `allow_fragments` is `False`, the tuple's last item is always `''`, whether or not *`url_string`* has a fragment. Items corresponding to missing parts are `''`. For example:

```
urlparse.urlsplit(
'http://www.python.org:80/faq.cgi?src=fie')
# Result is:
# ('http','www.python.org:80','/faq.cgi','src=fie','')
```

urlunsplit `urlunsplit(url_tuple)`

url_tuple is any iterable with exactly five items, all strings. Any return value from a `urlsplit` call is an acceptable argument for `urlunsplit`. `urlunsplit` returns a URL string with the given components and the needed separators, but with no redundant separators (e.g., there is no # in the result when the fragment, *url_tuple*'s last item, is `''`). For example:

```
urlparse.urlunsplit((
'http','www.python.org:80','/faq.cgi','src=fie',''))
# Result is: 'http://www.python.org:80/faq.cgi?src=fie'
```

`urlunsplit(urlsplit(x))` returns a normalized form of URL string *x*, which is not necessarily equal to *x* because *x* need not be normalized. For example:

```
urlparse.urlunsplit(
urlparse.urlsplit('http://a.com/path/a?'))
# Result is: 'http://a.com/path/a'
```

In this case, the normalization ensures that redundant separators, such as the trailing ? in the argument to `urlsplit`, are not present in the result.

The Third-Party requests Package

The third-party `requests` (*https://pypi.python.org/pypi/requests/*) package (very well documented online (*http://docs.python-requests.org/*)) supports both v2 and v3, and it's how we recommend you access HTTP URLs. As usual for third-party packages, it's best installed with a simple `pip install requests`. In this section, we summarize how best to use it for reasonably simple cases.

Natively, `requests` only supports the HTTP transport protocol; to access URLs using other protocols, you need to also install other third-party packages (known as *protocol adapters*), such as `requests-ftp` (*https://pypi.python.org/pypi/requests-ftp*) for FTP URLs, or others supplied as part of the rich, useful `requests-toolbelt` (*http://toolbelt.readthedocs.io/en/latest/index.html*) package of `requests` utilities.

`requests`' functionality hinges mostly on three classes it supplies: `Request`, modeling an HTTP request to be sent to a server; `Response`, modeling a server's HTTP response to a request; and `Session`, offering continuity across multiple requests, also known as a *session*. For the common use case of a single request/response interaction, you don't need continuity, so you may often just ignore `Session`.

Sending requests

Most often, you don't need to explicitly consider the `Request` class: rather, you call the utility function `request`, which internally prepares and sends the `Request`, and returns the `Response` instance. `request` has two mandatory positional arguments, both `str`s: `method`, the HTTP method to use, then `url`, the URL to address; and then, many optional named parameters (in the next section, we cover the most commonly used named parameters to the `request` function).

For further convenience, the `requests` module also supplies functions whose names are the HTTP methods `delete`, `get`, `head`, `options`, `patch`, `post`, and `put`; each takes a single mandatory positional argument, `url`, then the same optional named arguments as the function `request`.

When you want some continuity across multiple requests, call `Session` to make an instance *s*, then use *s*'s methods `request`, `get`, `post`, and so on, which are just like the functions with the same names directly supplied by the `requests` module (however, *s*'s methods merge *s*'s settings with the optional named parameters to prepare the request to send to the given `url`).

request's optional named parameters

The function `request` (just like the functions `get`, `post`, and so on—and methods with the same names on an instance *s* of class `Session`) accepts many optional named parameters—refer to the `requests` package's excellent online docs (*http://docs.python-requests.org/en/master/api/#requests.request*) for the full set, if you need advanced functionality such as control over proxies, authentication, special treatment of redirection, streaming, cookies, and so on. The most frequently used named parameters are:

`data`
: A `dict`, a sequence of key/value pairs, a bytestring, or a file-like object, to use as the body of the request

`headers`
: A `dict` of HTTP headers to send in the request

`json`
: Python data (usually a `dict`) to encode as JSON as the body of the request

`files`
: A `dict` with names as keys, file-like objects, or *file tuples* as values, used with the POST method to specify a multipart-encoding file upload; we cover the format of values for `files=` in the next section

`params`
: A `dict`, or a bytestring, to send as the query string with the request

`timeout`
: A `float` number of seconds, the maximum time to wait for the response before raising an exception

`data`, `json`, and `files` are mutually incompatible ways to specify a body for the request; use only one of them, and only for HTTP methods that do use a body, namely PATCH, POST, and PUT. The one exception is that you can have both `data=` passing a `dict`, and a `files=`, and that is very common usage: in this case, both the key/value pairs in the `dict`, and the files, form the body of the request as a single *multipart/form-data* whole, according to RFC 2388 (*https://www.ietf.org/rfc/rfc2388.txt*).

The files argument (and other ways to specify the request's body) When you specify the request's body with `json=`, or `data=` passing a bytestring or a file-like object (which must be open for reading, usually in binary mode), the resulting bytes are directly used as the request's body; when you specify it with `data=` (passing a `dict`, or a sequence of key/value pairs), the body is built as a *form*, from the key/value pairs formatted in *application/x-www-form-urlencoded* format, according to the relevant web standard (*https://url.spec.whatwg.org/#application/x-www-form-urlencoded*).

When you specify the request's body with `files=`, the body is also built as a form, in this case with the format set to *multipart/form-data* (the only way to upload files in a PATCH, POST, or PUT HTTP request). Each file you're uploading is formatted into its own part of the form; if, in addition, you want the form to give to the server further nonfile parameters, then in addition to `files=` also pass a `data=` with a `dict` value (or a sequence of key/value pairs) for the further parameters—those parameters get encoded into a supplementary part of the multipart form.

To offer you a lot of flexibility, the value of the `files=` argument can be a `dict` (its items are taken as an arbitrary-order sequence of name/value pairs), or a sequence of name/value pairs (in the latter case, the sequence's order is maintained in the resulting request body).

Either way, each value in a name/value pair can be a `str` (or, best,[3] a `bytes` or `bytearray`) to be used directly as the uploaded file's contents; or, a file-like object open for reading (then, `requests` calls `.read()` on it, and uses the result as the uploaded file's contents; we strongly recommend that, in such cases, you open the file in binary mode to avoid any ambiguity regarding content-length). When any of these conditions apply, `requests` uses the *name* part of the pair (e.g., the key into the `dict`) as the file's name (unless it can improve on that because the open file object is able to reveal its underlying filename), takes its best guess at a content-type, and uses minimal headers for the file's form-part.

Alternatively, the value in each name/value pair can be a tuple with two to four items: `fn, fp, [ft, [fh]]` (using square brackets as meta-syntax to indicate optional parts). In this case, *fn* is the file's name, *fp* provides the contents (in just the same way as in the previous paragraph), optional *ft* provides the content type (if missing, `requests` guesses it, as in the previous paragraph), and the optional `dict` *fh* provides extra headers for the file's form-part.

How to study examples of requests In practical applications, you don't usually need to consider the internal instance *r* of the class `requests.Request`, which func-

3 As it gives you complete, explicit control of exactly what octets are uploaded.

tions like `requests.post` are building, preparing, and then sending on your behalf. However, to understand exactly what `requests` is doing, working at a lower level of abstraction (building, preparing, and examining *r*—no need to send it!) is instructive. For example:

```
import requests

r = requests.Request('GET', 'http://www.example.com',
    data={'foo': 'bar'}, params={'fie': 'foo'})
p = r.prepare()
print(p.url)
print(p.headers)
print(p.body)
```

prints out (splitting the *p*.`headers` `dict`'s printout for readability):

```
http://www.example.com/?fie=foo
{'Content-Length': '7',
 'Content-Type': 'application/x-www-form-urlencoded'}
foo=bar
```

Similarly, when `files=` is involved:

```
import requests

r = requests.Request('POST', 'http://www.example.com',
    data={'foo': 'bar'}, files={'fie': 'foo'})
p = r.prepare()
print(p.headers)
print(p.body)
```

prints out (with several lines split for readability):

```
{'Content-Type': 'multipart/form-data;
  boundary=5d1cf4890fcc4aa280304c379e62607b',
  'Content-Length': '228'}
b'--5d1cf4890fcc4aa280304c379e62607b\r\nContent-Disposition: form-
data; name="foo"\r\n\r\nbar\r\n--5d1cf4890fcc4aa280304c379e62607b\r
\nContent-Disposition: form-data; name="fie"; filename="fie"\r
\n\r\nfoo\r\n--5d1cf4890fcc4aa280304c379e62607b--\r\n'
```

Happy interactive exploring!

The Response class

The one class from the `requests` module that you always have to consider is `Response`: every request, once sent to the server (typically, that's done implicitly by methods such as `get`), returns an instance *r* of `requests.Response`.

The first thing you usually want to do is to check *r*.`status_code`, an `int` that tells you how the request went, in typical "HTTPese": 200 means "everything's fine," 404 means "not found," and so on. If you'd rather just get an exception for status codes indicating some kind of error, call *r*.`raise_for_status()`; that does nothing if the request went fine, but raises a `requests.exceptions.HTTPError` otherwise. (Other exceptions, not corresponding to any specific HTTP status code, can and do get raised without requiring any such explicit call: e.g., `ConnectionError` for any kind of network problem, or `TimeoutError` for a timeout.)

Next, you may want to check the response's HTTP headers: for that, use `r.headers`, a `dict` (with the special feature of having case-insensitive string-only keys, indicating the header names as listed, e.g., in Wikipedia (*https://en.wikipedia.org/wiki/List_of_HTTP_header_fields*), per HTTP specs). Most headers can be safely ignored, but sometimes you'd rather check. For example, you may check whether the response specifies which natural language its body is written in, via `r.headers.get('content-language')`, to offer the user different presentation choices, such as the option to use some kind of natural-language translation service to make the response more acceptable to the user.

You don't usually need to make specific status or header checks for redirects: by default, `requests` automatically follows redirects for all methods except HEAD (you can explicitly pass the `allow_redirection` named parameter in the request to alter that behavior). If you do allow redirects, you may optionally want to check `r.history`, a list of all `Response` instances accumulated along the way, oldest to newest, up to but excluding `r` itself (so, in particular, `r.history` is empty if there have been no redirects).

In most cases, perhaps after some checks on status and headers, you'll want to use the response's body. In simple cases, you'll just access the response's body as a byte-string, `r.content`, or decoded via JSON (once you've determined that's how it's encoded, e.g., via `r.headers.get('content-type')`) by calling `r.json()`.

Often, you'd rather access the response's body as (Unicode) text, with property `r.text`. The latter gets decoded (from the octets that actually make up the response's body) with the codec `requests` thinks is best, based on the content-type header and a cursory examination of the body itself. You can check what codec has been used (or is about to be used) via the attribute `r.encoding`, the name of a codec registered with the `codecs` module, covered in "The codecs Module" on page 251. You can even *override* the choice of codec to use by *assigning* to `r.encoding` the name of the codec you choose.

We do not cover other advanced issues, such as streaming, in this book; if you need information on that, check `requests`' online docs (*http://docs.python-requests.org/en/master/user/quickstart/#raw-response-content*).

The urllib Package (v3)

Beyond `urllib.parse`, covered in "The urllib.parse (v3) / urlparse (v2) modules" on page 556, the `urllib` package in v3 supplies the module `urllib.robotparser` for the specific purpose of parsing a site's *robots.txt* file as documented in a well-known informal standard (*http://www.robotstxt.org/orig.html*) (in v2, use the standard library module `robotparser` (*https://docs.python.org/2/library/*

robotparser.html)); the module `urllib.error`, containing all exception types raised by other `urllib` modules; and, mainly, the module `urllib.request`, for opening and reading URLs.

The functionality supplied by v3's `urllib.request` is parallel to that of v2's `urrlib2` module, covered in "The urllib2 Module (v2)" on page 565, plus some functionality from v2's `urllib` module, covered in "The urllib Module (v2)" on page 562. For coverage of `urllib.request`, check the online docs (*https://docs.python.org/3/library/urllib.request.html#module-urllib.request*), supplemented with Michael Foord's HOWTO (*https://docs.python.org/3/howto/urllib2.html#urllib-howto*).

The urllib Module (v2)

The `urllib` module, in v2, supplies functions to read data from URLs. `urllib` supports the following protocols (schemes): *http*, *https*, *ftp*, *gopher*, and *file*. *file* indicates a local file. `urllib` uses *file* as the default scheme for URLs that lack an explicit scheme. You can find simple, typical examples of `urllib` use in Chapter 22, where `urllib.urlopen` is used to fetch HTML and XML pages that all the various examples parse and analyze.

Functions

The module `urllib` in v2 supplies a number of functions described in Table 19-1, with `urlopen` being the simplest and most frequently used.

Table 19-1.

quote `quote(`*`str`*`,safe='/')`

Returns a copy of *`str`* where special characters are changed into Internet-standard quoted form `%`*`xx`*. Does not quote alphanumeric characters, spaces, any of the characters `_,.-` (underscore, comma, period, hyphen), nor any of the characters in string `safe`. For example:

```
print(urllib.quote('zip&zap'))
# prints: zip%26zap
```

quote_plus `quote_plus(`*`str`*`, `*`safe`*`='/')`

Like `quote`, but also changes spaces into plus signs.

unquote `unquote(`*`str`*`)`

Returns a copy of *`str`* where each quoted form `%`*`xx`* is changed into the corresponding character. For example:

```
print(urllib.unquote('zip%26zap'))
# prints: zip&zap
```

unquote_plus `unquote_plus(`*`str`*`)`

Like `unquote`, but also changes plus signs into spaces.

urlcleanup `urlcleanup()`

Clears the cache of function `urlretrieve`, covered below.

urlencode `urlencode(query,doseq=False)`

Returns a string with the URL-encoded form of *`query`*. *`query`* can be either a sequence of (*`name, value`*) pairs, or a mapping, in which case the resulting string encodes the mapping's (*`key, value`*) pairs. For example:

```
urllib.urlencode([('ans',42),('key','val')])
# result is: 'ans=42&key=val'
urllib.urlencode({'ans':42, 'key':'val'})
# result is: 'key=val&ans=42'
```

The order of items in a dictionary is arbitrary. Should you need the URL-encoded form to have key/value pairs in a specific order, use a sequence as the *`query`* argument, as in the first call in this snippet.

When `doseq` is true, any *`value`* in *`query`* that is a sequence and is not a string is encoded as separate parameters, one per item in *`value`*. For example:

```
urllib.urlencode([('K',('x','y','z'))], True)
# result is: 'K=x&K=y&K=z'
```

When `doseq` is false (the default), each value is encoded as the `quote_plus` of its string form given by built-in `str`, regardless of whether the value is a sequence:

```
urllib.urlencode([('K',('x','y','z'))], False)
# result is: 'K=%28%27x%27%2C+%27y%27%2C+%27z%27%29'
```

urlopen `urlopen(urlstring,data=None,proxies=None)`

Accesses the given URL and returns a read-only file-like object *f*. *f* supplies file-like methods `read`, `readline`, `readlines`, and `close`, as well as two others:

`f``.geturl()`

Returns the URL of *f*. This may differ from *`urlstring`* by normalization (as mentioned for function `urlunsplit` earlier) and because of HTTP redirects (i.e., indications that the requested data is located elsewhere). `urllib` supports redirects transparently, and the method `geturl` lets you check for them if you want.

`f``.info()`

Returns an instance *m* of the class `Message` of the module `mimetools`, covered in "rfc822 and mimetools Modules (v2)" on page 604. *m*'s headers provide metadata about *f*. For example, `'Content-Type'` is the MIME type of the data in *f*, and *m*'s methods *`m`*`.gettype()`, *`m`*`.getmaintype()`, and *`m`*`.getsubtype()` provide the same information.

When *`data`* is None and *`urlstring`*'s scheme is *http*, `urlopen` sends a `GET` request. When *`data`* is not `None`, *`urlstring`*'s scheme must be *http*, and `urlopen` sends a `POST` request. *`data`* must then be in URL-encoded form, and you normally prepare it with the function `urlencode`, covered above.

`urlopen` can use proxies that do not require authentication. Set the environment variables `http_proxy`, `ftp_proxy`, and `gopher_proxy` to the proxies' URLs to exploit this. You normally perform such settings in your system's environment, in platform-dependent ways, before you start Python. On macOS only, `urlopen` transparently and implicitly retrieves proxy URLs from your Internet configuration settings. Alternatively, you can pass as argument *`proxies`* a mapping whose keys are scheme names, with the corresponding values being proxy URLs. For example:

```
f = urllib.urlopen('http://python.org',
proxies={'http':'http://prox:999'})
```

`urlopen` does not support proxies that require authentication; for such advanced needs, use the richer library module `urllib2`, covered in "The urllib2 Module (v2)" on page 565.

urlretrieve `urlretrieve(`*`urlstring`*`,filename=None,reporthook=None, data=None)`

Similar to `urlopen(`*`urlstring,data`*`)`, but meant for downloading large files. Returns a pair `(`*`f,m`*`)`, where *f* is a string that specifies the path to a file on the local filesystem, *m* an instance of class `Message` of module `mimetools`, like the result of method `info` called on the result value of `urlopen`, covered above.

When `filename` is `None`, `urlretrieve` copies retrieved data to a temporary local file, and *f* is the path to the temporary local file. When *`filename`* is not `None`, `urlretrieve` copies retrieved data to the file named *`filename`*, and *f* is *`filename`*. When `reporthook` is not `None`, it must be a callable with three arguments, as in the function:

```
def reporthook(block_count, block_size, file_size):
    print(block_count)
```

`urlretrieve` calls `reporthook` zero or more times while retrieving data. At each call, it passes *`block_count`*, the number of blocks of data retrieved so far; *`block_size`*, the size in bytes of each block; and *`file_size`*, the total size of the file in bytes. `urlretrieve` passes *`file_size`* as `-1` when it cannot determine file size, which depends on the protocol involved and on how completely the server implements that protocol. The purpose of `reporthook` is to allow your program to give graphical or textual feedback to the user about the progress of the file-retrieval operation that `urlretrieve` performs.

The FancyURLopener class

You normally use the module `urllib` in v2 through the functions it supplies (most often `urlopen`). To customize `urllib`'s functionality, however, you can subclass `urllib`'s `FancyURLopener` class and bind an instance of your subclass to the attribute `_urlopener` of the module `urllib`. The customizable aspects of an instance *f* of a subclass of `FancyURLopener` are the following:

prompt_user_passwd `f.prompt_user_passwd(host,realm)`

Returns a pair (*user*,*password*) that `urllib` is to use in order to authenticate access to *host* in the security *realm*. The default implementation in class `FancyURLopener` prompts the user for this data in interactive text mode. Your subclass can override this method in order to interact with the user via a GUI or to fetch authentication data from persistent storage.

version `f.version`

The string that *f* uses to identify itself to the server—for example, via the User-Agent header in the HTTP protocol. You can override this attribute by subclassing or rebind it directly on an instance of `FancyURLopener`.

The urllib2 Module (v2)

The `urllib2` module is a rich, highly customizable superset of the `urllib` module. `urllib2` lets you work directly with advanced aspects of protocols such as HTTP. For example, you can send requests with customized headers as well as URL-encoded POST bodies, and handle authentication in various realms, in both Basic and Digest forms, directly or via HTTP proxies.

In the rest of this section, we cover only the ways in which v2's `urllib2` lets your program customize these advanced aspects of URL retrieval. We do not try to impart the advanced knowledge of HTTP and other network protocols, independent of Python, that you need to make full use of `urllib2`'s rich functionality.

Functions

`urllib2` supplies a function `urlopen` that is basically identical to `urllib`'s `urlopen`. To customize `urllib2`, install, before calling `urlopen`, any number of handlers, grouped into an *opener* object, using the `build_opener` and `install_opener` functions.

You can also optionally pass to `urlopen` an instance of the class `Request` instead of a URL string. Such an instance may include both a URL string and supplementary information about how to access it, as covered in "The Request class" on page 566.

build_opener `build_opener(*handlers)`

Creates and returns an instance of the class `OpenerDirector` (covered in "The OpenerDirector class" on page 568) with the given *handlers*. Each handler can be a subclass of the class `BaseHandler`, instantiable without arguments, or an instance of such a subclass, however instantiated. `build_opener` adds instances of various handler classes provided by the module `urllib2` in front of the handlers you specify, in order to handle proxies; unknown schemes; the *http*, *file*, and *https* schemes; HTTP errors; and HTTP redirects. However, if you have instances or subclasses of said classes in *handlers*, this indicates that you want to override these defaults.

install_opener `install_opener(opener)`

Installs *opener* as the opener for further calls to `urlopen`. *opener* can be an instance of the class `OpenerDirector`, such as the result of a call to the function `build_opener`, or any signature-compatible object.

urlopen `urlopen(url,data=None)`

Almost identical to the `urlopen` function in the module `urllib`. However, you customize behavior via the opener and handler classes of `urllib2` (covered in "The OpenerDirector class" on page 568 and "Handler classes" on page 568) rather than via the class `FancyURLopener` as in the module `urllib`. The argument *url* can be a URL string, like for the `urlopen` function in the module `urllib`. Alternatively, *url* can be an instance of the class `Request`, covered in the next section.

The Request class

You can optionally pass to the function `urlopen` an instance of the class `Request` instead of a URL string. Such an instance can embody both a URL and, optionally, other information about how to access the target URL.

Request `class Request(urlstring,data=None,headers={})`

urlstring is the URL that this instance of the `Request` class embodies. For example, when there are no `data` and `headers`, calling:

```
urllib2.urlopen(urllib2.Request(urlstring))
```

is just like calling:

```
urllib2.urlopen(urlstring)
```

When `data` is not `None`, the `Request` constructor implicitly calls on the new instance *r* its method `r.add_data(data)`. `headers` must be a mapping of header names to header values. The `Request` constructor executes the equivalent of the loop:

```
for k,v in headers.items(): r.add_header(k,v)
```

The `Request` constructor also accepts optional parameters allowing fine-grained control of HTTP cookie behavior, but such advanced functionality is rarely necessary—the class's default handling of cookies is generally sufficient. For fine-grained, client-side control of cookies, see the online docs (*https://docs.python.org/2/library/cookielib.html*); we do not cover the `cookielib` module of the standard library in this book.

An instance *r* of the class `Request` supplies the following methods:

add_data `r.add_data(data)`

Sets *data* as *r*'s data. Calling `urlopen(r)` then becomes like calling `urlopen(r,data)`—that is, it requires *r*'s scheme to be *http* and uses a POST request with a body of *data*, which must be a URL-encoded string.

Despite its name, the method `add_data` does not necessarily *add* the *data*. If *r* already had data, set in *r*'s constructor or by previous calls to `r.add_data`, then the latest call to `r.add_data` *replaces* the previous value of *r*'s data with the new given one. In particular, `r.add_data(None)` removes *r*'s previous data, if any.

add_header `r.add_header(key,value)`

Adds a header with the given *key* and *value* to *r*'s headers. If *r*'s scheme is *http*, *r*'s headers are sent as part of the request. When you add more than one header with the same *key*, later additions overwrite previous ones, so out of all headers with one given *key*, only the one given last matters.

add_unredirected_header `r.add_unredirected_header(key,value)`

Like `add_header`, except that the header is added only for the first request, and is not used if the requesting procedure meets and follows any further HTTP redirection.

get_data `r.get_data()`

Returns the data of *r*, either `None` or a URL-encoded string.

get_full_url `r.get_full_url()`

Returns the URL of *r*, as given in the constructor for *r*.

get_host `r.get_host()`

Returns the `host` component of *r*'s URL.

get_method `r.get_method()`

Returns the HTTP method of *r*, either of the strings `'GET'` or `'POST'`.

get_selector `r.get_selector()`

Returns the selector components of *r*'s URL (path and all following components).

get_type `r.get_type()`

Returns the scheme component of *r*'s URL (i.e., the protocol).

has_data `r.has_data()`

Like `r.get_data() is not None`.

has_header `r.has_header(key)`

Returns `True` if *r* has a header with the given *key*; otherwise, returns `False`.

set_proxy `r.set_proxy(host,scheme)`

Sets *r* to use a proxy at the given *host* and *scheme* for accessing *r*'s URL.

The OpenerDirector class

An instance *d* of the class `OpenerDirector` collects instances of handler classes and orchestrates their use to open URLs of various schemes and to handle errors. Normally, you create *d* by calling the function `build_opener` and then install it by calling the function `install_opener`. For advanced uses, you may also access various attributes and methods of *d*, but this is a rare need and we do not cover it further in this book.

Handler classes

The `urllib2` module supplies a class called `BaseHandler` to use as the superclass of any custom handler classes you write. `urllib2` also supplies many concrete subclasses of `BaseHandler` that handle the schemes *gopher*, *ftp*, *http*, *https*, and *file*, as well as authentication, proxies, redirects, and errors. Writing custom `urllib2` handlers is an advanced topic, and we do not cover it further in this book.

Handling authentication

`urllib2`'s default opener does no authentication. To get authentication, call `build_opener` to build an opener with instances of `HTTPBasicAuthHandler`, `ProxyBasicAuthHandler`, `HTTPDigestAuthHandler`, and/or `ProxyDigestAuthHandler`, depending on whether you want authentication to be directly in HTTP or to a proxy, and on whether you need Basic or Digest authentication.

To instantiate each of these authentication handlers, use an instance *x* of the class `HTTPPasswordMgrWithDefaultRealm` as the only argument to the authentication handler's constructor. You normally use the same *x* to instantiate all the authentication handlers you need. To record users and passwords for given authentication realms and URLs, call `x.add_password` one or more times.

add_password `x.add_password(realm,URLs,user,password)`

Records in *x* the pair (*user*,*password*) as the credentials in the given *realm* for URLs given by *URLs*. *realm* is a string that names an authentication realm; when *realm* is `None`, it matches any realm not specifically recorded. *URLs* is a URL string or a sequence of URL strings. A URL *u* is deemed applicable for these credentials if there is an item *u1* of *URLs* such that the `location` components of *u* and *u1* are equal, and the `path` component of *u1* is a prefix of that of *u*. Other components (scheme, query, fragment) don't affect applicability for authentication purposes.

The following example shows how to use `urllib2` with basic HTTP authentication:

```
import urllib2

x = urllib2.HTTPPasswordMgrWithDefaultRealm( )
x.add_password(None, 'http://myhost.com/',
'auser', 'apassword')
auth = urlib2.HTTPBasicAuthHandler(x)
opener = urllib2.build_opener(auth)
urllib2.install_opener(opener)

flob = urllib2.urlopen('http://myhost.com/index.html')
for line in flob.readlines(): print line,
```

Other Network Protocols

Many, *many* other network protocols are in use—a few are best supported by Python's standard library, but, for most of them, you'll be happier researching third-party modules on PyPI (*https://pypi.python.org/pypi*).

To connect as if you were logging into another machine (or, into a separate login session on your own node), you can use the secure SSH (*https://en.wikipedia.org/wiki/Secure_Shell*) protocol, supported by the third-party module `paramiko` (*http://www.paramiko.org/*), or the higher abstraction layer wrapper around it, the third-party module `spur` (*https://github.com/mwilliamson/spur.py*). (You can also, with some likely security risks, still use classic telnet (*https://en.wikipedia.org/wiki/Telnet*), supported by the standard library module `telnetlib` (*https://docs.python.org/3/library/telnetlib.html*).)

Other network protocols include:

- NNTP (*https://en.wikipedia.org/wiki/Network_News_Transfer_Protocol*), to access the somewhat-old Usenet News servers, supported by the standard library module `nntplib` (*https://docs.python.org/3/library/nntplib.html*)
- XML-RPC (*https://en.wikipedia.org/wiki/XML-RPC*), for a rudimentary remote procedure call functionality, supported by `xmlrpc.client` (*https://docs.python.org/3/library/xmlrpc.client.html*) (`xmlrpc` (*https://docs.python.org/2/library/xmlrpclib.html*) in v2)

- gRPC (*http://www.grpc.io/*), for a more modern and advanced remote procedure call functionality, supported by the third-party module `grpcio` (*https://pypi.python.org/pypi/grpcio*)
- NTP (*http://www.ntp.org/*), to get precise time off the network, supported by the third-party module `ntplib` (*https://pypi.python.org/pypi/ntplib/*)
- SNMP (*https://en.wikipedia.org/wiki/Simple_Network_Management_Protocol*), for network management, supported by the third-party module `pysnmp` (*https://pypi.python.org/pypi/pysnmp*)

...among many others. No single book, including this one, could possibly cover all these protocols and their supporting modules. Rather, our best suggestion in the matter is a strategic one: whenever you decide that your application needs to interact with some other system via a certain networking protocol, don't rush to implement your own modules to support that protocol. Instead, search and ask around, and you're likely to find excellent existing Python modules already supporting that protocol.[4]

Should you find some bug or missing feature in such modules, open a bug or feature request (and, ideally, supply a patch or pull request that would fix the problem and satisfy your application's needs!). In other words, become an active member of the open source community, rather than just a passive user: you will be welcome there, meet your own needs, and help many other people in the process. "Give forward," since you cannot "give back" to all the awesome people who contributed to give you most of the tools you're using!

4 Even more important: if you think you need to invent a brand-new protocol and implement it on top of sockets, think again, and search carefully: it's far more likely that one or more of the huge number of existing Internet protocols meets your needs just fine!

20
Serving HTTP

When a browser (or any other web client) requests a page from a server, the server may return either static or dynamic content. Serving dynamic content involves server-side web programs generating and delivering content on the fly, often based on information stored in a database.

In the prehistory of the web, the standard for server-side programming was *CGI* (Common Gateway Interface), which required the server to run a separate program each time a client requested dynamic content. Process startup time, interpreter initialization, connection to databases, and script initialization add up to measurable overhead. Thus, CGI did not scale up well.

Nowadays, web servers support many server-specific ways to reduce overhead, serving dynamic content from processes that can serve for several hits rather than starting up a new CGI process per hit. Therefore, we do not cover CGI in this book. To maintain existing CGI programs, or port them to more modern approaches, consult the online docs for the standard library modules `cgi` (*https://docs.python.org/3/library/cgi.html*) and `http.cookies` (*https://docs.python.org/3/library/http.cookies.html*).[1]

HTTP has become even more fundamental to distributed systems design with the emergence of systems based on microservices, offering as it does a convenient way to transport between processes the JSON content that is frequently used. There are now thousands of publicly available HTTP data APIs on the Internet. While HTTP's

1 One historical legacy is that, in CGI, a server provided the CGI script with information about the HTTP request to be served mostly via the operating system's environment (in Python, that's `os.environ`); to this day, interfaces between web servers and application frameworks rely on "an environment" that's essentially a dictionary and generalizes and speeds up the same fundamental idea.

principles remain almost unchanged since its inception in the mid-1990s, it has been significantly enhanced over the years to extend its capabilities. For a more thorough grounding with excellent reference materials we recommend O'Reilly's *HTTP: The Definitive Guide.*

WSGI

Python's Web Server Gateway Interface (WSGI (*https://www.python.org/dev/peps/pep-3333/*)) is the standard by which all modern Python web development frameworks interface with underlying web servers or gateways. WSGI is not meant for direct use by your application programs; rather, you code your programs using any one of several higher-abstraction frameworks, and the framework, in turn, uses WSGI to talk to the web server.

You need to care about the details of WSGI only if you're implementing the WSGI interface for a web server that doesn't already provide it (should any such server exist), or if you're building a new Python web framework.[2] If so, study the WSGI PEP (*https://www.python.org/dev/peps/pep-3333/*), the docs for the standard library package `wsgiref` (*https://docs.python.org/3/library/wsgiref.html*), and the archive of wsgi.org (*http://wsgi.readthedocs.io/en/latest/*).

A few WSGI *concepts* may be important to you, if you use lightweight frameworks (i.e., ones that match WSGI closely). WSGI is an *interface*, and that interface has two sides: the *web-server/gateway* side, and the *application/framework* side.

The framework side's job is to provide a *WSGI application* object, a callable object (often the instance of a class with a `__call__` special method, but that's an implementation detail) respecting conventions in the PEP (*https://www.python.org/dev/peps/pep-3333/*); and to connect the application object to the server by whatever means the specific server documents (often a few lines of code, or configuration files, or just a convention such as naming the WSGI application object `application` as a top-level attribute in a module). The server calls the application object for each incoming HTTP request, and the application object responds appropriately, so that the server can form the outgoing HTTP response and send it on—all according to said conventions. A framework, even a lightweight one, shields you from such details (except that you may have to instantiate and connect the application object, depending on the specific server).

WSGI Servers

An extensive list of servers and adapters you can use to run WSGI frameworks and applications (for development and testing, in production web setups, or both) is

2 Please don't. As Titus Brown once pointed out, Python is (in)famous for having more web frameworks than keywords. One of this book's authors once showed Guido how to easily fix that problem when he was first designing Python 3—just add a few hundred new keywords—but, for some reason, Guido was not very receptive to this suggestion.

available online (*http://wsgi.readthedocs.io/en/latest/servers.html*)—extensive, but just partial. For example, it does not mention that Google App Engine (*https://cloud.google.com/appengine/docs/python/*)'s Python runtime is also a WSGI server, ready to dispatch WSGI apps as directed by the *app.yaml* configuration file.

If you're looking for a WSGI server to use for development, or to deploy in production behind, say, an nginx (*http://nginx.org/*)-based load balancer, you should be happy, at least on Unix-like systems, with Green Unicorn (*http://docs.gunicorn.org/*): pure Python goodness, supporting nothing but WSGI, very lightweight. A worthy (also pure Python and WSGI only) alternative, currently with better Windows support, is Waitress (*https://pylons.readthedocs.io/projects/waitress/*). If you need richer features (such as support for Perl and Ruby as well as Python, and many other forms of extensibility), consider the bigger, more complex uWSGI (*https://uwsgi-docs.readthedocs.io/*).[3]

WSGI also has the concept of *middleware*—a subsystem that implements both the server and application sides of WSGI. A middleware object "wraps" a WSGI application; can selectively alter requests, environments, and responses; and presents itself to the server as "the application." Multiple layers of wrappers are allowed and common, forming a "stack" of middleware, offering services to the actual application-level code. If you want to write a cross-framework middleware component, then you will, indeed, need to become a WSGI expert.

Python Web Frameworks

For a survey of most Python web frameworks, see the Python wiki page (*https://wiki.python.org/moin/WebFrameworks*). It's authoritative, since it's on the official python.org website, and community curated, so it will stay up to date as time goes by. As of this writing, it lists and points to 56 frameworks[4] that it identifies as "active," plus many more it identifies as "discontinued/inactive." In addition, it points to separate wiki pages about Python content management systems (*https://wiki.python.org/moin/ContentManagementSystems*), web servers (*https://wiki.python.org/moin/WebServers*), and web components (*https://wiki.python.org/moin/WebComponents*) and libraries thereof.

Full-Stack Versus Lightweight Frameworks

Roughly speaking, Python web frameworks can be classified as being either *full-stack* (trying to supply all the functionality you may need to build a web application) or *lightweight* (supplying just the minimum you need as a handy interface to web serving itself, and letting you pick and choose your own favorite, unrelated

3 Installing uWSGI on Windows currently requires compiling it with cygwin (*https://www.cygwin.com/*).

4 Since Python has barely more than 30 keywords, you can see why Titus Brown pointed out that Python has more web frameworks than keywords.

components for tasks such as interfacing to databases, covered in "The Python Database API (DBAPI) 2.0" on page 351, and templating, covered in "Templating" on page 624—as well as other tasks covered by web components, as mentioned in the next section). Of course, like all taxonomies, this one is imprecise and incomplete, and requires value judgments; however, it's one way to start making sense of those many dozens of Python web frameworks.

In this book, we cannot cover full-stack frameworks—each is far too vast (indeed, sometimes sprawling). Nevertheless, one of them might be the best approach for your specific applications, so we mention a few of the most popular ones, and recommend that you check out their websites that we link to.

When you use lightweight frameworks

By definition of "lightweight," if you need any database, templating, or other functionality not strictly related to HTTP, you'll be picking and choosing separate components for that purpose (we cover aspects of databases and templating in other chapters). However, the lighter-weight your framework, the more you may also want to use separate components for functionality "closer to home," such as authenticating a user or maintaining state across web requests by a given user. Many WSGI middleware (*http://wsgi.readthedocs.io/en/latest/libraries.html*) packages can help you with such tasks. Some excellent ones are quite focused—for example, Barrel (*https://pypi.python.org/pypi/barrel*) for access control, Beaker (*http://beaker.readthedocs.io/en/latest/*) for maintaining state in the form of lightweight sessions of several kinds, and so forth.

However, when we (the authors of this book) require good WSGI middleware for just about any purpose, almost invariably we first check Werkzeug (*http://werkzeug.pocoo.org/*), a collection of such components that's amazing in breadth and quality. We don't cover Werkzeug in this book (just as we don't cover other middleware), but we recommend it highly.

A Few Popular Full-Stack Frameworks

By far the most popular full-stack framework is Django (*https://www.djangoproject.com/*), which is vast and extensible. Django's so-called *applications* are in fact reusable (*https://www.djangoproject.com/*) subsystems, while what's normally called "an application," Django calls a *project*. Django requires its own unique mindset, but offers vast power and functionality in return.

An excellent full-stack alternative is web2py (*http://www.web2py.com/*), roughly as powerful, easier to learn, and well known for its dedication to backward compatibility (if it keeps up its great track record, any web2py application you code today will keep working indefinitely far in the future). Its documentation (*http://www.web2py.com/init/default/documentation*) is outstanding.[5]

A third worthy contender is TurboGears (*http://turbogears.org/*), which starts out as a lightweight framework, but achieves "full-stack" status by integrating other, independent third-party projects for the various other functionalities needed in most web apps, such as database interfacing and templating, rather than designing its own. Another, somewhat philosophically similar, "light but rich" framework is Pyramid (*https://trypyramid.com/*).

Some Popular Lightweight Frameworks

As mentioned, Python has multiple frameworks, including many lightweight ones. We cover four of the latter: Falcon, Flask, Bottle, and webapp2. In our coverage of each framework, we provide an example toy app that greets the users and reminds them of when they last visited the site, based on a `lastvisit` cookie. First, we show how to set the cookie in the main "greeter" function. However, an app would presumably want to set the `lastvisit` cookie no matter how the app was getting "visited." Instead of repeating the cookie setting in each and every appropriate method, these frameworks let you easily factor out the code to respect the key design principle of DRY (*https://en.wikipedia.org/wiki/Don%27t_repeat_yourself*) ("Don't Repeat Yourself"). So, we also provide an example of how to factor out the code for this purpose in each framework.

Falcon

Possibly the fastest (thus, by inference, lightest) Python web framework is Falcon (*https://falconframework.org/*). According to the benchmarks on its site, it runs 5 to 8 times faster than the most popular lightweight Python web framework, Flask, on both v2 and v3. Falcon is very portable, supporting Jython, or Cython for a further little speed-up, or PyPy for a huge boost—the latter making it, in all, 27 times faster than `Flask`. In addition to the project website (*https://falconframework.org/*), look at the sources on GitHub (*https://github.com/falconry/falcon*), the installation notes on PyPI (*https://pypi.python.org/pypi/falcon*), and the extensive docs (*http://falcon.readthedocs.io/en/latest/*). To run `Falcon` in Google App Engine locally on your computer (or on Google's servers at *appspot.com*), see Rafael Barrelo's useful GitHub page (*https://github.com/rafaelbarrelo/appengine-falcon-skeleton*).

The main class supplied by the `falcon` package is named `API`. An instance of `falcon.API` is a WSGI application, so a common idiom is a multiple assignment:

```
import falcon

api = application = falcon.API()
```

5 Quora (*https://www.quora.com/Is-web2py-a-good-Python-web-framework*) has a debate for and against web2py.

When you instantiate `falcon.API`, pass zero or more named parameters:

`media_type`
: Content type used in responses unless otherwise specified; defaults to `'application/json; charset=utf-8'`

`middleware`
: A *Falcon middleware* object, or a list of such objects, covered in "Falcon middleware" on page 581

`request_type`
: The class to use for requests; defaults to `falcon.request.Request`, but you might code a subclass of that class and use the subclass here

`response_type`
: The class to use for responses; defaults to `falcon.response.Response`, but you might code a subclass of that class and use the subclass here

`router`
: The class to use for routing; defaults to `falcon.routing.CompiledRouter`, not suitable to inherit from, but you could code your own router class, make it compatible by duck typing, and use your router class here

Once you have the `api` object, you can customize it in several ways, to handle errors and to add *sinks (*using regular expressions to intercept and dispatch a set of routes, for example by proxying to another site). We do not cover these advanced topics (nor custom request, response, and router types) in this book: the Falcon docs (*http://falcon.readthedocs.io/en/latest/index.html*) (particularly, as a reference, the Classes and Functions (*http://falcon.readthedocs.io/en/latest/api/index.html*) section) cover them well.

One customization method that you almost invariably do call on `api`, usually more than once, is necessary to add routing, and thus to get requests served:

add_route `add_route(`*`uri_template`*`,`*`resource`*`)`

`uri_template` is a string matching the URI to route; for example, `'/'` to route requests that ask for the root URL of the site. The template may include one or more *field expressions*—identifiers enclosed in braces (`{}`)—in which case the *responder methods* of the corresponding *`resource`* must accept arguments named like those identifiers, in order, after the mandatory arguments for request and response.

`resource` is an instance of a *Falcon resource* class, as covered in "Falcon resources" on page 576. Note that you pass a specific instance, which gets reused to serve all requests to the given URI, not the class itself: be very careful in your coding, especially about using instance variables.

Falcon resources A *Falcon resource class* is one that supplies methods, known as *responder methods*, whose names start with `on_` followed by an HTTP verb in lowercase; for example, the method on_get responds to the most common HTTP verb, GET.

Each responder method normally has a signature such as:

```
def on_get(self, req, resp): ...
```

accepting the request object and the response object as arguments. However, when the URI template routing to the resource includes field expressions, then responder methods need to accept extra arguments with names matching the identifiers in the field expressions. For example, if you route to the resource by calling `api.add_route('/foo/{bar}/{baz}', rsrc)`, then responder methods of the resource-class instance *rsrc* must have signatures such as:

```
def on_post(self, req, resp, bar, baz): ...
```

A resource does not have to supply responder methods for all HTTP verbs—if the resource is addressed by an HTTP verb it does not support (e.g., a POST to a route whose resource's class has no on_post method), Falcon detects that, and responds to the invalid request with HTTP status '405 Method Not Allowed'.

Falcon does not supply any class for resource classes to inherit from: rather, resource classes rely entirely on *duck typing* (i.e., they just define responder methods with the appropriate names and signatures) to fully support Falcon.

Falcon request objects The falcon.Request class supplies a large number of properties and methods, thoroughly documented in Falcon's docs (*http://falcon.readthedocs.io/en/latest/api/request_and_response.html*). The ones you'll be using most often are property cookies (*http://falcon.readthedocs.io/en/latest/api/cookies.html*), a dict mapping cookie names to values, and the methods get_header (*http://falcon.readthedocs.io/en/latest/api/request_and_response.html*) to get a header from the request (None, when the request had no such header), get_param (*http://falcon.readthedocs.io/en/latest/api/request_and_response.html*) to get a parameter from the request (None, when the request had no such parameter), and small variants such as get_param_as_int (*http://falcon.readthedocs.io/en/latest/api/request_and_response.html*) to get an int value for a request parameter that must be an integer.

Falcon response objects The falcon.Response class supplies many properties and methods, thoroughly documented in Falcon's docs (*http://falcon.readthedocs.io/en/latest/api/request_and_response.html*). Usually, you'll need to set many of the properties (except for ones controlling headers you're okay with being absent or taking on default values), and, often, call many of the methods. Here are the properties:

body
: Assign a Unicode string to encode in UTF-8 as the response body. If you have a bytestring for the body, assign it to data instead, for speed.

`cache_control`
: Assign to set the Cache-Control (*http://www.w3.org/Protocols/rfc2616/rfc2616-sec14.html#sec14.9*) header; when you assign a list of strings, Falcon joins them with `', '` to produce the header value.

`content_location`
: Assign to set the Content-Location (*http://www.w3.org/Protocols/rfc2616/rfc2616-sec14.html#sec14.14*) header.

`content_range`
: Assign to set the Content-Range (*http://www.w3.org/Protocols/rfc2616/rfc2616-sec14.html#sec14.16*) header.

`content_type`
: Assign to set the Content-Type (*http://www.w3.org/Protocols/rfc2616/rfc2616-sec14.html#sec14.17*) header; a typical value you'd assign to `resp.content_type` might be, for example, `'text/html; charset=ISO-8859-15'` when you're setting `resp.data` to an HTML document encoded in `ISO-8859-15` (defaults to `api.media_type`).

`data`
: Assign a bytestring to use the bytes as the response body.

`etag`
: Assign to set the ETag (*http://www.w3.org/Protocols/rfc2616/rfc2616-sec14.html#sec14.19*) header.

`last_modified`
: Assign to set the Last-Modified (*http://www.w3.org/Protocols/rfc2616/rfc2616-sec14.html#sec14.29*) header.

`location`
: Assign to set the Location (*http://www.w3.org/Protocols/rfc2616/rfc2616-sec14.html#sec14.30*) header.

`retry_after`
: Assign to set the Retry-After (*http://www.w3.org/Protocols/rfc2616/rfc2616-sec14.html#sec14.37*) header, typically in conjunction with setting `resp.status` to `'503 Service Unavailable'`.

`status`
: Assign a status-line string, defaulting to `'200 OK'` (for example, set `resp.status = '201 Created'` if an `on_post` method creates a new entity—see RFC 2616 (*http://www.w3.org/Protocols/rfc2616/rfc2616-sec10.html*) for all details on HTTP status codes and status lines).

`stream`
: Assign either a file-like object whose `read` method returns a string of bytes, or an iterator yielding bytestrings, when that's a more convenient way for you to express the response body than assigning to *`resp`*`.body` or *`resp`*`.data`.

`stream_len`
: Optionally, assign an `int`, the number of bytes in *`resp`*`.stream`, when you assign the latter; Falcon uses it to set the Content-Length (*http://www.w3.org/Protocols/rfc2616/rfc2616-sec14.html#sec14.13*) header (if not supplied, Falcon may use chunked encoding or other alternatives).

`vary`
: Assign to set the Vary (*http://www.w3.org/Protocols/rfc2616/rfc2616-sec14.html#sec14.44*) header.

Lightweight frameworks: you must know what you're doing!

You may have noticed that properly setting many of these properties requires you to understand HTTP (in other words, to know what you're doing), while a full-stack framework tries to lead you by the hand and have you do the right thing without really needing to understand how or why it is right—at the cost of time and resources, and of accepting the full-stack framework's conceptual map and mindset. ("You pays yer money and you takes yer choice"!) The authors of this book are enthusiasts of the knowledge-heavy, resources-light approach of lightweight frameworks, but we acknowledge that there is no royal road to web apps, and that others prefer rich, heavy, all-embracing full-stack frameworks. To each their own!

Back to `falcon.Response` instances, here are the main methods of an instance *`r`* of that class:

Table 20-1.

add_link	`r.add_link(`*`target`*`,`*`rel`*`,`*`title`*`=None,`*`title_star`*`=None,`*`anchor`*`=None,`*`hreflang`*`=None,`*`type_hint`*`=None)` Add a Link (*https://tools.ietf.org/html/rfc5988*) header to the response. Mandatory arguments are *`target`*, the target IRI for the link (Falcon converts it to a URI if needed), and *`rel`*, a string naming one of the many relations (*http://www.iana.org/assignments/link-relations/link-relations.xhtml*) catalogued by IANA, such as `'terms-of-service'` or `'predecessor-version'`. The other arguments (pass each of them as a named argument, if at all) are rarely needed, and are documented in the Falcon docs (*http://falcon.readthedocs.io/en/latest/api/request_and_response.html*) and RFC 5988 (*https://tools.ietf.org/html/rfc5988*). If you call `r.add_link` repeatedly, Falcon builds one `Link` header, with the various links you specify separated by commas.
append_header	`r.append_header(`*`name, value`*`)` Set or append an HTTP header with the given *`name`* and *`value`*. If a header of such *`name`* is already present, Falcon appends the *`value`* to the existing one, separated by a comma; this works for most headers, but not for *cookies*—for those, use the `set_cookie` method instead.
get_header	`r.get_header(`*`name`*`)` Return the string value for the HTTP header with the given *`name`*, or `None` if no such header is present.
set_cookie	`r.set_cookie(`*`name`*`,`*`value`*`,`*`expires`*`=None,`*`max_age`*`=None,`*`domain`*`=None,`*`path`*`=None,`*`secure`*`=True,`*`http_only`*`=True)` Set a `Set-Cookie` header on the response. Mandatory arguments are *`name`* (the cookie name) and *`value`*, a `str` (the cookie's value). The other arguments (pass each of them as a named argument, if at all) may be needed for extra security (and cookie persistence: if you set neither `expires` nor `max_age`, the cookie expires as soon as the browser session finishes), and are documented in the Falcon docs (*http://falcon.readthedocs.io/en/latest/api/request_and_response.html*) and RFC 6525 (*https://tools.ietf.org/html/rfc6265*). When you call `r.set_cookie` more than once, Falcon adds multiple `Set-Cookie` headers to the response.
set_header	`r.set_header(`*`name, value`*`)` Set an HTTP header with the given *`name`* and *`value`*. When a header with that *`name`* was already present, it's replaced.
set_headers	`r.set_headers(`*`headers`*`)` Set multiple HTTP headers as per `set_header`. *`headers`* is either an iterable of `(`*`name, value`*`)` pairs, or a mapping with *`name`* as the key, *`value`* as the corresponding value.

unset_cookie `r.unset_cookie(name)`

Remove the cookie named *name* from the response, if it's there; also add to the response a `Set-Cookie` header asking the browser to remove the cookie from its cache, if the cookie is in that cache.

Falcon middleware A *Falcon middleware class* is one that supplies one or more of three methods that examine, and potentially alter, incoming requests and outgoing responses. You pass in a list of instances of such classes as the *middleware* argument when you instantiate `falcon.API`, and those instances are given a chance to examine and alter all the incoming requests and outgoing responses. Multiple middleware class instances in the list get that chance in first-to-last order on incoming requests, then backward, last-to-first, on outgoing responses.

Falcon does not supply any class for middleware classes to inherit from: rather, middleware classes rely entirely on *duck typing* (i.e., they just define one or more of the three methods with appropriate name and signature). If a middleware class does not supply one or more of the three methods, Falcon treats its instances as if they supplied an empty implementation of the missing method(s), doing nothing.

The three methods Falcon middleware classes may supply are:

process_request `process_request(self,req,resp)`

Called *before* routing; if it changes *req*, that may affect routing.

process_resource `process_resource(self,req,resp,resource)`

Called *after* routing, but before processing. *resource* may be None if routing could not find a resource matching the request.

process_response `process_response(self,req,resp,resource)`

Called after the responder method, if any, returns. *resource* may be None if routing could not find a resource matching the request.

Example 20-1 shows a simple Falcon example.

Example 20-1. A Falcon example

```
import datetime, falcon
one_year = datetime.timedelta(days=365)

class Greeter(object):
    def on_get(self, req, resp):
        lastvisit = req.cookies.get('lastvisit')
        now = datetime.datetime.now()
        newvisit = now.ctime()
```

```
        thisvisit = '<p>This visit on {} UTC</p>'.format(newvisit)
        resp.set_cookie('lastvisit', newvisit,
                        expires=now+one_year, secure=False)
        resp_body = [
            '<html><head><title>Hello, visitor!</title>'
            '</head><body>']
        if lastvisit is None:
            resp_body.extend((
            '<p>Welcome to this site on your first visit!</p>',
            thisvisit,
            '<p>Please Refresh the web page to proceed</p>'))
        else:
            resp_body.extend((
            '<p>Welcome back to this site!</p>',
            '<p>You last visited on {} UTC</p>'.format(lastvisit),
            thisvisit))
        resp_body.append('</body></html>')
        resp.content_type = 'text/html'
        resp.stream = resp_body
        resp.stream_len = sum(len(x) for x in resp_body)

app = falcon.API()
greet = Greeter()
app.add_route('/', greet)
```

This Falcon example just shows how to use some of the fundamental building blocks that Falcon offers—the API, one resource class, and one instance, preparing the response (in this case, setting `resp.stream` is the natural way, since we have prepared in `resp_body` a list of string pieces of the response body; `resp.body = ''.join(resp_body)` would also be okay). The example also shows how to maintain a minimal continuity of state among multiple interactions with the server from the same browser by setting and using a cookie.

If this app had multiple resources and responder methods, presumably it would want to set the `lastvisit` cookie no matter through which resource and method the app was getting "visited." Here's how to code an appropriate middleware class and instantiate `falcon.API` with an instance of said class:

```
class LastVisitSettingMiddleware(object):
    def process_request(self, req, resp):
        now = datetime.datetime.now()
        resp.set_cookie('lastvisit', now.ctime(),
                        expires=now+one_year, secure=False)

lastvisitsetter = LastVisitSettingMiddleware()

app = falcon.API(middleware=[lastvisitsetter])
```

You can now remove the cookie setting from `Greeter.on_get`, and the app will keep working fine.

Flask

The most popular Python lightweight framework is Flask (*http://flask.pocoo.org/*). Although lightweight, it includes a development server and debugger, and explicitly relies on other well-chosen packages such as Werkzeug and jinja2 (both originally authored by Armin Ronacher, the author of Flask).

In addition to the project website (*http://flask.pocoo.org/*), look at the sources on GitHub (*https://github.com/pallets/flask*), the PyPI (*https://pypi.python.org/pypi/Flask*) entry, and the docs (*http://flask.pocoo.org/docs/*). To run Flask in Google App Engine (locally on your computer, or on Google's servers at *appspot.com*), see L. Henriquez and J. Euphrosine's GitHub page (*https://github.com/GoogleCloudPlatform/appengine-flask-skeleton*); or, for a somewhat richer and more structured approach, K. Gill's GitHub page (*https://github.com/kamalgill/flask-appengine-template*).

Serving HTTP

The main class supplied by the `flask` package is named `Flask`. An instance of `flask.Flask`, besides being a WSGI application itself, also wraps a WSGI application as its `wsgi_app` property. When you need to further wrap the WSGI app in some WSGI middleware, use the idiom:

```
import flask

app = flask.Flask(__name__)
app.wsgi_app = some_middleware(app.wsgi_app)
```

When you instantiate `flask.Flask`, always pass it as the first argument the application name (often just the `__name__` special variable of the module where you instantiate it; if you instantiate it from within a package, usually in *__init__.py*, `__name__.partition('.')[0]` works). Optionally, you can also pass named parameters such as `static_folder` and `template_folder` to customize where static files and jinja2 templates are found; however, that's rarely needed—the default values (folders named *static* and *templates*, respectively, located in the same folder as the Python script that instantiates `flask.Flask`) make perfect sense.

An instance *app* of `flask.Flask` supplies more than 100 methods and properties, many of them decorators to bind functions to *app* in various roles, such as *view functions* (serving HTTP verbs on a URL) or *hooks* (letting you alter a request before it's processed, or a response after it's built; handling errors; and so forth).

`flask.Flask` takes few parameters at instantiation (and the ones it takes are not ones that you usually need to compute in your code), and it supplies decorators you'll want to use as you define, for example, view functions. Thus, the normal pattern in `flask` is to instantiate *app* early, just as your application is starting up, so that the app's decorators, and other methods and properties, are available as you `def` view functions and so on.

As there's a single global *app* object, you may wonder how thread-safe it can be to access, mutate, and rebind *app*'s properties and attributes. No worry: they're *proxies* to actual objects living in the *context* of a specific request, in a specific thread or greenlet. Never type-check those properties (their types are in fact obscure proxy types), and you'll be fine; type checking is not a good idea in Python, anyway.

Flask also supplies many other utility functions and classes; often, the latter subclass or wrap classes from other packages to add seamless, convenient Flask integration. For example, Flask's `Request` and `Response` classes add just a little handy functionality by subclassing the corresponding Werkzeug classes.

Flask request objects The class `flask.Request` supplies a large number of properties, thoroughly documented in Flask's docs (*http://flask.pocoo.org/docs/api/#incoming-request-data*). The ones you'll be using most often are:

`cookies`
: A `dict` with the cookies from the request

`data`
: A string, the request's body (for POST and PUT requests)

`files`
: A `MultiDict` whose values are file-like objects, all files uploaded in the request (for POST and PUT requests), keys being the files' names

`headers`
: A `MultiDict` with the request's headers

`values`
: A `MultiDict` with the request's parameters (either from the query string or, for POST and PUT requests, from the form that's the request's body)

A `MultiDict` is like a `dict` except that it can have multiple values for a key. Indexing, and `get`, on a `MultiDict` instance *`m`*, return an arbitrary one of the values; to get the list of values for a key (an empty list, if the key is not in *`m`*), call *`m`*`.getlist(`*`key`*`)`.

Flask response objects Often, a Flask view function just returns a string (which becomes the response's body): Flask transparently wraps an instance *`r`* of `flask.Response` around the string, so you don't have to worry about the response class. However, sometimes you want to alter the response's headers; in this case, in the view function, call *`r`*`=flask.make_response(`*`astring`*`)`, alter `MultiDict` *`r`*`.headers` as you want, then `return` *`r`*. (To set a cookie, don't use *`r`*`.headers`; rather, call *`r`*`.set_cookie`, with arguments as mentioned in `set_cookie` in Table 20-1.)

Some of Flask's built-in integrations of other systems don't require subclassing: for example, the templating integration implicitly injects into the jinja2 context the Flask globals `config`, `request`, `session`, and `g` (the latter being the handy "globals catch-all" object `flask.g`, a proxy in application context, on which your code can store whatever you want to "stash" for the duration of the request being served), and the functions `url_for` (to translate an endpoint to the corresponding URL, same as `flask.url_for`) and `get_flashed_messages` (to support the advanced Flask concept of *flashed messages*, which we do not cover in this book; same as `flask.get_flashed_messages`). Flask provides convenient ways for your code to inject more filters, functions, and values into the jinja2 context, without any subclassing.

Most of the officially recognized or approved Flask extensions (*http://flask.pocoo.org/extensions/*) (over 50 at the time of this writing) adopt similar approaches, supplying classes and utility functions to seamlessly integrate other popular systems with your Flask applications.

Flask also introduces some advanced concepts of its own, such as signals (*http://flask.pocoo.org/docs/signals/*) to provide looser dynamic coupling in a "pub/sub" pattern, and blueprints (*http://flask.pocoo.org/docs/blueprints/*), offering a substantial subset of a Flask application's functionality to ease refactoring large applications in flexible ways. We do not cover these advanced concepts in this book.

Example 20-2 shows a simple Flask example.

Example 20-2. A Flask example

```
import datetime, flask
app = flask.Flask(__name__)
app.permanent_session_lifetime = datetime.timedelta(days=365)
app.secret_key = b'\xc5\x8f\xbc\xa2\x1d\xeb\xb3\x94;:d\x03'

@app.route('/')
def greet():
    lastvisit = flask.session.get('lastvisit')
    now = datetime.datetime.now()
    newvisit = now.ctime()
    template = '''
      <html><head><title>Hello, visitor!</title>
      </head><body>
      {% if lastvisit %}
        <p>Welcome back to this site!</p>
        <p>You last visited on {{lastvisit}} UTC</p>
        <p>This visit on {{newvisit}} UTC</p>
      {% else %}
        <p>Welcome to this site on your first visit!</p>
        <p>This visit on {{newvisit}} UTC</p>
        <p>Please Refresh the web page to proceed</p>
      {% endif %}
      </body></html>'''
    flask.session['lastvisit'] = newvisit
    return flask.render_template_string(
      template, newvisit=newvisit, lastvisit=lastvisit)
```

This Flask example just shows how to use some of the many building blocks that Flask offers—the `Flask` class, a view function, and rendering the response (in this case, using `render_template_string` on a jinja2 template; in real life, templates are usually kept in separate files rendered with `render_template`). The example also shows how to maintain continuity of state among multiple interactions with the server from the same browser, with the handy `flask.session` variable. (The example might alternatively have mimicked Example 20-1 more closely, putting together the HTML response in Python code instead of using jinja2, and using a cookie directly instead of the session; however, real-world Flask apps do tend to use jinja2 and sessions by preference.)

If this app had multiple view functions, no doubt it would want to set `lastvisit` in the session no matter through which URL the app was getting "visited." Here's how to code and decorate a hook function to execute after each request:

```
@app.after_request()
def set_lastvisit(response):
    now = datetime.datetime.now()
    flask.session['lastvisit'] = now.ctime()
    return response
```

You can now remove the `flask.session['lastvisit'] = newvisit` statement from the view function `greet`, and the app will keep working fine.

Bottle Another worthy lightweight framework is Bottle (*http://bottlepy.org/docs/dev/index.html*). Bottle is implemented as a single *bottle.py* file (of over 4,000 lines!). It has no dependencies beyond the standard library. Strictly speaking, Bottle requires no installation process: you can just download it to your current directory —for example, with **`curl --location -O http://bottlepy.org/bottle.py`**,[6] to get the latest development snapshot (although we recommend you install a stable release, as usual, with **`pip install bottle`**). Within that one *.py* file, Bottle supports both v2 and v3. It includes a web server useful for local development, and even a simple standalone template engine (*http://bottlepy.org/docs/dev/stpl.html*) based on embedding Python in your templates (although it also lets you use jinja2 or another external template engine you have installed).

In addition to the project website (*http://bottlepy.org/docs/stable/*), look at the source on GitHub (*https://github.com/bottlepy/bottle*). Bottle comes with adapters for many WSGI servers, including Google App Engine, but for a useful "skeleton" to run `bottle` on Google App Engine (locally on your computer, or on Google's servers at *appspot.com*), see L. Henriquez and J. Euphrosine's GitHub page (*https://github.com/GoogleCloudPlatform/appengine-bottle-skeleton*).

The main class supplied by the `bottle` package is named `Bottle`. An instance of `bottle.Bottle`, besides being a WSGI application itself, also wraps a WSGI application as its `wsgi` attribute. When you need to further wrap the WSGI app in some WSGI middleware, use the idiom:

6 Or **`wget http://bottlepy.org/bottle.py`**

```
import bottle

app = bottle.Bottle()
app.wsgi = some_middleware(app.wsgi)
```

When you instantiate `bottle.Bottle`, you can optionally pass the named parameters `catchall` and `autojson` (both default to `True`). When `catchall` is `True`, Bottle catches and handles all exceptions; pass it as `False` to let exceptions propagate (only useful when you wrap the WSGI app in some debugging middleware). When `autojson` is `True`, Bottle detects when a callback function returns a `dict`, and, in that case, serializes the `dict` with `json.dumps` as the response's body, and sets the response's `Content-Type` header to `'application/json'`; pass `autojson` as `False` to let such `dict`s propagate (only useful when you wrap the WSGI app in some middleware dealing with them).

An instance *app* of `bottle.Bottle` supplies dozens of methods and properties, including decorators to bind functions to *app* in various roles, such as *callback functions* (serving HTTP verbs on given URLs) or *hooks* (letting you alter a request before it's processed, or a response after it's built). The normal pattern in `bottle` is to instantiate *app* early, as your application is starting up, so the app's decorators, and other methods and properties, are available as you `def` callback functions and so on. Often, you don't even need to instantiate `bottle.Bottle` explicitly: Bottle makes a "default application object" for you, and module-level functions delegate to the default application's methods of the same name. When you want to access the default application object, call the function `bottle.default_app`. Relying on the default app is fine for small, simple web apps, although we recommend explicit instantiation as a more Pythonic style.

Bottle routing To route incoming requests to callback functions, Bottle supplies the function `route(path, method='GET', callback=None)`. You often use it as a decorator of the callback function, but, for flexibility, you also have the alternative of calling it directly and passing the callback function as the *callback* argument.

The *method* argument can be any HTTP method name (`'GET'`, `'DELETE'`, `'PATCH'`, `'POST'`, `'PUT'`) or a list of HTTP method names. Bottle also supplies functions that are synonyms of `route` but with a specified value for *method*—these functions are named like each HTTP method, lowercased (`get`, `delete`, `patch`, `post`, `put`).

path is a string matching the URI to route; for example, `'/'` to route requests that ask for the root URL of the site. The string may include one or more *wildcards*—identifiers enclosed in angle brackets <>—in which case the callback function must accept arguments named like those identifiers (when a path has no wildcards, Bottle calls the callback function it routes to without arguments). Each wildcard matches one or more characters of the URI, up to the first slash in the URI, excluded.

For example, when *path* is `'/greet/<name>/first'`, and the URI string is `'/greet/alex/first'`, the callback function must accept an argument named *name*, and Bottle calls the function with value `'alex'` for that argument.

For even more flexibility, the wildcard's identifier can be followed by a *filter*. For any identifier *ident*: `<ident:int>` matches digits and converts them to an `int`; `<ident:float>` matches digits and an optional dot and converts them to a `float`; `<ident:path>` matches characters *including* slashes (in a nongreedy way, if further parts follow); and `<ident:re:pattern>` matches the arbitrary regular expression pattern you indicate. Bottle even lets you code your own custom filters, although we do not cover this advanced subject in this book.

Bottle request objects The `bottle.Request` class supplies a large number of properties, thoroughly documented in Bottle's docs (*http://bottlepy.org/docs/dev/api.html#bottle.BaseRequest*). The ones you'll use most often are:

`body`
: A seekable file-like object, the request's body (for POST and PUT requests)

`cookies`
: A `FormsDict` with the cookies from the request

`files`
: A `FormsDict` whose values are file-like objects, all files uploaded in the request (for POST and PUT requests), keys being the files' names

`headers`
: A `WSGIHeaderDict` with the request's headers

`params`
: A `FormsDict` with the request's parameters (either from the query string, or, for POST and PUT requests, from the form that's the body)

A `FormsDict` is like a `dict` except that it can have multiple values for a key. Indexing, and the method `get`, on a `FormsDict` instance *f*, return an arbitrary one of the values; to get the whole list of values for a key (possibly an empty list), call `f.getall(key)`. A `WSGIHeaderDict` is like a `dict` except that it has `str` keys and values (bytes in v2, Unicode in v3) and keys are case-insensitive.

Signed cookies in `bottle.request.cookies` are not decoded: call `bottle.request.get_cookie(key, secret)` (which returns `None` when the cookie is missing or was not signed with the given *`secret`* string) to properly access a signed cookie in decoded form.

`bottle.request` is a thread-safe proxy to the request being processed.

Bottle response objects Often, a Bottle callback function just returns a result: Bottle transparently wraps an instance *`r`* of `bottle.Response` around a bytestring body (prepared depending on the result's type), so you don't have to worry about the response class.

The result can be a bytestring (used as the body), a Unicode string (encoded as per `Content-Type`, `utf8` by default), a `dict` (serialized with `json.dumps`—this also sets the content type to `'application/json'`), a file-like object (anything with a `read` method), or any iterable whose items are (byte or Unicode) strings.

When the result is an instance of class `HTTPError` or `HTTPResponse`, this indicates an error, just like raising such an instance does (the difference between the two classes is that, when you return or raise an instance of `HTTPError`, Bottle applies an *error handler*, while instances of `HTTPResponse` bypass error handling).

Serving HTTP

When your callback function wants to alter the response's headers, it can do so on `bottle.response` before returning the value for the response's body.

`bottle.response` is a thread-safe proxy to the response being prepared.

To set a cookie, don't use `bottle.response.headers`; rather, call `bottle.response.set_cookie`, with arguments as mentioned in `set_cookie` in Table 20-1, plus, optionally, a named argument `secret=...`, whose value is used to cryptographically *sign* the cookie: signing makes the cookie safe from tampering (although it does not hide its contents), and Bottle takes advantage of that to let you use an object of any type as the cookie's value and serialize it with `pickle` (the `pickle.dumps` result bytestring must fit in the 4 KB cookie limit).

Bottle templating Bottle supplies its own built-in Simple Templating System (*http://bottlepy.org/docs/dev/stpl.html*), which we do not cover in this book. However, using other templating engines, such as jinja2 (covered in "The jinja2 Package" on page 624) is also quite simple (provided that you have previously separately installed such engines in your Python installation or virtual environment).

By default, Bottle loads template files from either the current directory or its subdirectory *./views/* (you can change that by altering the list of strings `bottle.TEMPLATE_PATH`). To make a template object, call `bottle.template`: the first argument is either a template filename or a template string; every other positional argument is a `dict` cumulatively setting template variables, and so is every named argument, except, optionally, `template_adapter=...`, which lets you specify a template engine (defaulting to Bottle's own "simple templating"). `bottle.jinja2template` is the same function, but specifies the jinja2 adapter.

Once you have a template object, you can call its `render` method to obtain the strings it renders to—or, more often, you just return the template object from a callback function to have Bottle use the template object to build the response's body.

An even simpler way to use templating in a callback function is the decorator `bottle.view` (`bottle.jinja2view`, to use jinja2), which takes the same arguments as `bottle.template`: when a callback function is decorated this way, and the function returns a `dict`, then that `dict` is used to set or override template variables, and Bottle proceeds as if the function had returned the template.

In other words, the following three functions are equivalent:

```
import bottle

@bottle.route('/a')
def a():
    t = bottle.template('tp.html', x=23)
    return t.render()

@bottle.route('/b')
def b():
    t = bottle.template('tp.html', x=23)
    return t

@bottle.route('/c')
@bottle.view('tp.html')
def c():
    return {'x': 23}
```

If Bottle's built-in functionality (plus all the extras you can build up for yourself by explicit use of standard library and third-party modules) isn't enough, Bottle also lets you extend its own functionality via *plug-ins*. Bottle officially recognizes and lists (*http://bottlepy.org/docs/dev/plugins/index.html*) over a dozen reusable third-party plug-ins, and also documents (*http://bottlepy.org/docs/dev/plugindev.html*) how to write your own personal plug-ins. We don't cover Bottle plug-ins in this book.

Example 20-3 shows a simple Bottle example.

Example 20-3. A Bottle example

```
import datetime, bottle
one_year = datetime.timedelta(days=365)

@bottle.route('/')
def greet():
    lastvisit = bottle.request.get_cookie('lastvisit')
    now = datetime.datetime.now()
    newvisit = now.ctime()
    thisvisit = '<p>This visit on {} UTC</p>'.format(newvisit)
    bottle.response.set_cookie('lastvisit', newvisit,
                               expires=now+one_year)
    resp_body = ['<html><head><title>Hello, visitor!</title>'
                 '</head><body>']
    if lastvisit is None:
        resp_body.extend((
          '<p>Welcome to this site on your first visit!</p>',
          thisvisit,
          '<p>Please Refresh the web page to proceed</p>'))
    else:
        resp_body.extend((
          '<p>Welcome back to this site!</p>',
          '<p>You last visited on {} UTC</p>'.format(lastvisit),
```

```
            thisvisit))
    resp_body.append('</body></html>')
    bottle.response.content_type = 'text/html'
    return resp_body

if __name__ == '__main__':
    bottle.run(debug=True)
```


This Bottle example just shows how to use some of the many building blocks that Bottle offers—the default app object, one callback function, and one route, preparing the response (in this case, just returning a list of string pieces of the response body, which is, as often, a handy way to build things up). The example also shows how to maintain a minimal continuity of state among multiple interactions with the server from the same browser by setting and using a cookie.

If this app had multiple routes, no doubt it would want to set the `lastvisit` cookie no matter through which route the app was getting "visited." Here's how to code and decorate a hook function to execute after each request:

```
@bottle.hook('after_request')
def set_lastvisit():
    now = datetime.datetime.now()
    bottle.response.set_cookie('lastvisit', now.ctime(),
                               expires=now+one_year)
```

You can now remove the `bottle.response.set_cookie` call from the callback function `greet`, and the app will keep working fine.

webapp2

Last, but not least, is webapp2 (*https://webapp2.readthedocs.io/en/latest/*), which shares with Django and jinja2 the distinction of being bundled with Google App Engine (but of course, just like jinja2 and Django, can also perfectly well be used with other web servers). To install webapp2 with Google App Engine, see the main Quick Start (*http://bit.ly/2obTs5R*) guide; to install it independently of Google App Engine, see the alternative Quick Start (*http://bit.ly/2nBsZxd*) guide. You can also examine the source code (*http://bit.ly/2nkorZF*) and the PyPI entry (*http://bit.ly/2o8LQAY*).

The main class supplied by `webapp2` is named `WSGIApplication`. An instance of `webapp2.WSGIApplication` is a WSGI app, and you instantiate it with up to three named arguments: `routes`, a list of routing specifications; `debug`, a `bool` defaulting to `False` (pass as `True` to enable debugging mode); and `config`, a `dict` with configuration information for the application. Since `routes` is easier to express after you have defined the handlers you want to route to, the usual pattern in `webapp2` is to instantiate the WSGI application at the *end* of the module.

webapp2 request objects The `webapp2.Request` class (the current instance is available to your handler methods as `self.request`) supplies a large number of properties and methods, thoroughly documented in the webapp2 docs (*https://webapp2.readthedocs.io/en/latest/api/webapp2.html#request-and-response*). The ones you'll be using most often are three mappings: `cookies`, cookie names to values; `headers`, header names to values (case-insensitive); and `params`, request parameter names to values. Two handy methods are `get` (like `params.get`, but you can optionally pass the named argument `allow_multiple=True` to get a list of all values for the parameter) and `get_all` (like `get` with `allow_multiple=True`).

webapp2 response objects The `webapp2.Response` class (the current instance is available to your handler methods as `self.response`) supplies a large number of properties and methods, thoroughly documented in the webapp2 docs (*https://webapp2.readthedocs.io/en/latest/api/webapp2.html#request-and-response*). One you'll use often is the mapping property `headers`, which you use to set the response headers; however, for the specific purpose of setting cookies, use, instead, the method `set_cookie` (*http://webapp2.readthedocs.io/en/latest/guide/response.html?highlight=cookies#setting-cookies*). To set response status, assign to `status`—for example, `self.response.status = '404 Not Found'`.

To build up the response body, you normally call the response's `write` method (often more than once). Alternatively, assign to the attribute body a bytestring—or a Unicode string, which gets encoded as UTF-8, if the Content-Type header ends in `; charset=utf8` (or, equivalently, set the `charset` attribute to `'utf8'`).

webapp2 handlers webapp2 *handlers* are classes extending `webapp2.RequestHandler`. Handlers define methods named like (the lowercase version of) HTTP methods, such as `get` and `post`. Such methods access the current request as `self.request` and prepare the response as `self.response`.

A handler may optionally override the `dispatch` method, which gets called before the appropriate method (such as `get` or `post`) is determined. This lets the handler optionally alter the request, do custom dispatching, and also (typically after delegating to the superclass's `dispatch`) alter the resulting `self.response`. Such overriding is often done in a common base class: then, you inherit from that common base class in your actual handler classes.

webapp2 routes webapp2 supplies a `Route` class for sophisticated routing needs. However, in the majority of cases, you can think of a *route* as just a pair (*`template,handler`*).

The *`template`* is a string that may include identifiers enclosed in angle brackets <>. Such angle-bracket components match any sequence of characters (up to a slash, `/`, excluded) and pass the substring as a *named* argument to the handler's method.

Within the angle brackets, you might alternatively have a `:` (colon), followed by a regular expression pattern. In this case, the component matches characters per the pattern, and passes the substring as a *positional* argument to the handler's method.

Lastly, within the angle brackets, you may have an identifier, then a : (colon), then a regular expression pattern. In this case, the component matches characters per the pattern, and passes the substring as a *named* argument to the handler's method.

Positional arguments are passed only if no named ones are; if *`template`* has both kinds of components, the ones that would become positional arguments get matched, but their values are not passed at all to the handler's method. For example, if the template is `'/greet/<name>/<:.*>'`, the handler's method is called with named argument *`name`*, and without any positional argument corresponding to the trailing part of the URI.

Handler methods routed to by a route whose template includes angle-bracket components must accept the resulting positional or named parameters.

The *`handler`* is normally a *handler class* as covered in "webapp2 handlers" on page 592. However, there are alternatives, of which the most frequently used one is to have *`handler`* be a *string* identifying the handler class, such as `'my.module.the class'`. In this case, the relevant module is not imported until the handler class is specifically needed: if and when it's needed, webapp2 imports it on the fly (at most once).

webapp2 extras The webapp2.extras (*https://webapp2.readthedocs.io/en/latest/guide/extras.html*) package supplies several convenient modules to seamlessly add functionality to webapp2, covering authentication and authorization, integration with jinja2 and other templating engines, i18n, and *sessions* (with various possible backing stores) for easier maintenance of state than with just cookies.

Example 20-4 shows a simple webapp2 example.

Example 20-4. A webapp2 example

```
import datetime, webapp2
one_year = datetime.timedelta(days=365)

class Greeter(webapp2.RequestHandler):
    def get(self):
        lastvisit = self.request.cookies.get('lastvisit')
        now = datetime.datetime.now()
        newvisit = now.ctime()
        thisvisit = '<p>This visit on {} UTC</p>'.format(newvisit)
        self.response.set_cookie('lastvisit', newvisit,
                                 expires=now+one_year)
        self.response.write(
            '<html><head><title>Hello, visitor!</title>'
            '</head><body>')
        if lastvisit is None:
            self.response.write(
              '<p>Welcome to this site on your first visit!</p>')
            self.response.write(thisvisit)
```

```
            self.response.write(
              '<p>Please Refresh the web page to proceed</p>')
        else:
            self.response.write(
              '<p>Welcome back to this site!</p>')
            self.response.write(
              '<p>You last visited on {} UTC</p>'.format(lastvisit))
            self.response.write(thisvisit)
        self.response.write('</body></html>')

app = webapp2.WSGIApplication(
    [('/', Greeter),
    ]
)
```

This webapp2 example just shows how to use some of the many building blocks that webapp2 offers—the app object, one handler, and one route, preparing the response (in this case, just writing to it). The example also shows how to maintain a minimal continuity of state among multiple interactions with the server from the same browser by setting and using a cookie.

If this app had multiple routes, no doubt it would want to set the `lastvisit` cookie no matter through which route the app was getting "visited." Here's how to code a base handler class (derive every handler from it!), have it override `dispatch`, and use the override to always set the needed cookie:

```
class BaseHandler(webapp2.RequestHandler):
    def dispatch(self):
        webapp2.RequestHandler.dispatch(self)
        now = datetime.datetime.now()
        self.response.set_cookie('lastvisit', now.ctime(),
                                 expires=now+one_year)

class Greeter(BaseHandler): ...
```

You can now remove the `self.response.set_cookie` call from `Greeter.get`, and the app will keep working fine.

21 Email, MIME, and Other Network Encodings

What travels on a network are streams of bytes, also known in networking jargon as *octets*. Bytes can, of course, represent text, via any of several possible encodings. However, what you want to send over the network often has more structure than just a stream of text or bytes. The Multipurpose Internet Mail Extensions (MIME) and other encoding standards bridge the gap by specifying how to represent structured data as bytes or text. While often originally designed for email, such encodings are also used in the web and many other networked systems. Python supports such encodings through many library modules, such as `base64`, `quopri`, and `uu` (covered in "Encoding Binary Data as ASCII Text" on page 605), and the modules of the `email` package (covered in "MIME and Email Format Handling" on page 595).

MIME and Email Format Handling

The `email` package handles parsing, generation, and manipulation of MIME files such as email messages, Network News (NNTP) posts, HTTP interactions, and so on. The Python standard library also contains other modules that handle some parts of these jobs. However, the `email` package offers a complete and systematic approach to these important tasks. We suggest you use `email`, not the older modules that partially overlap with parts of `email`'s functionality. `email`, despite its name, has nothing to do with receiving or sending email; for such tasks, see the modules `poplib` and `smtplib`, covered in "Email Protocols" on page 552. `email` deals with handling MIME messages (which may or may not be mail) after you receive them, or constructing them properly before you send them.

Functions in the email Package

The `email` package supplies two factory functions that return an instance *m* of the class `email.message.Message`. These functions rely on the class `email.parser.Parser`, but the factory functions are handier and simpler. Therefore, we do not cover the `email.parser` module further in this book.

message_from_string `message_from_string(s)`

Builds *m* by parsing string *s*.

message_from_file `message_from_file(f)`

Builds *m* by parsing the contents of text file-like object *f*, which must be open for reading.

v3 only, also supplies two similar factory functions to build message objects from bytestrings and binary files:

message_from_bytes `message_from_bytes(s)`

Builds *m* by parsing bytestring *s*.

message_from_binary_file `message_from_binary_file(f)`

Builds *m* by parsing the contents of binary file-like object *f*, which must be open for reading.

The email.message Module

The `email.message` module supplies the class `Message`. All parts of the `email` package make, modify, or use instances of `Message`. An instance *m* of `Message` models a MIME message, including headers and a *payload* (data content). To create an initially empty *m*, call `Message` with no arguments. More often, you create *m* by parsing via the factory functions `message_from_string` and `message_from_file` of `email`, or by other indirect means such as the classes covered in "Creating Messages" on page 600. *m*'s payload can be a string, a single other instance of `Message`, or (for a multipart message) a list of other `Message` instances.

You can set arbitrary headers on email messages you're building. Several Internet RFCs specify headers for a wide variety of purposes. The main applicable RFC is RFC 2822 (*http://www.faqs.org/rfcs/rfc2822.html*). An instance *m* of the `Message` class holds headers as well as a payload. *m* is a mapping, with header names as keys and header value strings as values.

To make *m* more convenient, the semantics of *m* as a mapping are different from those of a `dict`. *m*'s keys are case-insensitive. *m* keeps headers in the order in which you add them, and the methods `keys`, `values`, and `items` return lists of headers in that order. *m* can have more than one header named *key*: *m*[*key*] returns an arbitrary such header (or None when the header is missing), and del *m*[*key*] deletes all of them (it's not an error if the header is missing).

To get a list of all headers with a certain name, call *m*.get_all(*key*). len(*m*) returns the total number of headers, counting duplicates, not just the number of distinct header names. When there is no header named *key*, *m*[*key*] returns None and does not raise KeyError (i.e., behaves like *m*.get(*key*)): del *m*[*key*] does nothing in this case, and *m*.get_all(*key*) returns an empty list. In v2, you cannot loop directly on *m*; loop on *m*.keys() instead.

An instance *m* of Message supplies the following attributes and methods that deal with *m*'s headers and payload.

add_header

m.add_header(*_name*,*_value*,***_params*)

Like *m*[*_name*]=*_value*, but you can also supply header parameters as named arguments. For each named argument *pname*=*pvalue*, add_header changes underscores to dashes, then appends to the header's value a parameter of the form:

```
; pname="pvalue"
```

When *pvalue* is None, add_header appends only a parameter ';*pname*'.

When a parameter's value contains non-ASCII characters, specify it as a tuple with three items, (*CHARSET*, *LANGUAGE*, *VALUE*). *CHARSET* names the encoding to use for the value, *LANGUAGE* is usually None or '' but can be set any language value per RFC 2231 (*http://www.rfc-base.org/rfc-2231.html*), and *VALUE* is the string value containing non-ASCII characters.

as_string

m.as_string(*unixfrom*=False)

Returns the entire message as a string. When *unixfrom* is true, also includes a first line, normally starting with 'From ', known as the *envelope header* of the message. The class's __str__ method is the same as as_string, but with *unixfrom* set to True in v2 only.

attach

m.attach(*payload*)

Adds *payload*, a message, to *m*'s payload. When *m*'s payload was None, *m*'s payload is now the single-item list [*payload*]. When *m*'s payload was a list of messages, appends *payload* to the list. When *m*'s payload was anything else, *m*.attach(*payload*) raises MultipartConversionError.

epilogue

The attribute *m*.epilogue can be None or a string that becomes part of the message's string-form after the last boundary line. Mail programs normally don't display this text. epilogue is a normal attribute of *m*: your program can access it when you're handling an *m* built by whatever means, and bind it when you're building or modifying *m*.

get_all `m.get_all(name,default=None)`

Returns a list with all values of headers named *name* in the order in which the headers were added to *m*. When *m* has no header named *name*, `get_all` returns *default*.

get_boundary `m.get_boundary(default=None)`

Returns the string value of the `boundary` parameter of *m*'s Content-Type header. When *m* has no Content-Type header, or the header has no `boundary` parameter, `get_boundary` returns *default*.

get_charsets `m.get_charsets(default=None)`

Returns the list *L* of string values of parameter `charset` of *m*'s Content-Type headers. When *m* is multipart, *L* has one item per part; otherwise, *L* has length `1`. For parts that have no Content-Type, no `charset` parameter, or a main type different from `'text'`, the corresponding item in *L* is *default*.

get_content_maintype `m.get_content_maintype(default=None)`

Returns *m*'s main content type: a lowercased string `'maintype'` taken from header Content-Type. For example, when Content-Type is `'text/html'`, `get_content_maintype` returns `'text'`. When *m* has no header Content-Type, `get_content_maintype` returns *default*.

get_content_subtype `m.get_content_subtype(default=None)`

Returns *m*'s content subtype: a lowercased string `'subtype'` taken from header Content-Type. For example, when Content-Type is `'text/html'`, `get_content_subtype` returns `'html'`. When *m* has no header Content-Type, `get_content_subtype` returns *default*.

get_content_type `m.get_content_type(default=None)`

Returns *m*'s content type: a lowercased string `'maintype/subtype'` taken from header Content-Type. For example, when Content-Type is `'text/html'`, `get_content_type` returns `'text/html'`. When *m* has no header Content-Type, `get_content_type` returns *default*.

get_filename `m.get_filename(default=None)`

Returns the string value of the `filename` parameter of *m*'s Content-Disposition header. When *m* has no Content-Disposition, or the header has no `filename` parameter, `get_filename` returns *default*.

get_param

`m.get_param(param,default=None,header='Content-Type')`

Returns the string value of parameter *param* of *m*'s header *header*. Returns the empty string for a parameter specified just by name (without a value). When *m* has no header *header*, or the header has no parameter named *param*, `get_param` returns *default*.

get_params

`m.get_params(default=None,header='Content-Type')`

Returns the parameters of *m*'s header *header*, a list of pairs of strings that give each parameter's name and value. Uses the empty string as the value for parameters specified just by name (without a value). When *m* has no header *header*, `get_params` returns *default*.

get_payload

`m.get_payload(i=None,decode=False)`

Returns *m*'s payload. When `m.is_multipart()` is `False`, *i* must be `None`, and `m.get_payload()` returns *m*'s entire payload, a string or `Message` instance. If *decode* is true and the value of header Content-Transfer-Encoding is either `'quoted-printable'` or `'base64'`, `m.get_payload` also decodes the payload. If *decode* is false, or header Content-Transfer-Encoding is missing or has other values, `m.get_payload` returns the payload unchanged.

When `m.is_multipart()` is `True`, *decode* must be false. When *i* is `None`, `m.get_payload()` returns *m*'s payload as a list. Otherwise, `m.get_payload(i)` returns the *i*th item of the payload, or raises `TypeError` if `i<0` or *i* is too large.

get_unixfrom

`m.get_unixfrom()`

Returns the envelope header string for *m*, or `None` when *m* has no envelope header.

is_multipart

`m.is_multipart()`

Returns `True` when *m*'s payload is a list; otherwise, `False`.

preamble

Attribute `m.preamble` can be `None` or a string that becomes part of the message's string form before the first boundary line. A mail program shows this text only if it doesn't support multipart messages, so you can use this attribute to alert the user that your message is multipart and a different mail program is needed to view it. `preamble` is a normal attribute of *m*: your program can access it when you're handling an *m* that is built by whatever means and bind, rebind, or unbind it when you're building or modifying *m*.

set_boundary

`m.set_boundary(boundary)`

Sets the `boundary` parameter of *m*'s Content-Type header to *boundary*. When *m* has no Content-Type header, raises `HeaderParseError`.

set_payload `m.set_payload(payload)`

Sets *m*'s payload to *payload*, which must be a string or list or `Message` instances, as appropriate to *m*'s Content-Type.

set_unixfrom `m.set_unixfrom(unixfrom)`

Sets the envelope header string for *m*. *unixfrom* is the entire envelope header line, including the leading `'From '` but *not* including the trailing `'\n'`.

walk `m.walk()`

Returns an iterator on all parts and subparts of *m* to walk the tree of parts depth-first (see "Recursion" on page 98).

The email.Generator Module

The `email.Generator` module supplies the class `Generator`, which you can use to generate the textual form of a message *m*. `m.as_string()` and `str(m)` may be sufficient, but `Generator` gives you more flexibility. You instantiate the `Generator` class with a mandatory argument and two optional arguments:

Generator `class Generator(outfp,mangle_from_=False,maxheaderlen=78)`

outfp is a file or file-like object that supplies method `write`. When *mangle_from_* is true, *g* prepends `'>'` to any line in the payload that starts with `'From '`, in order to make the message's textual form easier to parse. *g* wraps each header line, at semicolons, into physical lines of no more than *maxheaderlen* characters. To use *g*, call `g.flatten`:

```
g.flatten(m, unixfrom=False)
```

This emits *m* as text to *outfp*, like (but consuming less memory than) `outfp.write(m.as_string(unixfrom))`.

Creating Messages

The `email` package supplies modules with names that, in v2, start with `'MIME'`, each module supplying a subclass of `Message` named just like the module. In v3, the modules are in the subpackage `email.mime`, and the modules' names are lowercase (for example, `email.mime.text` in v3, instead of `email.MIMEText` in v2). Although imported from different modules in v2 and v3, the class names are the same in both versions.

These classes make it easier to create `Message` instances of various MIME types. The MIME classes are as follows:

MIMEAudio `class MIMEAudio(_audiodata,_subtype=None,_encoder=None, **_params)`

_audiodata is a bytestring of audio data to pack in a message of MIME type `'audio/_subtype'`. When *_subtype* is None, *_audiodata* must be parseable by standard Python library module `sndhdr` to determine the subtype; otherwise, `MIMEAudio` raises `TypeError`. When *_encoder* is None, `MIMEAudio` encodes data as Base64, typically optimal. Otherwise, *_encoder* must be callable with one parameter *m*, which is the message being constructed; *_encoder* must then call `m.get_payload()` to get the payload, encode the payload, put the encoded form back by calling `m.set_payload`, and set *m*'s `'Content-Transfer-Encoding'` header appropriately. `MIMEAudio` passes the *_params* dictionary of named-argument names and values to `m.add_header` to construct *m*'s `Content-Type`.

MIMEBase `class MIMEBase(_maintype,_subtype,**_params)`

Base class of all MIME classes, directly extends `Message`. Instantiating:

```
m = MIMEBase(main,sub,**parms)
```

is equivalent to the longer and less convenient idiom:

```
m = Message()
m.add_header('Content-Type','{}/{}'.
  format(main,sub),**parms)
m.add_header('Mime-Version','1.0')
```

MIMEImage `class MIMEImage(_imagedata,_subtype=None,_encoder=None, **_params)`

Like `MIMEAudio`, but with main type `'image'`; uses standard Python module `imghdr` to determine the subtype, if needed.

MIMEMessage `class MIMEMessage(msg,_subtype='rfc822')`

Packs *msg*, which must be an instance of `Message` (or a subclass), as the payload of a message of MIME type `'message/_subtype'`.

MIMEText `class MIMEText(_text,_subtype='plain',_charset='us-ascii', _encoder=None)`

Packs text string *_text* as the payload of a message of MIME type `'text/_subtype'` with the given `charset`. When *_encoder* is None, `MIMEText` does not encode the text, which is generally optimal. Otherwise, *_encoder* must be callable with one parameter *m*, which is the message being constructed; *_encoder* must then call `m.get_payload()` to get the payload, encode the payload, put the encoded form back by calling `m.set_payload`, and set *m*'s `'Content-Transfer-Encoding'` appropriately.

The email.encoders Module

The `email.encoders` module (in v3) supplies functions that take a *non-multipart* message *m* as their only argument, encode *m*'s payload, and set *m*'s headers appropriately. In v2, the module's name is titlecase, `email.Encoders`.

encode_base64 `encode_base64(m)`

Uses Base64 encoding, optimal for arbitrary binary data.

encode_noop `encode_noop(m)`

Does nothing to *m*'s payload and headers.

encode_quopri `encode_quopri(m)`

Uses Quoted Printable encoding, optimal for text that is almost but not fully ASCII (see "The quopri Module" on page 607).

encode_7or8bit `encode_7or8bit(m)`

Does nothing to *m*'s payload, and sets header Content-Transfer-Encoding to `'8bit'` when any byte of *m*'s payload has the high bit set; otherwise, to `'7bit'`.

The email.utils Module

The `email.utils` module (in v3) supplies several functions useful for email processing. In v2, the module's name is titlecase, `email.Utils`.

formataddr `formataddr(pair)`

pair is a pair of strings `(realname,email_address)`. `formataddr` returns a string *s* with the address to insert in header fields such as `To` and `Cc`. When *realname* is false (e.g., the empty string, `''`), `formataddr` returns *email_address*.

formatdate `formatdate(timeval=None,localtime=False)`

timeval is a number of seconds since the epoch. When *timeval* is `None`, `formatdate` uses the current time. When *localtime* is true, `formatdate` uses the local time zone; otherwise, it uses UTC. `formatdate` returns a string with the given time instant formatted in the way specified by RFC 2822.

getaddresses `getaddresses(L)`

Parses each item of *L*, a list of address strings as used in header fields such as `To` and `Cc`, and returns a list of pairs of strings `(name,email_address)`. When `getaddresses` cannot parse an item of *L* as an address, `getaddresses` uses `(None,None)` as the corresponding item in the list it returns.

mktime_tz `mktime_tz(t)`

t is a tuple with 10 items. The first nine items of *t* are in the same format used in the module `time`, covered in "The time Module" on page 363. `t[-1]` is a time zone as an offset in seconds from UTC (with the opposite sign from `time.timezone`, as specified by RFC 2822). When `t[-1]` is `None`, `mktime_tz` uses the local time zone. `mktime_tz` returns a float with the number of seconds since the epoch, in UTC, corresponding to the instant that *t* denotes.

parseaddr `parseaddr(s)`

Parses string *s*, which contains an address as typically specified in header fields such as `To` and `Cc`, and returns a pair of strings `(realname,email_address)`. When `parseaddr` cannot parse *s* as an address, `parseaddr` returns `('','')`.

parsedate `parsedate(s)`

Parses string *s* as per the rules in RFC 2822 and returns a tuple *t* with nine items, as used in the module `time`, covered in "The time Module" on page 363 (the items `t[-3:]` are not meaningful). `parsedate` also attempts to parse some erroneous variations on RFC 2822 that widespread mailers use. When `parsedate` cannot parse *s*, `parsedate` returns `None`.

parsedate_tz `parsedate_tz(s)`

Like `parsedate`, but returns a tuple *t* with 10 items, where `t[-1]` is *s*'s time zone as an offset in seconds from UTC (with the opposite sign from `time.timezone`, as specified by RFC 2822), like in the argument that `mktime_tz` accepts. Items `t[-4:-1]` are not meaningful. When *s* has no time zone, `t[-1]` is `None`.

quote `quote(s)`

Returns a copy of string *s*, where each double quote (`"`) becomes `'\"'` and each existing backslash is repeated.

unquote `unquote(s)`

Returns a copy of string *s* where leading and trailing double-quote characters (`"`) and angle brackets (`<>`) are removed if they surround the rest of *s*.

Example Uses of the email Package

The `email` package helps you both in reading and composing email and email-like messages (but it's not involved in receiving and transmitting such messages: those tasks belong to different and separate modules covered in Chapter 19). Here is an example of how to use `email` to read a possibly multipart message and unpack each part into a file in a given directory:

```
import os, email

def unpack_mail(mail_file, dest_dir):
    ''' Given file object mail_file, open for reading, and dest_dir, a
        string that is a path to an existing, writable directory,
        unpack each part of the mail message from mail_file to a
        file within dest_dir.
    '''
    with mail_file:
        msg = email.message_from_file(mail_file)
    for part_number, part in enumerate(msg.walk()):
        if part.get_content_maintype() == 'multipart':
            # we'll get each specific part later in the loop,
            # so, nothing to do for the 'multipart' itself
            continue
        dest = part.get_filename()
        if dest is None: dest = part.get_param('name')
        if dest is None: dest = 'part-{}'.format(part_number)
        # In real life, make sure that dest is a reasonable filename
        # for your OS; otherwise, mangle that name until it is
        with open(os.path.join(dest_dir, dest), 'wb') as f:
            f.write(part.get_payload(decode=True))
```

And here is an example that performs roughly the reverse task, packaging all files that are directly under a given source directory into a single file suitable for mailing:

```
def pack_mail(source_dir, **headers):
    ''' Given source_dir, a string that is a path to an existing,
        readable directory, and arbitrary header name/value pairs
        passed in as named arguments, packs all the files directly
        under source_dir (assumed to be plain text files) into a
        mail message returned as a MIME-formatted string.
    '''
    msg = email.Message.Message()
    for name, value in headers.items():
        msg[name] = value
    msg['Content-type'] = 'multipart/mixed'
    filenames = next(os.walk(source_dir))[-1]
    for filename in filenames:
        m = email.Message.Message()
        m.add_header('Content-type', 'text/plain', name=filename)
        with open(os.path.join(source_dir, filename), 'r') as f:
            m.set_payload(f.read())
        msg.attach(m)
    return msg.as_string()
```

rfc822 and mimetools Modules (v2)

The best way to handle email-like messages is with the `email` package. However, some other modules covered in Chapters 19 and 20, in v2 only, use instances of the class `rfc822.Message` or its subclass, `mimetools.Message`. This section covers the subset of these classes' functionality that you need to make effective use, in v2, of the modules covered in Chapters 19 and 20.

An instance *m* of the class `Message` in either of these v2-only modules is a mapping, with the headers' names as keys and the corresponding header value strings as values. Keys and values are strings, and keys are case-insensitive. *m* supports all mapping methods except `clear`, `copy`, `popitem`, and `update`. `get` and `setdefault` default to `''` instead of `None`. The instance *m* also supplies convenience methods (e.g., to combine getting a header's value and parsing it as a date or an address). For such purposes, we suggest you use the functions of the module `email.utils` (covered in "The email.utils Module" on page 602): use *m* just as a mapping.

When *m* is an instance of `mimetools.Message`, *m* supplies additional methods:

getmaintype `m.getmaintype()`

Returns *m*'s main content type, from header Content-Type, in lowercase. When *m* has no header Content-Type, `getmaintype` returns `'text'`.

getparam `m.getparam(param)`

Returns the value of the parameter named *param* of *m*'s Content-Type.

getsubtype `m.getsubtype()`

Returns *m*'s content subtype, taken from Content-Type, in lowercase. When *m* has no Content-Type, `getsubtype` returns `'plain'`.

gettype `m.gettype()`

Returns *m*'s content type, taken from Content-Type, in lowercase. When *m* has no Content-Type, `gettype` returns `'text/plain'`.

Encoding Binary Data as ASCII Text

Several kinds of media (e.g., email messages) can contain only ASCII text. When you want to transmit arbitrary binary data via such media, you need to encode the data as ASCII text strings. The Python standard library supplies modules that support the standard encodings known as Base64, Quoted Printable, and UU.

The base64 Module

The `base64` module supports the encodings specified in RFC 3548 as Base16, Base32, and Base64. Each of these encodings is a compact way to represent arbitrary binary data as ASCII text, without any attempt to produce human-readable results. `base64` supplies 10 functions: 6 for Base64, plus 2 each for Base32 and Base16. The 6 Base64 functions are:

b64decode `b64decode(`*`s`*`,`*`altchars`*`=None, `*`validate`*`=False)`

Decodes Base64-encoded bytestring *s*, and returns the decoded bytestring. *altchars*, if not `None`, must be a bytestring of at least two characters (extra characters are ignored) specifying the two nonstandard characters to use instead of + and / (potentially useful to deal with URL-safe or filesystem-safe Base64-encoded strings). *validate* can be passed only in v3: when `True`, when *s* contains any bytes that are not valid in Base64-encoded strings, the call raises an exception (by default, such bytes are just ignored and skipped). Also raises an exception when *s* is improperly padded according to the Base64 standard.

b64encode `b64encode(`*`s`*`, altchars=None)`

Encodes bytestring *s* and returns the bytestring with the corresponding Base64-encoded data. *altchars*, if not `None`, must be a bytestring of at least two characters (extra characters are ignored) specifying the two nonstandard characters to use instead of + and / (potentially useful to deal with URL-safe or filesystem-safe Base64-encoded strings).

standard_b64decode `standard_b64decode(`*`s`*`)`

Like `b64decode(s)`.

standard_b64encode `standard_b64encode(`*`s`*`)`

Like `b64encode(`*`s`*`)`.

urlsafe_b64decode `urlsafe_b64decode(`*`s`*`)`

Like `b64decode(`*`s`*`, '-_')`.

urlsafe_b64encode `urlsafe_b64encode(`*`s`*`)`

Like `b64encode(`*`s`*`, '-_')`.

The four Base16 and Base32 functions are:

b16decode `b16decode(`*`s`*`,`*`casefold`*`=False)`

Decodes Base16-encoded bytestring *s*, and returns the decoded bytestring. When *casefold* is `True`, lowercase characters can be part of *s* and are treated like their uppercase equivalents; by default, when lowercase characters are present, the call raises an exception.

b16encode `b16encode(`*`s`*`)`

Encodes bytestring *s* and returns the byte string with the corresponding Base16-encoded data.

b32decode `b32decode(s,casefold=False, map01=None)`

Decodes Base32-encoded bytestring *s*, and returns the decoded bytestring. When *casefold* is `True`, lowercase characters can be part of *s* and are treated like their uppercase equivalents; by default, when lowercase characters are present, the call raises an exception. When *map01* is `None`, characters `0` and `1` are not allowed in the input; when not `None`, it must be a single-character bytestring specifying what `1` is mapped to (lowercase `'l'` or uppercase `'L'`), while `0` is then always mapped to uppercase `'O'`.

b32encode `b32encode(s)`

Encodes bytestring *s* and returns the bytestring with the corresponding Base32-encoded data.

Email, MIME, and Encodings

In v3 only, the module also supplies functions to encode and decode the non-standard but popular encodings Base85 and Ascii85, which, while not codified in RFCs nor compatible with each other, can offer space savings of 15% by using larger alphabets for encoded bytestrings. See the online docs (*https://docs.python.org/3/library/base64.html#base64.a85encode*) for details on those functions.

The quopri Module

The `quopri` module supports the encoding specified in RFC 1521 as Quoted Printable (QP). QP can represent any binary data as ASCII text, but it's mainly intended for data that is mostly textual, with a small amount of characters with the high bit set (i.e., characters outside the ASCII range). For such data, QP produces results that are both compact and reasonably human-readable. The `quopri` module supplies four functions:

decode `decode(infile,outfile,header=False)`

Reads the binary file-like object *infile* by calling *infile*`.readline` until end of file (i.e., until a call to *infile*`.readline` returns an empty string), decodes the QP-encoded ASCII text thus read, and writes the decoded data to binary file-like object *outfile*. When *header* is true, `decode` also decodes _ (underscores) into spaces (per RFC 1522).

decodestring `decodestring(s,header=False)`

Decodes bytestring *s*, which contains QP-encoded ASCII text, and returns the bytestring with the decoded data. When *header* is true, `decodestring` also decodes _ (underscores) into spaces.

encode `encode(infile,outfile,quotetabs,header=False)`

Reads binary file-like object *infile* by calling *infile*`.readline` until end of file (i.e., until a call to *infile*`.readline` returns an empty string), encodes the data thus read in QP, and writes the encoded ASCII text to binary file-like object *outfile*. When *quotetabs* is true, `encode` also encodes spaces and tabs. When *header* is true, `encode` encodes spaces as _ (underscores).

encodestring `encodestring(s,quotetabs=False,header=False)`

Encodes bytestring *s*, which contains arbitrary bytes, and returns a bytestring with QP-encoded ASCII text. When *quotetabs* is true, `encodestring` also encodes spaces and tabs. When *header* is true, `encodestring` encodes spaces as _ (underscores).

The uu Module

The `uu` module supports the classic Unix-to-Unix (UU) encoding, as implemented by the Unix programs *uuencode* and *uudecode*. UU starts encoded data with a `begin` line, giving the filename and permissions of the file being encoded, and ends it with an `end` line. Therefore, UU encoding lets you embed encoded data in otherwise unstructured text, while Base64 encoding relies on the existence of other indications of where the encoded data starts and finishes. The `uu` module supplies two functions:

decode `decode(infile,outfile=None,mode=None)`

Reads the file-like object *infile* by calling *infile*.`readline` until end of file (i.e., until a call to *infile*.`readline` returns an empty string) or until a terminator line (the string `'end'` surrounded by any amount of whitespace). `decode` decodes the UU-encoded text thus read and writes the decoded data to the file-like object *outfile*. When *outfile* is `None`, `decode` creates the file specified in the UU-format `begin` line, with the permission bits given by *mode* (the permission bits specified in the `begin` line, when *mode* is `None`). In this case, `decode` raises an exception if the file already exists.

encode `encode(infile,outfile,name='-',mode=0o666)`

Reads the file-like object *infile* by calling *infile*.`read` (45 bytes at a time, which is the amount of data that UU encodes into 60 characters in each output line) until end of file (i.e., until a call to *infile*.`read` returns an empty string). It encodes the data thus read in UU and writes the encoded text to the file-like object *outfile*. `encode` also writes a UU `begin` line before the encoded text and a UU `end` line after the encoded text. In the `begin` line, `encode` specifies the filename as *name* and the mode as *mode*.

22
Structured Text: HTML

Most documents on the web use HTML, the HyperText Markup Language. *Markup* is the insertion of special tokens, known as *tags*, in a text document, to structure the text. HTML is, in theory, an application of the large, general standard known as SGML, the Standard General Markup Language. In practice, many documents on the web use HTML in sloppy or incorrect ways. Browsers have evolved heuristics over the years to compensate for this, but even so, it still happens that a browser displays a wrongly marked-up web page in weird ways (don't blame the browser, if it's a modern one: 9 times out of 10, the blame is on the web page's author).

HTML[1] is not suitable for much more than presenting documents on a browser. Complete, precise extraction of the information in the document, working backward from what most often amounts to the document's presentation, often turns out to be unfeasible. To tighten things up, HTML tried evolving into a more rigorous standard called XHTML. XHTML is similar to traditional HTML, but it is defined in terms of XML, and more precisely than HTML. You can handle well-formed XHTML with the tools covered in Chapter 23. However, as of this writing, XHTML does not appear to have enjoyed overwhelming success, getting scooped instead by the (non-XML) newest version, HTML5.

Despite the difficulties, it's often possible to extract at least some useful information from HTML documents (a task known as *screen-scraping*, or just *scraping*). Python's standard library tries to help, in both v2 and v3, supplying the `sgmllib`, `htmllib`, and `HTMLParser` modules in v2, and the `html` package in v3, for the task of parsing HTML documents, whether this parsing is for the purpose of presenting the documents, or, more typically, as part of an attempt to extract ("scrape") information. However, when you're dealing with somewhat-broken web pages, the third-party

1 Except perhaps for its latest version (HTML5) when properly applied

module BeautifulSoup usually offers your last, best hope. In this book, we mostly cover BeautifulSoup, ignoring most of the Python's standard library offerings "competing" with it.

Generating HTML, and embedding Python in HTML, are also reasonably frequent tasks. The standard Python library doesn't support HTML generation or embedding, but you can use Python string formatting, and third-party modules can also help. `BeautifulSoup` lets you alter an HTML tree (so, in particular, you can build one up programmatically, even "from scratch"); an alternative approach is *templating*, supported, for example, by the third-party module jinja2 (*http://jinja.pocoo.org/*), covered in "The jinja2 Package" on page 624.

The html.entities (v2: htmlentitydefs) Module

The `html.entities` module in Python's standard library (in v2, the module is named `htmlentitydefs`) supplies a few attributes, all of them mappings. They come in handy whatever general approach you're using to parse, edit, or generate HTML, including the BeautifulSoup package covered in "The BeautifulSoup Third-Party Package" on page 611.

`codepoint2name`
: A mapping from Unicode codepoints to HTML entity names. For example, `entities.codepoint2name[228]` is `'auml'`, since Unicode character 228, ä, "lowercase a with diaeresis," is encoded in HTML as `'ä'`.

`entitydefs`
: In v3, a mapping from HTML entity names to Unicode equivalent single-character strings. For example, in v3, `entities.entitydefs['auml']` is `'ä'`, and `entities.entitydefs['sigma']` is `'σ'`. In v2, the equivalence is limited to the Latin-1 (AKA ISO-8859-1) encoding, and HTML character references are used otherwise; therefore, in v2, `htmlentitydefs.entitydefs['auml']` is `'\xe4'`, and `htmlentitydefs.entitydefs['sigma']` is `'σ'`.

`html5` *(v3 only)*
: In v3 only, `html5` is a mapping from HTML5 named character references to equivalent single-character strings. For example, `entities.html5['gt;']` is `'>'` . The trailing semicolon in the key *does* matter—a few, but far from all, HTML5 named character references can optionally be spelled without a trailing semicolon, and, in those cases, both keys (with and without the trailing semicolon) are present in `entities.html5`.

`name2codepoint`
: A mapping from HTML entity names to Unicode codepoints. For example, `entities.name2codepoint['auml']` is 228.

The BeautifulSoup Third-Party Package

BeautifulSoup (*https://www.crummy.com/software/BeautifulSoup/*) lets you parse HTML even if it's rather badly formed—`BeautifulSoup` uses simple heuristics to compensate for likely HTML brokenness, and succeeds at this hard task with surprisingly good frequency. We strongly recommend BeautifulSoup version 4, also known as `bs4`, which supports both v2 and v3 smoothly and equally; we only cover `bs4` in this book (specifically, we document version 4.5 of `bs4`).

Installing versus importing BeautifulSoup

You install the module, for example, by running, at a shell command prompt, **`pip install beautifulsoup4`**; but when you import it, in your Python code, use `import bs4`. If you have both v2 and v3, you may need to explicitly use **`pip3`** to install to v3, and/or **`pip2`** for v2.

The BeautifulSoup Class

The `bs4` module supplies the `BeautifulSoup` class, which you instantiate by calling it with one or two arguments: first, *`htmltext`*—either a file-like object (which is read to get the HTML text to parse) or a string (which is the text to parse)—and next, an optional *`parser`* argument.

Which parser BeautifulSoup uses

If you don't pass a `parser` argument, `BeautifulSoup` "sniffs around" to pick the best parser (you may get a warning in this case). If you haven't installed any other parser, `BeautifulSoup` defaults to `html.parser` from the Python standard library (to specify that parser explicitly, use the string `'html.parser'`, which is the module's name in v3; that also works in v2, where it uses the module `HTMLParser`). To get more control, say, to avoid the differences between parsers mentioned in the `BeautifulSoup` documentation (*https://www.crummy.com/software/BeautifulSoup/bs4/doc/*), pass the name of the parser library to use as the second argument as you instantiate `BeautifulSoup`. Unless specified otherwise, the following examples use the default Python `html.parser`.

For example, if you have installed the third-party package `html5lib` (to parse HTML in the same way as all major browsers do, albeit slowly), you may call:

```
soup = bs4.BeautifulSoup(thedoc, 'html5lib')
```

When you pass `'xml'` as the second argument, you must have installed[2] the third-party package `lxml`, mentioned in "ElementTree" on page 630, and `BeautifulSoup`

2 The `BeautifulSoup` documentation (*https://www.crummy.com/software/BeautifulSoup/bs4/doc/*) provides detailed information about installing various parsers.

parses the document as XML, rather than as HTML. In this case, the attribute `is_xml` of *soup* is `True`; otherwise, *soup*`.is_xml` is `False`. (If you have installed `lxml`, you can also use it to parse HTML, by passing as the second argument `'lxml'`).

```
>>> import bs4
>>> s = bs4.BeautifulSoup('<p>hello', 'html.parser')
>>> sx = bs4.BeautifulSoup('<p>hello', 'xml')
>>> sl = bs4.BeautifulSoup('<p>hello', 'lxml')
>>> s5 = bs4.BeautifulSoup('<p>hello', 'html5lib')
>>> print(s, s.is_xml)
<p>hello</p> False
>>> print(sx, sx.is_xml)
<?xml version="1.0" encoding="utf-8"?>
<p>hello</p> True
>>> print(sl, sl.is_xml)
<html><body><p>hello</p></body></html> False
>>> print(s5, s5.is_xml)
<html><head></head><body><p>hello</p></body></html> False
```

Differences between parsers in fixing invalid HTML input

In the example, the `'html.parser'` tree builder inserts endtag `</p>`, missing from the input. As also shown, other tree builders go further in repairing invalid HTML input, adding required tags such as `<body>` and `<html>`, to different extents depending on the parser.

BeautifulSoup, Unicode, and encoding

`BeautifulSoup` uses Unicode, deducing or guessing the encoding[3] when the input is a bytestring or binary file. For output, the `prettify` method returns a Unicode string representation of the tree, including tags, with attributes, plus extra whitespace and newlines to indent elements, to show the nesting structure; to have it instead return a bytestring in a given encoding, pass it the encoding name as an argument. If you don't want the result to be "prettified," use the `encode` method to get a bytestring, and the `decode` method to get a Unicode string. For example, in v3:

```
>>> s = bs4.BeautifulSoup('<p>hello', 'html.parser')
>>> print(s.prettify())
<p>
 hello
</p>
>>> print(s.decode())
<p>hello</p>
```

3 As explained in the `BeautifulSoup` documentation (*https://www.crummy.com/software/BeautifulSoup/bs4/doc/*), which also shows various ways to guide or override `BeautifulSoup`'s guesses.

```
>>> print(s.encode())
b'<p>hello</p>'
```

(In v2, the last output would be just **<p>hello</p>**, since v2 does not use the `b'...'` notation to print bytestrings.)

The Navigable Classes of bs4

An instance *b* of class `BeautifulSoup` supplies attributes and methods to "navigate" the parsed HTML tree, returning instances of classes `Tag` and `NavigableString` (and subclasses of `NavigableString`: `CData`, `Comment`, `Declaration`, `Doctype`, and `ProcessingInstruction`—differing only in how they are emitted when you output them).

Navigable classes terminology

When we say "instances of `NavigableString`," we include instances of any of its subclasses; when we say "instances of `Tag`," we include instances of `BeautifulSoup`, since the latter is a subclass of `Tag`. We also call instances of navigable classes as *elements* or *nodes* in the tree.

Structured Text: HTML

Each instance of a "navigable class" lets you keep navigating, or dig for more information, with pretty much the same set of navigational attributes and search methods as *b* itself. There are differences: instances of `Tag` can have HTML attributes and children nodes in the HTML tree, while instances of `NavigableString` cannot (instances of `NavigableString` always have one text string, a parent `Tag`, and zero or more siblings, i.e., other children of the same parent tag).

All instances of navigable classes have attribute `name`: it's the tag string for `Tag` instances, `'[document]'` for `BeautifulSoup` instances, and `None` for instances of `NavigableString`.

Instances of `Tag` let you access their HTML attributes by indexing, or get them all as a `dict` via the `.attrs` Python attribute of the instance.

Indexing instances of Tag

When *t* is an instance of `Tag`, a construct like *t*`['foo']` looks for an HTML attribute named `foo` within *t*'s HTML attributes, and returns the string for the `foo` HTML attribute. When *t* has no HTML attribute named `foo`, *t*`['foo']` raises a `KeyError` exception; just like on a `dict`, call *t*`.get('foo',` *default*`=None)` to get the value of the default argument, instead of an exception, when *t* has no HTML attribute named `foo`.

A few attributes, such as `class`, are defined in the HTML standard as being able to have multiple values (e.g., `<body class="foo bar">...</body>`); in these cases, the indexing returns a `list` of values—for example, `soup.body['class']` would be `['foo', 'bar']` (again, you get a `KeyError` exception when the attribute isn't present at all; use the get method, instead of indexing, to get a default value instead).

To get a dict that maps attribute names to values (or, in a few cases defined in the HTML standard, lists of values), use the attribute *t*.attrs:

```
>>> s = bs4.BeautifulSoup('<p foo="bar" class="ic">baz')
>>> s.get('foo')
>>> s.p.get('foo')
'bar'
>>> s.p.attrs
{'foo': 'bar', 'class': ['ic']}
```

How to check if a Tag instance has a certain attribute

To check if a Tag instance *t*'s HTML attributes include one named 'foo', *don't* use if 'foo' in *t*:—the in operator on Tag instances looks among the Tag's children, *not* its attributes. Rather, use if 'foo' in *t*.attrs: or if *t*.has_attr('foo'):.

When you have an instance of NavigableString, you often want to access the actual text string it contains; when you have an instance of Tag, you may want to access the unique string it contains, or, should it contain more than one, all of them —perhaps with their text stripped of any whitespace surrounding it. Here's how.

Getting an actual string

If you have a NavigableString instance *s* and you need to stash or process its text somewhere, without further navigation on it, call str(*s*) (or, in v2, unicode(*s*)). Or, use *s*.encode(*codec*='utf8') to get a bytestring, and *s*.decode() to get text (Unicode). These give you the actual string, without references to the BeautifulSoup tree impeding garbage collection (*s* supports all methods of Unicode strings, so call those directly if they do all you need).

Given an instance *t* of Tag, you can get its single contained NavigableString instance with *t*.string (so *t*.string.decode() could be the actual text you're looking for). *t*.string only works when *t* has a single child that's a NavigableString, or a single child that's a Tag whose only child is a NavigableString; otherwise, *t*.string is None.

As an iterator on *all* contained (navigable) strings, use *t*.strings (''.join(*t*.strings) could be the string you want). To ignore whitespace around each contained string, use the iterator *t*.stripped_strings (it also skips strings that are all-whitespace).

Alternatively, call *t*.get_text()—it returns a single (Unicode) string with all the text in *t*'s descendants, in tree order (equivalently, access the attribute *t*.text). You can optionally pass, as the only positional argument, a string to use as a separator (default is the empty string `''`); pass the named parameter `strip=True` to have each string stripped of whitespace around it, and all-whitespace strings skipped:

```
>>> soup = bs4.BeautifulSoup('<p>Plain <b>bold</b></p>')
>>> print(soup.p.string)
None
>>> print(soup.p.b.string)
bold
>>> print(soup.get_text())
Plain bold
>>> print(soup.text)
Plain bold
>>> print(soup.get_text(strip=True))
Plainbold
```

The simplest, most elegant way to navigate down an HTML tree or subtree in `bs4` is to use Python's attribute reference syntax (as long as each tag you name is unique, or you care only about the first tag so named at each level of descent).

Structured Text: HTML

Attribute references on instances of BeautifulSoup and Tag

Given any instance *`t`* of a `Tag`, a construct like *`t`*`.foo.bar` looks for the first tag `foo` within *t*'s descendants, gets a `Tag` instance *`ti`* for it, looks for the first tag `bar` within *`ti`*'s descendants, and returns a `Tag` instance for the `bar` tag.

It's a concise, elegant way to navigate down the tree, when you know there's a single occurrence of a certain tag within a navigable instance's descendants, or when the first occurrence of several is all you care about, but beware: if any level of look-up doesn't find the tag it's looking for, the attribute reference's value is `None`, and then any further attribute reference raises `AttributeError`.

Beware typos in attribute references on Tag instances

Due to this BeautifulSoup behavior, any typo you may make in an attribute reference on a `Tag` instance gives a value of `None`, not an `AttributeError` exception—so be especially careful!

`bs4` also offers more general ways to navigate down, up, and sideways along the tree. In particular, each navigable class instance has attributes that identify a single "relative" or, in plural form, an iterator over all relatives of that ilk.

contents, children, descendants

Given an instance *`t`* of `Tag`, you can get a list of all of its children as *`t`*`.contents`, or an iterator on all children as *`t`*`.children`. For an iterator on all *descendants* (children, children of children, and so on), use *`t`*`.descendants`.

```
>>> soup = bs4.BeautifulSoup('<p>Plain <b>bold</b></p>')
>>> list(t.name for t in soup.p.children)
[None, 'b']
```

```
>>> list(t.name for t in soup.p.descendants)
[None, 'b', None]
```

The names that are None correspond to the NavigableString nodes; only the first of them is a *child* of the p tag, but both are *descendants* of that tag.

parent, parents

Given an instance *n* of any navigable class, its parent node is *n*.parent; an iterator on all ancestors, going up in the tree, is *n*.parents. This includes instances of NavigableString, since they have parents, too. An instance *b* of BeautifulSoup has *b*.parent None, and *b*.parents is an empty iterator.

```
>>> soup = bs4.BeautifulSoup('<p>Plain <b>bold</b></p>')
>>> soup.b.parent.name
'p'
```

next_sibling, previous_sibling, next_siblings, previous_siblings

Given an instance *n* of any navigable class, its sibling node to the immediate left is *n*.previous_sibling, and the one to the immediate right is *n*.next_sibling; either or both can be None if *n* has no such sibling. An iterator on all left siblings, going leftward in the tree, is *n*.previous_siblings; an iterator on all right siblings, going rightward in the tree, is *n*.next_siblings (either or both iterators can be empty). This includes instances of NavigableString, since they have siblings, too. An instance *b* of BeautifulSoup has *b*.previous_sibling and *b*.next_sibling both None, and both of its sibling iterators are empty.

```
>>> soup = bs4.BeautifulSoup('<p>Plain <b>bold</b></p>')
>>> soup.b.previous_sibling, soup.b.next_sibling
('Plain ', None)
```

next_element, previous_element, next_elements, previous_elements

Given an instance *n* of any navigable class, the node parsed just before it is *n*.previous_element, and the one parsed just after it is *n*.next_element; either or both can be None when *n* is the first or last node parsed, respectively. An iterator on all previous elements, going backward in the tree, is *n*.previous_elements; an iterator on all following elements, going forward in the tree, is *n*.next_elements (either or both iterators can be empty). Instances of NavigableString have such attributes, too. An instance *b* of BeautifulSoup has *b*.previous_element and *b*.next_element both None, and both of its element iterators are empty.

```
>>> soup = bs4.BeautifulSoup('<p>Plain <b>bold</b></p>')
>>> soup.b.previous_element, soup.b.next_element
('Plain ', 'bold')
```

As shown in the previous example, the b tag has no next_sibling (since it's the last child of its parent); however, as shown here, it does have a next_element—the node parsed just after it (which in this case is the 'bold' string it contains).

bs4 find... Methods ("Search Methods")

Each navigable class in bs4 offers several methods whose names start with find, known as *search methods*, to locate tree nodes that satisfy conditions you specify.

Search methods come in pairs—one method of each pair walks all the relevant parts of the tree and returns a list of nodes satisfying the conditions, and the other one stops and returns a single node satisfying the conditions as soon as it finds it (or None when it finds no such node). So, calling the latter method is like calling the former one with argument limit=1 , and indexing the resulting one-item list to get its single item, but a bit faster and more elegant.

So, for example, for any Tag instance *t* and any group of positional and named arguments represented by ..., the following equivalence always holds:

```
just_one = t.find(...)
other_way_list = t.find_all(..., limit=1)
other_way = other_way_list[0] if other_way_list else None
assert just_one == other_way
```

The method pairs are:

find, find_all
: *b*.find(...) *b*.find_all(...)

Searches the *descendants* of *b*, except that, if you pass as one of the named arguments recursive=False (available only for these two methods, not for other search methods), it searches *b*'s *children* only. These methods are not available on NavigableString instances, since they have no descendants; all other search methods are available on Tag and NavigableString instances.

Since find_all is frequently needed, bs4 offers an elegant shortcut: calling a tag is like calling its find_all method. That is, *b*(...) is the same as *b*.find_all(...).

Another shortcut, already mentioned in "Attribute references on instances of BeautifulSoup and Tag" on page 615, is that *b*.foo.bar is like *b*.find('foo').find('bar').

find_next, find_all_next
: *b*.find_next(...) *b*.find_all_next(...)

Searches the next_elements of *b*.

find_next_sibling, find_next_siblings
: *b*.find_next_sibling(...) *b*.find_next_siblings(...)

Searches the next_siblings of *b*.

find_parent, find_parents
: *b*.find_parent(...) *b*.find_parents(...)

Searches the parents of *b*.

find_previous, find_all_previous
`b.find_previous(...)` `b.find_all_previous(...)`

Searches the `previous_elements` of *b*.

find_previous_sibling, find_previous_siblings
`b.find_previous_sibling(...)`
`b.find_previous_siblings(...)`

Searches the `previous_siblings` of *b*.

Arguments of search methods

Each search method has three optional arguments: *`name`*, *`attrs`*, and *`string`*. *`name`* and *`string`* are *filters*, as described later in this section; *`attrs`* is a `dict`, also described later in this section. In addition, `find` and `find_all` only (not the other search methods) can optionally be called with the argument *`recursive`*`=False`, to limit the search to children, rather than all descendants.

Any search method returning a list (i.e., one whose name is plural or starts with `find_all`) can optionally have the named argument `limit`, whose value, if passed, is an integer, putting an upper bound on the length of the list it returns.

After these optional arguments, each search method can optionally have any number of arbitrary named arguments, whose name can be any identifier (except the name of one of the search method's specific arguments), while the value is a filter.

Search method arguments: filters A *filter* is applied against a *target* that can be a tag's name (when passed as the *`name`* argument); a `Tag`'s `string` or a `NavigableString`'s textual content (when passed as the *`string`* argument); or a `Tag`'s attribute (when passed as the value of a named argument, or in the *`attrs`* argument). Each filter can be:

A Unicode string
: The filter succeeds when the string exactly equals the target

A bytestring
: It's decoded to Unicode using `utf8`, and then the filter succeeds when the resulting Unicode string exactly equals the target

A regular expression object (AKA RE, as produced by `re.compile`*, covered in "Regular Expressions and the re Module" on page 253)*
: The filter succeeds when the `search` method of the RE, called with the target as the argument, succeeds

A list of strings
: The filter succeeds if any of the strings exactly equals the target (if any of the strings are bytestrings, they're decoded to Unicode using `utf8`)

A function object
: The filter succeeds when the function, called with the `Tag` or `NavigableString` instance as the argument, returns `True`

`True`
: The filter always succeeds

As a synonym of "the filter succeeds," we also say, "the target matches the filter."

Each search method finds the relevant nodes that match all of its filters (that is, it implicitly performs a logical and operation on its filters on each candidate node).

Search method arguments: name To look for `Tag`s whose `name` matches a filter, pass the filter as the first positional argument to the search method, or pass it as `name=`*`filter`*:

```
soup.find_all('b')  # or soup.find_all(name='b')
# returns all instances of Tag 'b' in the document
soup.find_all(['b', 'bah'])
# returns all instances of Tags 'b' and 'bah' in the document
soup.find_all(re.compile(r'^b'))
# returns all instances of Tags starting with 'b' in the document
soup.find_all(re.compile(r'bah'))
# returns all instances of Tags including string 'bah' in the document
def child_of_foo(tag):
  return tag.parent == 'foo'
soup.find_all(name=child_of_foo)
# returns all instances of Tags whose parent's name is 'foo'
```

Search method arguments: string To look for `Tag` nodes whose `.string`'s text matches a filter, or `NavigableString` nodes whose text matches a filter, pass the filter as `string=`*`filter`*:

```
soup.find_all(string='foo')
# returns all instances of NavigableString whose text is 'foo'
soup.find_all('b', string='foo')
# returns all instances of Tag 'b' whose .string's text is 'foo'
```

Search method arguments: attrs To look for tag nodes who have attributes whose values match filters, use a `dict` *d* with attribute names as keys, and filters as the corresponding values. Then, pass it as the second positional argument to the search method, or pass it as `attrs=`*d*.

As a special case, you can use, as a value in *d*, `None` instead of a filter; this matches nodes that *lack* the corresponding attribute.

As a separate special case, if the value *f* of `attrs` is not a `dict`, but a filter, that is equivalent to having an `attrs` of `{'class':` *f*`}`. (This convenient shortcut helps because looking for tags with a certain CSS class is a frequent task.)

You cannot apply both special cases at once: to search for tags without any CSS class, you must explicitly pass attrs={'class': None} (i.e., use the first special case, but not at the same time as the second one):

```
soup.find_all('b', {'foo': True, 'bar': None})
# returns all instances of Tag 'b' w/an attribute 'foo' and no 'bar'
```

Matching tags with multiple CSS classes

Differently from most attributes, a tag can have multiple values for its attribute 'class'. These are shown in HTML as a space-separated string (e.g., '<p class='foo bar baz'>...'), and in bs4 as a list of strings (e.g., *t*['class'] being ['foo', 'bar', 'baz']).

When you filter by CSS class in any search method, the filter matches a tag if it matches *any* of the multiple CSS classes of such a tag.

To match tags by multiple CSS classes, you can write a custom function and pass it as the filter to the search method; or, if you don't need other added functionality of search methods, you can eschew search methods and instead use the method *t*.select, covered in "bs4 CSS Selectors" on page 620, and go with the syntax of CSS selectors.

Search method arguments: other named arguments Named arguments, beyond those whose names are known to the search method, are taken to augment the constraints, if any, specified in attrs. For example, calling a search method with *foo*=*bar* is like calling it with attrs={'*foo*': *bar*}.

bs4 CSS Selectors

bs4 tags supply the methods select and select_one, roughly equivalent to find_all and find but accepting as the single argument a string that's a CSS selector (*http://www.w3schools.com/cssref/css_selectors.asp*) and returning the list of tag nodes satisfying that selector, or, respectively, the first such tag node.

bs4 supports only a subset of the rich CSS selector functionality, and we do not cover CSS selectors further in this book. (For complete coverage of CSS, we recommend the book *CSS: The Definitive Guide*, 3rd Edition [O'Reilly].) In most cases, the search methods covered in "bs4 find... Methods ("Search Methods")" on page 617 are better choices; however, in a few special cases, calling select can save you the (small) trouble of writing a custom filter function:

```
def foo_child_of_bar(t):
    return t.name=='foo' and t.parent and t.parent.name=='bar'
soup(foo_child_of_bar)
# returns tags with name 'foo' children of tags with name 'bar'
soup.select('foo < bar')
# exactly equivalent, with no custom filter function needed
```

An HTML Parsing Example with BeautifulSoup

The following example uses bs4 to perform a typical task: fetch a page from the web, parse it, and output the HTTP hyperlinks in the page. In v2, the code is:

```
import urllib, urlparse, bs4

f = urllib.urlopen('http://www.python.org')
b = bs4.BeautifulSoup(f)

seen = set()
for anchor in b('a'):
    url = anchor.get('href')
    if url is None or url in seen: continue
    seen.add(url)
    pieces = urlparse.urlparse(url)
    if pieces[0]=='http':
        print(urlparse.urlunparse(pieces))
```

In v3, the code is the same, except that the function urlopen now lives in the module urllib.request, and the functions urlparse and urlunparse live in the module urllib.parse, rather than in the modules urllib and urlparse, respectively, as they did in v2 (covered in "URL Access" on page 555)—issues not germane to BeautifulSoup itself.

The example calls the instance of class bs4.BeautifulSoup (equivalent to calling its find_all method) to obtain all instances of a certain tag (here, tag '<a>'), then the get method of instances of the class Tag to obtain the value of an attribute (here, 'href'), or None when that attribute is missing.

Generating HTML

Python does not come with tools specifically meant to generate HTML, nor with ones that let you embed Python code directly within HTML pages. Development and maintenance are eased by separating logic and presentation issues through *templating*, covered in "Templating" on page 624. An alternative is to use bs4 to create HTML documents, in your Python code, by altering what start out as very minimal documents. Since these alterations rely on bs4 *parsing* some HTML, using different parsers affects the output, as covered in "Which parser BeautifulSoup uses" on page 611.

Editing and Creating HTML with bs4

You can alter the tag name of an instance *t* of Tag by assigning to *t*.name; you can alter *t*'s attributes by treating *t* as a mapping: assign to an indexing to add or change an attribute, or delete the indexing—for example, del *t*['foo'] removes the attribute foo. If you assign some str to *t*.string, all previous *t*.contents (Tags and/or strings—the whole subtree of *t*'s descendants) are tossed and replaced with a new NavigableString instance with that str as its textual content.

Given an instance *s* of `NavigableString`, you can replace its textual content: calling `s.replace_with('other')` replaces *s*'s text with `'other'`.

Building and adding new nodes

Altering existing nodes is important, but creating new ones and adding them to the tree is crucial for building an HTML document from scratch.

To create a new `NavigableString` instance, just call the class, with the textual content as the single argument:

```
s = bs4.NavigableString(' some text ')
```

To create a new `Tag` instance, call the `new_tag` method of a `BeautifulSoup` instance, with the tag name as the single positional argument, and optionally named arguments for attributes:

```
t = soup.new_tag('foo', bar='baz')
print(t)
<foo bar="baz"></foo>
```

To add a node to the children of a `Tag`, you can use the `Tag`'s `append` method to add the node at the end of the existing children, if any:

```
t.append(s)
print(t)
<foo bar="baz"> some text </foo>
```

If you want the new node to go elsewhere than at the end, at a certan index among *t*'s children, call `t.insert(n, s)` to put *s* at index *n* in `t.contents` (`t.append` and `t.insert` work as if *t* was a list of its children).

If you have a navigable element *b* and want to add a new node *x* as *b*'s `previous_sibling`, call `b.insert_before(x)`. If instead you want *x* to become *b*'s `next_sibling`, call `b.insert_after(x)`.

If you want to wrap a new parent node *t* around *b*, call `b.wrap(t)` (which also returns the newly wrapped tag). For example:

```
print(t.string.wrap(soup.new_tag('moo', zip='zaap')))
<moo zip="zaap"> some text </moo>
print(t)
<foo bar="baz"><moo zip="zaap"> some text </moo></foo>
```

Replacing and removing nodes

You can call `t.replace_with` on any tag *t*: that replaces *t*, and all its previous contents, with the argument, and returns *t* with its original contents. For example:

```
soup = bs4.BeautifulSoup(
        '<p>first <b>second</b> <i>third</i></p>', 'lxml')
i = soup.i.replace_with('last')
soup.b.append(i)
```

```
print(soup)
<html><body><p>first <b>second<i>third</i></b> last</p></body></html>
```

You can call *t*.unwrap() on any tag *t*: that replaces *t* with its contents, and returns *t* "emptied," that is, without contents. For example:

```
empty_i = soup.i.unwrap()
print(soup.b.wrap(empty_i))
<i><b>secondthird</b></i>
print(soup)
<html><body><p>first <i><b>secondthird</b></i> last</p></body></html>
```

t.clear() removes *t*'s contents, destroys them, and leaves *t* empty (but still in its original place in the tree). *t*.decompose() removes and destroys both *t* itself, and its contents. For example:

```
soup.i.clear()
print(soup)
<html><body><p>first <i></i> last</p></body></html>
soup.p.decompose()
print(soup)
<html><body></body></html>
```

Lastly, *t*.extract() removes *t* and its contents, but—doing no actual destruction—returns *t* with its original contents.

Structured Text: HTML

Building HTML with bs4

Here's an example of how to use bs4's tree-building methods to generate HTML. Specifically, the following function takes a sequence of "rows" (sequences) and returns a string that's an HTML table to display their values:

```
def mktable_with_bs4(s_of_s):
  tabsoup = bs4.BeautifulSoup('<table>', 'html.parser')
  tab = tabsoup.table
  for s in s_of_s:
    tr = tabsoup.new_tag('tr')
    tab.append(tr)
    for item in s:
      td = tabsoup.new_tag('td')
      tr.append(td)
      td.string = str(item)
  return tab
```

Here is an example use of the function we just defined:

```
example = (
  ('foo', 'g>h', 'g&h'),
  ('zip', 'zap', 'zop'),
)
print(mktable_with_bs4(example))
# prints:
<table><tr><td>foo</td><td>g&gt;h</td><td>g&amp;h</td></tr>
<tr><td>zip</td><td>zap</td><td>zop</td></tr></table>
```

Note that bs4 automatically "escapes" strings containing mark-up characters such as <, >, and &; for example, `'g>h'` renders as `'g>h'`.

Templating

To generate HTML, the best approach is often *templating*. Start with a *template*, a text string (often read from a file, database, etc.) that is almost valid HTML, but includes markers, known as *placeholders*, where dynamically generated text must be inserted. Your program generates the needed text and substitutes it into the template.

In the simplest case, you can use markers of the form `{`*`name`*`}`. Set the dynamically generated text as the value for key `'`*`name`*`'` in some dictionary *d*. The Python string formatting method `.format` (covered in "String Formatting" on page 240) lets you do the rest: when *`t`* is the template string, *`t`*`.format(`*`d`*`)` is a copy of the template with all values properly substituted.

In general, beyond substituting placeholders, you also want to use conditionals, perform loops, and deal with other advanced formatting and presentation tasks; in the spirit of separating "business logic" from "presentation issues," you'd prefer it if all of the latter were part of your templating. This is where dedicated third-party templating packages come in. There are many of them, but all of this book's authors, having used and authored (*https://www.safaribooksonline.com/library/view/python-cookbook/0596001673/ch03s23.html*) some in the past, currently prefer jinja2 (*http://jinja.pocoo.org/docs/dev/*), covered next.

The jinja2 Package

For serious templating tasks, we recommend jinja2 (available on PyPI (*https://pypi.python.org/pypi/Jinja2*), like other third-party Python packages, so, easily installable with **`pip install jinja2`**).

The jinja2 docs (*http://jinja.pocoo.org/docs/dev/*) are excellent and thorough, covering the templating language (*http://jinja.pocoo.org/docs/dev/templates/*) itself (conceptually modeled on Python, but with many differences to support embedding it in HTML, and the peculiar needs specific to presentation issues); the API (*http://jinja.pocoo.org/docs/dev/api/*) your Python code uses to connect to jinja2, and expand (*http://jinja.pocoo.org/docs/dev/api/#custom-filters*) or extend (*http://jinja.pocoo.org/docs/dev/extensions/*) it if necessary; as well as other issues, from installation (*http://jinja.pocoo.org/docs/dev/intro/#installation*) to internationalization (*http://jinja.pocoo.org/docs/dev/extensions/#i18n-extension*), from sandboxing (*http://jinja.pocoo.org/docs/dev/sandbox/*) code to porting (*http://jinja.pocoo.org/docs/dev/switching/*) from other templating engines—not to mention, precious tips and tricks (*http://jinja.pocoo.org/docs/dev/tricks/*).

In this section, we cover only a tiny subset of `jinja2`'s power, just what you need to get started after installing it: we earnestly recommend studying `jinja2`'s docs to get the huge amount of extra information they effectively convey.

The jinja2.Environment Class

When you use `jinja2`, there's always an `Environment` instance involved—in a few cases you could let it default to a generic "shared environment," but that's not recommended. Only in very advanced usage, when you're getting templates from different sources (or with different templating language syntax), would you ever define multiple environments—usually, you instantiate a single `Environment` instance *`env`*, good for all the templates you need to render.

You can customize *`env`* in many ways as you build it, by passing named arguments to its constructor (including altering crucial aspects of templating language syntax, such as which delimiters start and end blocks, variables, comments, etc.), but the one named argument you'll almost always pass in real-life use is `loader=...`.

An environment's `loader` specifies where to load templates from, on request—usually some directory in a filesystem, or perhaps some database (you'd have to code a custom subclass of `jinja2.Loader` for the latter purpose), but there are other possibilities. You need a loader to let templates enjoy some of `jinja2`'s powerful features, such as *template inheritance* (which we do not cover in this book).

Structured Text: HTML

You can equip *`env`*, as you instantiate it, with custom filters, tests, extensions, and so on; each of those can also be added later, and we do not cover them further in this book.

In the following sections' examples, we assume *`env`* was instantiated with nothing but `loader=jinja2.FileSystemLoader('`*`/path/to/templates`*`')`, and not further enriched—in fact, for simplicity, we won't even make use of the loader. In real life, however, the loader is almost invariably set; other options, seldom.

`env``.get_template(`*`name`*`)` fetches, compiles, and returns an instance of `jinja2.Template` based on what *`env`*`.loader(`*`name`*`)` returns. In the following examples, for simplicity, we'll actually use the rarely warranted *`env`*`.from_string(`*`s`*`)` to build an instance of `jinja2.Template` from (ideally Unicode, though a bytestring encoded in `utf8` will do) string *s*.

The jinja2.Template Class

An instance *`t`* of `jinja2.Template` has many attributes and methods, but the one you'll be using almost exclusively in real life is:

render *`t`*`.render(...`*`context`*`...)`

The *`context`* argument(s) are the same you might pass to a `dict` constructor—a mapping instance, and/or named arguments enriching and potentially overriding the mapping's key-to-value connections.

`t``.render(`*`context`*`)` returns a (Unicode) string resulting from the *`context`* arguments applied to the template *`t`*.

Building HTML with jinja2

Here's an example of how to use a jinja2 template to generate HTML. Specifically, just like previously in "Building HTML with bs4" on page 623, the following function takes a sequence of "rows" (sequences) and returns an HTML table to display their values:

```
TABLE_TEMPLATE = '''\
<table>
{% for s in s_of_s %}
  <tr>
  {% for item in s %}
    <td>{{item}}</td>
  {% endfor %}
  </tr>
{% endfor %}
</table>'''

def mktable_with_jinja2(s_of_s):
    env = jinja2.Environment(
        trim_blocks=True,
        lstrip_blocks=True,
        autoescape=True)
    t = env.from_string(TABLE_TEMPLATE)
    return t.render(s_of_s=s_of_s)
```

The function builds the environment with option `autoescape=True`, to automatically "escape" strings containing mark-up characters such as <, >, and &; for example, with `autoescape=True`, `'g>h'` renders as `'g>h'`.

The options `trim_blocks=True` and `lstrip_blocks=True` are purely cosmetic, just to ensure that both the template string and the rendered HTML string can be nicely formatted; of course, when a browser renders HTML, it does not matter whether the HTML itself is nicely formatted.

Normally, you would always build the environment with option `loader=...`, and have it load templates from files or other storage with method calls such as *`t`* `=` *`env`*`.get_template(`*`template_name`*`)`. In this example, just in order to present everything in one place, we omit the loader and build the template from a string by calling method *`env`*`.from_string` instead. Note that `jinja2` is not HTML- or XML-specific, so its use alone does not guarantee validity of the generated content, which should be carefully checked if standards conformance is a requirement.

The example uses only the two most common features out of the many dozens that the `jinja2` templating language offers: *loops* (that is, blocks enclosed in `{% for ... %}` and `{% endfor %}`) and *parameter substitution* (inline expressions enclosed in `{{` and `}}`).

Here is an example use of the function we just defined:

```
example = (
  ('foo', 'g>h', 'g&h'),
```

```
  ('zip', 'zap', 'zop'),
)
print(mktable_with_jinja2(example))
# prints:
<table>
  <tr>
    <td>foo</td>
    <td>g&gt;h</td>
    <td>g&amp;h</td>
  </tr>
  <tr>
    <td>zip</td>
    <td>zap</td>
    <td>zop</td>
  </tr>
</table>
```

23
Structured Text: XML

XML, the *eXtensible Markup Language*, is a widely used data interchange format. On top of XML itself, the XML community (in good part within the World Wide Web Consortium [W3C]) has standardized many other technologies, such as schema languages, namespaces, XPath, XLink, XPointer, and XSLT.

Industry consortia have defined industry-specific markup languages on top of XML for data exchange among applications in their respective fields. XML, XML-based markup languages, and other XML-related technologies are often used for inter-application, cross-language, cross-platform data interchange in specific industries.

Python's standard library, for historical reasons, has multiple modules supporting XML under the `xml` package, with overlapping functionality; this book does not cover them all, so see the online documentation (*https://docs.python.org/3/library/xml.html*).

This book (and, specifically, this chapter) covers only the most Pythonic approach to XML processing: `ElementTree`, whose elegance, speed, generality, multiple implementations, and Pythonic architecture make it the package of choice for Python XML applications. For complete tutorials and all details on the `xml.etree.ElementTree` module, see the online docs (*https://docs.python.org/3/library/xml.etree.elementtree.html*) and the website of `ElementTree`'s creator (*http://effbot.org/zone/element-index.htm*), Fredrik Lundh, best known as "the effbot."[1]

1 Alex is far too modest to mention it, but from around 1995 to 2005 both he and Fredrik were, along with Tim Peters, the Python bots. Known as such for their encyclopedic and detailed knowledge of the language, the effbot, the martellibot, and the timbot have created software of immense value to millions of people.

This book takes for granted some elementary knowledge of XML itself; if you need to learn more about XML, we recommend the book *XML in a Nutshell* (O'Reilly).

Parsing XML from untrusted sources puts your application at risk for many possible attacks; this book does not cover this issue specifically, so see the online documentation (*https://docs.python.org/3/library/xml.html#xml-vulnerabilities*), which recommends third-party modules to help safeguard your application if you do have to parse XML from sources you can't fully trust. In particular, if you need an `ElementTree` implementation with safeguards against parsing untrusted sources, consider `defusedxml.ElementTree` (*https://pypi.python.org/pypi/defusedxml#defusedxml-elementtree*) and its C-coded counterpart `defusedxml.cElementTree` (*https://pypi.python.org/pypi/defusedxml#defusedxml-celementtree*) within the third-party package `defusedxml` (*https://pypi.python.org/pypi/defusedxml*).

ElementTree

Python and third-party add-ons offer several alternative implementations of the `ElementTree` functionality; the one you can always rely on in the standard library is the module `xml.etree.ElementTree`. In most circumstances, in v2, you can use the faster C-coded implementation `xml.etree.cElementTree`; in v3, just importing `xml.etree.ElementTree` gets you the fastest implementation available. The third-party package `defusedxml`, mentioned in the previous section of this chapter, offers slightly slower but safer implementations if you ever need to parse XML from untrusted sources; another third-party package, `lxml` (*http://lxml.de/*), gets you faster performance, and some extra functionality, via `lxml.etree` (*http://lxml.de/api.html*).

Traditionally, you get whatever available implementation of `ElementTree` you prefer, by a `from...import...as` statement such as:

```
from xml.etree import cElementTree as et
```

(or more than one such statement, with `try...except ImportError:` guards to discover what's the best implementation available), then use `et` (some prefer the uppercase variant, `ET`) as the module's name in the rest of your code.

`ElementTree` supplies one fundamental class representing a *node* within the *tree* that naturally maps an XML document, the class `Element`. `ElementTree` also supplies other important classes, chiefly the one representing the whole tree, with methods for input and output and many convenience ones equivalent to ones on its `Element` *root*—that's the class `ElementTree`. In addition, the `ElementTree` module supplies several utility functions, and auxiliary classes of lesser importance.

The Element Class

The `Element` class represents a node in the tree that maps an XML document, and it's the core of the whole `ElementTree` ecosystem. Each element is a bit like a mapping, with *attributes* that are a mapping from string keys to string values, and a bit like a sequence, with *children* that are other elements (sometimes referred to as the element's "subelements"). In addition, each element offers a few extra attributes and methods. Each `Element` instance *e* has four data attributes, or properties:

attrib A `dict` containing all of the XML node's attributes, with strings, the attributes' names, as its keys (and, usually, strings as corresponding values as well). For example, parsing the XML fragment `<a x="y">b</a>c`, you get an *e* whose `e.attrib` is `{'x': 'y'}`.

Avoid accessing attrib on Element instances, if feasible

It's normally best to avoid accessing `e.attrib` when possible, because the implementation might need to build it on the fly when you access it. *e* itself, as covered later in this section, offers some typical mapping methods that you might otherwise want to call on `e.attrib`; going through *e*'s own methods allows a smart implementation to optimize things for you, compared to the performance you'd get via the actual `dict e.attrib`.

tag The XML tag of the node, a string, sometimes also known as "the element's *type*." For example, parsing the XML fragment `<a x="y">b</a>c`, you get an *e* with `e.tag` set to `'a'`.

tail Arbitrary data (a string) immediately "following" the element. For example, parsing the XML fragment `<a x="y">b</a>c`, you get an *e* with `e.tail` set to `'c'`.

text Arbitrary data (a string) directly "within" the element. For example, parsing the XML fragment `<a x="y">b</a>c`, you get an *e* with `e.text` set to `'b'`.

e has some methods that are mapping-like and avoid the need to explicitly ask for the `e.attrib dict`:

clear `e.clear()`

`e.clear()` leaves *e* "empty," except for its `tag`, removing all attributes and children, and setting `text` and `tail` to None.

get `e.get(key, default=None)`

Like `e.attrib.get(key, default)`, but potentially much faster. You cannot use `e[key]`, since indexing on *e* is used to access children, not attributes.

items `e.items()`

Returns the list of `(name, value)` tuples for all attributes, in arbitrary order.

keys `e.keys()`

Returns the list of all attribute names, in arbitrary order.

set `e.set(key, value)`

Sets the value of attribute named *key* to *value*.

The other methods of *e* (including indexing with the `e[i]` syntax, and length as in `len(e)`) deal with all *e*'s children as a sequence, or in some cases—indicated in the rest of this section—with all descendants (elements in the subtree rooted at *e*, also known as *subelements* of *e*).

Don't rely on implicit bool conversion of an Element

In all versions up to Python 3.6, an `Element` instance *e* tests as false if *e* has no children, following the normal rule for Python containers' implicit `bool` conversion. However, it's documented that this behavior may change in some future version of v3. For future compatibility, if you want to check whether *e* has no children, explicitly check `if len(e) == 0:`—don't use the normal Python idiom `if not e:`.

The named methods of *e* dealing with children or descendants are the following (we do not cover XPath in this book: see the online docs (*https://docs.python.org/3/library/xml.etree.elementtree.html#elementtree-xpath*)):

append `e.append(se)`

Adds subelement *se* (which must be an `Element`) at the end of *e*'s children.

extend `e.extend(ses)`

Adds each item of iterable *ses* (every item must be an `Element`) at the end of *e*'s children.

find `e.find(match, namespaces=None)`

Returns the first descendant matching *match*, which may be a tag name or an XPath expression within the subset supported by the current implementation of `ElementTree`. Returns `None` if no descendant matches *match*. In v3 only, *namespaces* is an optional mapping with XML namespace prefixes as keys and corresponding XML namespace full names as values.

findall `e.findall(match, namespaces=None)`

Returns the list of all descendants matching *match*, which may be a tag name or an XPath expression within the subset supported by the current implementation of `ElementTree`. Returns `[]` if no descendants match *match*. In v3, only, *namespaces* is an optional mapping with XML namespace prefixes as keys and corresponding XML namespace full names as values.

findtext `e.findtext(match, default=None, namespaces=None)`

Returns the `text` of the first descendant matching *`match`*, which may be a tag name or an XPath expression within the subset supported by the current implementation of `ElementTree`. The result may be an empty string `''` if the first descendant matching *`match`* has no `text`. Returns *`default`* if no descendant matches *`match`*. In v3, only, *`namespaces`* is an optional mapping with XML namespace prefixes as keys and corresponding XML namespace full names as values.

insert `e.insert(index, se)`

Adds subelement *`se`* (which must be an `Element`) at index *`index`* within the sequence of *e*'s children.

iter `e.iter(tag='*')`

Returns an iterator walking in depth-first order over all of *e*'s descendants. When *`tag`* is not `'*'`, only yields subelements whose `tag` equals *`tag`*. Don't modify the subtree rooted at *e* while you're looping on `e.iter`.

iterfind `e.iterfind(match, namespaces=None)`

Returns an iterator over all descendants, in depth-first order, matching *`match`*, which may be a tag name or an XPath expression within the subset supported by the current implementation of `ElementTree`. The resulting iterator is empty when no descendants match *`match`*. In v3 only, *`namespaces`* is an optional mapping with XML namespace prefixes as keys and corresponding XML namespace full names as values.

itertext `e.itertext(match, namespaces=None)`

Returns an iterator over the `text` (not the `tail`) attribute of all descendants, in depth-first order, matching *`match`*, which may be a tag name or an XPath expression within the subset supported by the current implementation of `ElementTree`. The resulting iterator is empty when no descendants match *`match`*. In v3 only, *`namespaces`* is an optional mapping with XML namespace prefixes as keys and corresponding XML namespace full names as values.

remove `e.remove(se)`

Removes the descendant that `is` element *`se`* (as covered in Identity tests, in Table 3-2).

The ElementTree Class

The `ElementTree` class represents a tree that maps an XML document. The core added value of an instance *`et`* of `ElementTree` is to have methods for wholesale parsing (input) and writing (output) of a whole tree, namely:

Table 23-1. Elementree instance parsing and writing methods

parse `et.parse(source,parser=None)`

source can be a file open for reading, or the name of a file to open and read (to parse a string, wrap it in `io.StringIO`, covered in "In-Memory "Files": io.StringIO and io.BytesIO" on page 286), containing XML text. `et.parse` parses that text, builds its tree of `Elements` as the new content of *et* (discarding the previous content of *et*, if any), and returns the root element of the tree. *parser* is an optional parser instance; by default, `et.parse` uses an instance of class `XMLParser` supplied by the `ElementTree` module (this book does not cover `XMLParser`; see the online docs (*https://docs.python.org/3/library/xml.etree.elementtree.html#xmlparser-objects*)).

write `et.write(file,encoding='us-ascii',xml_declaration=None, default_namespace=None,method='xml',short_empty_elements=True)`

file can be a file open for writing, or the name of a file to open and write (to write into a string, pass as *file* an instance of `io.StringIO`, covered in "In-Memory "Files": io.StringIO and io.BytesIO" on page 286). `et.write` writes into that file the text representing the XML document for the tree that's the content of *et*.

encoding should be spelled according to the standard—for example, `'iso-8859-1'`, not `'latin-1'`, even though Python itself accepts both spellings for this encoding. In v3 only, you can pass *encoding* as `'unicode'` to output text (Unicode) strings, if `file.write` accepts such strings; otherwise, `file.write` must accept bytestrings, and that is the type of strings `et.write` outputs, using XML character references for characters not in the encoding—for example, with the default ASCII encoding, e with an acute accent, é, is output as `é`.

You can pass *xml_declaration* as `False` to not have the declaration in the resulting text, as `True` to have it; the default is to have the declaration in the result only when *encoding* is not one of `'us-ascii'`, `'utf-8'`, or (v3 only) `'unicode'`.

You can optionally pass *default_namespace* to set the default namespace for `xmlns` constructs.

You can pass *method* as `'text'` to output only the `text` and `tail` of each node (no tags). You can pass *method* as `'html'` to output the document in HTML format (which, for example, omits end tags not needed in HTML, such as `</br>`). The default is `'xml'`, to output in XML format.

In v3 only, you can optionally (only by name, not positionally) pass *short_empty_elements* as `False` to always use explicit start and end tags, even for elements that have no text or subelements; the default is to use the XML short form for such empty elements. For example, an empty element with tag a is output as `<a/>` by default, as `<a></a>` in v3 if you pass *short_empty_elements* as `False`.

In addition, an instance *et* of `ElementTree` supplies the method `getroot`—`et.getroot()` returns the root of the tree—and the convenience methods `find`, `findall`, `findtext`, `iter`, and `iterfind`, each exactly equivalent to calling the same method on the root of the tree—that is, on the result of `et.getroot()`.

Functions in the ElementTree Module

The `ElementTree` module also supplies several functions, described in Table 23-2.

Table 23-2.

Comment	`Comment(text=None)` Returns an `Element` that, once inserted as a node in an `ElementTree`, will be output as an XML comment with the given `text` string enclosed between '<!--' and '-->'. `XMLParser` skips XML comments in any document it parses, so this function is the only way to get comment nodes.
ProcessingInstruction	`ProcessingInstruction(`*`target`*`,text=None)` Returns an `Element` that, once inserted as a node in an `ElementTree`, will be output as an XML processing instruction with the given *`target`* and `text` strings enclosed between '<?' and '?>'. `XMLParser` skips XML processing instructions in any document it parses, so this function is the only way to get processing instruction nodes.
SubElement	`SubElement(`*`parent`*`,`*`tag`*`,attrib={},**`*`extra`*`)` Creates an `Element` with the given *tag*, attributes from `dict attrib` and others passed as named arguments in *`extra`*, and appends it as the rightmost child of `Element` *parent*; returns the `Element` it has created.
XML	`XML(`*`text`*`,parser=None)` Parses XML from the *`text`* string and returns an `Element`. `parser` is an optional parser instance; by default, `XML` uses an instance of the class `XMLParser` supplied by the `ElementTree` module (this book does not cover class `XMLParser`; see the online docs (*http://bit.ly/2nMPeRh*)).
XMLID	`XMLID(`*`text`*`,parser=None)` Parses XML from the *`text`* string and returns a tuple with two items: an `Element` and a `dict` mapping `id` attributes to the only `Element` having each (XML forbids duplicate `id`s). *`parser`* is an optional parser instance; by default, `XMLID` uses an instance of the class `XMLParser` supplied by the `ElementTree` module (this book does not cover the `XMLParser` class; see the online docs (*http://bit.ly/2nMPeRh*)).
dump	`dump(`*`e`*`)` Writes e, which can be an `Element` or an `ElementTree`, as XML to `sys.stdout`; it is meant only for debugging purposes.
fromstring	`fromstring(`*`text`*`,parser=None)` Parses XML from the *`text`* string and returns an `Element`, just like the `XML` function just covered.

fromstringlist

`fromstringlist(sequence,parser=None)`

Just like `fromstring(''.join(sequence))`, but can be a bit faster by avoiding the `join`.

iselement

`iselement(e)`

Returns `True` if *e* is an `Element`.

iterparse

`iterparse(source,events=['end'],parser=None)`

`source` can be a file open for reading, or the name of a file to open and read, containing an XML document as text. `iterparse` returns an iterator yielding tuples `(event, element)`, where *`event`* is one of the strings listed in argument *`events`* (which must be `'start'`, `'end'`, `'start-ns'`, or `'end-ns'`), as the parsing progresses and `iterparse` incrementally builds the corresponding `ElementTree`. *`element`* is an `Element` for events `'start'` and `'end'`, None for event `'end-ns'`, and a tuple of two strings `(namespace_prefix, namespace_uri)` for event `'start-ns'`. `parser` is an optional parser instance; by default, `iterparse` uses an instance of the class `XMLParser` supplied by the `ElementTree` module (this book does not cover class `XMLParser`; see the online docs (*http://bit.ly/2nMPeRh*)).

The purpose of `iterparse` is to let you iteratively parse a large XML document, without holding all of the resulting `ElementTree` in memory at once, whenever feasible. We cover `iterparse` in more detail in "Parsing XML Iteratively" on page 639.

parse

`parse(source,parser=None)`

Just like the `parse` method of `ElementTree`, covered in Table 23-1, except that it returns the `ElementTree` instance it creates.

register_namespace

`register_namespace(prefix,uri)`

Registers the string *`prefix`* as the namespace prefix for the string *`uri`*; elements in the namespace get serialized with this prefix.

tostring

`tostring(e,encoding='us-ascii,method='xml', short_empty_elements=True)`

Returns a string with the XML representation of the subtree rooted at `Element` *e*. Arguments have the same meaning as for the `write` method of `ElementTree`, covered in Table 23-1.

tostringlist

`tostringlist(e,encoding='us-ascii,method='xml', short_empty_elements=True)`

Returns a list of strings with the XML representation of the subtree rooted at `Element`*e*. Arguments have the same meaning as for the `write` method of `ElementTree`, covered in Table 23-1.

The ElementTree module also supplies the classes QName, TreeBuilder, and XMLParser, which we do not cover in this book. In v3 only, it also supplies the class XMLPullParser, covered in "Parsing XML Iteratively" on page 639.

Parsing XML with ElementTree.parse

In everyday use, the most common way to make an ElementTree instance is by parsing it from a file or file-like object, usually with the module function parse or with the method parse of instances of the class ElementTree.

For the examples in this chapter, we use the simple XML file found at *http://www.w3schools.com/xml/simple.xml*; its root tag is 'breakfast_menu', and the root's children are elements with the tag 'food'. Each 'food' element has a child with the tag 'name', whose text is the food's name, and a child with the tag 'calories', whose text is the string representation of the integer number of calories in a portion of that food. In other words, a simplified representation of that XML file's content of interest to the examples is:

```
<breakfast_menu>
  <food>
    <name>Belgian Waffles</name>
    <calories>650</calories>
  </food>
  <food>
    <name>Strawberry Belgian Waffles</name>
    <calories>900</calories>
  </food>
  <food>
    <name>Berry-Berry Belgian Waffles</name>
    <calories>900</calories>
  </food>
  <food>
    <name>French Toast</name>
    <calories>600</calories>
  </food>
  <food>
    <name>Homestyle Breakfast</name>
    <calories>950</calories>
  </food>
</breakfast_menu>
```

Since the XML document lives at a WWW URL, you start by obtaining a file-like object with that content, and passing it to parse; in v2, the simplest way is:

```
import urllib
from xml.etree import ElementTree as et

content = urllib.urlopen('http://www.w3schools.com/xml/simple.xml')
tree = et.parse(content)
```

and similarly, in v3, the simplest way uses the request module:

```
from urllib import request
from xml.etree import ElementTree as et

content = request.urlopen('http://www.w3schools.com/xml/simple.xml')
tree = et.parse(content)
```

Selecting Elements from an ElementTree

Let's say that we want to print on standard output the calories and names of the various foods, in order of increasing calories, with ties broken alphabetically. The code for this task is the same in v2 and v3:

```
def bycal_and_name(e):
  return int(e.find('calories').text), e.find('name').text

for e in sorted(tree.findall('food'), key=bycal_and_name):
  print('{} {}'.format(e.find('calories').text,
                       e.find('name').text))
```

When run, this prints:

```
600 French Toast
650 Belgian Waffles
900 Berry-Berry Belgian Waffles
900 Strawberry Belgian Waffles
950 Homestyle Breakfast
```

Editing an ElementTree

Once an `ElementTree` is built (be that via parsing, or otherwise), it can be "edited"—inserting, deleting, and/or altering nodes (elements)—via the various methods of `ElementTree` and `Element` classes, and module functions. For example, suppose our program is reliably informed that a new food has been added to the menu—buttered toast, two slices of white bread toasted and buttered, 180 calories—while any food whose name contains "berry," case-insensitive, has been removed. The "editing the tree" part for these specs can be coded as follows:

```
# add Buttered Toast to the menu
menu = tree.getroot()
toast = et.SubElement(menu, 'food')
tcals = et.SubElement(toast, 'calories')
tcals.text = '180'
tname = et.SubElement(toast, 'name')
tname.text = 'Buttered Toast'

# remove anything related to 'berry' from the menu
for e in menu.findall('food'):
    name = e.find('name').text
    if 'berry' in name.lower():
        menu.remove(e)
```

Once we insert these "editing" steps between the code parsing the tree and the code selectively printing from it, the latter prints:

```
180 Buttered Toast
600 French Toast
650 Belgian Waffles
950 Homestyle Breakfast
```

The ease of "editing" an `ElementTree` can sometimes be a crucial consideration, making it worth your while to keep it all in memory.

Building an ElementTree from Scratch

Sometimes, your task doesn't start from an existing XML document: rather, you need to make an XML document from data your code gets from a different source, such as a CSV document or some kind of database.

The code for such tasks is similar to the one we showed for editing an existing `ElementTree`—just add a little snippet to build an initially empty tree.

For example, suppose you have a CSV file, *menu.csv*, whose two comma-separated columns are the calories and name of various foods, one food per row. Your task is to build an XML file, *menu.xml*, similar to the one we parsed in previous examples. Here's one way you could do that:

```
import csv
from xml.etree import ElementTree as et

menu = et.Element('menu')
tree = et.ElementTree(menu)

with open('menu.csv') as f:
    r = csv.reader(f)
    for calories, namestr in r:
        food = et.SubElement(menu, 'food')
        cals = et.SubElement(food, 'calories')
        cals.text = calories
        name = et.SubElement(food, 'name')
        name.text = namestr

tree.write('menu.xml')
```

Parsing XML Iteratively

For tasks focused on selecting elements from an existing XML document, sometimes you don't need to build the whole `ElementTree` in memory—a consideration that's particularly important if the XML document is very large (not the case for the tiny example document we've been dealing with, but stretch your imagination and visualize a similar menu-focused document that lists millions of different foods).

So, again, what we want to do is print on standard output the calories and names of foods, this time only the 10 lowest-calorie foods, in order of increasing calories, with ties broken alphabetically; and *menu.xml*, which for simplicity's sake we now suppose is a local file, lists millions of foods, so we'd rather not keep it all in memory at once, since obviously we don't need complete access to all of it at once.

Here's some code that one might think would let us ace this task:

```
import heapq
from xml.etree import ElementTree as et

# initialize the heap with dummy entries
heap = [(999999, None)] * 10

for _, elem in et.iterparse('menu.xml'):
    if elem.tag != 'food': continue
    # just finished parsing a food, get calories and name
    cals = int(elem.find('calories').text)
    name = elem.find('name').text
    heapq.heappush(heap, (cals, name))

for cals, name in heap:
    print(cals, name)
```

Simple but memory-intensive approach

This approach does indeed work, but it consumes just about as much memory as an approach based on a full `et.parse` would!

Why does the simple approach still eat memory? Because `iterparse`, as it runs, builds up a whole `ElementTree` in memory, incrementally, even though it only communicates back events such as (by default) just `'end'`, meaning "I just finished parsing this element."

To actually save memory, we can at least toss all the contents of each element as soon as we're done processing it—that is, right after the call to `heapq.heappush`, add `elem.clear()` to make the just-processed element empty.

This approach would indeed save some memory—but not all of it, because the tree's root would end up with a huge list of empty children nodes. To be really frugal in memory consumption, we need to get `'start'` events as well, so we can get hold of the root of the `ElementTree` being built—that is, change the start of the loop to:

```
root = None
for event, elem in et.iterparse('menu.xml'):
    if event == 'start':
        if root is not None: root = elem
        continue
    if elem.tag != 'food': continue  # etc. as before
```

and then, right after the call to `heapq.heappush`, add `root.remove(elem)`. This approach saves as much memory as feasible, and still gets the task done!

Parsing XML within an asynchronous loop

While `iterparse`, used correctly, can save memory, it's still not good enough to use within an asynchronous (async) loop, as covered in Chapter 18. That's because `iterparse` makes blocking `read` calls to the file object passed as its first argument: such blocking calls are a no-no in async processing.

v2's `ElementTree` has no solution to offer to this conundrum. v3 does—specifically, it offers the class `XMLPullParser`. (In v2, you can get this functionality if you use the third-party package `lxml`, thanks to lxml.etree (*http://lxml.de/api/lxml.etree.XMLPullParser-class.html*).)

In an async arrangement, as covered in Chapter 18, a typical task is to write a "filter" component, which is fed chunks of bytes as they happen to come from some upstream source, and yields events downstream as they get fully parsed. Here's how `XMLPullParser` lets you write such a "filter" component:

```
from xml.etree import ElementTree as et

def filter(events=None):
    pullparser = et.XMLPullParser(events)
    data = yield
    while data:
        pullparser.feed(data)
        for tup in pullparser.read_events():
            data = yield tup
    pullparser.close()
    for tup in pullparser.read_events():
        data = yield tup
```

This assumes that `filter` is used via `.send(chunk)` calls to its result (passing new chunks of bytes as they are received), and `yields` `(event, element)` tuples for the caller to loop on and process. So, essentially, `filter` turns an async stream of chunks of raw bytes into an async stream of `(event, element)` pairs, to be consumed by iteration—a typical design pattern in modern Python's async programming.

V

Extending, Distributing, v2/v3 Migration

24
Extending and Embedding Classic Python

CPython runs on a portable, C-coded virtual machine. Python's built-in objects—such as numbers, sequences, dictionaries, sets, and files—are coded in C, as are several modules in Python's standard library. Modern platforms support dynamic-load libraries, with file extensions such as *.dll* on Windows, *.so* on Linux, and *.dylib* on Mac: building Python produces such binary files. You can code your own extension modules for Python in C, using the Python C API covered in this chapter, to produce and deploy dynamic libraries that Python scripts and interactive sessions can later use with the `import` statement, covered in "The import Statement" on page 174.

Extending Python means building modules that Python code can `import` to access the features the modules supply. *Embedding* Python means executing Python code from an application coded in another language. For such execution to be useful, Python code must in turn be able to access some of your application's functionality. In practice, therefore, embedding implies some extending, as well as a few embedding-specific operations. The three main reasons for wishing to extend Python can be summarized as follows:

- Reimplementing some functionality (originally coded in Python) in a lower-level language, hoping to get better performance
- Letting Python code access some existing functionality supplied by libraries coded in (or, at any rate, callable from) lower-level languages
- Letting Python code access some existing functionality of an application that is in the process of embedding Python as the application's scripting language

Embedding and extending are covered in Python's online documentation; there, you can find an in-depth tutorial (*https://docs.python.org/3/extending/index.html*) and an extensive reference manual (*https://docs.python.org/3/c-api/index.html*). Many details are best studied in Python's extensively documented C sources. Download Python's source distribution and study the sources of Python's core, C-coded extension modules, and the example extensions supplied for study purposes.

This chapter covers the basics of extending and embedding Python with C. It also mentions, but does not cover in depth, other ways to extend Python. Do notice that, as the online docs put it, several excellent third-party modules (such as Cython, covered in "Cython" on page 682, CFFI, mentioned at "Extending Python Without Python's C API" on page 681, and Numba (*http://numba.pydata.org/*) and SWIG (*http://www.swig.org/*), not covered in this book) "offer both simpler and more sophisticated approaches to creating C and C++ extensions for Python."

To extend or embed Python with the C API (or with most of the above-mentioned third-party modules), you need to know the C programming language. We do not cover C in this book; there are many good resources to learn C on the web (just make sure not to confuse C with its subtly different close relative C++, which is a different although similar language). In the rest of this chapter, we assume that you know C.

Extending Python with Python's C API

A Python extension module named *x* resides in a dynamic library with the same filename (*x.pyd* on Windows; *x.so* on most Unix-like platforms) in an appropriate directory (often the *site-packages* subdirectory of the Python library directory). You generally build the *x* extension module from a C source file *x.c* (or, more conventionally, *xmodule.c*) whose overall structure is:

```
#include <Python.h>

/* omitted: the body of the x module */

PyMODINIT_FUNC
PyInit_x(void)
{
    /* omitted: the code that initializes the module named x */
}
```

In v2, the module initialization function's name is `initx`; use C preprocessor constructs such as `#if PY_MAJOR_VERSION >= 3` if you're coding extensions meant to compile for both v2 and v3. For example, the module initialization function, for such a portable extension, might start:

```
PyMODINIT_FUNC
#if PY_MAJOR_VERSION >= 3
PyInit_x(void)
#else
initx(void)
```

```
#endif
{
```

When you have built and installed the extension module, a Python statement `import` *x* loads the dynamic library, then locates and calls the module initialization function, which must do all that is needed to initialize the module object named *x*.

Building and Installing C-Coded Python Extensions

To build and install a C-coded Python extension module, it's simplest and most productive to use the distribution utilities, `distutils` (*https://docs.python.org/2.7/distutils/setupscript.html#describing-extension-modules*) (or its improved third-party variant, `setuptools` (*https://pypi.python.org/pypi/setuptools*)). In the same directory as *x.c*, place a file named *setup.py* that contains the following statements:

```
from setuptools import setup, Extension
setup(name='x', ext_modules=[Extension('x',sources=['x.c'])])
```

From a shell prompt in this directory, you can now run:

```
C:\> python setup.py install
```

to build the module and install it so that it becomes usable in your Python installation. (You'll normally want to do this within a virtual environment, with **venv**, as covered in "Python Environments" on page 188, to avoid affecting the global state of your Python installation; however, for simplicity, we omit that step in this chapter.)

`setuptools` performs compilation and linking steps, with the right compiler and linker commands and flags, and copies the resulting dynamic library into the right directory, dependent on your Python installation (depending on that installation's details, you may need to have administrator or superuser privileges for the installation; for example, on a Mac or Linux, you may run **`sudo python setup.py install`**, although using **venv** instead is more likely to be what serves you best). Your Python code (running in the appropriate virtual environment, if needed) can then access the resulting module with the statement `import` *x*.

What C compiler do you need?

To compile C-coded extensions to Python, you normally need the same C compiler used to build the Python version you want to extend. For most Linux platforms, this means the free *gcc* compiler that normally comes with your platform or can be freely downloaded for it. (You might consider `clang` (*http://clang.llvm.org/*), widely reputed to offer better error messages.) On the Macintosh, *gcc* (actually a frontend to `clang`) comes with Apple's free XCode (AKA Developer Tools) integrated development environment (IDE), which you may download and install separately from Apple's App Store.

For Windows, you ideally need the Microsoft product known as VS2015 for v3, VS2010 for v2. However, other versions of Microsoft Visual Studio may also work.

Compatibility of C-coded extensions among Python versions

In general, a C-coded extension compiled to run with one version of Python has not been guaranteed to run with another. For example, a version compiled for Python 3.4 is only certain to run with 3.4, not with 3.3 or 3.5. On Windows, you cannot even try to run an extension with a different version of Python; elsewhere, such as on Linux or macOS, a given extension may happen to work on more than one version of Python, but you may get a warning when the module is imported, and the prudent course is to heed the warning: recompile the extension appropriately. (Since Python 3.5, you should be able to compile extensions forward-compatibly.)

At a C-source level, on the other hand, compatibility is almost always preserved within a major version (though not between v2 and v3).

Overview of C-Coded Python Extension Modules

Your C function `PyInit_x` generally has the following overall structure (from now on, we chiefly cover v3; see the v2 tutorial (*http://bit.ly/2mQDRs7*) and reference (*http://bit.ly/2mQHE95*) for slight differences):

```
PyMODINIT_FUNC
PyInit_x(void)
{
    PyObject* m = PyModule_Create(&x_module);
    // x_module is the instance of struct PyModuleDef describing the
    // module and in particular connecting to its methods (functions)

    // then: calls to PyModule_AddObject(m, "somename", someobj)
    // to add exceptions or other classes, and module constants.
    // And at last, when all done:
    return m;
}
```

More details are covered in "The Initialization Module" on page 650. `x_module` is a struct like:

```
static struct PyModuleDef x_module = {
   PyModuleDef_HEAD_INIT,
   "x",       /* the name of the module */
   x_doc,     /* the module's docstring, may be NULL */
   -1,        /* size of per-interpreter state of the module, or -1
                 if the module keeps state in global variables. */
   x_methods /* array of the module's method definitions */
};
```

and, within it, *`x_methods`* is an array of `PyMethodDef` structs. Each `PyMethodDef` struct in the *`x_methods`* array describes a C function that your module *x* makes available to Python code that imports *x*. Each such C function has the following overall structure:

```
static PyObject*
func_with_named_args(PyObject* self, PyObject* args, PyObject* kwds)
```

```
{
    /* omitted: body of function, accessing arguments via the Python C
       API function PyArg_ParseTupleAndKeywords, returning a PyObject*
       result, NULL for errors */
}
```

or a slightly simpler variant:

```
static PyObject*
func_with_positional_args_only(PyObject* self, PyObject* args)
{
    /* omitted: body of function, accessing arguments via the Python C
       API function PyArg_ParseTuple, returning a PyObject* result,
       NULL for errors */
}
```

How C-coded functions access arguments passed by Python code is covered in "Accessing Arguments" on page 653. How such functions build Python objects is covered in "Creating Python Values" on page 657, and how they raise or propagate exceptions back to the Python code that called them is covered in Chapter 5. When your module defines new Python types, AKA classes, your C code defines one or more instances of the struct `PyTypeObject`. This subject is covered in "Defining New Types" on page 674.

A simple example using all these concepts is shown in "A Simple Extension Example" on page 671. A toy-level "Hello World" example module could be as simple as:

```
#include <Python.h>

static PyObject*
hello(PyObject* self)
{
    return Py_BuildValue("s", "Hello, Python extensions world!");
}

static char hello_docs[] =
    "hello(): return a popular greeting phrase\n";

static PyMethodDef hello_funcs[] = {
    {"helloworld", (PyCFunction)hello, METH_NOARGS, hello_docs},
    {NULL}
};

static struct PyModuleDef hello_module = {
   PyModuleDef_HEAD_INIT,
   "hello",
   hello_docs,
   -1,
   hello_funcs
};

PyMODINIT_FUNC
PyInit_hello(void)
```

```
{
    return PyModule_Create(&hello_module);
}
```

The C string passed to Py_BuildValue is encoded in UTF-8, and the result is a Python str instance, which in v2 is also UTF-8 encoded. As previously mentioned, this is for v3. For the slight differences in module initialization in v2, see the online docs (*http://bit.ly/2nBj2jt*); for this trivial extension, all you need is to guard the whole definition of helloworld_module in a #if PY_MAJOR_VERSION >= 3 / #endif (since in v2 there is no such type as PyModuleDef), and change the module initialization function accordingly, to:

```
PyMODINIT_FUNC
#if PY_MAJOR_VERSION >= 3
PyInit_hello(void)
{
    return PyModule_Create(&hello_module);
#else
inithello(void)
{
    Py_InitModule3("hello",
        hello_funcs, hello_docs);
#endif
}
```

Save this as *hello.c* and build it through a *setup.py* script with distutils, such as:

```
from setuptools import setup, Extension
setup(name='hello',
      ext_modules=[Extension('hello',sources=['hello.c'])])
```

After you have run *python setup.py install*, you can use the newly installed module—for example, from a Python interactive session—such as:

```
>>> import hello
>>> print hello.hello()
Hello, Python extensions world!
>>>
```

Return Values of Python's C API Functions

All functions in the Python C API return either an int or a PyObject*. Most functions returning int return 0 in case of success and -1 to indicate errors. Some functions return results that are true or false: these functions return 0 to indicate false and an integer not equal to 0 to indicate true, and never indicate errors. Functions returning PyObject* return NULL in case of errors. See Chapter 5 for more details on how C-coded functions handle and raise errors.

The Initialization Module

The PyInit_*x* function must contain, at a minimum, a call to the function Py_Module_Create, (or, since 3.5, PyModuleDef_Init (*http://bit.ly/2mQJZAF*)), with, as the only parameter, the address of the struct PyModuleDef that defines the module's details. In addition, it may have one or more calls to the functions listed in Table 24-1, all returning -1 on error, 0 on success.

Table 24-1.

PyModule_AddIntConstant	`int PyModule_AddIntConstant(PyObject* module,char* name,long value)` Adds to the module *module* an attribute named *name* with integer value *value*.
PyModule_AddObject	`int PyModule_AddObject(PyObject* module,char* name,PyObject* value)` Adds to the module *module* an attribute named *name* with the value *value* and steals a reference to *value*, as covered in "Reference Counting" on page 652.
PyModule_AddStringConstant	`int PyModule_AddStringConstant(PyObject* module, char* name,char* value)` Adds to the module *module* an attribute named *name* with the string value *value* (encoded in UTF-8).

Sometimes, as part of the job of initializing your new module, you need to access something within another module—if you were coding in Python, you would just import othermodule, then access attributes of othermodule. Coding a Python extension in C, it can be almost as simple: call PyImport_Import for the other module, then PyModule_GetDict to get the other module's __dict__.

PyImport_Import `PyObject* PyImport_Import(PyObject* name)`

Imports the module named in Python string object *name* and returns a new reference to the module object, like Python's __import__(*name*). PyImport_Import is the highest-level, simplest, and most often used way to import a module.

PyModule_GetDict `PyObject* PyModule_GetDict(PyObject* module)`

Returns a borrowed reference (see "Reference Counting" on page 652) to the dictionary of the module *module*.

The PyMethodDef struct

To add functions to a module (or nonspecial methods to new types, as covered in "Defining New Types" on page 674), you must describe the functions or methods in an array of PyMethodDef structs, and terminate the array with a *sentinel* (i.e., a structure whose fields are all 0 or NULL). PyMethodDef is defined as follows:

```
typedef struct {
    char* ml_name;          /* Python name of function or method */
    PyCFunction ml_meth;    /* pointer to C function implementing it */
    int ml_flags;           /* flag describing how to pass arguments */
    char* ml_doc;           /* docstring for the function or method */
} PyMethodDef
```

You must cast the second field to `(PyCFunction)` unless the C function's signature is exactly `PyObject*` *`function`*`(PyObject*` *`self`*`, PyObject*` *`args`*`)`, which is the `typedef` for `PyCFunction`. This signature is correct when `ml_flags` is `METH_O`, which indicates a function that accepts a single argument, or `METH_VARARGS`, which indicates a function that accepts positional arguments. For `METH_O`, *`args`* is the only argument. For `METH_VARARGS`, *`args`* is a tuple of all arguments, to be parsed with the C API function `PyArg_ParseTuple`. However, `ml_flags` can also be `METH_NOARGS`, which indicates a function that accepts no arguments, or `METH_KEYWORDS`, which indicates a function that accepts both positional and named arguments. For `METH_NOARGS`, the signature is `PyObject*` *`function`*`(PyObject*` *`self`*`)`, without further arguments. For `METH_KEYWORDS`, the signature is:

```
PyObject* function(PyObject* self, PyObject* args, PyObject* kwds)
```

`args` is the tuple of positional arguments, and *`kwds`* is the dictionary of named arguments; both are parsed with the C API function `PyArg_ParseTupleAndKeywords`. In these cases, you do need to explicitly cast the second field to `(PyCFunction)`.

When a C-coded function implements a module's function, the `self` parameter of the C function is `NULL`, for any value of the `ml_flags` field. When a C-coded function implements a nonspecial method of an extension type, the `self` parameter points to the instance on which the method is being called.

Reference Counting

Python objects live on the heap, and C code sees them as pointers of the type `PyObject*`. Each `PyObject` counts how many references to itself are outstanding and destroys itself when the number of references goes down to `0`. To make this possible, your code must use Python-supplied macros: `Py_INCREF` to add a reference to a Python object and `Py_DECREF` to abandon a reference to a Python object. The `Py_XINCREF` and `Py_XDECREF` macros are like `Py_INCREF` and `Py_DECREF`, but you may also use them innocuously on a null pointer. The test for a nonnull pointer is implicitly performed inside the `Py_XINCREF` and `Py_XDECREF` macros, saving you the little bother of writing out that test explicitly when you don't know for sure whether the pointer might be null.

A `PyObject*` *`p`*, which your code receives by calling or being called by other functions, is known as a *new reference* when the code that supplies *`p`* has already called `Py_INCREF` on your behalf. Otherwise, it is known as a *borrowed reference*. Your code is said to *own* new references it holds, but not borrowed ones. You can call `Py_INCREF` on a borrowed reference to make it into a reference that you own; you must do this when you need to use the reference across calls to code that might cause the count of the reference you borrowed to be decremented. You must *always* call `Py_DECREF` before abandoning or overwriting references that you own, but *never* on references you don't own. Therefore, understanding which interactions transfer reference ownership and which ones rely on reference borrowing is absolutely crucial. For most functions in the C API, and for *all* functions that you write and Python calls, the following general rules apply:

- `PyObject*` arguments are borrowed references.
- A `PyObject*` returned as the function's result transfers ownership.

For each of the two rules, there are a few exceptions for some functions in the C API. `PyList_SetItem` and `PyTuple_SetItem` *steal* a reference to the item they are setting (but not to the list or tuple object into which they're setting it), meaning that they take ownership even though by general rules that item would be a borrowed reference. `PyList_SET_ITEM` and `PyTuple_SET_ITEM`, the C preprocessor macros, which implement faster versions of the item-setting functions, are also reference-stealers. So is `PyModule_AddObject`, covered in Table 24-1. There are no other exceptions to the first rule. The rationale for these exceptions, which may help you remember them, is that the object you just created will be owned by the list, tuple, or module, so the reference-stealing semantics save unnecessary use of `Py_DECREF` immediately afterward.

The second rule has more exceptions than the first one. There are several cases in which the returned `PyObject*` is a borrowed reference rather than a new reference. The abstract functions—whose names begin with `PyObject_`, `PySequence_`, `PyMapping_`, and `PyNumber_`—return new references. This is because you can call them on objects of many types, and there might not be any other reference to the resulting object that they return (i.e., the returned object might have to be created on the fly). The concrete functions—whose names begin with `PyList_`, `PyTuple_`, `PyDict_`, and so on—return a borrowed reference when the semantics of the object they return ensure that there must be some other reference to the returned object somewhere.

In this chapter, we show all cases of exceptions to these rules (i.e., return of borrowed references and rare cases of reference stealing from arguments) regarding all functions we cover. When we don't explicitly mention a function as being an exception, the function follows the rules: its `PyObject*` arguments, if any, are borrowed references, and its `PyObject*` result, if any, is a new reference.

Accessing Arguments

A function that has `ml_flags` in its `PyMethodDef` set to `METH_NOARGS` is called from Python with no arguments. The corresponding C function has a signature with only one argument, *`self`*. When `ml_flags` is `METH_O`, Python code calls the function with exactly one argument. The C function's second argument is a borrowed reference to the object that the Python caller passes as the argument's value.

When `ml_flags` is `METH_VARARGS`, Python code calls the function with any number of positional arguments, which the Python interpreter implicitly collects into a tuple. The C function's second argument is a borrowed reference to the tuple. Your C code then calls the `PyArg_ParseTuple` function:

PyArg_ParseTuple `int PyArg_ParseTuple(PyObject* tuple, char* format,...)`

Returns `0` for errors, and a value not equal to `0` for success. *`tuple`* is the `PyObject*` that was the C function's second argument. *`format`* is a C string that describes mandatory and optional arguments. The following arguments of `PyArg_ParseTuple` are addresses of C variables in which to put the values extracted from the tuple. Any `PyObject*` variables among the C variables are borrowed references. Table 24-2 lists the commonly used code strings, of which zero or more are joined to form string *`format`*.

Table 24-2. Format codes for PyArg_ParseTuple

Code	C type	Meaning
`c`	`int`	A Python `bytes`, `bytearray`, or `str` of length 1 becomes a C `int` (`char`, in v2).
`d`	`double`	A Python `float` becomes a C `double`.
`D`	`Py_Complex`	A Python `complex` becomes a C `Py_Complex`.
`f`	`float`	A Python `float` becomes a C `float`.
`i`	`int`	A Python `int` becomes a C `int`.
`l`	`long`	A Python `int` becomes a C `long`.
`L`	`long long`	A Python `int` becomes a C `long long` (`__int64` on Windows).
`O`	`PyObject*`	Gets non-`NULL` borrowed reference to Python argument.
`O!`	`type+PyObject*`	Like code `O`, plus type checking (see below).
`O&`	`convert+void*`	Arbitrary conversion (see below).
`s`	`char*`	Python string without embedded nulls to C `char*` (encoded in UTF-8).
`s#`	`char*+int`	Any Python string to C address and length.

Code	C type	Meaning
t#	char*+int	Read-only single-segment buffer to C address and length.
u	Py_UNICODE*	Python Unicode without embedded nulls to C.
u#	Py_UNICODE*+int	Any Python Unicode C address and length.
w#	char*+int	Read/write single-segment buffer to C address and length.
z	char*	Like s, but also accepts None (sets C char* to NULL).
z#	char*+int	Like s#, but also accepts None (sets C char* to NULL and int to 0).
(...)	as per ...	A Python sequence is treated as one argument per item.
|		All following arguments are optional.
:		Format end, followed by function name for error messages.
;		Format end, followed by entire error message text.

Code formats d to n (and rarely used other codes for unsigned chars and short ints) accept numeric arguments from Python. Python coerces the corresponding values. For example, a code of i can correspond to a Python float; the fractional part gets truncated, as if the built-in function int had been called. Py_Complex is a C struct with two fields named real and imag, both of type double.

O is the most general format code and accepts any argument, which you can later check and/or convert as needed. The variant O! corresponds to two arguments in the variable arguments: first the address of a Python type object, then the address of a PyObject*. O! checks that the corresponding value belongs to the given type (or any subtype of that type) before setting the PyObject* to point to the value; otherwise, it raises TypeError (the whole call fails, and the error is set to an appropriate TypeError instance, as covered in Chapter 5). The variant O& also corresponds to two arguments in the variable arguments: first the address of a converter function you coded, then a void* (i.e., any address). The converter function must have signature int *convert*(PyObject*, void*). Python calls your conversion function with the value passed from Python as the first argument and the void* from the variable arguments as the second argument. The conversion function must either return `0` and raise an exception (as covered in Chapter 5) to indicate an error, or return `1` and store whatever is appropriate via the `void*` it gets.

The code format `s` accepts a string from Python and the address of a `char*` (i.e., a `char**`) among the variable arguments. It changes the `char*` to point at the string's buffer, which your C code must treat as a read-only, null-terminated array of `char`s (i.e., a typical C string; however, your code must *not* modify it). The Python string must contain no embedded null characters; in v3, the resulting encoding is UTF-8. `s#` is similar, but corresponds to two arguments among the variable arguments: first the address of a `char*`, then the address of an `int`, which gets set to the string's length. The Python string can contain embedded nulls, and therefore so can the buffer to which the `char*` is set to point. `u` and `u#` are similar, but specifically accept a Unicode string (in both v3 and v3), and the C-side pointers must be `Py_UNICODE*` rather than `char*`. `Py_UNICODE` is a macro defined in *Python.h*, and corresponds to the type of a Python Unicode character in the implementation (this is often, but not always, a C `wchar_t`).

`t#` and `w#` are similar to `s#`, but the corresponding Python argument can be any object of a type respecting the buffer protocol, respectively read-only and read/write. Strings are a typical example of read-only buffers. `mmap` and `array` instances are typical examples of read/write buffers, and like all read/write buffers they are also acceptable where a read-only buffer is required (i.e., for a `t#`).

When one of the arguments is a Python sequence of known fixed length, you can use format codes for each of its items, and corresponding C addresses among the variable arguments, by grouping the format codes in parentheses. For example, code `(ii)` corresponds to a Python sequence of two numbers and, among the remaining arguments, corresponds to two addresses of `int`s.

The format string may include a vertical bar (`|`) to indicate that all following arguments are optional. In this case, you must initialize the C variables, whose addresses you pass among the variable arguments for later arguments, to suitable default values before you call `PyArg_ParseTuple`. `PyArg_ParseTuple` does not change the C variables corresponding to optional arguments that were not passed in a given call from Python to your C-coded function.

For example, here's the start of a function to be called with one mandatory integer argument, optionally followed by another integer argument defaulting to 23 if absent (rather like `def f(x, y=23):` in Python, except that the function must be called with positional arguments only and the arguments must be numeric):

```
PyObject* f(PyObject* self, PyObject* args) {
  int x, y=23;
  if(!PyArg_ParseTuple(args, "i|i", &x, &y)
    return NULL;
  /* rest of function snipped */
}
```

The format string may optionally end with `:name` to indicate that *name* must be used as the function name if any error messages result. Alternatively, the format string may end with `;text` to indicate that *text* must be used as the entire error message if `PyArg_ParseTuple` detects errors (this form is rarely used).

A function that has `ml_flags` in its `PyMethodDef` set to `METH_KEYWORDS` accepts positional and named arguments. Python code calls the function with any number of positional arguments, which the Python interpreter collects into a tuple, and named arguments, which the Python interpreter collects into a dictionary. The C function's second argument is a borrowed reference to the tuple, and the third one is a borrowed reference to the dictionary. Your C code then calls the `PyArg_ParseTupleAndKeywords` function.

PyArg_ParseTupleAndKeywords `int PyArg_ParseTupleAndKeywords(PyObject* tuple, PyObject* dict, char* format, char** kwlist,...)`

Returns `0` for errors, and a value not equal to `0` for success. *`tuple`* is the `PyObject*` that was the C function's second argument. *`dict`* is the `PyObject*` that was the C function's third argument. *`format`* is the same as for `PyArg_ParseTuple`, except that it cannot include the `(...)` format code to parse nested sequences. *`kwlist`* is an array of `char*` terminated by a `NULL` sentinel, with the names of the parameters, one after the other. For example, the following C code:

```
static PyObject*
func_c(PyObject* self, PyObject* args, PyObject* kwds)
{
    static char* argnames[] = {"x", "y", "z", NULL};
    double x, y=0.0, z=0.0;
    if(!PyArg_ParseTupleAndKeywords(
        args,kwds,"d|dd",argnames,&x,&y,&z))
        return NULL;
    /* rest of function snipped */
```

is roughly equivalent to this Python code:

```
def func_py(x, y=0.0, z=0.0):
    x, y, z = map(float, (x,y,z))
    # rest of function snipped
```

Creating Python Values

C functions that communicate with Python must often build Python values, both to return as their `PyObject*` result and for other purposes, such as setting items and attributes. The simplest and handiest way to build a Python value is most often with the `Py_BuildValue` function:

Py_BuildValue `PyObject* Py_BuildValue(char* format,...)`

format is a C string that describes the Python object to build. The following arguments of `Py_BuildValue` are C values from which the result is built. The `PyObject*` result is a new reference. Table 24-3 lists the commonly used code strings, of which zero or more are joined into string *format*. `Py_BuildValue` builds and returns a tuple if *format* contains two or more format codes, or if *format* begins with `(` and ends with `)`. Otherwise, the result is not a tuple. When you pass buffers—as, for example, in the case of format code `s#`—`Py_BuildValue` copies the data. You can therefore modify, abandon, or `free()` your original copy of the data after `Py_BuildValue` returns. `Py_BuildValue` always returns a new reference (except for format code `N`). Called with an empty *format*, `Py_BuildValue("")` returns a new reference to `None`.

Table 24-3. Format codes for Py_BuildValue

Code	C type	Meaning
`B`	`unsigned char`	A C `unsigned char` becomes a Python `int`.
`b`	`char`	A C `char` becomes a Python `int`.
`C`	`char`	A C `char` becomes a Python Unicode string of length `1` (v3 only).
`c`	`char`	A C `char` becomes a Python bytestring of length `1` (`bytes` in v3, `str` in v2).
`D`	`double`	A C `double` becomes a Python `float`.
`d`	`Py_Complex`	A C `Py_Complex` becomes a Python `complex`.
`H`	`unsigned short`	A C `unsigned short` becomes a Python `int`.
`h`	`short`	A C `short` becomes a Python `int`.
`I`	`unsigned int`	A C `unsigned int` becomes a Python `int`.
`i`	`int`	A C `int` becomes a Python `int`.
`K`	`unsigned long long`	A C `unsigned long long` becomes a Python `int` (if platform supports it).
`k`	`unsigned long`	A C `unsigned long` becomes a Python `int`.
`L`	`long long`	A C `long long` becomes a Python `int` (if platform supports it).

Code	C type	Meaning
`l`	`long`	A C `long` becomes a Python `int`.
`N`	`PyObject*`	Passes a Python object and *steals* a reference.
`O`	`PyObject*`	Passes a Python object and `INCREF`s it.
`O&`	`convert+void*`	Arbitrary conversion (see below).
`s`	`char*`	C `0`-terminated `char*` to Python string (bytes in v2, Unicode decoding with utf8 in v3), or `NULL` to `None`.
`s#`	`char*+int`	C `char*` and length to Python string (like `s`), or `NULL` to `None`.
`u`	`Py_UNICODE*`	C wide char (UCS-2 or UCS-4), null-terminated string to Python Unicode, or `NULL` to `None`.
`u#`	`Py_UNICODE*+int`	C wide char (UCS-2 or UCS-4) string and length to Python Unicode, or `NULL` to `None`.
`y`	`char*+int`	C char null-terminated string to `bytes`, or `NULL` to `None` (v3 only).
`y#`	`char*+int`	C char string and length to `bytes`, or `NULL` to `None` (v3 only).
`(...)`	As per `...`	Builds Python tuple from C values.
`[...]`	As per `...`	Builds Python list from C values.
`{...}`	As per `...`	Builds Python dictionary from C values, alternating keys and values (must be an even number of C values).

The code `O&` corresponds to two arguments among the variable arguments: first the address of a converter function you code, then a `void*` (i.e., any address). The converter function must have signature `PyObject*` *`convert`*`(void*)`. Python calls the conversion function with the `void*` from the variable arguments as the only argument. The conversion function must either return `NULL` and raise an exception (as covered in Chapter 5) to indicate an error, or return a new reference `PyObject*` built from data obtained through the `void*`.

The code {...} builds dictionaries from an even number of C values, alternately keys and values. For example, Py_BuildValue("{issi}",23,"zig","zag",42) returns a new PyObject* for {23:'zig','zag':42}.

Note the crucial difference between the codes N and O. N *steals* a reference from the corresponding PyObject* value among the variable arguments, so it's convenient to build an object including a reference you own that you would otherwise have to Py_DECREF. O does no reference stealing, so it's appropriate to build an object including a reference you don't own, or a reference you must also keep elsewhere.

Exceptions

To propagate exceptions raised from other functions you call, just return NULL as the PyObject* result from your C function. To raise your own exceptions, set the current-exception indicator, then return NULL. Python's built-in exception classes (covered in "Standard Exception Classes" on page 160) are globally available, with names starting with PyExc_, such as PyExc_AttributeError, PyExc_KeyError, and so on. Your extension module can also supply and use its own exception classes. The most commonly used C API functions related to raising exceptions are the following:

PyErr_Format

PyObject* PyErr_Format(PyObject* *type*,char* *format*,...)

Raises an exception of class *type*, which must be either a built-in such as PyExc_IndexError or an exception class created with PyErr_NewException. Builds the associated value from the format string *format*, which has syntax similar to C's printf's, and the following C values indicated as variable arguments above. Returns NULL, so your code can just use:

```
return PyErr_Format(PyExc_KeyError,
    "Unknown key name (%s)", thekeystring);
```

PyErr_NewException

PyObject* PyErr_NewException(char* *name*, PyObject* *base*,PyObject* *dict*)

Extends the exception class *base*, with extra class attributes and methods from dictionary *dict* (normally NULL, meaning no extra class attributes or methods), creating a new exception class named *name* (string *name* must be of the form "*modulename.classname*"), and returns a new reference to the new class object. When *base* is NULL, uses PyExc_Exception as the base class. You normally call this function during initialization of a module object. For example:

```
PyModule_AddObject(module, "error",
    PyErr_NewException(
    "mymod.error", NULL, NULL));
```

PyErr_NoMemory

`PyObject* PyErr_NoMemory()`

Raises an out-of-memory error and returns NULL, so your code can just use:

```
return PyErr_NoMemory();
```

PyErr_SetObject

`void PyErr_SetObject(PyObject* type, PyObject* value)`

Raises an exception of class *type*, which must be a built-in such as PyExc_KeyError or an exception class created with PyErr_NewException, with *value* as the associated value (a borrowed reference). PyErr_SetObject is a void function (i.e., returns no value).

PyErr_SetFromErrno

`PyObject* PyErr_SetFromErrno(PyObject* type)`

Raises an exception of class *type*, which must be a built-in such as PyExc_OSError or an exception class created with PyErr_NewException. Takes all details from errno, which C standard library functions and system calls set for many error cases, and the standard C library function strerror, which translates such error codes into appropriate strings. Returns NULL, so your code can just use:

```
return PyErr_SetFromErrno(PyExc_IOError);
```

PyErr_SetFromErrnoWithFilename

`PyObject* PyErr_SetFromErrnoWithFilename(PyObject* type,char* filename)`

Like PyErr_SetFromErrno, but also provides the string *filename* as part of the exception's value. When *filename* is NULL, works like PyErr_SetFromErrno.

Your C code may want to deal with an exception and continue, as a try/except statement would let you do in Python code. The most commonly used C API functions related to catching exceptions are the following:

PyErr_Clear

`void PyErr_Clear()`

Clears the error indicator. Innocuous if no error is pending.

PyErr_ExceptionMatches

`int PyErr_ExceptionMatches(PyObject* type)`

Call only when an error is pending, or the whole program might crash. Returns a value !=0 when the pending exception is an instance of the given *type* or any subclass of *type*, or 0 when the pending exception is not such an instance.

PyErr_Occurred `PyObject* PyErr_Occurred()`

Returns `NULL` if no error is pending; otherwise, a borrowed reference to the type of the pending exception. (*Don't* use the specific returned value; instead, call `PyErr_ExceptionMatches`, in order to catch exceptions of subclasses as well, as is normal and expected.)

PyErr_Print `void PyErr_Print()`

Call only when an error is pending, or the whole program might crash. Outputs a standard traceback to `sys.stderr`, then clears the error indicator.

If you need to process errors in highly sophisticated ways, study other error-related functions of the C API, such as `PyErr_Fetch`, `PyErr_Normalize`, `PyErr_GivenExceptionMatches`, and `PyErr_Restore` in the online docs (*https://docs.python.org/3/c-api/exceptions.html*). This book does not cover those advanced and rarely needed possibilities.

Abstract Layer Functions

The code for a C extension typically needs to use some Python functionality. For example, your code may need to examine or set attributes and items of Python objects, call Python-coded and Python built-in functions and methods, and so on. In most cases, the best approach is for your code to call functions from the *abstract layer* of Python's C API. These are functions that you can call on any Python object (functions whose names start with `PyObject_`), or on any object within a wide category, such as mappings, numbers, or sequences (with names starting with `PyMapping_`, `PyNumber_`, and `PySequence_`, respectively).

Many of the functions callable on specifically typed objects within these categories duplicate functionality that is also available from `PyObject_` functions. In these cases, you should almost invariably use the more general `PyObject_` function instead. We don't cover such almost-redundant functions in this book.

Functions in the abstract layer raise Python exceptions if you call them on objects to which they are not applicable. All of these functions accept borrowed references for `PyObject*` arguments and return a new reference (`NULL` for an exception) if they return a `PyObject*` result.

The most frequently used abstract-layer functions are listed in Table 24-4.

Table 24-4.

PyCallable_Check `int PyCallable_Check(PyObject* x)`

True when *x* is callable, like `callable(x)`.

PyIter_Check `int PyIter_Check(PyObject* x)`

True when *x* is an iterator.

PyIter_Next `PyObject* PyIter_Next(PyObject* x)`

Returns the next item from iterator *x*. Returns `NULL` *without* raising exceptions when *x*'s iteration is finished (i.e., when `next(x)` raises `StopIteration`).

PyNumber_Check `int PyNumber_Check(PyObject* x)`

True when *x* is a number.

PyObject_Call `PyObject* PyObject_Call(PyObject* f,PyObject* args,PyObject* kwds)`

Calls the callable Python object *f* with positional arguments in `tuple` *args* (may be empty, but never `NULL`) and named arguments in `dict` *kwds*. Returns the call's result. Like `f(*args,**kwds)`.

PyObject_CallObject `PyObject* PyObject_CallObject(PyObject* f,PyObject* args)`

Calls the callable Python object *f* with positional arguments in `tuple` *args* (may be `NULL`). Returns the call's result. Like `f(*args)`.

PyObject_CallFunction `PyObject* PyObject_CallFunction(PyObject* f, char* format,...)`

Calls the callable Python object *f* with positional arguments described by the format string *format*, using the same format codes as `Py_BuildValue`, covered in "Creating Python Values" on page 657. When *format* is `NULL`, calls *x* with no arguments. Returns the call's result.

PyObject_CallFunctionObjArgs `PyObject* PyObject_CallFunctionObjArgs(PyObject* f,..., NULL)`

Calls the callable Python object *f* with positional arguments passed as zero or more `PyObject*` arguments. Returns the call's result.

PyObject_CallMethod `PyObject* PyObject_CallMethod(PyObject* x,char* method,char* format,...)`

Calls the method named *method* of Python object *x* with positional arguments described by the format string *format*, using the same format codes as `Py_BuildValue`. When *format* is `NULL`, calls the method with no arguments. Returns the call's result.

PyObject_CallMethodObjArgs `PyObject* PyObject_CallMethodObjArgs(PyObject*` *x*`, char*` *method*`,...,` `NULL)`

Calls the method named *method* of Python object *x* with positional arguments passed as zero or more `PyObject*` arguments. Returns the call's result.

PyObject_DelAttrString `int PyObject_DelAttrString(PyObject*` *x*`,char*` *name*`)`

Deletes *x*'s attribute named *name*, like `del` *x*`.`*name*.

PyObject_DelItem `int PyObject_DelItem(PyObject*` *x*`,PyObject*` *key*`)`

Deletes *x*'s item with key (or index) *key*, like `del` *x*`[`*key*`]`.

PyObject_DelItemString `int PyObject_DelItemString(PyObject*` *x*`,char*` *key*`)`

Deletes *x*'s item with key *key*, like `del` *x*`[`*key*`]`.

PyObject_GetAttrString `PyObject* PyObject_GetAttrString(PyObject*` *x*`,char*` *name*`)`

Returns *x*'s attribute *name*, like *x*`.`*name*.

PyObject_GetItem `PyObject* PyObject_GetItem(PyObject*` *x*`,PyObject*` *key*`)`

Returns *x*'s item with key (or index) *key*, like *x*`[`*key*`]`.

PyObject_GetItemString `int PyObject_GetItemString(PyObject*` *x*`,char*` *key*`)`

Returns *x*'s item with key *key*, like *x*`[`*key*`]`.

PyObject_GetIter `PyObject* PyObject_GetIter(PyObject*` *x*`)`

Returns an iterator on *x*, like `iter(`*x*`)`.

PyObject_HasAttrString `int PyObject_HasAttrString(PyObject*` *x*`,char*` *name*`)`

True if *x* has an attribute *name*, like `hasattr(`*x*`,`*name*`)`.

PyObject_IsTrue `int PyObject_IsTrue(PyObject*` *x*`)`

True if *x* is true for Python, like `bool(`*x*`)`.

PyObject_Length `int PyObject_Length(PyObject*` *x*`)`

Returns *x*'s length, like `len(`*x*`)`.

PyObject_Repr `PyObject* PyObject_Repr(PyObject*` *x*`)`

Returns *x*'s detailed string representation, like `repr(`*x*`)`.

PyObject_RichCompare

`PyObject* PyObject_RichCompare(PyObject* x, PyObject* y,int op)`

Performs the comparison indicated by *op* between *x* and *y*, and returns the result as a Python object. *op* can be `Py_EQ`, `Py_NE`, `Py_LT`, `Py_LE`, `Py_GT`, or `Py_GE`, corresponding to Python comparisons *x*==*y*, *x*!=*y*, *x*<*y*, *x*<=*y*, *x*>*y*, or *x*>=*y*.

PyObject_RichCompareBool

`int PyObject_RichCompareBool(PyObject* x,PyObject* y,int op)`

Like `PyObject_RichCompare`, but returns `0` for false and `1` for true.

PyObject_SetAttrString

`int PyObject_SetAttrString(PyObject* x,char* name,PyObject* v)`

Sets *x*'s attribute named *name* to *v*, like `x.name=v`.

PyObject_SetItem

`int PyObject_SetItem(PyObject* x,PyObject* k, PyObject *v)`

Sets *x*'s item with key (or index) *key* to *v*, like `x[key]=v`.

PyObject_SetItemString

`int PyObject_SetItemString(PyObject* x,char* key, PyObject *v)`

Sets *x*'s item with key *key* to *v*, like `x[key]=v`.

PyObject_Str

`PyObject* PyObject_Str(PyObject* x)`

Returns *x*'s readable string form (Unicode in v3, bytes in v2), like `str(x)`. To get the result as bytes in v3, use `PyObject_Bytes`; to get the result as `unicode` in v2, use `PyObject_Unicode`.

PyObject_Type

`PyObject* PyObject_Type(PyObject* x)`

Returns *x*'s type object, like `type(x)`.

PySequence_Contains

`int PySequence_Contains(PyObject* x,PyObject* v)`

True if *v* is an item in *x*, like `v in x`.

PySequence_DelSlice

`int PySequence_DelSlice(PyObject* x,int start,int stop)`

Deletes *x*'s slice from *start* to *stop*, like `del x[start:stop]`.

PySequence_Fast

`PyObject* PySequence_Fast(PyObject* x)`

Returns a new reference to a tuple with the same items as *x*, unless *x* is a list, in which case returns a new reference to *x*. When you need to get many items of an arbitrary sequence *x*, it's fastest to call `t=PySequence_Fast(x)` once, then call `PySequence_Fast_GET_ITEM(t,i)` as many times as needed, and finally call `Py_DECREF(t)`.

PySequence_Fast_GET_ITEM

`PyObject* PySequence_Fast_GET_ITEM(PyObject* x, int i)`

Returns the *i* item of *x*, where *x* must be the result of `PySequence_Fast`, `x!=NULL`, and `0<=i<PySequence_Fast_GET_SIZE(t)`. Violating these conditions can cause program crashes. This approach is optimized for speed, not for safety.

PySequence_Fast_GET_SIZE

`int PySequence_Fast_GET_SIZE(PyObject* x)`

Returns the length of *x*. *x* must be the result of `PySequence_Fast`, `x!=NULL`.

PySequence_GetSlice

`PyObject* PySequence_GetSlice(PyObject* x, int start,int stop)`

Returns *x*'s slice from *start* to *stop*, like `x[start:stop]`.

PySequence_List

`PyObject* PySequence_List(PyObject* x)`

Returns a new list object with the same items as *x*, like `list(x)`.

PySequence_SetSlice

`int PySequence_SetSlice(PyObject* x,int start, int stop,PyObject* v)`

Sets *x*'s slice from *start* to *stop* to *v*, like `x[start:stop]=v`. Just as in the equivalent Python statement, *v* must also be a sequence.

PySequence_Tuple

`PyObject* PySequence_Tuple(PyObject* x)`

Returns a new reference to a tuple with the same items as *x*, like `tuple(x)`.

Other functions, whose names start with `PyNumber_`, let you perform numeric operations. Unary `PyNumber` functions, which take one argument `PyObject* x` and return a `PyObject*`, are listed in Table 24-5 with their Python equivalents.

Table 24-5. Unary PyNumber functions

Function	Python equivalent
PyNumber_Absolute	abs(x)
PyNumber_Float	float(x)
PyNumber_Int	int(x) (v2 only)
PyNumber_Invert	~x
PyNumber_Long	long(x) (int(x) in v3)
PyNumber_Negative	-x
PyNumber_Positive	+x

Binary PyNumber functions, which take two PyObject* arguments *x* and *y* and return a PyObject*, are similarly listed in Table 24-6.

Table 24-6. Binary PyNumber functions

Function	Python equivalent
PyNumber_Add	x + y
PyNumber_And	x & y
PyNumber_Divide	x // y
PyNumber_Divmod	divmod(x, y)
PyNumber_FloorDivide	x // y
PyNumber_Lshift	x << y
PyNumber_Multiply	x * y
PyNumber_Or	x | y
PyNumber_Remainder	x % y
PyNumber_Rshift	x >> y
PyNumber_Subtract	x - y

Function	Python equivalent
PyNumber_TrueDivide	x / y (nontruncating)
PyNumber_Xor	x ^ y

All the binary PyNumber functions have in-place equivalents whose names start with PyNumber_InPlace, such as PyNumber_InPlaceAdd and so on. The in-place versions try to modify the first argument in place, if possible, and in any case return a new reference to the result, be it the first argument (modified) or a new object. Python's built-in numbers are immutable; therefore, when the first argument is a number of a built-in type, the in-place versions work just the same as the ordinary versions. The function PyNumber_Divmod returns a tuple with two items (the quotient and the remainder) and has no in-place equivalent.

There is one ternary PyNumber function, PyNumber_Power:

PyNumber_Power `PyObject* PyNumber_Power(PyObject* x,PyObject* y, PyObject* z)`

When *z* is Py_None, returns *x* raised to the *y* power, like *x****y* or, equivalently, pow(*x*,*y*). Otherwise, returns *x****y*%*z*, like pow(*x*,*y*,*z*). The in-place version is named PyNumber_InPlacePower.

Concrete Layer Functions

Each specific type of Python built-in object supplies concrete functions to operate on instances of that type, with names starting with Py*type*_ (e.g., PyInt_ for functions related to Python ints). Most such functions duplicate the functionality of abstract-layer functions or auxiliary functions covered earlier in this chapter, such as Py_BuildValue, which can generate objects of many types. In this section, we cover just some frequently used functions from the concrete layer that provide unique functionality, or very substantial convenience or speed. For most types, you can check whether an object belongs to the type by calling Py*type*_Check, which also accepts instances of subtypes, or Py*type*_CheckExact, which accepts only instances of *type*, not of subtypes. Signatures are the same as for function PyIter_Check, covered in Table 24-4.

All functions whose name start with PyString are actually named PyBytes in v3 (and work on Python bytes objects, not str ones), but the names starting with PyString remain available (as synonyms implemented by C preprocessor macros) for convenience. Concrete-layer functions dealing with str in v3 and unicode in v2 have names starting with PyUnicode, but you're usually better off using the corresponding abstract-layer functions instead, so we don't cover the concrete-layer equivalents in this book.

PyDict_GetItem

`PyObject* PyDict_GetItem(PyObject* x,PyObject* key)`

Returns a borrowed reference to the item with key *key* of dictionary *x*.

PyDict_GetItemString

`int PyDict_GetItemString(PyObject* x,char* key)`

Returns a borrowed reference to the item with null-terminated string key *key* of dictionary *x*.

PyDict_Next

`int PyDict_Next(PyObject* x,int* pos,PyObject** k,PyObject** v)`

Iterates over items in dictionary *x*. You must initialize `*pos` to `0` at the start of the iteration: `PyDict_Next` uses and updates `*pos` to keep track of its place. For each successful iteration step, returns `1`; when there are no more items, returns `0`. Updates `*k` and `*v` to point to the next key and value, respectively (borrowed references), at each step that returns `1`. You can pass either *k* or *v* as `NULL` when you are not interested in the key or value. During an iteration, you must not change in any way the set of *x*'s keys, but you can change *x*'s values as long as the set of keys remains identical.

PyDict_Merge

`int PyDict_Merge(PyObject* x,PyObject* y,int override)`

Updates dictionary *x* by merging the items of dictionary *y* into *x*. *override* determines what happens when a key *k* is present in both *x* and *y*: when *override* is `0`, `x[k]` remains the same; otherwise, `x[k]` is replaced by the value `y[k]`.

PyDict_MergeFromSeq2

`int PyDict_MergeFromSeq2(PyObject* x,PyObject* y, int override)`

Like `PyDict_Merge`, except that *y* is not a dictionary but a sequence of sequences, where each subsequence has length 2 and is used as a `(key,value)` pair.

PyFloat_AS_DOUBLE

`double PyFloat_AS_DOUBLE(PyObject* x)`

Returns the C `double` value of Python `float` *x*, very fast, without any error checking.

PyList_New

`PyObject* PyList_New(int length)`

Returns a new, uninitialized list of the given *length*. You must then initialize the list, typically by calling `PyList_SET_ITEM` *length* times.

PyList_GET_ITEM

`PyObject* PyList_GET_ITEM(PyObject* x,int pos)`

Returns the *pos* item of list *x*, without any error checking.

PyList_SET_ITEM

`int PyList_SET_ITEM(PyObject*` *x*`,int` *pos*`,PyObject*` *v*`)`

Sets the *pos* item of list *x* to *v*, without any error checking. Steals a reference to *v*. Use only immediately after creating a new list *x* with `PyList_New`.

PyString_AS_STRING

`char* PyString_AS_STRING(PyObject*` *x*`)`

Returns a pointer to the internal buffer of string *x*, very fast, without any error checking. You must not modify the buffer in any way, unless you just allocated it by calling `PyString_FromStringAndSize(NULL,`*size*`)`.

PyString_AsStringAndSize

`int PyString_AsStringAndSize(PyObject*` *x*`,char**` *buffer*`,int*` *length*`)`

Puts a pointer to the internal buffer of string *x* in `*`*buffer*, and *x*'s length in `*` *length*. You must not modify the buffer in any way, unless you just allocated it by calling `PyString_FromStringAndSize(NULL,`*size*`)`.

PyString_FromFormat

`PyObject* PyString_FromFormat(char*` *format*`,...)`

Returns a Python string built from format string *format*, which has syntax similar to `printf`'s, and the following C values indicated as variable arguments (`...`) above.

PyString_FromStringAndSize

`PyObject* PyString_FromFormat(char*` *data*`,int` *size*`)`

Returns a Python string of length *size*, copying *size* bytes from *data*. When *data* is `NULL`, the Python string is uninitialized, and you must initialize it. You can get the pointer to the string's internal buffer by calling `PyString_AS_STRING`.

PyTuple_New

`PyObject* PyTuple_New(int` *length*`)`

Returns a new, uninitialized tuple of the given *length*. You must then initialize the tuple, typically by calling `PyTuple_SET_ITEM` *length* times.

PyTuple_GET_ITEM

`PyObject* PyTuple_GET_ITEM(PyObject*` *x*`,int` *pos*`)`

Returns the *pos* item of tuple *x*, without error checking.

PyTuple_SET_ITEM

`int PyTuple_SET_ITEM(PyObject*` *x*`,int` *pos*`, PyObject*` *v*`)`

Sets the *pos* item of tuple *x* to *v*, without error checking. Steals a reference to *v*. Use only immediately after creating a new tuple *x* with `PyTuple_New`.

A Simple Extension Example

Example 24-1 exposes the functionality of Python C API functions `PyDict_Merge` and `PyDict_MergeFromSeq2` for Python use. The `update` method of `dicts` works like `PyDict_Merge` with *`override`*=1, but Example 24-1 is slightly more general.

Example 24-1. A simple Python extension module merge.c

```
#include <Python.h>

static PyObject*
merge(PyObject* self, PyObject* args, PyObject* kwds)
{
    static char* argnames[] = {"x","y","override",NULL};
    PyObject *x, *y;
    int override = 0;
    if(!PyArg_ParseTupleAndKeywords(args, kwds, "O!O|i", argnames,
        &PyDict_Type, &x, &y, &override))
            return NULL;
    if(-1 == PyDict_Merge(x, y, override)) {
        if(!PyErr_ExceptionMatches(PyExc_TypeError))
            return NULL;
        PyErr_Clear();
        if(-1 == PyDict_MergeFromSeq2(x, y, override))
            return NULL;
    }
    return Py_BuildValue("");
}

static char merge_docs[] = "\
merge(x,y,override=False): merge into dict x the items of dict y (or\n\
  the pairs that are the items of y, if y is a sequence), with\n\
  optional override. Alters dict x directly, returns None.\n\
";

static PyObject*
mergenew(PyObject* self, PyObject* args, PyObject* kwds)
{
    static char* argnames[] = {"x","y","override",NULL};
    PyObject *x, *y, *result;
    int override = 0;
    if(!PyArg_ParseTupleAndKeywords(args, kwds, "O!O|i", argnames,
        &PyDict_Type, &x, &y, &override))
            return NULL;
    result = PyObject_CallMethod(x, "copy", "");
    if(!result)
        return NULL;
    if(-1 == PyDict_Merge(result, y, override)) {
        if(!PyErr_ExceptionMatches(PyExc_TypeError))
            return NULL;
        PyErr_Clear( );
```

```
        if(-1 == PyDict_MergeFromSeq2(result, y, override))
            return NULL;
    }
    return result;
}

static char mergenew_docs[] = "\
mergenew(x,y,override=False): merge into dict x the items of dict y\n\
  (or the pairs that are the items of y, if y is a sequence), with\n\
  optional override. Does NOT alter x, but rather returns the\n\
  modified copy as the function's result.\n\
";

static PyMethodDef merge_funcs[] = {
    {"merge", (PyCFunction)merge, METH_KEYWORDS, merge_docs},
    {"mergenew", (PyCFunction)mergenew, METH_KEYWORDS, mergenew_docs},
    {NULL}
};

static char merge_module_docs[] = "Example extension module";

static struct PyModuleDef merge_module = {
   PyModuleDef_HEAD_INIT,
   "merge",
   merge_module_docs,
   -1,
   merge_funcs
};

PyMODINIT_FUNC
PyInit_merge(void)
{
    return PyModule_Create(&merge_module);
}
```

This example declares as `static` every function and global variable in the C source file except `PyInit_merge` (in v3; it would be named `initmerge` in v2), which must be visible from the outside so Python can call it. Since the functions and variables are exposed to Python via `PyMethodDef` structures, Python does not need to see their names directly. Therefore, declaring them `static` is best: this ensures that their names don't accidentally end up in the whole program's global namespace, as might otherwise happen on some platforms, possibly causing conflicts and errors.

The format string `"O!O|i"` passed to `PyArg_ParseTupleAndKeywords` indicates that the function `merge` accepts three arguments from Python: an object with a type constraint, a generic object, and an optional integer. At the same time, the format string indicates that the variable part of `PyArg_ParseTupleAndKeywords`'s arguments must contain four addresses in the following order: the address of a Python type object, two addresses of `PyObject*` variables, and the address of an `int` variable. The `int` variable must be previously initialized to its intended default value, since the corresponding Python argument is optional.

And indeed, after the *argnames* argument, the code passes &PyDict_Type (i.e., the address of the dictionary type object). Then it passes the addresses of the two PyObject* variables. Finally, it passes the address of the variable *override*, an int that was previously initialized to 0, since the default, when the *override* argument isn't explicitly passed from Python, is "no overriding." If the return value of PyArg_ParseTupleAndKeywords is 0, then the code immediately returns NULL to propagate the exception; this automatically diagnoses most cases where Python code passes wrong arguments to our new function merge.

When the arguments appear to be okay, it tries PyDict_Merge, which succeeds if *y* is a dictionary. When PyDict_Merge raises a TypeError, indicating that *y* is not a dictionary, the code clears the error and tries again, this time with PyDict_MergeFromSeq2, which succeeds when *y* is a sequence of pairs. If that also fails, it returns NULL to propagate the exception. Otherwise, it returns None in the simplest way (i.e., with return Py_BuildValue("")) to indicate success.

The mergenew function basically duplicates merge's functionality; however, mergenew does not alter its arguments, but rather builds and returns a new dictionary as the function's result. The C API function PyObject_CallMethod lets mergenew call the copy method of its first Python-passed argument, a dictionary object, and obtain a new dictionary object that it then alters (with exactly the same logic as the merge function). It then returns the altered dictionary as the function result (thus, there's no need to call Py_BuildValue in this case).

The code of Example 24-1 must reside in a source file named *merge.c*. In the same directory, create the following script named *setup.py*:

```
from setuptools import setup, Extension
setup(name='merge',
      ext_modules=[Extension('merge',sources=['merge.c'])])
```

Extend and Embed Python

Now, run **python setup.py install** at a shell prompt in this directory (with a user ID having appropriate privileges to write into your Python installation, or use **sudo** on Unix-like systems if necessary—or, best, use a virtual environment!). This command builds the dynamically loaded library for the merge extension module, and copies it to the appropriate directory for your Python installation. Now Python code (in the appropriate virtual environment, if you have, as recommended, used venv) can use the module. For example:

```
import merge
x = {'a':1,'b':2 }
merge.merge(x,[['b',3],['c',4]])
print(x)                              # prints: {'a':1, 'b':2, 'c':4 }
print(merge.mergenew(x,{'a':5,'d':6},override=1))
# prints: {'a':5, 'b':2, 'c':4, 'd':6 }
print(x)                              # prints: {'a':1, 'b':2, 'c':4 }
```

This example shows the difference between `merge` (which alters its first argument) and `mergenew` (which returns a new object and does not alter its argument). It also shows that the second argument can be either a dictionary or a sequence of two-item subsequences. It also demonstrates the default operation (where keys that are already in the first argument are left alone) versus the `override` option (where keys coming from the second argument take precedence, as in Python dictionaries' `update` method).

Defining New Types

In your extension modules, you often want to define new types and make them available to Python. A type's definition is held in a struct named `PyTypeObject`. Most of the fields of `PyTypeObject` are pointers to functions. Some fields point to other structs, which in turn are blocks of pointers to functions. `PyTypeObject` also includes a few fields that give the type's name, size, and behavior details (option flags). You can leave almost all fields of `PyTypeObject` set to `NULL` if you do not supply the related functionality. You can point some fields to functions in the Python C API in order to supply fundamental object functionality in standard ways.

The best way to implement a type is to copy from the Python sources one of three files in the directory *Modules*, which Python supplies exactly for such didactical purposes, and edit it. The files are named *xxlimited.c* (v3 only), *xxmodule.c*, and *xxsubtype.c* (the latter focused on subclassing built-in types, with two types, one each subclassing from `list` and `dict`, respectively).

See the online docs (*https://docs.python.org/3/c-api/typeobj.html*) for detailed documentation on `PyTypeObject` and other related structs. The file *Include/object.h* in the Python sources contains the declarations of these types, as well as several important comments that you would do well to study.

Per-instance data

To represent each instance of your type, declare a C struct that starts, right after the opening brace, with the macro `PyObject_HEAD`. The macro expands into the data fields that your struct must begin with in order to be a Python object. These fields include the reference count and a pointer to the instance's type. Any pointer to your structure can be correctly cast to a `PyObject*`. You can choose to look at this practice as a kind of C-level implementation of a (single) inheritance mechanism.

The `PyTypeObject` struct defining your type's characteristics and behavior must contain the size of your per-instance struct, as well as pointers to the C functions you write to operate on your structure. Thus, you normally place the `PyTypeObject` toward the end of your C-coded module's source code, after the definitions of the per-instance struct, and of all the functions operating on instances of the per-instance struct. Each *x* pointing to a `struct` starting with `PyObject_HEAD`, and in particular each `PyObject*` *x*, has a field *x*`->ob_type` that is the address of the `PyTypeObject` structure that is *x*'s Python type object.

The PyTypeObject definition

Given a per-instance struct such as:

```
typedef struct {
    PyObject_HEAD
    /* other data needed by instances of this type, omitted */
} mytype;
```

the related PyTypeObject struct, almost invariably, begins in a way similar to:

```
static PyTypeObject t_mytype = {
/* tp_head */       PyObject_HEAD_INIT(NULL)   /* use NULL for MSVC++ */
/* tp_internal */   0,                    /* must be 0 */
/* tp_name */       "mymodule.mytype", /* type name, including module */
/* tp_basicsize */  sizeof(mytype),
/* tp_itemsize */   0,                    /* 0 except variable-size type */
/* tp_dealloc */    (destructor)mytype_dealloc,
/* tp_print */      0,                    /* usually 0, use str instead */
/* tp_getattr */    0,                    /* usually 0 (see getattro) */
/* tp_setattr */    0,                    /* usually 0 (see setattro) */
/* tp_compare*/     0,                    /* see also richcompare */
/* tp_repr */       (reprfunc)mytype_str,  /* like Python's __repr__ */
    /* rest of struct omitted */
```

For portability to Microsoft Visual C++, the PyObject_HEAD_INIT macro at the start of the PyTypeObject must have an argument of NULL. During module initialization, you must call PyType_Ready(&t_mytype), which, among other tasks, inserts in t_mytype the address of its type (the type of a type is also known as a *metatype*), normally &PyType_Type. Another slot in PyTypeObject pointing to another type object is tp_base, which comes later in the structure. In the structure definition itself, you must have a tp_base of NULL, again for compatibility with Microsoft Visual C++. However, before you invoke PyType_Ready(&t_mytype), you can optionally set t_mytype.tp_base to the address of another type object. When you do so, your type inherits from the other type, just as a class coded in Python can optionally inherit from a built-in type. For a Python type coded in C, "inheriting" means that, for most fields of PyTypeObject, if you set the field to NULL, PyType_Ready copies the corresponding field from the base type. A type must explicitly assert in its field tp_flags that it's usable as a base type; otherwise, no type can inherit from it.

The tp_itemsize field is of interest only for types that, like tuples, have instances of different sizes, and can determine instance size once and forever at creation time. Most types just set tp_itemsize to 0. The fields tp_getattr and tp_setattr are generally set to NULL because they exist only for backward compatibility; modern types use the fields tp_getattro and tp_setattro instead. The tp_repr field is typical of most of the following fields, which are omitted here: the field holds the address of a function, which corresponds directly to a Python special method (here, __repr__). You can set the field to NULL, indicating that your type does not supply the special method, or else set the field to point to a function with the needed functionality. If you set the field to NULL but also point to a base type from the tp_base slot, you inherit the special method, if any, from your base type. You often need to cast your functions to the specific `typedef` type that a field needs (here, the `reprfunc` type for the `tp_repr` field) because the `typedef` has a first argument `PyObject* self`, while your functions—being specific to your type—normally use more specific pointers. For example:

```
static PyObject* mytype_str(mytype* self) { ... /* rest omitted */
```

Alternatively, you can declare `mytype_str` with a `PyObject* self`, then use a cast `(mytype*)self` in the function's body. Either alternative is acceptable style, but it's more common to locate the casts in the `PyTypeObject` declaration.

Instance initialization and finalization

The task of finalizing your instances is split among two functions. The `tp_dealloc` slot must never be `NULL`, except for immortal types (i.e., types whose instances are never deallocated). Python calls `x->ob_type->tp_dealloc(x)` on each instance *x* whose reference count decreases to `0`, and the function thus called must release any resource held by object *x*, including *x*'s memory. When an instance of `mytype` holds no other resources that must be released (in particular, no owned references to other Python objects that you would have to `DECREF`), `mytype`'s destructor can be extremely simple:

```
static void mytype_dealloc(PyObject *x)
{
    x->ob_type->tp_free((PyObject*)x);
}
```

The function in the `tp_free` slot has the specific task of freeing *x*'s memory. Often, you can just put in slot `tp_free` the address of the C API function `_PyObject_Del`.

The task of initializing your instances is split among three functions. To allocate memory for new instances of your type, put in slot `tp_alloc` the C API function `PyType_GenericAlloc`, which does absolutely minimal initialization, clearing the newly allocated memory bytes to `0` except for the type pointer and reference count. Similarly, you can often set field `tp_new` to the C API function `PyType_GenericNew`. In this case, you can perform all per-instance initialization in the function you put in slot `tp_init`, which has the signature:

```
int init_name(PyObject *self,PyObject *args,PyObject *kwds)
```

The positional and named arguments to the function in slot `tp_init` are those passed when calling the type to create the new instance, just as, in Python, the positional and named arguments to `__init__` are those passed when calling the class. Again, as for types (classes) defined in Python, the general rule is to do as little initialization as feasible in `tp_new` and do as much as possible in `tp_init`. Using `PyType_GenericNew` for `tp_new` accomplishes this. However, you can choose to define your own `tp_new` for special types, such as ones that have immutable instances, where initialization must happen earlier. The signature is:

```
PyObject* new_name(PyObject *subtype,PyObject *args,PyObject *kwds)
```

The function in `tp_new` returns the newly created instance, normally an instance of *subtype* (which may be a subtype of yours). The function in `tp_init`, on the other hand, must return `0` for success, or `-1` to indicate an exception.

If your type is subclassable, it's important that any instance invariants be established before the function in `tp_new` returns. For example, if it must be guaranteed that a certain field of the instance is never `NULL`, that field must be set to a non-`NULL` value by the function in `tp_new`. Subtypes of your type might fail to call your `tp_init` function; therefore, such indispensable initializations, needed to establish type invariants, should always be in `tp_new` for subclassable types.

Attribute access

Access to attributes of your instances, including methods (as covered in "Attribute Reference Basics" on page 110), goes through the functions in slots `tp_getattro` and `tp_setattro` of your `PyTypeObject` struct. Normally, you use the standard C API functions `PyObject_GenericGetAttr` and `PyObject_GenericSetAttr`, which implement standard semantics. Specifically, these API functions access your type's methods via the slot `tp_methods`, pointing to a sentinel-terminated array of `PyMethodDef` structs, and your instances' members via the slot `tp_members`, a sentinel-terminated array of `PyMemberDef` structs:

```
typedef struct {
    char* name;      /* Python-visible name of the member */
    int type;        /* code defining the data-type of the member */
    int offset;      /* member's offset in the per-instance struct */
    int flags;       /* READONLY for a read-only member */
    char* doc;       /* docstring for the member */
} PyMemberDef;
```

As an exception to the general rule that including *Python.h* gets you all the declarations you need, you have to include *structmember.h* explicitly in order to have your C source see the declaration of `PyMemberDef`.

type is generally `T_OBJECT` for members that are `PyObject*`, but many other type codes are defined in *Include/structmember.h* for members that your instances hold as C-native data (e.g., `T_DOUBLE` for `double` or `T_STRING` for `char*`). For example, say that your per-instance struct is something like this:

```
typedef struct {
    PyObject_HEAD
    double datum;
    char* name;
} mytype;
```

Expose to Python the per-instance attributes *datum* (read/write) and *name* (read-only) by defining the following array and pointing your `PyTypeObject`'s `tp_members` to it:

```
static PyMemberDef[] mytype_members = {
    {"datum", T_DOUBLE, offsetof(mytype, datum), 0, "Current datum"},
    {"name", T_STRING, offsetof(mytype, name), READONLY, "Datum name"},
    {NULL}
};
```

Using `PyObject_GenericGetAttr` and `PyObject_GenericSetAttr` for `tp_getattro` and `tp_setattro` also provides further possibilities, which we do not cover in detail in this book. `tp_getset` points to a sentinel-terminated array of `PyGetSetDef` structs, the equivalent of having `property` instances in a Python-coded class. If your `PyTypeObject`'s field `tp_dictoffset` is not equal to `0`, the field's value must be the offset, within the per-instance struct, of a `PyObject*` that points to a Python dictionary. In this case, the generic attribute access API functions use that dictionary to allow Python code to set arbitrary attributes on your type's instances, just like for instances of Python-coded classes.

Another dictionary is per-type, not per-instance: the `PyObject*` for the per-type dictionary is slot `tp_dict` of your `PyTypeObject` struct. You can set slot `tp_dict` to `NULL`, and then `PyType_Ready` initializes the dictionary appropriately. Alternatively, you can set `tp_dict` to a dictionary of type attributes, and then `PyType_Ready` adds other entries to that same dictionary, in addition to the type attributes you set. It's generally easier to start with `tp_dict` set to `NULL`, call `PyType_Ready` to create and initialize the per-type dictionary, and then, if need be, add any further entries to the dictionary via explicit C code.

Field `tp_flags` is a `long` whose bits determine your type struct's exact layout, mostly for backward compatibility. Set this field to `Py_TPFLAGS_DEFAULT` to indicate that you are defining a normal, modern type. Set `tp_flags` to `Py_TPFLAGS_DEFAULT|Py_TPFLAGS_HAVE_GC` if your type supports cyclic garbage collection. Your type should support cyclic garbage collection if instances of the type contain `PyObject*` fields that might point to arbitrary objects and form part of a reference loop. To support cyclic garbage collection, it's not enough to add `Py_TPFLAGS_HAVE_GC` to field `tp_flags`; you also have to supply appropriate functions, indicated by the slots `tp_traverse` and `tp_clear`, and register and unregister your instances appropriately with the cyclic garbage collector. Supporting cyclic garbage collection is an advanced subject, and we don't cover it further in this book; see the online docs (*https://docs.python.org/3/c-api/gcsupport.html*). Similarly, we don't cover the advanced subject of supporting weak references, also well covered online (*https://docs.python.org/3/extending/newtypes.html#weakref-support*).

The field `tp_doc`, a `char*`, is a null-terminated character string that is your type's docstring. Other fields point to structs (whose fields point to functions); you can set each such field to `NULL` to indicate that you support none of those functions. The fields pointing to such blocks of functions are `tp_as_number`, for special methods typically supplied by numbers; `tp_as_sequence`, for special methods typically supplied by sequences; `tp_as_mapping`, for special methods typically supplied by mappings; and `tp_as_buffer`, for the special methods of the buffer protocol.

For example, objects that are not sequences can still support one or a few of the methods listed in the block to which `tp_as_sequence` points, and in this case the `PyTypeObject` must have a non-`NULL` field `tp_as_sequence`, even if the block of function pointers it points to is in turn mostly full of `NULL`s. For example, dictionaries supply a `__contains__` special method so that you can check if *x* `in` *d* when *d* is a dictionary. At the C code level, the method is a function pointed to by the field `sq_contains`, which is part of the `PySequenceMethods` struct to which the field `tp_as_sequence` points. Therefore, the `PyTypeObject` struct for the `dict` type, named `PyDict_Type`, has a non-`NULL` value for `tp_as_sequence`, even though a dictionary supplies no other field in `PySequenceMethods` except `sq_contains`, and therefore all other fields in `*(PyDict_Type.tp_as_sequence)` are `NULL`.

Type definition example

Example 24-2 is a complete Python extension module that defines the very simple type `intpair`, each instance of which holds two integers named `first` and `second`.

Example 24-2. Defining a new intpair type

```
#include "Python.h"
#include "structmember.h"

/* per-instance data structure */
typedef struct {
    PyObject_HEAD
    int first, second;
} intpair;

static int
intpair_init(PyObject *self, PyObject *args, PyObject *kwds)
{
    static char* nams[] = {"first","second",NULL};
    int first, second;
    if(!PyArg_ParseTupleAndKeywords(args, kwds, "ii", nams, &first, &second))
        return -1;
    ((intpair*)self)->first = first;
    ((intpair*)self)->second = second;
    return 0;
}

static void
intpair_dealloc(PyObject *self)
{
    self->ob_type->tp_free(self);
}

static PyObject*
intpair_str(PyObject* self)
{
```

```
    return PyString_FromFormat("intpair(%d,%d)",
        ((intpair*)self)->first, ((intpair*)self)->second);
}

static PyMemberDef intpair_members[] = {
    {"first", T_INT, offsetof(intpair, first), 0, "first item" },
    {"second", T_INT, offsetof(intpair, second), 0, "second item" },
    {NULL}
};

static PyTypeObject t_intpair = {
    PyObject_HEAD_INIT(0)                   /* tp_head */
    0,                                      /* tp_internal */
    "intpair.intpair",                      /* tp_name */
    sizeof(intpair),                        /* tp_basicsize */
    0,                                      /* tp_itemsize */
    intpair_dealloc,                        /* tp_dealloc */
    0,                                      /* tp_print */
    0,                                      /* tp_getattr */
    0,                                      /* tp_setattr */
    0,                                      /* tp_compare */
    intpair_str,                            /* tp_repr */
    0,                                      /* tp_as_number */
    0,                                      /* tp_as_sequence */
    0,                                      /* tp_as_mapping */
    0,                                      /* tp_hash */
    0,                                      /* tp_call */
    0,                                      /* tp_str */
    PyObject_GenericGetAttr,                /* tp_getattro */
    PyObject_GenericSetAttr,                /* tp_setattro */
    0,                                      /* tp_as_buffer */
    Py_TPFLAGS_DEFAULT,
    "two ints (first,second)",
    0,                                      /* tp_traverse */
    0,                                      /* tp_clear */
    0,                                      /* tp_richcompare */
    0,                                      /* tp_weaklistoffset */
    0,                                      /* tp_iter */
    0,                                      /* tp_iternext */
    0,                                      /* tp_methods */
    intpair_members,                        /* tp_members */
    0,                                      /* tp_getset */
    0,                                      /* tp_base */
    0,                                      /* tp_dict */
    0,                                      /* tp_descr_get */
    0,                                      /* tp_descr_set */
    0,                                      /* tp_dictoffset */
    intpair_init,                           /* tp_init */
    PyType_GenericAlloc,                    /* tp_alloc */
    PyType_GenericNew,                      /* tp_new */
    _PyObject_Del,                          /* tp_free */
};
```

```
static PyMethodDef no_methods[] = { {NULL} };

static char intpair_docs[] =
    "intpair: data type with int members .first, .second\n";

static struct PyModuleDef intpair_module = {
   PyModuleDef_HEAD_INIT,
   "intpair",
   intpair_docs,
   -1,
   no_methods
};

PyMODINIT_FUNC
PyInit_intpair(void)
{
    PyObject* this_module = PyModule_Create(&intpair_module);
    PyType_Ready(&t_intpair);
    PyObject_SetAttrString(this_module, "intpair", (PyObject*)&t_intpair);
    return this_module;
}
```

The `intpair` type defined in Example 24-2 gives just about no substantial benefits when compared to an equivalent definition in Python, such as:

```
class intpair(object):
    __slots__ = 'first', 'second'
    def __init__(self, first, second):
        self.first = first
        self.second = second
    def __repr__(self):
        return 'intpair(%s,%s)' % (self.first, self.second)
```

The C-coded version does, however, ensure that the two attributes are integers, truncating float or complex number arguments as needed (in Python, you could approximate that functionality by passing the arguments through `int`—but it still wouldn't be quite the same thing, as Python would then also accept argument values such as string `'23'`, while the C version wouldn't). For example:

```
import intpair
x=intpair.intpair(1.2,3.4)                  # x is: intpair(1,3)
```

The C-coded version of `intpair` occupies a little less memory than the Python version. However, the purpose of Example 24-2 is purely didactic: to present a C-coded Python extension that defines a simple new type.

Extending Python Without Python's C API

You can code Python extensions in other classic compiled languages besides C. For Fortran, we recommend Pearu Peterson's F2PY (*https://pypi.python.org/pypi/F2PY/*

Extend and Embed Python

2.45.241_1926). It is now part of NumPy (*http://www.numpy.org/*), since Fortran is often used for numeric processing. If, as recommended, you have installed `numpy`, then you don't need to also separately install `f2py`.

For C++, you can of course use the same approaches as for C (adding `extern "C"` where needed). Many C++-specific alternatives exist, but, out of them all, SIP (*https://riverbankcomputing.com/software/sip/intro*) appears to be the only one to be still actively maintained and supported.

A popular alternative is Cython (*http://cython.org/*)—a "Python dialect" focused on generating C code from Python-like syntax, with a few additions centered on precise specification of the C-level side of things. We highly recommend it, and cover it in "Cython" on page 682.

Yet another alternative is CFFI (*https://pypi.python.org/pypi/cffi*)—originated in the PyPy project, and perfect for it, but also fully supporting CPython. The "ABI online" mode of CFFI matches the standard Python library module `ctypes` (*https://docs.python.org/3/library/ctypes.html*), mentioned in the next section, but CFFI has vast added value, especially the ability to generate and compile C code ("offline," in CFFI's terminology) as well as interfacing at the stabler API, rather than ABI, level.

ctypes

The `ctypes` (*https://docs.python.org/3/library/ctypes.html*) module of the Python standard library lets you load existing C-coded dynamic libraries, and call—in your Python code—functions defined in those libraries. The module is rather popular, because it allows handy "hacks" without needing access to a C compiler or even a third-party Python extension. However, the resulting program can be quite fragile, very platform-dependent, and hard to port to other versions of the same libraries, as it relies on details of their *binary* interfaces.

We recommend avoiding `ctypes` in production code, and using instead one of the excellent alternatives covered or mentioned in this chapter, particularly `CFFI` or, even better, `cython`.

Cython

The Cython (*http://cython.org/*) language, a "friendly fork" of Greg Ewing's pyrex (*http://www.cosc.canterbury.ac.nz/greg.ewing/python/Pyrex/*), is often the most convenient way to write extensions for Python. Cython is a nearly complete subset of Python (with a declared intention of eventually becoming a complete superset of it[1], with the addition of optional C-like types for variables: you can automatically compile Cython programs (source files with extension *.pyx*) into machine code (via an

1 Mostly v2 by default, but you can run Cython with the **`-3`** switch, or include **`# cython: language_level=3`** at the top of the source, to have Cython support v3 instead—strings being Unicode, print being a function, and so forth.)

intermediate stage of generated C code), producing Python-importable extensions. See the preceding URL for deep, thorough, excellent documentation of all details of Cython programming; in this section, we cover only a few essentials to help you get started with Cython.

Cython implements almost all of Python, with four marginal, minor differences (*http://docs.cython.org/en/latest/src/userguide/limitations.html*) that the Cython authors do not intend to fix, and a few more small differences that are considered bugs in current Cython and the authors plan to fix soon (it would be pointless to list them here, as it's quite possible that by the time you read this they may be fixed).

So, Cython is a vast subset indeed of Python. More importantly, Cython adds to Python a few statements that allow C-like declarations, enabling generation of efficient machine code (via a C-code generation step). Here is a simple example; code it in source file *hello.pyx* in a new empty directory:

```
def hello(char *name):
    return 'Hello, ' + name + '!'
```

This is almost exactly like Python—except that parameter `name` is preceded by a `char*`, declaring that its type must always be a C `0`-terminated string (but, as you see from the body, in Cython, you can use its value as a normal Python string).

When you install Cython (by the download-then-**`python setup.py install`** route, or just **`pip install cython`**), you also gain a way to build Cython source files into Python dynamic-library extensions through the `distutils` approach. Code the following in file *setup.py* in the new directory:

```
from setuptools import setup
from Cython.Build import cythonize

setup(name='hello',ext_modules=cythonize('hello.pyx'))
```

Now run **`python setup.py install`** in the new directory (ignore compilation warnings; they're fully expected and benign). Now you can import and use the new module—for example, from an interactive Python session:

```
>>> import hello
>>> hello.hello('Alex')
'Hello, Alex!'
```

Given how we've coded this Cython, we *must* pass a string to `hello.hello`; passing no arguments, >1 argument, or a nonstring, raises an exception:

```
>>> hello.hello()
Traceback (most recent call last):
  File "<stdin>", line 1, in ?
TypeError: function takes exactly 1 argument (0 given)
>>> hello.hello(23)
Traceback (most recent call last):
  File "<stdin>", line 1, in ?
TypeError: argument 1 must be string, not int
```

The cdef and cpdef Statements and Function Parameters

You can use the keyword `cdef` mostly as you would `def`, but `cdef` defines functions that are internal to the extension module and are not visible on the outside, while `def` functions can also be called by Python code that imports the module. `cpdef` functions can be called both internally (with speed very close to `cdef` ones) and by external Python (just like `def` ones), but are otherwise identical to `cdef` ones.

For any kind of function, parameters and return values with unspecified types—or, better, ones explicitly typed as `object`—become `PyObject*` pointers in the generated C code (with implicit and standard handling of reference incrementing and decrementing). `cdef` functions may also have parameters and return values of any other C type; `def` functions, in addition to untyped (or, equivalently, `object`) arguments, can only accept `int`, `float`, and `char*` types. For example, here's a `cdef` function to specifically sum two integers:

```
cdef int sum2i(int a, int b):
    return a + b
```

You can also use `cdef` to declare C variables—scalars, arrays, and pointers like in C:

```
cdef int x, y[23], *z
```

and `struct`, `union`, `enum` Pythonically (colon on head clause, then indent):

```
cdef struct Ure:
    int x, y
    float z
```

(Afterward, refer to the new type by name only—e.g., *`Ure`*. Never use the keywords `struct`, `union`, and `enum` except in the `cdef` declaring the type.)

External declarations

To interface with external C code, you can declare variables as `cdef extern`, with the same effect that `extern` has in the C language. More commonly, the C declarations of some library you want to use are in a *.h* C header file; to ensure that the Cython-generated C code includes that header file, use the following `cdef`:

```
cdef extern from "someheader.h":
```

and follow with a block of indented `cdef`-style declarations (*without* repeating the `cdef` in the block). Only declare functions and variables that you want to use in your Cython code. Cython does not read the C header file—it trusts your Cython declarations in the block, not generating any C code for them. Cython implicitly uses the Python C API, covered at the start of this chapter, but you can explicitly access any of its functions. For example, if your Cython file contains:

```
cdef extern from "Python.h":
    object PyString_FromStringAndSize(char *, int)
```

the following Cython code can use PyString_FromStringAndSize. This may come in handy, since, by default, C "strings" are deemed to be terminated by a zero character—but with this function you may instead explicitly specify a C string's length and also get any zero character(s) it may contain.

Conveniently, Cython lets you group such declarations in *.pxd* files (roughly analogous to C's *.h* files, while *.pyx* Cython files are roughly analogous to C's *.c* files). *.pxd* files can also include `cdef inline` declarations, to be inlined at compile time. A *.pyx* file can import the declarations in a *.pxd* one by using keyword `cimport`, analogous to Python's `import`.

Moreover, Cython comes with several prebuilt *.pxd* files in its directory *Cython/includes*. In particular, the *.pxd* file *cpython* already has all the `cdef extern from "Python.h"` you might want: just `cimport cpython` to access them.

cdef classes

A `cdef class` statement lets you define a new Python type in Cython. It may include `cdef` declarations of attributes (which apply to every instance, not to the type as a whole), which are normally invisible from Python code; however, you can specifically declare attributes as `cdef public` to make them normal attributes from Python's viewpoint, or `cdef readonly` to make them visible but read-only from Python (Python-visible attributes must be numbers, strings, or `object`s).

A `cdef class` supports special methods (with some caveats), properties (with a special syntax), and inheritance (single inheritance only). To declare a property, use the following within the body of the `cdef class`:

```
property name:
```

followed by indented `def` statements for methods `__get__(self)` and optionally `__set__(self, value)` and `__del__(self)`.

A `cdef class`'s `__new__` is different from that of a normal Python class: the first argument is `self`, the new instance, already allocated and with its memory filled with `0`s. Cython always calls the special method `__cinit__(self)` right after the instance allocation, to allow further initialization; `__init__`, if defined, is called next. At object destruction time, Cython calls special method `__dealloc__(self)` to let you undo whatever allocations `__new__` and/or `__cinit__` have done (`cdef class`es have no `__del__` special method).

There are no *righthand-side* versions of arithmetic special methods, such as `__radd__` to go with `__add__`, like in Python; rather, if (say) `a+b` can't find or use `type(a).__add__`, it next calls `type(b).__add__(a, b)`—note the order of arguments (*no* swapping!). You may need to attempt some type checking to ensure that you perform the correct operation in all cases.

To make the instances of a `cdef class` into iterators, define a special method `__next__(self)`, like in v3 (even when you're using Cython with v2).

Here is a Cython equivalent of Example 24-2:

```
cdef class intpair:
    cdef public int first, second
    def __init__(self, first, second):
        self.first = first
        self.second = second
    def __repr__(self):
        return 'intpair(%s,%s)' % (self.first, self.second)
```

Like the C-coded extension in Example 24-2, this Cython-coded extension also offers no substantial advantage with respect to a Python-coded equivalent. However, the simplicity and conciseness of the Cython code is much closer to that of Python than to the verbosity and boilerplate needed in C, yet the machine code generated from this Cython file is very close to what gets generated from the C code in Example 24-2.

The ctypedef Statement

You can use the keyword `ctypedef` to declare a name (synonym) for a type:

```
ctypedef char* string
```

The for...from Statement

In addition to the usual Python `for` statements, Cython has another form of `for`:

```
for variable from lower_expression<=variable<upper_expression:
```

This is the most common form, but you can use either < or <= on either side of the *`variable`* after the `from` keyword; alternatively, you can use > and/or >= to have a backward loop (you cannot mix a < or <= on one side and > or >= on the other).

The `for...from` statement is much faster than the usual Python `for` *`variable`* `in range(...):`, when the variable and loop boundaries are C-kind `int`s. However, in modern Cython, `for` *`variable`* `in range(...):` is optimized to near equivalence to `for...from`, so the classic Pythonic `for` *`variable`* `in range(...):` can usually be chosen for simplicity and readability.

Cython Expressions

In addition to Python expression syntax, Cython can use some, but not all, of C's additions to it. To take the address of variable *`var`*, use `&`*`var`*, like in C. To dereference a pointer *`p`*, however, use *`p`*`[0]`; the equivalent C syntax `*`*`p`* is not valid Cython. Where in C you would use *`p`*`->`*`q`*, use *`p`*`.`*`q`* in Cython. The null pointer uses the Cython keyword `NULL`. For char constants, use the syntax `c'x'`. For casts, use angle brackets—such as `<int>`*`somefloat`* where in C you would code `(int)`*`somefloat`*; also, use casts only on C values and onto C types, *never* with Python values and types (let Cython perform type conversion for you automatically when Python values or types occur).

A Cython Example: Greatest Common Divisor

Euclid's algorithm for GCD (Greatest Common Divisor) of two numbers is quite simple to implement in pure Python:

```
def gcd(dividend, divisor):
    remainder = dividend % divisor
    while remainder:
        dividend = divisor
        divisor = remainder
        remainder = dividend % divisor
    return divisor
```

The Cython version is very similar:

```
def gcd(int dividend, int divisor):
    cdef int remainder
    remainder = dividend % divisor
    while remainder:
        dividend = divisor
        divisor = remainder
        remainder = dividend % divisor
    return divisor
```

On a Macbook Air laptop, `gcd(454803,278255)` takes about 1 microsecond in the Python version, while the Cython version takes 0.22 microseconds. A speed-up of four-plus times for so little effort can be well worth the bother (assuming, of course, that this function takes up a substantial fraction of your program's execution time!), even though the pure Python version has practical advantages (it runs in Jython, IronPython, or PyPy just as well as in CPython; it works with `long`s just as well as with `int`s; it's effortlessly cross-platform; and so on).

Embedding Python

If you have an application already written in C or C++ (or another classic compiled language), you may want to embed Python as your application's scripting language. To embed Python in languages other than C, the other language must be able to call C functions (how you do that varies, not just by language, but by specific implementation of the language: what compiler, what linker, and so on). In the following, we cover the C view of things; other languages, as mentioned, vary widely regarding what you have to do in order to call C functions from them.

Installing Resident Extension Modules

In order for Python scripts to communicate with your application, your application must supply extension modules with Python-accessible functions and classes that expose your application's functionality. When, as is normal, these modules are linked with your application (rather than residing in dynamic libraries that Python can load when necessary), register your modules with Python as additional built-in modules by calling the `PyImport_AppendInittab` C API function:

PyImport_AppendInittab `int PyImport_AppendInittab(char* name,void (*initfunc)(void))`

name is the module name, which Python scripts use to `import` the module. *initfunc* is the module initialization function, taking no argument and returning no result, as covered in "The Initialization Module" on page 650 (i.e., *initfunc* is the module's function that would be named `init`*name* for a normal extension module in a dynamic library in v2). Call `PyImport_AppendInittab` *before* `Py_Initialize`.

Setting Arguments

You may want to set the program name and arguments, which Python scripts can access as `sys.argv`, by calling either or both of the following C API functions:

Py_SetProgramName `void Py_SetProgramName(char* name)`

Sets the program name, which Python scripts can access as `sys.argv[0]`. Must be called *before* `Py_Initialize`.

PySys_SetArgv `void PySys_SetArgv(int argc,char** argv)`

Sets the program arguments, which Python scripts can access as `sys.argv[1:]`, to the *argc* `0`-terminated strings in array *argv*. Must be called *after* `Py_Initialize`.

Python Initialization and Finalization

After installing extra built-in modules and optionally setting the program name, your application initializes Python. At the end, when Python is no longer needed, your application finalizes Python. The relevant functions in the C API are as follows:

Py_Finalize `void Py_Finalize(void)`

Frees all memory and other resources that Python is able to free. You should not make any other Python C API call after calling this function.

Py_Initialize `void Py_Initialize(void)`

Initializes the Python environment. Make no other Python C API call before this one, except `PyImport_AppendInittab` and `Py_SetProgramName`.

Running Python Code

Your application can run Python source code from a character string or from a file. To run or compile Python source code, choose the mode of execution as one of the following three constants defined in *Python.h*:

`Py_eval_input`
: The code is an expression to evaluate (like passing `'eval'` to the Python built-in function `compile`).

`Py_file_input`
: The code is a block of one or more statements to execute (like `'exec'` for `compile`; just like in that case, a trailing `'\n'` must close compound statements).

`Py_single_input`
: The code is a single statement for interactive execution (like `'single'` for `compile`; implicitly outputs the results of expression statements).

Running Python source code is similar to passing a source code string to Python's `exec` or `eval`, or, in v2, a source code file to the built-in function `execfile`. Two general functions you can use for this task are the following:

PyRun_File `PyObject* PyRun_File(FILE* fp,char* filename,int start, PyObject* globals,PyObject* locals)`

fp is a file of Python source code open for reading. *filename* is the name of the file, to use in error messages. *start* is one of the constants `Py_..._input` that define execution mode. *globals* and *locals* are `dicts` (may be the same dictionary twice) to use as global and local namespace for the execution. Returns the result of the expression when *start* is `Py_eval_input`, a new reference to `Py_None` otherwise, or `NULL` to indicate that an exception has been raised.

PyRun_String `PyObject* PyRun_String(char* astring,int start, PyObject* globals,PyObject* locals)`

Like `PyRun_File`, but the source is in the null-terminated string *astring*.

The dictionaries *locals* and *globals* are often new, empty `dicts` (conveniently built by `Py_BuildValue("{}")`) or the dictionary of a module. `PyImport_Import` is a convenient way to get an existing module object; `PyModule_GetDict` gets a module's dictionary.

When you want to create a new module object on the fly, often in order to populate it with `PyRun_` calls, use the `PyModule_New` C API function:

PyModule_New `PyObject* PyModule_New(char& name)`

Returns a new, empty module object for a module named *name*. Before the new object is usable, you must add to the object a string attribute named `__file__`. For example:

```
PyObject* newmod = PyModule_New("mymodule");
PyModule_AddStringConstant(newmod,"__file__","<synth>");
```

After this code runs, the module object *newmod* is ready; you can obtain the module's dictionary with `PyModule_GetDict(newmod)` and pass the `dict` to such functions as `PyRun_String` as the *globals* and possibly the *locals* argument.

To run Python code repeatedly, and to separate the diagnosis of syntax errors from that of runtime exceptions raised by the code when it runs, you can compile the Python source to a code object, then keep the code object and run it repeatedly. This is just as true when using the C API as when dynamically executing in Python, as covered in "Dynamic Execution and exec" on page 383. Two C API functions you can use for this task are the following:

Py_CompileString `PyObject* Py_CompileString(char* code,char* filename, int start)`

code is a null-terminated string of source code. *filename* is the name of the file to use in error messages. *start* is one of the constants that define execution mode. Returns the Python code object that contains the bytecode, or `NULL` for syntax errors.

PyEval_EvalCode `PyObject* PyEval_EvalCode(PyObject* co,PyObject* globals, PyObject* locals)`

co is a Python code object, as returned by `Py_CompileString`, for example. *globals* and *locals* are dictionaries (may be the same dictionary twice) to use as global and local namespace for the execution. Returns the result of the expression when *co* was compiled with `Py_eval_input`, a new reference to `Py_None` otherwise, or `NULL` to indicate the execution has raised an exception.

25 Distributing Extensions and Programs

Python's `distutils` is part of the standard library, underlying the tools used for packaging and distributing Python programs and extensions. However, we don't recommend that you use `distutils` directly: use, instead, newer third-party tools. In most cases, you'll want to use `setuptools` and `wheels` to create *wheels*, then use `twine` to upload them to your favorite repository (usually PyPI, the Python Package Index, aka The Cheeseshop (*https://wiki.python.org/moin/CheeseShop*)) and `pip` to download and install them. If you do not have `pip` installed (it comes with v2 and v3), see pip's installation page (*http://bit.ly/2o9pAH4*). Be sure to use the most upgraded version of `pip`, by running **`pip install --upgrade pip`**. On Windows, run **`py -m pip install -U pip setuptools`** and then make sure `pip` is in your system PATH, similar to ensuring Python is on your PATH (*http://bit.ly/2mQEItb*).

In this chapter, we cover the simplest uses of `setuptools` and `twine` for the most common packaging needs. For more in-depth or advanced explanation, see the Python Packaging User Guide (*https://packaging.python.org/*). At the time of writing, the new PEP 518 (*https://www.python.org/dev/peps/pep-0518/*) specifies protocols for distributing extensions and programs with other build tools, but these are not yet supported, so we do not cover them in this book.

If you are looking to create and distribute complicated cross-platform or cloud-based apps, you may wish to explore Docker (*https://www.docker.com/*) containers; if you want a complete package manager, especially if you're doing data science/engineering, consider conda (*http://bit.ly/2mQFsOM*) (the base of both Miniconda (*http://bit.ly/1HVwnq5*) and Anaconda (*https://docs.continuum.io/*)); if you'd like a script installer that also manages your virtual environments, consider pipsi (*http://bit.ly/2nwZ085*).

setuptools

`setuptools` is a rich and flexible set of tools to package Python programs and extensions for distribution; we recommend that you use it in preference to the standard library's `distutils`.

The Distribution and Its Root

A *distribution* is the set of files to package into a single archive file for distribution purposes. A distribution may include Python packages and/or other Python modules (as covered in Chapter 6), as well as, optionally, Python scripts, C-coded (and other) extensions, data files, and auxiliary files with metadata. A distribution is said to be *pure* when all code it includes is Python, and *nonpure* when it includes non-Python code (usually, C-coded extensions). A distribution is *universal* when it is pure and can be used with either v2 or v3 without `2to3` conversion.

You usually place all the files of a distribution in a directory, known as the *distribution root*, and in subdirectories of the distribution root. Mostly, you can arrange the subtree of files and directories rooted at the distribution root to suit your needs. However, as covered in "Packages" on page 184, a Python package must reside in its own directory (unless you are creating namespace packages, covered in "Namespace Packages (v3 Only)" on page 186), and a package's directory must contain a file named *__init__.py* (and subdirectories with *__init__.py* files for the package's subpackages, if any) as well as other modules that belong to that package.

A distribution must include a *setup.py* script, and should include a *README* file (preferably in reStructuredText (*http://docutils.sourceforge.net/rst.html*) [*.rst*] format); it may also contain a *requirements.txt*, a *MANIFEST.in*, and a *setup.cfg*, covered in the following sections.

Testing your package during development

If you wish to test your package while still developing it, you may install it locally with **`pip install -e`**; the **`-e`** flag stands for "editable," and all details are well explained in the online docs (*http://bit.ly/2oiS0vq*).

The setup.py Script

The distribution root directory must contain a Python script that by convention is named *setup.py*. The *setup.py* script can, in theory, contain arbitrary Python code. However, in practice, *setup.py* always boils down to some variation of this:

```
from setuptools import setup, find_packages

setup( many named arguments go here )
```

You should also import `Extension` if your *setup.py* deals with a nonpure distribution. All the action is in the parameters you supply in the call to `setup`. It is fine, of course, to have a few statements before the call to `setup` in order to arrange `setup`'s arguments in clearer and more readable ways than could be managed by having everything inline as part of the setup call. For example, a *long_description* string may be provided from its own separate file, as in, for example:

```
with open('./README.rst') as f:
    long_desc=f.read()
```

The setup function accepts only named arguments, and there are a large number of such arguments that you could potentially supply. Named arguments to setup fall primarily into three groups: metadata about the distribution, information about which files are in the distribution, and information about dependencies. A simple example is the *setup.py* for Flask (covered in "Flask" on page 583), showing some of this metadata:

```
""" __doc__ for long_description goes here; omitted. """

import re
import ast
from setuptools import setup

_version_re = re.compile(r'__version__\s+=\s+(.*)')
with open('flask/__init__.py', 'rb') as f:
    version = str(ast.literal_eval(_version_re.search(
        f.read().decode('utf-8')).group(1)))

setup(
    name='Flask',
    version=version,
    url='http://github.com/pallets/flask/',
    license='BSD',
    author='Armin Ronacher',
    author_email='armin.ronacher@active-4.com',
    description='A microframework based on Werkzeug, Jinja2 '
                'and good intentions',
    long_description=__doc__,
    packages=['flask', 'flask.ext'],
    include_package_data=True,
    zip_safe=False,
    platforms='any',
    install_requires=[
        'Werkzeug>=0.7',
        'Jinja2>=2.4',
        'itsdangerous>=0.21',
        'click>=2.0',
    ],
    classifiers=[
        'Development Status :: 4 - Beta',
        'Environment :: Web Environment',
        'Intended Audience :: Developers',
        'License :: OSI Approved :: BSD License',
        'Operating System :: OS Independent',
        'Programming Language :: Python',
```

```
            'Programming Language :: Python :: 2',
            'Programming Language :: Python :: 2.6',
            'Programming Language :: Python :: 2.7',
            'Programming Language :: Python :: 3',
            'Programming Language :: Python :: 3.3',
            'Programming Language :: Python :: 3.4',
            'Programming Language :: Python :: 3.5',
            'Topic :: Internet :: WWW/HTTP :: Dynamic Content',
            'Topic :: Software Development :: Libraries :: Python Modules'
        ],
        entry_points='''
            [console_scripts]
            flask=flask.cli:main
        '''
    )
```

Metadata about the distribution

Provide metadata about the distribution, by supplying some of the following named arguments when you call the `setup` function. The value you associate with each argument name you supply is a string, intended mostly to be human-readable; the specifications about the string's format are mostly advisory. The explanations and recommendations about the metadata fields in the following list are also non-normative and correspond only to common, but not universal, conventions. Whenever the following explanations refer to "this distribution," the phrase can be taken to refer to the material included in the distribution rather than to the packaging of the distribution. The following metadata arguments are required:

`author`
: The name(s) of the author(s) of material included in this distribution. You should always provide this information: authors deserve credit for their work.

`author_email`
: Email address(es) of the author(s) named in the argument `author`. You should usually provide this information; however, you may optionally direct people toward a `maintainer` and provide `maintainer_email` instead.

`classifiers`
: A list of Trove strings to classify your package; each string must be one of those listed at List Classifiers (*https://pypi.python.org/pypi?%3Aaction=list_classifiers*) on PyPI.

`description`
: A concise description of this distribution, preferably fitting within one line of 80 characters or less.

`long_description`
: A long description of this distribution, typically as provided in the *README* file, preferably in *.rst* format.

`license`
: The licensing terms of this distribution, in a concise form that typically references the full license text included as another distributed file or available at a URL.

`name`
: The name of this distribution as a valid Python identifier (see PEP 426 #name (*https://www.python.org/dev/peps/pep-0426/#name*) for criteria). If you plan to upload your project to PyPI, this name must not conflict with any project already in the PyPI database.

`url`
: A URL at which more information can be found about this distribution, or `None` if no such URL exists.

`version`
: The version of this distribution, normally structured as *`major.minor`* or even more finely. See PEP 440 (*https://www.python.org/dev/peps/pep-0440/*)for recommended versioning schemes.

The following optional arguments may also be provided, if appropriate:

`keywords`
: A list of strings that would likely be searched for by somebody looking for the functionality provided by this distribution. You should provide this information so users can find your package on PyPI or other search engines.

`maintainer`
: The name(s) of the current maintainer(s) of this distribution. You should provide this information when the maintainer is different from the author.

`maintainer_email`
: Email address(es) of the maintainer(s) named in argument `maintainer`. You should provide this information only when you supply the `maintainer` argument and the maintainer is willing to receive email about this work.

`platforms`
: A list of platforms on which this distribution is known to work. You should provide this information when you have reason to believe this distribution may not work everywhere. This information should be reasonably concise, so the field often references information at a URL or in another distributed file.

Distribution contents

A distribution can contain a mix of Python source files, C-coded extensions, and data files. `setup` accepts optional named arguments that detail which files to put in the distribution. Whenever you specify file paths, the paths must be relative to the distribution root directory and use `/` as the path separator. `setuptools` adapts location and separator appropriately when it installs the distribution. Wheels, in particular, do not support absolute paths: all paths are relative to the top-level directory of your package.

The named arguments `packages` and `py_modules` do not list file paths, but rather Python packages and modules, respectively. Therefore, in the values of these named arguments, don't use path separators or file extensions. If you list subpackage names in argument `packages`, use Python dot syntax instead (e.g., *`top_package.sub_package`*).

Python source files By default, `setup` looks for Python modules (listed in the value of the named argument `py_modules`) in the distribution root directory, and for Python packages (listed in the value of the named argument `packages`) as subdirectories of the distribution root directory.

Here are the `setup` named arguments you will most frequently use to detail which Python source files are part of the distribution:

entry_points `entry_points={'`*`group`*`':['`*`name=P.m:obj`*`',],}`

`entry_points` is a `dict` holding one or more *groups*; each *`group`* has a list of *`name=value`* strings. *`name`* is an identifier, while *`value`* is a Python module *`P.m`* (the package part *`P.`* is optional), followed by a function, class, or other object, *`obj`* within *m*, with a colon `:` as the separator between module and object.

The *`group`* may be a plug-in, parser, or other service. See Dynamic Discovery of Services and Plugins (*http://bit.ly/2oiqcrd*) for further information on this use. However, the most common use of `entry_points` is to create executable scripts: `console_scripts` and `gui_scripts` are the most common *group* arguments. See "What are entry_points?" on page 697.

packages `packages=find_packages()|[`*`list of package name strings`*`]`

You can import and use `find_packages` from `setuptools` to automatically locate and include packages and subpackages in your distribution root directory. Alternatively, you may provide a list of packages. For each package name string *p* in the list, `setup` expects to find a subdirectory *p* in the distribution root directory and includes in the distribution the file *p/__init__.py*, which must be present, as well as any other file *p/*.py* (i.e., all the modules of package *p*). `setup` does not search for subpackages of *p*: unless you use `find_packages`, you must explicitly list all subpackages, as well as top-level packages, in the value of the named argument `packages`. We recommend using `find_packages`, to avoid having to update `packages` (and potentially miss a package) as your distribution grows:

find_packages `find_packages(where='.', exclude=())`

where indicates the directory which `find_packages` walks (subdirectories included) to find and include all packages (and modules within those packages); by default, it's `'.'`, the usual notation for "current directory," meaning, in this case, the distributions's root directory. `exclude` lists names and wildcards (e.g., `'tests'` or `'*.test'`) to be removed from the list of packages to be returned (note that `exclude` is executed last).

py_modules `py_modules=[` *`list of module name strings`* `]`

For each module name string *m* in the list, `setup` expects to find the file *m.py* in the distribution root directory and includes *m.py* in the distribution. Use `py_modules`, instead of `find_packages`, when you have a very simple package with only a few modules and no subdirectories.

What are entry_points? `entry_points` are a way to tell the installer (usually `pip`) to register plug-ins, services, or scripts with the OS and, if appropriate, to create a platform-specific executable. The primary `entry_points` *`group`* arguments used are `console_scripts` (replaces the named argument `scripts`, which is deprecated) and `gui_scripts`. Other plug-ins and services (e.g., parsers), are also supported, but we do not cover them further in this book; see the Python Packaging User Guide (*https://packaging.python.org/*) for more detailed information.

When `pip` installs a package, it registers each entry point *`name`* with the OS and creates an appropriate executable (including an *.exe* launcher on Windows), which you can then run by simply entering **`name`** at the terminal prompt, rather than, for example, having to type **`python -m mymodule`**.

Scripts are Python source files that are meant to be run as main programs (see "The Main Program" on page 180), generally from the command line. Each script file should have as its first line a shebang line—that is, a line starting with `#!` and containing the substring `python`. In addition, each script should end with the following code block:

```
if __name__ == '__main__':
    mainfunc()
```

To have `pip` install your script as an executable, list the script in `entry_points` under `console_scripts` (or `gui_scripts`, as appropriate). In addition to, or instead of, the main function of your script, you can use `entry_points` to register other functions as script interfaces. Here's what `entry_points` with both `console_scripts` and `gui_scripts` defined might look like:

```
entry_points={
    'console_scripts': ['example=example:mainfunc',
                        'otherfunc=example:anotherfunc',
                       ],
    'gui_scripts': ['mygui=mygui.gui_main:run',
                   ],
    },
```

After installation, type **example** at the terminal prompt to execute *mainfunc* in the module *example*. If you type **otherfunc**, the system executes *anotherfunc*, also in the module *example*.

Data and other files To put files of any kind in the distribution, supply the following named arguments. In most cases, you'll want to use package_data to list your data files. The named argument data_files is used for listing files that you want to install to directories *outside* your package; however, we do not recommend you use it, due to complicated and inconsistent behavior, as described here:

data_files data_files=[*list of pairs(target_directory, list_of_files)*]

The value of named argument data_files is a list of pairs. Each pair's first item is a string and names a *target directory* (i.e., a directory where setuptools places data files when installing the distribution); the second item is the list of file path strings for files to put in the target directory.

At installation time, installing from a wheel places each target directory as a subdirectory of Python's sys.prefix for a pure distribution, or of Python's sys.exec_prefix for a nonpure distribution; installing from *sdist* with pip uses setuptools to place target directories relative to site_packages, but installing without pip and with distutils has the same behavior as wheels. Because of such inconsistencies, we do not recommend you use data_files.

package_data package_data={*k*:*list_of_globs*, ...}

The value of named argument package_data is a dict. Each key is a string and names a *package* in which to find the data files; the corresponding value is a list of glob patterns for files to include. The patterns may include subdirectories (using relative paths separated by a forward slash, /, even on Windows). An empty package string, '', recursively includes all files in any subdirectory that matches the pattern—for example, '': ['*.txt'] includes all *.txt* files anywhere in the top-level directory or subdirectories. At installation time, setuptools places each file in appropriate subdirectories relative to site_packages.

C-coded extensions To put C-coded extensions in the distribution, supply the following named argument:

ext_modules `ext_modules=[` *`list of instances of class`* `Extension ]`

All the details about each extension are supplied as arguments when instantiating the `setuptools.Extension` class. `Extension`'s constructor accepts two mandatory arguments and many optional named arguments. The simplest possible example looks something like this:

```
ext_modules=[Extension('x',sources=['x.c'])]
```

The `Extension` class constructor is:

Extension `class Extension(`*`name, sources, **kwds`*`)`

> *`name`* is the module name string for the C-coded extension. *`name`* may include dots to indicate that the extension module resides within a package. *`sources`* is the list of C source files that must be compiled and linked in order to build the extension. Each item of *`sources`* is a string that gives a source file's path relative to the distribution root directory, complete with the file extension *.c*. *`kwds`* lets you pass other, optional named arguments to `Extension`, as covered later in this section.

The `Extension` class also supports other file extensions besides *.c*, indicating other languages you may use to code Python extensions. On platforms having a C++ compiler, the file extension *.cpp* indicates C++ source files. Other file extensions that may be supported, depending on the platform and on various add-ons to `setuptools`, include *.f* for Fortran, *.i* for SWIG, and *.pyx* for Cython files. See "Extending Python Without Python's C API" on page 681 for information about using different languages to extend Python.

In most cases, your extension needs no further information besides mandatory arguments *`name`* and *`sources`*. Note that you need to list any *.h* headers in your *MANIFEST.in* file. `setuptools` performs all that is necessary to make the Python headers directory and the Python library available for your extension's compilation and linking, and provides whatever compiler or linker flags or options are needed to build extensions on a given platform.

When additional information is required to compile and link your extension correctly, you can supply such information via the named arguments of the class `Extension`. Such arguments may potentially interfere with the cross-platform portability of your distribution. In particular, whenever you specify file or directory paths as the values of such arguments, the paths should be relative to the distribution root directory. However, when you plan to distribute your extensions to other platforms, you should examine whether you really need to provide build information via named arguments to `Extension`. It is sometimes possible to bypass such needs by careful coding at the C level.

Here are the named arguments that you may pass when calling `Extension`:

`define_macros = [ (`*`macro_name,macro_value`*`) ... ]`
: Each of the items *`macro_name`* and *`macro_value`* is a string, respectively the name and value of a C preprocessor macro definition, equivalent in effect to the C preprocessor directive: `#define` *`macro_name macro_value`*.

  `macro_value` can also be `None`, to get the same effect as the C preprocessor directive: `#define` *`macro_name`*.

`extra_compile_args = [`*`list of compile_arg strings`*`]`
: Each of the strings listed as the value of `extra_compile_args` is placed among the command-line arguments for each invocation of the C compiler.

`extra_link_args = [`*`list of link_arg strings`*`]`
: Each of the strings listed as the value of `extra_link_args` is placed among the command-line arguments for the linker.

`extra_objects = [`*`list of object_name strings`*`]`
: Each of the strings listed as the value of `extra_objects` names an object file to link in. Do not specify the file extension as part of the object name: `distutils` adds the platform-appropriate file extension (such as *.o* on Unix-like platforms and *.obj* on Windows) to help you keep cross-platform portability.

`include_dirs = [`*`list of directory_path strings`*`]`
: Each of the strings listed as the value of `include_dirs` identifies a directory to supply to the compiler as one where header files are found.

`libraries = [`*`list of library_name strings`*`]`
: Each of the strings listed as the value of `libraries` names a library to link in. Do not specify the file extension or any prefix as part of the library name: `distutils`, in cooperation with the linker, adds the platform-appropriate file extension and prefix (such as *.a*, and a prefix *lib*, on Unix-like platforms, and *.lib* on Windows) to help you keep cross-platform portability.

`library_dirs = [ `*`list of directory_path strings`*`]`
: Each of the strings listed as the value of `library_dirs` identifies a directory to supply to the linker as one where library files are found.

`runtime_library_dirs = [ `*`list of directory_path strings`*`]`
: Each of the strings listed as the value of `runtime_library_dirs` identifies a directory where dynamically loaded libraries are found at runtime.

undef_macros = [*list of macro_name strings*]
: Each of the strings *macro_name* listed as the value of undef_macros is the name for a C preprocessor macro definition, equivalent in effect to the C preprocessor directive: #undef *macro_name*.

Dependencies and requirements

You may optionally list dependencies with named arguments in *setup.py* or in a requirements file (see "The requirements.txt File" on page 701):

install_requires install_requires=['*pkg*',['*pkg2*>=n.n']]

install_requires takes a list of package names as strings, with specific version requirements n.n optionally provided (see PEP 440 (*https://www.python.org/dev/peps/pep-0440/#version-specifiers*) for details on how version specifiers are handled). Provide the broadest version requirements possible for your program. Use this named argument to supply dependencies that are the minimum necessary for your program to run. pip automatically calls pip install pkg on each argument pkg to install the dependency.

extras_require extras_require={'*rec*':['*pkgname*']]

extras_require takes a dict of recommended additional dependencies: 'rec' as a string key describing the recommendation (e.g., 'PDF'), 'pkgname' as the value. pip does not automatically install these dependencies, but the user may opt in to installing *rec* at installation time of the main package, *mpk*, with **pip install *mpk*[rec]**.

The requirements.txt File

You may optionally provide a *requirements.txt* file. If provided, it contains pip install calls, one per line. This file is particularly useful for re-creating a particular environment for installation, or forcing the use of certain versions of dependencies.

When the user enters the following at a command prompt, pip installs all items listed in the file; however, installation is *not* guaranteed to be in any particular order:

```
pip install -r requirements.txt
```

install_requires vs. extras_require or requirements.txt

pip only automatically discovers and installs dependencies listed in install_requires. extras_require entries must be manually opted in to at installation time, or be used in the install_requires of another package's *setup.py* (e.g., your package is being used as a library by others). *requirements.txt* must be manually run by the user. For detailed usage, see the pip docs (*https://pip.pypa.io/en/latest/user_guide/#requirements-files*).

The MANIFEST.in File

When you package your source distribution, `setuptools` by default inserts the following files in the distribution:

- All Python (*.py*) and C source files explicitly listed in `packages` or found by `find_packages` in *setup.py*
- Files listed in `package_data` and `data_files` in *setup.py*
- Scripts or plug-ins defined in `entry_points` in *setup.py*
- Test files, located at *test/test*.py* under the distribution root directory, unless excluded in `find_packages`
- Files *README.rst* or *README.txt* (if any), *setup.cfg* (if any), and *setup.py*

To add yet more files in the source distribution, place in the distribution root directory a *manifest template* file named *MANIFEST.in*, whose lines are rules, applied sequentially, about files to add (`include`) or subtract (`prune`) from the list of files to place in the distribution. See the Python docs (*https://docs.python.org/3/distutils/sourcedist.html#specifying-the-files-to-distribute*) for more info. If you have any C extensions in your project (listed in *setup.py* named argument `ext_modules`), the path to any *.h* header files must be listed in *MANIFEST.in* to ensure the headers are included, with a line like `graft /dir/*.h`, where *`dir`* is a relative path to the headers.

The setup.cfg File

setup.cfg supplies appropriate defaults for options to build-time commands. For example, you can add the following lines to *setup.cfg* to always build *universal wheels* (see "Creating wheels" on page 704):

```
[bdist_wheel]
universal=1
```

Distributing Your Package

Once you have your *setup.py* (and other files) in order, distributing your package requires the following steps:

1. Create ("package up") the distribution into a wheel or other archive format.

2. Register your package, if necessary, to a repository.

3. Upload your package to a repository.

Create the Distribution

In the past, a packaged "source" distribution (*sdist*) made with `python setup.py sdist` was the most useful file you could produce with `distutils`. When you are distributing packages with C extensions for flavors of Linux, you still want to create an *sdist*. And when you absolutely require absolute paths (rather than relative paths) for installation of certain files (listed in the `data_files` argument to *setup.py*), you need to use an *sdist*. (See the discussion on `data_files` (*https://packaging.python.org/distributing*) in the Python Packaging User Guide.) But when you are packaging pure Python, or platform-dependent C extensions for macOS or Windows, you can make life much easier for most users by also creating "built" wheels of your distribution.

Wheels make the Python world go round

Wheels are the new, improved way to package up your Python modules and packages for distribution, replacing the previously favorite packaging form known as *eggs*. Wheels are considered "built" distributions, meaning your users don't have to go through a "build" step in order to install them. Wheels provide for faster updates than eggs and may be multiplatform compatible because they do not include *.pyc* files. In addition, your users don't need a compiler for C extensions on Mac and Windows machines. Finally, wheels are well-supported by PyPI and preferred by `pip`.

To build wheels, install the `wheel` package by running the following command on a terminal: **`pip install wheel`**.

Pure wheels Wheels are considered *pure* if they only contain Python code, and *nonpure* if they contain extensions coded in C (or other programming languages). Pure wheels can be *universal* if the code can be run with either v2 or v3 without needing `2to3` conversion, as covered in "v2 source with conversion to v3" on page 716. Universal *wheels* are cross-platform (but beware: not all Python built-ins work in exactly the same way on all platforms). Version-specific, pure Python wheels are also cross-platform but require a particular version of Python. When your pure distribution requires `2to3` conversion (or has different v2 and v3 requirements, e.g., *setup.py* arguments specified in `install_requires`), you need to create two wheels, one for v2 and one for v3.

Nonpure wheels For a pure distribution, supplying wheels is just a matter of convenience for the users. For a nonpure distribution, making built forms available may be more than just an issue of convenience. A nonpure distribution, by definition, includes code that is not pure Python—generally, C code. Unless you supply a built form, users need to have the appropriate C compiler installed in order to build and install your distribution. In addition, installing a source distribution may be rather intricate, particularly for end users who may not be experienced programmers. It is therefore recommended to provide both an *sdist*, in *.tar.gz* format, and a wheel (or several) for nonpure packages. For that, you need to have the necessary C compiler installed. Nonpure wheels work only on other computers with the same platform (e.g., macOS, Windows) and architecture (e.g., 32-bit, 64-bit) as they were built on.

Creating wheels In order to create a wheel, in many cases, all you need to run is a single line. For a pure (Python only), universal (works on both v2 and v3 without conversion) distribution, just type the following at your distribution's top-level directory:

```
python setup.py bdist_wheel --universal
```

This creates a wheel that can be installed on any platform. When you are creating a pure package that works on both v2 and v3 but requires `2to3` conversion (or has different arguments in *setup.py* to, for example, `install_requires` for v2 and v3), create two wheels, one for v2 and one for v3, as follows:

```
python2 setup.py bdist_wheel
python3 setup.py bdist_wheel
```

For a pure package that can *only* work on v2 or *only* on v3, use only the appropriate Python version to create the single wheel. Version-specific pure wheels work on any platform with the appropriate version of Python installed.

Don't use --universal with nonpure or version-specific packages

`bdist_wheel --universal` *doesn't* detect whether your package is nonpure or version-specific. In particular, if your package contains C-extensions, you *shouldn't* create a universal wheel: `pip` would override your platform wheel or sdist to install the universal wheel instead.

Nonpure wheels can be created for macOS or for Windows, but only for the platform being used to create them. Running **`python setup.py bdist_wheel`** (without the `--universal` flag) automatically detects the extension(s) and creates the appropriate wheel. One benefit of creating a wheel is that your users are able to **`pip install`** the package, regardless of whether they have a C compiler themselves, as long as they're running on the same platform as you used to create the wheel.

Nonpure Linux wheels

Unfortunately, distributing nonpure Linux wheels isn't quite as simple as distributing pure ones, due to variations among Linux distributions, as described in PEP 513 (*https://www.python.org/dev/peps/pep-0513/#id35*). PyPI does not accept nonpure Linux wheels unless they are tagged *manylinux*. The complex process to create these cross-distribution wheels currently involves Docker images and `auditwheel`; check out the manylinux (*https://github.com/pypa/manylinux*) docs for more information.

Once you run **`python setup.py bdist_wheel`**, you will have a wheel named something like *mypkg-0.1-py2.py3-none-any.whl* in a (new, if you've run *setup.py* for the first time) directory called *dist/*. For more information on wheel naming and tagging conventions, see PEP 425 (*https://www.python.org/dev/peps/pep-0425/*). To check which files have been inserted after building the wheel, without installing or uncompressing it, you can use:

```
unzip -l mypkg
```

because a wheel file is just a *zip* archive with appropriate metadata.

Creating an sdist

To create an *sdist* (source distribution) for your project, type the following in the top level of your package directory:

```
python setup.py sdist
```

This creates a *.tar.gz* file (if it creates a *.zip* on Windows, you may need to use **--formats** to specify the archive format).

.tar.gz preferred by PyPI

Do not attempt to upload both a *.zip* and a *.tar.gz* file to PyPI; you'll get an error. Instead, stick with *.tar.gz* for most use cases.

Your *.tar.gz* file may then be uploaded to PyPI or otherwise distributed. Your users will have to unpack and install with, typically, **python setup.py install**. More information on source distributions is available in the online docs (*https://docs.python.org/3.5/distutils/sourcedist.html#*).

Registering and Uploading to a Repository

Once you've created a wheel or an sdist, you may choose to upload it to a repository for easy distribution to your users. You can upload to a local repository, such as a company's private repository, or you may upload to a public repository such as PyPI. In the past, *setup.py* was used to build and immediately upload; however, due to issues with security, this is no longer recommended. Instead, you should use a third-party module such as `twine` (or `Flit` for extremely simple packages, as covered in the Flit docs (*https://pypi.python.org/pypi/flit*)). There are plans to eventually merge `twine` into `pip`: check the Python Packaging User Guide (*https://packaging.python.org/*) for updated information.

Using `twine` is fairly straightforward. Run **pip install twine** to download it. You'll need to create a *~/.pypirc* file (which provides repository information), and then it's a simple command to register or upload your package.

Your ~/.pypirc file

`Twine` recommends that you have a *~/.pypirc* file (that is, a file named *.pypirc*, residing in your home directory) that lists information about the repositories you want to upload to, including your username and password. Since *.pypirc* is typically stored "in clear," you should set permissions to `600` (on Unix-like systems), or leave the password off and be prompted for it each and every time you run `twine`. The file should look something like this:

```
[distutils]
index-servers=
    testpypi
    pypi
    warehouse
    myrepo

[testpypi]
repository=https://testpypi.python.org/pypi
username=yourusername
password=yourpassword

[pypi]
repository=https://pypi.python.org/pypi
username=yourusername
password=yourpassword

[warehouse]
repository=https://upload.pypi.org/legacy/
username=yourusername
password=yourpassword

[myrepo]
repository=https://otherurl/myrepo
username=yourusername
password=yourpassword
```

Register and upload to PyPI

If you've never used PyPI, create a user account with a username and password. (You may do this during the register step, but it's best to do it online at PyPI (*https://pypi.python.org/pypi*).) You should also create a user account on testpypi (*https://testpypi.python.org/pypi*), to practice uploading packages to a temporary repository before uploading them to the public repository.

If you are uploading your package to PyPI, you may need to register the package before you upload it the first time. Use the appropriate command to specify the wheel or sdist you're registering (simply using `dist/*` does not work):

```
twine register -r repo dist/mypkg.whl # for a wheel
```

or:

```
twine register -r repo dist/mydist.tar.gz # for an sdist
```

`repo` is the particular repository where you're registering your package, as listed in your *~/.pypirc* file. Alternatively, you may provide the repository URL on the command line with the flag **`--repository-url`**.

Warehouse is the new backend to PyPI. Registration will no longer be required. You can add it to your *~/.pypirc* now, as shown in the preceding example. Running `twine` without `-r` should upload to the correct version of PyPI by default.

Once your package is registered, you may upload it with the following command at the top level of your package; `twine` finds and uploads the latest version of your distribution to the repo specified in your *.pypirc* (or alternatively, you may provide the repository URL on the command line with flag **`--repository-url`**):

```
twine upload -r repo dist/*
```

At this point, your users will be able to use **`pip install`** ***`yourpkg`*** **`--user`** (or just **`pip install`** into a virtual environment; it's wiser for them to avoid a nonvenv `pip install`, which affects the whole Python installation for all users) to install your package.

The Python Packaging Authority (PyPA (*https://www.pypa.io/en/latest/*)) continues to improve Python packaging and distribution. Please join in the effort (*https://www.pypa.io/en/latest/help/*) by contributing to the codebase or documentation, posting bug reports, or joining in the discussions on packaging.

v2/v3 Migration and Coexistence

The earliest release of Python 3 (the precursor of what we call v3 in this book) first appeared in 2008, specifically as "Python 3.0": that release was not a production-quality one, nor was it meant to be. Its main purpose was to let people start adapting to changes in syntax and semantics; some parts of the implementation were unsatisfactory (particularly the I/O facilities, now much improved). As we're writing this chapter, the current releases are 2.7.12 and 3.5.2, with a 3.6.0 release just out in December 2016, very close to the deadline for us to finish this book (as a result, while we mention 3.6's highlights as being "new in 3.6," that's in good part based on a beta version of 3.6: we can't claim thorough coverage of 3.6).

Python's core developers have done a lot of work to backport v3 features into v2, but this activity has now ended, and v2 is feature-frozen (some v3 standard library backports to v2 are available for **`pip install`**, as repeatedly mentioned earlier in this book). v2 is getting only security bug-fix releases, and even those are due to stop once v2 maintenance formally ends in 2020. Guido van Rossum's PyCon NA keynote (*https://www.youtube.com/watch?v=0Ef9GudbxXY*) in 2014 explicitly ruled out any 2.8 release; should you choose to stick with v2, after 2020 you will be on your own.

For those who have mastered Python's build system, or who are able to hire third-party developers to support their v2 use, "sticking with v2" may remain a viable strategy even after 2020. However, for most readers, the first task to address will likely be converting existing v2 code to v3.

Preparing for Python 3

Before starting a coexistence or conversion project, if you are not thoroughly familiar with both versions of Python, it will be helpful to read the official guide Porting Python 2 Code to Python 3 (*https://docs.python.org/3/howto/pyporting.html*) in the Python documentation. Among other things, this makes the same recommendation we do about v2 (i.e., only support Python 2.7[1]).

Make sure that your tests cover as much of your project as possible, so that interversion errors are likely to be picked up during testing. Aim for at least 80% testing coverage; much more than 90% can be difficult to achieve, so don't spend too much effort to reach a too-ambitious standard (although *mocks*, mentioned in "Unit Testing and System Testing" on page 456, can help you increase your unit-testing coverage breadth, if not depth).

You can update your v2 codebase semi-automatically, using either Python 2's `2to3` utility or the *`modernize`* (*http://python-modernize.readthedocs.io/en/latest/*) or *`futurize`* (*http://python-future.org/overview.html#automatic-conversion-to-py2-3-compatible-code*) packages that build on it (the porting guide mentioned previously has good advice about choosing between the latter two, which we discuss briefly in "v2/v3 Support with a Single Source Tree" on page 724). A continuous integration environment helps you verify that you are using best-practice coding standards. Also, use tools like coverage (*https://pypi.python.org/pypi/coverage*) and flake8 (*https://pypi.python.org/pypi/flake8*) to roughly quantify your code quality.

Even while you are still using v2, you can start to check some of the issues that a transition to v3 involves, by using the **`-3`** command-line option when starting the Python interpreter. This makes it warn about "Python 3.x incompatibilities that `2to3` will not trivially fix." Also, add the **`-Werror`** flag to convert warnings to errors, thus ensuring you don't miss them. Don't assume, however, that this technique tells you *everything* you need to know: it can't detect some subtle issues, such as data from files opened in text mode being treated as bytes.

Whenever you use automatic code conversion, review the output of the conversion process. A dynamic language like Python makes it impossible to perform a perfect translation; while testing helps, it can't pick up all imperfections.

Readers with large codebases or a serious interest in multiversion compatibility should also read *Porting to Python 3* (*http://python3porting.com/*) by Lennart Regebro (available both electronically and in print). Python 2.7 had not yet appeared when the second edition of that book was produced, but its feature set was fairly well known, and the book contains much useful and detailed advice that we do not repeat here. Instead, we cover the main points where incompatibilities are likely to

1 As further encouragement, Python 2.6 is deprecated on PyPI and pip.

arise in “Minimizing Syntax Differences” on page 711, and some of the tools that can assist your conversion task.

Imports from __future__

`__future__` is a standard library module containing a variety of features, documented in the online docs (*https://docs.python.org/3/library/__future__.html*), to ease migration between versions. It is unlike any other module, because importing features can affect the syntax, not just the semantics, of your program. Such imports must be the initial executable statements of your code.

Each “future feature” is activated using the statement:

```
from __future__ import feature
```

where *feature* is the feature you want to use. In particular, we recommend placing the following line at the top of your v2 modules for best compatibility.

```
from __future__ import (print_function, division,
                        absolute_import)
```

Under v2, it establishes compatibility with v3’s printing, division, and import mechanisms.

Minimizing Syntax Differences

There are a number of differences between Python 3.5 (referred to in this book as v3) and earlier Python 3 versions. While it is possible to accommodate these earlier versions, in the interest of brevity we have excluded such techniques. In addition, by v2 we always mean 2.7.x, not any previous versions of Python 2.

Avoid “Old-Style” Classes

While the update to the object model in Python 2.2 was largely backward compatible, there are some important, subtle areas of difference, particularly if you use multiple inheritance. To ensure that these differences don’t affect you, make sure that your v2 code uses only new-style classes.

The simplest way to do this is to have your classes explicitly inherit from `object`. You may want to adjust the order of other base classes, if any, to ensure that the intended methods are referenced. Most software needs little adjustment, but the more complex your multiple inheritance hierarchy, the more detailed the work.

You may choose to add `__metaclass__ = type` to the top of your modules to ensure “bare” classes (ones without bases) in your code are new-style, as covered in “How Python v2 Determines a Class’s Metaclass” on page 142: the statement is innocuous in v3.

print as a Function

One of the most visible differences between v2 and v3 is the move from `print` as a *statement* to `print` as a *function*. To minimize breakage, always use the `print` function, enabling it with the `__future__` imports recommended earlier. (We assume this import in all of the code examples in this book.) In v2, print statements used a trailing comma to suppress newlines; in v3, use `end="  "` to override the default `end="\n"`.

String Literals

When v3 first came out, literals like `b'bytestring'` for bytestring objects were incompatible with v2, but this syntax has now been backported and is available in both versions. Similarly, the v2 Unicode string literal format `u'Unicode string'` was not available in early v3 implementations, but its inclusion in v3 was recommended in PEP 414 (*https://www.python.org/dev/peps/pep-0414/*) and is now implemented, making it easier to support both languages with a common source tree without radical changes to all string literals.

If your code's string literals are mostly Unicode, but not flagged as such, you may use `from __future__ import unicode_literals`, which causes the v2 interpreter to treat all ambiguous literals as though they were prefixed with a `u` (just like the v3 interpreter always does).

Numeric Constants

In v2, integer literals beginning with `0` were treated as octal. This was confusing to beginners (and occasionally to more experienced programmers). Although v2 still allows this, it has become a syntax error in v3; avoid this notation altogether.

Use instead the more recent notation for octal numbers, better aligned with the notation for binary and hexadecimal numbers. In Table 26-1 the base is indicated by a letter following an initial `0` (`b` for binary, `o` for octal, `x` for hexadecimal).

Table 26-1. Preferred integer literal representations

Base	Representations of decimal 0, 61 and 200
Binary	`0b0`, `0b111101`, `0b11001000`
Octal	`0o0`, `0o75`, `0o310`
Hexadecimal	`0x0`, `0x3d`, `0xc8`

Long integer representations in older v2 implementations required the use of a trailing `L` or `l`; for compatibility, that syntax is still accepted in v2. It is no longer necessary (and it's a syntax error in v3); make sure that none of your code uses it.

Text and Binary Data

Perhaps the most troublesome conversion area for most projects is v3's insistence on the difference between binary and textual data, using bytestrings for the former and Unicode strings for the latter. The `bytes` and `bytearray` types are available in v2 (`bytes` being an alias for `str`, rather than a backport). Ensure that all string literals in v2 code use version-compatible syntax, as discussed in "String Literals" on page 712, and keep the two types of data separate.

Untangling strings

Too many v2 programs don't take care to differentiate between two very different kinds of strings: bytestrings and Unicode strings. Where text is concerned, remember to "decode on input, encode on output." There are many different ways to *represent* (encode) Unicode on external devices: all encodings have to be decoded on input to convert them to Unicode, which is how you should hold all text inside your program.

Avoid using the `bytes` type as a function with an integer argument. In v2 this returns the integer converted to a (byte)string because `bytes` is an alias for `str`, while in v3 it returns a bytestring containing the given number of null characters. So, for example, instead of the v3 expression `bytes(6)`, use the equivalent `b'\x00'*6`, which seamlessly works the same way in each version.

Another consequence of the v2 alias: indexing a bytestring in v2 returns a one-byte string, while in v3 it returns the integer value of the indexed byte. This means that some comparisons are byte-to-byte in v2 and byte-to-integer in v3, which can lead to incompatible results. You should at least test your code with Python's **-bb** command-line option, which warns when such comparisons are made.

Never Sort Using cmp

The `cmp` named argument to sorting functions and methods has been removed in v3; don't use it in your code...it's not a good idea in v2, either. The `cmp` argument had to be a function that took two values as arguments and returned either `-1`, `0`, or `+1` according to whether the first argument was less than, equal to, or greater than the second. This can make sorting slow, as the function may have to be called with each pair of items to compare in the sort, leading to a large number of calls.

The `key=` argument, by contrast, takes a single item to sort and returns an appropriate sort key: it is called only once for each item in the sequence to sort. Internally, the sorting algorithm creates a (*key*, *value*) tuple for each value in the input sequence, performs the sort, then strips keys off to get a sequence of just the values. The following example shows how to sort a list of strings *by length* (shortest first, strings of equal length in the same order as in the input):

```
>>> names = ['Victoria', 'Brett', 'Luciano', 'Anna', 'Alex', 'Steve']
>>> names.sort(key=len)
```

```
>>> names
['Anna', 'Alex', 'Brett', 'Steve', 'Luciano', 'Victoria']
```

Because Python's sort algorithm is *stable* (i.e., it leaves items that compare equal in the same order in the output as in the input), names of the same length are not necessarily in alphabetical order (rather, the input order is preserved on output for strings with equal key values). This is why `'Anna'` appears before `'Alex'` in the output. You could change this by including the value as a secondary sort key, used to discriminate between items whose primary sort keys compare as equal:

```
>>> names.sort(key=lambda x: (len(x), x))
>>> names
['Alex', 'Anna', 'Brett', 'Steve', 'Luciano', 'Victoria']
```

Sometimes it's faster to rely on Python's sorting stability: sort the list twice, first alphabetically (i.e., on the minor sort key), then by length (the major sort key). Empirically, on the list in this example, we've measured that the "sort twice" approach is about 25% faster than the "sort once with a `lambda` as `key`" approach (remember that avoiding `lambda`, when feasible, often optimizes your code).

except Clauses

If an `except` clause needs to work with the exception value, use the modern syntax `except ExceptionType as v`. The older form `except ExceptionType, v` is a syntax error in v3, and is anyway less readable in v2.

Division

Prepare for conversion by ensuring that all integer divisions use the `//` (truncating division) operator. In v2, `12 / 5` is 2; in v3 the value of the same expression is `2.4`. This difference could cause problems. In both versions, `12 // 5` is `2`, so it's best to convert your code to use explicit truncating division where appropriate.

For division where you actually *want* a floating-point result, in v2 you probably either used a floating-point integer constant in an expression like `j/3.0`, or applied the `float` function to one of the operands as in `float(j)/3`. You can take this opportunity to simplify your v2 code by adding `from __future__ import division` at the top of your modules to ensure that v2 division acts like v3 division, allowing you to simply code `j/3`. (Be sure to perform this simplification pass on your code only *after* you've changed all the existing `/` operators to `//` for those cases where you *want* truncating division.)

Incompatible Syntax to Avoid for Compatibility

One of the most irksome parts of maintaining a dual-version codebase is forcing yourself *not* to use some of the new features of v3. These have typically been added to the language to make it easier to use, so avoiding them inevitably makes the programming task a little more difficult.

Along with the differences described previously, other v3 features you need to avoid include: function annotations, covered in “Function Annotations and Type Hints (v3 Only)” on page 88; the `nonlocal` statement, covered in “Nested functions and nested scopes” on page 93; keyword-only arguments, covered in ““Keyword-only” Parameters (v3 Only)” on page 86; and `metaclass=` in class statements, covered in “The class Statement” on page 102. Also, list comprehensions in v3 have their own scope, unlike in v2, covered in List comprehensions and variable scope on page 79. Last but not least, anything we've marked throughout the book as “new in 3.6” is obviously a must-avoid in v2.

Choosing Your Support Strategy

You need to decide how you are going to use Python, depending on your specific requirements. Choice of strategy is constrained in various ways, and each strategy has upsides and downsides. You need to be pragmatic when deciding which version(s) you are going to support, and how.

One strategy that is likely to prove counterproductive is to maintain parallel source trees (such as two separate branches in the same code repository) for the two separate versions. The Python core development team maintained two separate source trees of CPython, 2.* and 3.*, for years, and that required a good deal of otherwise unnecessary work.

If your codebase is mature and changes infrequently, parallel source trees can be a viable strategy. But if there is substantial activity, you will almost certainly find the work required to maintain two branches irksome and wasteful. You also have to maintain two separate distributions, and ensure that users get the version they need. If you decide to do this, be prepared to expend extra effort. However, we recommend you choose one of the following options instead.

Steady As She Goes—v2-only Support

If you have a very large corpus of v2 code, we might heretically suggest that you simply continue to use v2. To do so, you must be ready to stay out of mainstream Python development, but this lets you keep using libraries not ported to v3 (though their number is happily dwindling). You do also avoid a large conversion task.

This strategy is clearly better suited to programs with a limited lifetime, and to environments where locally compiled interpreters are in use. If you need to run on a supported Python platform after 2020 (when long-term developer support for v2 ends), then you should plan to bite the bullet and convert to v3 well before then.

v2/v3 Migration

v2/v3 Support with Conversion

When developing from a single source tree, you have to decide whether that source will be in v2 or v3. Both strategies are workable, and conversion utilities exist to go either way, which lets you choose whether to maintain a v2 or a v3 codebase.

You need to use a script, unless you have very few files in your project; the complexity of that script is increased if you want to increase speed by converting only those files that have changed since your last test run. The conversions still take time, which can slow down development iteration if you decide (as you really should) to test both versions each and every time.

The *tox package (https://tox.readthedocs.io/en/latest/)* is useful to manage and test multiversion code. It lets you test your code under a number of different virtual environments, and supports not only v2 and v3 but also several earlier implementations, as well as Jython and PyPy.

v2 source with conversion to v3

If you have a large v2 codebase, then a good start to the migration task is rejigging your source so it can be converted automatically into v3. The Python core developers were farsighted enough to include automatic translation tools as a part of the first v3 release, and this support continues right up the the present day in the form of the `2to3` utility. `2to3` also provides a `lib2to3` library containing *fixers*, functions that handle specific constructs requiring conversion. Other conversion utilities we discuss later in this chapter also leverage `lib2to3`.

The first task is to assemble your source code and prepare it for conversion to Python 3. Fortunately, nowadays, this is not difficult, as core and distribution developers have thoughtfully provided conversion routines. Installing a Python 3.5 version (*https://www.continuum.io/downloads*) of Anaconda, for example, lets you (in a command-line environment where tab completion is available) enter **`2to3`** and hit the Tab key to reveal:

```
(s3cmdpy3) airhead:s3cmd sholden$ 2to3
2to3       2to3-2     2to3-2.7  2to3-3.4  2to3-3.5  2to32.6
```

Note, though, that not all of these come from Anaconda (the system in use had a number of Pythons on the system path), as the following directory listing shows:

```
airhead:s3cmd sholden$ for f in 2to3 2to3- 2to3-2 2to3-2.7
                                2to3-3.4 2to3-3.5 2to32.6
do
 ls -l $(which $f)
done
lrwxr-xr-x  1 sholden  staff  8 Mar 14 21:45 /Users/sholden/
Projects/Anaconda/bin/2to3 -> 2to3-3.5
lrwxr-xr-x  1 sholden  admin  36 Oct 24 12:30 /usr/local/bin/
2to3-2 -> ../Cellar/python/2.7.10_2/bin/2to3-2
lrwxr-xr-x  1 sholden  admin  38 Oct 24 12:30 /usr/local/bin/
2to3-2.7 -> ../Cellar/python/2.7.10_2/bin/2to3-2.7
lrwxr-xr-x  1 sholden  admin  38 Sep 12  2015 /usr/local/bin/
2to3-3.4 -> ../Cellar/python3/3.4.3_2/bin/2to3-3.4
-rwxr-xr-x  1 sholden  staff  121 Mar 14 21:45 /Users/sholden/
Projects/Anaconda/bin/2to3-3.5
lrwxr-xr-x  1 root  wheel  73 Aug  6  2015 /usr/bin/
```

```
2to32.6 -> ../../System/Library/Frameworks/Python.framework/
Versions/2.6/bin/2to32.6
```

The Anaconda install supplies `2to3.5`, and a symbolic link from `2to3` in the same directory; the remainder are from other installs. As long as the Python executable directory is at the beginning of your system path, the default `2to3` is the one targeting that installation: you'll be converting to the v3 supported by it.

v3 source with conversion to v2

If you are coding in v3 but want to support v2 too, use `3to2`, aka `lib3to2`, documented online (*https://pypi.python.org/pypi/3to2*). `3to2` uses the same *fixers* as `lib2to3`, reversing them to create a backward-compatible version of your code. `3to2` either produces working v2 code, or provides error messages describing why it can't. Some features in v3 are unavailable in v2: differences may be subtle—test your code in both versions.

2to3 Conversion: A Case Study

The most frequent conversion use case at this time is the v2 programmer wishing to convert to v3. Here we outline the procedure for conversion, with notes from real experience. It's not as easy as it used to be to find v2-only modules, but there are still some around. We landed on the `voitto` (*https://github.com/japsu/voitto*) package, which was released to the world in 2012 and appears to have had little or no attention since. As with many older projects, there is no documentation about how the tests should be run.

First, we cloned the repository and created a v2 virtual environment to allow verification and testing of the downloaded package. We then installed the `nose` testing framework, installed `voitto` as an editable package, and ran `nosetests` to execute the package's tests. Many older, unmaintained packages suffer from bit rot, so this *is* a necessary step. This involved the following commands:

```
$ virtualenv --python=$(which python2) ../venv2
Running virtualenv with interpreter /usr/local/bin/python2
New python executable in ↵
/Users/sholden/Projects/Python/voitto/venv2/bin/python2.7
Also creating executable in ↵
/Users/sholden/Projects/Python/voitto/venv2/bin/python
Installing setuptools, pip, wheel...done.
$ source ../venv2/bin/activate
(venv2) $ pip install nose
Collecting nose
  Using cached nose-1.3.7-py2-none-any.whl
Installing collected packages: nose
Successfully installed nose-1.3.7
(venv2) $ pip install -e .
Obtaining file:///Users/sholden/Projects/Python/voitto
Installing collected packages: voitto
  Running setup.py develop for voitto
```

```
Successfully installed voitto-0.0.1
(venv2) $ nosetests
....
----------------------------------------------------------------------
Ran 4 tests in 0.023s

OK
```

After verifying that the tests succeed, we created a Python3 virtual environment and ran the tests after again reinstalling dependencies. The error tracebacks have been trimmed here to retain only the significant information:

```
(venv2) $ deactivate
$ pyvenv ../venv3
$ source ../venv3/bin/activate
(venv3) $ pip install nose
Collecting nose
  Using cached nose-1.3.7-py3-none-any.whl
Installing collected packages: nose
Successfully installed nose-1.3.7
(venv3) airhead:voitto sholden$ pip install -e .
Obtaining file:///Users/sholden/Projects/Python/voitto
Installing collected packages: voitto
  Running setup.py develop for voitto
Successfully installed voitto
(venv3) $ nosetests
EEE
======================================================================
ERROR: Failure: NameError (name 'unicode' is not defined)
----------------------------------------------------------------------
Traceback (most recent call last):
 ...
  File "/Users/sholden/Projects/Python/voitto/tappio/lexer.py",
  line 43, in build_set
    assert type(ch) in (str, unicode)
NameError: name 'unicode' is not defined

======================================================================
ERROR: Failure: ImportError (No module named 'StringIO')
----------------------------------------------------------------------
Traceback (most recent call last):
 ...
  File "/Users/sholden/Projects/Python/voitto/tests/script_import_test.py",
  line 23, in <module>
    from StringIO import StringIO
ImportError: No module named 'StringIO'

======================================================================
ERROR: Failure: SyntaxError (invalid syntax (tappio_test.py, line 173))
----------------------------------------------------------------------
Traceback (most recent call last):
 ...
```

```
  File "/Users/sholden/Projects/Python/voitto/tests/tappio_test.py",
  line 173
    print Parser(lex.lex_string(input)).parse_document()
               ^
SyntaxError: invalid syntax

----------------------------------------------------------------------
Ran 3 tests in 0.014s

FAILED (errors=3)
```

As you can see, the program needs some adaptation to the v3 environment: `unicode` is not a valid type in v3, the `StringIO` module has been renamed, and the `print` statement needs to be transformed into a function call.

Initial run of 2to3

`2to3` has a number of different modes of operation. The most useful way to get a handle on the likely difficulty of a conversion is to simply run it on the project's root directory. The command

```
2to3 .
```

scans all code ands report on suggested changes in the form of difference listings (diffs), summarizing which files likely need changing. Here is that summary:

```
RefactoringTool: Files that need to be modified:
RefactoringTool: ./setup.py
RefactoringTool: ./tappio/__init__.py
RefactoringTool: ./tappio/lexer.py
RefactoringTool: ./tappio/models.py
RefactoringTool: ./tappio/parser.py
RefactoringTool: ./tappio/writer.py
RefactoringTool: ./tappio/scripts/extract.py
RefactoringTool: ./tappio/scripts/graph.py
RefactoringTool: ./tappio/scripts/indent.py
RefactoringTool: ./tappio/scripts/merge.py
RefactoringTool: ./tappio/scripts/missing_accounts.py
RefactoringTool: ./tappio/scripts/move_entries.py
RefactoringTool: ./tappio/scripts/print_accounts.py
RefactoringTool: ./tappio/scripts/print_earnings.py
RefactoringTool: ./tappio/scripts/renumber.py
RefactoringTool: ./tests/helpers.py
RefactoringTool: ./tests/script_import_test.py
RefactoringTool: ./tests/tappio_test.py
RefactoringTool: ./voitto/__init__.py
RefactoringTool: ./voitto/helpers/io.py
RefactoringTool: ./voitto/helpers/tracer.py
RefactoringTool: Warnings/messages while refactoring:
RefactoringTool: ### In file ./tappio/scripts/missing_accounts.py ###
RefactoringTool: Line 36: You should use a for loop here
```

v2/v3 Migration

The diffs show that approximately 20 source files are being recommended for change. As the old saying goes, why keep a dog and bark yourself? We can have `2to3` actually *make* the recommended changes by adding the **`-w`** flag to the command line. Normally `2to3` creates a backup file by renaming the original file from *.py* to *.py.bak*. Operating under a version-control system renders this unnecessary, however, so we can also add the **`-n`** flag to inhibit the backups:

```
(venv3) $ 2to3 -wn .
```

Here are the changes that `2to3` makes—we don't mention the filenames. Many of the changes are similar in nature, so we don't provide an exhaustive commentary on each one. As detailed next, many of the changes might be suboptimal; `2to3` is much more focused on producing working code than in optimizing its performance (remember the "golden rule of programming," covered in "Optimization" on page 479). Optimization is best treated as a separate step, once the code has been successfully converted and is passing its tests. The lines to be removed are preceded by minus signs (-), the replacement code by plus signs (+):

```
- assert type(ch) in (str, unicode)
+ assert type(ch) in (str, str)
```

v3, of course, does not define `unicode`, so `2to3` has converted it to `str` but failed to recognize that this no longer requires the tuple-membership test. Since the statement should work, however, leave this optimization for later.

```
- token = self.token_iterator.next()
+ token = next(self.token_iterator)
```

Several similar changes of this nature were recommended. In all cases the `next` method from v3, now renamed `__next__`, could simply transliterate the method call. However, `2to3` has chosen to produce better code, compatible across both versions, by using the `next` function instead.

```
- for account_number, cents in balances.iteritems():
+ for account_number, cents in balances.items():
```

Again several similar changes are recommended. In this case the converted code has a slightly different effect if run under v2, since the original was specifically coded to use an iterator rather than the list that (under v2) the `items` method produces. While this may use more memory, it shouldn't affect the result.

```
- map(all_accounts.update, flat_accounts.itervalues())
+ list(map(all_accounts.update, iter(flat_accounts.values())))
```

This is an interesting change because the original code was rather dubious—this is the line where the migration tool advised use of a `for` loop instead. Under v2, `map` returns a list while the v3 `map` is an iterator. Not only has the `itervalues` call been changed to `values` (because v3's `values` method produces an iterator; the `iter` call is redundant, though innocuous), but a `list` call has also been placed around the result to ensure that a list is still produced. It might appear that the application of the `list` function serves no useful purpose, but removing the call would mean that the `all_accounts.update` function would only be applied to accounts as they were consumed from the iterator.

In fact the original code is somewhat dubious, and misused the `map` function. It would really have been little more complex, and far more comprehensible, to write

```
for ac_value in iter(flat_accounts.values()):
    all_accounts.update(ac_value)
```

as `2to3` advised. We leave this optimization for now, though, since despite its dubious nature the code as produced still works.

```
- print "{account_num}: ALL  {fmt_filenames}".format(**locals())
+ print("{account_num}: ALL  {fmt_filenames}".format(**locals()))
```

`2to3` ensures that all `print` statements are converted to function calls, and is good at making such changes.

```
- from StringIO import StringIO
+ from io import StringIO
```

The `StringIO` functionality has been moved to the `io` library in v3. Note that `2to3` does not necessarily produce code that is compatible across both versions; it pursues its principal purpose, conversion to v3—although in this case, as in previous ones, v2 is also happy with the converted code (since `StringIO` can also be accessed from `io` in v2, specifically in 2.7).

```
- assert_true(callable(main))
+ assert_true(isinstance(main, collections.Callable))
```

This change is a throwback because earlier v3 implementations removed the `callable` function. Since this was reinstated since v3.2, the conversion isn't really necessary, but it's harmless in both v2 and v3.

```
- except ParserError, e:
+ except ParserError as e:
```

This change also provides compatible syntax, good in both v2 and v3.

The `2to3` conversion detailed in this initial run of `2to3` does not, however, result in a working program. Running the tests still gives two errors, one in the `lexer_single` test and one in `writer_single`. Both complain about differing token lists. This is the first (we've inserted line breaks to avoid too-wide code boxes running off the page):

```
...
  File "/Users/sholden/Projects/Python/voitto/tests/tappio_test.py",
        line 54, in lexer_single
    assert_equal(expected_tokens, tokens)
AssertionError: Lists differ: [('integer', '101')] !=
                              [<Token: integer '101'>]

First differing element 0:
('integer', '101')
```

```
<Token: integer '101'>

- [('integer', '101')]
+ [<Token: integer '101'>]
```

The second one is similar:

```
...
  File "/Users/sholden/Projects/Python/voitto/tests/tappio_test.py",
       line 188, in writer_single
    assert_equal(good_tokens, potentially_bad_tokens)
AssertionError: Lists differ:
  [<Tok[1169 chars]ce_close ''>, <Token: brace_close ''>,
   <Token: brace_close ''>] != [<Tok[1169 chars]ce_close ''>,
   <Token: brace_close ''>, <Token: brace_close ''>]

First differing element 0:
<Token: brace_open ''>
<Token: brace_open ''>

Diff is 1384 characters long. Set self.maxDiff to None to see it.
```

These were both traced to the token list comparison routine itself, which the original code provides in the form of a `__cmp__` method for the `Token` class, reading as follows:

```
def __cmp__(self, other):
    if isinstance(other, Token):
        return cmp((self.token_type, self.value),
                   (other.token_type, other.value))
    elif (isinstance(other, list) or
          isinstance(other, tuple)) and len(other) == 2:
        return cmp((self.token_type, self.value), other)
    else:
        raise TypeError('cannot compare Token to {!r}'.format(
                                                   type(other)))
```

This method is not used in v3, which relies on so-called *rich comparison* methods. Since no `__eq__` is found, equality checks falls back to those inherited from `object`, which unfortunately don't measure up. The fix is to replace the `__cmp__` method with an `__eq__` method. This suffices to implement the equality checks required in the tests; the new code is:

```
def __eq__(self, other):
    if isinstance(other, Token):
        return (self.token_type, self.value) ==
               (other.token_type, other.value)
    elif (isinstance(other, list) or
          isinstance(other, tuple)) and len(other) == 2:
        return (self.token_type, self.value) == tuple(other)
    else:
        raise TypeError('cannot compare Token to {!r}'.format(
                                                   type(other)))
```

This final change is all that is required to have all tests pass under v3:

```
(ve35) airhead:voitto sholden$ nosetests
....
----------------------------------------------------------------------
Ran 4 tests in 0.028s

OK
```

Retaining v2 compatibility

While we now have working v3 code, running the tests under v2 shows that we have broken backward compatibility, and the `writer_test` now fails:

```
File "/Users/sholden/Projects/Python/voitto/tappio/writer.py",
       line 48, in write
    self.stream.write(str(token))
TypeError: unicode argument expected, got 'str'
```

It would be unfair to complain about the fact the `2to3` conversion breaks compatibility, since maintaining compatibility is no part of its purview. Happily, it is relatively easy to take this v3 code and make it also compatible with v2. The process does, for the first time, require writing some code that introspects to determine the particular version of Python. We discuss version compatibility further in "v2/v3 Support with a Single Source Tree" on page 724.

The issue is that the original code does not explicitly flag string literals as Unicode, so under v2 they are treated as being of type `str` rather than the required `unicode` type. It would be tedious to make this conversion manually, but there's a solution in the `__future__` module: the `unicode_literals` import. When this import is present in a v2 program, string literals are implicitly treated as Unicode strings, which is exactly the change we want. We therefore added the line

```
from __future__ import unicode_literals
```

as the first executable line in each module.

Note that this is not always the panacea it might appear to be (and it certainly doesn't offer an immediate fix here, as we'll shortly see). Although it's helpful in this case, when programs have mixed binary and textual string data there is no one representation to serve both purposes, and many developers prefer to take things gradually. The changes can introduce regressions in Python 2, which have to be addressed. Not only that, but all docstrings implicitly then become Unicode, which prior to 2.7.7 would have caused syntax errors.

This change alone actually *increases* the number of failing tests to three, and the error is the same in all cases:

```
File "/Users/sholden/Projects/Python/voitto/tappio/lexer.py",
      line 45, in build_set
  assert type(ch) in (str, str)
```

You can see that the change that `2to3` made to remove the `unicode` type has come back to bite us because, while it suffices in v3, under v2 we need to explicitly allow strings of type `unicode`. We can't just revert that change, since that type isn't available under v3: attempts to reference it raise a `NameError` exception.

What we need is a type that is compatible with both versions. The `six` module (covered later) does introduce such a type, but, rather than carry the overhead of the entire module, in this case we chose to write a simple compatibility module at *tappio/compat.py* that creates an appropriate definition of the name `unicode` for the version it's running on. Following the advice of the porting guide, we use feature detection rather than querying version information. *compat.py* reads as follows:

```
try:
    unicode = unicode
except NameError:
    unicode = str
```

The alert reader might ask themselves why it is necessary to bind the `unicode` name rather than simply referencing it. The reason is that in v2 the `unicode` on the RHS comes from the built-in namespace, and so, without the assignment, it would not be available for import from the module.

The modules *tappio/writer.py* and *tappio/lexer.py* were modified to import `unicode` from `tappio.compat`. In *writer.py*, `str(token)` was changed to `unicode(token)`. In *lexer.py*, `isinstance(ch, str)` was reverted to `isinstance(ch, unicode)`. After these changes, all tests pass under both v2 and v3.

v2/v3 Support with a Single Source Tree

As the preceding exercise demonstrates, you can write Python that executes correctly in both environments. But this means taking some care when writing code, and you usually need to add some code specifically to provide compatibility between the two environments. Python's official Porting HOWTO (*https://docs.python.org/3.5/howto/pyporting.html*) document includes practical advice on interversion compatibility with a rather broader focus than ours.

A number of libraries have been produced to support single-source development, including `six`, `python-modernize`, and `python-future`. The last two each allow you to fix v2 code and add appropriate imports from `__future__` to get necessary bits and pieces of v3 functionality.

six

The `six` library (*https://pythonhosted.org/six/*) was the earliest project to provide such compatibility adaptation, but some people feel that it is too bulky, and convenience can also be an issue. It has been, however, successfully used in large projects such as Django (*https://docs.djangoproject.com/en/dev/topics/python3/*) to provide version compatibility, so you can trust that the library is capable of doing all you need.

six is particularly valuable when you need to retain compatibility with earlier v2 implementations, since it was produced when 2.6 was current and therefore also takes into account the extra issues that 2.6 compatibility raises. However, we recommend you target only Python 2.7, not earlier versions, in such compatibility quests: the task is hard enough without having to make it even harder.

python-modernize

The python-modernize library appeared when Python 3.3 was current. This library provides good compatibility between 2.6, 2.7, and 3.3 by providing a thin wrapper around 2to3, and is used in much the same way. The author, Armin Ronacher, describes its use, and gives porting advice useful to anyone considering dual-version support, in *Porting to Python Redux (http://lucumr.pocoo.org/2013/5/21/porting-to-python-3-redux/)*.

python-modernize uses six as a base and operates much like 2to3, reading your code and writing out a version that's easier to maintain as a dual-source codebase. Install it in a virtual environment with **pip install modernize**. Its output tends to move code stylistically toward v3.

python-future

The most recent tool for single-source support is the Python-Future (*http://python-future.org/*) library: install it in a virtual environment with **pip install future**. If you (as we recommend) support only v2 (Python 2.7) and v3 (Python 3.5 and newer), it stands alone, without external dependencies. With the addition of importlib, unittest2, and argparse, it can extend support to 2.6, should you absolutely require that.

Translation happens in two stages: the first stage uses only "safe" fixers that are extremely unlikely to break your code, and does not attempt to use any compatibility functions from the future package. The output from stage one is still v2 code with calls to v2 standard functions; the purpose of the two-stage approach is to remove uncontroversial changes, so that the second stage can focus on those more likely to cause breakage.

The second-stage changes add dependencies on the future package, and converts the source to v3 code that also runs on v2 by using the dependencies. Existing users of v2 might find that the converted output style is more like the code they are used to.

future also comes with a pasteurize command that claims to convert v3 code into v2 code. We found, however, that its default mode was unable to duplicate the v2 compatibility changes we discussed at the end of "Retaining v2 compatibility" on page 723.

v3-only Support

For anyone creating new Python projects with no dependencies on v2-only libraries, the preferred strategy is: write in v3, and never look back! Of course, if you produce libraries or frameworks meant for use under both versions, then you don't have this luxury: you need to provide the compatibility your consumers require.

Bear in mind the limited lifetime remaining for v2: the v3-only strategy is becoming more viable by the month. More and more v3 code is being produced daily, and over time the new code will tend to dominate. You can also expect more projects to drop v2 support, as many significant scientific projects indicate in the *Python 3 Statement (http://www.python3statement.org/)*. So, if you choose to produce only v3 code, the number of complaints is more likely to go down than up over time. Stick to your guns, and reduce your maintenance load!

Index

Symbols

A

B

C

D

E

F

G

H

I

J

K

L

M

N

O

P

Q

R

S

T

U

V

W

X

Z

About the Authors

Alex Martelli has been programming for over 30 years, mainly in Python for the recent half of that time. He wrote the first two editions of *Python in a Nutshell* and co-authored the first two editions of the *Python Cookbook*. He's a PSF Fellow, and won the 2002 Activators' Choice Award and the 2006 Frank Willison Memorial Award for contributions to the Python community. He's active on Stack Overflow and a frequent speaker at technical conferences. He's been living in Silicon Valley with his wife Anna for 12 years, and working at Google throughout this time, currently as Senior Staff Engineer leading "long tail" tech support for the Google Cloud Platform.

Anna Martelli Ravenscroft is an experienced speaker and trainer, with a background developing curricula for a wide range of topics, from church, to regional transit, to disaster preparedness; developing web applications for therapy, learning, and fitness; and writing and reviewing technical books, articles, and presentations. While not a professional programmer, Anna is a Python enthusiast, and an active member of the Open Source community: she's a PSF Fellow, and winner of the 2013 Frank Willison Memorial Award for contributions to the Python community. Anna co-authored the second edition of the *Python Cookbook*. Anna lives in Silicon Valley with her husband Alex, two dogs, one cat, and eight chickens.

Steve Holden celebrates his half-century as a programmer with the publication of this book, the last 20 years using Python as his principal programming language. In 2002 Steve wrote *Python Web Programming*; from 2003 to 2005 he chaired the first three PyCon conferences in the USA. He has served as both a director and chairman of the Python Software Foundation, of which he is now a Fellow; he won the 2007 Frank Willison Memorial Award for contributions to the Python community; and is a well-known speaker to Python audiences. Steve currently lives in London, where he is the CTO of a small startup.

Colophon

The animal on the cover of *Python in a Nutshell*, Third Edition, is an African rock python (*Python sebae*), one of approximately 18 species of python. Pythons are nonvenomous constrictor snakes that live in tropical regions of Africa, Asia, Australia, and some Pacific Islands. Pythons live mainly on the ground, but they are also excellent swimmers and climbers. Both male and female pythons retain vestiges of their ancestral hind legs. The male python uses these vestiges, or spurs, when courting a female.

The python kills its prey by suffocation. While the snake's sharp teeth grip and hold the prey in place, the python's long body coils around its victim's chest, constricting tighter each time it breathes out. They feed primarily on mammals and birds. Python attacks on humans are extremely rare.

Many of the animals on O'Reilly covers are endangered; all of them are important to the world. To learn more about how you can help, go to *animals.oreilly.com*.

The cover image is a 19th-century engraving from the Dover Pictorial Archive. The cover fonts are URW Typewriter and Guardian Sans. The text font is Adobe Minion Pro; the heading font is Adobe Myriad Condensed; and the code font is Dalton Maag's Ubuntu Mono.

CPSIA information can be obtained
at www.ICGtesting.com
Printed in the USA
BVHW040929070619
550449BV00012B/70/P